# COMPUTERS

## ARE YOUR FUTURE

2005

2004

2003

2002

BRIEF EDITION

# COMPUTERS
## ARE YOUR FUTURE

2005

2004

2002

## BILL DALEY

PEARSON

Prentice
Hall

Upper Saddle River, New Jersey

*Computers Are Your Future 2005*
**Brief edition / William Daley**

**Publisher and Vice President:** Natalie E. Anderson
**Executive Editor:** Jodi McPherson
**Project Manager, Editorial:** Jodi Bolognese
**Project Manager, Supplements:** Melissa Edwards
**Development Editors:** Jodi Bolognese and Christine Wright
**Editorial Assistants:** Alana Meyer and Jasmine Slowik
**Senior Media Project Manager:** Cathi Profitko
**Marketing Manager:** Emily Williams Knight
**Associate Director, IT Product Development:** Melonie Salvati
**Manager, Production:** Gail Steier de Acevedo
**Senior Production Project Manager:** April Montana
**Manufacturing Buyer:** Natacha St. Hill Moore
**Manager Print Production:** Christy Mahon
**Design Manager:** Maria Lange
**Cover Art Director:** Michael Fruhbeis
**Interior Design:** Quorum Creative Services
**Cover Design:** DePinho Graphic Design
**Composition:** Quorum Creative Services
**Full Service Management:** Pre-Press Company, Inc.
**Photo Research:** Shirley Webster
**Printer/Binder:** R.R. Donnelly and Sons Company/ Willard
**Cover Printer:** Phoenix Color

Credits and acknowledgments borrowed from other sources and reproduced, with permission, in this textbook appear on page C.1.

Microsoft Excel, Solver, and Windows are registered trademarks of Microsoft Corporation in the U.S.A. and other countries. Screen shots and icons reprinted with permission from the Microsoft Corporation. This book is not sponsored or endorsed by or affiliated with Microsoft Corporation.

Selected screen shots supplied courtesy of Prentice-Hall, Inc.

10 9 8 7 6 5 4 3 2 1
ISBN 0-13-113979-7

*To Dr. Charles Neyhart—my mentor and friend.*

Thank you for believing in me, and for your counsel.

Your help and guidance have significantly contributed to producing "A" work.

And thank you for your decision to allow me to teach;

it has made all the difference in the world.

&

*To Sharon*

Thank you for your love and unending support.

I could not have accomplished this without you.

You are my sweetie, my partner, and my best friend.

I love you with all that I am.

—Bill Daley

# Acknowledgements

I am grateful for the assistance of the following reviewers of this edition:

**Gary R. Armstrong**, Shippensburg University
**Wayne E. Ballentine**, University of Houston, Downtown
**Judith F. Bennett**, Sam Houston State University
**Deborah Buell**, University of Houston, Downtown
**Judy Cestaro**, California State University, San Bernardino
**Joseph DeLibero**, Arizona State University
**Annette Duvall**, Albuquerque T-VI
**Deena Engel**, New York University
**Tracey L. Fisher**, Butler County Community College
**Linda Foster-Turpen**, Albuquerque T-VI
**Susan Fry**, Boise State University
**Marta Gonzalez**, Hudson County Community College
**Cheryl Jordan**, San Juan College
**Bhushan Kapoor**, California State University at Fullerton
**Trudy McNew Gift**, Hagerstown Community College
**Diane Stark**, Phoenix College
**Mary Ann Zlotow**, College of DuPage

I am grateful for the assistance of the following reviewers of the fifth edition:

**Judith F. Bennett**, Sam Houston State University
**Judy Clark**, Northwest Missouri State University
**Mark DuBois**, Illinois Central College
**Gina M. Dunatov**, DeVry College
**Alan D. Evans**, Montgomery County Community College
**Michelle M. Hansen**, Davenport University
**Shelly Hawkins**, Western Washington University
**Cheryl Jordan**, San Juan College
**Bhushan Kapoor**, California State University at Fullerton
**Emilio A. Laca**, University of California at Davis

I am grateful for the assistance of the following reviewers of the fourth edition:

**Beverly Amer,** Northern Arizona University
**Dennis Anderson,** Pace University
**Bob Bretz**, Western Kentucky University
**Joseph DeLibero**, Arizona State University
**Mark DuBois**, Illinois Central College
**Said Fares**, Valdosta State University
**Nancy Grant**, Community College of Allegheny County
**Carolyn Hardy**, Northwest Missouri State University
**Michelle Hulett**, Southwest Missouri State University
**Emilio A. Laca**, University of California at Davis
**Kuber Maharjan**, Purdue University
**Karen Norwood**, McLennan Community College
**Anthony J. Nowakowski**, Buffalo State College
**Chuck Riden**, Arizona State University
**John Ross**, Fox Valley Technical College
**Ray Smith**, Salt Lake City Community College
**Steve Smith**, El Paso Community College
**Lynn Wermers**, North Shore Community College
**Linda Woolard**, Southern Illinois University

What a team! You are about to begin a journey through "my" book. But I want you to know that authoring is not a solo occupation. Here's a brief description of Prentice Hall's team approach to producing this book. I was hired by an executive editor and then assigned an assistant editor to work with on a daily basis. I also have a development editor who ensures that what I write is as good as it can be. All work eventually makes it to a copy editor. Meanwhile a photo researcher is busy obtaining the photos for the book, and others are getting permissions for any copyrighted work I use or quote. All of the manuscript and photos then go to a compositor and then through an iterative editing process. Overall workflow is managed by a project manager and a production manager. I have been so fortunate to work with people who are at the top of their profession!

My most heartfelt appreciation goes to Jodi Bolognese, who both served as the editorial project manager and contributed development editor work on nearly half of the chapters. Her greatest attribute is that she always does what she says she's going to do, and usually does it sooner than promised. What a dream it has been to work with Jodi! Special thanks go to Christine Wright, Development Editor. Christine provided expert advice and insight into better ways to organize and describe the content of the book. She brought many years of professional experience to the project. April Montana, Senior Project Manager of Production, saw the book through the complex production process with the coolness and calmness that comes only from a consummate professional. I also sincerely appreciate the artistic flair with which Debbie Iverson of Quorum Creative Services composed the text, photos, and artwork in this book. Jennifer Carley and the dedicated folks at Pre-Press provided the best copyediting and proofreading an author could hope for. Their attention to detail has helped ensure that you are reading the cleanest textbook on the market today. Shirley Webster, Photo Researcher, worked long and hard hours in researching the photos. She is a joy to work with and has provided photos that accurately depict the topics in the text. Jodi McPherson is my Executive Editor. She believed that I could write this book before I knew it was a possibility. Thank you, Jodi, for believing in me and for your unabashed support of my work. Finally, I would like to express my deepest appreciation to everyone in my Prentice Hall family. Quality comes from caring; Prentice Hall is a company of people who care.

—Bill Daley

# Preface

## About This Edition

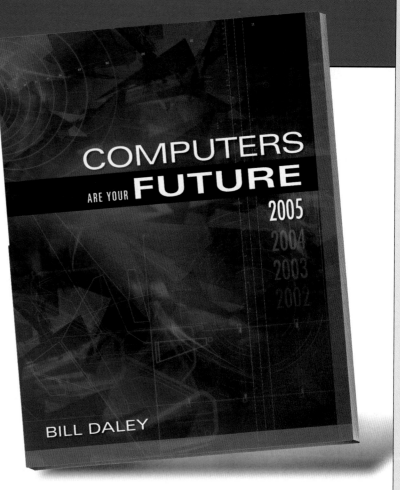

We've worked to produce a book that will meet your needs and the needs of your students. We listened to our reviewers, we listened at roundtable discussions, and most important, we dedicated our best people and resources to this project. Here are some things we think you should know about the revision of *Computers in Your Future*:

- Title change: *Computers Are Your Future*. You want a book to reflect the diverse students you now teach. Students today aren't wowed by technology—it's part of their daily lives. From the time they're in grade school, they look at a computer like a toaster—just another common home appliance. We've revised the book to match what we believe they already know with what you've told us they should know.

- You want the new edition to be more current and streamlined than the sixth edition—but without forcing changes in the way you're teaching the course. We've significantly reorganized the table of contents, cut redundancy across chapters, and focused on producing a vibrant and active flow to the content.

- You want new chapters on wired and wireless communications, and on enterprise computing. We've conducted the research and written Chapters 8 and 14.

- You want a concepts book with great learning tools that hold your students' interest and reinforce critical material—but without causing them to lose focus. We've removed the encyclopedic dryness and condensed the key terms down to those that are truly "key."

- You want a text-specific, interactive Web site that enhances your students' learning with valuable additional resources and practice exercises—and for your students to be led intuitively to key information that is concise, intelligent, and clearly laid out. Wait until you experience what we've created!

Now available as an annual edition, ***Computers Are Your Future 2005*** brings a new design, new and updated coverage, new *Spotlight*, *Currents*, and *Impacts* features, and an updated accompanying Web site. This text is ready for the challenge of teaching even your most diversified class—without sacrificing quality, integrity, or choice. *Computers Are Your Future 2005* comes in three versions—Brief (Chapters 1–8), Introductory (1–12), or Complete (1–14)—to meet the needs of your classroom.

# The 2005 edition offers you flexibility and currency.

CURRENTS boxes examine issues in computing as well as cutting-edge computer technology. Students learn about what's going to change the face of computing by the time they become professionals. Currents boxes include: emerging technologies, ethics, privacy, piracy, communications, and wireless technology.

Computer FLUENCY continues to be emphasized in the 2005 edition. It's one thing to be computer literate, but it's quite another to be computer fluent. Computer-literate people are skilled computer and Internet users; computer-fluent people are able to navigate the digital world easily. Their knowledge of the underlying concepts and principles of computers and the Internet gives them tremendous advantage. The more computer-fluent people work with computer technology, the deeper and richer their understanding grows. They also understand enough about computing to recognize the risks, as well as the benefits, of technology.

TechTV links and references appear in every chapter. TechTV provides Web-based VIDEOS that are current, rich, and interesting. These are the same videos found on the 24-hour TechTV cable news channel.

SPOTLIGHT sections highlight innovative thinking in each subject area—for example, emerging technologies, ethics, crime, and security; as well as buying and upgrading your computer system and file management.

IMPACTS boxes offer chapter-by-chapter insights on societal implications of computing. Students are introduced to thought-provoking bites of information to stimulate class discussion or team debates on all aspects of technology's impact on life today.

CUTTING-EDGE topics covered include: Microsoft Office 2003, ethics, e-commerce, security, privacy, communications trends and infrastructure, and multimedia.

Chapters are significantly UPDATED. Chapter 1 is revised to engage the student and to provide a vivid outline of the book's content. Chapters 2 through 4 are revised and updated. Chapters 5 and 6 combine content that used to be distributed in other chapters. Chapters 7 through 9 are heavily revised, with additional coverage of privacy, security, and intellectual property issues. Chapters 10 through 12 are updated to include the latest practices in programming, managing data, and systems. Chapter 13 is totally revised and updated. And Chapter 14, on enterprise computing, is brand new.

# For the Instructor

## INSTRUCTOR RESOURCES

The new and improved Prentice Hall Instructor's Resource CD-ROM includes the tools you expect from a Prentice Hall Computer Concepts text, like:

- The Instructor's Manual in Word and PDF formats
- Solutions to all questions and exercises from the book and Web site
- Multiple, customizable PowerPoint slide presentations for each chapter
- Computer concepts animations
- TechTV videos
- Image library of all of the figures from the text

This CD-ROM is an interactive library of assets and links. This CD writes custom "index" pages that can be used as the foundation of a class presentation or online lecture. By navigating through this CD, you can collect the materials that are most relevant to your interests, edit them to create powerful class lectures, copy them to your own computer's hard drive, and/or upload them to an online course management system.

## TESTGEN SOFTWARE

TestGen Software: TestGen is a test generator that lets you view and easily edit testbank questions, transfer them to tests, and print in a variety of formats suitable to your teaching situation. The program also offers many options for organizing and displaying testbanks and tests. A built-in random number and text generator makes it ideal for creating multiple versions of tests that involve calculations and provides more possible test items than testbank questions. Powerful search and sort functions let you easily locate questions and arrange them in the order you prefer.

QuizMaster, also included in this package, allows students to take tests created with TestGen on a local area network. The QuizMaster utility built into TestGen lets instructors view student records and print a variety of reports. Building tests is easy with TestGen, and exams can be easily uploaded into WebCT, Blackboard, and CourseCompass.

## TRAINING AND ASSESSMENT
http://www.phgenit.com

Prentice Hall offers performance-based training and assessment in one product—Train&Assess IT. The training component offers computer-based training that a student can use to preview, learn, and review Microsoft Office application skills. Web- or CD-ROM-delivered, Train IT offers interactive, multimedia, computer-based training to augment classroom learning. Built-in prescriptive testing suggests a study path based not only on student test results but also on the specific textbook chosen for the course.

The assessment component offers computer-based testing that shares the same user interface as Train IT and is used to evaluate a student's knowledge about specific topics in Word, Excel, Access, PowerPoint, Outlook, the Internet, and computing concepts. It does this in a task-oriented environment to demonstrate students' proficiency as well as comprehension of the topics. More extensive than the testing in Train IT, Assess IT offers more administrative features for the instructor and additional questions for the student.

Assess IT also allows professors to test students out of a course, place students in appropriate courses, and evaluate skill sets.

## TOOLS FOR ONLINE LEARNING

### Companion Web Site
**www.prenhall.com/cayf2005**

This text is accompanied by a companion Web site at www.prenhall.com/cayf2005. Features of this new site include an interactive study guide, downloadable supplements, online end-of-chapter materials, additional Internet exercises, TechTV videos, Web-resource links such as Careers in IT and crossword puzzles, plus technology updates and bonus chapters on the latest trends and hottest topics in information technology. All links to Web exercises will be constantly updated to ensure accuracy.

### EXPLORE IT
**http://www.prenhall.com/exploreitlabs**

Prentice Hall offers computer-based training just for computer literacy. Designed to cover some of the most difficult concepts, as well as some current topical areas—EXPLORE IT is a Web- and CD-ROM-based product designed to complement a course. Available for free with any Prentice Hall title, our new lab coverage includes: troubleshooting, programming logic, mouse and keyboard basics, databases, building a Web page, hardware, software, operating systems, building a network, and more!

### ONLINE Courseware for Blackboard, WebCT, and CourseCompass

Now you have the freedom to personalize your own online course materials!

Prentice Hall provides the content and support you need to create and manage your own online course in WebCT, Blackboard, or Prentice Hall's own CourseCompass. Content includes lecture material, interactive exercises, e-commerce case videos, additional testing questions, and projects and animations.

### CourseCompass
**www.coursecompass.com**

CourseCompass is a dynamic, interactive online course-management tool powered exclusively for Pearson Education by Blackboard. This exciting product allows you to teach market-leading Pearson Education content in an easy-to-use, customizable format.

### Blackboard
**www.prenhall.com/blackboard**

Prentice Hall's abundant online content, combined with Blackboard's popular tools and interface, results in robust Web-based courses that are easy to implement, manage, and use—taking your courses to new heights in student interaction and learning.

### WebCT
**www.prenhall.com/webct**

Course-management tools within WebCT include page tracking, progress tracking, class and student management, a grade book, communication tools, a calendar, reporting tools, and more. GOLD LEVEL CUSTOMER SUPPORT, available exclusively to adopters of Prentice Hall courses, is provided free of charge upon adoption and provides you with priority assistance, training discounts, and dedicated technical support.

TechTV is the San Francisco-based cable network that showcases the smart, edgy and unexpected side of technology. By telling stories through the prism of technology, TechTV provides programming that celebrates its viewers' passion, creativity and lifestyle.

TechTV's programming falls into three categories:

1. **Help and Information**, with shows like *The Screen Savers*, TechTV's daily live variety show featuring everything from guest interviews and celebrities to product advice and demos, *Tech Live*, featuring the latest news on the industry's most important people, companies, products and issues, and *Call for Help*, a live help and how-to show providing computing tips and live viewer questions.

2. **Cool Docs**, with shows like *The Tech Of...*, a series that goes behind the scenes of modern life and shows you the technology that makes things tick, *Performance*, an investigation into how technology and science are molding the perfect athlete, and *Future Fighting Machines*, a fascinating look at the technology and tactics of warfare.

3. **Outrageous Fun**, with shows like *X-Play*, exploring the latest and greatest in videogaming, and *Unscrewed with Martin Sargent*, a new late-night series showcasing the darker, funnier world of technology.

For more information, log onto **www.techtv.com** or contact your local cable or satellite provider to get TechTV in your area.

# For the Student

Welcome to **Computers Are Your Future 2005**! The following pages are designed to help you get the most out of the material and make the learning process rewarding. We call your attention to areas that may help you as you read through the book. Please read on, and enjoy!

**SPOTLIGHT** sections highlight important ideas about computer-related topics and provide indepth, useful information to take your learning to the next level.

IMPACTS

Milestones

## How "Human" Can Robots Become?

Robots have come a long way since the term was first used to describe man-made laborers in a 1921 play by Czech author Karel Capek. Once found only in scientific labs, today robots paint cars for auto manufacturers, help surgeons conduct surgery, and make trips to outer space.

Robots are entering our homes, too. Can't have a pet in your dorm room? How about AIBO, the doglike "Entertainment Robot" from Sony (Figure 1.13a)? According to Sony, AIBO has "the five instincts of love, curiosity, movement, hunger, and sleep" as well as the "emotions of happiness, sadness, anger, surprise, fear, and dislike." How can you tell what AIBO is "feeling"? According to the Japanese company, AIBO conveys its "feelings" through melodies, body language, and lights in its eyes and on its tail. You can even train AIBO to do tricks. Best of all, AIBO doesn't need to be house-trained!

Even more humanlike is the Japanese-made PaPeRo (short for **Pa**rtner-type **Pe**rsonal **Ro**bot) (Figure 1.13b). PaPeRo's colorful, rounded canister shape may not look huggable at first, but when treated with kindness, it's irresistible. PaPeRo can welcome you home after a long day, and when you're away, it wanders around looking for human companionship. If it doesn't find any, it takes a nap. PaPeRo even has the ability to recognize voice patterns; if these patterns are unfriendly, it runs away.

While PaPeRo is a humanlike toy, robots are taking the place of humans in industry in many ways. In 2001, IBM conducted an experiment in

which robots participated in simulated trading of commodities such as pork bellies and gold. By using specially designed algorithms, the robots performed the same tasks as human commodity brokers—and made seven percent more money than their human counterparts! Can you imagine a future in which robots make economic decisions? It would certainly give the stock exchange floor a new look. (And speaking of which, are robots capable of insider trading? Would you need a "robot," or just a computer?)

Researchers are also working on a robot that changes its shape to accomplish a specific task. The shape-changing robot has pieces that are moved around by a computer-managed algorithm. Such shape-changing robots will one day walk, crawl, carry tools, and fit into tight spaces humans can't.

Lockstep logic is wonderful for a machine, but humans rely on intuitive and often illogical decisions. Will robots ever act nonrationally? A team of researchers at MIT is working on a "sociable humanoid robot" able to learn from and interact with humans. Called Kismet, the big-eyed robot uses algorithms based on what we know about child development to react in a human way. According to MIT's research team, Kismet can perceive a variety of social cues from its "parent" through its eyes and ears, and can then deliver feedback through its facial expression, posture, and "voice." So will robots ever act illogically? With humans as surrogate parents, anything is possible.

**FIGURE 1.13** (a) AIBO and (b) PaPeRo are popular home robots.

**IMPACTS** boxes in each chapter illustrate thought-provoking cultural, ethical, and societal implications of computing.

these words aren't in its massive, built-in dictionary. But many correctly spelled words, such as proper nouns (the names of people and places), aren't likely to be found in the computer's dictionary. For this reason, the program won't make any changes without asking you to confirm them.

• **Storage** Once you've corrected the spelling in your document, you save the revised document to disk.

CURRENTS

Debates

## Platform Passion: Macs versus PCs

As you almost certainly know, as a computer user, you have two major platforms to choose from: Macintosh and PC. The debate over which platform is best has raged on for years, and if market power is anything, PCs are winning by a landslide. But Apple hangs in there with its slew of adherents who choose to "think different." What's the difference between the platforms? Although you'd never know from listening to people who love or hate Macs, there's not much difference, really. At least not in terms of power capacity. Still, the debate goes on.

On the one side, Mac lovers say their machines are easier to set up and use. Macs come with everything you need built right in—all you have to do is plug them in and you're on your way. Mac lovers also point to the fact that Apple has developed some incredibly advanced technology. (Even PC users will agree to that.) Apple offers its users cutting-edge, easy-to-use applications such as iMovie, iTunes, iPhoto, and iDVD. And Mac's FireWire technology has spread to PCs: first it was available as an option and now it may be becoming a standard.

It's not just the system and the software Mac users love. Most Macophiles love their one-button mice as well as their many shortcut keys. Not to mention the Apple design; many Mac adherents love the look of the Mac above all else. Today, you'll find Macs being used in most primary and elementary schools in the United States. (OS X is virtually crash-proof!) In addition, certain professions, such as publishing, advertising, and design, rely almost exclusively on Macs.

On the other hand, PCs still dominate, and the race isn't even close. PCs claim the largest chunk of the marketplace and are the choice of corporate America. And thanks to economies of scale, they also tend to be cheaper, in terms of both their hardware and software. Indeed, software is a big plus for PC users, who have far more to choose from than their Mac counterparts. Because so many more people buy the software, it tends to be better, and it is often developed and published more quickly than similar software for Macs. And as much as Mac lovers claim the one-button mouse is the way to go, PC users love their two-button mouse, which offers more choices in hand.

And as for design? Step aside, Mac. Make way for new PCs on the market. In the fall of 2002, Gateway introduced its new all-in-one computer that hopes to steal market share from Apple's iMac G4 (Figure 2.8).

In recent years, Apple has tried to woo PC users by playing on the idea that Macs are easier to use. Meanwhile, Mac's OS X could improve the number of software products developed for Macs, and that includes games, one reason PCs lead in the marketplace. However, as Apple moves into the PC market with its recent UNIX innovations, it may make itself more vulnerable to the viruses that have been mostly a PC headache in the past. In any case, Macs have a long way to go to catch up to PCs—and few users from either camp see that happening any time soon.

**CURRENTS** boxes in each chapter examine cutting-edge issues in computing and computer technology.

**FIGURE 2.8** Gateway claims its all-in-one computer (a) is better and cheaper than its Mac counterpart (b).

**TECHTALK** margin notes define commonly used computer jargon.

**DESTINATIONS** margin notes direct you to related Web sites where you can explore chapter topics in more depth.

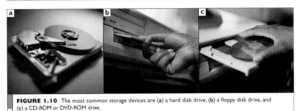

**FIGURE 1.10** The most common storage devices are **(a)** a hard disk drive, **(b)** a floppy disk drive, and **(c)** a CD-ROM or DVD-ROM drive.

very simple processing operations at very high speeds. To check your document's spelling, the program begins by constructing a list of all the words in your document. Then it compares these words, one by one, with a huge list of

### Techtalk

**peripheral**
A computer device that is not an essential part of the computer; that is, any device that is not the memory or microprocessor. Peripheral devices can be external—such as a mouse, keyboard, printer, monitor, external Zip drive, or scanner—or internal, such as a CD-ROM drive, CD-R drive, or internal modem.

---

# Computer Fundamentals

Learning computer and Internet concepts is partly about learning new terms. So let's start with the most basic term of all: *computer.*

### UNDERSTANDING THE COMPUTER: BASIC DEFINITIONS

A **computer** is a machine that performs four basic operations: input, processing, output, and storage (Figure 1.4). Together, these four operations are called the **information**

**processing cycle.** Input, processing, output, storage—that's what computers do. The processing function relies upon input, output is dependant upon the results of processing, and storage is where output may be kept for later use. Since these operations are dependent upon each other, the information processing cycle is always performed in order.

You'll often hear the term *computer system,* which is normally shortened to *system.* This term is more inclusive than *computer.* A **computer system** is a collection of related components that have been designed to work together smoothly. These components can be broken down into two major categories: hardware and software. A computer system's **hardware** includes the physical components of the

### Destinations

To learn more about the time line of computer development, see the excellent Timeline of Computer History at **www.computer.org/ computer/timeline/**

---

**FIGURE 1.2** Workers with computer and Internet skills tend to make more money and have more satisfying careers than do workers without such skills.

decisions you make will be major life decisions; others will have minor consequences. But there will always be facts to gather, opinions to hear, and choices to weigh. Learning about and understanding computers and technology will help you make informed choices.

How can you judge the direction and speed with which technology is moving? What knowledge can you gain that will prepare you to capitalize on technological advancements? What current knowledge in your life can you use for perspective?

Consider this: You were most likely born in the mid-1980s. Many of your parents were born in the mid-1960s. Think of the changes that have occurred as a result of technological innovation during the most recent 40 years. When your parents were born there were no telephone answering machines, no cell phones, no calculators, and no personal computers. People wrote letters by hand or with a typewriter, kept track of numbers and data in ledgers, and communicated in person or through the use of the telephone. In fact, telephones were physically connected—there were no wireless phones until the 1970s or cell phones until the 1980s.

When you were born the Internet (including e-mail) was restricted to use by the United States government and to institutions of higher education, cell phones were just beginning to be used, and fax

machines were the fastest way for most people to share documents throughout the world. The World Wide Web would not come into existence until after you started grade school, and e-commerce didn't exist until you were almost 10. Today, millions of people use the Internet not only in their professional lives in business, government, and education but also in their personal lives. Cell phones are a seemingly necessary part of everyday life, fax machines are becoming obsolete, and e-commerce was responsible for more than three billion dollars in transactions last year.

Today it's becoming harder and harder to find an activity that doesn't involve computers and technology (Figure 1.1). Clearly, you'd be wise to learn all you can about computers, the Internet, and the World Wide Web. You should know how to use a computer, the Internet, and popular software such as Microsoft Word or Excel. At work, computer and Internet skills are needed to succeed in almost every occupational area. Studies consistently show that workers with computer and Internet skills tend to make more money and have more satisfying careers than do workers who don't have such skills (Figure 1.2).

But skills alone aren't enough. To be a fully functioning member of today's computerized world, you also should learn the concepts that underlie computer and Internet technology, such as the distinction

### techtv

To learn more about technology and your future, see the video clip with futurist Alvin Toffler at: **www.prenhall.com /cayf2005**

**TECHTV** margin notes give you links to our Web site, where you can view video clips on chapter-specific subjects.

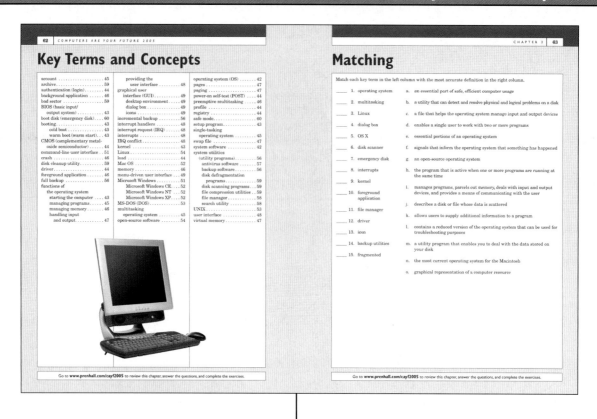

**END-OF-CHAPTER MATERIAL** includes updated multiple-choice, matching, fill-in, and short-answer questions, as well as Web research projects so you can prepare for tests.

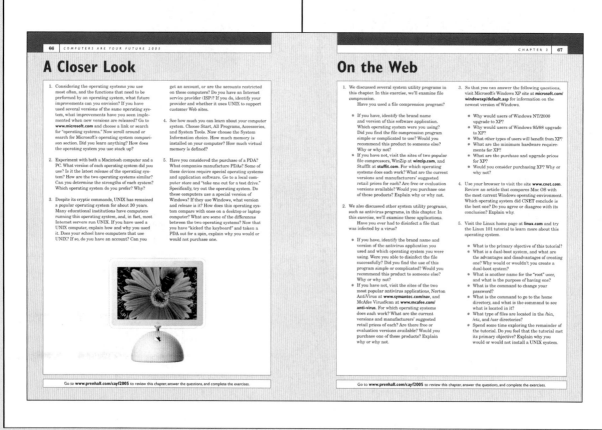

**EXPLORE IT LABS** present you with an interactive look into the world of computer concepts. These labs bring challenging topics in computer concepts to life through interactivity and assess your knowledge via a Quiz section, which can be e-mailed, saved to disk, or printed.

# Table of Contents

## At a Glance

# Table of Contents

# COMPUTERS

## ARE YOUR FUTURE

### 2005

# Computers, the Web, & You

## What You'll Learn . . .

■ **Explain the importance of computers in your world.**

■ **Define the word *computer* and name the four basic operations that a computer performs.**

■ **Explain the two main components of a computer system: hardware and software.**

■ **Explain the difference between system software and application software.**

■ **Provide examples of hardware devices that handle input, processing, output, and storage tasks.**

■ **Give an example of the information processing cycle in action.**

■ **Explain advantages, disadvantages, and ethical considerations involved with computer usage.**

■ **Discuss the two major categories and the various types of computers.**

■ **Define the Internet and list the most popular uses of the Internet.**

# Computers, the Web, & You

You're here. Your computer's here. Out there's the Web. What do you need to know to get you from here to there? Not much, you might be thinking. You've used a computer for ages. You've seen and explored the Web. You IM friends and family, download MP3s, and burn CDs every day. You've been there and done that. What more could you possibly need to know? What more is there to know?

Sure, you can perform all of those tasks. But your future isn't just about performing tasks. That's part of it, but hardly all of it. Your future is about having choices and making decisions.

The reason to learn more about any subject is to equip yourself with the knowledge and skills you will need to make more informed decisions. Some

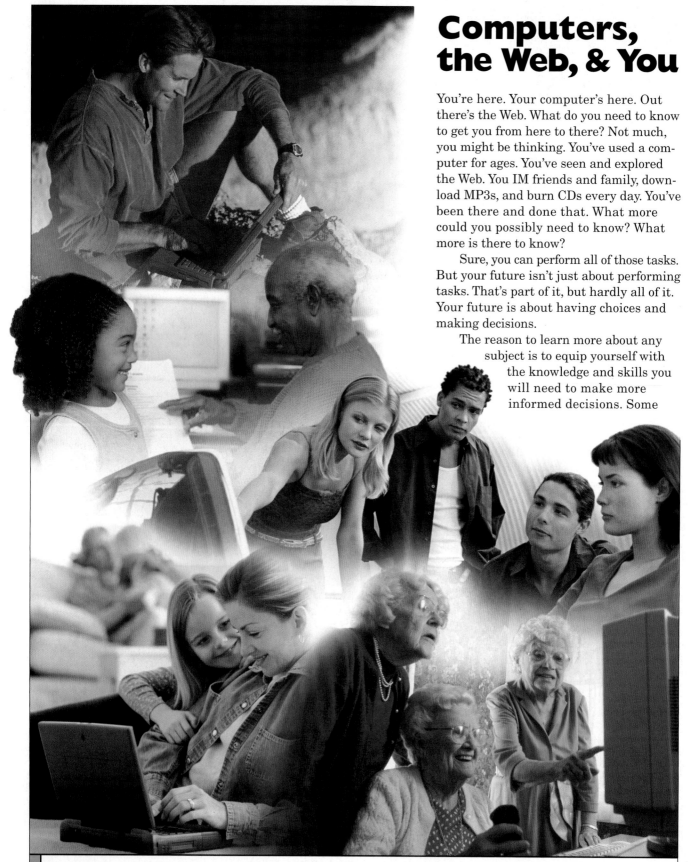

**FIGURE 1.1** Computers were once considered to be tools for an information age; today they are simply a part of our everyday environment.

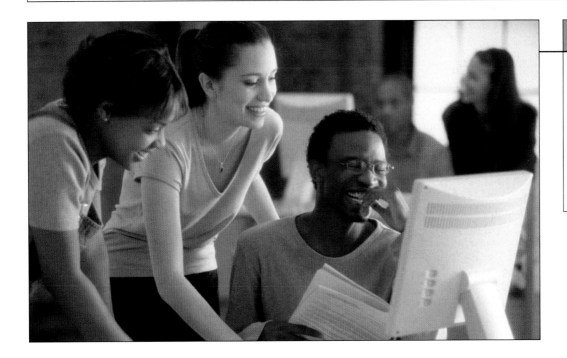

**FIGURE 1.2**
Workers with computer and Internet skills tend to make more money and have more satisfying careers than do workers without such skills.

decisions you make will be major life decisions; others will have minor consequences. But there will always be facts to gather, opinions to hear, and choices to weigh. Learning about and understanding computers and technology will help you make informed choices.

How can you judge the direction and speed with which technology is moving? What knowledge can you gain that will prepare you to capitalize on technological advancements? What current knowledge in your life can you use for perspective?

Consider this: You were most likely born in the mid-1980s. Many of your parents were born in the mid-1960s. Think of the changes that have occurred as a result of technological innovation during the most recent 40 years. When your parents were born there were no telephone answering machines, no cell phones, no calculators, and no personal computers. People wrote letters by hand or with a typewriter, kept track of numbers and data in ledgers, and communicated in person or through the use of the telephone. In fact, telephones were physically connected—there were no wireless phones until the 1970s or cell phones until the 1980s.

When you were born the Internet (including e-mail) was restricted to use by the United States government and to institutions of higher education, cell phones were just beginning to be used, and fax machines were the fastest way for most people to share documents throughout the world. The World Wide Web would not come into existence until after you started grade school, and e-commerce didn't exist until you were almost 10. Today, millions of people use the Internet not only in their professional lives in business, government, and education but also in their personal lives. Cell phones are a seemingly necessary part of everyday life, fax machines are becoming obsolete, and e-commerce was responsible for more than three billion dollars in transactions last year.

Today it's becoming harder and harder to find an activity that doesn't involve computers and technology (Figure 1.1). Clearly, you'd be wise to learn all you can about computers, the Internet, and the World Wide Web. You should know how to use a computer, the Internet, and popular software such as Microsoft Word or Excel. At work, computer and Internet skills are needed to succeed in almost every occupational area. Studies consistently show that workers with computer and Internet skills tend to make more money and have more satisfying careers than do workers who don't have such skills (Figure 1.2).

But skills alone aren't enough. To be a fully functioning member of today's computerized world, you also should learn the concepts that underlie computer and Internet technology, such as the distinction

To learn more about technology and your future, see the video clip with futurist Alvin Toffler at: **www.prenhall.com/cayf2005**

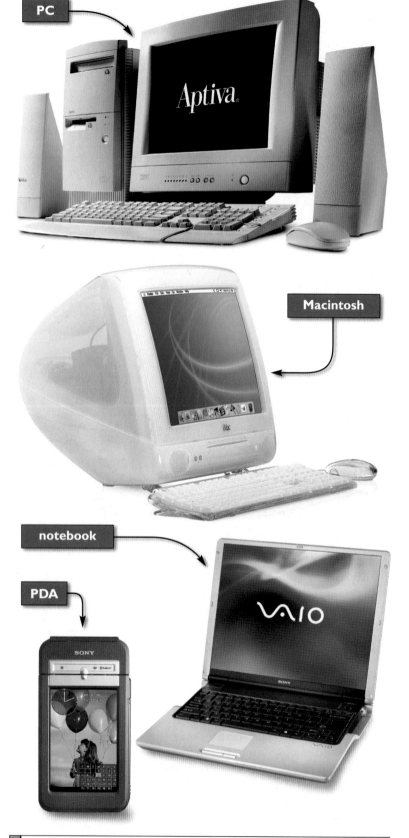

between hardware and software and how to manage the plethora of files that are created each day. As computers and the Internet play an increasingly direct and noticeable role in our personal lives, balancing their proper and improper use also becomes increasingly difficult. Should you shop on the Internet on company or school time? Is your credit card information, Social Security number, or personal communication safe from intrusion or misuse? In the past, the only way to shop during work or school was to leave the premises, and the only time you needed to worry about your personal information was if your wallet or mail were stolen!

You will make decisions about using technology, whether as a consumer in your personal life or as a business person in your professional life (Figure 1.3). How much power and speed do you need to perform everyday tasks? How soon do you need it? What will a bigger, faster computer enable you to do better? What types of technology tools do you need? Do you need advanced training or just enough for a beginner? This text and course provide answers to these questions as well as the knowledge and skills required to make informed decisions about technology in all areas of your life. Once you understand these concepts, you'll be able to:

- decide whether to purchase new equipment or upgrade specific components

- judge the likely impact of computer innovations on your personal and business life

- sort through the difficult ethical and moral challenges that computer use places before us

It is true that the more you work with computer technology, the deeper and richer your understanding should grow. Instead of being intimidated by new technologies, you will become quietly confident in your abilities. As your confidence and knowledge grow, you will become more and more adept in your use of computers.

In order to gain confidence in using computers, let's start out by describing the machine that's at the center of what you need to know.

**FIGURE 1.3** In addition to possessing skills, you will need to make decisions about technology.

# Computer Fundamentals

Learning computer and Internet concepts is partly about learning new terms. So let's start with the most basic term of all: *computer*.

## UNDERSTANDING THE COMPUTER: BASIC DEFINITIONS

A **computer** is a machine that performs four basic operations: input, processing, output, and storage (Figure 1.4). Together, these four operations are called the **information** **processing cycle**. Input, processing, output, storage—that's what computers do. The processing function relies upon input, output is dependant upon the results of processing, and storage is where output may be kept for later use. Since these operations are dependent upon each other, the information processing cycle is always performed in order.

You'll often hear the term *computer system*, which is normally shortened to *system*. This term is more inclusive than *computer*. A **computer system** is a collection of related components that have been designed to work together smoothly. These components can be broken down into two major categories: hardware and software. A computer system's **hardware** includes the physical components of the

## Destinations

To learn more about the time line of computer development, see the excellent Timeline of Computer History at **www.computer.org/ computer/timeline/**

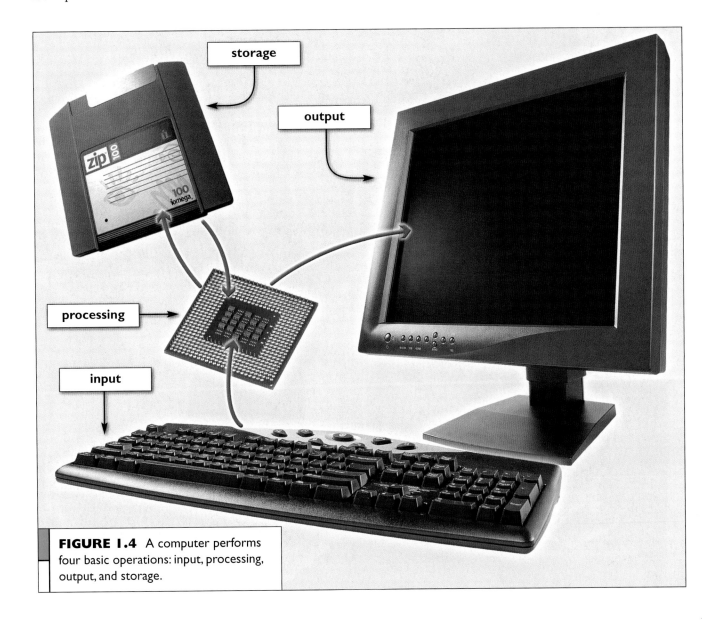

storage

output

processing

input

**FIGURE 1.4** A computer performs four basic operations: input, processing, output, and storage.

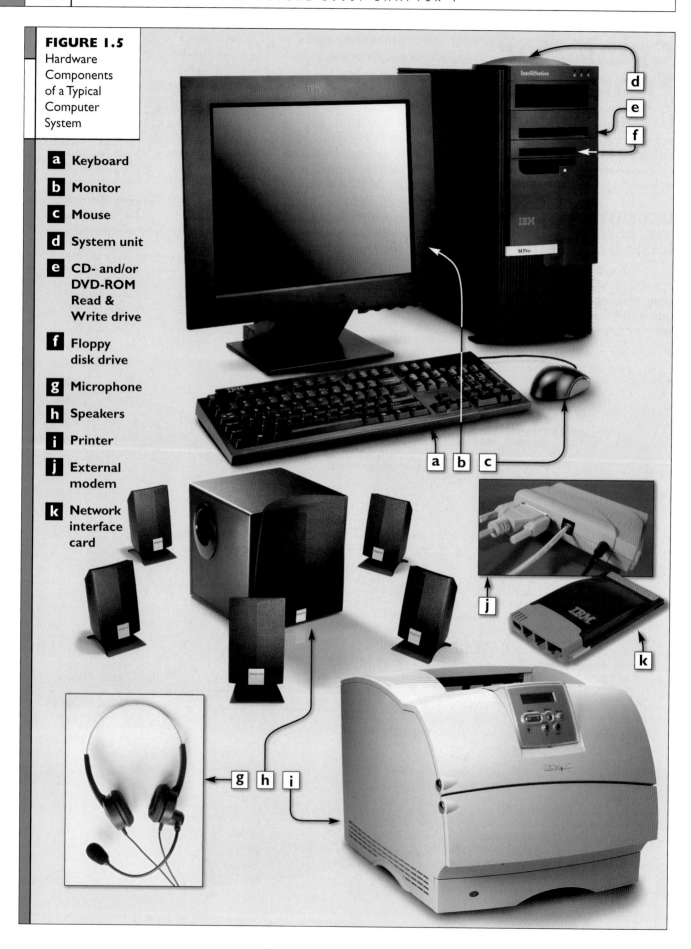

**FIGURE 1.5**
Hardware Components of a Typical Computer System

**a** Keyboard

**b** Monitor

**c** Mouse

**d** System unit

**e** CD- and/or DVD-ROM Read & Write drive

**f** Floppy disk drive

**g** Microphone

**h** Speakers

**i** Printer

**j** External modem

**k** Network interface card

computer, including the computer itself as well as keyboards, monitors, speakers, and so on (Figure 1.5).

In order for a computer system's hardware to function, a computer needs a program. A **program** is a list of instructions that tells the computer how to perform the four operations in the information processing cycle in order to accomplish a task. **Software** includes all of the programs that give the computer its instructions. You can divide software into two categories: system software and application software. **System software** includes all the programs that help the computer function properly, the most important being the operating system (OS) such as Microsoft Windows as well as system utilities like Help and Add/Remove Programs. **Application software** consists of all the programs you can use to perform a task including word processing, spreadsheet, database, presentation, e-mail, and Web browser software.

You might compare a computer system to an aquarium. The computer hardware is like the fish tank, the operating system is like the water, and the software applications are like the fish (Figure 1.6). You wouldn't put fish in an empty aquarium. Fish can't survive without water, just as software applications can't function without an operating system. And without the water and fish, an aquarium is an empty box, just like computer hardware isn't much use without an operating system and applications.

Now that we have the basic terms under our belt, let's take a closer look at the operations in the information processing cycle and which hardware devices are involved in each step.

**FIGURE 1.6**
You might compare your computer system to an aquarium.

## INPUT: GETTING DATA INTO THE COMPUTER

In the first operation, called **input**, the computer accepts data. The term **data** refers to unorganized raw facts, which can be made up of words, numbers, images, sounds, or a combination of these.

**Input devices** enable you to enter data into the computer for processing. The most common input devices are the keyboard and mouse (Figure 1.7). Microphones, disc drives, and devices such as scanners and digital cameras provide alternative ways of getting data into the computer.

## PROCESSING: TRANSFORMING DATA INTO INFORMATION

In the second operation, called **processing**, computers transform data into information. They don't really "think" at all. They are

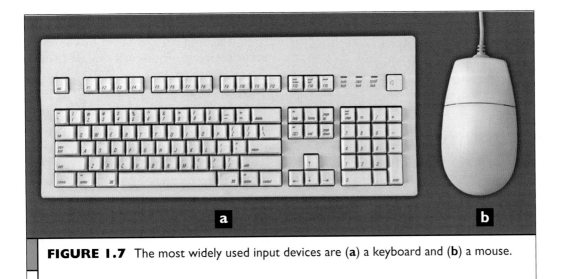

**FIGURE 1.7** The most widely used input devices are (**a**) a keyboard and (**b**) a mouse.

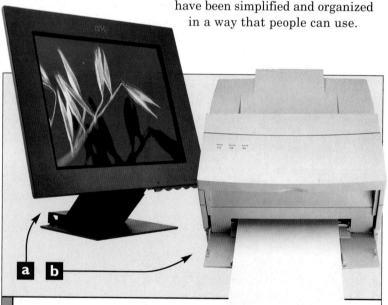

only capable of simple, repetitive processing actions organized into an algorithm—a series of steps that result in the solution to a problem. During processing, the computer's processing circuitry, called the **central processing unit** (**CPU**) or **microprocessor** (or just **processor** for short), performs operations on the entered or input data (Figure 1.8). The processor is located within the computer system's case, also called the **system unit**.

Since the CPU needs to juggle multiple input/output requests at the same time, it uses memory chips to store program instructions and data. Memory is essential to the smooth operation of the CPU. A typical computer includes several different types of memory, but the most important of these is **random access memory** (**RAM**), which temporarily stores the programs and data with which the CPU interacts.

**FIGURE 1.8**
The CPU (microprocessor or processor) performs operations on input data.

### OUTPUT: DISPLAYING INFORMATION

In the third operation, called **output**, the computer provides the results of the processing operation in a way that people can understand. The processed data become **information**—which refers to data that have been simplified and organized in a way that people can use.

**Output devices** show the results of processing operations. The most common output devices are a monitor and a printer—or, if the computer is processing sounds, you may hear the results on the computer's speakers (Figure 1.9).

### STORAGE: HOLDING PROGRAMS AND DATA FOR FUTURE USE

In the fourth operation, called **storage**, the computer saves the results of processing so that they can be used again later. **Storage devices** are used to hold all of the programs and data that the computer system uses. Most computers are equipped with the following storage devices: a hard disk drive, floppy disk drive, and CD-ROM drive and/or DVD-ROM drive (Figure 1.10). These devices are commonly nonremovable and mounted inside the system unit.

Although communications hasn't traditionally been a part of the information processing cycle, there can be another step involved.

### COMMUNICATIONS: MOVING DATA BETWEEN COMPUTERS

**Communications**, often a fifth operation in the information processing cycle, involves moving data around within the computer or between computers at very high speeds. To move data between computers, **communications devices** are necessary. Communications devices enable computers to connect to a computer network. A **network** is a group of two or more computer systems that are connected together, usually for the purpose of sharing input/output devices and other resources.

Most computers are equipped with a **modem**, which enables the computer to access other computers and the Internet via telephone lines, cable, and even wireless connections (Figure 1.11). Most modems are housed inside the system unit.

Now that we understand how hardware and software work in the information processing cycle and where they are located in a typical computer system, let's

**FIGURE 1.9** The most common output devices are (**a**) a monitor and (**b**) a printer.

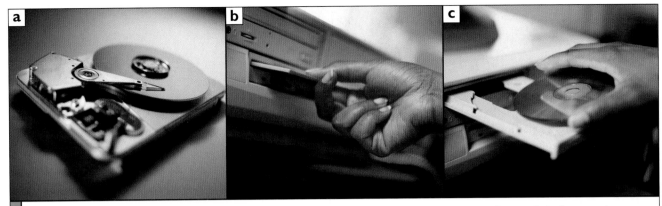

**FIGURE 1.10** The most common storage devices are (**a**) a hard disk drive, (**b**) a floppy disk drive, and (**c**) a CD-ROM or DVD-ROM drive.

**FIGURE 1.11** A modem is a communications device.

look at an example of how the computer uses the basic functions of input, processing, output, and storage.

## THE INFORMATION PROCESSING CYCLE IN ACTION

Even if you haven't wondered what goes on "behind the scenes" when using a computer, the following example illustrates your role and the computer's role in each step of the information processing cycle (Figure 1.12).

- **Input** You've just finished writing a research paper for one of your classes. You think it's probably riddled with misspellings and grammatical errors, so you run your word processing program's spell checker on it. In this example, your entire word processed document is the input.

- **Processing** A spell checker makes use of the computer's ability to perform

very simple processing operations at very high speeds. To check your document's spelling, the program begins by constructing a list of all the words in your document. Then it compares these words, one by one, with a huge list of correctly spelled words. If you've used a word that isn't in the dictionary, the program puts the word into a list of apparent misspellings.

Be aware that the computer isn't really "checking spelling" when it performs this operation. The computer can't check your spelling because it doesn't possess the intelligence to do so. All it can do is tell you which of the words you've used aren't in the dictionary. Ultimately, only you can decide whether a given word is misspelled.

- **Output** The result of the processing operation is a list of apparent misspellings. The word "apparent" is important here because the program doesn't actually know whether the word is misspelled. It is able to tell only that

## Techtalk

**peripheral**
A computer device that is not an essential part of the computer; that is, any device that is not the memory or microprocessor. Peripheral devices can be external—such as a mouse, keyboard, printer, monitor, external Zip drive, or scanner—or internal, such as a CD-ROM drive, CD-R drive, or internal modem.

| FIGURE 1.12 **The Information Processing Cycle in Action** | |
|---|---|
| **Input** | Entire word processed document |
| **Processing** | Constructing and comparing a list of misspelled words |
| **Output** | List of misspelled words |
| **Storage** | Corrected and revised document |

**IMPACTS**

## Miilestones

# How "Human" Can Robots Become?

Robots have come a long way since the term was first used to describe man-made laborers in a 1921 play by Czech author Karel Capek. Once found only in scientific labs, today robots paint cars for auto manufacturers, help surgeons conduct surgery, and make trips to outer space.

Robots are entering our homes, too. Can't have a pet in your dorm room? How about AIBO, the doglike "Entertainment Robot" from Sony (Figure 1.13a)? According to Sony, AIBO has "the five instincts of love, curiosity, movement, hunger, and sleep" as well as the "emotions of happiness, sadness, anger, surprise, fear, and dislike." How can you tell what AIBO is "feeling"? According to the Japanese company, AIBO conveys its "feelings" through melodies, body language, and lights in its eyes and on its tail. You can even train AIBO to do tricks. Best of all, AIBO doesn't need to be house-trained!

Even more humanlike is the Japanese-made PaPeRo (short for **P**artner-type **P**ersonal **Ro**bot) (Figure 1.13b). PaPeRo's colorful, rounded canister shape may not look huggable at first, but when treated with kindness, it's irresistible. PaPeRo can welcome you home after a long day, and when you're away, it wanders around looking for human companionship. If it doesn't find any, it takes a nap. PaPeRo even has the ability to recognize voice patterns; if these patterns are unfriendly, it runs away.

While PaPeRo is a humanlike toy, robots are taking the place of humans in industry in many ways. In 2001, IBM conducted an experiment in

**FIGURE 1.13** (a) AIBO and (b) PaPeRo are popular home robots.

which robots participated in simulated trading of commodities such as pork bellies and gold.

By using specially designed algorithms, the robots performed the same tasks as human commodity brokers—and made seven percent more money than their human counterparts! Can you imagine a future in which robots make economic decisions? It would certainly give the stock exchange floor a new look. (And speaking of which, are robots capable of insider trading? Would you need a "robot," or just a computer?)

Researchers are also working on a robot that changes its shape to accomplish a specific task. The shape-changing robot has pieces that are moved around by a computer-managed algorithm. Such shape-changing robots will one day walk, crawl, carry tools, and fit into tight spaces humans can't.

Lockstep logic is wonderful for a machine, but humans rely on intuitive and often illogical decisions. Will robots ever act nonrationally? A team of researchers at MIT is working on a "sociable humanoid robot" able to learn from and interact with humans. Called Kismet, the big-eyed robot uses algorithms based on what we know about child development to react in a human way. According to MIT's research team, Kismet can perceive a variety of social cues from its "parent" through its eyes and ears, and can then deliver feedback through its facial expression, posture, and "voice." So will robots ever act illogically? With humans as surrogate parents, anything is possible.

these words aren't in its massive, built-in dictionary. But many correctly spelled words, such as proper nouns (the names of people and places), aren't likely to be found in the computer's dictionary. For this reason, the program won't make any changes without asking you to confirm them.

- **Storage** Once you've corrected the spelling in your document, you save the revised document to disk.

In sum, computers transform data (here, a document full of misspellings) into information (a document that is free of misspellings).

Because you now understand the fundamental elements of a computer system and the four major functions of the information processing cycle, you should be able to adapt to new computer technologies with ease and grasp the risks as well as the benefits of these new technologies.

## RESPONSIBLE COMPUTING: ADVANTAGES, DISADVANTAGES, AND ETHICAL CONSIDERATIONS OF COMPUTER USAGE

Computer users need to take into account the advantages, disadvantages, and ethical considerations of using a computer system.

### Advantages and Disadvantages of Using Computers

A computer system conveys certain advantages such as speed, memory, storage, hardware reliability, and accuracy to its users. With these advantages come some disadvantages as well (Figure 1.14). Disadvantages include information overload, the expense of computer equipment, data inaccuracy, and our increasing dependence on unreliable software. Computer technology is growing at such an incredible rate that we are spending more and more time just trying to keep up. The following paragraphs explore various facts and considerations about computer systems.

A computer can process data at very high speeds. The most brilliant human mathematicians can perform only a few dozen operations per second, whereas an inexpensive computer can perform hundreds of millions—even billions—of them in a second.

If computers capable of processing data at impressive speeds did not already exist, we would have to invent them. According to one recent estimate, humans will create more information in the next three years than they have in all the previous centuries of our existence on this planet. In fact, people are generating so much information today that they often succumb to information overload, the feelings of anxiety and incapacity experienced when people are presented with more information than they can reasonably handle.

Computers can store and recall enormous amounts of data and information in a variety of formats including words, graphic images, and video clips. A computer's ability to work with all types of data is the first major reason for its remarkable penetration into almost every occupational area and nearly two-thirds of U.S. households. Even an inexpensive desktop computer can store and provide quick access to a 32-volume encyclopedia, the entire collected works of Shakespeare, a world atlas, an unabridged dictionary, and much more.

Although RAM can provide very fast access to these resources, it's also expensive. As a result, most computers are equipped with enough RAM to hold programs and data while the computer works with them, but no more. In addition, programs and data in RAM can be lost if the power is switched off. The alternative is storage devices, which are typically much slower than RAM, but offer increased storage capacity at a more affordable price.

Not only do they hold and generate huge amounts of information, computers are exceptionally reliable and accurate, too. Even the least expensive personal computers perform several million operations per second, and can do so for years without making an error caused by the computer's physical components. For example, you can equip a computer to transcribe your speech with an accuracy of 95 percent or more—which is better than most people's typing accuracy. In fact, almost all "computer errors" are actually caused by flaws in software or mistakes in the data people supply to computers. Computers store these mistakes for long

**FIGURE 1.14 Advantages and Disadvantages of a Computer System**

| Advantages | Disadvantages |
|---|---|
| Speed | Information Overload |
| Memory | Expensive |
| Storage | Data Inaccuracy |
| Hardware Reliability and Accuracy | Software Unreliability |

## Nanotechnology: Atoms Shaping the Future of Computers

In the early days of computing, room-sized noisy machines spindled and punched cards to perform their calculations. Today, computers are smaller than the palm of your hand and can accomplish a wide array of tasks. But what will computers be like in the future?

What would you say if you were told that various products would one day be able to manufacture themselves, or that computers would work billions of times faster than they do now? How about that there would be an end to famine and disease? And what if it were possible for extinct animals and plants to live again? What about distant planets, now uninhabitable, being made to look earthlike? All of these things and more may one day be possible with nanotechnology.

Merriam-Webster's defines nanotechnology as "the art of manipulating materials on an atomic or molecular scale especially to build microscopic devices (as robots)." Nanotechnology is based on a unit of measure called a nanometer, which is a billionth of a meter. The atoms and molecules used to perform certain tasks in nanotechnology, or nanorobots, will one day be able to perform an array of tasks. And because of their size, they'll be able to do things we never before thought possible.

The tie between medical and corporate research in nanotechnology is already strong. In fact, breakthroughs in nanomedicine and uses for medical nanorobots will most likely come first. For instance, medical nanorobots may one day be able to destroy fatty deposits in the bloodstream or be used to organize cells to restore artery walls, thereby preventing heart attacks. Nanorobots may also one day help improve our immune system by disabling or getting rid of viruses within our bodies. Cancer research may also use nanorobots to one day deliver drugs to specific areas of the body.

Meanwhile, NASA recently funded research to create nanoparticles and nanocapsules. While this research will be invaluable medically, NASA is interested in using the technology in space travel and long-term space habitation as well. NASA is concerned about the effect of radiation on its astronauts. They believe that nanomedicine could be the answer for radiation protection, self-diagnosis of disease in space, and delivery of medication during long space missions, among other things. Nanotechnology may also be able to alter the properties of known materials, making them lighter and stronger for lengthy space flights.

Nanotechnology sounds complex, and it is, but its possibilities and implications are truly endless. In fact, nanotechnology has been called the most important technological breakthrough since steam power. Looking for a new career? With corporate and medical research and development on parallel "nanopaths," they may create a high demand for nanotechnicians in your lifetime.

**techtv**

To learn more about nanotechnology, see the video clip with nanotechnologist Ralph Merkle at: **www.prenhall.com/ cayf2005**

periods of time, and then replicate those errors with amazing speed.

Even though computers have strengths and weaknesses, there are additional points to consider in your quest to become a responsible user.

### Don't Be Intimidated by Hardware

Many people feel threatened by computers because they fear that computers are too complicated. But without humans, computers have no intelligence at all. The processing operations they perform are almost ridiculously simple. The average insect is a genius compared with a computer.

As you learned earlier, one of the computer's strengths is that it performs these simple operations quickly and reliably. So there is nothing scary about computer hardware. Without a person and a program to tell it what to do, the computer is no more frightening—or useful—than an empty fish tank.

Computer hardware components should be treated with the same respect that you would give to any electronic device. Be mindful that electronic devices are sensitive to dust, moisture, static electricity, and magnetic interference. Treat the physical components of your computer with respect and you will get the most return for your money.

The disturbing thing about computers isn't the computers themselves but what people might do with them—which leads to the next point.

## Take Ethics Seriously

**Ethics** is the behavior associated with your moral beliefs. You learned what is right and wrong from your parents, teachers, and spiritual leaders. By this stage of your life you know what is right and wrong. It is important for you to recognize that the power of computers and the Internet is a relatively new ethical realm. In fact, a new branch of philosophy called *computer ethics* deals with computer-related moral dilemmas and also defines ethical principles for computer professionals.

Responsible computing requires that you understand the advantages and disadvantages of using the computer, as well as the potential that computer misuse could subject others to harm. Every day there are stories in the news of people misusing computerized data. Names and e-mail addresses are distributed freely without permission or regard for privacy. Viruses are launched against unsuspecting victims. Credit card information is stolen and fraudulently used. Computerized dialing machines call thousands of households an hour with unwanted solicitations. Children and women are stalked. Pornography abounds. Illegitimate copies of software are installed every day. Professional musicians lose tens and hundreds of thousands of dollars a year in unpaid royalties due to sharing programs and digital copying. Homework assignments are copied and then modified to appear as though they are original work. The Internet is a hotbed of illicit and sometimes illegal documents. The list of ethical considerations goes on and on.

Computers are very powerful tools. They can be used to magnify many aspects of our lives including unethical behavior. The Spotlight following this Chapter provides an in-depth discussion of computer ethics.

## Recognize the Risks of Using Flawed Software

Computer hardware can be amazingly reliable, but software is another matter.

All programs contain errors, and this is why: Computers can perform only a limited series of simple actions. Many programs contain millions of lines of

programming code (Figure 1.15). In general, each line of a program tells the computer to perform an action, such as adding two numbers or comparing them. Consider this: The program that allows you to withdraw cash from an ATM contains only 90,000 lines of code. But when you file your taxes, the IRS program that gives you your refund contains 1,000 times that—100 million lines of code!

With so many lines of code, errors inevitably occur—and they are impossible to eradicate completely. On average, commercial programs contain between 14 and 17 errors for every thousand lines of code. This means that an ATM is likely to have 1,350 errors in its code, and the IRS program code might have as many as one and a half million or more errors! Thankfully, most errors simply cause programs to run slowly or to perform unnecessary tasks, but some errors do cause miscalculations or other inconveniences.

Another phenomenon worth mentioning is that the more lines of code you add, the more complex the program becomes—and the harder it is to eradicate the errors. Just for fun, calculate how many hours it would take to read through 900,000 lines of programming code at one line per second. How many errors would you be likely to spot? (hours = 900,000/60/60) (errors = 900,000/1,000*15)

The fact that every computer program contains errors means that all computer

**Techtalk**

**bug**
An error or defect in software or hardware that causes a program to malfunction. The term derives from an incident in the very early days of computing when pioneer programmer Grace Hopper witnessed a moth fly into the computer she was manipulating, causing her program to crash.

**FIGURE 1.15 Programs often contain millions of lines of code**

| Program | Lines of Programming Code |
|---|---|
| Bank ATM | 90,000 |
| Air Traffic Control | 900,000 |
| Microsoft Windows 98 | 18 million |
| Microsoft Windows 2000 | 27 million |
| Microsoft Office XP | 35 million (estimated) |
| Internal Revenue Service (IRS) | 100 million (all programs) |

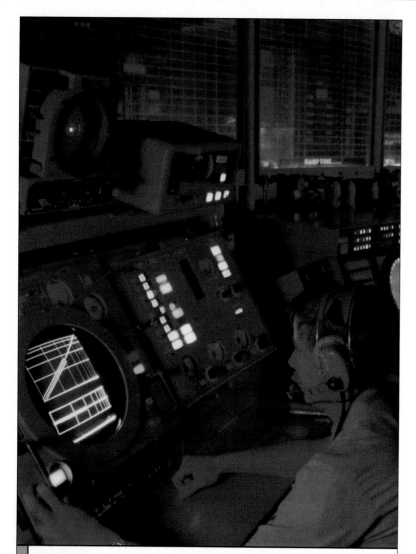

**FIGURE 1.16** The air traffic control system has a remarkable safety record.

human lives depend, such as an air traffic control system or a computerized signaling system used for high-speed commuter trains. When these systems fail, human lives are at stake (Figure 1.16). Safety-critical systems are designed to much higher quality standards and have backup systems that kick in if the main computer goes down.

Throughout our discussion to this point, we've been talking about computers in general. We now need to examine specific types of computers that can be used in a wide variety of tasks and job situations.

# Types of Computers

Computers come in all sizes, from large to small. It's convenient to divide them into two categories: computers for individuals (Figure 1.17) and computers for organizations (Figure 1.18).

## COMPUTERS FOR INDIVIDUALS

A **personal computer**, also called a microcomputer, is designed to meet an individual's computing needs. The two most commonly used types of personal computers are Apple Computer's Macintosh systems and the more numerous IBM-compatible personal computers, also called PCs, made by many manufacturers. These machines are called "IBM compatible" because the first such computer was made by IBM. Personal computers have steadily dropped in price, even as they have become more powerful and more useful.

Designed for use at a desk or in an office environment, a **desktop computer** is a personal computer that runs programs designed to help individuals accomplish their work more productively or to gain access to the Internet.

A **notebook computer** is small enough to fit in a briefcase. Many notebook computers are as powerful as desktop computers and include nearly all of a personal computer's components, such as stereo sound, a CD-ROM drive, and a modem.

**Laptop computers** are like notebook computers, except that they are a bit too

use entails a certain level of risk. A bug might occur when you least expect it and cause your computer to freeze up. You may be forced to restart your computer, losing your unsaved work.

The foregoing explains why it's not a good idea to put off writing a paper until the night before your assignment is due. Bugs in a word processing program aren't usually life threatening, but computers are increasingly being used in mission-critical and safety-critical systems. Mission-critical systems are essential to an organization's viability, such as a company's computerized cash register system. If the system goes down, the organization can't function—and the result is often a very expensive fiasco. A safety-critical system is one on which large to fit into a briefcase. Fewer laptops are being sold now that the smaller notebooks have become so powerful.

**Subnotebooks** are notebook computers that omit some components (such as a CD-ROM drive) to cut down on weight and size. A significant advantage is that some of them weigh less than three pounds. One disadvantage is that users must often carry along external disk drives with their attendant wiring.

A type of notebook computer that has an LCD screen upon which the user can write using a special-purpose pen, or stylus, is referred to as a **tablet PC**. The handwriting is converted to standard text through handwriting recognition, or it can remain as handwritten text. Tablet PCs also typically have a keyboard and/or a mouse for input.

**Personal digital assistants** (**PDAs**), sometimes called **handheld computers**, pack much of a notebook's power into a much lighter package. Most include built-in software for appointments, scheduling, and e-mail, and **pen computers** accept handwritten input.

**All-in-one computers**, such as the Apple e-Mac, are essentially a monitor with everything else built in. The only external devices are a keyboard and a mouse. The microprocessor, memory, storage, and speakers are all contained within the monitor case. This design may be the wave of the future.

**Network computers** (**NCs**) provide much of a personal computer's functionality but at a lower price. Because they get their software from a computer network, they don't need disk drives. In the consumer market, NCs such as WebTV enable consumers to use their televisions to connect to the Internet.

**Internet appliances** are computers with minimal memory, disk storage, and processing power designed to connect to a network, especially the Internet. The idea behind Internet appliances and network computers is that many users who are connected to a network don't need all the computer power they get from a typical personal computer. Instead, they can rely on the power of the network servers.

**Professional workstations** provide powerful tools for engineers, architects, circuit designers, financial analysts, and

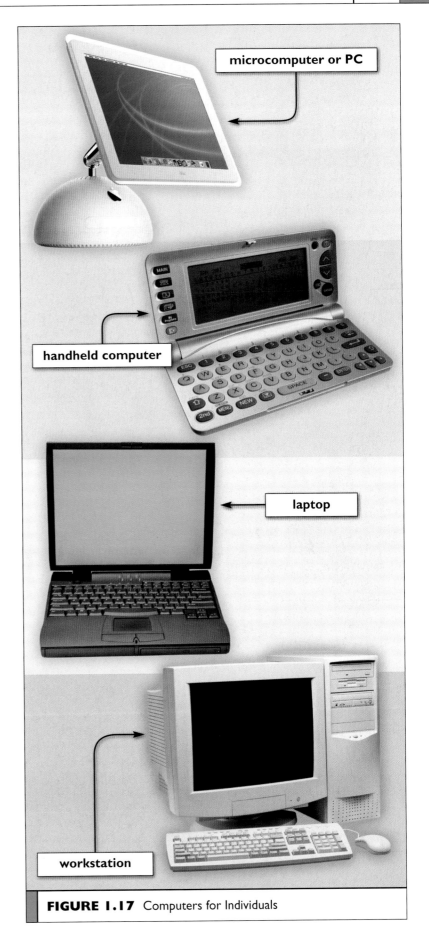

**FIGURE 1.17** Computers for Individuals

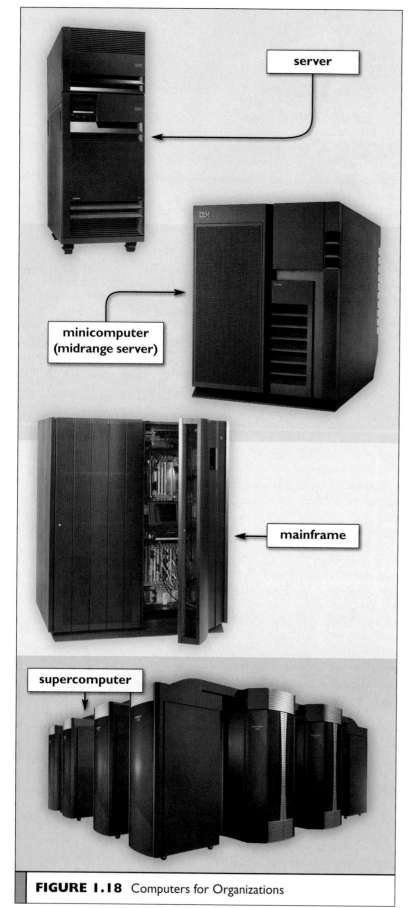

**FIGURE 1.18** Computers for Organizations

other professionals who need exceptionally powerful processing and output capabilities. They're the most expensive type of computers made for individuals.

## COMPUTERS FOR ORGANIZATIONS

**Servers** are computers that are not designed for individual use. They make programs and data available for people who are connected to a computer network. Employees use **clients**, which can be either computers or software the computers are running, to contact the server and obtain the needed information. This use of desktop clients and centralized servers is called **client/server computing**. It plays an important role in today's businesses.

**Minicomputers** can handle the computing needs of a smaller corporation or organization. They enable dozens, hundreds, or even thousands of people to use them simultaneously by means of **terminals** (remote keyboard and display units) or personal computers.

**Mainframes** are designed to handle gigantic processing jobs in large corporations or government agencies, such as handling an airline's reservations. Some mainframes are designed to be used by hundreds of thousands of people. People connect with mainframes using terminals as well as personal computers. Mainframes are usually stored in special, secure rooms that have a controlled climate.

**Supercomputers** are ultrafast computers designed to process huge amounts of scientific data and then display the underlying patterns that have been discovered. In 2000, IBM announced that it had built a supercomputer capable of executing 12 trillion calculations per second. Known as the ASCI White, the supercomputer covers an area the size of two basketball courts and is used by the Department of Energy. In March of 2002, Japan's NEC Corporation announced it had created an even faster supercomputer. The system, known as "the Earth Simulator," takes up the space of four tennis courts and is said to be five times faster than the ASCI White.

Whatever type of computer you decide to use or purchase, the Internet and Web are the destinations most computer users seek.

# The Internet and World Wide Web

As you may already know, the **Internet** is a huge global information space made up of thousands of privately owned computers and networks (Figure 1.19). Every computer connected to the Internet can exchange data with any other computer on the Internet. Today, hundreds of thousands of networks and nearly 50 million computers of all types and sizes are directly connected to the Internet.

Most users still connect to the Internet by means of a dial-up connection, which requires a modem and a telephone line, but access to broadband cable is increasing each day. What makes the Internet so appealing for so many is the variety of ways you can use the network:

- **E-mail** (short for **electronic mail**) is a software application that enables you to send and receive messages via the network (Figure 1.20). E-mail is fast becoming indispensable for individuals as well as businesses, and it is

**FIGURE 1.19**
The Internet spans the entire globe.

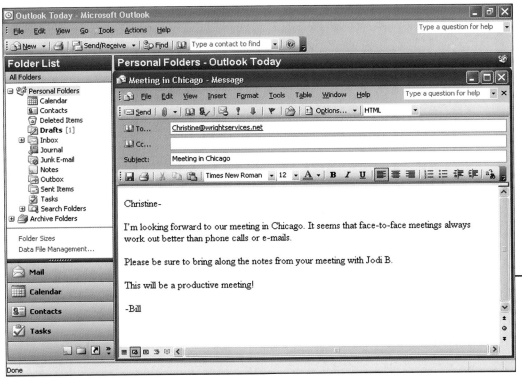

**FIGURE 1.20**
E-mail is an extremely popular form of interpersonal written communication.

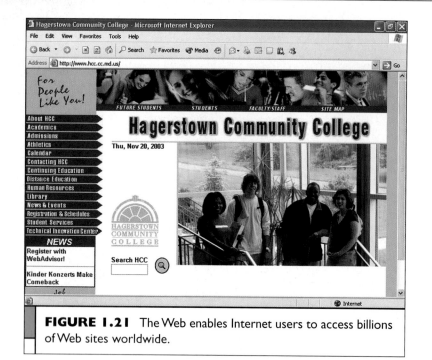

**FIGURE 1.21** The Web enables Internet users to access billions of Web sites worldwide.

Markup Language), which supports links to other documents, as well as graphics, audio, and video files. This means you can jump from one document to another simply by clicking the links. The Web enables Internet users to access billions of Web sites worldwide (Figure 1.21). A **Web site** is a computer that is accessible to the Internet which houses a collection of related Web documents made available to the public.

- **Electronic commerce** (**e-commerce**) involves all kinds of traditional business transactions, including buying, selling, renting, borrowing, and lending. Much e-commerce occurs in what you've heard referred to as the dot-com world, the universe of Web sites with the suffix *com* appended to their names. Web-based retail sites, called e-tailers, sell books, CDs, clothes, and much more.

- **Instant messaging systems**, such as Microsoft's Windows Messenger, let you know when a friend or business associate is online (connected to the Internet). You can then contact this person and exchange messages instantly (Figure 1.22).

well on its way to replacing the postal system as the medium of choice for interpersonal written communication.

- The **World Wide Web** (**Web** or **WWW**) is a portion of the Internet containing billions of documents. These documents are formatted in HTML (Hypertext

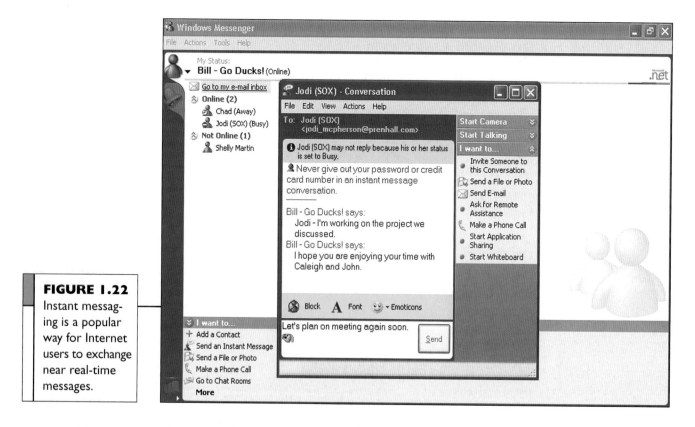

**FIGURE 1.22**
Instant messaging is a popular way for Internet users to exchange near real-time messages.

# Summary
# COMPUTERS, THE WEB, & YOU

- It is important to understand the fundamentals of computers and technology because computers are a part of our environment. Computer users must be able to adapt to new computer technologies with ease and grasp the risks as well as the benefits of these new technologies.

- A computer is a machine that performs the following four operations: input, processing, output, and storage. These four operations are called the *information processing cycle*.

- A computer system is a collection of related components that have been designed to work together. It includes both the computer's hardware (its physical components) and its software (the programs that run on it).

- System software refers to the programs that help the computer function properly, such as the operating system and system utilities. Application software enables users to perform useful tasks.

- In a typical computer system, a keyboard and a mouse provide input capabilities, while the processing is done by the microprocessor (CPU) and RAM (random access memory). You see the results (output) on a monitor, and you typically use a hard disk for long-term storage.

- Spell checking a word processed document exemplifies the information processing cycle. The input consists of the original document, which contains spelling mistakes. In processing, the computer detects and flags possible spelling errors by checking every word in the document against a massive spelling dictionary. Output consists of a list of words that the spell checker doesn't find in its library. User interaction is required to confirm whether the apparent misspelling needs to be corrected. The user saves the corrected document to storage for future use.

- Responsible computing requires that you understand the advantages and disadvantages of using the computer, as well as the potential that computer misuse could subject yourself and others to harm.

- The two major categories of computers are for individuals and organizations. Types of computers for individuals include personal computers, desktop computers, notebook, subnotebook, and laptop computers, handheld computers like personal digital assistants (PDAs), pen computers and tablet PCs, network computers (NCs), and Internet appliances. Servers, minicomputers, mainframes, and supercomputers are types of computers for organizations.

- The Internet is a global network of computers and networks. Popular uses of the Internet include e-mail, the Web, e-commerce, and instant messaging systems.

Go to **www.prenhall.com/cayf2005** to review this chapter, answer the questions, and complete the exercises.

# Key Terms and Concepts

Go to **www.prenhall.com/cayf2005** to review this chapter, answer the questions, and complete the exercises.

# Matching

Match each key term in the left column with the most accurate definition in the right column.

_____ 1. program

_____ 2. processing

_____ 3. hardware

_____ 4. software

_____ 5. modem

_____ 6. server

_____ 7. peripheral

_____ 8. e-mail

_____ 9. terminal

_____ 10. data

_____ 11. RAM

_____ 12. desktop computer

_____ 13. output

_____ 14. information

_____ 15. mainframe

a. a computer device that is not part of the essential computer

b. remote keyboard and display unit

c. unorganized raw facts

d. a software application that enables Internet users to send and receive messages

e. organized and useful, or meaningful facts

f. a list of instructions that describes how to perform input, processing, output, and storage operations to accomplish a task

g. includes all the programs that give the computer its instructions

h. the computer's physical components

i. temporarily stores programs and data for the CPU

j. a computer that is designed for use in an office environment

k. a computer that is used by large companies or government agencies

l. transforming data into information

m. enables a computer to access other computers and the Internet via a telephone line

n. makes programs and data available for people connected to a computer network

o. the results of processing operations

# Multiple Choice

Circle the correct choice for each of the following.

1. What are the four basic operations performed by a computer?
   a. processing, communication, storage, data creation
   b. input, processing, output, storage
   c. input, output, storage, communication
   d. input, printing, storage, retrieval

2. Which of the following is a common input device?
   a. keyboard
   b. printer
   c. disk drive
   d. monitor

3. Which of the following is not a type of output device?
   a. monitor
   b. speakers
   c. printer
   d. mouse

4. Which of the following is not a type of storage?
   a. floppy drive
   b. DVD-ROM
   c. microphone
   d. hard disk

5. Which type of memory temporarily stores the programs and data with which the central processing unit interacts?
   a. read only memory
   b. random access memory
   c. refreshable auxiliary memory
   d. read alone memory

6. Which of the following is an example of a computer that is designed to process huge amounts of data within a large organization?
   a. notebook computer
   b. mainframe computer
   c. minicomputer
   d. desktop computer

7. What does the acronym PDA stand for?
   a. personal data aid
   b. professional digital attachment
   c. personal digital assistant
   d. programmable data acquisition

8. Which device enables the computer to access other computers and the Internet via telephone lines?
   a. server
   b. Internet
   c. World Wide Web
   d. modem

9. Which of the following computers is not designed for individual use?
   a. workstation
   b. laptop
   c. server
   d. tablet PC

10. Which of these personal computing devices allows you to write on the screen with a special pen or stylus?
    a. tablet PC
    b. notebook
    c. subnotebook
    d. laptop

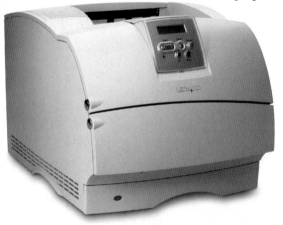

# Fill-In

In the blanks provided, write the correct answer for each of the following.

1. A _____ is a machine that performs four basic operations: input, processing, output, and storage.

2. A _____ is a list of instructions that tells the computer how to perform.

3. _____ includes the physical components of the computer, including the computer itself as well as keyboard, monitor, and speakers.

4. _____ is used to temporarily store the programs and data with which the CPU interacts.

5. The most common _____ are the keyboard, mouse, and microphone.

6. The most common output devices are a _____ and _____ .

7. A type of notebook computer that is actually smaller that a notebook computer is called a _____ .

8. _____ show the results of processing operations.

9. _____ are used to hold all of the programs and data that the computer system uses.

10. Most computers are equipped with a _____, which enables the computer to access other computers and the Internet via telephone lines.

11. _____ consists of all the programs you can use to perform a task such as writing a research paper or browsing the Web.

12. _____ includes all the programs that help the computer function properly, the most important being the operating system (OS) such as Microsoft Windows.

13. _____ is the behavior associated with your moral beliefs.

14. _____ are personal computers designed for use at a desk or in an office environment.

15. The _____ is a portion of the Internet containing billions of documents.

# Short Answer

1. What do you think about using copied software? Explain.

2. What is the difference between hardware and software?

3. What is the difference between system software and application software? Provide an example of each.

4. Is it ethical to download music files? Explain.

5. Describe your experiences with the Internet. Specifically, identify the browser and e-mail software applications that you have used. Have you used other Internet-related software? If you have, describe these applications.

6. Select a course that you are taking this semester. List two course activities that could require the use of a computer, and identify two different software applications that would be needed to complete these activities.

Go to **www.prenhall.com/cayf2005** to review this chapter, answer the questions, and complete the exercises.

# A Closer Look

1. Obtain a copy of your institution's "acceptable use" policy for computers. What restrictions does the institution place upon your computer use that you might not encounter when using your own computer or a commercial connection? What advantages do you receive by connecting to the Internet through your institution instead of through a commercial connection? Are there time restrictions? Are there volume restrictions? Are there any content restrictions? Are there ethical concerns when using the school's system that you wouldn't have if you were using your own system?

2. Institutions usually provide on-campus Internet connections. Contact your institution's computing services and see if they provide off-campus Internet connections. If they do provide this connectivity, do students pay an extra fee for this service, or is it funded by general student fees? If your school does not provide off-campus Internet access, how do you connect to the Internet, and what are the monthly fees?

3. For various reasons, most individuals use either a desktop or, if they want or need more portability, a laptop computer. Use the Internet or contact a local vendor and compare the prices for comparably equipped desktop and laptop computers. Based on your needs and finances, explain which computer you would buy, and give reasons to support your purchase. Why or why would you not consider purchasing a sub-notebook or handheld computer in place of a desktop or laptop?

4. Have you ever made a copy of software that you've bought for yourself? Did you ever give a copy of it away? Although purchasers are permitted to make a backup copy of software that they have purchased, they are not allowed to make additional copies and distribute them to others. What are your feelings about software piracy, that is, making illegal copies of software? Originally, software applications were installed from a series of floppy disks. However, since most software is now supplied on CD-ROMs, copies must be created using a "CD burner." Do you own or have access to one of these burners?

5. Obtain a local or regional newspaper and find one or more advertisements for computers and peripherals for sale. Write on the photos in the ads—identifying the input, processing, output, and storage devices. Compare a desktop computer with a laptop or PDA. Which input, processing, output, and storage (IPOS) devices look the same? Which are different?

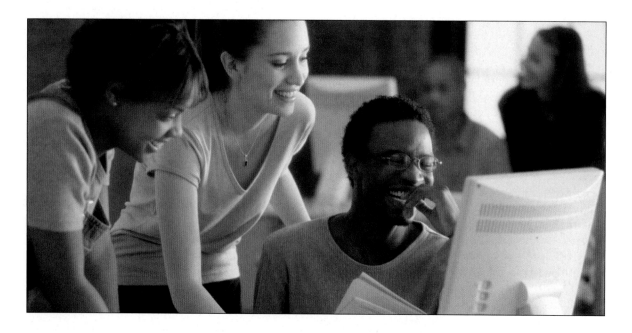

# On the Web

1. The speed at which the Internet is growing is phenomenal, and the number of users can only be estimated. To compare the growth of the Internet with that of other media, visit the Computer Almanac site at **www-2.cs.cmu.edu/afs/ cs.cmu.edu/user/bam/www/numbers.html**. This site is an online treasury of statistical information about computers. How many years did it take radio to have 50 million listeners? How many years did it take television to achieve 50 million viewers? How many years did it take the Web to reach 50 million U.S. users? (This is a lengthy Web site, so use your browser's *find on page* feature, and search for "50 million.")

2. Major software companies frequently release new versions of their popular software packages. At the time you read this book, Microsoft should have just released or be near release of its new Office product. To see if this software is worth its several hundred–dollar price tag, visit Microsoft's comparison site at **http://microsoft.com/office/ evaluation/indepth/compare.asp** and identify a new feature in each of the following areas:

   - Productivity and Efficiency
   - Access to Information
   - Reliability, Data Recovery, and Security
   - Collaborative Document Review
   - Collaborating with Others: Integration with SharePoint Team Services
   - Connecting and Coordinating with Others

   Which two of the new features are most important to you? Explain why you would or would not purchase or upgrade to this product.

3. Easter eggs are special, fun screens or information that software developers put into commercial versions of software. Many different programs include Easter eggs. You can find out about some existing Easter eggs at The Easter Egg Archive at **www.eeggs.com**. How difficult is it to display Easter eggs in some programs? Using the information from the Web site, can you locate any Easter eggs in the programs on your computer? Which Easter eggs surprised you the most?

4. Compared with the other types of computers, supercomputers are very small in number. Some major universities (such as the University of Tokyo), specialized governmental organizations (such as NASA), and businesses (such as Verizon) use these extremely fast and expensive computers. Visit the list of the world's most powerful computing sites to see some other types of organizations, agencies, and companies that have supercomputers. Begin your search at: **www.top500.org**.

   - What is the minimum processing speed needed to be included in this list?
   - What are the type and speed of the supercomputer that is used by George Lucas's Industrial Light and Magic (ILM) company to make movie special effects?
   - What are the types of supercomputers that CitiBank uses to maintain its many accounts?
   - What are the types and speeds of supercomputers that AOL uses to maintain its vast databases?
   - What are the types and speeds of supercomputers that the FBI uses to maintain its enormous number of records?

5. Using media such as radio, television, newspapers, and, of course, the Internet, people are able to obtain information about current events. The Internet Public Library maintains a worldwide list of newspapers at **www.ipl.org**. This site allows international students attending schools in the United States to read (in their native languages) about events that are happening in their countries. This site also allows U.S. students to read (in English) about global political, financial, or cultural events from the perspective of other nations. Can you think of other reasons why someone would read "foreign" newspapers?

   Find the headline or lead story from the following newspapers:

   - The *Cape Argus*, published in Cape Town, South Africa
   - The *Viet Nam News*, published in Hanoi, Vietnam
   - The *Buenos Aires Herald*, published in Buenos Aires, Argentina
   - The *Moscow Times*, published in Moscow, Russia
   - The *Kuwait Times*, published in Kuwait City, Kuwait

Go to **www.prenhall.com/cayf2005** to review this chapter, answer the questions, and complete the exercises.

# Spotlight
# *Ethics*

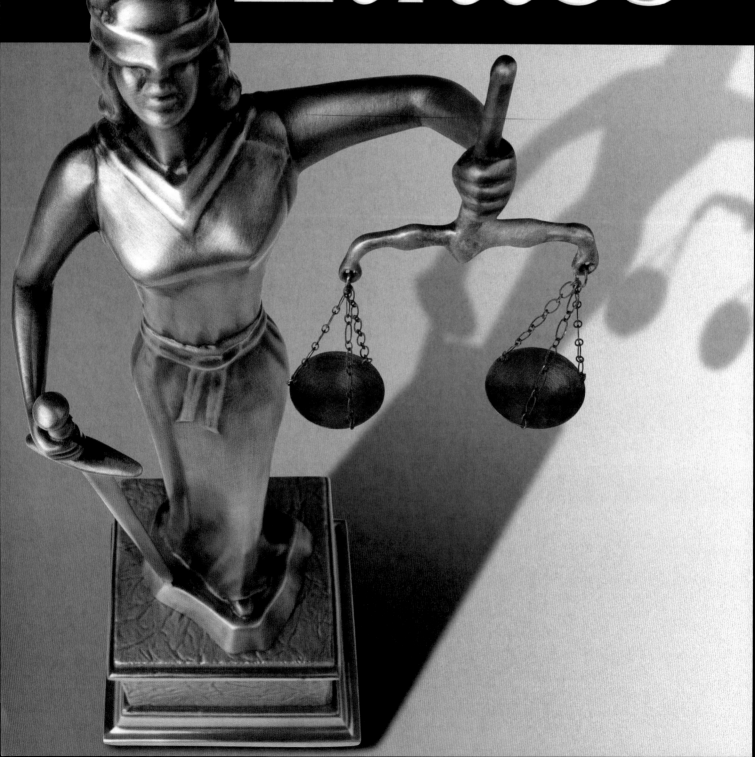

# STANDARDS OF INFORMATION AGE CONDUCT

Ethics IS THE BRANCH OF PHILOSOPHY CONCERNED WITH DETERMINING WHAT'S RIGHT AND WRONG. BY LAYING DOWN COMMONLY ACCEPTED RULES, OR ETHICAL PRINCIPLES, ETHICISTS WORK TO CONSTRUCT A FRAMEWORK INTO WHICH WE CAN PLACE DILEMMAS TO HELP US MAKE GOOD DECISIONS. IT SOUNDS SIMPLE ENOUGH, BUT THE DIFFICULTY OF MAKING ETHICAL DECISIONS LIES IN UNTRIED CIRCUMSTANCES. PEOPLE MUST TRY TO FIGURE OUT HOW THE EXISTING RULES, OR ETHICAL PRINCIPLES, APPLY TO A NEW SITUATION.

AS WE DISCUSSED IN CHAPTER 1, INFORMATION TECHNOLOGY CHANGES VERY RAPIDLY. SINCE COMPUTER USERS ENCOUNTER NEW SITUATIONS ON A DAILY BASIS, ETHICS IS ESPECIALLY IMPORTANT IN THE WORLD OF COMPUTERS. THE RESULT OF THIS MORAL GRAY AREA IS A NEW BRANCH OF PHILOSOPHY CALLED COMPUTER ETHICS. **COMPUTER ETHICS** DEALS WITH COMPUTING-RELATED MORAL DILEMMAS AND ALSO DEFINES ETHICAL PRINCIPLES FOR COMPUTER PROFESSIONALS. THIS SPOTLIGHT EXAMINES SOME OF THE MOST COMMON ISSUES IN COMPUTER ETHICS, FROM LEGAL PROBLEMS, IN WHICH ETHICS ARE DETERMINED BY LAW, TO MORAL DILEMMAS WHERE THE DIFFERENCE BETWEEN RIGHT AND WRONG ISN'T SO EASY TO DISCERN.

## Avoiding Computer-Related Legal Problems

Every day, newspapers carry stories about people getting into trouble by using their computers to conduct personal business while they're at work. In many cases, the offenders used company computers to browse the Web and send personal e-mail on company time, or to commit crimes such as cyberstalking or distributing pornography. While most companies have an acceptable computer use policy, you should be aware that using a computer for nonbusiness-related tasks is generally banned within an organization.

What other kinds of things can cause computer users problems? Let's start with a problem that gets many college students into serious trouble: plagiarism.

## PLAGIARISM

The term we often use in discussing rights of writers is **intellectual property**. The use of someone else's intellectual property is called **plagiarism.** Plagiarism predates computers; in fact, it has been practiced for thousands of years. But computers—and especially the Internet—make the temptation and ease of plagiarizing even greater. It's not only very easy to copy and paste from the Internet, but some sites are actually set up specifically to sell college-level papers to the lazy or desperate. Selling the papers isn't plagiarism, but turning in the work as your own is.

Imagine this scenario. It's four in the morning, and you have a paper due for your nine o'clock class. While searching for sources on the Internet, you find a Web site with a nice little essay on your topic. There's no copyright notice. What's wrong with downloading the text, reworking it a bit, and handing it in? Plenty.

Plagiarism is a serious offense. How serious? At some colleges, the first offense can get you thrown out of school (Figure 1A). You might think it's rare for plagiarizers to be caught, but the truth is that college instructors are often able to detect plagiarism in students' papers without much effort. The tip-off can be a change in the sophistication of phraseology, writing that is a little too polished, or errors in spelling and grammar that are identical in two or more papers. There are even software programs that can scan through text and then compare it to a library of known phrases. If a paper has one or more recognizable phrases, it is marked for closer inspection. Furthermore, even if your actions are not discovered now, someone could find out later, and the evidence could void your degree and even damage your career.

The more well known you are, the more you're at risk of your plagiarism being uncovered. Take noted historian and Pulitzer Prize–winning author Doris Kearns Goodwin, for example. In 2002, she was accused of plagiarizing part of her best-selling 1987 book *The Fitzgeralds and the Kennedys*. Although she claimed her plagiarizing was inadvertent and due to inadequate research methods, she suffered a significant decline in credibility and even felt obligated to leave her position at the PBS news program *NewsHour with Jim Lehrer*. It took 15 years for Goodwin's plagiarism to come to light.

Plagiarism may cause legal problems, too. Plagiarizing copyrighted material is called **copyright infringement**, and if you're caught, you can be sued and may have to pay damages in addition to compensating your victim for any financial losses due to your theft of the material. If you're tempted to copy anything from the Web, bear in mind that the United States is a signatory to international copyright regulations, which specify that an author does *not* need to include an explicit copyright notice to be protected under the law.

Does this mean you can't use the Internet source you found? Of course not. But to do so you must follow certain citation guidelines. In college writing it's fine to make use of someone else's effort as long as you use your own words and give credit where credit is due. If you use a phrase or a few sentences from the source, use quotation marks. Attach a bibliography, and list the source. For Internet sources you should list the Web site's address or uniform resource locator (URL), the date the article was published (if available), the date and time you accessed the site, the name of the article, and the author's name.

## SOFTWARE PIRACY

You need to have Microsoft Office 11 for your computer class. A friend has a copy that she got from her mom's office. You've just installed a copy on your computer. Have you done something wrong? Yes, of course you have! In fact, so has your friend. It is illegal for her to

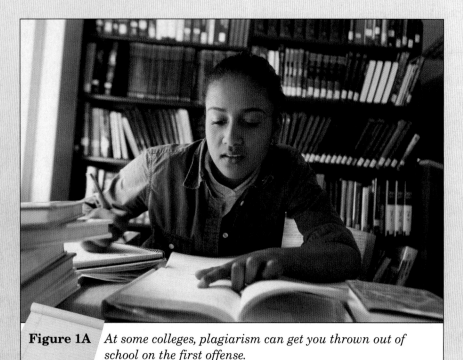

**Figure 1A** *At some colleges, plagiarism can get you thrown out of school on the first offense.*

have a copy of the software from her mom's office in the first place.

Some programs, however, are placed in the **public domain**, which means anyone is free to copy the program, or even modify it, if they want. However, don't assume that a program is in the public domain unless you see a note (often in the form of a "read me" text file) that explicitly identifies the file as copyright free.

Some programs are made available under the provisions of the Free Software Foundation's **General Public License (GPL)**. This license specifies that anyone may freely copy, use, and modify the software, but no one can sell it for profit. Much Linux software, for example, is available under the provisions of GPL.

Unlike public domain software, **shareware** programs are copyrighted. This means you can't copy or modify the program without permission from the owner. You can almost always find the owner and licensing information by accessing the Help menu or by locating and reading a "read me" file that is usually placed in the same directory as the program.

You may, however, freely copy trial versions of shareware programs. Shareware authors make evaluation versions of their programs available on a try-before-you-buy basis. When the evaluation period expires, you must pay the **registration fee** or delete the software from your disk. If you continue using the software past this date without paying the fee, you're violating the author's copyright.

Most commercial software is copyrighted; to use it, you must purchase the program. What you're really purchasing is a **software license**, which outlines what you can and can't do. Generally, software publishers grant you the right to make backups of the program disks. You may also be allowed to install the software on multiple machines, as long as it's clear that

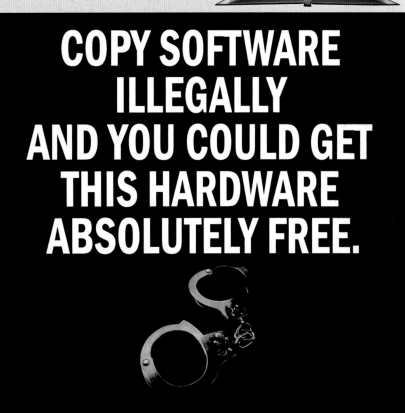

**Figure 1B**  *The Software Publisher's Association (SPA) is trying to raise consciousness about software piracy.*

you're only using one copy of the software at a time. Things you cannot do might include providing the program to others or modifying the program's function.

Increasingly, software is becoming **machine dependent**. This means that the program captures a machine ID during the installation process and writes that ID back to the installation disc or to the software company's server during a mandatory online registration process. Should you attempt to install the program on another

machine, the code will be checked and the installation will terminate.

Organizations with many computers can often purchase software for all their computers at a reduced price per unit. This type of agreement, called a **site license**, is a contract with the software publisher; the contract allows multiple copies of software to be made for use in the organization. Taking copies outside the organization usually violates the contract.

The copying and use of copyrighted software is rampant among college students and within organizations. Software manufacturers are working very hard to develop **copyright protection schemes** to thwart the illegal use of their programs. Although early versions of these schemes caused slowdowns on legitimate users' machines, recent versions do not do so.

The solution to the problem, perhaps, is for individuals to do the right thing and purchase every program they use. This isn't always easy, as a "free" copy can be very attractive, but doing the right thing tends to pay off in the long run.

Now that you understand the various ways in which software publishers make programs available, you can tell whether you're guilty of **software piracy** (Figure 1B). All of the following actions are illegal:

- *Incorporating all or part of a GPL program in a commercial program that you offer for sale.*

- *Continuing to use a shareware program past the evaluation program's expiration date without paying the registration fee.*

- *Violating the terms of a software license, even if you've paid for the program. For example, many licenses forbid you to install and use more than one copy at a time, so you're guilty of an infringement if you have copies of the same program on your desktop and notebook computers.*

- *Making copies of site-licensed programs for your personal use at home.*

- *Giving or selling copies of commercial programs to others.*

How serious is software piracy? The information technology industry loses billions of dollars a year in revenues; and if you're caught, you may be charged with a felony. If you're convicted of a felony, you could spend time in jail, lose the right to vote, and ruin your chances for a successful career.

Do you have pirated programs on your computer? The police aren't likely to storm into your residence hall and take you away, kicking and screaming. Most software piracy prosecutions target individuals who are trying to distribute or sell infringing copies or companies that have illegally made multiple copies for their employees. At Bates College, some students were arrested after investigators discovered that they were distributing copies of Microsoft Office 2000 from a Web site based on the college's server. They were charged with aggravated invasion of computer privacy, a crime that carries a maximum sentence of five years in prison, a $5,000 fine, or both. If you have any pirated software, you should remove these programs from your computer right away for two simple reasons: it's illegal, and it's wrong.

## COPYRIGHT INFRINGEMENT

Increasing numbers of Internet users seem to believe that sharing illegally made copies of copyrighted music is permissible because so many people are doing it, especially on college campuses. At the University of Oregon, a student was charged with criminal copyright infringement—a federal crime—after making thousands of MP3s available on his Web site. He faced potential penalties of up to three years in prison and $250,000 in fines. At Carnegie Mellon University, 71 students were disciplined for posting illegally duplicated music files on their sites.

**Figure 1C** *Bands like Metallica fought to have illegal downloads banned from the Internet. In 2000, Metallica sued Napster, a once-popular site for free music downloads. Thanks to lobbying by Metallica and other musicians, free downloads are harder to find on the Web.*

Copyright violators are endlessly creative when it comes to rationalizing their illegal behavior. You may hear that it's okay to download a copyrighted MP3 file as long as you keep it no longer than 24 hours, but that's false. If you upload music copied from a CD you've paid for, you're still violating the law. Spreading a band's copyrighted music around isn't justified by saying it's "free advertising"; if the group wants advertising, they'll arrange it themselves (Figure 1C). And don't fall into the trap of thinking that sharing MP3s is legal as long as you don't charge any money for them. Any time you're taking royalties away from copyright holders, it's illegal.

You'll often hear people use the term **fair use** to justify illegal copying. The fair use doctrine does justify *limited* uses of copyrighted material without payment to or permission from the copyright holder, but use is sharply limited in purpose and scope. The fair use doctrine holds that a *brief* selection from a copyrighted work may be excerpted for the purposes of commentary, parody, news reporting, research, and education. Such excerpts are short—generally, no more than five percent of the original work—and they shouldn't compromise the commercial value of the work. In general, the reproduction of an entire work is almost never justifiable by means of the fair use doctrine.

# Introducing Ethics

Unlike the legal issues discussed above, right and wrong are not so easily defined when it comes to ethics (Figure 1D). As this Spotlight's opening suggests, computers cause new ethical problems by pushing people into unprecedented situations. Computer ethics explores the ways that ethical principles can be used to think through the moral dilemmas caused by computer use.

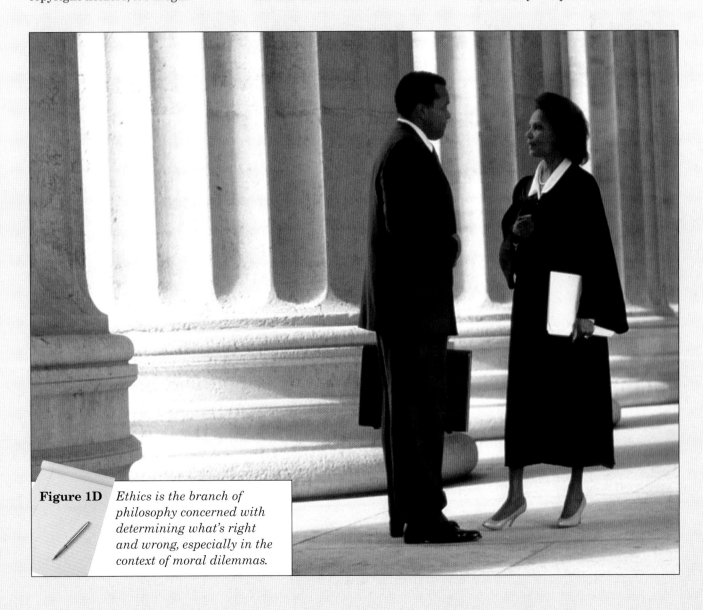

**Figure 1D** *Ethics is the branch of philosophy concerned with determining what's right and wrong, especially in the context of moral dilemmas.*

## MORAL DILEMMAS

It's easy to say that you don't need to worry about ethics; you'll just do the right thing. But that's just the trouble with moral dilemmas. When you're in one, it's difficult to tell what's right and what's wrong (Figure 1E).

Moral dilemmas arise in two situations:

- **When it's not clear which, if any, moral rule applies.** Can you imagine an electronic love triangle? That's just what resulted from an incident on the WELL, a computer network based in northern California. A male user was involved in electronic romances with at least two female users. Neither woman was aware of the other, nor had any of these people ever met. Do real-life courtship rules apply to an online chat group? Are these relationships real?

- **When two or more rules apply and they conflict.** You've just discovered that your friend is making and selling CDs containing pirated copies of your school's site-licensed software. You've told your friend that it's wrong and he should stop, but he persists. The copies could get your school—and your friend—in a lot of trouble. What's more important: your loyalty to your friend or your obligations to your school?

When you find yourself in the middle of a moral dilemma, it's a lonely feeling—people disagree about what you should do. Ethical principles come in handy because they help you think through your options.

## ETHICAL PRINCIPLES

An **ethical principle** is a principle that helps people evaluate and resolve moral dilemmas. Over the centuries, philosophers have come up with many ethical principles. To some, it's disconcerting to find that these principles sometimes conflict. The truth is that an ethical principle is only a tool you can use to think through a difficult situation. In the end, you must make your choice and live with the consequences.

Three of the most useful ethical principles are:

- **An act is ethical if, were everyone to act the same way, society as a whole would benefit.** Here's a good argument against software piracy. If everyone stole software, programmers would have little incentive to develop innovative programs. When we refuse to tolerate software piracy, everyone wins.

- **An act is ethical if it treats people as an end in themselves, rather than as a means to an end.** If the cybernetic two-timer had spent more time thinking about the fact that people with feelings were on the other end of the chat line, he might not have been so eager to play his little game. In this view, the fact that the relationships took place by means of the computer becomes irrelevant. He was using the relationships as a means to another end: his own gratification. From this perspective, his actions are unethical.

- **An act is ethical if impartial observers would judge that it is fair to all parties concerned.** If the acceptable use policy in a business or institution clearly states that the use of e-mail for personal communications is not allowed, and you learn that some of your e-mail has been monitored, the monitoring is ethical. You might not agree on grounds that your e-mail is private, but someone without any personal feelings at stake would be better able to judge the fairness of your situation. Since the impartial observer is not involved in the day-to-day activities of your group, he or she would be able to judge that the monitoring was ethical because the company's rules are stated in the acceptable use policy.

## THINKING THROUGH MORAL DILEMMAS

If you find yourself in a moral dilemma related to computer use, talk to people you trust. Make sure you have all the facts. Think through alternative courses of

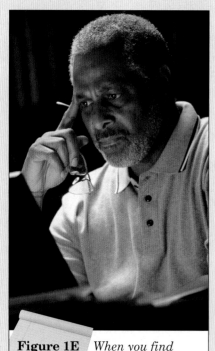

**Figure 1E** *When you find yourself in the middle of a moral dilemma, it can be difficult to tell what's right and what's wrong.*

action, based on different principles. Find a solution you can be proud of.

It isn't always easy to discern the right thing to do. Even when you know what's right, it's not always easy to act on it. Peer pressure is a tremendous force. Why should you be the one to do the right thing when everyone else is getting away with using copied software and music files? The next section might help.

# Computer Ethics for Computer Users

How do these ethics concepts apply to you, the college computer user? They all boil down to one word: respect. Use campus computers in a way that shows respect for yourself, for others, and for academic integrity.

- **Respect yourself.** If you obtain an account and password to use the campus computer system, don't give your password to others. They could do something that gets you in trouble. In addition, don't say or do anything on the Internet that could reflect poorly on you, even if you think no one will ever find out.

- **Respect others.** Obviously, you shouldn't use a computer to threaten or harass anyone. You should also avoid using more than your share of computing resources, such as disk space. If you publish a Web page on your college's computers, remember that your page's contents affect the college's public image.

- **Respect academic integrity.** Always give credit for text

you've copied from the Internet. Ask permission before you copy pictures. Don't copy or distribute software unless the license specifically says you can.

Your college probably has its own code of conduct for computer users. Read it carefully, and follow the rules.

## TEN COMMANDMENTS FOR COMPUTER ETHICS

The Computer Ethics Institute of the Brookings Institution, located in Washington, D.C., has developed the following "Ten Commandments" for computer users, programmers, and system designers:

1. *Don't use a computer to harm other people.*
2. *Don't interfere with other people's computer work.*
3. *Don't snoop around in other people's files.*
4. *Don't use a computer to steal.*
5. *Don't use a computer to bear false witness.*
6. *Don't copy or use proprietary software for which you have not paid.*
7. *Don't use other people's computer resources without authorization or proper compensation.*
8. *Don't appropriate other people's intellectual output.*
9. *Do think about the social consequences of the program you write or the system you design.*
10. *Do use a computer in ways that show consideration and respect for your fellow humans.*

## NETIQUETTE

General principles such as the "Ten Commandments for Computer Ethics" are useful for overall guidance, but they don't provide specific help for the special situations you'll run into online—such as an unwanted sexual advance in a MUD (multiuser dungeon) game. As a result, computer and Internet users have developed a lengthy series of specific behavior guidelines for the various Internet services available, such as e-mail, mailing lists, Usenet, Internet Relay Chat (IRC), MUDs, and MOOs (MUD object oriented). Called **netiquette**, these guidelines provide specific pointers on how to show respect for others—and for yourself—while you're online.

Here's a sample, based on Arlene Rinaldi's "Netiquette Home Page" (**www.fau.edu/netiquette/net/netiquette.html**) and other Internet sources:

- **Mailing lists.** After you join a mailing list, read the discussion for a couple of days to see what kinds of questions are welcomed and how to participate meaningfully. If the list has a FAQ (Frequently Asked Questions) document posted on the Web, be sure to read it before posting a question to the list; it may already have been answered in the FAQ. Bear in mind that some people using the list may not speak English as their native tongue, so don't belittle people for spelling errors. Don't post inflammatory messages; never post in anger. If you agree with something, don't post a message that says "Me too"—you're just wasting everyone's time. If you need to unsubscribe from the list, don't post messages requesting that somebody do this for you; find out how to send the correct command to the list server.

- **E-mail.** Check your e-mail daily, and respond promptly to the messages you've been sent. Download or delete messages once you've read them so that you don't exceed your disk usage quota. Remember that e-mail isn't private; you should never send a message that contains anything you wouldn't want others to read. Always speak of others professionally and courteously; e-mail is easily forwarded, and the person you're describing may eventually see the message. Check your computer frequently for viruses that can propagate by means of e-mail messages. Keep your messages short and to the point; focus on one subject per message. Don't type in all capital letters; this comes across as SHOUTING. Spell check your e-mail as you would any other written correspondence, especially in professional settings. Watch out for sarcasm and humor in e-mail; often, it fails to come across as a joke. Be mindful when you request a return receipt; some people consider this to be an invasion of privacy.

- **Internet Relay Chat (IRC).** Learn what commonly used IRC abbreviations such as BRB (Be Right Back) mean so that you don't pester others to explain them. In a new channel, listen to the discussion for a while so you can figure out how to join in meaningfully. Don't flood the channel with text so that others can't communicate, and lay off the colors, beeps, and scripts that interfere with the flow of dialogue. Don't harass other users with unwanted invitations. If somebody tells you to type in a command, don't do it—it may be a trick. Learn how to use the ignore command if someone is bothering you.

# Computer Ethics for Computer Professionals

Suppose you hire an engineer to build a bridge. Within months it collapses, injuring several people. It turns out that your so-called engineer never took any courses in bridge construction. And as you investigate further, you learn that the engineer received a 15 percent kickback from his recommended contractor who sold you substandard materials. For these reasons, you probably wouldn't have very much confidence in the next engineer you hire.

As this example suggests, no profession can stay in business for long without a rigorous (and enforced) code of professional ethics. That's why professional engineers subscribe to ethical **codes of conduct**. Many such codes exist; they're developed by professional associations, such as the Association for Computing Machinery (ACM). These codes expressly forbid actions such as those undertaken by this engineer. Figure 1F is an excerpt from the Code of Ethics of the Institute for Certification of Computing Professionals.

## SAFETY FIRST

Computer ethicists try to specify ethical codes for computer professionals. Most of these codes closely resemble engineering ethical codes, and for good reason. Like engineers, computer professionals create products that affect many people and may expose them to risk of personal injury or even death. Increasingly, computers and computer programs figure prominently in safety-critical systems,

## CODES OF CONDUCT AND GOOD PRACTICE FOR CERTIFIED COMPUTING PROFESSIONALS

The essential elements related to conduct that identify a professional activity are:

- *a high standard of skill and knowledge*

- *a confidential relationship with people served*

- *public reliance upon the standards of conduct in established practice*

- *the observance of an ethical code*

**Figure 1F**   *Excerpt from the Code of Ethics of the Institute for Certification of Computing Professionals*

including transportation monitoring (such as air-traffic control) and patient monitoring in hospitals and institutions.

At the core of every engineering or computer code of ethics, therefore, is a professional person's highest and indispensable aim: to preserve and protect human life and to avoid harm or injury. If we, the public, are to trust professional people, we must be able to believe that they have the ethics needed to protect our safety and welfare—even if doing so means the professional person suffers financially.

## ADDITIONAL ETHICAL RESPONSIBILITIES

Safety is important, but the public also has a right to expect additional ethical responsibilities in a professional person. Professionals in any branch of computing should have the following qualities:

- **Competence.** Professionals keep up with the latest knowledge in their fields by reading professional journals, attending conferences, and taking refresher courses as needed. In addition, professionals perform services only in their areas of competence. They make sure all their work meets the highest possible standards of quality.

- **Responsibility.** Professionals are loyal to their clients or employers. They don't disclose confidential information concerning a project, even if they leave a client or firm's employment. Professionals are also honest: if a project seems likely to fail, they say so. They turn down work if accepting it would place them in a conflict of interest.

- **Integrity.** Professionals express opinions only when they're based on fact. They are impartial in their judgment and don't change their judgment in response to external pressure.

## THE ACM CODE OF CONDUCT

Of all the computing associations' codes of conduct, the one developed by the Association for Computing Machinery (ACM) is considered the most innovative and far-reaching. According to the ACM code, a computing professional:

1. *contributes to society and human well-being*
2. *avoids harm to others*
3. *is honest and trustworthy*
4. *is fair and takes action not to discriminate on the basis of race, sex, religion, age, disability, or national origin*
5. *honors property rights, including copyrights and patents*
6. *gives proper credit when using the intellectual property of others*
7. *respects the right of other individuals to privacy*
8. *honors confidentiality*

Like previous engineering codes of conduct, the ACM code places public safety and well-being at the top of the list. Unlike previous codes, it adds a new and important dimension of professionalism: active intervention to prevent sexual, racial, and other forms of discrimination.

## PROGRAMMER LIABILITY

Even the most ethical programmer can produce a program with errors. Most complex programs have so many possible combinations of conditions that to test for every combination isn't feasible. In some cases, the tests would take years; in other cases, no one could think of a test for all the possibilities. All experienced programmers know that all programs of any size have bugs. But if the program results in injury or death, who's at fault?

Consider the following situation. An airplane flying in poor visibility uses a computer to guide the plane. The air-traffic control system is also computer-based. The plane crashes. The investigation discloses minor bugs in both computer programs. If the plane's computer had been dealing with a person in the tower rather than a computer, or if the air-traffic control program had been interacting with a human pilot, the crash would not have occurred. Where does the liability lie for the loss of life and property?

Because bugs are inevitable and programmers can't predict all the different ways programs interact with their environment, most computer experts believe that it's wrong to single out programmers for blame. Software companies are at fault, too, if they fail to test and document their products. And the organization that buys the software may share part of the blame if they fail to train personnel to use the system and understand its possible shortcomings.

Recognizing these facts, a new field called **software engineering** attempts to apply the principles of mainstream engineering to software production. Among other things, these principles call for an external, impartial review of a project at various stages before completion. Computer scientists are also working on **fault-tolerant systems**, which can keep working even if they encounter a glitch.

## COMPUTER ETHICS IN BUSINESS

To serve its clients effectively, a business or organization must protect its data from loss and damage, from misuse and error, and from unauthorized access.

**Figure 1G** *A backup system can help to protect the information assets of a business. It would be unethical to not keep regular backups because the loss of the company's data could negatively impact the stakeholders in the business.*

Protecting data from loss is often simply a matter of utilizing proper **backup procedures**. Backup procedures involve making copies of data files for protection against data loss. Without backup procedures, an organization may place its customers' information at risk (Figure 1G). What would happen to a bank, for example, if it lost all its data and didn't have backups?

In contrast, protecting data from misuse or error is often more difficult. Misuse can arise, for example, from not using the appropriate software or not using the software properly. Data that hasn't been properly maintained can have serious effects on the individual or organization it relates to. Errors in data can and do occur. It is the ethical responsibility of any organization dealing with data to ensure that its data is as correct as possible.

Another type of data misuse occurs when an employee or company fails to keep data confidential. A breach of confidentiality occurs when an employee looks up data about a person in a database and uses that information for something other than what was intended. For example, according to a recent press report, some IRS employees routinely looked up the tax returns of neighbors and celebrities. Thanks to public outcry, such actions are now grounds for termination.

Companies may punish employees for looking up customer data, but many of them think nothing of selling it to third parties. A mail-order company, for example, can gain needed revenue by selling customer lists to firms trying to market related products. Privacy advocates believe that it's unethical to divulge customer data without first asking the customer's permission.

## WHISTLE-BLOWING

What happens when a company's profit-seeking goals conflict with a computer professional's code of conduct? For example, the ACM Code of Ethics tells computing professionals to respect people's privacy. What if you're hired to write software that gathers information about customers without their knowledge?

People who have dealt with situations like this agree that none of the options are attractive. You can quit and look for another job. You can refuse to perform the requested task, but you'll probably be fired. Or, if the requested task poses a danger to the public or appears to be illegal, you can report the company's intentions to regulatory agencies or the press, an action called **whistle-blowing**. Although some laws exist that protect whistle-blowers, most wind up unemployed—and permanently blacklisted. And what if your whistle-blowing actions cause the government to shut down your company, harming not only you but all your coworkers as well? Often, there's no clear-cut solution.

## ETHICS IN YOUR FUTURE

As this discussion illustrates, codes of ethics don't solve every ethical problem. They provide guidance, but they can't save you from moral dilemmas. In the end, you must think through your dilemmas, weigh your options against ethical principles, and make your own decisions.

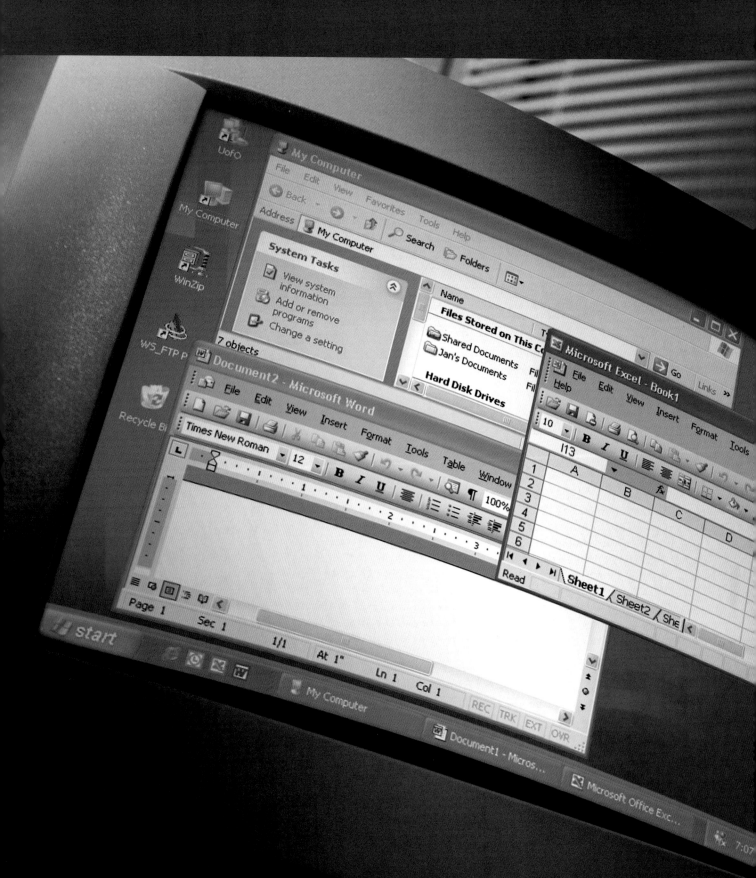

# System Software:
# The Operating Environment

## What You'll Learn . . .

- List the two major components of a computer's operating system software.

- Explain why a computer isn't useful without an operating system.

- List the five basic functions of an operating system.

- Explain what happens when you turn on a computer.

- List the three major types of user interfaces.

- Discuss the strengths and weaknesses of the most popular operating systems.

- List the seven system utilities that are considered essential.

- Discuss data backup procedures.

Without software—the set of instructions that tells the computer what to do—a computer is just an expensive collection of wires and components. Chances are you've already worked with one type of software: application software. Application software helps you accomplish a task, such as writing a college essay or balancing your checkbook. The other major type of software is system software. **System software** includes all the programs that are needed to enable a computer and its peripheral devices to function smoothly. Although some system software works "behind the scenes," or without a user's knowledge, some of it requires your guidance and control.

System software has two major components: (1) the operating system and (2) system utilities that provide various maintenance functions. Learning how to use an operating system and system utilities is the first step you need to take toward the mastery of any computer system. Mastering a computer system is not unlike understanding the fundamentals of any system. The more you know about managing the

water, filters, plants, and water temperature in your aquarium, the healthier and happier your fish tend to be. It's the same with computers; the more you know about and understand the operating system, the better your computer will serve you. In this chapter you'll learn what operating systems do, look at the most popular operating systems, and learn which utilities you should use to ensure that your computing experience is safe and enjoyable.

# The Operating System (OS): The Computer's Traffic Cop

The **operating system** (**OS**) is essentially a set of programs designed to work with a

**FIGURE 2.1** An operating system works at the intersection of application software, the user, and the computer's hardware. It starts the computer, manages programs, manages memory to applications, handles internal messages from input and output devices, and provides a means of communicating with the user.

operating system

specific type of hardware, such as a PC or a Macintosh. Its most important role lies in coordinating the various functions of the computer's hardware. The operating system also provides support for running application software. An operating system (OS) performs five basic functions. The operating system starts the computer, manages programs, manages memory, handles messages from input and output devices, and provides a means of communicating with the user (Figure 2.1). The operating system is most often found on a hard disk, although on some small handheld computers you'll find the operating system on a memory chip.

Imagine the traffic in a downtown New York City intersection at rush hour, and you'll have a good idea of what it's like inside a computer. Electrons are whizzing around at incredible speeds transported this way and that by the operating system (OS), the electronic equivalent of a harried traffic cop. Impatient peripherals and programs are honking electronic "horns," trying to get the cop's attention. As if the scene weren't chaotic enough, the "mayor" (the user) wants to come through right now. Keeping traffic running smoothly is the computer's operating system—just like a traffic cop, standing at the intersection of the computer's hardware, application programs, and the user.

Let's examine the five functions of an OS more closely.

## STARTING THE COMPUTER

When you start or restart a computer, it reloads the operating system into the computer's memory. This process is called **booting**, after the notion that the computer "pulls itself up by its bootstraps." In a **cold boot**, you start the computer after the power has been switched off. In a **warm boot** (also called a warm start), you restart a computer that is already on. Warm boots are often necessary after installing new software or after an application crashes or stops working. In PCs, you can initiate a warm boot by pressing Ctrl + Alt + Del (hold down the Ctrl and Alt keys, and press Del) or by pressing the Reset button that is usually located on the front of the system unit.

In both types of booting, the computer copies the kernel along with other essential portions of the operating system from the hard disk into the computer's memory, where it remains while your computer is powered on and functioning. The **kernel** is the central part of the operating system and starts applications, manages devices and memory, and performs other essential functions. The kernel is *memory resident*, which means it "resides" in memory at all times. Because the kernel takes up space in memory, it must be kept as small as possible. Less frequently used portions of the operating system, called nonresident, are stored on the hard disk and retrieved as needed.

A cold or warm boot is a step-by-step process. The following sections discuss the steps followed by the computer after you initiate a cold or warm boot.

### Step 1: The BIOS (Basic Input/Output System) and Setup Program

When you first turn on or reset a PC, electricity flows from the power supply through the CPU, which resets and searches for the BIOS. The **BIOS (basic input/output system)** is the part of the system software that equips the computer with the instructions needed to accept keyboard input and display information on-screen. The BIOS is encoded, or permanently written, in the computer's ROM. ROM, or read-only memory, is a kind of memory that is permanent and unchanging. Programs such as the BIOS that are encoded in ROM are meant to be reliably used over and over again. Once the BIOS is located, you may briefly see the BIOS screen, a text-only screen that provides information about the BIOS.

While the BIOS information is visible, you can access the computer's setup program by pressing a special key, such as Del or F8. (You'll see an on-screen message indicating which key to press to access the setup program.) The **setup program** includes many settings that control the computer's hardware. You should *not* alter or change *any* of these settings unless you are instructed to do so by technical support personnel. We'll look more closely at the setup program in the "Loading the Operating System" section.

### Step 2: The Power-On Self-Test (POST)

After the BIOS instructions are loaded into memory, a series of tests are conducted to make sure that the computer and associated peripherals are operating correctly. Collectively, these tests are known as the **power-on self-test** (**POST**). Among the components tested are the computer's main memory (random access memory, or RAM), the keyboard and mouse, disk drives, and the hard disk. If the computer encounters an error, you'll hear a beep and see an on-screen error message. Often, you can correct such problems by making sure components such as keyboards are plugged in securely.

Should any of the power-on self-tests fail, you may see an error message, and the computer will stop. Some failures are so serious that the computer cannot display a message; instead, it sounds a certain number of beeps. To help the technician repair the computer, write down any messages you see and try to remember how many beeps you heard.

### Step 3: Loading the Operating System

Once the power-on self-test is successfully completed, the BIOS initiates a search for the operating system. Options (or settings) in the setup program determine where BIOS looks for the operating system. (These settings are set by default but can be modified by the user.) The settings are stored in a type of nonvolatile memory called **CMOS** (**complementary metal-oxide semiconductor**). CMOS is a special type of memory used to store essential startup configuration options, such as the amount of memory that has been installed in the computer.

On most PCs, BIOS first looks for the operating system on the computer's hard disk. When BIOS finds the operating system, it loads the operating system's kernel into the computer's memory. (To **load** a program means to transfer it from a storage device like the hard disk to memory.) At this point, the operating system takes control of the computer and begins loading system configuration information.

### Step 4: System Configuration

In Microsoft Windows, configuration information about installed peripherals and software is stored in a database called the **registry**. The registry also contains information about your system configuration choices, such as background graphics and mouse settings.

Once the operating system's kernel has been loaded, it checks the system's configuration to determine which drivers and other utility programs are needed. A **driver** is a utility program that is needed to make a peripheral device function correctly. If a peripheral device that is already installed on the system requires a driver to operate, that peripheral's driver will be installed and loaded automatically. If not, you may be prompted to insert a disk containing the needed driver.

Operating systems are equipped with Plug and Play (PnP) capabilities, which automatically detect new PnP-compatible peripherals that you may have installed while the power was switched off, load the necessary drivers, and check for conflicts with other devices. Peripheral devices equipped with PnP features identify themselves to the operating system.

### Step 5: Loading System Utilities

Once the operating system has detected and configured all of the system's hardware, it loads system utilities such as speaker volume control, antivirus software, and a PC card unplugging utility. In Microsoft Windows, you can view any available custom configuration choices by right-clicking one of the small icons located on the right side of the Windows taskbar. You can access additional system configuration choices in the Control Panel (Figure 2.2).

### Step 6: Authenticating Users

When the operating system finishes loading, you may see a dialog box asking you to type a user name and password. This process is called **authentication** (or **login**). In authentication, you verify that you are indeed the person who is authorized to use the computer.

Consumer-oriented operating systems such as Microsoft Windows and Mac OS do not demand that you supply a user name and password to use the computer. However, you can set up profiles on these systems. Associated with a user name and, optionally, a password, a **profile** is a record of a specific user's preferences for

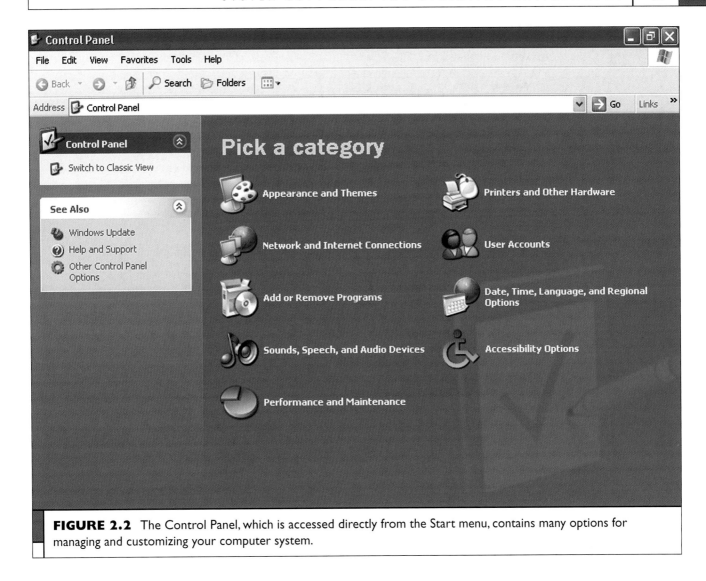

**FIGURE 2.2**  The Control Panel, which is accessed directly from the Start menu, contains many options for managing and customizing your computer system.

the desktop theme, icons, and menu styles. If you set up a profile for yourself, you'll see your preferences on-screen after you log in. You can also allow other users to create and log on to their profiles, and they'll see their preferences without disturbing yours.

On multiuser computer systems, you must have an account on the computer. Your **account** consists of your user name, your password, and your storage space, called a home directory. The account is usually created by the computer's system administrator, the person who's responsible for managing the use of the computer in multiuser systems. To access your account, you must supply your user name and password.

Now that the OS is loaded and running, let's look at another important task that the OS handles: managing programs.

## MANAGING PROGRAMS

An important operating system function—and the one that most dramatically affects an operating system's overall quality—is the way it runs and manages programs. In the early days of personal computing, **single-tasking operating systems** could run only one application program at a time. This was often inconvenient. In order to switch between programs you had to quit one program before you could start the second one.

Today, many users work with five or more applications simultaneously. **Multitasking operating systems** enable a user to work with two or more programs at the same time. In multitasking operating systems, the computer doesn't actually run two programs at once; rather, it switches between them as needed. From

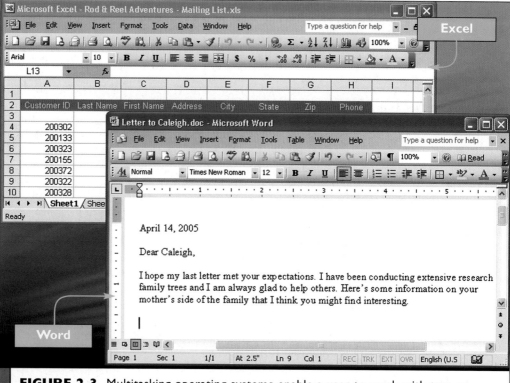

**FIGURE 2.3** Multitasking operating systems enable a user to work with two or more programs at once. Here the user is switching between Word and Excel. The Word application is the foreground application—as indicated by the darkened blue title bar at the top of its window. The Excel application is the background application—as indicated by its grayed out title bar.

the user's perspective, one application (called the **foreground application**) is active, while another (the **background application**) is inactive (Figure 2.3). Multitasking operating systems are now the norm.

A clear measure of the stability of an operating system is the technique it uses to handle multitasking. If one of the running programs invades another's memory space, one or both of the programs will become unstable or, at the extreme, **crash** (stop working).

A better and more recent type of multitasking, called **preemptive multitasking**, enables the operating system to regain control if an application stops running. You may lose any unsaved work in the application that crashed, but the failure of one application does not bring the whole system down. Personal computer operating systems that use preemptive multitasking include Linux, recent versions of Mac OS, and all current versions of Microsoft Windows.

Now that you have an overview of how the operating system manages programs, let's take a look at how it manages its primary storage function: memory.

## MANAGING MEMORY

If the operating system had to constantly access program instructions from their storage location on your computer's hard disk, programs would run very slowly. There needs to be a buffer of some kind that can help make the processing of instructions more fluid. Computers use a temporary storage medium, called **memory**, to function as this buffer. Memory is managed by the computer's operating system. For example, the operating system gives each running program its own portion of memory, and attempts to keep the programs from interfering with each other's use of memory.

Most of today's operating systems can make the computer's main memory

(RAM) seem larger than it really is. This trick is accomplished by means of **virtual memory**, a method of using the computer's hard disk as an extension of RAM. In virtual memory, program instructions and data are divided into units of fixed size, called **pages**. If memory is full, the operating system starts storing copies of pages in a hard disk file, called the **swap file**. When the pages are needed, they are copied back into memory (Figure 2.4). The transferring of files from storage to memory and back is called **paging**.

Although virtual memory enables users to work with more memory than the amount installed on the computer's motherboard (main circuit board), paging slows the computer down. Disks are much slower than RAM. For this reason, adding more RAM to your computer is often the best way to improve its performance. With sufficient RAM, the operating system makes minimal use of virtual memory.

Once the computer's operating system is up and running and managing programs and memory, it needs to be able to accept data and commands—and to represent the results of processing operations.

## HANDLING INPUT AND OUTPUT

How does your computer "know" that you want to get it to do something? How does it show you the results of its work? The operating system handles these functions, input and output, as well as enabling communication with input and output devices.

Most operating systems come with drivers for popular input and output devices. Drivers are programs that contain specific information about a particular brand and model of input or output device. They enable communication between the operating system and the input and output components of a computer system. Printers, scanners, monitors, speakers, and the mouse all have driver programs. Drivers that are not included with the operating system software are supplied by the device manufacturers themselves, and are often available on their corporate Web sites. You might need to obtain drivers for any device that was manufactured after your operating system was released. For example, there is no way the operating system can contain the appropriate driver for a printer that

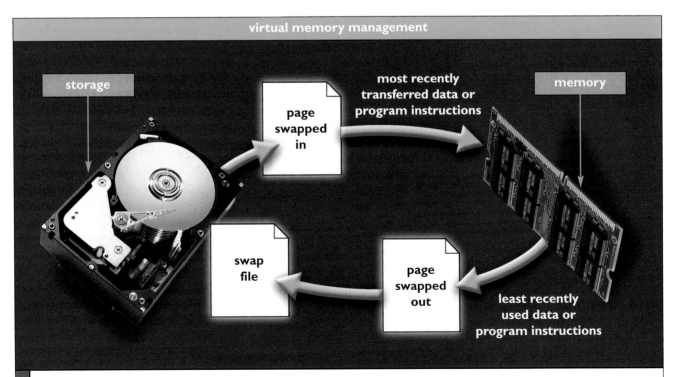

**FIGURE 2.4** In virtual memory, program instructions and data are divided into units of fixed size, called pages. If virtual memory is full, the operating system starts storing copies of pages in a hard disk file called the swap file. When the pages are needed, they're copied back into memory.

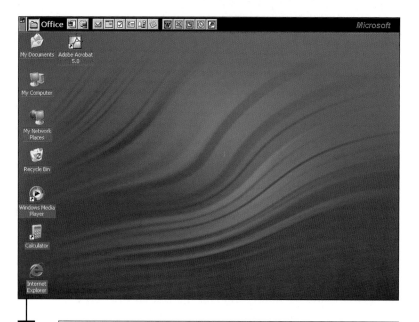

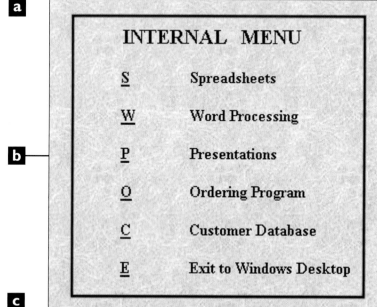

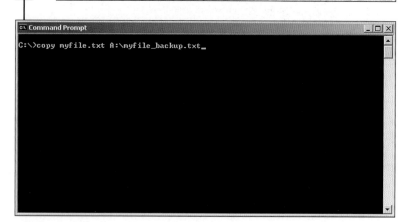

**FIGURE 2.5** Examples of (**a**) graphical, (**b**) menu-driven, and (**c**) command-line user interfaces.

wasn't on the market when the operating system was being created.

Input and output devices generate **interrupts**, signals that inform the operating system that something has happened (for example, the user has pressed a key, the mouse has moved to a new position, or a document has finished printing). The operating system provides **interrupt handlers**, miniprograms that kick in immediately when an interrupt occurs.

Communication between input or output devices and the computer's CPU is handled by **interrupt request (IRQ)** lines. Most PCs have a fixed number (16) of IRQs, numbered 0 through 15. If two devices are configured to use the same IRQ but aren't designed to share an IRQ line, the result is a serious system failure called an **IRQ conflict**. In most cases, an IRQ conflict makes the system so unstable that it cannot function. To remedy an IRQ conflict, you may need to shut down the computer and remove peripheral devices, one by one, until you determine which one is causing the conflict. Happily, Plug and Play–compatible operating systems and peripherals have made IRQ conflicts much less common. Still, this is a phenomenon worth mentioning because it helps in your ability to solve the problems you encounter when using a computer.

Now it is time to explore the different interfaces that are used to provide interaction with you, the user.

## PROVIDING THE USER INTERFACE

From the user's perspective, the most important piece that an operating system provides is the **user interface**, the part of the operating system that you see and interact with and by which users and programs communicate with each other.

### User Interface Functions
User interfaces typically enable you to do the following:

- Start (launch) application programs.

- Manage disks and files. You can format new disks, copy files from one disk to another, rename files, and delete files.

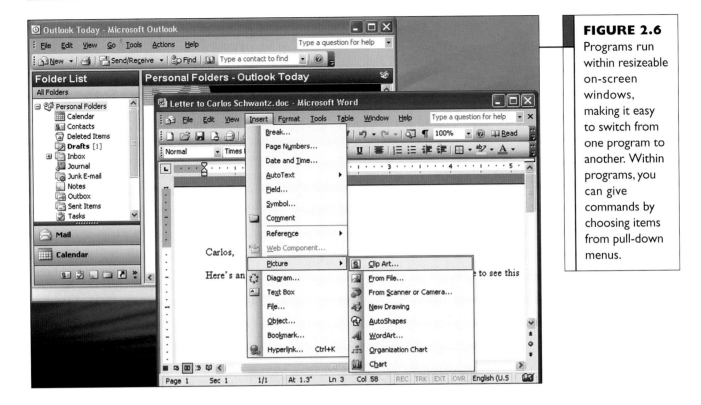

**FIGURE 2.6**
Programs run within resizeable on-screen windows, making it easy to switch from one program to another. Within programs, you can give commands by choosing items from pull-down menus.

- Shut down the computer safely by following an orderly shutdown procedure. (You shouldn't just switch the computer off; doing so may leave scrambled data on the computer's hard disk.)

### Types of User Interfaces

The three types of user interfaces are graphical, menu-driven, and command-line (Figure 2.5).

By far the most popular user interface, a **graphical user interface** (**GUI**, pronounced "gooey"), is a program interface that takes advantage of the computer's graphics capabilities to make the program easier to use. On today's PCs and Macintoshes, GUIs are used to create the **desktop environment**, which appears after the operating system finishes loading into memory. In a desktop environment, computer resources (such as programs, data files, and network connections) are represented by small pictures, called **icons**. You can initiate many actions by clicking an icon. Programs run within resizeable on-screen windows, making it easy to switch from one program to another (Figure 2.6). Within programs, you can give commands by choosing items from pull-down menus, some of which display dialog boxes. In a **dialog box**, you can

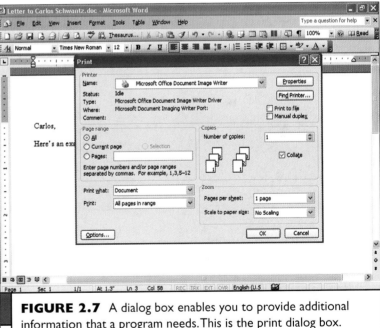

**FIGURE 2.7** A dialog box enables you to provide additional information that a program needs. This is the print dialog box.

supply additional information that the program needs (Figure 2.7). Although GUIs are easy to use, they make heavy demands on a computer's processing circuitry and can slow the computer down considerably.

**Menu-driven user interfaces** enable you to avoid memorizing keywords and syntax. On-screen, text-based menus show

**CURRENTS**

**Debates**

# Platform Passion: Macs versus PCs

As you almost certainly know, as a computer user, you have two major platforms to choose from: Macintosh and PC. The debate over which platform is best has raged on for years, and if market power is anything, PCs are winning by a landslide. But Apple hangs in there with its slew of adherents who choose to "think different." What's the difference between the platforms? Although you'd never know from listening to people who love or hate Macs, there's not much difference, really. At least not in terms of power capacity. Still, the debate goes on.

On the one side, Mac lovers say their machines are easier to set up and use. Macs come with everything you need built right in—all you have to do is plug them in and you're on your way. Mac lovers also point to the fact that Apple has developed some incredibly advanced technology. (Even PC users will agree to that.) Apple offers its users cutting-edge, easy-to-use applications such as iMovie, iTunes, iPhoto, and iDVD. And Mac's FireWire technology has spread to PCs: first it was available as an option and now it may be becoming a standard.

It's not just the system and the software Mac users love. Most Macophiles love their one-button mice as well as their many shortcut keys. Not to mention the Apple design; many Mac adherents love the look of the Mac above all else. Today, you'll find Macs being used in most primary and elementary schools in the United States. (OS X is virtually crash-proof!) In addition, certain professions, such as publishing, advertising, and design, rely almost exclusively on Macs.

On the other hand, PCs still dominate, and the race isn't even close. PCs claim the largest chunk of the marketplace and are the choice of corporate America. And thanks to economies of scale, they also tend to be cheaper, in terms of both their hardware and software. Indeed, software is a big plus for PC users, who have far more to choose from than their Mac counterparts. Because so many more people buy the software, it tends to be better, and it is often developed and published more quickly than similar software for Macs. And as much as Mac lovers claim the one-button mouse is the way to go, PC users love their two-button mouse, which offers more choices in hand.

And as for design? Step aside, Mac. Make way for new PCs on the market. In the fall of 2002, Gateway introduced its new all-in-one computer that hopes to steal market share from Apple's iMac G4 (Figure 2.8). In recent years, Apple has tried to woo PC users by playing on the idea that Macs are easier to use. Meanwhile, Mac's OS X could improve the number of software products developed for Macs, and that includes games, one reason PCs lead in the marketplace. However, as Apple moves into the PC market with its recent UNIX innovations, it may make itself more vulnerable to the viruses that have been mostly a PC headache in the past. In any case, Macs have a long way to go to catch up to PCs—and few users from either camp see that happening any time soon.

a b

**FIGURE 2.8 Gateway claims its all-in-one computer (a) is better and cheaper than its Mac counterpart (b).**

all the options available at a given point. With most systems, you select an option with the arrow keys, and then press Enter. Some systems enable you to click the desired option with the mouse or to choose a letter with the keyboard.

**Command-line user interfaces** require you to type commands using keywords that tell the operating system what to do (such as "format" or "copy") one line at a time. You must observe complicated rules of syntax that specify exactly what you can type in a given place. For example, the following command

```
copy a:myfile.txt c:myfile.txt
```

copies a file from the disk in drive A to the disk in drive C, not the other way around.

Command-line operating systems aren't popular with most users because they require memorization, and it's easy to make a typing mistake. While the commands are usually very simple, such as *copy* and *paste*, some are more cryptic, such as *dir* to view the directory structure, and *md* to make a new directory. Some experienced users actually prefer command-line operating systems, however, because you can operate the computer quickly after you've memorized the keywords and syntax.

Now that you've seen how the operating system makes itself available to you, let's explore the most popular operating systems in depth.

# Exploring Popular Operating Systems: A Guided Tour

All of today's popular operating systems are strongly influenced by two very different predecessors: UNIX, and the first GUI-based operating system developed at Xerox's Palo Alto Research Center (PARC). In various ways, current operating systems represent numerous successful attempts to pull together the ideas pioneered in these systems.

We will begin our tour with Microsoft Windows, and will then look at the Macintosh operating system, DOS, UNIX, and Linux. While it is true that your choice of which operating system to use is very limited, it is important for you to know how the various systems have evolved over time, and what their strengths and weaknesses are.

## MICROSOFT WINDOWS

**Microsoft Windows** is by far the most popular operating system. Over the years, it has gone through many iterations (Figure 2.9), and it is now considered *the* operating system of PCs worldwide. When you purchase a computer it comes with an operating system installed. Microsoft makes agreements with the major computer manufacturers to provide Windows on almost all of the personal computers that are made today. Some manufacturers offer a choice of operating system, but the Windows operating environment is and will remain the standard for years to come.

Let's start by looking at the most recent version, Windows XP, and then we'll look at the other operating systems you might encounter on today's personal and corporate computers.

**FIGURE 2.9** Windows Time Line

| Year Released | Version |
|---|---|
| 2001 | Windows XP |
| 2000 | Windows 2000/ME |
| 1998 | Windows 98 |
| 1995 | Windows 95 |
| 1993 | Windows NT |
| 1992 | Windows 3.1 |
| 1990 | Windows 3.0 |
| 1987 | Windows 2.0 |
| 1985 | Windows 1.0 |

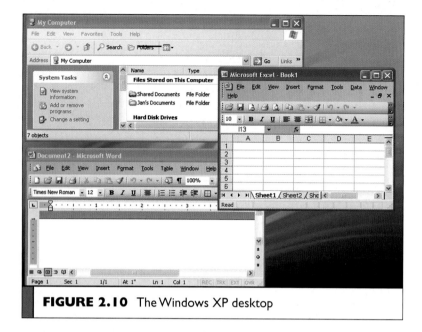

**FIGURE 2.10** The Windows XP desktop

## Destinations

Explore the features of Microsoft's latest Windows offerings at the Windows home page at **www.microsoft .com/windows/ default.mspx**.

For the latest news and developments in Linux, visit "Linux Today" at **linuxtoday.com**. Linux beginners can get assistance at Linuxnewbie.org at **www.linuxnewbie .org** and at Linux Start at **www.linuxstart .com**.

### Microsoft Windows XP

Released in the fall of 2001, **Microsoft Windows XP** (Figure 2.10) is the first Microsoft operating system family that uses the same underlying code for all three versions (consumer, corporate desktop, and server). XP is short for "experience," reflecting Microsoft's view that users want computers with rich audio and visual features. Microsoft Windows XP Home Edition, an improved version of Windows 2000 Professional that is designed for home users, replaces all previous versions of Windows designed for home users. Microsoft Windows XP Professional and Microsoft Windows XP Server are updated versions of the Windows 2000 Professional and Server products, respectively. XP Professional is designed for desktop computer users in networked corporate settings, while XP Server is designed to make information and services available on corporate computer networks.

### Microsoft Windows NT

To go head-to-head with the powerful UNIX client/server systems that once dominated corporate computing, Microsoft developed **Microsoft Windows NT**. Unlike Windows 95 and Windows 98, Windows NT is specifically designed for client/server systems. To support client/server computing, Windows NT is made up of two components: Windows NT Workstation and Windows NT Server.

Windows NT is a sophisticated operating system oriented to business needs. The Windows NT Workstation module is designed for individual desktop computers. On-screen, it looks like Windows 95, but it isn't as easy to use. The real benefits of Windows NT Workstation emerge in a networked corporate environment, where NT desktops link to servers running Windows NT Server.

In a corporate network, Windows NT Server provides the following benefits:

**Security**  Controls individual workstation access to networked resources, such as a database containing sensitive financial information.

**Remote Administration**  Enables the network administrator to set options remotely for each user's computer, such as specifying which applications the user can start.

**Directory Services**  Provides a "map" to all the files and applications available on the network.

**Web Server**  Makes Web pages available to internal intranet users or the external World Wide Web.

### Microsoft Windows CE

Designed for hot-selling PDAs, **Microsoft Windows CE** is a "light" version of Windows. Windows CE is designed to run simplified versions of Windows programs, such as Microsoft's own Office applications, which are available in "pocket" versions for Windows CE. This enables users to create documents on a PDA and transfer them to a desktop computer for further processing and printing.

For mobile computing, Windows CE includes an interactive scheduling calendar, an address book for contacts, e-mail, and Web browsing. Users can quickly synchronize the corresponding utilities on their desktop computers. CE includes handwriting recognition and support for voice recording as well (Figure 2.11).

## MAC OS

**Mac OS** introduced the graphical user interface to the world. The original Macintosh operating system was released in 1984. It

**FIGURE 2.11** Windows CE brings Windows and Office functionality to the PDA.

consisted of the operating system (called the System) and a separate shell (called the Finder). By the late 1980s, the Mac's operating system was the most technologically advanced in personal computing, but Apple Computer was unable to capitalize on its lead, and Mac OS (as it came to be called after System 7.5) lost market share to Microsoft Windows. Still, Mac OS is widely considered to be the easiest operating system for beginning computer users. In 1998, Apple was reinvigorated by the return of founder Steve Jobs. A new version of the operating system, called Mac OS X, was released in 2000 and brought Mac OS up to the technical standards of Microsoft Windows (Figure 2.12).

that continues to define what an operating system should do and how it should work. UNIX (pronounced "you-nix") was the first operating system with preemptive multitasking, and it was designed to work efficiently in a secure, centrally administered computer network. Other important UNIX innovations include the concepts of file directories and path names.

If UNIX is so great, why didn't it take over the computer world? One reason is the lack of compatibility among the many different versions of UNIX. Another reason is that it's difficult to use. UNIX, like DOS, defaults to a command-line user interface, which is challenging for new computer users. In the past few years, a number of

## MS-DOS

**MS-DOS** (or DOS, which is short for Disk Operating System) is an operating system for Intel-based PCs that uses a command-line user interface. Developed by Bill Gates's and Paul Allen's fledgling Microsoft Corporation for the original IBM PC in 1981, MS-DOS was marketed by IBM in a virtually identical version, called PC-DOS. The command-line interface is difficult to learn, and the syntax and commands are not easy for the casual user to remember. It is unlikely that you will ever encounter a command-line interface on a modern personal computer.

## UNIX

Developed at AT&T's Bell Laboratories, **UNIX** is a pioneering operating system

**FIGURE 2.12** Released in 2000, Mac OS X brought Mac OS up to the technical standards of Microsoft Windows.

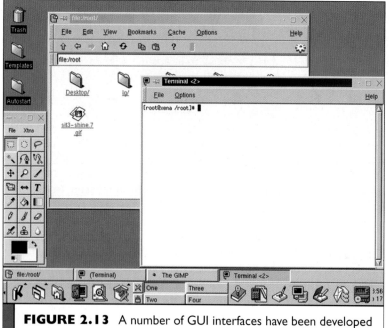

**FIGURE 2.13** A number of GUI interfaces have been developed for UNIX in the past few years, improving the usability of this operating system.

**techtv**

To learn more about the powerful but virtually unheard of alternative operating system FreeBSD, see the video clip at **www.prenhall.com/cayf2005**.

GUI interfaces have been developed for UNIX, improving its usability (Figure 2.13).

## LINUX

A new "flavor" of UNIX, called **Linux** (pronounced "linn-ux"), is the fastest-growing new operating system for Intel-based personal computers. (Versions of Linux have also been created for other PCs, including Macintoshes.) Linux is **open-source software**, meaning its

source code (the code of the program itself) is available for all to see and use. What makes Linux so attractive? Two things: it's powerful and it's free. Linux brings all the maturity and sophistication of UNIX to the PC. Linux includes all the respected features of UNIX, including multitasking, virtual memory, Internet support, and a graphical user interface. Created in 1991 by a Finnish university student named Linus Torvalds, Linux has since been developed by thousands of the world's best programmers, who have willingly donated their time to make sure that Linux is a very good version of UNIX. According to Linux backers, they may have created the best version of UNIX in existence. According to one estimate, more than 257 million systems are running Linux (Figure 2.14).

Although Linux is powerful and free, many corporate chief information officers (CIOs) shy away from adopting Linux precisely because it isn't a commercial product with a stable company behind it. Also, Linux can't run the popular Microsoft Office applications, which most corporate users prefer. But Linux is gaining acceptance.

The beauty of Linux, and its development model, is that it doesn't run on any particular type of computer: it runs on them all. Linux has been translated to run on systems as small as PDAs and as large as homegrown supercomputers.

All of the operating systems just discussed work in tandem with helper programs, called utilities, to keep the computer system running smoothly.

**FIGURE 2.14** Linux may soon be appearing on a computer near you.

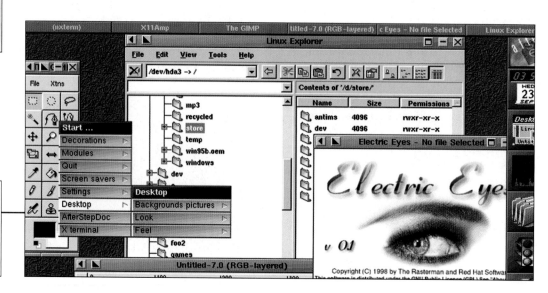

**IMPACTS**

**Milestones**

# Could the Future Be Nothing But Net?

Standardized protocols and a universal common denominator are the hallmarks of the Information Age. Cyberspace transactions must share a common set of rules or there would be constant electronic chaos; and computing systems with differing operating systems and software must be able to share documents and data with each other, or there would be no value derived from using cyberspace. The following three profiles—of Marc Andreessen, Linus Torvalds, and Bill Gates— will help you to see what lies ahead in the Information Age (Figure 2.15).

While an undergraduate at the University of Illinois in 1992, Marc Andreessen led a group of students to create Mosaic, the first graphical-interface Web browser. Mosaic was a point-and-click, user-friendly technology that became instantly popular; however, it was the school's property. Subsequently, Andreessen and others formed the Netscape Communications Corporation and created a new browser called Mozilla, which became Netscape Navigator. Within a year and a half of its introduction, Netscape became the most rapidly assimilated product in history, with 65 million users. Andreessen's vision is the cornerstone of the popularity and usability of the Web, and represents the first piece of our Information Age triad: universal interface.

Around the same time that Andreessen was creating his browser, Finnish university student Linus Torvalds was working on a new operating system that he hoped would offer users a free alternative to UNIX. The story of Linux begins with Torvalds' being unable to afford to run UNIX on his home computer—starting prices for UNIX were $5,000, and it required a $10,000

workstation. So Torvalds decided to write his own version from scratch—something quite revolutionary. Operating systems are typically created by large teams of software engineers working for large corporations. That concept was turned upside down in 1991 when Torvalds introduced Linux, his freeware operating system, to the world.

Torvalds posted his fledgling operating system, named Linux version .02, on an Internet newsgroup and invited people to download it and make it better. Many people who downloaded Linux made modifications to the program. The community approach to Linux has made it a marvel of the computer world and has made Torvalds a folk legend. So, an open-source, universally available operating system is the second piece of our puzzle.

The story of Bill Gates and Microsoft is pretty well known. What you might not know is that on February 14, 2002, Bill Gates officially unveiled Microsoft's vision for the future: the .NET strategy, which is a comprehensive package of development tools aimed at facilitating the seamless sharing of documents and data across cyberspace. If Gates's vision comes to fruition, our third piece will be complete: any computer (using any operating system and software) will be able to share documents and data (in their native format) across cyberspace.

While Andreessen, Torvalds, and Gates could be looked at as professional adversaries, together they have thrown open the doors of computers and the Internet to everyday users. Their extraordinary Web browser, operating system, and software have become daily tools for millions—even billions—of ordinary people around the world. The future of the Information Age will be interesting!

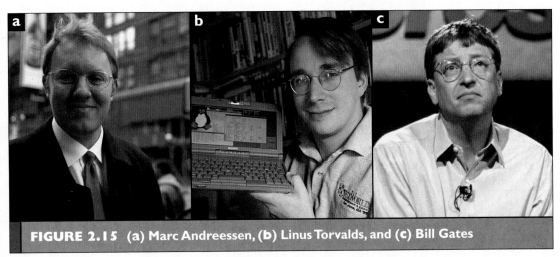

**FIGURE 2.15** (a) Marc Andreessen, (b) Linus Torvalds, and (c) Bill Gates

# System Utilities: Tools for Housekeeping

Providing a necessary addition to an operating system, **system utilities** (also called **utility programs**) are used to keep the computer system running smoothly. Sometimes these programs are included in the operating system, and sometimes they're provided by software vendors. The following sections discuss the utilities that are considered essential to the effective management of a computer system. System utility programs do things such as perform backups of system and application files, provide antivirus protection, scan and defragment disks and files, search for and manage files, and compress files so that they take up less space. We'll progress through the utility programs and then end with a short section on troubleshooting.

## BACKUP SOFTWARE

**Backup software** is an essential part of safe, efficient computer usage. It copies data from the computer's hard disk to backup devices, such as tape cartridges or a Zip drive. Should the hard disk fail, you can recover the data from the backup disk (Figure 2.16).

A backup begins with a **full backup**, in which a "mirror image" is made of the entire hard disk's contents. Subsequently, the software performs an incremental backup at specified intervals (such as once per day). In an **incremental backup**, the backup software copies only those files that have been created or changed since the last backup occurred. In this way, the backup disks always contain an up-to-date copy of all programs and data. In the event of a hard disk or computer system failure, the backup disk can be used to restore the data by copying it from the disk to a new hard disk.

Even if you don't have backup software, you can still make backup copies of your important files: just copy them to a disk. When you finish working on an assignment,

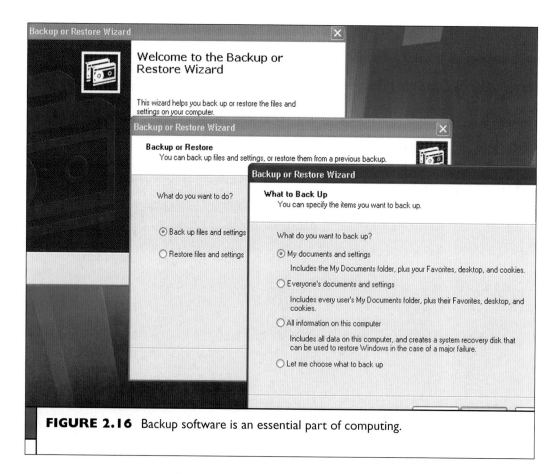

**FIGURE 2.16** Backup software is an essential part of computing.

always copy the data to a disk, and put the disk away for safekeeping. Don't ever rely on a hard disk to keep the only copies of your work.

## ANTIVIRUS SOFTWARE

**Antivirus software** protects a computer from computer viruses (Figure 2.17). This software works by examining all the files on a disk, looking for the telltale "signatures" of virus code. One limitation of such programs is that they can detect only those viruses whose "signatures" are in their databases. Most antivirus programs enable you to download the signatures of new viruses from a Web site. New viruses, however, appear every day. If your system becomes infected by a virus that's not in the system's database, it may not be detected. Due to this shortcoming, many antivirus programs also include monitoring programs that can detect and stop the destructive operations of unknown viruses.

Viruses are insidious and spread like wildfire. Consider the following scenario.

You're in a large lecture section of 100 students. Your teacher is very knowledgeable and you trust e-mail content that you receive from him or her. A former student of your professor receives an e-mail from a friend, opens it, and finds an attachment with an alluring filename, such as "Spring Break." The former student opens the attachment and notices that nothing seems to happen. Thinking nothing of it, the student goes about her Web browsing and homework assignments. The attachment, however, *is* doing something. It is sending a copy of itself to everyone in the student's e-mail address box—including your professor.

Your professor opens the mail from the former student and is pleased to find an attachment that apparently contains a picture of the student's spring break and so opens it. The attachment appears to do nothing, and the professor goes about his or her business. Now, for the interesting part: Each of the 100 students in the class receives an e-mail from the professor. Each has no idea that the attachment is a virus, and most open it. Now the attachment is propagating to the e-mail address lists of

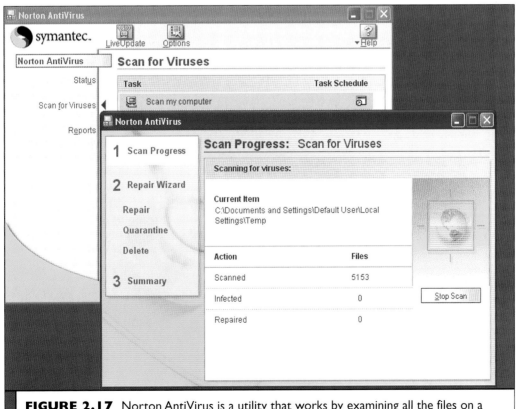

**FIGURE 2.17** Norton AntiVirus is a utility that works by examining all the files on a disk, looking for the telltale "signatures" of virus code.

each of the students. The attachment is received by parents, friends, professors, and fellow students. Many open the attachment, and the process accelerates very rapidly.

Some viruses do their damage immediately, while others hide themselves on your hard disk and then wait for a trigger time to do their work. Regardless, viruses spread quickly and can affect thousands, even millions, of users in a short period of time. This is why it is important that you install and use antivirus software. It only takes one nasty virus to cause you a lot of grief.

## FILE MANAGERS

Another important system utility is the **file manager** (My Computer in Windows), a utility program that enables you to deal with the data stored on your disk (Figure 2.18). The file manager enables you to perform various operations on the files and folders created on your computer's storage devices. You use file managers to make copies of your files, to manage how and where they are stored, and to delete unwanted files. File management is covered in depth in the Spotlight that follows Chapter 5.

## SEARCHING

On a large hard disk with thousands of files, the task of finding a needed file can be time-consuming and frustrating if attempted manually. For this reason, most operating systems include a **search utility**, which enables you to search an entire hard disk for a file. In Microsoft Windows, Search enables you to search for files in a number of ways, including by name, date, and size (Figure 2.19). A similar Mac OS utility, called Find File, offers the same features.

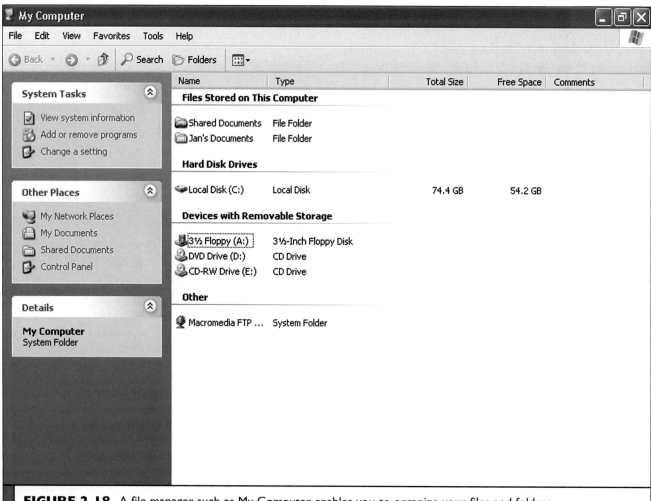

**FIGURE 2.18** A file manager such as My Computer enables you to organize your files and folders.

## FILE COMPRESSION UTILITIES

To exchange programs and data efficiently, particularly by means of the Internet, **file compression utilities** (Figure 2.20) can reduce the size of a file by as much as 80 percent without harming the data. Most file compression utilities work by searching the file for frequently repeated but lengthy data patterns and substituting short codes for these patterns. When the file is decompressed, the utility restores the lengthier pattern where each code is encountered. Popular compression utilities include WinZip for the PC and StuffIt for Macintosh systems.

Most compression utilities can also create archives. An **archive** is a single file that contains two or more files, stored in a special format. Archives are handy for storage as well as file exchange purposes because as many as several hundred separate files can be stored in a single, easily handled unit. WinZip combines compression and archiving functions.

## DISK SCANNING PROGRAMS

A **disk scanning program** or disk scanner can detect and resolve a number of physical and logical problems that occur as your computer stores files on a disk. A physical problem involves an irregularity in the drive's surface, which results in a **bad sector** (a portion of the disk that is unable to store data reliably). The scanner can fix the problem by locking out the bad sector so that it's no longer used. Logical problems are usually caused by a power outage that occurs before the computer is able to finish writing data to the disk. **Disk cleanup utilities** can save disk space by removing files that you no longer need.

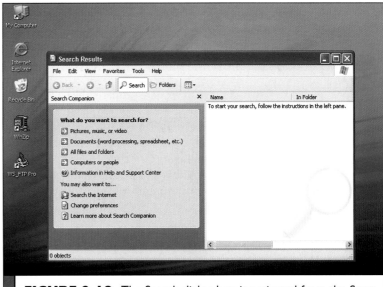

**FIGURE 2.19** The Search dialog box is activated from the Start menu. This tool can help you locate your work in many different ways.

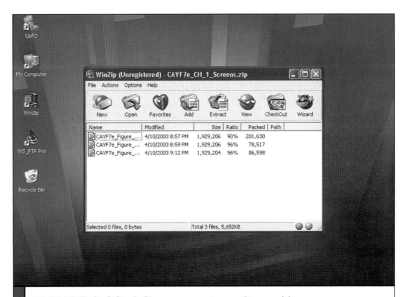

**FIGURE 2.20** A file compression utility enables you to create archives and compressed files.

## DISK DEFRAGMENTATION PROGRAMS

As you use a computer, it creates and erases files on the hard disk. The result is that the disk soon becomes a patchwork of files, with portions of files scattered here and there. This slows disk access because the system must look in several locations to find all of a file's segments. A disk with data scattered around in this way is referred to as fragmented. A fragmented disk isn't dangerous—the location of all the data is known, thanks to the operating system's tracking mechanisms—but periodic maintenance is required to restore the disk's performance. **Disk defragmentation programs** are used to reorganize the data on the disk so that it is stored in adjoining sectors (Figure 2.21).

Besides system utilities, there are additional ways to safeguard your data or take care of operating problems.

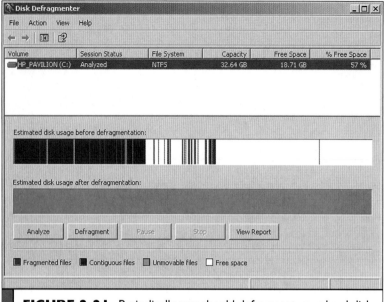

**FIGURE 2.21** Periodically, you should defragment your hard disk to ensure top performance. In Windows XP the defragmentation utility is found using this menu sequence: Start, All Programs, Accessories, System Tools, Disk Defragmenter.

## TROUBLESHOOTING

Almost every user of a computer system experiences trouble from time to time. Whether the trouble stems from starting the computer or running programs or adding hardware or software, users need troubleshooting tips to get them through a crisis.

If your computer fails to start normally, you may be able to get it running by using a **boot disk** (also called an **emergency disk**) in the floppy disk drive. The emergency disk loads a reduced version of the operating system that can be used for troubleshooting purposes. An emergency disk sometimes comes with a new computer but oftentimes is something that you need to create yourself. Consult the documentation that came with your computer, or choose Help from the My Computer program to learn about this process.

In Microsoft Windows, configuration problems that can occur after adding a new peripheral device such as a Zip drive to your system can often be resolved by starting the computer in Windows' **safe mode**, an operating mode in which Windows loads a minimal set of drivers that are known to function correctly. Within safe mode, you can use the Control Panel to determine which devices are causing the problem. You access safe mode by pressing the F8 key repeatedly during the initial start-up process. It is often the case that you can start the computer in safe mode, which will reset or report any conflicting programs or device drivers, and then simply shut it down and let it boot up normally.

System slowdown can sometimes occur. There are many things that can cause this problem, but usually it stems from the fact that you have changed a piece of hardware or software. Or there might be a gradual change overall in your system that degrades performance. A variety of situations can cause changes in system performance. Here are some things to watch for:

- Viruses can cause system slowdown, so be sure to scan for them.

- If you've recently added memory to your system you may need to double-check that it is configured properly.

- Your processor could be overheating. Check to be sure your CPU fan is still operating. If your system detects that your CPU fan has failed, the system will automatically slow down your processor.

- The BIOS settings may have been inadvertently changed if your system has been infected with a virus or if you tried to change something else in the BIOS. Check the backup of your last BIOS settings and options to be sure nothing has been changed. Also check hard disk modes, as well as your memory and cache timings.

- Fragmented files can cause system slowdown. If you have not defragmented your hard disk in a while, try doing so.

The best way to ensure that your system runs optimally is to never change more than one thing at a time. That way, if the system has troubles, you can undo your last action or installation and see if the problem goes away.

# Summary

## SYSTEM SOFTWARE: THE OPERATING ENVIRONMENT

- System software has two major components: (1) the operating system and (2) system utilities that provides various maintenance functions.

- Without software—the set of instructions that tells the computer what to do—a computer is just an expensive collection of wires and components. The operating system (OS) coordinates the various functions of the computer's hardware as well as provides support for running application software.

- An operating system works at the intersection of application software, the user, and the computer's hardware. Its five basic functions are starting the computer, managing programs, managing memory, handling internal messages from input and output devices, and providing a means of communicating with the user.

- When you start or restart a computer, it reloads the operating system into the computer's memory. There are six steps that the computer goes through at startup: loading the BIOS, the power-on self-test, loading the operating system, configuring the system, loading system utilities, and authenticating users.

- The three major types of user interfaces are graphical user interfaces (GUIs), menu-driven user interfaces, and command-line user interfaces.

- The two major operating systems for the personal computer are Microsoft Windows and Macintosh OS X. The major strength of Windows is that it has been dominant in the market for more than 15 years and is installed and maintained on most of the personal computers in the world. The major strength of OS X is that it has been modified and upgraded for more than 20 years and is the most stable.

- Essential system utilities include backup software, antivirus software, file managers, searching, file compression utilities, disk scanning programs, and disk defragmentation programs.

- A sound backup procedure begins with a full backup of an entire hard disk and continues with periodic incremental backups of just those files that have been created or altered since the last backup occurred.

Go to **www.prenhall.com/cayf2005** to review this chapter, answer the questions, and complete the exercises.

# Key Terms and Concepts

Go to **www.prenhall.com/cayf2005** to review this chapter, answer the questions, and complete the exercises.

# Matching

Match each key term in the left column with the most accurate definition in the right column.

_____ 1. operating system

_____ 2. multitasking

_____ 3. Linux

_____ 4. dialog box

_____ 5. OS X

_____ 6. disk scanner

_____ 7. emergency disk

_____ 8. interrupts

_____ 9. kernel

_____ 10. foreground application

_____ 11. file manager

_____ 12. driver

_____ 13. icon

_____ 14. backup utilities

_____ 15. fragmented

a. an essential part of safe, efficient computer usage

b. a utility that can detect and resolve physical and logical problems on a disk

c. a file that helps the operating system manage input and output devices

d. enables a single user to work with two or more programs

e. essential portions of an operating system

f. signals that inform the operating system that something has happened

g. an open-source operating system

h. the program that is active when one or more programs are running at the same time

i. manages programs, parcels out memory, deals with input and output devices, and provides a means of communicating with the user

j. describes a disk or file whose data is scattered

k. allows users to supply additional information to a program

l. contains a reduced version of the operating system that can be used for troubleshooting purposes

m. a utility program that enables you to deal with the data stored on your disk

n. the most current operating system for the Macintosh

o. graphical representation of a computer resource

# Multiple Choice

Circle the correct choice for each of the following.

1. Which kind of software enables a computer and its peripheral devices to function smoothly?
   a. application
   b. system
   c. defragmentation
   d. file management

2. Which of the following is not typically handled by the operating system?
   a. managing programs
   b. dealing with I/O devices
   c. publishing Web pages
   d. interacting with the user

3. What is the name of the type of memory that is created if random access memory is full?
   a. read-only memory
   b. on-the-fly memory
   c. add-on memory
   d. virtual memory

4. Which version of Windows is designed for PDAs?
   a. Windows CE
   b. Windows NT
   c. Windows ME
   d. Windows PDA

5. Which of the following is a key component of a graphical user interface?
   a. command words
   b. icons
   c. keyboard
   d. virtual memory

6. Which operating system is considered to be the easiest for beginners?
   a. OS X
   b. Linux
   c. Windows XP
   d. UNIX

7. What term is used to describe the central part of the operating system that starts applications, manages devices and memory, and performs other essential functions?
   a. master
   b. kernel
   c. general
   d. boss

8. Which of the following operating systems is ideally suited for a networked corporate environment?
   a. Windows XP
   b. Linux
   c. Windows NT
   d. Windows CE

9. If your computer fails to start normally, you may need to use one of these.
   a. emergency disk
   b. system utility
   c. file utility
   d. nonemergency disk

10. Linus Torvalds is credited with what?
    a. developing multithreading
    b. creating the Linux operating system
    c. designing the first GUI
    d. leading the team that wrote the first Mac operating system

# Fill-In

In the blanks provided, write the correct answer for each of the following.

1. _____ user interfaces are the most popular interfaces.

2. When multiple programs are running on a computer, the one being used at the current time is known as the _____ application.

3. If an operating system uses virtual memory when memory is full, the operating system starts storing parts of memory in a(n) _____ on the hard drive.

4. Files can be located by using the _____ utility.

5. Unlike Windows 95 and Windows 98, _____ is specifically designed for client/server systems.

6. _____ is a free and powerful operating system that brings all the maturity and sophistication of UNIX to the PC.

7. If a file's data is not stored in contiguous locations on a disk, it is said to be _____.

8. _____ software protects a computer from viruses.

9. A(n) _____ is used to copy and delete files.

10. _____ are programs that can reduce the size of a file by as much as 50 percent without harming the data.

11. A(n) _____ is a single file that contains two or more files.

12. A(n) _____ is a portion of a disk that is unable to store data reliably.

13. _____ is a special type of memory that is used to store essential start-up configuration options.

14. _____ is an operating system for Intel-based PCs that uses a command-line user interface.

15. _____ enable a single user to work with two or more programs at the same time.

# Short Answer

1. Explain the purpose of the power-on self-test (POST). In addition to a computer system, do you know of any other systems that perform a POST?

2. Which operating system is installed on your computer or the computer that you use most often? Do you know if it is a legitimate copy? Visit **www.microsoft.com** and search for your operating system. Now use the search box to search for the term "legitimate." Read one or more articles on operating system software legitimacy.

3. What are the advantages of multitasking? Describe the multitasking that happens during one of your typical computer sessions. How would things be different if you could run only one program at a time?

4. What is the purpose of a driver? Have you ever had to install a driver when connecting a new peripheral device to a computer? If you did, what was the device, and was the driver supplied by the operating system or by the device manufacturer?

5. Explain the differences between a full backup and an incremental backup. Which peripheral devices are commonly used for backups? Have you ever lost important files because you did not back them up? If you have done a backup, did you copy the entire disk or just selected files? When was the last time you performed a backup?

Go to **www.prenhall.com/cayf2005** to review this chapter, answer the questions, and complete the exercises.

# A Closer Look

1. Considering the operating systems you use most often, and the functions that need to be performed by an operating system, what future improvements can you envision? If you have used several versions of the same operating system, what improvements have you seen implemented when new versions are released? Go to **www.microsoft.com** and choose a link or search for "operating systems." Now scroll around or search for Microsoft's operating system comparison section. Did you learn anything? How does the operating system you use stack up?

2. Experiment with both a Macintosh computer and a PC. What version of each operating system did you use? Is it the latest release of the operating system? How are the two operating systems similar? Can you determine the strengths of each system? Which operating system do you prefer? Why?

3. Despite its cryptic commands, UNIX has remained a popular operating system for about 30 years. Many educational institutions have computers running this operating system, and, in fact, most Internet servers run UNIX. If you have used a UNIX computer, explain how and why you used it. Does your school have computers that use UNIX? If so, do you have an account? Can you get an account, or are the accounts restricted on these computers? Do you have an Internet service provider (ISP)? If you do, identify your provider and whether it uses UNIX to support customer Web sites.

4. See how much you can learn about your computer system. Choose Start, All Programs, Accessories, and System Tools. Now choose the System Information choice. How much memory is installed on your computer? How much virtual memory is defined?

5. Have you considered the purchase of a PDA? What companies manufacture PDAs? Some of these devices require special operating systems and application software. Go to a local computer store and "take one out for a test drive." Specifically, try out the operating system. Do these computers use a special version of Windows? If they use Windows, what version and release is it? How does this operating system compare with ones on a desktop or laptop computer? What are some of the differences between the two operating systems? Now that you have "kicked the keyboard" and taken a PDA out for a spin, explain why you would or would not purchase one.

# On the Web

1. We discussed several system utility programs in this chapter. In this exercise, we'll examine file compression.

    Have you used a file compression program?

   - If you have, identify the brand name and version of this software application. Which operating system were you using? Did you find the file compression program simple or complicated to use? Would you recommend this product to someone else? Why or why not?
   - If you have not, visit the sites of two popular file compressors, WinZip at **winzip.com**, and StuffIt at **stuffit.com**. For which operating systems does each work? What are the current versions and manufacturers' suggested retail prices for each? Are free or evaluation versions available? Would you purchase one of these products? Explain why or why not.

2. We also discussed other system utility programs, such as antivirus programs, in this chapter. In this exercise, we'll examine these applications.

    Have you ever had to disinfect a file that was infected by a virus?

   - If you have, identify the brand name and version of the antivirus application you used and which operating system you were using. Were you able to disinfect the file successfully? Did you find the use of this program simple or complicated? Would you recommend this product to someone else? Why or why not?
   - If you have not, visit the sites of the two most popular antivirus applications, Norton AntiVirus at **www.symantec.com/nav**, and McAfee VirusScan at **www.mcafee.com/anti-virus**. For which operating systems does each work? What are the current versions and manufacturers' suggested retail prices of each? Are there free or evaluation versions available? Would you purchase one of these products? Explain why or why not.

3. So that you can answer the following questions, visit Microsoft's Windows XP site at **microsoft.com/windowsxp/default.asp** for information on the newest version of Windows.

   - Why would users of Windows NT/2000 upgrade to XP?
   - Why would users of Windows 95/98 upgrade to XP?
   - What other types of users will benefit from XP?
   - What are the minimum hardware requirements for XP?
   - What are the purchase and upgrade prices for XP?
   - Would you consider purchasing XP? Why or why not?

4. Use your browser to visit the site **www.cnet.com**. Review an article that compares Mac OS with the most current Windows operating environment. Which operating system did CNET conclude is the best one? Do you agree or disagree with its conclusion? Explain why.

5. Visit the Linux home page at **linux.com** and try the Linux 101 tutorial to learn more about this operating system.

   - What is the primary objective of this tutorial?
   - What is a dual-boot system, and what are the advantages and disadvantages of creating one? Why would or wouldn't you create a dual-boot system?
   - What is another name for the "root" user, and what is the purpose of having one?
   - What is the command to change your password?
   - What is the command to go to the home directory, and what is the command to see what is located in it?
   - What type of files are located in the /bin, /etc, and /usr directories?
   - Spend some time exploring the remainder of the tutorial. Do you feel that the tutorial met its primary objective? Explain why you would or would not install a UNIX system.

# Application Software:
## Tools for Productivity

## What You'll Learn . . .

- Understand how system software supports application software.

- List the most popular types of horizontal applications.

- Discuss the advantages and disadvantages of standalone programs, integrated programs, and suites.

- Discuss the advantages of Web technology and file compatibility.

- Explain the concept of software versions.

- Differentiate between commercial software, shareware, freeware, and public domain software.

- Describe the essential concepts and skills of using application software.

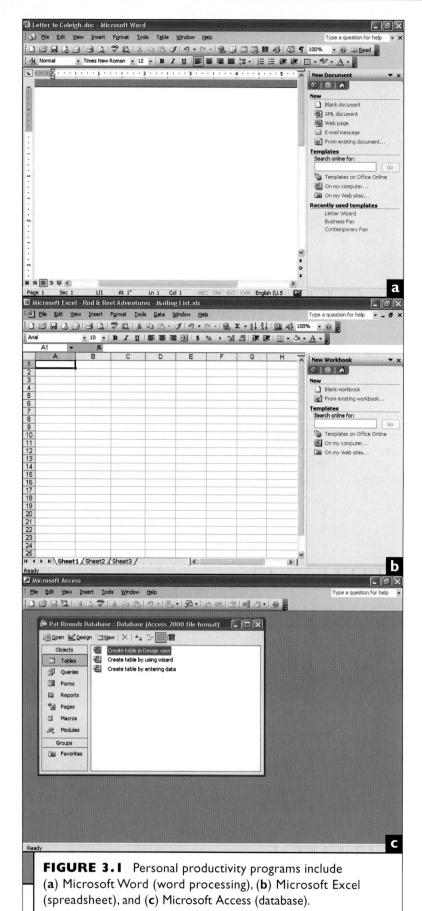

**FIGURE 3.1** Personal productivity programs include (**a**) Microsoft Word (word processing), (**b**) Microsoft Excel (spreadsheet), and (**c**) Microsoft Access (database).

The term **application software** refers generally to all the programs that enable you to *apply* the computer to the work you do. In this sense, application software is in contrast to system software, the programs that help the computer to function properly. Application software enables you to work efficiently with documents created in almost any line of work, including invoices, letters, reports, proposals, presentations, customer lists, newsletters, tables, and flyers. Referring back to our aquarium analogy, applications are the fish that swim in the water (operating system). The operating system provides the environment in which the applications run. It supports the functions of input, processing, output, and storage—while the applications support the function of accomplishing tasks. Applications can do such things as create work product, inform, enable communication, and entertain.

In this chapter, you'll learn how to make sense of the world of application software—including the various types and how to install, maintain, and upgrade the programs that work for you each day.

# Types of Application Software

Application software falls into two general categories: horizontal applications and vertical applications. **Horizontal applications** are used *across* the departments or functional divisions of a company and are also popular in the consumer market. These general-purpose programs address the needs of many people, such as writing (word processing), working with numbers (spreadsheets), and keeping track of information (databases). For instance, Marketing, Finance, Accounting, and Management all need to produce written documents, so a word processor is a horizontal application. **Vertical applications** are designed for a particular type of business or for a specific division in a company. An example of a vertical application would be an accounting program or a customer resource management program for a sales force.

## HORIZONTAL APPLICATIONS: GENERAL-PURPOSE PROGRAMS

The most popular general-purpose programs are called **personal productivity programs**, which, as the name implies, help individuals do their work more effectively and efficiently. General-purpose programs include: productivity, multimedia and graphics, Internet, and home or educational programs. These horizontal applications are likely to be found on home and business users' personal computers.

Productivity programs such as word processors, spreadsheets, and databases are all horizontal applications (Figure 3.1). Their value to us is that they perform their functions regardless of the subject matter. For instance, a word processor is equally valuable for typing a term paper for your writing class and for typing a term paper for your marketing class.

Programs such as personal information managers (for use with electronic address books and for scheduling) as well as presentation graphics programs, which enable you to develop slides and transparencies for presentations, are also considered personal productivity software. PowerPoint is an example of a popular presentation graphics program (Figure 3.2).

**Multimedia and graphics software** includes professional desktop publishing programs (such as QuarkXPress), image-editing programs (such as Photoshop), three-dimensional rendering programs (such as computer-aided design [CAD] programs), and video-editing programs. One consideration to keep in mind is that these programs tend to use lots of disk space and often require extra memory to run efficiently. Be sure to read the Minimum System Requirements on the package and to realize that the numbers truly are *minimums*.

**Internet programs**, such as e-mail and instant messaging programs, Web browsers, and videoconferencing software will be discussed in more detail in Chapters 7 and 8. For now you can simply remember that they are general-purpose programs because they help us to communicate, learn, and interact.

General-purpose software also includes **home and educational programs**, such as personal finance software, home design and landscaping software, computerized reference information (such as encyclopedias and street maps), and games.

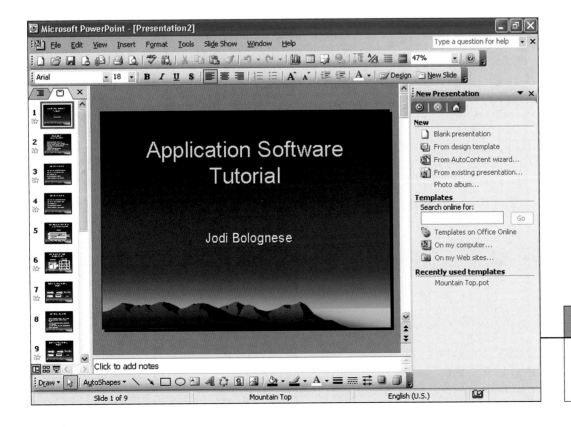

**FIGURE 3.2**
PowerPoint is a popular presentation graphics program.

Figure 3.3 lists the various forms of horizontal application software.

## VERTICAL APPLICATIONS: TAILOR-MADE PROGRAMS

If you can't find general-purpose horizontal applications to meet your computing needs, you might consider vertical applications that are tailor-made for specialized fields as well as the consumer market. For example, programs are available to handle the billing needs of medical offices, manage restaurants, and track occupational injuries (Figure 3.4).

Vertical applications designed for professional and business use often cost much more than horizontal applications. In fact, some of these programs cost $10,000 or more. The high price is due to the costs of developing the programs and the small size of most vertical markets.

If the right application isn't available, programmers can create custom software to meet your needs.

### Custom vs. Packaged Software

In the world of application software, a distinction can be made between custom software and packaged software (also called off-the-shelf software or shrink-wrapped software).

**Custom software** is developed by programmers to meet the specific needs of an organization. Custom software is expensive, but sometimes an organization's needs are so specialized that no alternative exists. An example of a custom software package might be the grade tracking

### FIGURE 3.3  Horizontal Application Software

| Personal Productivity Software | Multimedia and Graphics Software | Internet Software | Home and Educational Software |
|---|---|---|---|
| Word Processing | Professional Desktop Publishing Programs | E-mail Programs | Personal Finance Software |
| Spreadsheet | Professional Image-Editing Programs | Web Browsers | Tax Preparation Software |
| Database | Three-Dimensional Rendering Programs | Instant Messaging Software | Personal Desktop Publishing Programs |
| Presentation Graphics | Video-Editing Programs | Videoconferencing Software | Personal Image-Editing Programs |
| Personal Information Management | | | Home Design and Landscaping Software |
| | | | Computer-Assisted Tutorials |
| | | | Computerized Reference Information (such as Encyclopedias and Street Maps) |
| | | | Games |

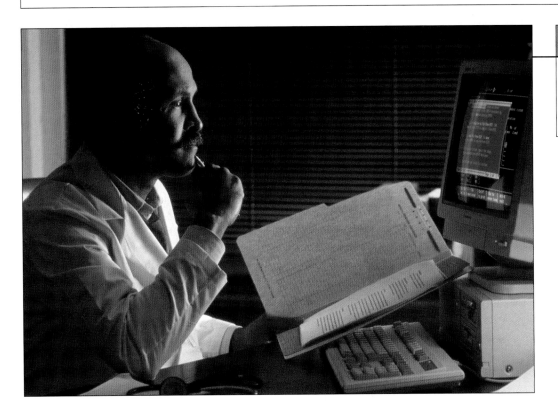

**FIGURE 3.4**
Medical offices use vertical applications to handle their billing.

software that has been programmed to suit the needs of your college registrar's office. Custom software is almost always a vertical application.

**Packaged software**, in contrast, is aimed at a mass market that includes home as well as business users. Although packaged software can be customized, it is designed to be immediately useful in a wide variety of contexts. An example of packaged software is the presentation software program your professor may use to create class presentations. The payoff comes with the price: packaged software is much cheaper than custom software.

# Integrated Programs and Suites: The All-in-One Approach

Before suites came along, you could only buy standalone programs. A **standalone program** is a program that is complete

unto itself—fully self-contained. Microsoft Word and Excel are examples of standalone programs. You can purchase and install them separately, and they function perfectly well all by themselves. Standalone programs required a lot of storage overhead, however. For example, if you purchased Word and installed it and then purchased Excel and installed it, neither program would know about the other, nor would they share any resources such as menus, drivers, graphics libraries, and tools. Obviously, this was a very inefficient way to install and use software when the programs had so many features they could share.

**Integrated programs** offer all the functions of the leading productivity programs in a single, easy-to-use program. Integrated programs such as Microsoft Works are generally aimed at beginning users. They offer easy-to-learn and easy-to-use versions of basic productivity software. All the functions, called **modules**, share the same interface, and you can switch between them quickly. The individual modules, however, may be short on features compared with standalone programs or office suites. The lack of features may make these easy programs seem more difficult when you start exploring the program's more advanced capabilities.

Microsoft Works contains a word processor that is very similar to Word, a spreadsheet program that is very similar to Excel, a database program, a calendar, and other productivity tools. Integrated programs are not available as standalone programs—you cannot purchase the spreadsheet program in Works as a standalone product.

A **software suite** (sometimes called an **office suite**) is an interconnected bundle of programs that share resources with each other and are designed to help workers accomplish the tasks they perform in a typical office environment. If Microsoft Windows is your desktop, then Microsoft Office is the set of tools that you typically use at work. A suite may include as many as five or more productivity applications. Today, most personal productivity software is sold in office suites, such as Corel WordPerfect Office 2002, Lotus SmartSuite, and the market leader, Microsoft Office (Figure 3.5).

The advantage of a software suite is that the individual applications share common program code, interface tools, drivers, and graphics libraries. For instance, if you purchased Word and Excel as standalone applications, each one would require you to install a printer. Each one would have its own dictionary, thesaurus, toolbars, and graphics library. When you use Word and Excel as a part of Microsoft Office, all of these features are shared.

Office suites typically include a full-featured version of leading word processing, spreadsheet, presentation graphics, database, and personal information manager (PIM) programs (Figure 3.6).

**FIGURE 3.5**
Microsoft Office is the most popular office suite.

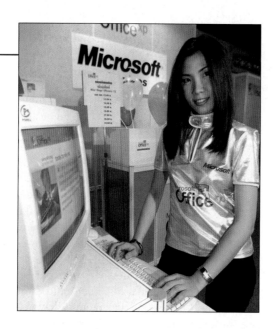

- **Word processing programs** enable you to create, edit, and print your written work. They also offer commands that enable you to format your documents so that they have an attractive appearance. Although some people still prefer to use other writing tools, word processing programs are the most often used office suite software.

- **Spreadsheet programs** present users with a grid of rows and columns, the

**FIGURE 3.6  Office Suites (Microsoft Windows)**

|  | **Microsoft Office** | **WordPerfect Office 2002** | **Lotus SmartSuite** |
|---|---|---|---|
| **Word Processing** | Microsoft Word | WordPerfect | Word Pro |
| **Spreadsheet** | Microsoft Excel | Quattro Pro | Lotus 1-2-3 |
| **Database** | Microsoft Access | Paradox | Lotus Approach |
| **Presentation Graphics** | Microsoft PowerPoint | Corel Presentations 10 | Freelance Graphics |
| **Personal Information Managers (PIMs)** | Microsoft Outlook | Corel Central | Lotus Organizer |

# Software Piracy: "Warez" Can Get You into Big Trouble

**CURRENTS**

**Ethical Debates**

It's called *warez,* and there's one important thing to know about it: it's illegal. The term *warez* (pronounced "wares") is widely used in the computer underground to describe illegal copies of commercial programs, such as Adobe Photoshop or Microsoft Office. Thanks to the Internet, trafficking in illegally duplicated software is rampant and increasing rapidly. According to a recent estimate, U.S. software firms lose $3 billion per year due to unauthorized software duplication; at this clip, the cost to the U.S. economy amounts to more than 100,000 jobs and $1 billion in lost tax revenues.

Much warez trafficking on the Internet takes place on Internet Relay Chat (IRC), in which it's hard to trace the actions of individuals. It's hard, but not impossible, as 25 individuals learned recently. All 25 were named in a lawsuit filed by the Business Software Association (BSA), an industry association that fights software piracy. The lawsuit's filing was accompanied by FBI-conducted raids at residences throughout the United States, in which computer equipment and software were confiscated. In addition to their civil liability under the lawsuit, each of the accused individuals is subject to up to $100,000 in civil penalties for *each* case of infringement that can be proven by prosecutors. Criminal penalties can include fines of up to $250,000 and jail terms of up to five years.

What about casual trading—just sharing programs without asking for money? That's illegal, too—and equally dangerous. Thanks to the No Electronic Theft (NET) Act, signed into law by President Clinton in 1997, it's no longer necessary for prosecutors to prove a profit motive in cases of criminal copyright infringement.

Despite enforcement efforts, software piracy is still rampant in the United States, where an estimated 25 percent of all business software programs in current use are thought to be illegally obtained. But the situation is much worse overseas. In China, as much as 96 percent of the software in current use is illegally obtained, thanks to the existence of several dozen large CD duplication factories that, until recently, operated with impunity. More recently, China's bid to gain entry into international trade associations has led to a crackdown against the duplication factories, but unauthorized software duplication is still the norm, rather than the exception. Unauthorized duplication is hurting China's emerging software industry, too; Beijing's Kingsoft Company, one of China's largest software producers, estimates that for every legal copy of its software, three pirated copies are in existence. As a result of piracy, the Chinese software market isn't growing and many publishers are driven into bankruptcy.

---

computer equivalent of an accountant's worksheet. By embedding formulas within the cells, you can create "live" worksheets in which changing one of the values forces the entire spreadsheet to be recalculated. Spreadsheets are indispensable tools for anyone who works with numbers.

- **Presentation graphics programs** enable you to create transparencies, slides, and handouts for presentations.

- **Database programs** give you the tools necessary to store data in an organized form, as well as to retrieve this data in such a way that it can be meaningfully summarized and displayed.

- **Personal information managers** provide you with calendars, contact managers, task reminders, and e-mail.

### WEB TECHNOLOGY: A NEW WAY TO SHARE FILES

The new wave in office suites is **Web technology**, which, for application software, means the capability to save your files in a form that contains the HTML (Hypertext Markup Language) codes that underlie Web documents. Why save in HTML? The answer boils down to one costly process: file conversion.

Many large organizations have been spending millions of dollars dealing with

To learn more about warez and software piracy, see the video clip at **www.prenhall.com/ cayf2005.**

file incompatibility problems caused by the use of proprietary file formats. Proprietary means that the file formats are limited to a specific vendor's software or computer model. For instance, if you don't have Microsoft Word installed on your system, you can't view a Word file unless you have a conversion program. The use of proprietary file formats imposes severe burdens, unless everyone in the company is using the same product. Even then, you encounter file incompatibility problems because software publishers introduce new file formats in new versions that support new features. Programs that can save data to HTML form eliminate file conversion costs because the file can be read by anyone with a Web browser.

File conversion costs come into play, too, when companies want to publish documents on the Web for use on the Internet or on

internal corporate intranets. To put any document on the Web generally requires saving the document in plain text format and then reformatting it from scratch for Web publishing. The capability to save documents in HTML format eliminates these costs.

Microsoft Word, Excel, and PowerPoint include the *Save as Web Page* feature within the File menu. We will explore Web pages in depth in Chapter 7.

On February 14, 2002, Microsoft formally unveiled its new long-term vision of the PC as a globally connected device (Figure 3.7). The strategy, called .NET (pronounced "dot NET"), is to accomplish the creation of universal communications between disparate and diverse computers. According to Microsoft, .NET is a set of software technologies "for connecting your world of information, people, systems, and devices." Microsoft hopes that .NET will

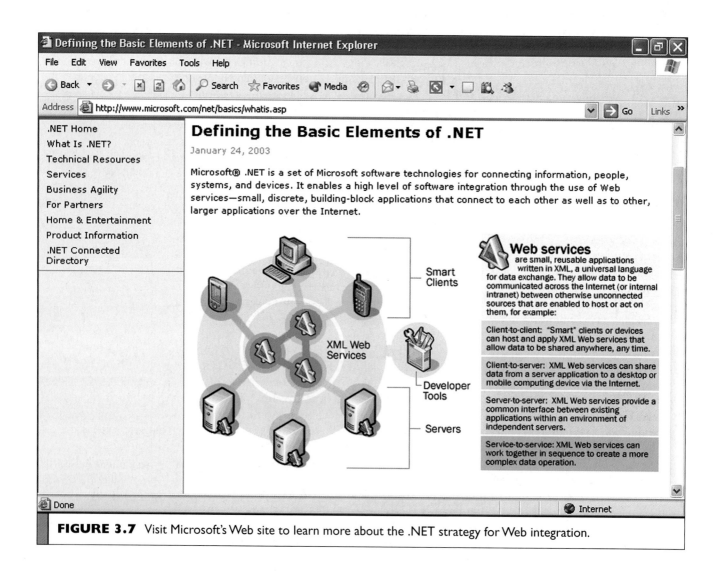

**FIGURE 3.7** Visit Microsoft's Web site to learn more about the .NET strategy for Web integration.

increase software compatibility through the use of XML Web services, which are applications that connect to each other as well as to other applications via the Internet. There is no doubt that in the next five years there will be significant changes in the way we share communications and information with each other across the Internet.

Now that you are familiar with the many types of application software and how the software can be packaged, let's look at some other considerations to keep in mind when choosing application software.

# System Requirements and Software Versions

When you buy software, your computer system will need to meet the program's **system requirements**, the minimum level of equipment that a program needs in order to run. For example, a given program may be designed to run on a PC with a Pentium class microprocessor, a CD-ROM drive, at least 16 MB of RAM, and 125 MB of free hard disk space. If you're shopping for software, you'll find the system requirements printed somewhere on the outside of the box. Although a program will run on a system that meets the minimum requirements, you'd be wise to exceed them, especially when it comes to memory and disk space.

You've no doubt noticed that most program names include a number, such as 6.0, or a year, such as 2004. Software publishers often bring out new versions of their programs, and these numbers help you determine whether you have the latest version. In a version number, the whole number (such as 6 in 6.0) indicates a major program revision. A decimal number indicates a **maintenance release** (a minor revision that corrects bugs or adds minor features). The year 2004 would indicate the year that the software was published—but would not provide an indication of how many versions of the software there were previously.

Software publishers sometimes offer **time-limited trial versions** of commercial programs on the Internet, which expire or stop working when a set trial period (such as 60 or 90 days) ends. You can download, install, and use these programs for free, but after the time limit is up, you can no longer use them.

Beta versions of forthcoming programs are sometimes available for free. A **beta version** is a preliminary version of a program in the final phases of testing. Beta software is known to contain bugs (errors) and should be installed and used only with caution.

## SOFTWARE UPGRADES

**Software upgrading** describes the process of keeping your version of an application current with the marketplace. Some upgrades are small changes called patches; sometimes they are major fixes called service releases or service packs. Service releases keep the current version up to date. The ultimate upgrade is when you purchase and install the next version or release of a program. For instance, you might have recently upgraded from Microsoft Office XP to Microsoft Office 2003.

So, how do you know if you should purchase the next version of a software application or if there is a patch or fix available that will make your current version perform better? Well, when it comes to upgrading you should look at two things: is your current version so out of date that you are having compatibility problems, or are there features in the newer version that you find attractive? As for patches, you should visit the software manufacturer's Web site occasionally to see if there are service releases or patches. Microsoft software has a built-in capability to automatically check with Microsoft's Web site to determine if there are any updates available.

## DISTRIBUTION AND DOCUMENTATION

Before the Internet came along, most software was available only in shrink-wrapped boxes that contained floppy disks or CD-ROMs with the program installation files. Now, many software publishers are using the Internet as a means of distributing programs and program updates. Doing so is much cheaper for the company and often more convenient for the consumer than physically delivering a program in a box.

If you buy software in a shrink-wrapped package, you typically get at least some printed **documentation** in the form of tutorials and reference manuals that explain how to use the program. Downloaded software contains "read me" files and help files. A "read me" file is a plain text document that is readable by any text-reading program and that contains information the software manufacturer thinks you'll find helpful. You'll also find **help screens** in programs that enable you to consult all or part of the documentation on-screen (Figure 3.8). You may also find additional information at the software publisher's Web site.

Now that you've chosen the right application software version, considered upgrades, and looked over the documentation, let's look at some other considerations you might have when using application software.

# Software Licenses and Registration

A **software license** is a document distributed with a program that gives you the right to install and use the program on only *one* computer (Figure 3.9). If you want to install the program on more than

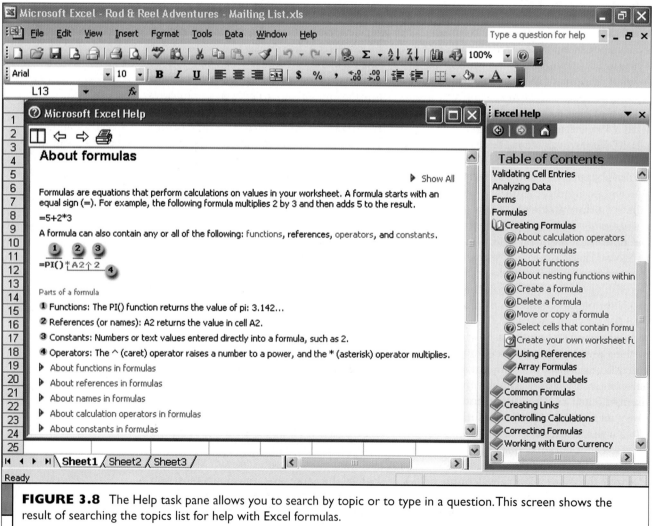

**FIGURE 3.8** The Help task pane allows you to search by topic or to type in a question. This screen shows the result of searching the topics list for help with Excel formulas.

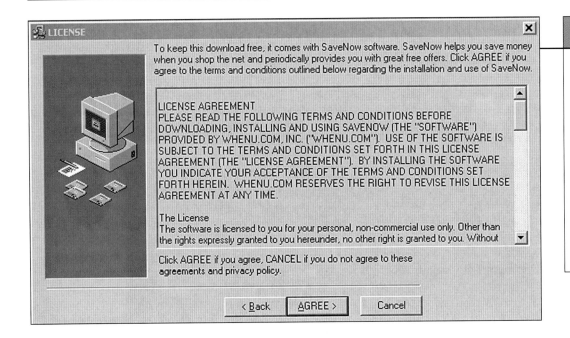

**FIGURE 3.9**
A software license gives you the right to install and use a program on only one computer. If you want to install the program on more than one computer, you must purchase additional licenses.

one computer, you must purchase additional licenses; otherwise, you violate the publisher's copyright.

Organizations such as colleges and universities often purchase **site licenses**, which enable them to install copies of a program on a specified number of computers. Site licenses offer large organizations licenses at a slightly reduced cost.

As for warranty, most software publishers will be happy to replace the program disk if it's defective, but that's it. The license expressly denies any liability on the publisher's part for any damages or losses suffered through the use of the software. If you buy a program containing bugs, and if these bugs wipe out your data, it's your tough luck. Or that's what software companies would like you to believe. In the past, these licenses haven't stood up in court; judges and juries have agreed that the products were sold with an implied warranty of fitness for a particular use. Under consideration by U.S. state legislatures is a controversial model act, called the Uniform Computer Information Transactions Act (UCITA), which would give these licenses the force of law.

When you purchase a program, you'll also be asked to register your software by filling out a registration form. (If your computer is connected to the Internet, you can often do this online; otherwise, you need to mail the registration form to the software publisher.)

Generally, registration is worth the trouble. After you're registered, you'll receive automatic notification of software upgrades. Sometimes, you'll have a chance to upgrade to new versions at a price lower than the one offered to the general public.

## COMMERCIAL SOFTWARE, SHAREWARE, FREEWARE, AND PUBLIC DOMAIN SOFTWARE

Most computer software is copyrighted, which means that you can't make copies for other people without infringing on the program's copyright (such infringements are called **software piracy** and are a federal offense in the United States). There are three types of copyrighted software: commercial software, shareware, and freeware. **Commercial software** is software you must pay for before using—such as Microsoft Office, Adobe Acrobat, and Mac OS X. **Shareware** refers to software that you can use on a "try before you buy" basis (Figure 3.10). If you like the program after using it for a specified trial period, you must pay a registration fee or you violate the copyright. **Freeware** refers to software given away for free, with the understanding that you can't turn around and sell it for profit. Included in the freeware category are programs distributed under the Free Software Foundation's General Public License (GPL), such as the Linux operating

**Destinations**

How will UCITA affect you? Learn more about the UCITA controversy at UCITA online at **www.ucita online.com**.

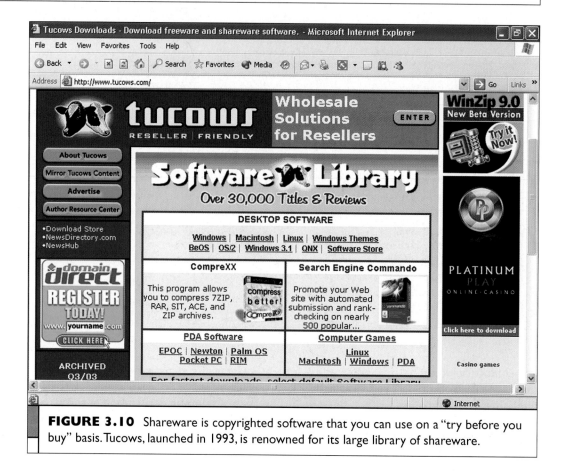

**FIGURE 3.10** Shareware is copyrighted software that you can use on a "try before you buy" basis. Tucows, launched in 1993, is renowned for its large library of shareware.

system discussed in Chapter 2. There is one type of software that is not copyrighted. **Public domain software** is expressly free from copyright, and you can do anything you want with it, including modifying or selling it to others. Public domain software typically includes games, loan analyzers, and small utility programs.

When a program includes some type of measure to ensure that you don't make unauthorized copies of it, it is called **copy-protected software**. Copy-protected software isn't popular with users because it often requires extra steps to install and usually requires a call to technical support if any program files become corrupted. Perhaps the loudest objection to copy-protected software, though, is that the copy protection schemes are beginning to work. It is becoming difficult to "share" a copy of major software programs with friends and family or "lend" it to them.

Copyright or not, you're always better off owning a legitimate copy of the software you're using. It's the right thing to do and offers you the greatest opportunity to derive benefits from the software. You're entitled

to full customer support services should anything go wrong, as well as any add-ons or enhancements the company offers.

Now that you know what to look for when you are purchasing application software, let's look at what to do with that software once you have it.

# Installing and Managing Application Software

To use your computer successfully, you'll find it useful to understand the essential concepts and acquire the skills of using application software, including installing applications, launching applications, understanding application windows, using menus and toolbars, and working with documents. The following sections briefly outline these concepts and skills.

**Ethical Debates**

# Digital Piracy: What's the Big Deal?

Most of us wouldn't consider walking into a store and stealing a laptop computer. But when it comes to software (or music or videos) for that laptop, well that's a different story. How many people do you know who have "borrowed" (that means stolen!) software, or who have downloaded copyrighted music off the Web illegally? If you ask around, you'll find that you're surrounded by users who don't see the big deal in stealing digital data.

Why is this? It may be that when you buy a computer or a CD, you buy a physical, tangible thing that you'll own. But when you buy software, you're only purchasing the right to *use* the software, not the copyright. So if you install software onto your computer and then install it onto a friend's computer, you're stealing. And if you download music illegally off the Web, you're stealing too. Just like you'd be stealing if you grabbed a laptop computer or CD off the shelf in a store. You may not see it that way, but the companies creating and distributing the software and other digital data do, as does the law.

Certainly, it's tempting for users to steal software and music. Consider a school system with 1,000 computers, all of which need to have Microsoft Word. Legitimate licensing could amount to quite a hefty bill, to say the least. Do you think it's okay for a school system to have unlicensed software on its computers? After all, the software is benefiting students. If you think the law bends for schools—and many school administrators do—think again. These same school administrators may one day be holding letters from software companies requesting an inspection to determine whether pirated software is running on their school's machines. If piracy is discovered, schools can face steep fines.

Maybe you're thinking, well, what if the school system just buys 500 copies of the software instead of the full 1,000? They're still paying for a lot of software; what's the big deal if they don't pay for it all? If you do a little calculating, though, you'll find that this kind of rationalization is expensive. Let's assume the value of each copy is $50. This means that the school is stealing $25,000 worth of software. Multiply that to include other schools in the district, state, country, and world, and suddenly billions of dollars of programs are being stolen.

And when it comes to music, you may think it's no big deal to download your new favorite song off the Web, or to burn a copy of your friend's CD on your CD burner. Who isn't tempted by free music (especially college students who often already have to pinch a penny)? But what about the artist who wrote or performed the song? Or the record company that paid for the song to be produced, and all the other people down the line who rely on honest consumers to purchase the actual CD? Sure, the $15 you've saved isn't much in the grand scheme of things for them, but if just 100,000 other people burn that same CD instead of buying it, that's a million and a half dollars of lost sales for your favorite artist.

Will you get caught? Maybe not. But technology offers us many ethical choices, and in the long run, digital piracy hurts us all.

## INSTALLING APPLICATIONS

Before you can use an application, you must install it on your computer. **Installing** an application involves more than transferring the software from the distribution medium, such as a CD-ROM, to your computer's hard disk. The program must also be configured properly to run on your system. Installation software makes sure that this configuration is performed properly. Most programs come with an installation or setup utility, which makes this job quite easy.

If the software was obtained from the Internet, you must first decompress it. Many programs from the Internet include decompression software; you simply open the file you obtained, and the decompression occurs automatically. After the program has been installed, you will see its name in menus or on the desktop, and you can start using it.

If you later decide that you don't want to use an application, you shouldn't just delete it from your hard disk. Always uninstall the application using the Windows utility called Add or Remove Programs that

techtv™

To learn more about how to uninstall programs, see the video clip at **www.prenhall.com/cayf2005**.

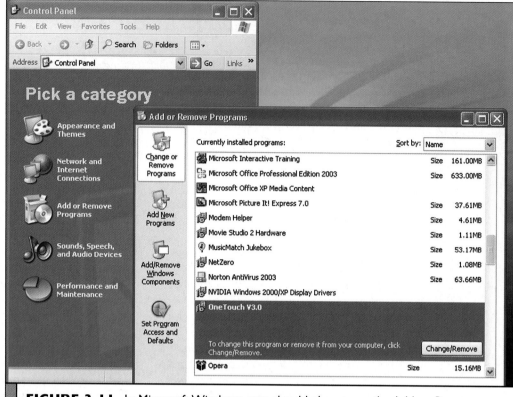

**FIGURE 3.11** In Microsoft Windows, you should always use the Add or Remove Programs utility to remove unwanted software. This utility is accessed from the Start, Control Panel menu sequence.

is provided for this purpose (Figure 3.11). **Uninstalling** not only removes the application's files from your hard disk, but also removes the program from the registry.

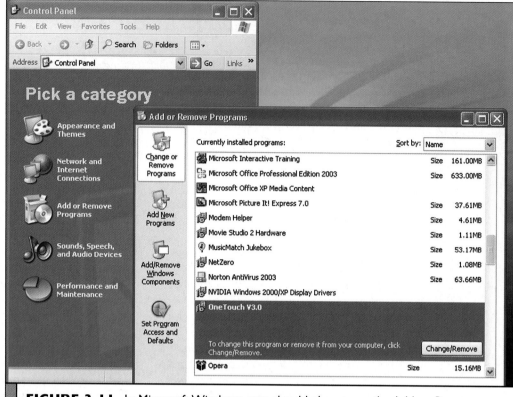

**FIGURE 3.12** Choose Start, All Programs to access the programs that are installed on your computer.

## LAUNCHING APPLICATIONS

Once you have installed an application, you can launch it. **Launching** an application transfers the program code from your computer's hard disk to memory, and the application appears on-screen. There are many ways to launch programs. The most reliable way in Microsoft Windows is to click the Start menu, point to All Programs, and choose the application you want to launch (Figure 3.12). In Mac OS, you locate the application's folder and double-click the application's icon. Application icons are also often available on the desktop, in the taskbar at the bottom of the desktop, and from toolbars.

## UNDERSTANDING THE APPLICATION'S WINDOW

When the application appears on-screen (Figure 3.13), you'll see some or all of the following features within the **application window**, the area that encloses and displays the application:

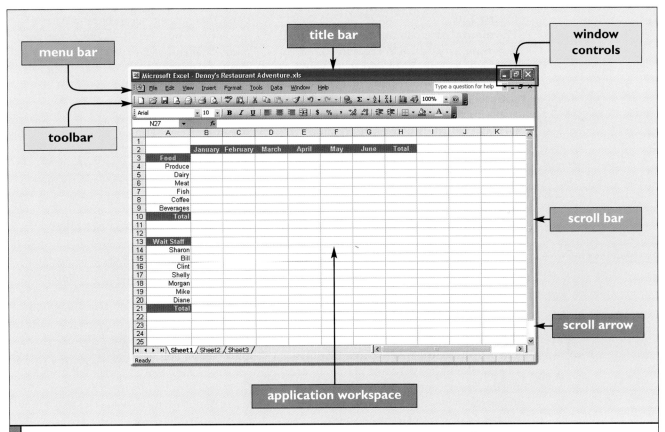

**FIGURE 3.13** These window features are found in most Microsoft Windows applications.

### Title Bar

The **title bar** usually contains the name of the application as well as the name of the file you are working on, if any. If you haven't yet saved the file, you'll see a generic file name, such as Untitled or Document1.

### Window Controls

Within the title bar, you'll also find **window controls**, which enable you to **maximize** or enlarge the window so that it fills the whole screen, **minimize** or hide the window so that it's reduced to the size of an icon or button, **restore** or change the window to the preceding unmaximized size, and close the window once you've finished using it.

### Window Borders

In Microsoft Windows, you can change the size of a window by dragging a vertical **window border** left or right, or a horizontal border up or down (Figure 3.14). If you click and drag a window corner, you can size the window horizontally and vertically at the same time. In Mac OS, click

and drag the size box, which is positioned in the window's lower right corner, to size the window on-screen.

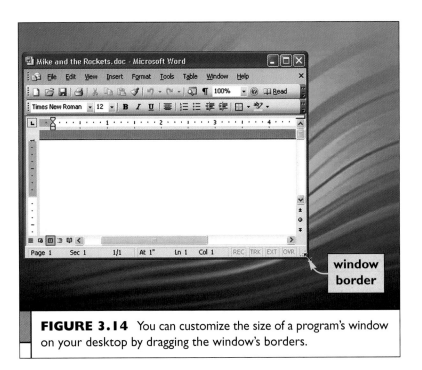

**FIGURE 3.14** You can customize the size of a program's window on your desktop by dragging the window's borders.

### Menu Bar

The **menu bar** contains the names of **pull-down menus**, which are rectangular lists, such as File, Edit, View, and so on, containing the names of the commands you can use with the application. A **command** performs a specific type of action, such as printing or formatting text. In Microsoft Windows, the menu bar is positioned beneath the title bar. In Mac OS, the menu bar is positioned at the top of the screen.

### Toolbar

The **toolbar** contains pictures, called icons, which depict the actions performed by the most commonly used commands, such as scissors for cut and a printer for printing. Most applications have more than one toolbar.

### Application Workspace

The **application workspace** displays the document you are working on. In computing, a **document** is any type of product you create with the computer, including written work, an electronic spreadsheet, or a graphic.

### Scroll Bars and Scroll Arrows

If the document with which you are working is larger than can be displayed in a single screen, such as a document that is more than one page long, you'll see one or more scroll bars. You can use scroll bars and scroll arrows to move (scroll) through the document. Typically, you can click the scroll arrows to move line-by-line or drag the scroll bar to move longer distances faster.

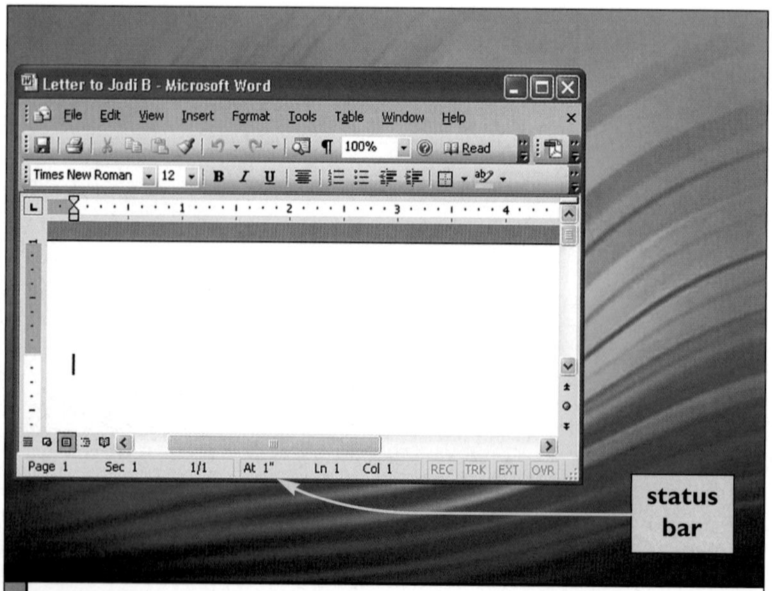

### Status Bar

The **status bar** (Figure 3.15), located at the bottom of the document window, displays information about the program as well as the program's messages to you, the user.

## UNDERSTANDING MENUS

A **menu** is a list of words that signify categories of tasks you can accomplish within an application. When you go to a restaurant, the menu has a section for appetizers, the entrée, beverages, and dessert. Applications have menus that allow you to manage and modify the work you are accomplishing. Although applications organize menus in varying ways, many applications make use of the following standard menu names:

### File

On the **File menu**, you'll find options for creating new documents, opening existing documents, closing documents, saving documents, saving documents with a new file name or new location, printing documents, and quitting the application.

### Edit

On the **Edit menu**, you'll find options for deleting text, cutting text to a temporary storage location called the **Clipboard**, pasting text from the Clipboard to a specific location in the document, undoing and redoing actions, and finding text within the document. In Mac OS, this menu also contains the Preferences options, which enable you to choose program preferences.

### View

The **View menu** contains options that enable you to choose how your document is displayed and to manage how toolbars and other features appear on your screen. Typically included are zoom options, expressed as a magnification percentage; various page views such as print layout and Web layout; and options that enable you to hide or display toolbars.

status bar

**FIGURE 3.15** The status bar is an often overlooked document information source.

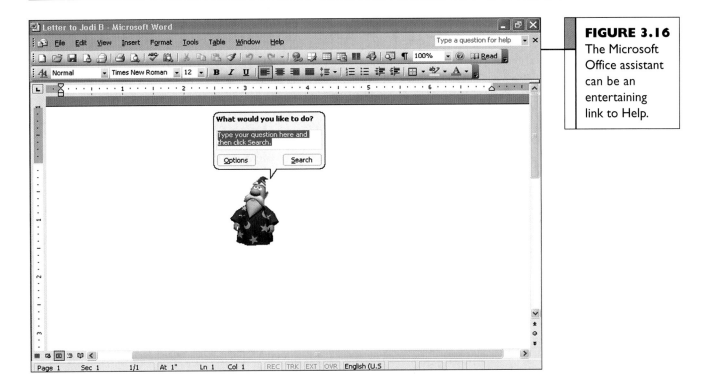

**FIGURE 3.16**
The Microsoft Office assistant can be an entertaining link to Help.

## Format

The **Format menu** allows you to modify such features as the font style, paragraph settings, borders and shading, bullets and numbering, styles, and themes.

## Tools

The **Tools menu** typically includes useful utilities, such as a spell checker. In Microsoft Windows, it also includes Options, a command that enables you to choose program preferences.

## Help

On the **Help menu**, you'll find the various options available for getting help with the program, which typically include a table of contents of frequently requested items and a searchable index to all available items (Figure 3.16). If you are connected to the Internet, you may be able to access additional help resources on the Web. Some applications provide animated assistants that enable you to type a question and view a list of possibly relevant responses. If the assistant annoys you, you can hide it.

## USING POPUP MENUS

In addition to menus and toolbars, most applications enable you to display popup

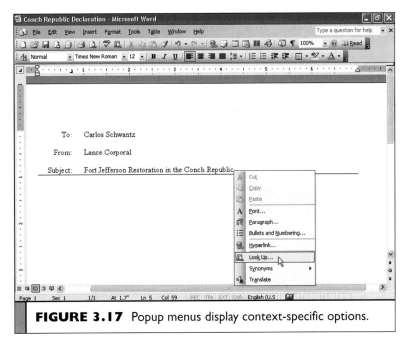

**FIGURE 3.17** Popup menus display context-specific options.

menus (Figure 3.17). Typically, a **popup menu**, also called a **context menu,** appears when you click the right mouse button. (On the Macintosh, you can display a popup menu by holding the mouse button down.) Popup menus list the commands that are available for the area where you clicked the mouse button. For example, if you right-click the application workspace within Microsoft Word, you'll see a menu of text-editing and text-formatting commands.

## CREATING DOCUMENTS

When you create a new document, you can start with a new, blank document or a template (Figure 3.18). A **template** is a generic version of a document that has already been started for you. For example, word processing programs typically include templates for faxes, letters, memos, reports, manuals, brochures, and many more types of documents. The template may include text, appropriate formats, graphics, or all of these.

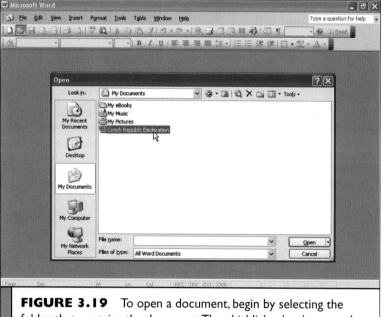

**FIGURE 3.18** Templates provide consistent background content and formatting for standardized documents.

**FIGURE 3.19** To open a document, begin by selecting the folder that contains the document. Then highlight the document's name, and click Open.

## OPENING AN EXISTING DOCUMENT

To **open** an existing document means to locate the document and load it into the application workspace. To do so, you'll use the Open dialog box. Figure 3.19 shows the typical appearance of an Open dialog box in Microsoft Windows. Begin by selecting the folder that contains the document. Next, highlight the document's name. Click Open to transfer the document to the application workspace.

## CHOOSING OPTIONS

Applications typically enable you to choose **options**, which specify how you want the program to operate (Figure 3.20). Your choices can change the program's **defaults**, which are the settings that are in effect unless you deliberately override them. For example, Microsoft Word enables you to choose an option that allows you to display white text against a blue background, a setting that some writers find to be a bit easier on the eyes.

When you start working with a newly installed application, check the options menu for a setting—usually called **autosave**—that automatically saves your work at a specified interval. With this option enabled, you'll be assured that you won't lose more than a few minutes' worth of work should the program fail for some reason.

## USING WIZARDS

To guide you through lengthy or complex operations, some applications include wizards. A **wizard** is a series of dialog boxes that guides you through a step-by-step procedure that is designed to result in the solution to a task—such as creating a calendar or meeting agenda. When you finish making choices in each dialog box, click Next to go on to the next step (Figure 3.21). You can locate wizards by accessing the File, New, General Templates menu sequence. Wizards are not templates, but they are stored in the same location.

## SAVING YOUR WORK

**Saving** your work refers to the process of transferring the document from the computer's temporary memory, or RAM, to a permanent storage device, such as a hard disk. In Microsoft Windows, documents are saved by default to a folder called My Documents unless you specify another folder from within the Tools, Options menu.

Each time you save your work for the first time you'll see the **Save As** dialog box because the operating system needs to know where and with what name you wish to store your work. For now, let's assume that you wish to store your documents in the default My Documents folder on your hard disk. The next thing you'll need to do is to give your document a **filename**, the name that the storage device uses to identify the file uniquely. The name must differ from all the other filenames used within the same folder or directory. In Microsoft Windows, you can use up to 250 characters in a filename, including spaces. Filenames in Microsoft Windows cannot include any of the following characters: forward slash (/), backslash ( \ ), greater than sign (>), less than sign (<), asterisk (*), question mark (?), quotation mark ("), pipe symbol ( | ), colon (:), or semicolon (;). In Mac OS, you can use up to 31 characters in a filename, including spaces and all characters except a colon (Figure 3.22).

Microsoft Windows filenames typically include a period and an **extension**, an addition to the filename of up to three characters in length. Typically, extensions are used to identify the type of data that the file contains, as well as the application that created the file. The applications in Microsoft Office automatically assign an extension when you save your document for the first time. For example, Microsoft Word automatically assigns the .doc extension. In Mac OS, extensions are not needed because Macintosh files include a code representing the name of the application that created the file. However, if you're a Mac user and you want to send files to PC users, it's a good idea to add the extension to the end of your filename to avoid

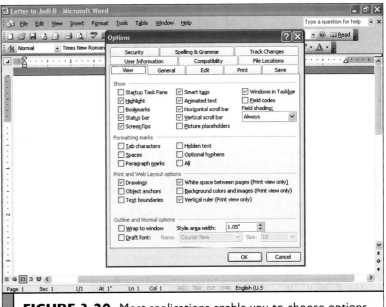

**FIGURE 3.20** Most applications enable you to choose options for program defaults by using the Tools, Options menu sequence.

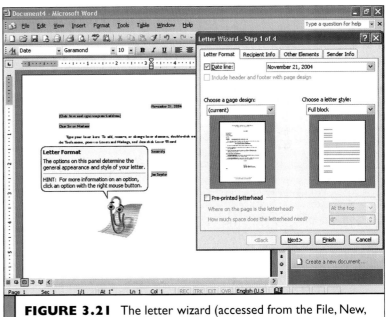

**FIGURE 3.21** The letter wizard (accessed from the File, New, General Templates menu sequence) can help you create a letter.

conversion problems. Figure 3.23 lists the most commonly used extensions and their file types.

Once you've successfully saved your document, you can always save another copy elsewhere by using the Save As command, which enables you to save the document using a new location, a new filename, or both.

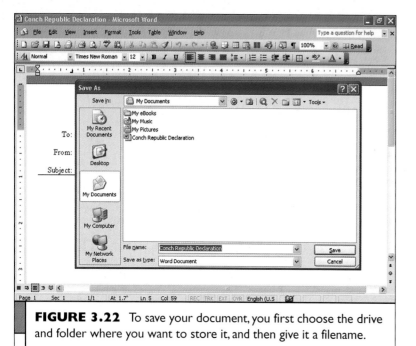

**FIGURE 3.22** To save your document, you first choose the drive and folder where you want to store it, and then give it a filename.

**FIGURE 3.23 Commonly Used File Extensions**

| Extension | File Type |
|---|---|
| .exe | application |
| .doc | Microsoft Word |
| .xls | Microsoft Excel |
| .ppt | Microsoft PowerPoint |
| .mbd | Microsoft Access |
| .pdf | Adobe |
| .txt | SimpleText |
| .htm or .html | Web pages |
| .rtf | Rich Text Format |

Many computer users never figure out the difference between Save and Save As. It is actually quite simple: Save takes what is in memory and writes it to the same storage device and folder, with the same filename that it had when it was opened in the application. In other words, the content in memory replaces the content in storage. Save As, on the other hand, brings up a dialog box that offers all of the choices you had when you first saved a file. You may choose a different device or a different folder, or simply modify the filename. Modifying the filename is a good way to save various versions of your work—just in case something happens to what is in memory and you need to go back to a previous version.

## EXITING THE APPLICATION

When you've finished using the application, don't just switch off the computer. Exit the application by choosing the Exit command from the File menu. By doing so you ensure that the application will warn you if you've failed to save some of your work. In addition, you'll save any options you set while using the program.

## SHUTTING DOWN YOUR SYSTEM

When you've finished using the computer, be sure to shut it down properly. Don't just switch off the power without going through the shutdown procedure properly. In Microsoft Windows XP, click Start, and choose Turn Off Computer. In Mac OS, click Special, and choose Shut Down. If you switch the power off without shutting down, the operating system may fail to write certain system files to the hard disk. The next time you start the computer, the operating system will need to run the disk scanning utility to check for file fragments. File fragments that result from improper shutdown could leave you with permanent damage to system or personal files.

An alternative to completely shutting down your system is to put it on Standby. In Microsoft Windows XP, **Standby** is a low-power state that allows you to restore your system to full power quickly without going through the lengthy boot process. Standby is accessed in the same way as Turn Off, from the Start, Turn Off Computer menu sequence. In Mac OS, this option is called **Sleep**.

# Summary

## APPLICATION SOFTWARE: TOOLS FOR PRODUCTIVITY

- System software provides the environment in which application software performs tasks. Applications create work product, inform, enable communication, and entertain.

- The four types of horizontal applications are personal productivity programs, multimedia and graphics software, Internet programs, and home and educational programs.

- Most people who need personal productivity software purchase an office suite because they can save money by doing so. A potential downside is that suites tend to take up lots of disk space and may include software that you don't need or want. Integrated programs are aimed at beginning users and may not include features some users will want later. A standalone program provides just the software tool that you need, but is often nearly as expensive as a complete suite.

- Office suites that incorporate Web technology are becoming popular. These programs can save data to HTML, eliminating file conversion costs because files can be read by anyone with a Web browser. The HTML format also enables the sharing of files that may otherwise be incompatible.

- Software publishers often bring out new versions of their programs. In a version number, the whole number (such as 6 in 6.0) indicates a major program revision. A decimal number indicates a maintenance release (a minor revision that corrects bugs or adds minor features). For example: Office XP is technically Office 10, while Office 2003 is Office 11. These numbers help you determine whether you have the latest version.

- You must pay for commercial software before you can use it. Shareware is copyrighted but distributed on a "try before you buy" basis. Freeware is copyrighted but available for free, as long as you don't turn around and sell it. Public domain software is not copyrighted.

- To use your computer successfully, you need to learn the essential concepts and skills of using application software, including installing applications, launching applications, understanding and using application windows, using menus and toolbars, and working with documents.

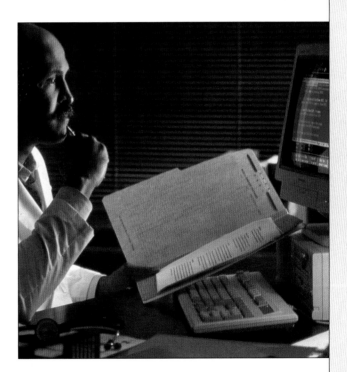

# Key Terms and Concepts

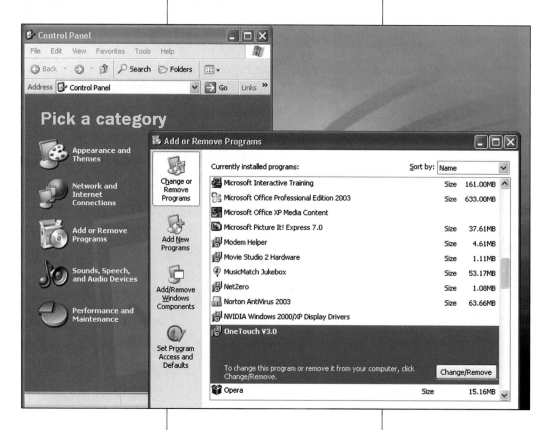

Go to **www.prenhall.com/cayf2005** to review this chapter, answer the questions, and complete the exercises.

# Matching

Match each key term in the left column with the most accurate definition in the right column.

_____ 1. application software

_____ 2. vertical application

_____ 3. horizontal application

_____ 4. standalone program

_____ 5. site license

_____ 6. freeware

_____ 7. shareware

_____ 8. copy-protected software

_____ 9. documentation

_____ 10. status bar

_____ 11. popup menu

_____ 12. autosave

_____ 13. open

_____ 14. save

_____ 15. software piracy

a. software that is designed for a particular line of business or for a division

b. also known as a context menu

c. displays information about the application, as well as the application's messages to the user

d. all the programs that enable computer users to apply the computer to the work they do

e. copyrighted software that is free

f. printed materials in the form of tutorials and reference manuals that explain how to use a program

g. an option that allows you to save your work automatically at specified intervals

h. to locate a document and load it into the application workspace

i. copyrighted software that you can use on a "try before you buy" basis

j. infringing on a program's copyright by making copies for other people

k. self-contained software application that serves one function

l. software that is used across the functional divisions of a company

m. gives you permission to install copies of a program on a specified number of computers

n. to transfer a document from memory to a storage device such as a hard or floppy disk

o. includes some type of measure to ensure that you don't make unauthorized copies of the software

Go to **www.prenhall.com/cayf2005** to review this chapter, answer the questions, and complete the exercises.

# Multiple Choice

Circle the correct choice for each of the following.

1. Which of the following is a horizontal application?
   a. computer-aided design software
   b. software to manage a video store
   c. motel management software
   d. word processing programs

2. What do you purchase when you buy a software program?
   a. the unlimited rights to the program and its source code
   b. the right to use the software in accordance with the publisher's software license
   c. a box and a distribution medium such as a disc or CD-ROM
   d. a warranty that guarantees the software will do what you want it to do

3. What term is used to describe keeping your software version current with the marketplace?
   a. upgrading
   b. currency
   c. downgrading
   d. currency release

4. Microsoft Office is an example of what type of program?
   a. standalone
   b. integrated
   c. suite
   d. vertical

5. Which feature should you use if you don't want to shut your computer down completely?
   a. Wait
   b. Wait and Watch
   c. Standby
   d. Conserve

6. Window controls allow users to do which of the following?
   a. maximize a window
   b. minimize a window
   c. close a window
   d. all of the above

7. Integrated programs can be separated into these:
   a. defaults
   b. modules
   c. templates
   d. commands

8. Which of the following is not typically included in software suites?
   a. FTP client
   b. word processing
   c. database
   d. spreadsheet

9. What are maintenance releases?
   a. major revisions to an application
   b. minor revisions to an application
   c. entirely new versions of an application
   d. none of the above

10. The capability to save application files in HTML provides what benefit?
    a. a common format for sharing data with others
    b. the capability to publish on the Web
    c. no need to convert application files
    d. all of the above

# Fill-In

In the blanks provided, write the correct answer for each of the following.

1. _____ applications are typically more expensive than horizontal applications.

2. _____ software is expensive and requires the services of a professional programmer or programming team.

3. _____ is copyrighted software given away for free.

4. A(n) _____ is an addition to a filename that can be used to identify the type of data that the file contains, and sometimes the application that created the file.

5. _____ allow you to choose the way you want a program to operate.

6. _____ software is copyrighted software that you must pay for before you can use it.

7. _____ contain pictures, called icons, that depict the actions performed by the most commonly used commands.

8. The _____ usually contains the name of the application as well as the name of the file you are working on.

9. A(n) _____ combines individual programs into a coordinated package in which they share the user interface, drivers, and libraries.

10. If you want to install a program on a number of machines in your organization, you can purchase a(n) _____.

11. A(n) _____ version is a preliminary version of a program in the final phases of testing.

12. A(n) _____ is a generic version of a document that has already been started for you.

13. The _____ command enables you to save a document using a new filename, a new location, or both.

14. To guide you through lengthy or complex operations, some applications display _____, which are a series of dialog boxes that guide you through a step-by-step procedure.

15. In office suites, _____ uses hypertext markup language to alleviate file compatibility problems.

# Short Answer

1. Name the product and type of application for any beta version of software you have used. Since beta versions may contain errors, describe any problems that you encountered. What procedures did you follow to report any problems to the software producer? If you have not used a beta version, look for the answers to the questions on a beta version FAQs Web page. (Use a search engine for "beta version").

2. What are the differences between shareware, freeware, and public domain software? If you have ever used any of this software, identify the name of the product and type of application. Describe your experience. If you have not used

any of these programs, then use the Web to locate a program and report on what you are able to learn.

3. What are the benefits of registering your software? Do you regularly register your software applications? Why or why not?

4. Identify a software application you needed to uninstall, and explain why it was necessary to remove it. If the application did not uninstall completely, what directories or files still remained?

5. Why should you use the operating system's Turn Off or Shut Down command to turn off your computer? Under what circumstances have you ever just turned off the power?

# A Closer Look

1. A full-function version of a shareware application can be downloaded, installed, and run on your computer for free for a specified period of time. Although your computer will not self-destruct, the application will no longer function after the time interval expires. Have you used this method to evaluate software? Did you eventually purchase the full product? As a consumer, what do you think about this method of distributing and selling software?

2. Interview a faculty member from your major or intended major department to find out what career-specific applications are used by professionals in that discipline. If this is impractical, use the Web to find the information. Identify the discipline and type of applications, and explain how each application is used.

3. As you read in this chapter, a software license gives you the right to install and use a program on only *one* computer. If you want to install a program on more than one computer, you must purchase additional licenses. If you don't, you are in violation of the publisher's copyright. Read the software licenses that are provided with two major application software programs. Identify the product, version, and company. What do the licenses provide you? Are you protected by the licenses? Which product gives you more protection? How would you change them if you could?

4. Presentation software, such as PowerPoint, is typically included with office suites. This kind of software enables you to develop slides and transparencies for presentations. Do any of your instructors use presentation software in their classroom lectures or demonstrations? Have you ever used presentation software in support of a presentation? If so, identify the application and explain why you like or dislike the software.

5. Businesses and institutions frequently use site licenses to purchase multiple copies of software applications. Contact your computing services center to find out if your school uses this method of purchasing software. If it does, identify the applications for which site licenses are purchased. Is student home use of software applications included in the license? What is the primary advantage of purchasing site licenses for an application?

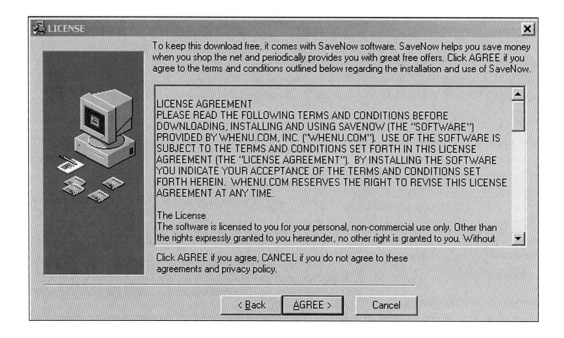

# On the Web

1. In July 1999, the National Conference of Commissioners on Uniform State Laws proposed the controversial Uniform Computer Information Transactions Act (UCITA) as the standard for state laws on software transactions. To learn more about this potential legislation, visit *InfoWorld's* UCITA Web site at **www.infoworld.com/ucita**. Identify two consequences that would result from passing this act. List the names of two organizations and two companies that support the UCITA, and list the names of two organizations and two companies that oppose it. Read the section about UCITA and national security. What is the problem with UCITA with regard to national security? Do you believe UCITA should be done away with? Explain why or why not.

2. Visit **www.microsoft.com**. Locate and select the Office link. Find the links for Product Information and then System Requirements. Prepare a list that compares the minimum system requirements with those that are on the computer you use most often. Be sure to list the version of Office that you are assessing.

3. Do you want some free or inexpensive software? Since the Internet is frequently used for distributing shareware and freeware applications, check out **www.yahoo.com**. Type "freeware" (without the quotes) in the Search box at the top of the window. Browse some of the more than 5.9 million sites that your search returns. Pick one or two to write about. Be sure your description includes the product name, file size, function, and whatever caution you would exercise in using it.

4. Microsoft offers two software suites: Office for business and higher education markets, and Works for home and K–12 educational customers. Which, if either, of these products does your school use? Did you use either of these when attending K–12 schools? Go to Microsoft's Works site at **works.msn.com** to learn about this product. What is the current version of the Works suite? Name the applications that are included in this version. Which are already available as free downloads from Microsoft's Web site? What components are included with Works Suite 2002? What is the estimated retail price of the Works suite? Explain why you would or would not purchase this product.

5. The major competitors of Microsoft Office are Corel WordPerfect Office 2002 and Lotus SmartSuite Millennium Edition 9.6.

   - Visit the Corel Web site at **www.corel.com**. Identify the application areas and product names that are included in the professional version of Corel's office suite. What are the suggested full and upgrade prices? Are there different prices for digital and boxed versions? Is a free trial version available?
   - Visit the IBM Lotus Software Web site at **www.lotus.com**. Identify the application areas and product names that are included in the professional version of Lotus' office suite. What are the suggested full and upgrade prices? Is a free trial version available?
   - Explain why you would or would not purchase either of these products.

Go to **www.prenhall.com/cayf2005** to review this chapter, answer the questions, and complete the exercises.

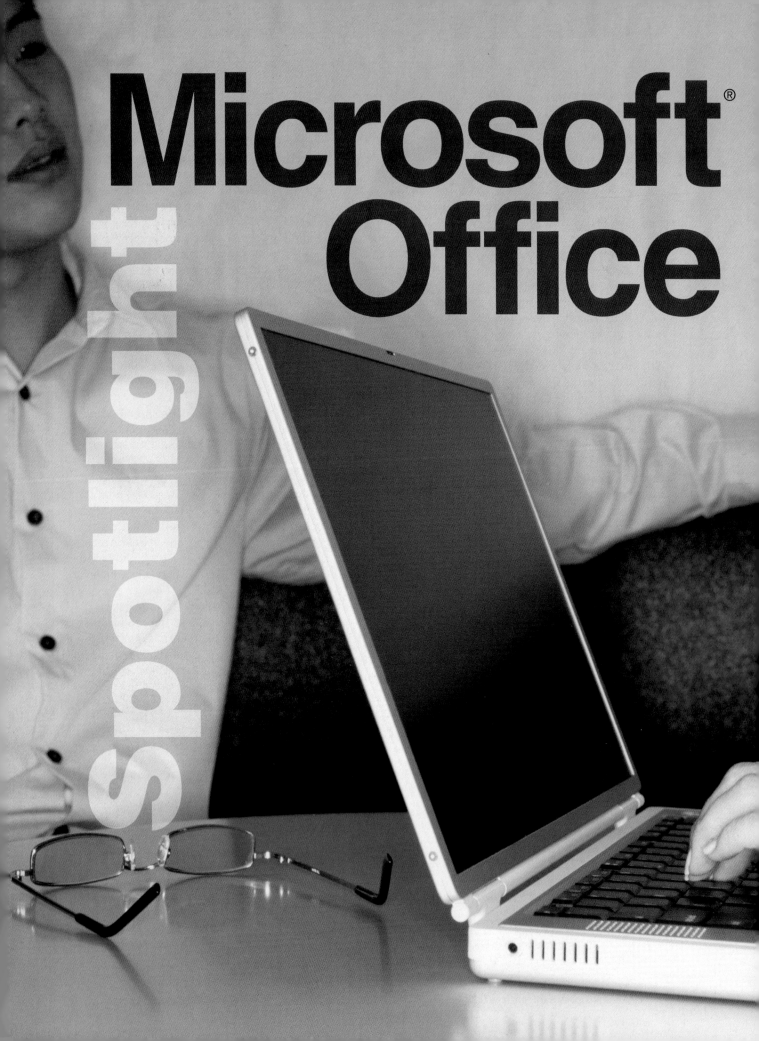

*You're at work and your boss tells you she needs you to create a presentation for her to deliver at the annual stockholders' meeting in two days. Although you know creating a professional presentation is a challenge, this is the opportunity you've been waiting for—you were hired in part because of your abilities to use productivity software programs.*

*You get started right away by using Microsoft Access to generate reports that provide you with important information regarding your company's activities throughout the year. You then import the data you have extracted from Access into Microsoft Excel so that you can perform some statistical analysis and produce a number of key charts and graphs for stockholders. Now that you've got the background materials covered, you open Microsoft Word. Into your Word document, you copy your Excel charts and a number of the Access reports you have generated. You also type and format the meeting agenda that your boss will distribute to the attendees. Now comes*

**FIGURE 2A**
The ability to use software programs such as those in Microsoft Office will help you gain a competitive edge in many careers.

*the fun part: you open PowerPoint and create a professional, visually appealing presentation using the Word, Excel, and Access documents you've already created. As you put the finishing touches on your presentation—embedding an MP3 file into the introduction slide—you realize you've finally been able to use the skills you've worked so hard to acquire.*

*All of the programs you've used to help you create your presentation are components of a suite of software programs called* **Microsoft Office.** *This Spotlight explores the various programs, features, and uses of Microsoft Office (Figure 2A).*

# Introducing Office

Microsoft was the first company to develop the concept of an office suite. In Chapter 3 we defined a suite as an interconnected bundle of programs that share resources with each other and are designed to help workers accomplish the tasks they perform in a typical office environment. If Microsoft Windows is your desktop, then an office suite is the set of tools that you typically use at work.

In the early 1990s Microsoft started bundling two standalone programs: Word and Excel. Word was the word processing program that Microsoft used to compete with the early market leader, WordPerfect. Likewise, Excel competed with Lotus 1-2-3. Soon, both Word and Excel left their competition far behind.

Before suites came along, you could only buy standalone programs. In those days you could purchase Word and install it and purchase Excel and install it, and neither program would know about the

other, nor would they share any resources such as menus, drivers, graphics libraries, and tools. Obviously, this was a very inefficient way to install and use software when the programs had so many features they could share.

When Microsoft recognized that its programs could share all of these features if they were bundled together, Office was born. At first, the bundled programs shared only the menu system and toolbars. Eventually, however, the programs were able to share graphics libraries, drawing tools, printer and other device drivers, and more.

Microsoft Office is sold in three versions: Standard, Professional, and Developer. The Standard version includes Word, Excel, Outlook (for managing e-mail and contacts), and PowerPoint. (Office for the Macintosh uses a program called Entourage for managing e-mail and contacts.) The Professional version includes the Standard version programs as well as Access and the FrontPage Web site creation and management program. It also includes additional tools and documentation for building, deploying, and managing Office-based solutions. The Developer version includes everything in the Professional version as well as a Visual Basic programmer's tool set and other programs that are used in creating and managing Office files. Released in 2003, Office 2003 is the most recent version of Office on the market (Figure 2B).

In the following sections we'll look more closely at how Office components can help you represent your thoughts, ideas, and solutions in a professional way.

**FIGURE 2B**
Microsoft Office 2003 is the result of many generations of Office.

## THE SHARED OFFICE INTERFACE AND TOOLS

Microsoft programs share a common **user interface**, the part of the operating system through which users interact with the computer. You learned about the user interface and the terms that are used to describe it in Chapter 3. Office applications use many interface objects that are similar to those of Windows.

The topmost area of each program interface is called the **title bar**. It includes the program icon, the name of the program being used, the name of the file that is open in the program, and the minimize, restore, and close buttons. The bottom part of the program interface, called the **status bar**, contains specific information about your activities within the program, such as the current page number and number of pages in your document (Figure 2C).

The shared interface also includes the menu bar and toolbars. The **menu bar** is made up of pull-down menus that include top-level headings such as File, Edit, View, Insert, Format, Tools, and Help. When you click a menu heading, a pull-down list appears, allowing you to choose among a number of tasks that you can complete. For instance, you might choose the File menu and then the Open command to bring up the Open dialog box.

**Toolbars** consist of icons that act as shortcuts to using the pull-down menus (Figure 2D). For instance, if you click the printer icon on the standard toolbar, your file is sent directly to the printer. (If you work on a Mac and click the printer icon, the print dialog box appears.) The printer icon takes the place of the File, Print, OK menu sequence you would use via the menu bar. To launch or activate the various toolbars, select View, Toolbars from the menu bar.

Two toolbars, the **Standard toolbar** and **Formatting toolbar**, are loaded by default in Word, Excel, and PowerPoint. The Standard toolbar includes icons that allow you to open, close, print, spell check, copy, paste, and save your file, as well as several more options. The Formatting toolbar includes icons that allow you to choose the document font, font size, style (bold, italic, or underlined), indentation, bullet style, and more. Dozens of other toolbars are available within the various Office applications, and you can also customize existing toolbars or create your own toolbars

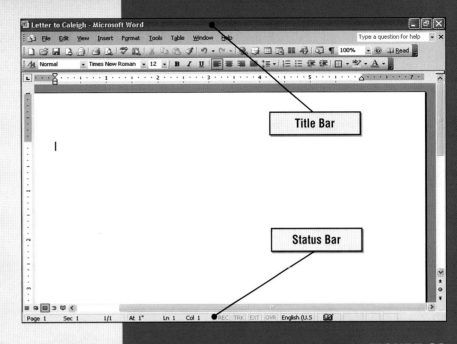

**FIGURE 2C**

The title and status bars provide information about the program and allow you to resize the program window on your desktop.

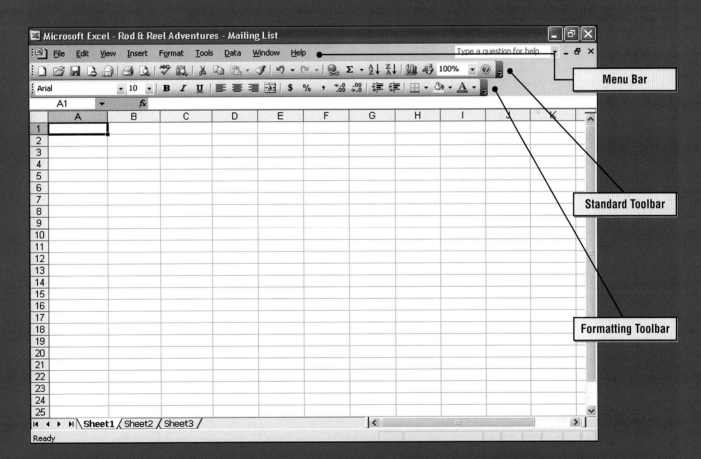

**FIGURE 2D**

Toolbars include icons that act as shortcuts to program menu choices, while menu bar sequences often allow you to make choices about the function or feature you're invoking.

**FIGURE 2E**
The Clip Organizer is an efficient way to insert images.

to suit your needs. To do so, choose the View, Toolbars, Customize menu sequence.

### Other Shared Resources and Features

Office applications share a number of other resources, including the Clip Organizer, print drivers, and the Office Clipboard. Recent versions of Office offer such shared features as the task pane and smart tags, as well as templates and wizards.

The **Clip Organizer** is a repository of clip art and images

that you can insert into a document or presentation (Figure 2E). You can access the Clip Organizer by selecting Insert, Picture, Clip Art from the menu bar. Whereas each standalone program accessed its own separate gallery of images, in Office all the applications share the same gallery.

Another shared feature of Office applications is the use of drivers. For instance, when you install a printer, some of the files that are placed on your hard drive are called print drivers. Print drivers contain the printer's instruction set. In the early days of computing, you needed to select a printer for each application you wished to use. Today, print drivers

are installed from the Windows operating environment Control Panel and are shared by all of the programs installed on your PC. The Macintosh OS has always had this feature, but it wasn't available for the PC until Microsoft recognized that the operating environment, rather than the program, should control the printer.

Office applications also share the Clipboard. The **Office Clipboard** temporarily stores in memory whatever you've cut or copied from a document and makes those cut or copied items available for use within any Office application. For example, you can create a financial summary in Excel, copy it to the Clipboard, and then paste it into Word.

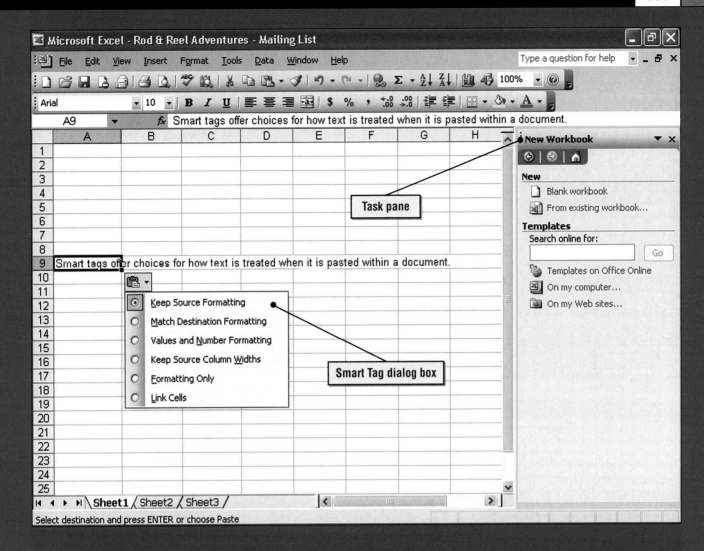

FIGURE 2F
The task pane provides options for creating work, and smart tags offer choices for how text is treated when it's pasted within an application or between applications.

Another shared feature, which first appeared in Office XP, is the task pane (Figure 2F). The **task pane** usually appears on the right side of the window whenever an application is first opened. It contains options for opening work, creating new work, and formatting work, among other things. You can close the task pane by clicking the X in the top right corner, and open it again by choosing View, Task Pane from the menu bar.

Most Office applications also have smart tags (Figure 2F). **Smart tags** are icons that are attached to items that you've pasted, or text and data that the program recognizes as a place where you might want to choose different options. When you click a smart tag, a small menu of choices appears. For example, when you copy text from one place in a Word document and paste it to another place, or if you switch over into an Excel spreadsheet and paste the text there, a smart tag appears, listing options for how the pasted text should be treated. In this example, the options would be to keep the formatting from Word or change the formatting to that of the destination cell in Excel.

You can turn off both the task pane and the smart tags features by selecting Tools, Options, View from the menu bar.

Other shared features within Office applications include templates and wizards. **Templates** are document frameworks that are created once and then used many times. For example, you might create a personal letterhead template. **Wizards** provide a stepwise process for solving a problem. The mail merge wizard is used to create multiple documents by merging a document template with a data source.

Now that you've gotten an overview of Office, let's explore each of the applications individually.

# Microsoft® Word

Microsoft Word is a very powerful word processing program. In fact, it's so powerful that it rivals software made especially for desktop publishing. As with other Office applications, its interface includes the title bar, Standard toolbar, Formatting toolbar, and status bar. The remainder of the screen is basically a blank sheet of paper upon which you can create documents (Figure 2G).

Using Word at its most basic level is extraordinarily simple; you just type text into the Word document and press the print button on the Standard toolbar to send your document to the printer. Word features automatic text and page wrapping, a find and replace utility, and the ability to cut, copy, and paste both within the document and between documents or other programs. To improve the presentation and professional look of your documents, there are editing and formatting tools such as inserting headers/footers, page breaks, page numbers, and dates. Word also includes a number of other features that can enhance your ability to present your thoughts in a formal way. For example, you can embed pictures, graphics, charts, tables, and other objects into your document. You can work with columns and set tabs to align text. You can print your document in portrait or landscape orientation. It's almost true that if you can imagine it, you can do it in Word.

Word also comes with a library of templates (Figure 2H). Fax cover sheets are a good example of template use. The Office applications that have templates store them in a special folder that you access by selecting File, New from the menu bar. The task pane opens and you see a selection of templates to choose from.

In addition to the templates that Microsoft provides, you can

**FIGURE 2G**
The Word interface is very simple and intuitive.

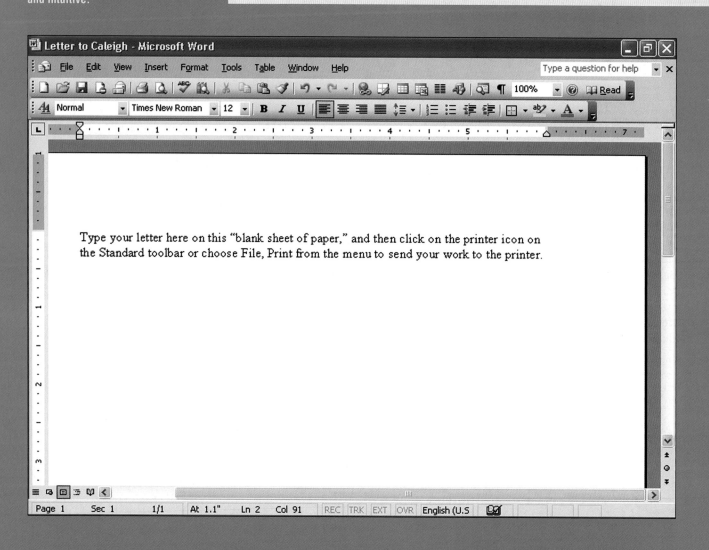

also save files as templates yourself. For example, if you use the same format repeatedly in your college papers, you can save your paper format as a template. That way, the next time you write a paper you won't have to re-create all of the margins or indentations. To create a template, open the file you'd like to save as a template and select File, Save As from the menu bar. In the dialog box that appears, select Template from the Save As Type pull-down menu at the bottom of the dialog box. Now, every time you wish to use your template, you can access it by selecting File, New from the menu bar, or directly from the task pane.

If you're using a PC, the files that you create in Word include the .doc extension by default. (If you're using a Mac, no such extension is needed.) Word can also save your documents as plain text (.txt), Web pages (.htm), Rich Text Format (.rtf), or in a format that can be read by previous versions of Word and competing products, such as WordPerfect. You will learn about other Office program extensions as you continue reading this Spotlight.

Now that you have a basic understanding of what Word can do for you, you're ready to move on to other Office applications. The following section will introduce you to Excel.

**FIGURE 2H**
Templates are very useful for providing a standardized framework for new documents.

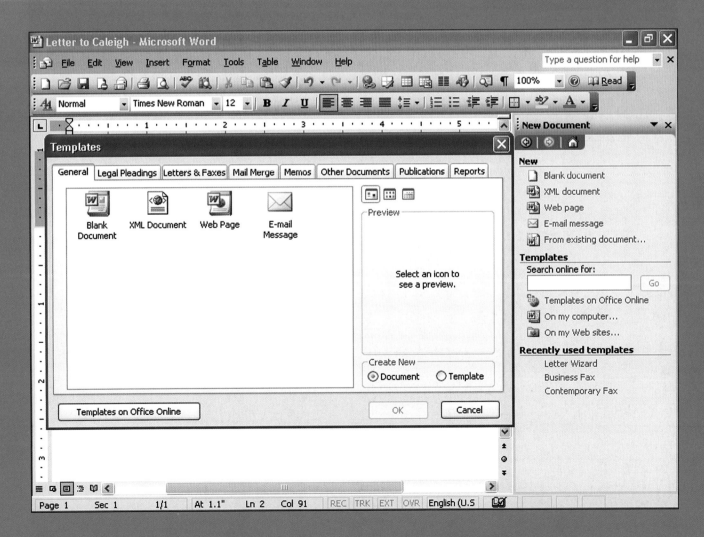

# Microsoft® Excel

Microsoft Excel is the most popular spreadsheet program in the world. The primary function of a spreadsheet program is to store and manipulate numbers. You use a spreadsheet either to record things that have actually happened or predict things that might happen through a method called **modeling** or what-if analysis. Projected income statements are a good example of spreadsheet modeling. You plug in your assumptive values, and the model provides the prediction. If your assumptions are correct, the model will closely match the actual outcome. If not, then you can learn from your experience and perhaps make better assumptions in the future.

Excel's user interface is very similar to that of Word. One major difference is that in Excel, the menu bar has a choice for Data, whereas Word has a choice for Tables. The Standard and Formatting toolbars are almost identical. Like Word, Excel has a status bar at the bottom of the screen, along with scroll bars that enable you to move your view vertically and horizontally.

In Excel, each file is called a **workbook**. A workbook may contain as many as 255 **sheets**. Each sheet is composed of **columns** and **rows**, the intersections of which are called **cells** (Figure 2I).

Spreadsheets have a fixed maximum size, which is 256 columns wide (column A through column IV) and 65,536 rows deep. This may not seem important, but you might consider the number of available columns to be a limitation if you wished to have a column for every day of the year or the rows a limitation if you wished to list 100,000 items. Interestingly, there is no limit to the number of pages you can create in a Word document, or the number of slides you can create in a PowerPoint presentation, or the amount of data you can store in

## FIGURE 2I

Spreadsheets are composed of cells, on sheets, in workbooks.

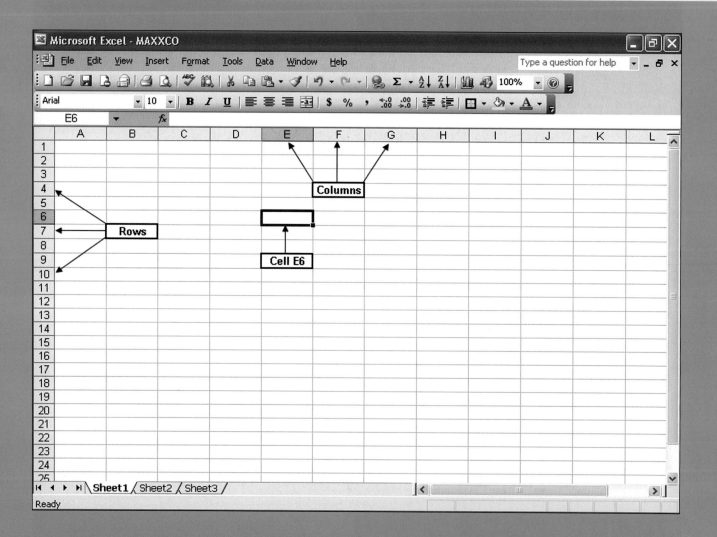

tables in Access. But Excel does have limits. In fact, you can have only as many as 255 sheets in a workbook—a limit that most of us will never encounter, but a limit just the same.

Everything you do in Excel must be contained in a cell. Nothing can occupy more than one cell. A cell is identified by its column letter and then its row number. The columns in a spreadsheet are identified by the letters of the alphabet, and the rows by numbers. For example, A1, B3, and AC342 each represent an individual cell.

A **range** (two or more cells selected at the same time) of cells is identified by the addresses of the top left and bottom right cells, separated by a colon. For example, the range from cell A1 to cell D5 would be represented as A1:D5.

Cells are used for storing text, numbers, and formulas. Text entries, also referred to as **labels**, are used to identify numeric entries. For example, you might type the label "First month's rent" in cell A5 and then place the value "$650" next to it in cell B5. Labels are also used to identify typed-in numbers and the results of formulas. A **formula** is a combination of numeric constants, cell references, arithmetic operators, and/or functions that display the result of a calculation. Excel interprets a cell entry as a formula if the entry is preceded by the equals sign (=). Formulas come in two types: mathematic expressions and functions. In a **mathematic formula**, the mathematic order of operations is followed; that is, values in parentheses are acted upon first, followed by exponentiation, multiplication, division, addition, and subtraction (PEMDAS or Please Excuse My Dear Aunt Sallie). For example: =6*(4–2)/3+2 is equal to 6—because 4 minus 2 is 2, and 6 times 2 is 12, and 12 divided by 3 is 4, and 4 plus 2 is 6.

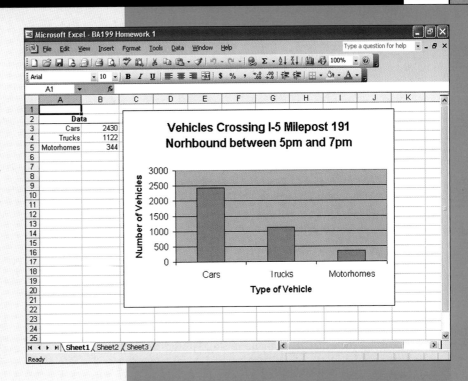

**FIGURE 2J**
An Excel chart can add emphasis to your reports.

The other type of a formula is called a function. A **function** is a very powerful type of formula because it includes the ability to perform operations on multiple inputs. As an example, the payment function is able to take the rate of interest, time period, and amount borrowed to produce the payment amount on a loan. Like mathematic formulas, functions begin with the equals sign. However, they then list the name of the function (such as PMT for calculating payments on a loan) and an argument set, which is placed within parentheses. An **argument set** contains the passable parameters or variables in a function. In the loan example above, the argument set contains the rate of interest, the time period of the loan, and the amount borrowed. For example, =PMT(.005,48,18000) would return the payment for a loan of $18,000 at an interest rate of 6 percent for 48 months.

Excel also has features for creating **charts**, which are a graphical representation of data (Figure 2J). Charts are based upon data sets and the labels that identify the data. There are two primary kinds of charts: bar charts and area charts or pie charts. **Bar charts** show each element in comparison to the other elements in a numeric way. **Area charts** or **pie charts** show each element as a percentage of the sum of all the elements. Several other tools are also available for developing, managing, and assessing data. You can create pivot tables and charts or sorted reports with subtotals, and you can use the database feature to extract information from your data set.

To learn more about creating charts and reports in Excel, consult the online help at **www.microsoft.com** or the Excel Help wizard.

So, Word provides you a tool to accomplish work up to and including desktop publishing, and you can use Excel to work with numbers. Now we'll take a look at the Office application for managing databases.

# Microsoft® Access

Database concepts are very simple: you capture data, store them, manipulate them, and create a report. This collection of data is referred to as a **database**. Microsoft Access, which is available in the Professional and Developer Office suites, is a database management system (DBMS). A **database management system** (**DBMS**) is a software application that is designed to manage the functions of capturing, storing, manipulating, and reporting data and information. In short, a database management system manages databases.

The Access interface is similar to that of Word and Excel, but is also different in many ways. The opening interface includes the menu bar, a Standard toolbar, and the task pane on the right-hand side (Figure 2K). In Access, you must always work on an existing or new database that you've named and saved to disk. There is no default blank database screen analogous to the blank document in Word or the blank worksheet in Excel. Access must always work between storage and memory—you cannot work within the program without first establishing a file on disk.

Two types of databases exist: flat file and relational. The difference between them is defined by the number of tables they contain. A **table** holds data in cells, which are formed by the intersection of a column and row. A **flat file database** is a database that has only one table. A **relational database**, on the other hand, is one in which there is more than one table. Access is a relational DBMS.

**FIGURE 2K**

The Access opening interface is rather stark in comparison to Word and Excel.

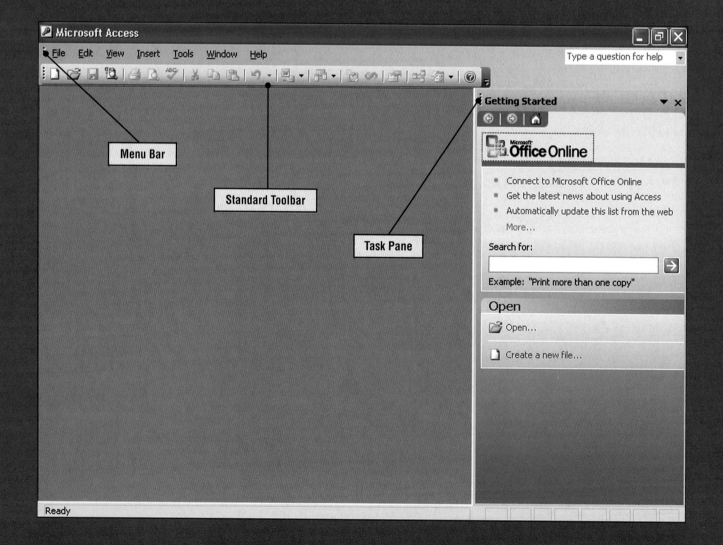

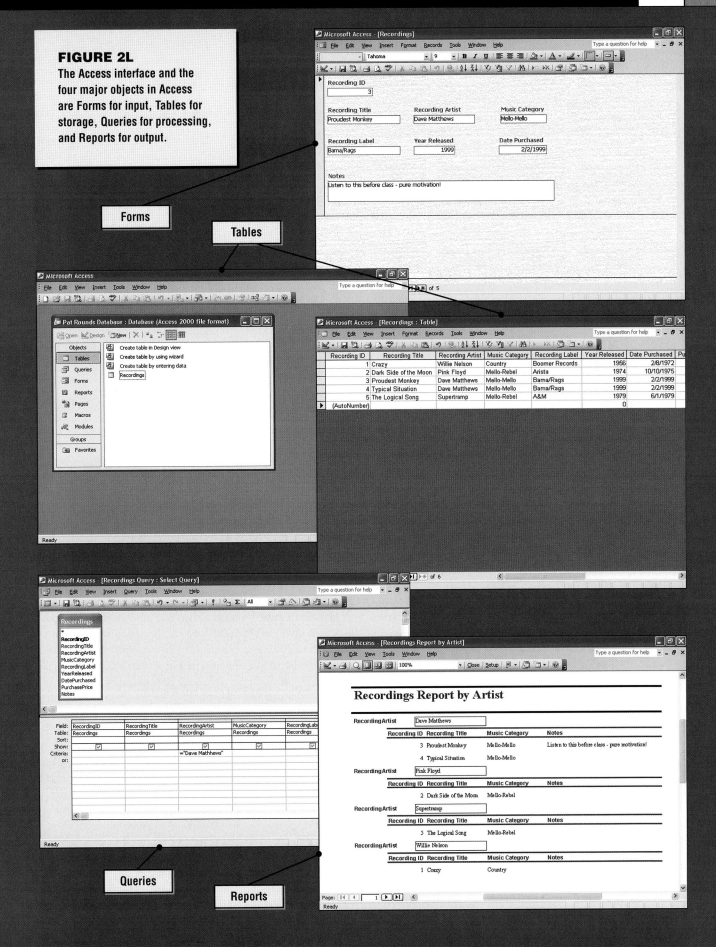

**FIGURE 2L**

The Access interface and the four major objects in Access are Forms for input, Tables for storage, Queries for processing, and Reports for output.

Forms

Tables

Queries

Reports

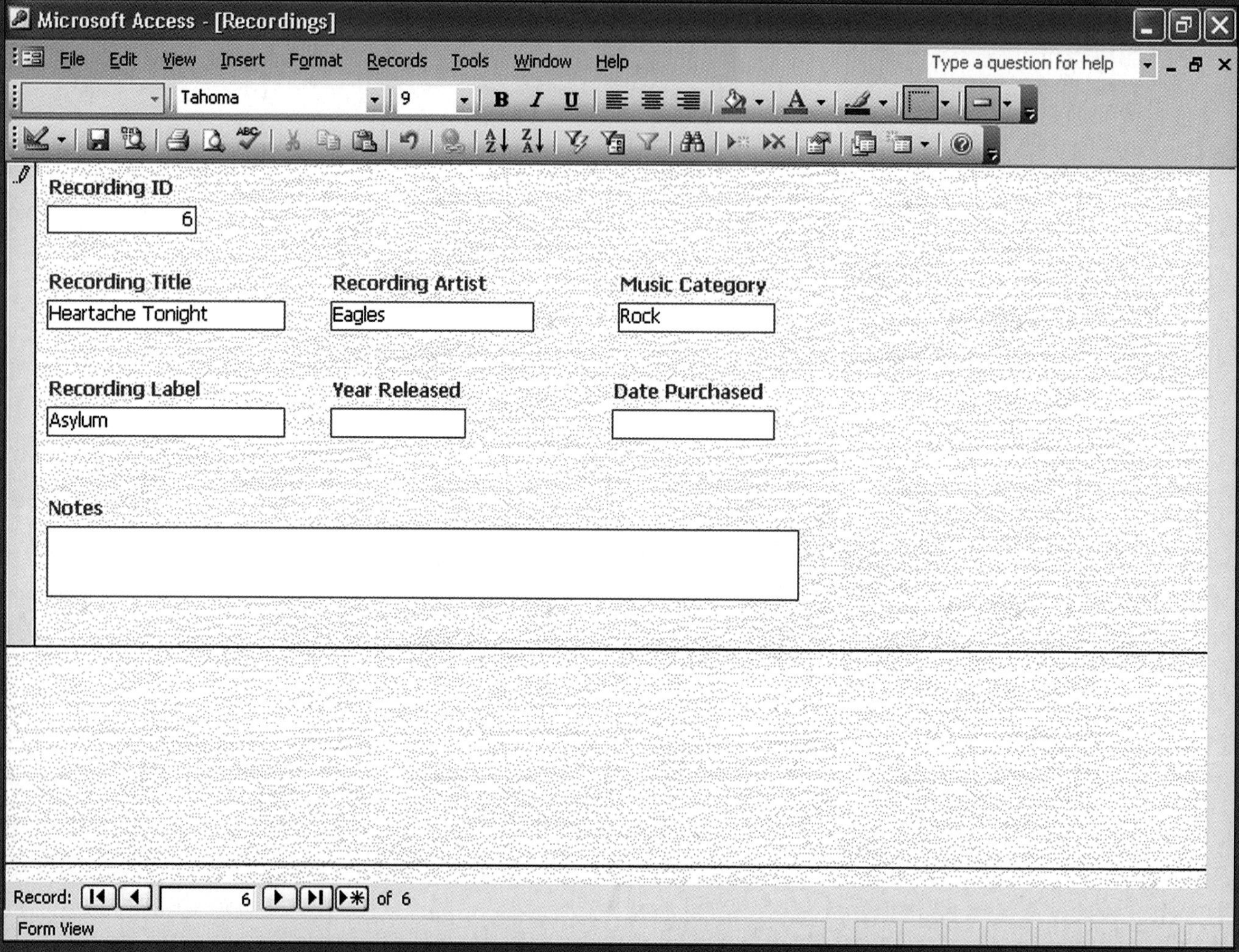

**FIGURE 2M**
The Form object provides a sophisticated interface to the records that are stored in tables.

Access is designed to work with and manage data. **Data** are raw facts that become information when they are organized in such a way so as to be useful and provide meaning. Access uses objects to manage and present data. In Access an **object** is a subprogram that manages one aspect of database management. For instance, you use the **Form object** to collect data, the **Table object** to store data, the **Query object** to ask questions of the database, and the **Report object** to present your

data (Figure 2L, Figure 2M). The functions of these four objects match your computer's input, storage, processing, and output functions. (The order is usually input, processing, output, and storage, but in a database management system the input has to be stored before it can be processed.) A relatively new feature in Access is the **Data Access Page object**, which is used to post data to the Web so that others can retrieve it.

The columns of a table are referred to as fields. A **field** is a collection of data that are of the same type. For instance, fields might hold last names, first names, addresses, and so forth. The rows of a table are referred to as records. A **record** is a collection of field data that rep-

resent a person, place, or thing. You might think of your checkbook; the fields are the check number, date, recipient, and amount. Each check is a record of a transaction.

Access is capable of importing data from many sources, including, of course, Microsoft Excel. If the data isn't imported, then a form is usually used for data entry. A **form** is a formatted document containing blank fields that users can fill in with data. You have filled out physical and electronic forms many times in your life. Forms should be organized so that the person who is typing in the data can easily move from one field to the next in a logical order.

To be useful, the data must usually be processed using the Query object. The Query object allows you to ask questions of a data set. A **data set** describes the contents of a table. Let's say you have a data set that includes the names and addresses of family, friends, and business associates. You want to send a mailing to your family to let them know how school has been going. To find the names and addresses of just your family members, you would run a query on your data set and set the filtering parameter to include only those names that have a field entry under the field name "family."

A **filter** is a pattern through which data are passed. Only data that matches the pattern are allowed to pass through the filter. In this case you are asking the data set to provide you with your family members and no one else. The filtering parameter is that the query will only return records where the field for "family" is checked. In a large organization with a multi-table database that has tens of thousands of records, queries are very important.

When you use Access, you need to present the results of your query in a manner that is not only useful but is professional in appearance—in short, you

must design a report. The Report object is the only object that most of us see. We receive reports from databases all of the time. Junk mail, a utility bill, and credit card solicitations all come from reports that are generated from massive data sets.

Access is the only Office program that doesn't include the Save As feature to save files. You may use Save As to save an *object* within your database, but you can't save an open database to another location or give it another name. This can be a concern because Access is a complex program and it's possible you'll make mistakes that can cost you a lot of lost time and energy if you have to restore your entire database back to the way it was before you made the mistake. Most database managers, therefore, create intermediate copies of their work, just in case something goes wrong with the copy they're working on.

Let's look at an example. When you work in an application such as Word, the work you accomplish is all in memory until you initially save it to disk. Once you've saved your work to disk, the subsequent work you perform is in memory

until you either save over the work you've saved before (using the Save command), or choose a new folder and/or filename for your added work (using the Save As command).

As you just learned, because you can't use the Save or Save As command in Access, if you make a mistake, the work you have in memory is often the same as the work you have on disk. Access doesn't continually save everything you do, but it writes to disk often enough to make it very difficult to predict whether your actions have been recorded over your previously saved work. This means that it's possible for you to lose your entire database if you don't have a backup copy. The solution is to always make a copy of your work *before* a work session and then work on that copy.

To learn more about how to use Access, visit the online help provided at **www.microsoft.com**. You can also use the Access wizards to learn how to create the objects that you'll need to manage whatever projects you may undertake.

Let's now look at a program that's a favorite among many college students: PowerPoint.

# Microsoft® PowerPoint®

Microsoft PowerPoint is a popular program used to create and deliver presentations. The task pane on the right side of the screen allows you to choose to open an existing presentation, a new blank presentation, or a new presentation based on a design template, or to use a wizard to create a presentation by answering questions or choosing from a list of topics.

PowerPoint opens to a blank slide that is in the Title slide format

(Figure 2N). A **slide** is the canvas upon which you organize text boxes and graphics to represent your ideas or points. There are currently 27 slide layouts from which you can choose. Each layout has text or graphics boxes into which you can type text or embed graphics. While it is true that the various boxes are in a set position on the slide canvas, you may modify or move them around on the slide if you wish. Each slide layout

is named; a Title slide has two text boxes: the top box is for the title of your presentation, and the bottom box is for a subtitle or your name. You might choose Title and Text as the layout for your second slide as it has a text box for your title at the top of the slide and a bulleted list text box for your major presentation points on the lower portion of the slide.

A PowerPoint template contains preformatted fonts, text and graphic

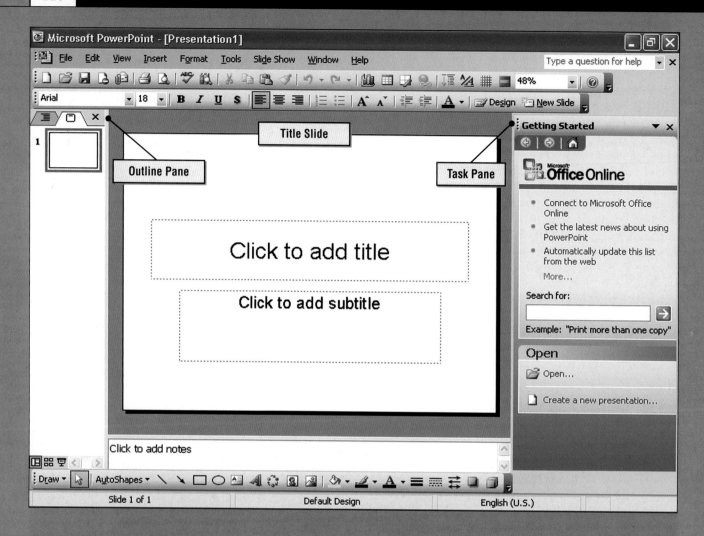

**FIGURE 2N**
The initial PowerPoint screen features the outline pane on the left, a blank title slide in the center, and the task pane on the right.

locations, and color schemes. **Design templates** are professionally created slide designs that can be applied to a presentation. You might create your slides in the blank presentation (black and white with no special fonts or effects) and then apply various design templates until you achieve the desired effect (Figure 2O).

The AutoContent Wizard is an interactive tool that guides you through the process of creating a presentation. It includes presentation categories for home and business projects, as well as the Carnegie Coach. The Carnegie Coach provides presentation outlines on a wide variety of topics—everything from selling your ideas to introducing and thanking a speaker. The coach suggests the content, and you simply customize it with the details for your particular presentation.

Once you've written your outline, you are ready to create your presentation. The two easiest ways to do so are to use the wizard or to begin with a blank presentation. Using the wizard will result in slides that have a design template applied and at least the beginnings of your presentation embedded. You would then add and remove content to complete your work. If you begin with a blank presentation, you will perform an iterative process of typing in your text, choosing whether or not to include graphics, inserting a new slide that is based on a slide layout template, and then repeating.

It's very easy to get caught up in all of the bells and whistles available in PowerPoint. Ultimately, though, *you* are the presenter and therefore *you* must command your audience. A good PowerPoint presentation should serve as a backdrop to your presentation (Figure 2P).

Be forewarned: presentations almost never look the same on a video projector as they do on your computer screen. With this in mind, it's a good idea to try out your presentation in the room where you'll give it. If you allow yourself plenty of time, you'll be able to change the design template

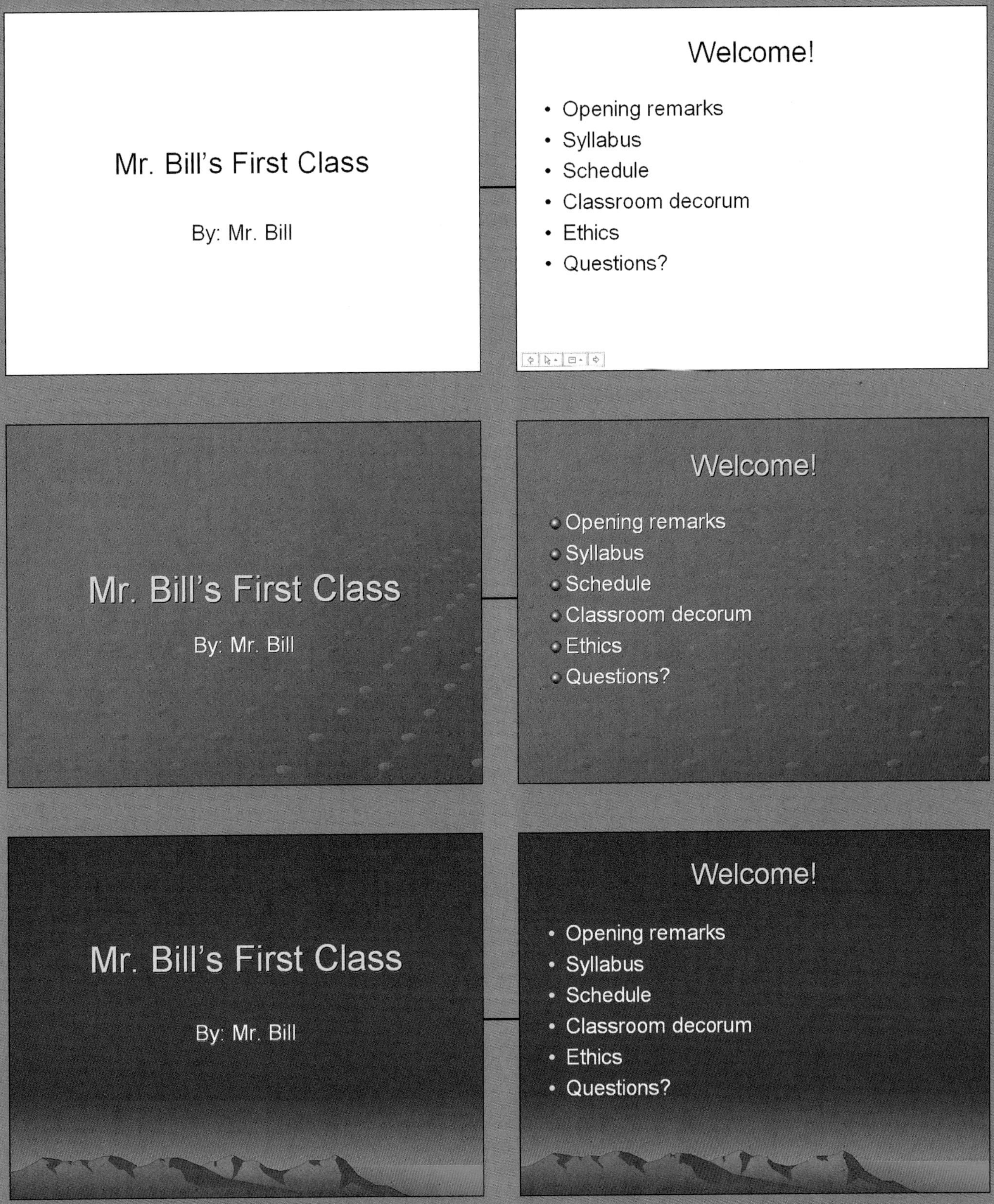

**FIGURE 20**
Design templates provide a robust way to present a feeling along with your message.

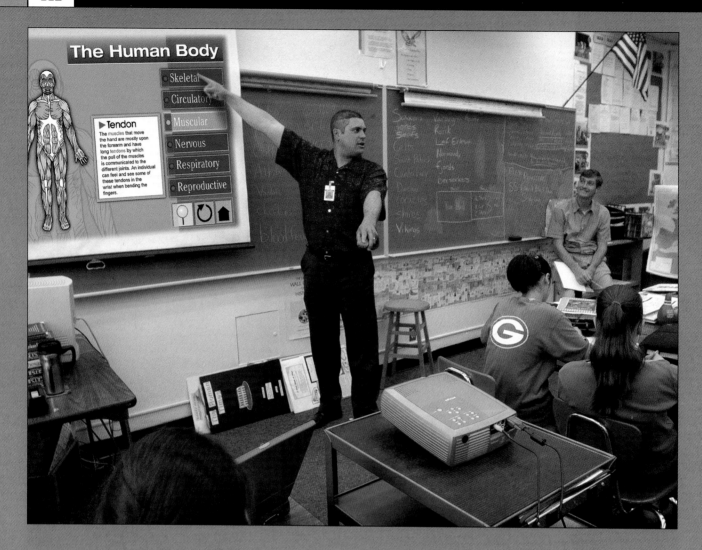

to colors that will work best in the room. Professional presenters often purchase digital light projectors and use them to consistently project their presentations, thus eliminating the variability found in using whatever system is installed in the room.

Let's now move on to a program that will help you communicate with others and manage your busy schedule: Outlook.

# Microsoft® Outlook

Microsoft Outlook is an e-mail and organizational communications tool that you can use to send and receive mail, maintain a personal calendar, schedule meetings with coworkers, and store information about your personal contacts. Figure 2Q shows the Outlook interface.

When you use the e-mail function of Outlook, you obviously need to know the recipient's e-mail address. E-mail addresses are composed of two parts: the name of the mailbox owner and the address where the mailbox resides. Mailbox addresses follow the same syntax as Web addresses, usually a server name followed by the domain type. For example, an e-mail address might look like **president@whitehouse.gov**.

Outlook also has an autocomplete feature that suggests the completion of an address

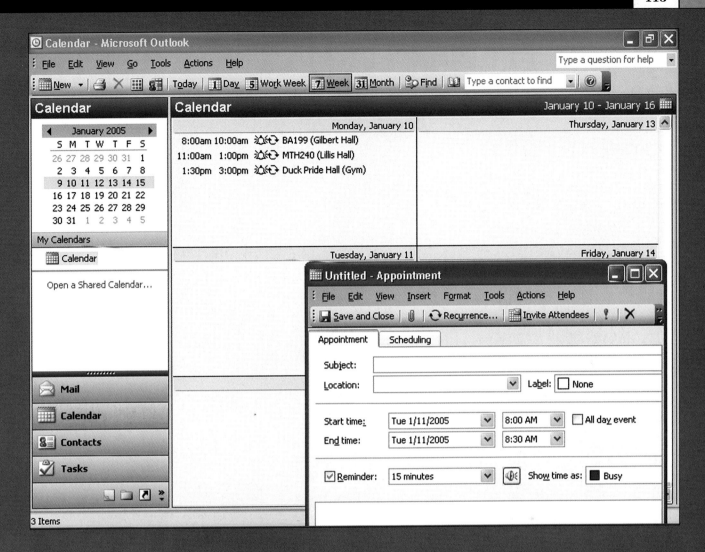

FIGURE 2Q
The Outlook calendar is a good way to manage your busy college schedule.

you've already used as you type on the To: line. For example, if you begin typing the address **myfriend@yahoo.com**, the auto-complete feature suggests the complete address when you type the third letter, f, in myfriend. If the suggestion is correct, press the Enter key to insert the address. If the suggestion is not what you intend, then simply keep typing the correct address.

One feature of Outlook that is very helpful is the ability to create folders, which you can use to organize your saved e-mail messages. For example, you could create a Family folder for family mail, a separate folder for each of your classes, and perhaps a Friends folder for personal messages you've received from friends. Placing mail that you've read into these folders will then help you keep your inbox uncluttered.

You may find the Outlook calendar helpful in managing all of the activities associated with school, work, and socializing. The calendar is very easy to use and even features an alarm to alert you 10 or 15 minutes before a scheduled event.

The best way to learn how to use Outlook is to experiment with it. Also remember that you can use the Help program to learn how to use the various features Outlook includes. You'll be surprised at just how easy it is to manage Outlook.

# Summary

Microsoft Office offers versatility, flexibility, and customization for your desktop. The tools, templates, wizards, and integration will serve you well in communicating your ideas to others.

# Inside the System Unit

## What You'll Learn . . .

- Understand how computers represent data.

- Understand the measurements used for transferring or storing data.

- Describe the various physical connectors on the exterior of the system unit and explain their use.

- List the components found inside the system unit and explain their use.

- List the components found on the computer's motherboard and explain the role they play in the functioning of the computer's systems.

- Discuss (in general terms) how a computer's central processing unit (CPU) processes data.

- Explain the factors that determine a microprocessor's performance.

- List the various types of memory found in a computer system and explain the purpose of each.

### Destinations

For a great Web guide to personal computer hardware, see "PC Guide" at **www.pcguide.com/intro/over.htm**. Author Charles Kozierok presents a free, detailed survey of PC system components, including special sections on system care, system enhancement, and troubleshooting. If you're thinking about upgrading your system or if you want to understand what a particular component does, this site is a great place to start.

# Describing Hardware Performance

Before we launch into our discussion of the system unit and its components, it's important that you understand a few things about hardware performance. As you learned in Chapter 1, computers perform four basic functions: inputting data, processing these data, displaying the results using output devices, and storing the results for subsequent use. Computer hardware, especially the system unit, is involved in all of these functions.

When we talk about hardware *performance*, we're referring to how fast the computer can obtain, process, display, and store these data. To communicate knowledgeably with others about the capabilities of computer hardware, you need to learn the terminology that's used to describe *how* computers represent data as well as *how much* data computers can transfer or store.

Computer performance is often considered to be approximate to the speed of the processor—but the processor's capabilities are only part of the complete picture. Imagine that you have an engine that produces 500 horsepower. If you put this engine in your stock sedan and apply that horsepower aggressively, you'll soon begin to break things. The stock transmission, drive train, and axles are not designed to handle so much power. Your tires and wheels may not be able to handle the transfer of energy to the pavement. You will have an engine that you cannot fully use. It's the same with computers—all of the components need to be matched.

Now that you have a brief overview of hardware performance, let's look at how computers represent data.

# How Computers Represent Data

To understand computer hardware, you need to understand the basic concepts of digital computing—and that means you need to know the essentials of how computers represent data.

In order for a computer to work with data, the data must be represented inside the computer. Computers can't do anything without data to work with. In the next section, you'll learn that the technique used to represent data within the computer—by means of digits—explains a great deal about both the strengths and the limitations of modern computers.

## REPRESENTING DATA AS NUMBERS

We're all used to counting with decimal numbers, which consist of 10 digits (0, 1, 2, 3, 4, 5, 6, 7, 8, 9). Computers count with **binary numbers**, which consist of only two digits (0 and 1). A binary number is called a binary digit, or bit for short. A **bit** is the smallest unit of information that a computer can work with (Figure 4.1).

You can think of a bit as being similar to a light switch: it has only two possible states and is always in one or the other. If you have one light switch, you have the possibility that the switch is on or that it is off. If you have two light switches, then you have four possibilities: both switches are on, both switches are off, the first switch is on and the second switch is off, or the first switch is off and the second switch is on. Three switches allow for eight possibilities, and so on—up to eight switches, which results in 256 possible combinations.

A **byte** consists of 8 bits and represents one unit of storage. Since it takes 8 bits (on/off switches) to make a byte, and 8 bits result in 256 possible on/off combinations, you'll see the number 256 appearing behind the scenes in many computer functions and applications. A single

**FIGURE 4.1**
A binary number is called a binary digit, or bit for short. A bit is the smallest unit of information with which a computer can work.

| Binary digit | 0 | 1 |
|---|---|---|
| Bit | ○ | ● |
| Status | On | Off |

**FIGURE 4.2  Measurements that Describe Units of Data**

| Measurement | Abbreviation | Approximate Amount | Exact Amount | Text |
|---|---|---|---|---|
| **Bit** | b | | 1/8th of a byte | none |
| **Byte** | B | | 1 byte | one character |
| **Kilobyte** | KB or K | 1 thousand bytes | 1,024 bytes | one page |
| **Megabyte** | MB or M | 1 million bytes | 1,048,576 bytes | 1,000 pages |
| **Gigabyte** | GB or G | 1 billion bytes | 1,043,741,824 bytes | 1,000 books |
| **Terabyte** | TB or T | 1 trillion bytes | 1,099,511,627,776 bytes | 1 million books |

byte usually represents one character of data, such as the essential numbers (0–9), the basic letters of the alphabet in English and European languages, and the most common punctuation symbols. For this reason, you can use the byte as a baseline for understanding just how much information a computer is storing. For example, a typical college essay contains 250 words per page, and each word contains (on average) 5.5 characters. So the page contains about 1,375 characters. In other words, you need about 1,375 bytes of storage for one page of a college paper.

Bits (1s and 0s) are commonly used for measuring the data transfer rate (the number of bits transmitted per second) of computer communications devices such as modems, whereas bytes are commonly used to measure data storage. To describe rapid data transfer rates, the measurements **kilobits per second (Kbps), megabits per second (Mbps),** and **gigabits per second (Gbps)** are used. These rates correspond (roughly) to one thousand, one million, and one billion bits per second. Remember that these terms refer to *bits* per second, not *bytes* per second. A modem that can transfer 53 Kbps (about 53,000 bits per second) is transferring only about 8,000 bytes per second, or about five pages of text.

The measurements **kilobyte (K or KB), megabyte (M or MB), gigabyte (G or GB),** and **terabyte (T or TB)** are used to describe the amount of data we are managing either in memory or in

longer-term storage on disk. Figure 4.2 shows how much data is approximately equivalent to each multiple of a thousand. Because computer data is stored using binary numbers, a kilobyte is not exactly one thousand bytes, nor is a megabyte exactly one million bytes. However, the exact amount is close enough that you can think in these rounded, approximate terms (one thousand, one million, or one billion) for most purposes.

## NUMBERING SYSTEMS

Binary numbers are difficult to work with because so many digits are required to represent even a small number. (In the binary numbering system, for example, the decimal number 14 is represented as 1110.) Also, it's tedious to translate binary numbers into their decimal equivalents. For these reasons, programmers like to translate binary numbers into **hexadecimal** (called **hex** for short), a numbering system with a base of 16. These numbers use the symbols 0 through 9 and A through F to make a total of 16 symbols. It's easy to translate binary numbers into the much more readable hexadecimal ones. For example, a commonly used code for the letter K, 01001011, quickly translates to 4B (Figure 4.3).

Computers would be impossible to use if they just spat out binary numbers at us. Fortunately, thanks to character code, we can understand computer output.

**FIGURE 4.3** Counting with Binary, Decimal, and Hexadecimal Numbers

| Decimal Number | Binary Number | Hexa-decimal Number |
|---|---|---|
| 0 | 0 | 0 |
| 1 | 1 | 1 |
| 2 | 10 | 2 |
| 3 | 11 | 3 |
| 4 | 100 | 4 |
| 5 | 101 | 5 |
| 6 | 110 | 6 |
| 7 | 111 | 7 |
| 8 | 1000 | 8 |
| 9 | 1001 | 9 |
| 10 | 1010 | A |
| 11 | 1011 | B |
| 12 | 1100 | C |
| 13 | 1101 | D |
| 14 | 1110 | E |
| 15 | 1111 | F |

## REPRESENTING CHARACTERS: CHARACTER CODE

**Character code** translates between the numerical world of the computer and the letters, numbers, and symbols we're accustomed to using. You need not be intimidated by this new term. You already know the English alphabet and are at least aware that other cultures have their own alphabets. Computers can recognize several different character codes—just as you or a friend might know more than one alphabet. Let's take a look at the most common character codes used with today's computers.

## ASCII and EBCDIC

The most widely used character code is the **American Standard Code for Information Interchange** (**ASCII**), pronounced "ask-ee," which is used on minicomputers, personal computers, and computers designed to make information available on the Internet. IBM mainframe computers and some other systems use a different code, called **Extended Binary Coded Decimal Interchange Code** (**EBCDIC**), pronounced "ebb-see-dic."

Originally, ASCII and EBCDIC used a total of 7 bits to represent **characters** (letters, numbers, and punctuation marks). Seven bits allow the computer to encode a total of 128 characters, which is enough for the numbers 0–9, uppercase and lowercase letters A–Z, and a few punctuation symbols. This 128-bit code is suitable, however, only for English language–speaking users. Looking for a wider market for their personal computers, both IBM and Apple expanded the amount of space reserved for the character code to 8 bits, equivalent to 1 byte. However, these **extended character sets** (characters added to the standard 7-bit set) are not standardized; the Macintosh and PC versions differ. This explains why you may encounter some character representation errors if you try to open a Macintosh document on an IBM PC. (There's less of a problem going the other way because the Macintosh comes with translation software that automatically translates IBM PC characters.) You may see errors if the document contains special characters such as foreign language characters or special punctuation marks.

## Unicode

Although ASCII and EBCDIC contain some foreign language symbols, both are clearly insufficient in a global computer market. **Unicode** solves this problem for most languages by expanding the number of available bits to 16. Because 16 bits are enough to code more than 65,000 characters, Unicode can represent many, if not most, of the world's languages. At this writing, nearly 40,000 characters have been encoded. Some languages are not represented because more research is needed to determine how best to encode their scripts. Examples of as-yet-unsupported languages are Cherokee, Mongolian, and Sinhala (the

IMPACTS

IT History

# The Evolution of the Intel Microprocessor

The IBM PC, introduced in 1981, used the Intel 8088, an 8-bit processor running initially at 4.77 MHz. A major limitation of this processor was its maximum memory size of 1 MB. Another major limitation was that programs could directly access the computer's memory. If you tried to run more than one program at a time, one of the programs might overwrite the other one's portion of memory, causing a crash.

To deal with this problem, in 1982, Intel introduced the 80286, which had two modes. The first mode, called real mode, emulated the 8088. The second mode, called protected mode, introduced two major technical improvements. In protected mode, programs could use up to a gigabyte of RAM. Also, the processor gave programs a certain section of memory and prevented other programs from using the same section. This allocation reduced the number of system failures when users tried to run more than one program. The 80286 was followed in 1985 by the 80386, also called the 386, Intel's first 32-bit microprocessor.

The IBM PC's operating system, MS-DOS, runs in real mode and can't take advantage of the benefits of protected mode. The reason for the popularity of Microsoft Windows lies in its capability to switch the 80386 and later processors into protected mode, enabling users to make full use of more than 640 KB of memory and providing protection for multitasking, in which the processor runs more than one program at once by switching among them.

By the time the 80486 came along in 1989, several manufacturers had created clones of Intel processors, and a court ruled that Intel could not protect the 80386 nomenclature. So the 80486 came to be called the Intel 486. In 1993, Intel released the first Pentium microprocessors, which used a 64-bit data bus (described later in this chapter). Pentium is derived from the Latin word for *five*. (This chip would have been called the 80586 if Intel had stuck with the old numbering system). The Pentium chip was followed in 1995 by the Pentium Pro, an advanced Pentium design intended for use in servers and engineering workstations. In 1997, the Pentium MMX was introduced, containing a new set of 57 multimedia instructions. These instructions enabled Pentium MMX–based systems to run games and multimedia applications more quickly (Figure 4.4).

The year 1998 saw the first of a series of Pentium II processors, which incorporated the Pentium Pro's advanced design as well as MMX graphics and the games circuitry of earlier chips. A low-priced version of the Pentium II, called Celeron, reduced costs by cutting down on the amount of secondary processor memory. An advanced version of the Pentium II, the Xeon, was designed for professional applications. In 1999, Intel released the Pentium III (Figure 4.5), an upgraded version of the Pentium II with clock speeds of up to 1,000 MHz (1 gigahertz or GHz). However, Intel's main competitor, Advanced Micro Devices (AMD), beat Intel to the 1-GHz mark with the company's Athlon processor (Figure 4.6).

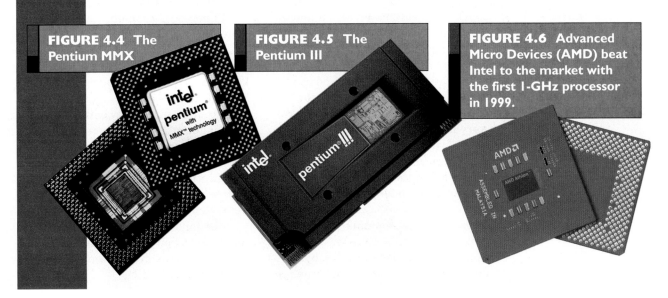

**FIGURE 4.4** The Pentium MMX

**FIGURE 4.5** The Pentium III

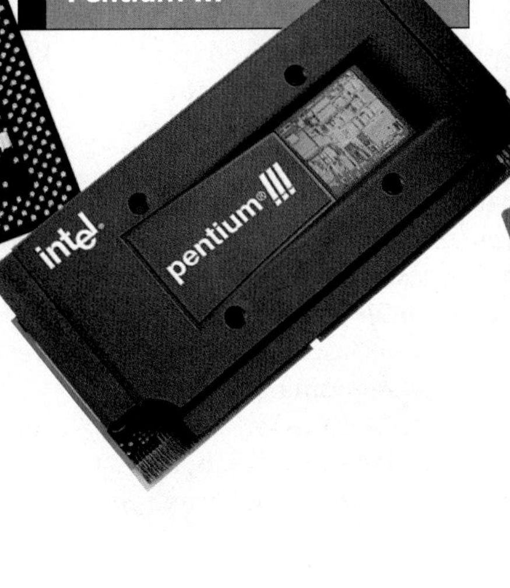


**FIGURE 4.6** Advanced Micro Devices (AMD) beat Intel to the market with the first 1-GHz processor in 1999.

most widely spoken language in the island nation Sri Lanka).

### Parity

No matter which coding system is used to represent characters in the computer's memory, the code must be stored correctly in order to avoid errors. To check each character, computers are designed to add an additional bit to each character code. This extra bit, called a **parity bit**, is generated by an automatic operation that adds all the bits in the character's code. It records a 0 or a 1 to make the total number of bits odd (**odd parity**) or even (**even parity**). If one of the bits in the code has been changed due to a storage error, the computer generates a **parity error**. Some systems stop processing data if a parity error occurs because the error may indicate a component failure that could scramble all the data. Most personal computers, however, are configured so that **parity checking** (the procedure followed to check for parity errors) is turned off. Although parity errors are rare, they do sometimes occur. But they rarely cause problems serious enough to warrant shutting down the computer, which could cause users to lose hours of work.

### REPRESENTING VERY LARGE AND VERY SMALL NUMBERS

Although character codes are useful for representing textual data and whole numbers (0 through 9), they are not useful for numbers that have fractional parts, such as 1.25. To represent and process numbers with fractions, as well as extremely large numbers, computers use floating-point notation. The term *floating-point* suggests how this notation system works: no fixed number of digits is before or after the decimal point, so the computer can work with very large, as well as very small, numbers. Floating-point notation requires special processing circuitry, which is generally provided by the floating-point unit (FPU). Almost a standard in the circuitry of today's microprocessors, the FPU on older computers was sometimes a separate chip, called the math coprocessor.

Now that you understand bits, bytes, and other important hardware performance terminology, we can take a close look at the system unit, where these terms will come into play.

# Introducing the System Unit

The **system unit** is a boxlike case that houses the computer's main hardware components (Figure 4.7). The system unit is more than just a case—it provides a sturdy frame for mounting internal components, including storage devices and connectors for input and output devices; protects these components from physical damage; and keeps them cool. A good case also provides room for system upgrades, such as additional disk drives.

System units come in a variety of styles. In some desktop computing systems, the system unit is a separate metal or plastic box that's designed to sit on top of a desk. Ideally, the case should have a small **footprint** (the amount of room taken up by the case on the desk). Desktop computer cases are wide and deep, but not very tall. A small case may not have enough room for add-on components. One solution to this problem is the **tower case**, a system unit case that is designed to sit on the floor next to a desk. The tower case is tall and deep, and a little wider than a desktop case is tall. Smaller versions of tower cases are called **minitower cases**.

In notebook computers and personal digital assistants (PDAs) the system unit contains all of the computer's components, including input components (such as a keyboard or pen interface) and the display. Some desktop computers, such as Apple's iMac, contain the display within the system unit (Figure 4.8).

System units also vary in what is called their form factor. A **form factor** is a specification for how internal components, such as the motherboard, are mounted in the system unit.

The following sections explore what can be found on the outside as well as the inside of the system unit of a typical desktop computer.

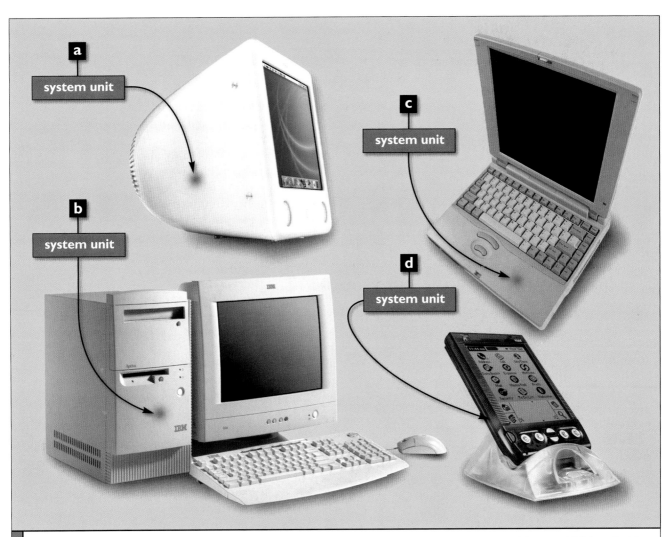

**FIGURE 4.7 a–d** Every kind of computer has a system unit: (**a**) Apple iMac, (**b**) desktop, (**c**) laptop, (**d**) handheld.

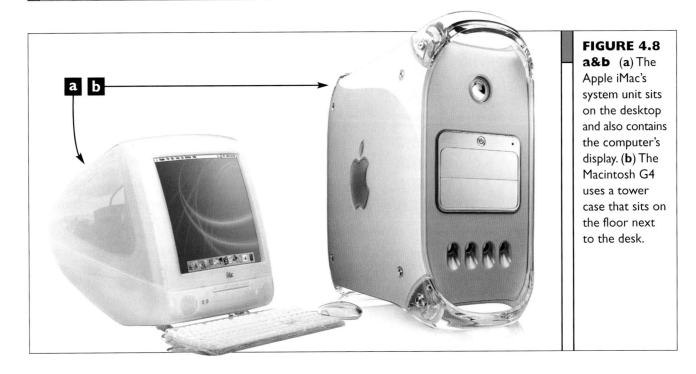

**FIGURE 4.8 a&b** (**a**) The Apple iMac's system unit sits on the desktop and also contains the computer's display. (**b**) The Macintosh G4 uses a tower case that sits on the floor next to the desk.

# What's on the Outside of the Box?

You'll find the following features on the outside of a typical desktop computer's system unit:

- the front panel with various buttons and lights

- the power switch

- connectors and ports for plugging in keyboards, mice, monitors, and other peripheral devices

### The Front Panel

On the front panel of most computers, you'll find a **reset switch** (which enables you to restart your computer in the event of a failure), a **drive activity light** (a light that tells when your hard disk is accessing data), and a **power-on light** (a light that tells you whether the power is on). You may also find a key lock you can use to prevent others from operating the machine. Do not press the reset switch unless you are certain that your computer is no longer responding to input. Always try pressing the Control, Alt, and Delete keys simultaneously to activate the Windows Task Manager and attempt to shut down your system normally. If you have any unsaved work and you press the reset switch, you will most likely lose it.

### The Power Switch

The **power switch** is usually located on the front of the computer. In earlier days it was placed on the back of the system unit because of the fear that you might accidentally press it and inadvertently shut down your system. Computers don't handle sudden power losses well. For example, a power outage caused by a service interruption could scramble the data on your hard drive. Likewise, just turning off your computer instead of shutting it down properly can leave the system unstable and possibly unable to restart. You should always follow the appropriate shutdown procedure to shut off your computer.

### Connectors and Ports

A **connector** is a physical receptacle that is designed for a specific type of plug that fits into the connector (and is sometimes secured by thumbscrews). **Expansion cards** (also called expansion boards, adapter cards, or adapters) are plug-in adapters used to connect the computer with various peripherals. Connectors on the outside of the case enable you to connect peripheral devices, such as a printer, keyboard, or mouse (Figure 4.9). Connectors are described as being male connectors (which have external pins) or female connectors (which have receptacles for external pins).

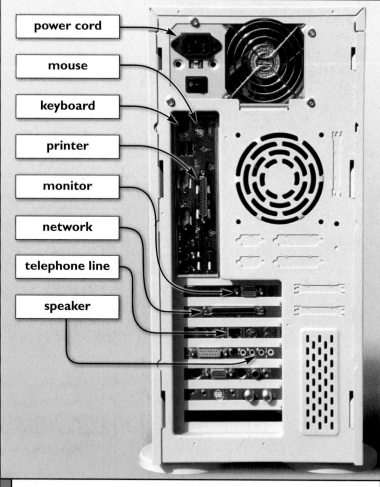

**FIGURE 4.9** The connectors on the outside of a system unit enable you to connect peripherals such as a printer, a keyboard, or a mouse.

Figure 4.10 summarizes the connectors you may find on the computer's case. Most of these connectors are on the back of the case, but sometimes you'll find one or more of them on the front.

People often call these connectors *ports*, but this usage is not necessarily accurate. A **port** is an electronically defined pathway, called an **interface**, for getting information into and out of the computer. In order to function, a port must be linked to a specific receptacle. This is done by the computer system's start-up and configuration software. In the following section, the term *port* is used as if it were synonymous with connector, in line with everyday usage, but it's important to keep the distinction in mind. Let's now look at the types of ports found on the exterior of a typical computer system's case.

## Parallel Ports

A **parallel port** sends and receives data 8 bits at a time over eight separate wires. This allows data to be transferred very quickly; however, the cable required is more bulky because of the number of individual wires it must contain. Parallel ports are typically used to connect a PC to a printer and are rarely used for much else.

On PCs, access to the parallel port is provided by means of a 25-pin (DB-25) female connector. Macs use a 6-pin (mini-DIN) connector.

The newest parallel ports, called enhanced parallel ports (EPPs) and extended capabilities ports (ECPs), offer higher speeds than traditional parallel ports. In addition, they enable two-way communication between the printer and computer. If the printer encounters an error, it can send back a detailed message explaining what went wrong and how to fix it.

## Serial Ports

A **serial port** sends and receives data one bit at a time (Figure 4.11). This is how data streams need to be sent and received across communications lines, whether they are telephone lines, coaxial or television cable type lines, fiber optics, or satellite. While a serial port takes eight times as long as a parallel port to transfer each byte of data, it can achieve two-way communication

| Connector | Use |
|---|---|
| DB-25, 25-pin female | parallel port for printer |
| DB-25, 25-pin male | serial port for printers, modems, or scanners |
| DIN, 6-pin female | mouse or keyboard |
| DB-15, 15-pin female | VGA video (monitor) |
| RJ-11 | phone line |
| RJ-45 | local area network (LAN) |
| stereo miniplug female | microphone, speakers, or headphones |
| USB | port for many devices on PCs and Macintoshes |
| FireWire | port for cameras and portable storage |

**FIGURE 4.10** Most of these connectors are on the back of the computer's case, but some of them may be in front.

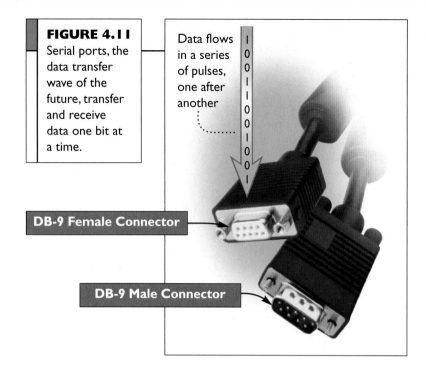

**FIGURE 4.11** Serial ports, the data transfer wave of the future, transfer and receive data one bit at a time.

Data flows in a series of pulses, one after another

DB-9 Female Connector

DB-9 Male Connector

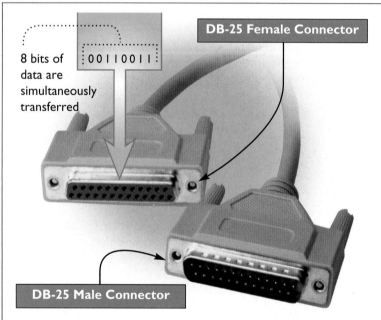

8 bits of data are simultaneously transferred

DB-25 Female Connector

DB-25 Male Connector

**FIGURE 4.12** Parallel cables transfer 8 bits of information simultaneously and are used for printers.

with only three separate wires—one to send, one to receive, and a common signal ground wire. This feature is a tremendous advantage when transferring data more than a dozen feet or so because it uses a maximum of three wires instead of eight and it meets the criteria of sending streams of bits instead of bytes.

Serial ports weren't considered very important when computers had fewer capabilities for communicating or working with lots of different peripherals. But today, serial port use is proliferating at an increasing rate because the computer is no longer a standalone device—but a connected device that facilitates communications, data transfer, and the use of many types of peripherals.

IBM PC and compatible computers are typically equipped with at least two serial ports and one parallel port. Even though these two types of ports are used for communicating with external devices, they work in different ways.

On IBM-compatible PCs, there are four serial ports: COM1, COM2, COM3, and COM4. However, a PC may have only one or two physical connectors for serial devices. In addition, some expansion boards contain serial ports that connect directly to the computer's internal wiring.

The difference between a serial port and a parallel port is similar to the difference between a one-lane road and a freeway. You might imagine a serial port's relationship to transferring data as that of a one-lane road with lots of cars moving along like a procession of ants. Unlike a serial port, which can transfer only 1 bit of information at a time, parallel ports can transfer 8 bits of information (a byte) simultaneously (Figure 4.12).

**Universal Serial Bus (USB) Ports**
**USB 1.1** **Universal serial bus (USB) ports** use an external (between the computer and peripheral devices—not between devices within the system unit) bus standard that supports data transfer rates of 12 Mbps. A single USB port can be used to connect up to 127 peripheral devices, such as mice, modems, and keyboards.

Beginning in 1996, a few computer manufacturers started including USB support in their new machines. It wasn't until the release of the best-selling iMac in 1998, though, that USB became widespread. Now, USB ports are expected to completely replace other serial and parallel ports as technology continues to move forward (Figure 4.13). Primarily, USB allows **hot swapping**, or connecting and disconnecting devices without shutting down your

**FIGURE 4.13** USB ports and connectors will be the standard for years to come.

**Destinations**

To learn more about PC interfaces, including serial and parallel ports, see **www.howstuff works.com**. Type "ports" in the search box that is located near the top right corner of the screen.

computer. This is convenient when you're using devices that you often want to disconnect, such as a digital camera.

An additional advantage of USB is its built-in Plug and Play (PnP) support. With PnP, the computer automatically detects the brand, model, and characteristics of the device when you plug it in, and configures the system accordingly.

**USB 2.0** Also referred to as *Hi-Speed USB*, USB 2.0 is an external bus that supports data rates of up to 480 Mbps (four hundred eighty million bits per second). USB 2.0 is an extension of USB 1.1. Hewlett-Packard, Intel, Lucent, Microsoft, NEC, and Philips jointly led the initiative to develop a higher data transfer rate than the 1.1 specification to meet the bandwidth demands of developing technologies. USB 2.0 is fully compatible with USB 1.1 and uses the same cables and connectors. The USB 2.0 specification was released in April 2000.

### SCSI Ports

A **SCSI** (short for **small computer system interface** and pronounced "scuzzy") **port** is a type of parallel interface that is found increasingly on PCs. Unlike a standard parallel port, a SCSI port enables users to connect up to eight SCSI-compatible devices, such as printers, scanners, and digital cameras, in a daisy-chain series. The most recent SCSI standard, called SCSI-2, can transfer data at very fast rates.

External connectors for SCSI peripherals vary. Some SCSI adapters have 50- or 68-pin connectors with a click-in locking mechanism for the plug, while others use a standard 50-pin (D50) connector.

Some high-end systems use a SCSI-2 or SCSI-3 connection, which is made internally, to connect the computer's hard disk. (A high-end system is a computer priced higher than systems with a typical configuration.) These hard disks often offer the best performance because data can be retrieved and deposited faster.

### 1394 Ports (FireWire)

You have probably heard the term *FireWire* if you have any interest in digital video— or maybe you know it as Sony i.Link or as IEEE 1394, the official name for the standard. Originally created by Apple and standardized in 1995 as the specification IEEE 1394 High Performance Serial

## Techtalk

### PCMCIA

Short for Personal Computer Memory Card International Association, PCMCIA refers to the input/output (I/O) bus design that this organization invented. Developed for notebook computers, PCMCIA provides one or more slots for credit card–sized adapters, such as modems and networking cards. Originally, these cards were called PCMCIA cards—but just try pronouncing that phrase! Today, PCMCIA cards are simply called PC cards.

Bus, **FireWire** is very similar to USB in that it offers a high-speed connection for dozens of peripheral devices (up to 63 of them).

On non-Apple systems, this port is called a **1394 port** after the international standard that defines this port. Like USB, FireWire enables hot swapping and PnP. However, it is more expensive than USB and is used only for certain high-speed peripherals, such as digital video cameras, that need greater throughput (data transfer capacity) than USB provides. With the advent of USB 2.0 and the promise of an even faster USB interface in the future, use of the 1394 FireWire standard will most likely fade away.

### IrDA Ports

Some keyboards, mice, and printers are designed to communicate using an IrDA port. IrDA is an abbreviation of the Infrared Data Association, which created the IrDA standard. **IrDA ports** use infrared signals to communicate between peripheral devices and between those devices and the system unit. This method is also used by television and other remote control devices. No physical connection is required, but the transmitter must be in the direct line of sight of the receiver, a transparent panel mounted on the computer's surface.

### Video Connectors

Most computers use a **video adapter** (also called a **video card**) to generate the output that is displayed on the computer's screen (also referred to as the computer monitor). On the back of the adapter, you'll find a standard **VGA** (Video Graphics Array) **connector**, a 15-pin male connector that is designed to work with standard monitor cables.

Some computers have the video circuitry built into the motherboard. This type of video circuitry is called **on-board video**. On such systems, the video connector is found on the back of the case.

### Additional Ports and Connectors

You may find the following additional ports and connectors on the exterior of a computer's case or on one of the computer's expansion cards:

- **Telephone connector** The standard modem interface, this connector (called RJ-11) is a standard modular telephone jack that will work with an ordinary telephone cord.

- **Network connector** Provided with networking adapters, this connector (called RJ-45) looks like a standard telephone jack, but it's bigger and capable of much faster data transfer.

- **PC card slots** On notebook computers, one or more PC card slots are provided for plugging in PC cards. A **PC card** is a credit card–sized adapter that provides notebook users with the ability to use modems, networking, and additional functions. Like USB devices, PC cards can be inserted or removed while the computer is running.

- **Sound card connectors** PCs equipped with a **sound card** (an adapter that provides stereo sound and sound synthesis), as well as Macs with built-in sound, offer two or more sound connectors. These connectors, also called jacks, accept the same stereo miniplug used by portable CD players. Most sound cards provide four connectors: Mic (microphone input), Line In (accepts input from other audio devices), Line Out (sends output to other audio devices), and Speaker (sends output to external speakers).

- **Game card** Game cards provide a connector for high-speed access to the CPU and RAM for graphics-intensive interaction.

- **TV/sound capture board connectors** If your computer is equipped with TV and video capabilities, you'll see additional connectors that look like those found on a television monitor. These include a connector for a coaxial cable, which can be connected to a video camera or cable TV system.

It's important to remember that a connector isn't the same thing as a port. The connector is the physical device—the plug-in—while the port is the interface—the matching of input and output flows. A port almost always uses a connector, but a connector isn't always a port. For example, a USB port uses a USB connector, but a telephone jack is just a connector—not a port.

Now that you know what's on the outside of the system unit, let's look at an overview of what's inside.

# Inside the System Unit

Most computer users don't need to open their system unit: they receive their computer in a ready-to-use package. However, if you ever do need to open your system unit, bear in mind that the computer's components are sensitive to static electricity. If you touch certain components while you're charged with static electricity, you could destroy them. Always disconnect the power cord before removing your computer's case, and discharge your personal

static electricity by touching something that's well grounded, such as a water faucet. If it's one of those dry days when you're getting shocked every time you touch a doorknob, don't work on your computer's internal components.

If you do open your system unit, you'll see the following components (Figure 4.14):

- **Motherboard** The motherboard contains the computer's central processing unit (CPU). You'll learn more about the motherboard and CPU later in the chapter; for now remember that the CPU *is* the computer in the strict sense of the term; all other components (such as disk drives, monitors, and printers) are peripheral to, or outside of, the CPU.

- **Power supply** A computer's **power supply** transforms the alternating current (AC) available from standard wall outlets into the direct current (DC) needed for the computer's operation. It also steps the voltage down to the low voltage required by the

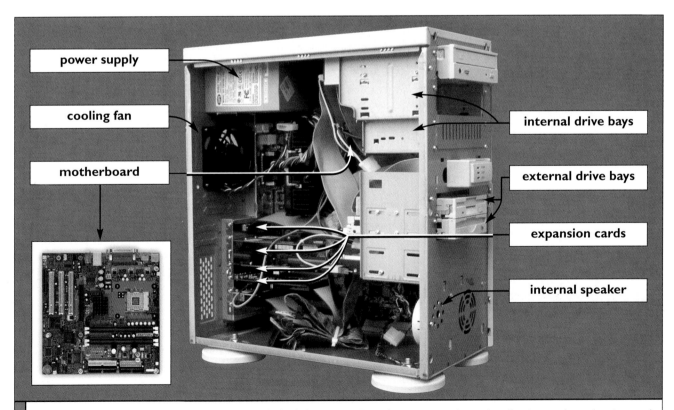

**FIGURE 4.14** Inside the system unit, you'll find the motherboard, power supply, cooling fan, internal speaker, internal drive bays, external drive bays, and various expansion cards (such as the sound card and network interface card).

**FIGURE 4.15** Expansion cards allow you to add enhancements to your system.

motherboard. Power supplies are rated according to their peak output in watts. A 250-watt power supply is adequate for most desktop systems, but 300 watts provides a margin of safety if you plan to add many additional components.

- **Cooling fan** The computer's components can be damaged if heat accumulates within the system unit. A **cooling fan** is therefore used to keep the system unit cool. Often, the fan is part of the power supply, although some high-powered systems include auxiliary fans to provide additional cooling.

- **Internal speaker** The computer's **internal speaker** isn't designed for high-fidelity reproduction. It's useful only for the beeps you hear when the computer encounters an error. Macintoshes come with built-in stereo sound, but to produce good sound from a PC, you need to upgrade the system with sound components (including a sound card and speakers).

- **Drive bays** **Drive bays** are designed to accommodate the computer's disk drives, such as the hard disk drive, floppy disk drive, and CD-ROM or DVD-ROM drive. Internal drive bays are used for hard disks, in which the disk is permanently contained within the drive's case. Therefore, they do not enable outside access. External drive bays mount drives so that they are accessible from the outside (a necessity if you need to insert and remove disks from the drive). External drive bays vary by size. Some bays are designed to accommodate 5.25-inch drives (for CD-ROMs and DVD-ROMs), whereas others are designed for 3.5-inch drives (for floppy and Zip disks).

- **Expansion cards** The system unit also contains slots that will accept additional circuit boards, or expansion cards. Examples of expansion cards are memory modules, sound cards, modem cards, network interface cards, and video cards (Figure 4.15).

Now that you have a good overview of the internal components of the system unit, let's look more closely at the most important component: the computer's motherboard.

# What's on the Motherboard?

Think of a motherboard as a scale model of a futuristic city with many modular plug-in buildings, each using power from a common electrical system. Multiple-lane highways of various widths transport data between the buildings. The motherboard is the data and power infrastructure for the entire computer (Figure 4.16).

The **motherboard** is a large printed circuit board (PCB), a flat piece of plastic or fiberglass that contains thousands of electrical circuits etched into the board's surface. The circuits connect numerous plug-in receptacles, which accommodate the computer's most important components (such as the microprocessor). The motherboard provides the centralized physical and electrical connection point for the computer's most important components. Most of the components on the motherboard are integrated circuits. An **integrated circuit** (**IC**), also called a **chip**, can carry electrical current and contains millions of transistors. A **transistor** is an electronic switch (or gate) that controls the flow of electrical signals to the circuit. Much of what a computer does boils down to using such electronic switches to route data in different ways, according to the software's instructions. Encased in black plastic blocks or enclosures, most chips are packaged to fit specially designed receptacles or slots on the motherboard's surface.

So, what do these chips do? Let's look at some of the most important components you'll see on the motherboard: the central processing unit (or microprocessor), the system clock, the chipset, input/output (I/O) buses, and memory.

## THE CENTRAL PROCESSING UNIT: THE MICROPROCESSOR

The **central processing unit** (**CPU**) is a **microprocessor** (or **processor** for short), an integrated circuit chip that is capable of processing electronic signals. It interprets the instructions given to it by software and carries out these instructions by processing data and controlling the rest of the computer's components. No other single element of a computer determines its overall performance as much as the CPU. Because the computer's microprocessor is so important, let's spend some time looking at it in detail before moving on to the remaining components of the motherboard.

**Destinations**

The Intel Museum's "How Chips Are Made" provides a nicely illustrated overview of the chip fabrication process. The Intel Museum is located at **www.intel.com/ intel/intelis/ museum/index.htm**.

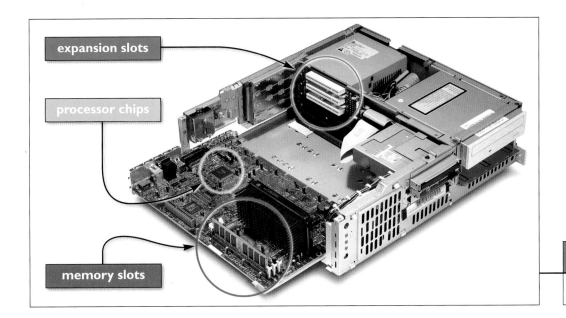

expansion slots

processor chips

memory slots

**FIGURE 4.16**
A Typical PC Motherboard

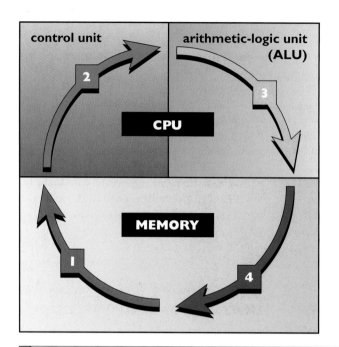

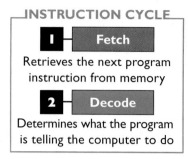

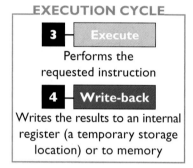

**FIGURE 4.17** The control unit manages four basic operations: fetch, decode, execute, and write-back.

Although microprocessors are complex devices, the underlying ideas are easy to understand. When you're ready to consider buying a computer, you'll need to understand the capabilities and limitations of a given microprocessor.

**Processor Slots and Sockets**

An integrated circuit (IC) of fabulous complexity, a microprocessor is designed to plug into a motherboard in much the same way that other ICs do. However, motherboard designers have created special slots and sockets to accommodate microprocessors. Part of the reason is simply that microprocessors are larger and have more pins than do most other chips. In addition, microprocessors generate so much heat that they could destroy themselves or other system components. The microprocessor is generally covered by a **heat sink**, which drains heat away from the chip. To accomplish this, the heat sink may contain a small auxiliary cooling fan. The latest high-end microprocessors include their own built-in refrigeration systems, which are needed to keep these speedy processors cool.

**The Instruction Set**

Every processor can perform a fixed set of operations, such as retrieving a character from the computer's memory or comparing two numbers to see which is larger. Each of these operations has its own unique number, called an instruction. A processor's list of instructions is called its **instruction set**. Different processors have different instruction sets. Because each processor has a unique instruction set, programs devised for one computer type won't run on another. For example, a program written for the Apple Macintosh will not run on an IBM PC. A program that can run on a given computer is said to be compatible with that computer's processor. Alternatively, if that program is compatible, it's said to be a native application for a given processor design.

**The Control Unit and the Arithmetic-Logic Unit**

CPUs contain two subcomponents: the control unit and the arithmetic-logic unit (ALU). The **control unit** extracts instructions from memory and decodes and executes them. Under the direction of a program, the control unit manages four basic operations (Figure 4.17):

- **Fetch** Retrieves the next program instruction from the computer's memory.

- **Decode** Determines what the program is telling the computer to do.

- **Execute** Performs the requested instruction, such as adding two numbers or deciding which one of them is larger.

- **Write-back** Writes the results to an internal register (a temporary storage location) or to memory.

This four-step process is called a **machine cycle**, or **processing cycle**, and consists of two phases: the **instruction cycle** (fetch and decode) and the **execution cycle** (execute and write-back). Today's microprocessors can go through this entire four-step process billions of times per second. The **arithmetic-logic unit** (**ALU**), as its name implies, can perform arithmetic or logical operations. **Arithmetic operations** include addition, subtraction, multiplication, and division. **Logical operations** involve comparing two data items to see which one is larger or smaller.

Some operations require the control unit to store data temporarily. **Registers** are temporary storage locations in the microprocessor that are designed for this purpose. For example, one type of register stores the location from which data was retrieved from memory. Registers also store results of intermediate calculations.

## MICROPROCESSOR PERFORMANCE

The number of transistors available has a huge effect on the performance of a processor. The greater the number and the closer their proximity to each other are crucial physical factors in processing speed. Also important to performance are factors such as the data bus width and word size, operations per microprocessor cycle, parallel processing, and type of chip. In the following sections you will explore these factors that contribute to microprocessor performance.

**FIGURE 4.18** Word Size Capacity (in bits) of Popular Operating Systems

| Operating System | Word Size | When in Time? |
|---|---|---|
| CP/M | 8 | Past |
| MS-DOS | 8 | Past |
| Windows 3.1 | 16 | Past |
| Windows 95/98/NT/2000/XP | 32 | Current |
| Windows XP 64 Bit Edition 2003 | 64 | Current |
| Linux | 64 | Current |
| Mac OS X (with Velocity Engine chip) | 128 | Current |

### Data Bus Width and Word Size

The **data bus**, a highway of parallel wires, connects the internal components of the microprocessor. The bus is a pathway for the electronic impulses that form bytes. The more lanes this highway has, the faster data can travel. Data bus width is measured in bits (8, 16, 32, or 64).

The width of a CPU's data bus partly determines the maximum number of bits the CPU can process at once (its **word size**). Data bus width also affects the CPU's overall speed, because a CPU with a 32-bit data bus is capable of shuffling data around twice as fast as a CPU with a 16-bit data bus. The terms *8-bit CPU, 16-bit CPU, 32-bit CPU,* and *64-bit CPU* are used to sum up the maximum number of bits a given CPU can handle at a time.

A CPU's word size is important because it determines which operating systems the CPU can use and which software can be run. Figure 4.18 lists the word size requirements of past and current operating systems.

Today's personal computer market is dominated by 32-bit CPUs and 32-bit operating systems. However, 64-bit CPUs and 64-bit operating systems are beginning to enter the marketplace. Intel's 64-bit Itanium processor, introduced in late 2000, brought 64-bit computing to the PC market for the first time. In 2003 Mac

**Destinations**

To learn more about the 64-bit version of the Microsoft Windows operating system, visit **www.microsoft.com/ windowsxp/64bit/ default.asp**.

**CURRENTS**

**Emerging Technologies**

# Dreams of Homework Machines?
# Computers in Your Pocket?

Now, don't deny that you have dreamed of owning a machine of some sort that could do your homework and class assignments for you. You may have even written about a "homework machine" in elementary school. Well, keep dreaming—such machines are not here yet. But personal digital assistants, or PDAs—those small, handheld computing devices—come pretty close.

PDAs have been used successfully in the corporate world for years and have more recently entered the realm of everyday student life—and for good reason. PDAs can fit in your pocket, remind you when and where a class or meeting is taking place, and keep those little gems you think up and don't want to forget from vanishing into thin air. With PDAs, you can take notes in class and, with special software, even give yourself pop quizzes throughout the day. They can also connect you with the Internet, where you can access your library's online catalog and other useful sites.

Today, many colleges and universities are requiring that their students own a computer. As most students know, real estate on a classroom desk is limited, so having a small computer is important. With note-book-sized desks, laptops leave little room for other student needs, such as textbooks. That's where PDAs come in handy.

With PDAs, you can leave your laptop at home and still carry a great deal of computing power in a small system unit. Inexpensive accessories like folding, detachable keyboards enable you to take notes easily in class. And once you've finished

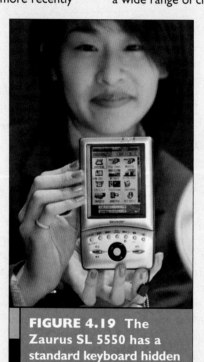

**FIGURE 4.19  The Zaurus SL 5550 has a standard keyboard hidden under a sliding cover.**

using your PDA, you can download the information you've stored on it to your traditional computer. Desktops and laptops now offer docking bays for PDAs along with the traditional USB, FireWire, or other port hookups for transferring data. In addition, infrared data beaming between PDA devices allows for easy wireless exchange of information (and, of course, games).

If you're considering buying a PDA, you'll have a wide range of choices: monochrome or color screen, battery or rechargeable, from Palm to Sony. Priced anywhere between $99 and $599 and up, depending on which options you choose, PDAs combine small size, low price, and portability. What PDA is right for you? Obviously, the higher-end PDAs, such as the Zaurus SL 5550 (Figure 4.19), have more functions, including MP3 players, color screens, high resolution, super-fast processors, and wireless connectivity. But even the cheaper PDAs pack a lot of computing punch into a small container.

PDAs are not all about hardware, of course. Specially designed software can turn your PDA into a true technical marvel. Most software for PDAs is reasonably priced, and some can be downloaded as shareware from the Internet. (For information on software that is specially targeted toward students, visit **www.palmgear.com** and search under the keywords *students* and *school*.)

No, they're not homework machines just yet, but PDAs are more than just paperless storage islands for information. They're great homework tools.

OS X was using a 128-bit word size and 64-bit versions of the popular Linux and Microsoft Windows operating systems were also released.

**The System Clock**

Within the computer, events happen at a pace controlled by a tiny electronic "drummer" on the motherboard called the system

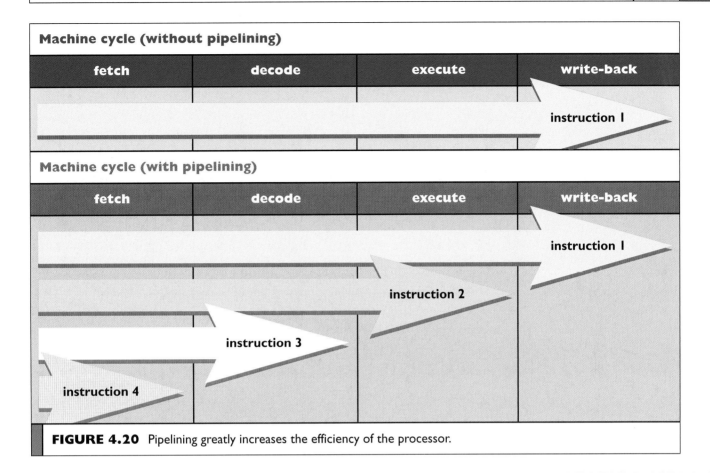

**FIGURE 4.20** Pipelining greatly increases the efficiency of the processor.

clock. The **system clock** is an electronic circuit that generates pulses at a rapid rate and synchronizes the computer's internal activities. These electrical pulses are measured in billions of cycles per second (GHz) and referred to as a processor's **clock speed**. Any computer you purchase today will have a clock speed of more than 1 GHz. A hertz is an electrical cycle per second. So, a 3-GHz processor is capable of processing three billion cycles in one second. As a frame of reference, can you figure out how many seconds there are in the average human life span? The answer may surprise you (77yrs*365.25days* 24hrs*60min*60sec)! Note that the system clock does not keep track of the day or time—this chore is handled by CMOS, which we discussed in Chapter 2.

### Operations per Cycle

The number of operations per clock tick (one pulse of the system clock) also affects microprocessor performance. You might think that a CPU can't perform more than one instruction per clock tick, but thanks to new technologies, that's not true. Any CPU that can execute more than one instruction per clock cycle is referred to as **superscalar**, and its design is called a **superscalar architecture**. Today's fastest CPUs, such as the Pentium 4, use superscalar architectures. One of the design tricks that makes superscalar architectures possible is called **pipelining**, a processing technique that feeds a new instruction into the CPU at every step of the processing cycle so that four or more instructions are worked on simultaneously (Figure 4.20).

Pipelining resembles an auto assembly line in which more than one car is being worked on at once. Before the first instruction is finished, the next one is started. But what if the CPU needs the results of a completed instruction to process the next one? This problem is called **data dependency**. It can cause a pipeline stall, in which the assembly line is held up until the results are known. To cope with this problem, advanced CPUs use a technique called **speculative execution** in which the processor executes

## Destinations

To learn more about the technologies used to speed processor performance, see MicroDesign-Resources' clearly written technical guide "PC Processor Microarchitecture" at **www.mdron line.com**. It's not exactly light reading, but there's plenty to intrigue the technically inclined.

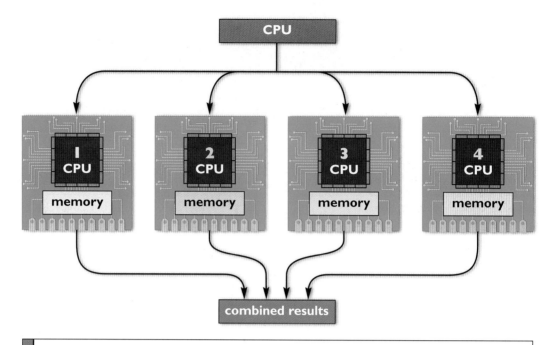

**FIGURE 4.21**   Parallel processing computers have multiple processors that run simultaneously.

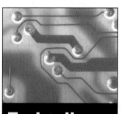

and temporarily stores the next instruction in case it proves useful. CPUs also use a technique called **branch prediction**, in which the processor tries to predict what will likely happen (with a surprisingly high degree of accuracy).

### Parallel Processing

Another way to improve CPU performance doesn't involve making CPUs faster. It involves using more than one of them at the same time. A **parallel processing** computer has more than one processor running simultaneously, in parallel (Figure 4.21).

### RISC and CISC

Another aspect of microprocessor design that you might find useful is the distinction between RISC and CISC processor architecture.

**RISC** stands for **reduced instruction set computer**. A RISC chip offers a bare-bones instruction set. For this reason, RISC chips are less complex, less expensive to produce, and more efficient in power usage. The drawback of the RISC design is that the computer must combine or repeat operations to complete many processing operations. RISC chips also place extra

demands on programmers, who must consider how to get complex results by combining simple instructions.

Until the mid-1980s, the tendency among computer manufacturers was to build increasingly complex CPUs that had ever-larger sets of instructions. At that time, however, a number of computer manufacturers decided to reverse this trend by building CPUs capable of executing only a very limited set of instructions. One advantage of reduced instruction set computers is that they can execute their instructions very fast because the instructions are so simple. Another, perhaps more important, advantage is that RISC chips require fewer transistors, which makes them cheaper to design.

Since the emergence of RISC computers, conventional computers have been referred to as CISCs. **CISC** stands for **complex instruction set computer**. A CISC chip includes many special-purpose circuits that carry out instructions at high speeds. CISC chips, however, are complex and expensive to produce, and they run hot because they consume a lot of current.

There is still considerable controversy among experts about the ultimate value of RISC architectures. Its proponents argue that RISC machines are both cheaper and faster, and are therefore the machines of the future. Skeptics note that by making the hardware simpler, RISC architectures put a greater burden on the software. They argue that this is not worth the trouble because conventional microprocessors are becoming increasingly fast and cheap anyway.

To some extent, the argument is becoming moot because CISC and RISC implementations are becoming more and more alike. Many of today's RISC chips support as many instructions as yester-day's CISC chips. And today's CISC chips use many techniques formerly associated with RISC chips.

## Popular Microprocessors

The most commonly used microprocessors are those in IBM PC compatibles and Macintoshes. The chips powering most PCs are made by Intel Corporation, although AMD, Cyrix Corporation, and other firms make Intel-compatible chips. Figure 4.22 shows how popular personal computer microprocessors have improved since the days of the first PC. In 2001, Intel released

## Destinations

For the latest information on the hottest and fastest processors, take a look at the aptly named "Chip Geek" at **www.ugeek.com/ procspec/ procmain.htm**. You'll find the latest news on new, super-fast processors, including performance comparisons, reviews, and tips on putting together the ultimate high-speed system.

For help on comparing microprocessor performance, take a look at the "Processor Buyer's Guide" at **www.buybuddy.com**. You'll find up-to-date information on the latest processors, as well as tips on how to compare them meaningfully.

**FIGURE 4.22** The Evolution of Intel Microprocessors

| Year | Chip | Bus Width | Clock Speed | Transistors |
|------|------|-----------|-------------|-------------|
| 1971 | 4004 | 4 bits | 740 KHz | 2,300 |
| 1974 | 8080 | 8 bits | 2 MHz | 6,000 |
| 1979 | 8088 | 8 bits | Up to 8 MHz | 29,000 |
| 1982 | 80286 | 16 bits | Up to 12 MHz | 134,000 |
| 1985 | 80386 | 32 bits | Up to 33 MHz | 275,000 |
| 1989 | Intel 486 | 32 bits | Up to 100 MHz | 1.6 million |
| 1993 | Pentium (original) | 32 bits | Up to 200 MHz | 3.3 million |
| 1995 | Pentium Pro | 32 bits | 200 MHz and higher | 5.5 million |
| 1997 | Pentium MMX | 32 bits | 233 MHz and higher | 4.5 million |
| 1998 | Pentium II | 32 bits | 233 MHz and higher | 7.5 million |
| 1998 | Xeon | 32 bits | 400 MHz and higher | 7.5 million |
| 1998 | Celeron | 32 bits | 400 MHz and higher | 7.5–19 million |
| 1999 | Duron | 32 bits | 600 MHz and higher | 18 million |
| 1999 | Pentium III | 32 bits | 450 MHz and higher | 9.5–28.1 million |
| 2000 | Pentium 4 | 32 bits | 1.4 GHz and higher | 34 million |
| 2000 | Itanium | 64 bits | 800 MHz and higher | 25 million |

microprocessors are RISC chips that run earlier Macintosh software by emulating the earlier processor's characteristics. Figure 4.24 shows how these processors have improved since the first ones appeared in 1979. Note that Apple Computer gives its own name to the PowerPC chips: Motorola's 750 is the same thing as Apple's G3, while Motorola's 7400 becomes the G4 in Apple's marketing.

## THE CHIPSET AND INPUT/OUTPUT (I/O) BUS

Another important motherboard component is the chipset. The **chipset** is a collection of chips that are designed to work together (that's why they're called a "set"). They provide the switching circuitry that the microprocessor needs in order to move data to and from the rest of the computer. One of the jobs handled by the chipset involves linking the microprocessor to the computer's input/output (I/O) buses.

An **input/output (I/O) bus** extends the computer's internal data pathways beyond the boundaries of the microprocessor so that the microprocessor can communicate with input and output devices. Typically, an I/O bus contains **expansion slots**, which are receptacles designed to accommodate plug-in expansion cards.

Today's PCs and Macs use the **Personal Computer Interface (PCI) bus**, which supports PnP. Many motherboards still contain an Industry Standard Architecture (ISA) bus and make one or two ISA slots available. The Accelerated Graphics Port (AGP) is a bus designed for video buses. Input/output (I/O) buses extend adapters.

### Benchmarks

As the previous discussion suggests, two 200-MHz processors made by different manufacturers may perform very differently, depending on variations in bus width and architecture. To provide some basis for comparison, benchmarks have been developed. A **benchmark** is a test that puts a processor through a series of operations so different processors can be compared. The idea sounds good, but a variety of benchmarks are available, and some do a better job than others of measuring the real-world

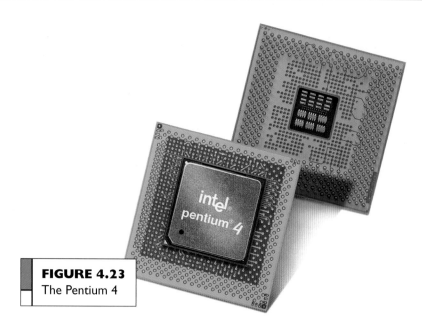

**FIGURE 4.23**
The Pentium 4

**FIGURE 4.24** The Evolution of Motorola Microprocessors

| Year | Chip | Bus Width | Clock Speed |
|------|------|-----------|-------------|
| 1979 | 68000 | 16 bits | 8 MHz |
| 1984 | 68020 | 32 bits | Up to 40 MHz |
| 1988 | 68040 | 64 bits | Up to 120 MHz |
| 1994 | PowerPC 603 | 64 bits | Up to 160 MHz |
| 1995 | PowerPC 603e | 64 bits | Up to 300 MHz |
| 1995 | PowerPC 604e | 64 bits | Up to 300 MHz |
| 1998 | PowerPC 750 (G3) | 64 bits | 200 MHz and higher |
| 2000 | PowerPC 7400 (G4) | 64 bits | 400 MHz and higher |
| 2003 | G4 (Velocity Eng) | 128 bits | 1.4 GHz and higher |

a version of the Pentium 4 microprocessor running at a clock speed of 2 GHz, the first commercially available chip to attain that speed (Figure 4.23).

Providing the CPU for Macintoshes over the years are chips made by Motorola Corporation. They fall into two processor families: the 68000 series (68000 to 68040) and the PowerPC family. PowerPC

conditions that a processor is likely to encounter. Another problem is that benchmarks don't test only the CPU, but may react to other system components.

Although benchmark tests provide information about processor performance, they may fail to describe a computer system's overall performance accurately. Real-world benchmark tests measure a system's overall performance in running complex applications.

The microprocessor is one of several chips on the computer's motherboard. Among the other chips are those that provide the computer's memory.

## MEMORY

The CPU needs to interact with multiple input/output requests at the same time. That's the job performed by the computer's memory. **Memory** is a general term used for the devices that enable the computer to retain information. Memory chips store program instructions (the tools) and data (the parts) so that the CPU can access them quickly. As you'll see in this section, the computer's motherboard contains several different types of memory, each optimized for its intended use.

### RAM (Random Access Memory)

The large memory modules housed on the computer's motherboard contain the computer's random access memory (RAM). A volatile memory technology, **random access memory** (**RAM**) stores information temporarily so that it's directly and speedily available to the microprocessor. This information includes software as well as the data to be processed by the software. In volatile memory like RAM, the memory's contents are erased when the computer's power is switched off. However, volatile memory technologies provide much higher data transfer rates. RAM is designed for fast operation because the processor acts directly on the information stored in RAM.

Why is it called *random access* memory? The term *random access* doesn't imply that the memory stores data randomly. A better term would be *address* because each memory location has one—just like a post office box. Using this address, called a **memory**

address, the processor can store and retrieve data by going directly to a single location in memory (Figure 4.25).

Of the various types of RAM available, today's computers use a type of RAM called **dynamic RAM** (also called **DRAM**). DRAM (pronounced "dee-RAM") must be energized constantly or it loses its contents.

An improved type of DRAM is **synchronous DRAM** (**SDRAM**). SDRAM's operations are very fast because they are synchronized to the pulses of the computer's system clock. **Rambus DRAM** (**RDRAM**) uses a narrow but very fast bus to connect to the microprocessor, which enables Rambus DRAM chips to send and receive data within one clock cycle. **Double data rate** (**DDR**) **SDRAM** is a type of SDRAM that can both send and receive data within a single clock cycle. The newest and fastest PCs contain either Rambus DRAM or DDR SDRAM memory chips.

How much RAM does a computer need? In general, the more memory, the better. For today's Microsoft Windows, Linux, and Macintosh operating systems, 128 MB of

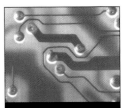

## Techtalk

**PC 100 SDRAM**
A type of SDRAM that is capable of keeping up with the latest and fastest motherboards, which have bus speeds of 100 MHz.

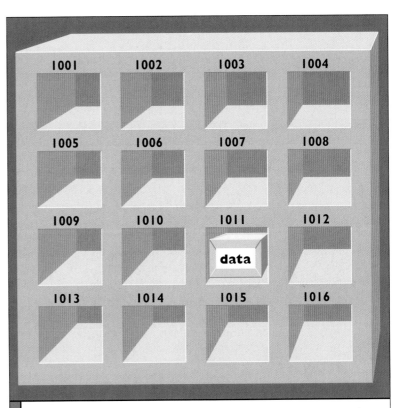

**FIGURE 4.25** Random access memory stores data in specific, addressed locations for easy access and retrieval.

## Destinations

To learn more about RAM, see Kingston Technology's "Ultimate Memory Guide," at **www.kingston.com/ tools/umg/default. asp**, which thoroughly explains how memory works, what memory technologies are available, and how to select the best RAM chips for your computer system.

RAM is a practical working minimum, but the computer will not run well with so little memory. Oftentimes these operating systems use virtual memory in addition to RAM. Through virtual memory, the computer can use the hard disk as an extension of RAM. It does this when RAM gets full (which can easily happen if you run two or more programs at once). Disk drives are much slower than RAM so when virtual memory kicks in, the computer slows down to a frustratingly slow pace. To avoid using virtual memory, you're better off with 256 MB of RAM, and increasingly, systems are sold with 512 MB of RAM.

### ROM (Read-Only Memory)

If everything in RAM is erased when the power is turned off, how does the computer start again? The answer is **read-only memory** (**ROM**), a type of memory on which instructions have been prerecorded. The instructions to start the computer are stored in read-only memory chips. Once instructions have been written onto a ROM chip, they cannot be removed and can only be read. In contrast to RAM, ROM is nonvolatile memory, which retains information even when the power is switched off.

### Cache Memory

RAM is fast, but it isn't fast enough to support the processing speeds of today's super-fast microprocessors, such as the Motorola G4 or Pentium 4. To enable these microprocessors to function at maximum speed, computer designers use **cache memory**. (The term *cache* is pronounced "cash.") Cache memory is much faster than RAM, but it's also more expensive. Although generally no larger than 512 KB, cache memory greatly improves the computer system's overall performance. The processor can use the cache to store frequently accessed program instructions and data.

Two types of cache memory are available. The first type, called **primary cache**, or level 1 (L1) cache, is included in the microprocessor chip. The second type, called **secondary cache**, or level 2 (L2) cache, is included on a separate printed circuit board. To improve secondary cache performance, the latest microprocessors are provided in plastic modules that contain a special type of secondary cache, called **backside cache**. Keeping the secondary cache as close as possible to the processor improves performance (Figure 4.26).

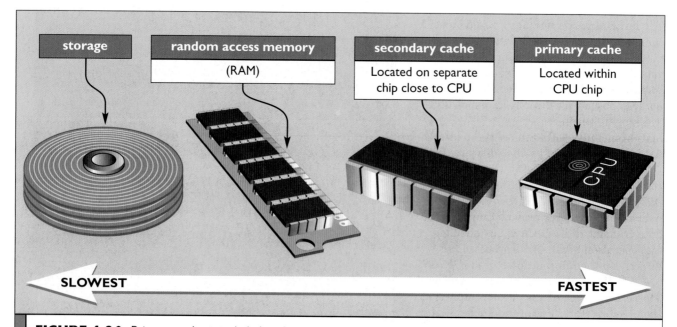

**FIGURE 4.26** Primary cache is included in the microprocessor chip. Secondary cache is included on a separate printed circuit board. Keeping the secondary cache as close as possible to the processor improves performance.

# Summary

## INSIDE THE SYSTEM UNIT

- The basic unit of information in a computer is the bit, a single-digit binary number (either 1 or 0). An 8-bit sequence of numbers, called a byte, is sufficient to represent the basic letters, numbers, and punctuation marks in most European languages.

- Data transfer rates of communications devices, such as modems, are measured in bits per second (bps), including Kbps (approximately one thousand bits per second), Mbps (approximately one million bits per second), and Gbps (approximately one billion bits per second). Data storage capacity is measured in bytes, such as kilobyte (K or KB, approximately one thousand bytes), megabyte (M or MB, approximately one million bytes), gigabyte (G or GB, approximately one billion bytes), and terabyte (T or TB, approximately one trillion bytes).

- Almost all computers have serial ports (for mice, external modems, and some printers), parallel ports (mainly for printers), and a video port. Some computers also have a SCSI port (for SCSI devices such as scanners), a USB port (for USB peripherals, including USB digital cameras and USB printers), a 1394 (FireWire) port (for FireWire peripherals such as digital video cameras), an IrDA port (for infrared keyboards and mice), input and output jacks for microphones and speakers, a telephone connector, or a network connector.

- The system unit contains the motherboard, which acts as the central connector for the processor, memory, and circuits within the computer. It also contains the power supply (which converts AC power to DC current), a cooling fan to keep the processor and circuits cool, and an internal speaker (which emits beeps and a few basic tones). Additionally, the system unit holds drive bays for data storage and retrieval devices, and expansion cards for additional memory, a modem, sound, video, and games.

- The computer's motherboard contains the microprocessor (the CPU— the 'brains' of the computer), the system clock (which generates pulses to synchronize the computer's activities), the chipset (chips that help the processor move data around), and memory modules. Also provided are slots that give expansion cards access to the computer's input/output (I/O) bus, which provides access to the CPU and other system services to devices such as modems, sound cards, game controllers, and more.

- A computer's central processing unit (CPU) processes data in a four-step cycle called a machine cycle using two components, called the control unit and the arithmetic-logic unit (ALU). The control unit follows a program's instructions and manages four basic operations: fetch, decode, execute, and write-back. The arithmetic-logic unit can perform arithmetic operations or logical operations.

- Factors that affect a microprocessor's performance include the data bus width (how many bits it can process at once), clock speed (the number of operations the chip can execute per clock cycle), and the chip architecture (RISC vs. CISC).

- A computer's memory includes several different components. The computer's main memory, random access memory (RAM) is used to hold programs, data, and instructions for quick use by the processor. Read-only memory (ROM) is used to hold prerecorded start-up operating instructions. Primary cache memory operates at very high speeds and keeps frequently accessed data available to the processor. Secondary cache memory enhances processor performance.

Go to **www.prenhall.com/cayf2005** to review this chapter, answer the questions, and complete the exercises.

# Key Terms and Concepts

# Matching

Match each key term in the left column with the most accurate definition in the right column.

_____ 1. parallel port

_____ 2. expansion card

_____ 3. RAM

_____ 4. character code

_____ 5. byte

_____ 6. parallel processing

_____ 7. Motorola

_____ 8. USB port

_____ 9. pipelining

_____ 10. register

_____ 11. parity bit

_____ 12. fetch

_____ 13. instruction set

_____ 14. cache memory

_____ 15. RJ-11

a. describes a computer that has many processors running at the same time

b. 8 bits

c. connector used to connect a telephone line to a computer

d. additional memory that is used to improve the computer system's overall performance

e. retrieve the next program instruction from memory

f. a processing technique that feeds new instructions into the CPU at every step of the processing cycle

g. a port used for peripherals such as printers that require a high-speed connection

h. high-speed temporary storage location in the CPU

i. an extra bit that is used for error checking

j. a processor's list of instructions

k. a printed circuit board designed to fit into an expansion bus's receptacles that allows additional components to be connected to a computer

l. stores information temporarily so that it's directly and speedily available to the microprocessor

m. a code that translates between the numerical words of the computer and the letters, numbers, and symbols that we are accustomed to using

n. the company that manufacturers the processors for Macintosh computers

o. a port that can connect more than one device at a time

# Multiple Choice

Circle the correct choice for each of the following.

1. This is not typically located outside the
   system unit.
   a. port
   b. power switch
   c. console
   d. motherboard

2. What are the plug-in adapters that are used to
   connect the computer with various peripherals?
   a. compatibility cards
   b. pi adapters
   c. expansion cards
   d. compatibility sockets

3. About how many bytes are in a kilobyte?
   a. 100
   b. 1,000
   c. 1,100
   d. 1,500

4. What does SCSI mean?
   a. standard computer system interface
   b. small computer system interface
   c. serial computer system interface
   d. sequential computer system interface

5. Which of the following is not a variation of the
   Intel Pentium CPU?
   a. PowerPC
   b. Pentium II
   c. Xeon
   d. Celeron

6. This is not a type of memory.
   a. RAM
   b. ALU
   c. cache
   d. ROM

7. What does an ALU do?
   a. arithmetic operations
   b. advanced logic operations
   c. asynchronous operations
   d. accelerated level utilization

8. Which of these extracts instructions from
   memory and decodes and executes them?
   a. control unit
   b. RAM
   c. ROM
   d. data bus

9. This is the name given to an electronic circuit
   that carries data from one computer component
   to another.
   a. trace
   b. data lead
   c. bus
   d. chip

10. What do you call the ability of a computer to run
    more than one processor at a time?
    a. multiple processing
    b. parallel processing
    c. serial processing
    d. dual processing

# Fill-In

In the blanks provided, write the correct answer for each of the following.

1. A(n) _____ is a physical receptacle designed for a specific type of plug.

2. _____ is another name for the IEEE 1394 port that is used for high-speed video input.

3. _____ is a type of memory on which instructions have been prerecorded.

4. _____ allows external components to be plugged and unplugged while the computer is running.

5. _____ means that a processor can run more than one program at the same time.

6. The most widely used character code is _____.

7. A(n) _____ contains millions of transistors.

8. _____ is the number of bits a CPU can process at once.

9. The _____ contains almost all of a computer's central processing unit on a single chip.

10. A(n) _____ is an electronically defined pathway for getting information into and out of a computer.

11. The _____ enables a computer to perform mathematical operations more quickly.

12. Programmers use the _____ numbering system, which is based on 16.

13. A test that puts a processor through a series of operations to provide a basis for comparison is called a _____.

14. The _____ is an input/output bus that is designed to connect devices to notebook computers.

15. The _____ is an electronic circuit that generates rapid pulses.

# Short Answer

1. Describe the components of a computer system, including those that can be found inside and outside of the system unit.

2. Explain the difference between RAM and ROM. Why are both types of memory used in a computer?

3. What are buses used for? What types of buses are in a computer system?

4. What elements affect the performance of a computer system?

5. What is the difference between a serial port and a parallel port? Why are keyboards connected to the serial port? (Note: some keyboards, as well as mice, are connected to USB ports.)

6. What advantage does Unicode have over the ASCII and EBCDIC codes?

7. Explain why a megabyte is not exactly 1,000,000 bytes.

Go to **www.prenhall.com/cayf2005** to review this chapter, answer the questions, and complete the exercises.

# A Closer Look

1. You have read about a variety of input/output ports, so now let's look at an actual computer to see which ones are installed. Using your own computer or a campus one, determine the number and types of ports that are available, and specifically identify the external devices that are connected to each port.

2. All computers, regardless of their size or manufacturer, follow the same four steps in the machine, or processing, cycle. Identify and explain the purpose of each of these steps. Most of the newer processors use pipelining. Explain how pipelining enhances the overall processing speed. Give a noncomputer example of pipelining (that is, an activity that you have personally performed that requires multiple steps to complete and in which you can begin the next step before the current one is completed).

3. Many vehicle owners take active steps to protect their investments. They follow manufacturers' maintenance schedules, obtain insurance against damage or loss, and even install antitheft devices. Let's see how individuals and institutions protect their computer investments. If you own a computer, especially a laptop, what measures do you take to protect it from theft while on campus or when traveling? Is your computer covered by homeowner's or renter's insurance? If it is covered, what, if any, is the amount of the deductible? How does your school ensure that public computers and computer components are not stolen? Are there any special security provisions in place for computer laboratories? How are faculty and staff office computers protected? Check with your campus security and find out if any computers have been stolen in the past month. Do you feel that the laboratory and office computers and components are adequately protected from theft?

4. Although conventional computer memory (RAM) has increased in size and speed, most new computer systems use cache memory. What is the purpose of cache memory? Explain the difference between level 1 (L1) and level 2 (L2) cache. Although it was not discussed in the textbook, there is a third level of cache memory called L3. See what information you can find about this additional level of cache.

5. Besides the size and speed improvements in processors, there have been corresponding improvements to the system buses. However, the bus improvements have not been as dramatic as those for processors. The size of data buses in the first generation of personal computers was 8 bits, and they operated at a speed of 2 or 4 MHz. Find the current size and speed for the high-end Intel Pentium 4 and Motorola PowerPC data buses. How do the bus speeds compare with the processor speeds? This disparity is one of the reasons for cache memory.

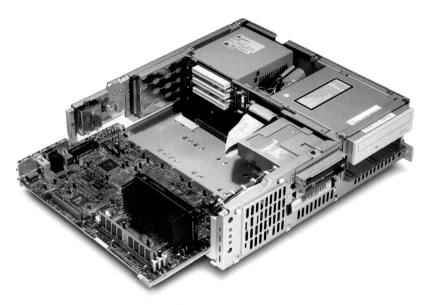

# On the Web

1. Since technology changes rapidly, some of the information printed in a textbook is no longer up to date. Currently, the fastest Intel processor for a personal computer is the Pentium 4 with a clock speed of more than 3 GHz, and the fastest Motorola processor is the G4 with a clock speed of more than 1.4 GHz. Visit Intel at **www.intel.com/home/desktop/pentium4** and Apple at **www.apple.com/powermac/processor.html** to find their fastest processors. Which would you purchase? (Remember that processor speed alone does not determine which computer is faster.)

2. Unlike today's computers, in which memory chips are located on the motherboard, memory for the first microcomputers (circa 1978) was located on separate expansion cards, and 4 KB (not 4 MB) cost $295! Warm up your calculator, and divide the cost by the number of bytes to determine the cost per byte of storage. Visit **www.cnet.com** and find the current price for 256 MB of RAM. Once again divide the cost by the number of bytes, and determine the cost per byte. Using 1978 prices, how much would 256 MB of RAM cost today?

3. Serial ports allow you to connect a mouse, cameras, external DVD drives, and lots of other devices to your computer.

   Visit **computer.howstuffworks.com/serial-port.htm** to learn more about how serial ports work and what they can do for you. You might write a short paper on the difference between USB and USB.2.

4. Due to the high cost of a new car, many people buy used ones. Have you considered purchasing a used or refurbished computer? Just as with automobiles, you can purchase a computer from a company or from an individual. What are some advantages and disadvantages of purchasing a used or refurbished car from a company or individual? Visit the refurbished laptop site, **buycsn.com**, and select a specific laptop computer. Identify the computer, its specifications, and cost. Now review this chapter, and then write a short paper that shows that you understand at least six key terms from the chapter as they apply to purchasing a used computer.

5. Go to **computer.howstuffworks.com/motherboard.htm** to see what else you can learn about motherboards. Watch for key terms you learned in this chapter. Write a short paper that clearly explains what the motherboard does and how it performs at least one function within the system unit. For instance, the motherboard acts as the connection point for electrical circuits within the system unit.

# Input/Output and Storage

## What You'll Learn . . .

- Explain the purpose of special keys on the keyboard and list the most frequently used pointing devices.

- Discuss input devices used to get audio and digital data into the computer.

- List the characteristics that determine a monitor's quality, the various types of monitors, and the advantages and disadvantages of each.

- Identify the two major types of printers and indicate the advantages and disadvantages of each.

- Distinguish between memory and storage.

- Discuss how storage devices are categorized.

- List the performance characteristics of hard drives.

- Explain how data is stored on both hard and floppy disks.

- List and compare the various optical storage media available for personal computers.

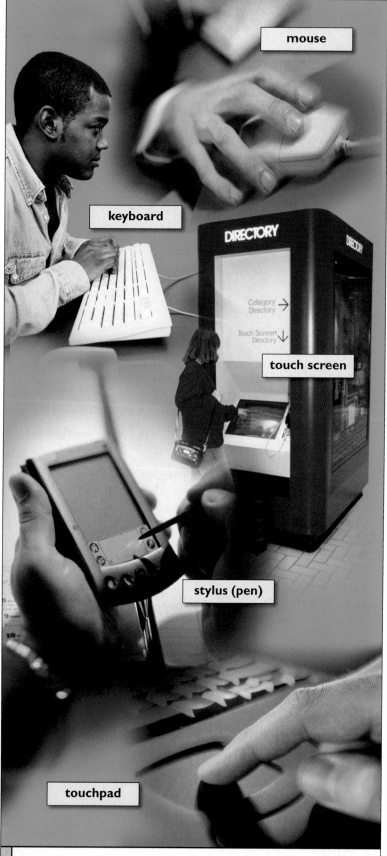

mouse

keyboard

DIRECTORY

DIRECTORY

Category
Directory →

Touch Screen
Directory ↓

touch screen

stylus (pen)

touchpad

**FIGURE 5.1** Input devices enable you to get data, programs, commands, and responses into the computer's memory.

Now that you've learned about the hardware and software that make the computer valuable to you, let's take a look at the practical impact of inputting data and commands, receiving audio and visual output, and storing your work. When you're using the computer, your attention is focused on the input and output devices you're using—typically, a keyboard, a mouse, and a monitor. Input devices enable you to direct the activity of the computer. They can be compared to human senses in that they enable the computer to see, hear, and even detect odors. Output devices transform processed digital information into forms that make sense to humans. They put our senses into contact with processed data, engaging our eyes, our ears, and even our sense of touch. Finally, storage devices provide nonvolatile (permanent) storage for the programs and data we work with.

In this chapter, you'll learn about input devices, output devices, why storage is necessary, and what types of devices you can use to store your data.

# Input Devices: Giving Commands

**Input** refers to any data or instructions that you enter into the computer's memory. As discussed in Chapter 1, there are two main types of input: data and instructions. This section will discuss **input devices**, the hardware components that enable you to get data and instructions into the computer's memory (Figure 5.1).

## KEYBOARDS

Despite all of the high tech input devices on the market, the **keyboard** is still the best way to get data into the computer.

How do keyboards work? When you press one of the keys, the keyboard sends a digital impulse through a cable (usually a USB cable) to the computer. When the computer receives the impulse, it displays a character such as a letter, number,

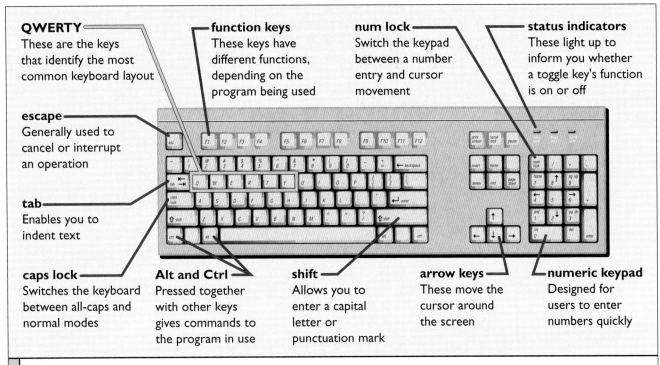

**QWERTY**
These are the keys that identify the most common keyboard layout

**function keys**
These keys have different functions, depending on the program being used

**num lock**
Switch the keypad between a number entry and cursor movement

**status indicators**
These light up to inform you whether a toggle key's function is on or off

**escape**
Generally used to cancel or interrupt an operation

**tab**
Enables you to indent text

**caps lock**
Switches the keyboard between all-caps and normal modes

**Alt and Ctrl**
Pressed together with other keys gives commands to the program in use

**shift**
Allows you to enter a capital letter or punctuation mark

**arrow keys**
These move the cursor around the screen

**numeric keypad**
Designed for users to enter numbers quickly

**FIGURE 5.2** Most computers use the standard QWERTY keyboard layout. This enhanced QWERTY keyboard also includes a number of special keys and a numeric keypad.

punctuation mark, or symbol on-screen. The character appears at the on-screen location of the **cursor** (also called the **insertion point**), which shows where text will appear when you type. The cursor may be a blinking vertical line, a blinking underscore, or a highlighted box.

### Using a Keyboard

All keyboards include keys that allow you to type in letters, punctuation marks, and numbers, as well as an assortment of other special keys that enable you to backspace over or delete characters, use a 10-key number pad, navigate software programs, and give commands to the operating system. Desktop PCs typically come equipped with an enhanced keyboard, which has 101 keys (Figure 5.2, Figure 5.3). The Macintosh equivalent, called the extended keyboard, has almost the exact same key layout.

Let's look at some of the special keys on the keyboard. If you don't want to type where the cursor is located, you can use the mouse or **cursor-movement keys** (also called **arrow keys**) to move the cursor around.

A **toggle key** is a key named after a type of electrical switch that has only two positions: on and off. For example, the

Caps Lock key functions as a toggle key. It switches the caps lock mode on and off. When the caps lock mode is engaged, you do not have to press the Shift key to enter capital letters. To turn off the caps lock mode, just press the Caps Lock key again.

Above the letters and numbers on the keyboard you'll find **function keys** (labeled F1 through F10 or F15), which are used to provide different commands depending on the program in use. Near the function keys, you'll also notice the Esc key, which is short for Escape. The Esc key's function also depends on which program you're using, but it's generally used to interrupt or cancel an operation.

Some keys have no effect unless you hold them down and press a second key. These are called **modifier keys** because they modify the meaning of the next key you press. You'll use modifier keys in keyboard shortcuts, which provide quick keyboard access to menu commands. See Figure 5.4 for a list of standard keyboard shortcuts.

### Using Alternative Keyboards

Although most desktop computers come equipped with a keyboard that is connected by means of a keyboard cable, some

**Destinations**

For a list of keyboard shortcuts for many Microsoft products, see Microsoft's "Keyboard Assistance" at **www.microsoft.com/enable/products/keyboard/keyboardsearch.asp.**

**FIGURE 5.3** Special Keys on the PC Enhanced Keyboard

| Key Name | Typical Function |
|---|---|
| Alt | In combination with another key, enters a command (example: Alt + X). |
| Backspace | Deletes the character to the left of the cursor. |
| Caps Lock | Toggles caps lock mode on or off. |
| Ctrl | In combination with another key, enters a command (example: Ctrl + C). |
| Delete | Deletes the character to the right of the cursor. |
| Down arrow | Moves the cursor down. |
| End | Moves the cursor to the end of the current line. |
| Esc | Cancels the current operation or closes a dialog box. |
| F1 | Displays on-screen help. |
| Home | Moves the cursor to the beginning of the current line. |
| Insert | Toggles between insert and overwrite mode, if these modes are available in the program you're using. |
| Left arrow | Moves the cursor left. |
| Num Lock | Toggles the numeric keypad's num lock mode, in which the keypad enters numbers. |
| Page Down | Moves down one screenful or one page. |
| Page Up | Moves up one screenful or one page. |
| Pause/Break | Suspends a program. (This key is not used by most applications.) |
| Popup menu key | Displays the popup menu for the current context (Windows only). |
| Print Screen | Captures the screen image to a graphics file, or prints the current screen on the printer. |
| Right arrow | Moves the cursor right. |
| Up arrow | Moves the cursor up. |
| Windows key | Displays the Start menu in Microsoft Windows. |

computers are equipped with an infrared port that enables them to use a **wireless keyboard** (also called a **cordless keyboard**). These keyboards use infrared or radio waves to send signals to the computer.

Also popular among handheld computer users are **portable keyboards**, which are small folding keyboards you can connect to your handheld. Portable keyboards enable you to type as you

### FIGURE 5.4 Standard Keyboard Shortcuts

| PC Shortcut | Mac Shortcut | Purpose |
|---|---|---|
| Ctrl + A | ⌘ + A | Selects all available items. |
| Ctrl + B | ⌘ + B | Bolds all selected items. |
| Ctrl + C | ⌘ + C | Copies text to the Clipboard. |
| Ctrl + F | ⌘ + F | Finds text. |
| Ctrl + I | ⌘ + I | Italicizes selected text. |
| Ctrl + J | ⌘ + J | Justifies text. |
| Ctrl + N | ⌘ + N | Creates a new document. |
| Ctrl + O | ⌘ + O | Opens an existing document. |
| Ctrl + P | ⌘ + P | Prints an existing document. |
| Ctrl + Q | ⌘ + Q | Quits the application. |
| Ctrl + S | ⌘ + S | Saves the existing document. |
| Ctrl + U | ⌘ + U | Underlines the selected items. |
| Ctrl + V | ⌘ + V | Pastes the contents of the Clipboard. |
| Ctrl + X | ⌘ + X | Cuts selected items. |

would using a normal desktop or notebook computer (Figure 5.5).

### Health Risks of Keyboard Use

Be aware that prolonged keyboard use can cause **carpal tunnel syndrome** (also known as cumulative trauma disorder or repetitive strain injury). This type of injury is caused by repeated motions that damage sensitive nerve tissue. Sometimes these injuries are so serious that they require surgery. To help prevent these problems, ergonomic keyboards are available. **Ergonomic keyboards** such as the Microsoft Natural Keyboard keep your wrists straight, reducing (but not eliminating) your chance of an injury.

Now that we've discussed the basics of using keyboards, let's move on to another type of equipment commonly used for input: pointing devices.

**FIGURE 5.5** Portable keyboards are popular among handheld users because they allow users to type information quickly and easily.

### THE MOUSE AND OTHER POINTING DEVICES

A **pointing device** gives you control over the movements of the on-screen pointer. The **pointer** is an on-screen symbol that signifies the type of command, input, or response you can give. Pointing devices such as a mouse also enable you to initiate

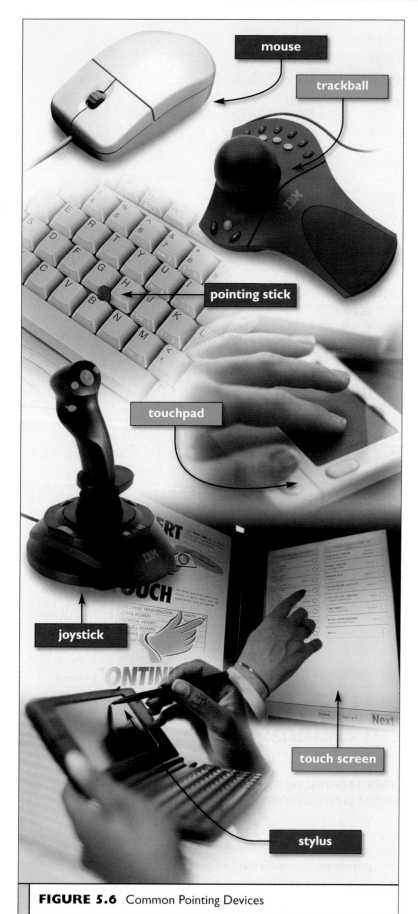

**FIGURE 5.6** Common Pointing Devices

actions, such as clicking, double-clicking, selecting, and dragging. By means of these actions, you can give commands and responses to whatever program the computer is running. Pointing devices can also be used to provide input. For example, pointing devices can be used in graphics programs to draw and paint on-screen, as if you were using a pencil or brush (Figure 5.6).

### The Mouse

The most widely used pointing device is the mouse, which is standard equipment on today's computer systems. As you probably know, a **mouse** is a palm-sized pointing device that is designed to move about on a clean, flat surface called a **mouse pad**. As you move the mouse, its movements are mirrored by the on-screen pointer. To initiate actions, use the mouse buttons.

**Types of Mice** Developed by Microsoft, the **wheel mouse** includes a rotating wheel that can be used to scroll text vertically within a document or Web page (Figure 5.7). Another type of mouse, called the **cordless mouse** (also called a **wireless mouse**) uses invisible infrared signals to connect to the computer's infrared (IrDA) port.

### Mouse Alternatives

Although the mouse is by far the most popular pointing device, some people prefer alternatives such as trackballs, pointing sticks, or touchpads. These alternatives are especially attractive when desktop space is limited—or nonexistent, as in most of the places where people use notebook computers. Additional input devices, such as joysticks, touch screens, styluses, and light pens, are also available for special purposes such as playing games, using automated teller machines, and managing personal digital assistants.

**Trackball** Trackballs are basically mice flipped on their backs. Instead of moving the mouse, you directly move the rotating ball. Trackballs usually come with one or more buttons that work in the same way as mouse buttons.

**Pointing Stick** A **pointing stick** is a small, stubby pointing nub that protrudes from the computer's keyboard. Because pointing sticks are pressure-sensitive, you use them by pushing them in various directions with your finger. Separate buttons are usually used to initiate clicking and dragging motions in conjunction with the pointing stick.

**Touchpad** Many notebook computers use a touchpad for a pointing device. A **touchpad** (also called a **trackpad**) is a pressure-sensitive device that responds to your finger's movement over the pad's surface.

**Joystick** A **joystick** is an input device with a large vertical lever that can be moved in any direction. Although joysticks can be used as pointing devices, they're most often used to control the motion of an on-screen object in a computer game or training simulator.

**Touch Screen** A **touch screen** uses a pressure-sensitive panel to detect where a user has tapped the display screen with a fingertip. Since touch screens are reliable, easy to use, and virtually impossible to steal, they are often used in kiosks. A **kiosk** is a booth that provides a computer service of some type, such as an automated teller machine (ATM). Though most frequently seen in banks, touch screen kiosks are used for many purposes, such as providing information to tourists and at airport e-ticket terminals.

**Pen Computing** Although touch screens are easy to use, human fingers are much bigger than an on-screen pointer. As a result, software designers must provide fewer options and larger, on-screen buttons. These characteristics of touch screens make them best suited to simple, special-purpose programs. For more detailed work, light pens can be used. **Light pens** contain a light source that triggers the touch screen's detection mechanism (Figure 5.8). You may already have used a light pen to sign your name electronically when using a credit card for a purchase. This is just one example of pen computing, the branch of computing that involves the above-mentioned light pens as well as styluses and PDAs.

A **stylus**, which looks like an ordinary pen, except that the tip is dry and semiblunt, is commonly found on personal digital assistants (PDAs). Styluses are also often used in computer-aided design (CAD) applications and other graphics applications with a graphics tablet, a digitizing tablet consisting of a grid on which users design things such as cars, buildings, medical devices, and robots.

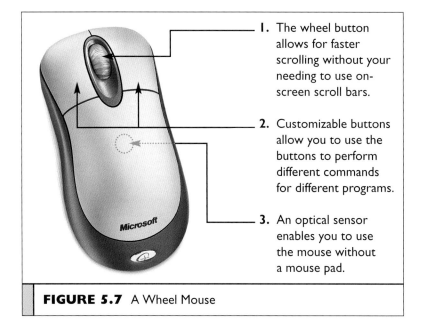

1. The wheel button allows for faster scrolling without your needing to use on-screen scroll bars.

2. Customizable buttons allow you to use the buttons to perform different commands for different programs.

3. An optical sensor enables you to use the mouse without a mouse pad.

**FIGURE 5.7** A Wheel Mouse

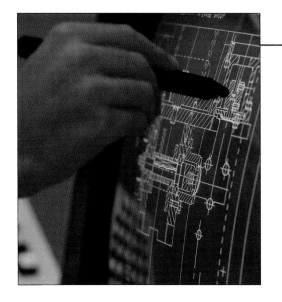

**FIGURE 5.8** Light pens provide a way to get input into a touch screen system.

You've learned about different types of keyboards and pointing devices, but what if you can't or don't use input devices that you hold in your hands? The next sections will offer some alternatives.

## AUDIO INPUT: SPEECH RECOGNITION AND SOUND CARDS

**Speech recognition**, also called **voice recognition**, is a type of input in which the computer recognizes spoken words. Depending on the context, the words may be interpreted as part of a command (such

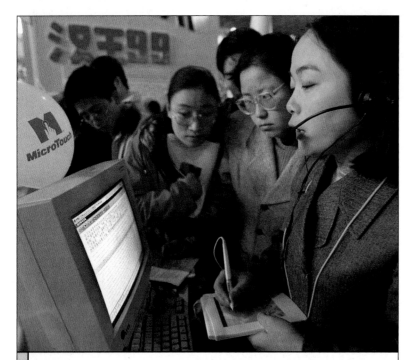

**FIGURE 5.9** Speech-recognition technology enables users to use spoken words to command the computer and enter textual data.

## Destinations

For the latest on speech-recognition technology, including reviews of the latest software, visit "21st Century Eloquence" at **www.voicerecog nition.com.**

as "Open Microsoft Word") or as data input. If the words are interpreted as data, they appear within a document as if you had typed them at the keyboard (Figure 5.9).

Past speech-recognition systems used discrete speech recognition, in which you had to speak each word separately. In contrast, today's continuous speech–recognition software enables users to speak without pausing between words.

Computers equipped with sound cards can accept sound input from a microphone. In PCs, a **sound card** is an expansion board designed to record and play back sound files. (Sound is built into Macintosh computers.) **Sound files** contain digitized sound data, which is saved in one of several standardized sound formats. These formats specify how sounds should be digitally represented, and generally include some type of data compression that reduces the size of the file. Examples of popular sound file formats are the Windows WAV format (the standard Microsoft Windows stereo sound file format), and **Moving Picture Experts Group** (**MPEG**) audio formats (called **MP2** and **MP3**). The MPEG formats are used frequently because they reduce file size significantly without sacrificing audio quality.

Now that you understand the main kinds of audio input, let's explore another technology that is transforming the IT industry: digital input.

## DIGITAL INPUT: DIGITAL CAMERAS AND DIGITAL VIDEO

It seems as though it was just yesterday when using digital computer data was so difficult that only computer scientists were able to accomplish the feat. But today's digital technology is so easy to use that even your family photo albums may be digitized.

### Digital Cameras

One of the hottest products on today's consumer market is the digital camera (Figure 5.10). A **digital camera** is a camera that uses digital technology to store and display images instead of recording them on film. As a result, the shots you take need to be stored in the camera until you can transfer them to a computer for long-term storage or printing.

What sets digital cameras apart from traditional cameras is their inner workings—specifically, how the image is saved. In digital cameras, the captured image's light falls on a charge-coupled device (CCD), a photosensitive computer chip that transforms light patterns into pixels (individual dots).

In most cases, you'll need to download the image data to a computer for safekeeping and printing. Some cameras are designed to connect to a computer by means of a serial or USB cable. Others can transfer data into your computer by means of an infrared port. Another technology often used to input digital image data into the computer is flash memory storage, which will be discussed later in this chapter.

### Digital Video

In the past, most full-motion images were captured and stored by means of analog techniques. In order to input analog video to the computer, a video capture board is required. A **video capture board** (also called a **video capture card**) transforms an analog video into its digital counterpart. Because a digital video file for even a short video requires a great deal of storage space, most video capture boards are equipped to perform on-the-fly data compression to reduce file size.

Increasingly popular are **digital video cameras**, which use digital rather than analog technologies to store recorded video images. Like digital cameras, digital video cameras can connect to a computer; often, this is done by means of a USB port. Because the signal produced by a digital video camera conforms to the computer's digital method of representing data, no video capture board is necessary. Most digital video cameras can take still images as well as movies.

A **Web cam** is an inexpensive, low-resolution analog or digital video camera that is designed to sit on top of the computer monitor. The images are small, jerky, and subject to delays. Still, thousands of Internet users employ Web cams and programs such as Microsoft's NetMeeting to stay in touch with friends and family.

## ALTERNATIVE INPUT DEVICES

Though keyboards, pointing devices, and audio and digital input devices are most commonly used to input data to the computer, a number of specialized input devices are used in the realms of business, industry, and science. This section introduces some of these alternative input devices and their uses.

### Scanners
**Scanners** are designed to copy anything that's printed on a sheet of paper, including

**FIGURE 5.10** Digital cameras are among the hottest items on today's consumer market.

artwork, handwriting, printed documents, and typed documents. Flatbed scanners work on a single sheet of paper at a time (Figure 5.11a). Sheet-fed scanners draw in the sheets to be copied by means of a roller mechanism. Handheld scanners can be used to copy smaller originals, such as photographs (Figure 5.11b).

Most scanners come with **optical character recognition** (**OCR**) software that automatically decodes scanned text into a text file. This technology has improved so much that most printed or typed documents can be scanned into text files, eliminating the need to retype such documents to get them into the computer.

## Destinations

For reviews, comparisons, and price information for digital cameras, see the "Digital Camera Buyer's Guide," at **www.digital-camerastore.com.**

**Earthcam.com** provides a large number of links to Web cams that are positioned throughout the world.

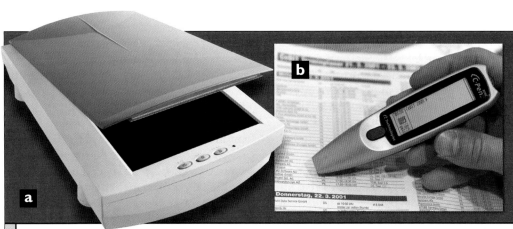

**FIGURE 5.11 a&b** (a) Flatbed scanners work on a single piece of paper at a time. (b) Handheld scanners are used most often to scan text into a microcomputer.

### Fax Machines

**Facsimile (fax) machines** transmit scanned images of documents via the telephone system (Figure 5.12). Fax machines do not require the use of a computer. However, you can set up a computer to simulate a fax machine. To do so, you'll need fax software and a fax modem. A **fax modem** is a communications device that enables a computer to send and receive faxes via the telephone system. When the fax modem is connected to a telephone line and the fax software is running, the computer can receive incoming faxes. The incoming document is displayed on-screen, and it can be printed or saved.

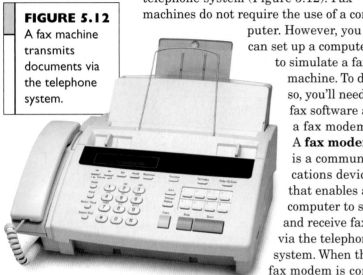

**FIGURE 5.12**
A fax machine transmits documents via the telephone system.

### MICR Systems, Bar Code Readers, and Optical Mark Readers

One of the earliest scanning systems was developed by the banking industry in the 1950s for processing checks. The **magnetic-ink character recognition (MICR) system** is used to encode the bank, branch, account number, and check number on each check. After the customer has used a check, all the bank has to enter manually is the amount.

In many retail and grocery stores, employees use a **bar code reader**, a handheld or desktop-mounted scanning device, to read an item's universal product code (UPC). The UPC is a pattern of bars printed on merchandise that links to a store's computer system to retrieve information about the item and its price. Today, bar codes are used to update inventory and ensure correct pricing. For example, Federal Express uses a bar code system to identify and track each package shipped.

In class, every time you take a test on a Scantron form, you're creating input suitable for an **optical mark reader (OMR)**. An OMR is a scanning device that senses the magnetized marks from your #2 pencil to determine which responses are marked.

Almost any type of questionnaire can be designed for OMR devices, making it helpful to researchers who need to tabulate responses to large surveys.

We're constantly finding more ways to tell the computer what we want it to do. Today we're using biological feedback, chemical detectors, and gesture recognition as useful input sources. Some day we may even be able to control the computer by just thinking about what we want it to do.

Now that we know how to get our data into a computer system, let's look at how that data is presented back to us with output devices.

# Output Devices: Engaging Our Senses

**Output devices** enable people to see, hear, and even feel the results of processing operations. The most widely used output devices are monitors and printers. We'll begin this section by looking at monitors, and examine printers, sound systems, and alternative output devices in subsequent sections.

## MONITORS

**Monitors** (also called **displays**) display output. The on-screen display enables you to see how applications are processing your data, but it's important to remember that the screen display isn't a permanent record. To drive home this point, screen output is sometimes called soft copy, as opposed to hard copy (printed output). To make permanent copies of your work, you should save it to a storage device or print it.

Monitors are categorized by the technology used to generate their images, the colors they display, their screen size, and additional performance characteristics.

### Types of Monitors

The large monitors you see that look like television screens connected to desktop computers are **cathode-ray tube (CRT)** monitors (Figure 5.13). In a color monitor, three guns (corresponding to the colors red, green, and blue) are combined in varying intensities to produce on-screen colors. CRT monitors are inexpensive compared with other types of monitors, but they consume more energy and take up more desktop space.

The thinner monitors used on notebook and newer desktop computers are known as **liquid crystal displays** (**LCDs**) or **flat-panel displays**. The least expensive LCDs are called passive-matrix LCDs (also called dual scans) and may generate image flaws, such as an unwanted shadow next to a column of color, and they are too slow for full-motion video. Active-matrix LCDs use transistors to control the color of each on-screen pixel. Other flat-panel display technologies include gas plasma displays and field emission displays (FEDs). An intriguing new technology, FEDs look like LCDs, except a tiny CRT produces each on-screen pixel.

Compared with CRT-based monitors, LCD monitors consume less electricity and take up much less room. These features make LCD monitors ideal for portable computers, including notebook computers, personal digital assistants (PDAs), Web-enabled devices such as digital cellular telephones that have the ability to connect to the Internet, and e-book readers. An **e-book reader** is a book-sized device that displays an **e-book**, a book that has been digitized and distributed by means of a

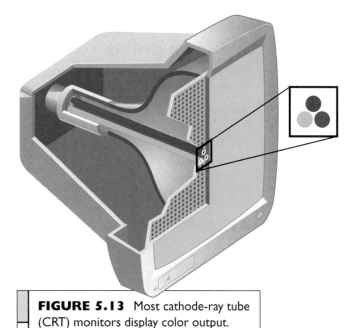

**FIGURE 5.13** Most cathode-ray tube (CRT) monitors display color output.

digital storage medium (such as flash memory or a CD-ROM disc) (Figure 5.14).

### Screen Size
Monitors are also categorized by their size. For CRTs, the **quoted size** is the size of the CRT's front surface measured diagonally. But some of this surface is hidden and unavailable for display purposes. For this reason, it's important to distinguish between the monitor's quoted size and the **viewable area**, the area available for viewing. Figure 5.15 shows typical relationships between quoted size and viewable

**techtv**

To learn more about monitors, see the video clip at www.prenhall.com/ cayf2005.

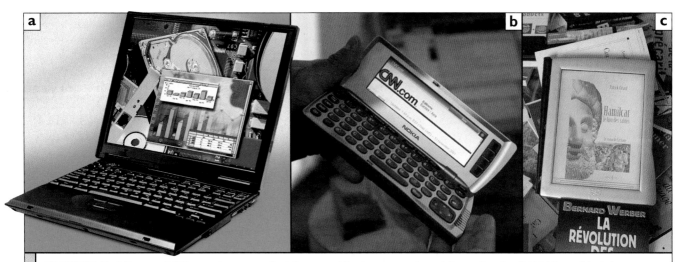

**FIGURE 5.14 a–c** LCD monitors are ideal for portable devices such as (**a**) notebooks, (**b**) Web-enabled devices, and (**c**) e-books.

**FIGURE 5.15 Quoted Monitor Size and Actual Viewable Area**

| Monitor Size | Viewable Area |
|---|---|
| 21 inches | 20 inches |
| 19 inches | 17 inches |
| 17 inches | 16 inches |
| 15 inches | 14 inches |

area. Vendors now provide both sizes, thanks to a consumer lawsuit.

How big should your monitor be? Increasingly, 17-inch monitors are considered standard. For desktop publishing and other applications where full-page displays are needed, 21-inch monitors are preferred. An alternative to a 21-inch display is a type of 17-inch display that can rotate to a vertical position and display a full page.

### Resolution

The term **resolution** generally refers to an image's sharpness. Video adapters conform to standard resolutions that are expressed by the number of dots (pixels) that can be displayed horizontally, followed by an "x" and the number of lines that can be displayed vertically (for example, 1024 x 768). Figure 5.16 lists common PC resolutions.

**FIGURE 5.16 Common PC Resolutions**

| |
|---|
| 640 x 480 |
| 800 x 600 |
| 1024 x 768 |
| 1280 x 1024 |

For color graphics displays, **video graphics adapter** (**VGA**) is the lowest-resolution standard (640 x 480). Most of today's computers default to **Super VGA** (1024 x 768).

### Refresh Rate

Another important measurement of video adapter quality is the refresh rate generated at a given resolution. **Refresh rate** refers to the frequency with which the screen image is updated, and it's measured in hertz (Hz), or cycles per second. Below 60 Hz, most people notice an annoying, eye-straining flicker. Very few people notice flicker when the refresh rate exceeds 72 Hz.

### Televisions as Monitors

The use of TVs for computer output is certain to become more common once High Definition Television (HDTV) comes into widespread use. **High Definition Television** (**HDTV**) is the name given to several standards for digital television displays. Although all HDTV devices support higher resolution than today's nondigital standard, the technology has been slow to develop because of high cost and lack of international agreement regarding standards.

Now that we've discussed monitors and soft copy, let's move on to devices that produce hard-copy output: printers.

## PRINTERS

**Printers** produce permanent versions (what we referred to earlier as *hard copy*) of the output that's visible on the computer's display screen. Some of the most popular printers are inkjet printers and laser printers (Figure 5.17).

**Inkjet printers** (also called **bubble-jet printers**) are the least expensive and can print in color, which makes them popular choices for home users. Although inkjet printers are inexpensive and produce excellent output, they are slow, and per-page costs may exceed the costs of running a laser printer due to the generally high cost of ink cartridges.

**Laser printers** work like copy machines. Under the printer's computerized control, a laser beam creates electrical charges on a rotating print drum. These charges attract toner, which is transferred to the paper and fused to its surface by a heat process. In contrast to inkjets, laser printers print faster: some can crank out 60 or more pages per minute. Although they are more expensive initially than inkjet printers, laser printers generally have lower per-page costs.

Dot-matrix printers, which were once the most popular type of printer used with personal computers, are decreasing in use. Large computers use line printers that can crank out hard copy at a rate of 3,000 lines per minute. Although their print quality is below that of inkjet and laser printers, these printers are mainly used for printing backup copies of large amounts of data.

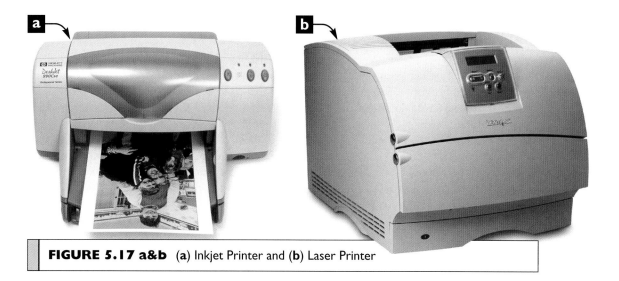

**FIGURE 5.17 a&b** (a) Inkjet Printer and (b) Laser Printer

The best color printers are **thermal transfer printers**. These printers use a heat process to transfer colored dyes or inks to the paper's surface. The best thermal transfer printers are called dye sublimation printers. These printers are slow and expensive, but they produce results that are difficult to distinguish from high-quality color photographs. Less expensive are snapshot printers, which are thermal transfer printers designed to print the output of digital cameras.

### Plotters

A **plotter**, like a printer, produces hard-copy output. Most form an image by

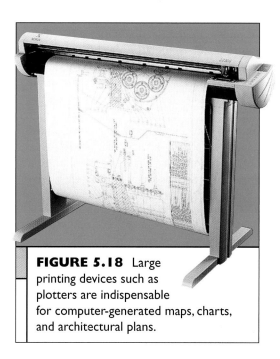

**FIGURE 5.18** Large printing devices such as plotters are indispensable for computer-generated maps, charts, and architectural plans.

physically moving a pen over a sheet of paper. A continuous-curve plotter is used to draw maps from stored data (Figure 5.18). Computer-generated maps can be retrieved and plotted or used to show changes over time.

Now that you've learned about visual output, the next section will discuss output we can hear.

## AUDIO OUTPUT: SOUND CARDS AND SPEAKERS

Introduced earlier as input devices, sound cards function as output devices too. In fact, sound cards and speakers, the two accessories needed to listen to computer-generated sound, are now standard equipment on new computer systems.

Sound cards can play the contents of digitized recordings, such as music recorded in the Windows WAV or MPEG sound file formats. Some do this job better than others. Quality enters into the picture most noticeably when the sound card reproduces files containing Musical Instrument Digital Interface (MIDI) information. **Musical Instrument Digital Interface (MIDI)** files are text files that tell a synthesizer when and how to play individual musical notes. (A synthesizer produces music by generating musical tones.) Better sound cards use wavetable synthesis, in which the sound card generates sounds using ROM-based recordings of actual musical instruments. The latest sound cards include surround-sound effects.

## ALTERNATIVE OUTPUT DEVICES

This section explores common output devices that you might add to your system, such as data projectors, fax machines, and multifunction devices.

### Data Projectors

Data projectors take a computer's video output and project this output onto a screen so that an audience can see it. For example, an **LCD projector** enables a speaker to project the computer's screen display on a screen similar to the one used with a slide projector, making it ideal for presentations to small audiences. In contrast, the latest technology, **digital light processing (DLP) projectors**, employs millions of microscopic mirrors embedded in a microchip to produce a bright, sharp image. This image is visible even in a brightly lit room, and it is sharp enough to be used with very large screens, such as those found at rock concerts and large auditoriums. Because of the complexity of these projectors, they are often expensive and built directly into an arena or auditorium.

### Fax and Multifunction Devices

As you learned earlier in this chapter, computers equipped with a fax modem and fax

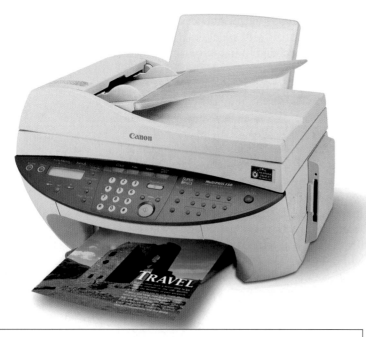

**FIGURE 5.19** A multifunction device combines an inkjet or laser printer with a scanner, a fax machine, and a copier.

software can receive incoming faxes. They can also send faxes as output. To send a fax with the computer, save your document using a special format that is compatible with the fax program. The fax program can then send this document through the telephone system to a distant fax machine. This output function is helpful because it is no longer necessary to print the document locally in order to send it as a fax.

In addition, **multifunction devices** combine inkjet or laser printers with a scanner, a fax machine, and a copier, enabling home office users to obtain all these devices without spending a great deal of money (Figure 5.19).

Now that you've learned about a variety of output devices, let's look at how you can store data for later use.

# Storage: Holding Data for Future Use

**Storage** (also called **mass storage** and **auxiliary storage**) refers collectively to all the various media on which a computer system can store software and data. Organizations are increasingly turning to computer storage systems to store all of their computer software, data, and information. The reason? Storing information on paper is expensive and offers no opportunity for electronic manipulation and sharing. As you'll learn in this section, a simple storage device can store the same information for about $10 per gigabyte that would cost $10,000 to store on paper. In fact, storage devices are increasing in capacity to the point that they can hold an entire library's worth of information. Read on to learn why storage is necessary, what kinds of storage devices are out there, and which will best fit your computing needs.

## MEMORY VS. STORAGE

To understand the distinction between memory and storage, think of the last time you worked at your desk. In your file drawer, you store all your personal items

# Wearables: The Fashion of Technology

**CURRENTS**

**Emerging Technologies**

All dressed, you head down the street in your "wearables." As you walk to the library, you e-mail a friend on your wrist pad, asking her to meet you for lunch later. At the library, the network automatically recognizes you by your ring. You search your pocket for your stylus, find it, and point at a library computer screen. The computer acknowledges you, and viewing through your monocle, you access your documents, open one, and begin jotting down notes by waving your pen in the air. Leaving the library, you call three of your friends. You visually chat together through your monocle and earpiece until your next class. You are seamlessly network-connected throughout your day by your wearable fashions.

Sound intriguing but unbelievable? Some of these technologies already exist. Take the Xybernaut company's "Poma," which combines a head-mounted display with a portable, lightweight CPU and an optical pointing device. Selling for about $1,500, Poma gives you wearable computer access to the Internet, e-mail, Word files, and games. It's also compatible with wearable keyboards and other input devices.

In fact, Xybernaut wearable computers may one day be used by astronauts in space (Figure 5.20). They have already been selected to be used in field tests for a research project dedicated to

exploring the planet Mars. It is hoped that the equipment will enable the one-day Mars explorers to learn how to use hands-free computing in their work. The wearable computers may also someday be used to enable two-way video- and audio-conferencing from Mars to the Earth.

Most wearable technologies to date have been incorporated into headsets and glasses, backpacks and fanny packs, rings and wristbands, and multipocketed pants. Recently, however, Santa Fe Science and Technologies created a commercial fiber that is similar to nylon but conducts electricity. Called "Smart Thread," this fiber can be woven into clothing like traditional threads, but it gives clothing computerlike abilities. The possibilities of Smart Thread are limitless. No more heavy packs for soldiers, who will instead be able to wear lightweight computers. Emergency search and rescue teams may one day wear computers that could connect them to a command center. Smart Thread could also be woven into a child's clothing to act as a tracking device. The possibilities are endless.

Products using Smart Thread are still two or three years away, but soon you may be wearing your computer, cell phone, music device, and other technologies as if they were everyday clothing. Get ready for wearables with style!

**FIGURE 5.20 Xybernaut equipment is helping would-be Mars explorers learn to use hands-free computing technology.**

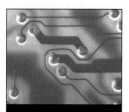

**Techtalk**

**storage media**
The things, such as floppy disks, hard disks, CDs, and DVDs, that store software and data—even when the computer is turned off. *Media* is plural; the singular is *medium*.

and papers, such as your checking account statements. The file drawer is good for long-term storage. When you decide to work on one or more of these items, you take it out of storage and put it on your desk. The desktop is a good place to keep the items you're working with; they're close at hand and available for use right away.

Computers work the same way. When you want to work with the contents of a file, the computer transfers the file to a temporary workplace: the computer's memory. Memory is a form of storage, but it is temporary. For the purpose of this section we will use the term *storage* to mean that which is long term.

## WHY IS STORAGE NECESSARY?

Why don't computers just use memory to hold all those files? Here are some reasons:

- **Storage devices retain data when the current is switched off.** The computer's random access memory (RAM) is **volatile**. This means that when you switch off the computer's power, all the information in RAM is irretrievably lost. On the other hand, storage devices are **nonvolatile**. They do not lose data when the power goes off.

- **Storage devices are cheaper than memory.** RAM is designed to operate very quickly so that it can keep up with the computer's CPU. For this reason, RAM is expensive—much more

expensive than storage (Figure 5.21). In fact, most computers are equipped with just enough RAM to accommodate all the programs a user wants to run at once. In contrast, a computer system's storage devices hold much more data and software than the computer's memory does. Today, you can buy a storage device capable of storing four gigabytes (GB) of software and data for about the same amount you'll pay for 256 megabytes (MB) of RAM.

- **Storage devices play an essential role in system startup operations.** When you start your computer, the BIOS (basic input/output system) reads essential programs into the computer's RAM, including one that begins loading essential system software from the computer's hard disk.

- **Storage devices are needed for output.** When you've finished working, you use the computer's storage system as an output device in an operation called saving. When you save a document, the computer transfers your work from the computer's memory to a read/write storage device, such as a hard or floppy disk. If you forget to save your work, it will be lost when you switch off the computer's power. Remember, the computer's RAM is volatile!

For all these reasons, demand for increased storage capacity is soaring. According to one estimate, the need for digital storage is increasing 60 percent each year, and the pace shows no signs of slowing down.

Now that you understand the importance of storage, let's look at the devices and media used to hold your data.

# Storage Devices

**Storage devices** are categorized in various ways, including the type of operations they can perform, the method used to access the information they contain, the technology they use, and where they're

**FIGURE 5.21** Memory vs. Storage

| | Device | Access Speed | Cost per MB |
|---|---|---|---|
| **MEMORY** | Cache Memory | Fastest | Highest |
| | RAM | Fast | High |
| **STORAGE** | Hard Disk | Medium | Medium |
| | CD-ROM Disc | Slow | Low |
| | Backup Tape | Very Slow | Lowest |

located in the storage hierarchy. Capacity and speed are also important factors with storage devices. The following sections explain these points.

### Sequential vs. Random Access Storage

Storage devices are categorized according to the way they retrieve the requested data. In a **sequential storage device**, such as a tape backup unit, the computer has to go through a fixed sequence of stored items to get to the one that's needed. Like a cassette tape, it forces you to fast forward or rewind to get to the data you want. Sequential storage devices are slow but inexpensive.

A **random access storage device** can go directly to the requested data without having to go through a sequence. For example, a disk drive is a storage device that has a read/write head. By moving across the disk, the read/write head can get to the requested data's location quickly. Random access storage devices are faster but more expensive than sequential storage devices.

### STORAGE TECHNOLOGIES: MAGNETIC AND OPTICAL

Two storage technologies are in widespread use: magnetic storage and optical storage. Most storage devices use one technology or the other; occasionally, they are combined.

**Magnetic storage devices** use disks or tapes that are coated with magnetically sensitive material. In all magnetic storage devices, the basic principle is the same: an electromagnet, called a **read/write head**, records information by transforming electrical impulses into a varying magnetic field. As the magnetic materials pass beneath the read/write head, this varying field forces the particles to rearrange themselves in a meaningful pattern of positive and negative magnetic indicators. This operation is called writing. In reading, the read/write head senses the recorded pattern and transforms this pattern into electrical impulses.

The two most common types of magnetic media are magnetic tape, which is used with sequential storage devices, and **magnetic disks**, which are used with random access devices. Popular magnetic

storage media include hard disks, floppy disks, and Zip disks.

**Optical storage devices** use tightly focused laser beams to read microscopic patterns of data encoded on the surface of plastic discs (Figure 5.22). Microscopic indentations, called **pits**, absorb the laser's light in certain areas. The drive's light-sensing device receives no light from these areas, so it sends a signal to the computer corresponding to a 0 in the computer's binary numbering system. Flat, reflective areas, called **lands**, bounce the light back to a light-sensing device, which sends a signal equivalent to a 1.

CD-ROM discs are read-only media. However, several types of optical read/write media are available, including one-time recordable CD-ROM (CD-R) discs, rewritable CD-ROM (CD-RW) discs, and DVD-ROM discs.

How much data can an optical medium store? Scientists believe that the physics of light limit optical media to a maximum of 5 gigabits of storage per square inch. However, new optical technologies (discussed later in this chapter) break this barrier by using discs with more than one layer.

## Destinations

Looking for the latest news and information concerning storage media? SearchStorage.com at **searchstorage. techtarget.com** offers a wealth of information about storage technologies, including product reviews, background information, storage-related software, online discussions, and troubleshooting tips.

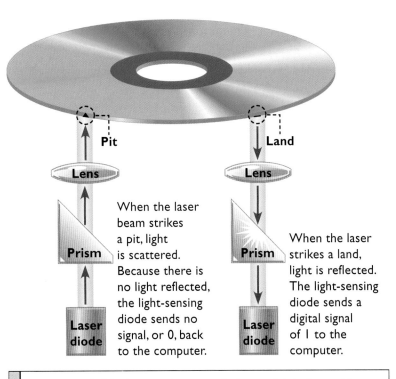

When the laser beam strikes a pit, light is scattered. Because there is no light reflected, the light-sensing diode sends no signal, or 0, back to the computer.

When the laser strikes a land, light is reflected. The light-sensing diode sends a digital signal of 1 to the computer.

**FIGURE 5.22** In optical storage devices, a tightly focused laser beam reads data encoded on the disc's surface. Some optical devices can write data as well as read it.

## Techtalk

**disk or disc?**
If the subject is magnetic media, the correct spelling is disk. Disc is used to describe optical media.

**Magneto-optical (MO) drive** storage devices combine the two basic technologies. They contain both magnetic and optical technology so that future MO discs no larger than today's CD-ROMs will contain up to 100 GB of storage.

## THE STORAGE HIERARCHY

Storage devices fit into one of three levels in the **storage hierarchy**:

Online storage is the most important component of the storage hierarchy. Also called **primary storage**, **online storage** consists of the storage devices that are actively available to the computer system and do not require any action on the part of the user. The computer's hard disk is a personal computer's online storage system.

**Near-online storage**, also called **secondary storage**, consists of storage that isn't directly available but can be made available easily by some simple action on the user's part, such as inserting a disk. Examples of near-online storage devices for personal computers are floppy and CD-ROM drives.

**Offline storage** (also called tertiary storage or archival storage) consists of storage that is not readily available. Offline storage media, such as magnetic tapes, are used for infrequently accessed data that needs to be kept for archival purposes.

## STORAGE CAPACITY AND SPEED

Storage capacity is measured in bytes. Capacities range from the floppy disk's 1.44 MB to huge room-filling arrays of storage devices capable of storing a dozen or more terabytes of data. To provide this much storage with print-based media, you'd need to cut down several million trees.

A storage device's most important performance characteristic is the speed with which it retrieves desired data. The amount of time it takes for the device to begin reading data is its **access time** (Figure 5.23). For disk drives, the access time includes the **seek time**, the time it takes the read/write head to locate the data before reading begins.

### FIGURE 5.23 Access Time: Memory vs. Storage

| Device | Typical Access Time |
|---|---|
| Static RAM (SRAM) | 5–15 nanoseconds |
| Dynamic RAM (DRAM) | 50–70 nanoseconds |
| Solid state disk (SSD) | 0.1 millisecond |
| Hard disk drive | 6–12 milliseconds |
| CD-ROM drive | 80–800 milliseconds |

The following sections will explore the different types of storage devices you can utilize to store your programs and data.

## HARD DISKS

On almost all computers, the **hard disk** is by far the most important online storage device. A hard disk is a high-capacity, high-speed storage device that usually consists of several fixed, rapidly rotating disks called **platters**. Most hard disks are fixed disks, which use platters that are sealed within the mechanism's case.

In the early days of personal computing, hard disks were optional. Programs were small enough to fit on floppy disks (discussed in the next section), and users rarely created files that exceeded a floppy disk's capacity. In contrast, today's computer systems require a hard disk, one with at least several gigabytes of storage.

### How Hard Disks Work

Magnetic read/write heads move across the surface of a disk coated with magnetically sensitive material. A hard disk contains two or more vertically stacked platters, each with two read/write heads (one for each side of the disk). The platters spin so rapidly that the read/write head floats on a thin cushion of air, at a distance 300 times smaller than the width of a human hair. To protect the platter's surface, hard disks are enclosed in a sealed container.

How does the read/write head know where to look for data? To answer this question, you need to know a little about how stored data is organized on a disk. Like a vinyl record, disks contain circular bands called **tracks**. Each track is divided into pie-shaped wedges called **sectors**. Two or more sectors combine to form a **cluster** (Figure 5.24).

To keep track of where specific files are located, the computer's operating system records a table of information on the disk. This table contains the name of each file and the file's exact location on the disk. On Microsoft Windows systems, this table is called the **file allocation table** or **FAT**.

Hard disks can be divided into partitions. A **partition** is a section of a disk set aside as if it were a physically separate disk. Partitions are often used to enable computers to work with more than one operating system. For example, Linux users often create one partition for Linux and another for Microsoft Windows. In this way, they can work with programs developed for either operating system.

To communicate with the CPU, hard disks require a hard disk controller. A **hard disk controller** is an electronic circuit board that provides an interface between the CPU and the hard disk's electronics. The controller may be located on the computer's motherboard, on an expansion card, or within the hard disk.

If hard disks develop a defect or the read/write head encounters an obstacle, such as a dust or smoke particle, the head bounces on the disk surface, preventing the computer from reading or writing data to one or more sectors of the disk. Hard disks can absorb minor jostling without suffering damage, but a major jolt—such as one caused by dropping the computer while the drive is running—could cause a head crash to occur. Head crashes are one of the causes of **bad sectors**—areas of the disk that have become damaged and can no longer hold data reliably. If you see an on-screen message indicating that a disk has a bad sector, try to copy the data off the disk and don't use it to store new data.

### Factors Affecting Hard Disk Performance

A hard disk's performance is determined by two factors: positioning performance and transfer performance.

**Positioning performance** refers to how quickly the disk can position the read/write head so that it can begin

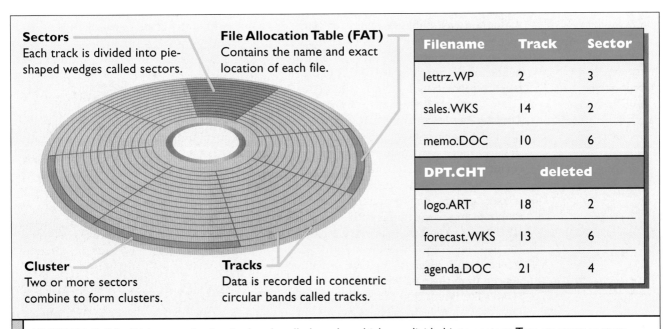

**Sectors**
Each track is divided into pie-shaped wedges called sectors.

**File Allocation Table (FAT)**
Contains the name and exact location of each file.

| Filename | Track | Sector |
|----------|-------|--------|
| lettrz.WP | 2 | 3 |
| sales.WKS | 14 | 2 |
| memo.DOC | 10 | 6 |
| DPT.CHT | deleted | |
| logo.ART | 18 | 2 |
| forecast.WKS | 13 | 6 |
| agenda.DOC | 21 | 4 |

**Cluster**
Two or more sectors combine to form clusters.

**Tracks**
Data is recorded in concentric circular bands called tracks.

**FIGURE 5.24** Disks contain circular bands called tracks, which are divided into sectors. Two or more sectors combine to form a cluster.

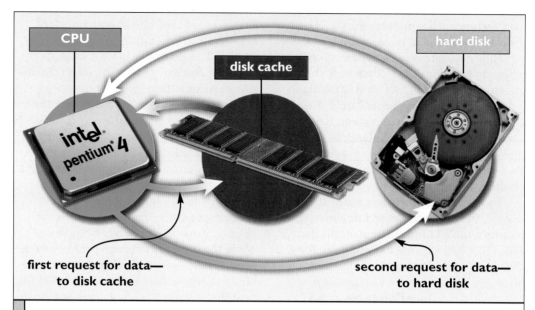

**first request for data— to disk cache**

**second request for data— to hard disk**

**FIGURE 5.25** Disk cache, a type of RAM, dramatically improves hard disk performance. When the CPU needs to get information from the disk, it looks in the disk cache first.

## Destinations

For an excellent Web-based tutorial on varieties of RAID, see Advanced Computer & Network Corporation's "RAID Technology" at **www.acnc.com/ raid.html**.

transferring data. This aspect of a disk's performance is measured by the disk's seek time, which, as you learned earlier, is the amount of time required to move the read/write head to the required position.

**Transfer performance** refers to how quickly the disk is able to transfer data from the disk to memory. One way to improve transfer performance is to increase the speed with which the disk spins, which makes data available more quickly to the read/write heads. Another way is to improve the spacing of data on the disk so that the heads can retrieve several blocks of data on each revolution.

**Disk Caches: Improving A Hard Disk's Performance** To improve hard disk performance, most computers have a type of cache memory called disk cache (Figure 5.25). A **disk cache** is a type of RAM (random access memory) that is used to store the program instructions and data you are working with. When the CPU needs to get information, it looks in the disk cache first. If it doesn't find the information it needs, it retrieves the information from the hard disk.

**RAID Devices: Protecting Against Data Loss** A device that groups two or more hard disks that contain exactly the same data is called **RAID**, which is short for **redundant array of independent disks** (Figure 5.26). The key word in this

phrase is redundant, which means "extra copy." No matter how many disks a RAID device contains, the computer "thinks" it's dealing with just one disk. Should one of the disks fail, there's no interruption of service. All the disks contain an exact copy of all the data, so one of the other disks kicks in and delivers the requested data.

RAID devices offer a high degree of **fault tolerance**; that is, they keep working even if one or more components fail.

**FIGURE 5.26** RAID devices help protect against data loss.

# September 11:
# Business the Day After

**IMPACTS**

**Safety and Security**

September 11, 2001, was a day of extraordinary human tragedy for America. Terrorists not only took many lives, they also tried to knock the United States off its economical feet. As the country attempted to recover, Americans realized that the way to prove to terrorists that they weren't going to succeed in quashing the American spirit was to get back to business as quickly as possible.

One company hit especially hard was bond house and financial services firm Cantor Fitzgerald, along with its sister companies eSpeed and TradeSpark, which operated from the top floors of One World Trade Center. More than 650 of its employees perished in the WTC disaster, including half of its senior leadership staff. However, because of the dedication of its surviving employees, as well as its redundant and concurrent backup computing centers in Rochelle, New Jersey, and London, England, Cantor Fitzgerald was miraculously up and running just two days after the attack.

September 11 forced companies not just in New York City but across the United States to take a closer look at their backup capabilities—not just *whether* they had a backup system, but also *where* it was located. In fact, many of the companies at the Trade Towers did have backup systems on September 11, but many of these companies relied on systems at the other Tower or at another nearby building in the area affected by the attack. The disaster changed all that. The idea governing backup systems today is not just

to ensure redundancy of data, but to ensure that backup data is stored in geographically dispersed places. Most important, these facilities must be located far from major cities, which are seen as potential terrorist targets. Thus, in the aftermath of September 11, many companies are moving their backup centers to suburban areas with independent utility and transportation systems. The New York Stock Exchange, for example, is planning on creating a backup trading floor in Westchester, New York, to ensure trading can continue in case of an emergency.

Some redundancy centers are used solely in case of an emergency and serve only as storage facilities, complete with their own electrical generators and telecommunications grids. Others are fully functioning business facilities that act as satellite offices while they also duplicate all company data. Because such "mirroring" of data needs to be performed in an organized fashion, professional backup and security companies have experienced an increased demand for their services in the wake of September 11. Meanwhile, some building companies are now advertising themselves as specialists in constructing backup buildings.

Back at Ground Zero, cleanup is complete, and the rebuilding goes on. Companies once located in the WTC are now located across New York and its surroundings. Whether these companies will ever return to downtown Manhattan is uncertain. What is certain is that the change in business landscape has made backup computing systems a necessity.

For this reason, RAID devices are widely used wherever a service interruption could prove costly, hazardous, or inconvenient to customers. Most of the major Web sites use RAID devices to ensure the constant availability of their Web pages. Most personal computer users don't need RAID devices as long as they back up their data regularly.

## Removable Hard Disks

Most hard disks are fixed disks, a type of hard disk that is nonremovable. **Removable hard disks** enclose the platters within a cartridge, which can be inserted into a drive bay and removed. Removable hard

disks are a near-online storage medium. Their popularity and survival will depend upon their costs and versatility versus that of memory-based storage devices.

## Internet Hard Drives

An **Internet hard drive** is storage space on a server that is accessible from the Internet. Usually, a computer user subscribes to the storage service and agrees to rent a block of storage space for a specific period of time. You might store files there that you wish to share with family and friends. Instead of sending attachments with your e-mail, you might simply post the files to your storage device and then allow them to be viewed or retrieved by others. You might create backup copies of critical files or of all the data on your hard disk.

The key advantage of this remote storage is the ability to access data from multiple locations. You're able to access your files from any device that can access the Internet, so everything you store on the site is available to you at any time. Some disadvantages are that your data may not be secure, the storage device might corrupt or lose your data, and the company may go out of business.

While hard disks are currently the most important storage media within your computer, the disks explored in the next section are examples of portable storage.

## FLOPPY AND ZIP DISKS AND DRIVES

A **disk** (also called a **diskette**) is a portable storage medium that provides personal computer users with convenient, near-online storage. Disks are housed in a variety of cases, but all contain a circular plastic disk coated with a magnetically sensitive film, the same material that's on a cassette tape. Disks are designed to work with **disk drives**, which allow the computer to read the disks. Disk drives come in internal versions (mounted in one of the system unit's drive bays) as well as external versions, which are often used with laptops.

### Floppy Disk Drives

As we mentioned earlier, all disks are read and written to by disk drives. A **floppy disk drive** is a mechanism that enables a computer to read and write data to floppy disks. In desktop computer systems, a disk drive is installed in one of the system unit's drive bays. In laptops, the drive is also sometimes provided by means of an external unit that plugs into the system's case (Figure 5.27).

The disk that has been around the longest is the **floppy disk**, a magnetic disk used to store and transport files. Introduced by IBM in the 1970s, floppy disks were originally packaged in 8-inch flexible, or "floppy," packages. Even though most of today's floppy disks are packaged in 3.5-inch hard plastic cases, the term "floppy" is still commonly used.

Almost all floppy disks you see being used today are of the high density (HD) type, giving them more storage capacity than their predecessors—up to 1.2 MB for Macintosh disks and up to 1.44 MB for PC disks. However, as computer programs (and users' data files) have grown significantly in size, floppies are becoming less useful. For this reason, several companies are no longer including a floppy drive with their new systems but offer alternatives that have much higher storage capacities.

### Zip Disk Drives

A **Zip disk drive** is almost identical to a floppy disk drive except that it is designed

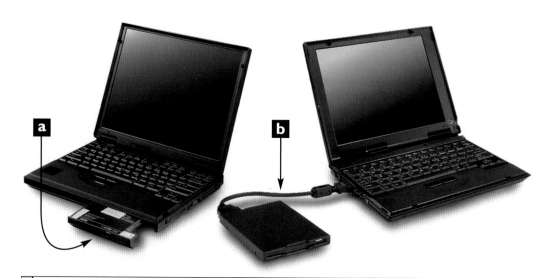

**FIGURE 5.27 a&b**  (a) A Floppy Disk Drive and (b) an External Floppy Disk Drive

to hold the slightly thicker and larger Zip disks. Iomega's **Zip disk**, an increasingly popular magnetic portable storage medium, is capable of storing up to 750 MB of data (Figure 5.28) by means of data compression. This technique converts data to use less space while being stored, and then converts the data back to full size when it is read from the disk, enabling disks to store more data than ever before.

### Protecting Your Data on Disks

Disks are portable media, which means that you can remove a disk from one computer and insert it into another. Accordingly, disks are designed to keep your data safe. A sliding metal shutter protects the disk from fingerprints, dust, and dirt. Still, the metal shutter can't protect your disks entirely. The following are a few tips for handling disks:

- Don't touch the surface of the disk. Fingerprints can contaminate the disk and cause errors.

- Don't expose disks to magnetic fields. Because data is magnetically encoded on the disks, direct exposure may cause loss of data.

- To avoid contamination, don't eat or drink around disks.

- To avoid condensation, keep disks away from humidity.

- Don't expose disks to excessive temperatures.

### MAGNETIC TAPE

**Magnetic tape** was once the most commonly used sequential storage medium. You've probably seen film clips of 1960s-era "electronic brains," with big banks of whirling reel-to-reel tapes. The earliest personal computers came with cassette tape drives. Although tapes store data sequentially, making access times slow, they're still useful for storing very large amounts of data that don't need to be accessed frequently. Many organizations create a tape backup for each day of the

**FIGURE 5.28** Zip disks offer an easy-to-use personal storage solution designed to make it easier for consumers to move, protect, share, and back up information on their computers.

month and then an archive tape on the last day of the month. They then reuse the daily tapes during subsequent months—ending the year with 12 monthly archive tapes. Tapes may become obsolete in the future.

Now that we've learned about the basics of magnetic storage media and devices, let's turn our attention to optical storage.

### CD AND DVD TECHNOLOGY

The most popular and least expensive type of optical disc standard is **CD-ROM** (Figure 5.29). Short for **compact disc–read-only memory**, these CDs are read-only discs. This means that the data recorded upon them is meant to be read many times but

**FIGURE 5.29** The CD-ROM is the most popular and least expensive optical disc. CD-ROM drives come standard on today's personal computers.

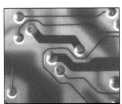

**Techtalk**

**network effect** Term used by economists to describe the rewards consumers get when they purchase a popular product rather than a less popular one, even if the less popular product offers superior technology. In computer markets, network effects are powerful due to compatibility issues. For instance, in the area of high-capacity portable storage, the Zip disk has roughly 80 percent of the market, while all competitors have less than 20 percent. If you adopt the Zip disk technology, you're more likely to be able to share data with others who also have Zip disks than with those who do not.

cannot be changed. Examples are music CDs or a software installation disc.

Because most software is distributed by means of CD-ROM discs, CD-ROM drives are standard and necessary equipment for today's personal computers. CD-ROM discs are capable of storing up to 650 MB of data, the equivalent of more than 400 floppy disks. These discs provide the ideal medium for distributing operating systems, large applications, office suites, and multimedia products involving thousands of large graphics or audio files.

As is the case with disks, it's important that you handle CD-ROM discs carefully. The following are a few things to remember about caring for CDs:

- Do not expose discs to excessive heat or sunlight.

- Do not touch the underside of discs. Hold them by their edges.

- Do not write on the label side of discs with a hard instrument, such as a ballpoint pen.

- Do not eat, drink, or smoke near discs.

- To avoid contamination, do not stack discs.

- Store discs in jewel boxes (plastic protective cases) when they are not being used.

**FIGURE 5.30** DVD-ROM drives read CD-ROM discs as well as DVD-ROM discs.

## CD-R and CD-RW Discs and Recorders

Declining prices have placed read/write CD technologies, called CD-R and CD-RW, within the budget of many computer owners. For this reason, CD-R and CD-RW discs are a popular, cost-effective alternative medium for archival and storage purposes.

**CD-R drives**, short for compact disc–recordable, can read standard CD-ROM discs and write data to CD-R discs. **CD-R discs** are compact disc–recordable storage media that are "write-once" technology: after you've saved data to the disc, you can't erase or write over it. An advantage of CD-R discs is that they aren't expensive; in quantities of 20 or more, they're often available for less than $1 per disc.

**CD-RW drives** (short for compact disc–rewritable) provide full read/write capabilities using erasable **CD-RW discs**, which are more expensive than CD-R discs but allow data that has been saved to be erased and rewritten.

## DVD-ROM Discs and Drives

The newest optical disc format, **digital video disc** (**DVD**), also called digital versatile disk, is capable of storing up to 17 GB of data—enough for an entire digitized movie. **DVD-ROM drives** (DVD–read-only memory) can transfer data from **DVD-ROM discs** at high speeds (up to 12 Mbps; comparable to the data transfer rates of hard drives). In addition, DVD-ROM drives are downwardly compatible with CD-ROM (Figure 5.30).

**DVD-R discs** (DVD–recordable) operate the same way as CD-R discs; you write to them once and read from them many times. **DVD+RW discs** (DVD rewritable) allow you to write, erase, and read from the disc many times. A relatively new read/write drive, called **DVD-RAM** (DVD–random access memory), enables computer users to burn DVD-ROM discs containing up to nearly 5 GB of data. Like most new technologies (including DVD-ROM), a profusion of incompatible formats has made consumers reluctant to embrace DVD-RAM, but it is expected to take off once clear standards emerge.

The future of CD-ROM drives and discs is already marked. In the home entertainment market, the DVD player has decimated the market for CD players.

As the technology develops and DVD drives become less and less expensive, the use of CD-ROM drives will decline. In fact, the day will come in the not so distant future when we'll use DVD-read/write drives in the same manner that we once used the ubiquitous floppy disk drive.

## STORAGE HORIZONS

In response to the explosive demand for more storage capacity, designers are creating storage devices that store more data and retrieve this data more quickly. Exemplifying these trends are FMD-ROM discs and solid state storage devices.

### FMD-ROM

A single optical disc, scientists believe, can store no more than about 5 gigabits per square inch. But why not create transparent discs with more than one layer? Here's the idea: each layer contains data, but the layer is transparent enough to allow a laser beam to shine through. The laser beam focuses on only one layer at a time. If this sounds futuristic, take a look at a DVD-ROM disc. It contains two layers—which is why DVD-ROMs store so much more data than their single-layer predecessor, the CD-ROM.

On an **FMD-ROM** (short for **fluorescent multilayer disc–read-only memory**) disc each storage layer is coated with a fluorescent substance. When the laser beam strikes each layer, the light that is bounced back is also fluorescent. This type of light can pass undisturbed through the disc's many layers. Research indicates that FMD-ROM discs of up to 100 layers are possible. While no larger than today's CD-ROM, such discs could each contain up to one terabyte of data.

The first efforts to bring this technology to market stalled in 2002, but the idea is sound and there will surely be others who will try. A trillion bytes on a single disk—imagine the possibilities!

### Solid State Storage Devices
A **solid state storage device** consists of nonvolatile memory chips, which retain the data stored in them even if the chips are disconnected from a computer or other device. The term *solid state* indicates that these devices have no moving parts; they consist only of semiconductors. Solid state storage devices have a number of important advantages over mechanical storage devices such as disk drives: they are small, lightweight, highly reliable, and portable. Among the solid state storage devices in common use are PC cards, flash memory cards, and smart cards.

**PC Cards**  A **PC card** (also called a **PCMCIA card**) is a credit card–sized computer accessory typically used with notebook computers (Figure 5.31). PC cards can serve a variety of functions. For example, some PC cards are modems, others are network adapters, and still others provide additional memory or storage capacity.

When used as storage devices, PC cards are most commonly used to transfer data from one PC card slot–equipped computer to another. For example, a notebook computer user can store documents created on a business trip on a solid state memory card and then transfer these documents to a desktop computer (as long as it is equipped with a PC card reader).

PC cards are standardized by the Personal Computer Memory Card International Association (PCMCIA), a consortium of industry vendors. As a result, a notebook computer equipped with a PC card slot can use PC cards from any PC card vendor.

**FIGURE 5.31** PC cards are about the size of a credit card and fit into PC card slots, which are included with most notebooks.

**FIGURE 5.32** Flash memory cards are thin, portable solid state storage systems.

**Flash Memory Cards** Increasingly popular among digital camera users are flash memory cards, which use nonvolatile flash memory chips (Figure 5.32). **Flash memory cards** are wafer-thin, highly portable solid state storage systems that are capable of storing as much as 1 GB of data. Flash memory cards are also used with digital cellular phones, portable MP3 music players, digital video cameras, and other portable digital devices. In order to use a flash memory card with one of these devices, the device must have a compatible **flash memory reader** (a slot or compartment into which the flash memory card is inserted.)

SmartMedia flash memory cards are among the smallest solid state storage systems available, but their small size and relative simplicity place limits on their storage capacity (up to 128 MB). Increasingly popular are CompactFlash cards. CompactFlash cards are thicker than SmartMedia cards, enabling CompactFlash cards to contain up to 1 GB of data. Recently introduced is Sony's Memory

**FIGURE 5.33** Smart cards combine flash memory with a tiny micro-processor.

Stick, a chewing gum–sized flash memory card, currently available in capacities of up to 128 MB. Memory Stick readers are found mainly in Sony-made devices, although a few other manufacturers are beginning to use Sony's technology.

**Smart Cards** A **smart card** is a credit card–sized device that combines flash memory with a tiny microprocessor, enabling the card to process as well as store information (Figure 5.33). Smart cards have many applications. For example, tomorrow's credit cards will utilize smart card technology to provide far more convenience, functionality, and safety than today's credit cards can provide. One smart card will replace the collection of credit cards, club cards, store cards, and travel mileage cards that the average consumer carries around today. By inserting the card into a compatible reader, users will be able to access their account information by means of a secure Internet connection. Because smart cards use encryption and other measures for security, they'll be all but impossible to misuse if they're stolen.

Many applications for smart cards already exist, and more are on the way. Where a computer network contains highly confidential data, smart cards can be used to provide network users with a highly secure means of verifying their identity; unlike a typed user name and password, the identifying information on the smart card cannot easily be stolen or duplicated. **Digital cash systems**, in widespread use in Europe and Asia, enable users to purchase a prepaid amount of electronically stored money, which can be used to pay the small amounts required for parking, bridge tolls, transport fares, museum entrance fees, and similar charges.

But some believe that digital cash systems pose a significant danger to basic freedoms. A world in which every cash transaction, no matter how minute, is traced is one in which every person's purchases—no matter how tiny—can be assembled and scrutinized. In short order, an investigator could put together a list of the magazines and newspapers you purchase and read, where and when you paid bridge tolls and subway fares, and what you had for lunch.

# Summary
## INPUT/OUTPUT AND STORAGE

- The computer keyboard's special keys include cursor movement keys (arrow keys and additional keys such as Home and End), the numeric keypad (for entering numerical data), toggle keys (for switching keyboard modes on and off, such as Num Lock and Caps Lock), function keys (defined for different purposes by application programs), modifier keys such as Ctrl and Alt (for use with keyboard shortcuts), and special keys for use with Microsoft Windows. The most frequently used pointing device is the mouse. Alternatives include trackballs, pointing sticks, touchpads, joysticks, touchscreens, styluses, and light pens.

- One type of audio input is speech recognition, which enables users to dictate words to a computer. Another is sound cards, which utilize data compression to digitize sound files. Visual input is entered into the computer by digital cameras. Digital video cameras digitize full-motion images such as animations, videos, and movies; and videoconferencing and Web cams enable people to use computers to simulate face-to-face, real-time conversations.

- Among factors determining a monitor's quality are the amount of VRAM on the video card and the adapter's refresh rate. A monitor's quality is also determined by its screen size (the larger, the better), its dot pitch (a dot pitch of .28 mm or lower is good), and its ability to work with adapters that have a high refresh rate (72 Hz or higher). CRT monitors are inexpensive compared with other types of monitors, but they consume more energy and take up more room on the desk. LCD or flat-panel displays are more expensive, but they take up much less room and are easier on the eyes.

- Printers use either inkjet or laser technology. Inkjet printers produce excellent quality text and color photographs for a reasonable price. Laser printers produce excellent quality text and graphics, but color models are expensive.

- Memory uses costly, high-speed components to make software and data available for the CPU's use. Memory needs to have enough capacity to hold the software and data that are currently in use. RAM is volatile and doesn't retain information when the computer is switched off. In contrast, storage is slower and less costly, but it offers far greater capacity. Storage devices are nonvolatile; they retain information even when the power is switched off. Storage devices play important input and output roles by transferring information into memory and saving and storing your work.

- Storage devices are categorized by the type of operations they can perform (read-only or read/write), the type of data access they provide (sequential or random access), the type of technology they use (magnetic or optical), and their location in the storage hierarchy (online, near-online, or offline).

- A hard disk's performance is measured by its positioning performance (how quickly the drive can position the read/write head to begin transferring data) and its transfer performance (how quickly the drive sends the information once the head has reached the correct position).

- Disks store data in circular bands called tracks. Each track is divided into pie-shaped wedges called sectors. The sectors are combined into clusters, which provide the basic unit for data storage. To access data on the drive, the drive's actuator moves the read/write head to the track that contains the desired data. Hard disks store data in much the same way floppies do, except the hard disk contains multiple platters. Because hard disks offer so much storage space, it is sometimes convenient to divide them into sections, called partitions, which appear to the operating system as if they were separate disks.

- CD-ROM discs and drives are standard equipment in today's computer systems, largely because most software is now distributed on CD-ROM discs. CD-ROM is a read-only technology. CD-R drives can record once on inexpensive CD-R discs; CD-RW drives can write repeatedly to erasable CD-RW discs, which are more expensive. Read-only DVD-ROM discs offer much more storage capacity. A read/write version, DVD-RAM, has been slow to catch on due to standardization squabbles.

Go to **www.prenhall.com/cayf2005** to review this chapter, answer the questions, and complete the exercises.

# Key Terms and Concepts

Go to **www.prenhall.com/cayf2005** to review this chapter, answer the questions, and complete the exercises.

# Matching

Match each key term in the left column with the most accurate definition in the right column.

_____ 1. near-online storage

_____ 2. data compression

_____ 3. fault tolerance

_____ 4. refresh rate

_____ 5. speech recognition

_____ 6. plotter

_____ 7. thermal transfer printer

_____ 8. seek time

_____ 9. read-only

_____ 10. digital light processing (DLP)

_____ 11. sound card

_____ 12. head crash

_____ 13. RAID

_____ 14. sector

_____ 15. track

a. the ability to keep working even if one or more components fail

b. a device that groups two or more hard disks that contain exactly the same data

c. unable to be written to

d. storage that is not directly available

e. physical contact between the read/write head and a hard disk

f. a circular band on a disk

g. an area on a disk that is a pie-shaped wedge

h. the time it takes the read/write head to locate data before reading or writing begins

i. an expansion board that can record and play sound files

j. reduces the size of a file

k. an output device that draws images on paper using pens

l. a type of input in which the computer recognizes spoken words

m. the frequency with which a screen image is updated

n. printer that produces images that are similar to high-quality color photographs

o. projectors that use millions of microscopic mirrors to project an image

# Multiple Choice

Circle the correct choice for each of the following.

1. Which of the following is a popular input device?
   a. synthesizer
   b. monitor
   c. plotter
   d. mouse

2. Which of the following expansion boards accepts analog or digital video signals and transforms them into digital data?
   a. digital camera
   b. sound card
   c. Web cam
   d. video capture board

3. Which of the following printers is considered the best color printer?
   a. dot-matrix printer
   b. heat transfer printer
   c. line printer
   d. color laser printer

4. When used with digital cameras and scanners, CCD represents what?
   a. color-coded display
   b. charge-coupled device
   c. common color display
   d. comprehensive capture device

5. This storage device does not use magnetic-sensitive materials for recording information.
   a. CD-ROM drive
   b. tape drive
   c. hard disk drive
   d. floppy disk drive

6. Which of the following is not a random access storage medium?
   a. tape
   b. CD-ROM
   c. hard disk
   d. floppy disk

7. This technology allows CDs to be rewritten.
   a. CD-RAM
   b. CD-ROM
   c. CD-RW
   d. CD-R

8. What does FAT mean?
   a. floppy advanced transfer
   b. fixed all-purpose tape
   c. fast access time
   d. file allocation table

9. This type of storage device retains its information, even when the power is switched off.
   a. sequential
   b. nonvolatile
   c. solid state
   d. volatile

10. Why is FMD-ROM a promising technology?
    a. It provides fast access to data.
    b. It allows multiple layers on which data can be stored.
    c. It creates network connections to CD-ROM jukeboxes.
    d. It stores redundant data on different DVD-ROMs.

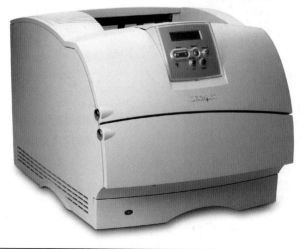

# Fill-In

In the blanks provided, write the correct answer for each of the following.

1. _____ are mice flipped on their backs.

2. A(n) _____ is a mechanism that enables a computer to read and write data to floppy disks.

3. A(n) _____ is a pointing device that is commonly used to control the motion of on-screen objects in computer games.

4. _____ devices combine an inkjet or laser printer with a scanner, a fax machine, and a copier.

5. A(n) _____ uses a lens to capture an image, but stores it in digital form rather than recording the image on film.

6. The amount of time it takes for a storage device to begin reading data is its _____.

7. _____ storage, (also called tertiary storage) is storage that is not readily available.

8. A(n) _____ uses a transparent pressure-sensitive panel to detect where users have tapped the display screen with their fingers.

9. A(n) _____ is made up of several fixed, rapidly rotating disks.

10. _____ are small folding keyboards you can connect to your handheld.

11. _____ is memory that is used to improve hard disk performance.

12. Damaged areas on a disk are called _____.

13. A(n) _____ is a credit card–sized device that combines flash memory with a tiny microprocessor.

14. A(n) _____ is storage space on a server that is accessible from the Internet.

15. _____ synthesis is used by sound cards to generate actual musical instrument sounds.

# Short Answer

1. If you have used a laptop computer, which of the various pointing devices—trackball, touchpad, or pointing stick—have you used? Which input device do you prefer to use? Explain why. Would you consider using an external mouse? Why or why not?

2. What is the difference between memory and storage?

3. Many instructors use blackboards, whiteboards, or overhead projectors to display course material. In addition to these, do any of your instructors use data projectors to complement the presentation of their lectures or labs? If they do use them, are they LCD or DLP projectors? What types of software do they use? What are your feelings about using this technology to deliver classroom instruction?

4. What is the difference between a sequential storage device and a random access storage device? Give an example of each.

5. Explain the difference between inkjet and laser printers. What are the pros and cons of each?

# A Closer Look

1. The ability to store data for long periods of time is extremely important. For example, how long would you want your school transcripts stored? Discuss the inability of computers to store data permanently. Describe the two major hindrances of computers storing and accessing data "forever," and give an example of each. Is paper a good storage medium? Why or why not?

2. When hard disks first became available, their storage capacities were around 5 MB, and at the time this seemed like an enormous amount of storage. Since many applications and certain data files now use tens of megabytes of storage, current personal computers come with hard disks that are measured in gigabytes. Select any brand of personal computer and determine the hard disk capacity for the least and most expensive computer models. Do you think that you would ever fill the hard disk on even the least expensive model?

   If necessary, use the Internet to find the storage requirements for the following popular applications:

   - Any version of Microsoft Office
   - Adobe Photoshop
   - Netscape Navigator

   Certain data files also require large amounts of storage. What types of files do you think would require several megabytes of storage?

3. Until the release of the first Macintosh computer in 1984, a mouse was just a rodent that ate cheese. With the advent of cordless technology, users of mice (and keyboards) are no longer tethered to their computers. Explain how cordless mice and keyboards work. Check newspaper advertisements, or call or visit a local vendor and compare the purchase prices of conventional mice and keyboards with the cost of cordless ones. Based on cost and convenience, explain why you would or would not upgrade to a cordless mouse or keyboard or purchase one with a new computer.

4. In order to provide equal opportunities to all citizens, the Americans with Disabilities Act (ADA) was passed on July 26, 1990. Consequently, as part of this act, your institution must provide computer access to persons with disabilities. Contact your school's computing services or visit some campus computer facilities to determine what types of special software and input or output devices have been installed or modified specifically to accommodate users with sight, hearing, and motor impairments. Explain how these devices are used to enter or display data.

5. Many instructors prefer that students submit assignments in hard-copy form. Visit your school or department computer facilities to determine what types of printers are available for student use. Do students have access to dot-matrix, inkjet, or laser printers? Which, if any, of the printers are capable of color output? Are printing services free? If not, what are the printing costs? If you have a personal computer, which type of printer do you have? Explain why you prefer to use your own or your school's printers.

# On the Web

1. Although Iomega was not the first company to market removable hard disks, it has been the most successful. Visit Iomega's Web site at **iomega.com/na/landing.jsp** to learn more about its products. What is the storage capacity of its Zip disks? What are two of the ways to connect a Zip drive to a computer? Write a short paragraph about your findings. Be sure to include your thoughts on how the use of a removable storage device might or might not fit into your computing practices.

2. Since a DVD-ROM can store up to 14 times the amount of information that a CD-ROM can hold, DVD-ROM drives have replaced CD-ROM drives on some new computers. Visit CNET's DVD site at **www.cnet.com** and find the best price for the fastest DVD-ROM drive. (Hint: click re-sort by price.) In addition to video information, what other types of information could be stored on a DVD-ROM? Explain why you would or would not purchase a new computer with a DVD-ROM drive or upgrade your present CD-ROM drive to a DVD-ROM one.

3. One method for increasing your storage capacity is to use Internet storage (sometimes called online storage). Have you ever considered using this option? Visit the WebWizards site at **www.webwizards.net/useful/wbfs.htm** to learn more about Internet storage sites. Which two major Internet service providers also offer Internet storage? List at least one advantage and one disadvantage of using Internet storage. In addition to storage, what other services do these sites provide? Some sites provide free storage, while others charge a fee. Select a free one, and describe the following:

   - the registration process
   - the amount of free storage space
   - additional services that are provided

   Would you consider using the selected site? Explain why or why not.

4. Since most new computers now include a CD-ROM drive, a good set of speakers, and perhaps even a subwoofer, users are able to play their music CDs and enjoy high-quality music while working on their computers. With the advent of MP3 files, users can now download these files, save them on a hard drive, and play high-quality music directly on their computers. Have you ever downloaded and played MP3 files? Why do you think that MP3 files are not saved on floppy disks? Unlike CDs, which are portable and can be used in any CD player, MP3 files reside on the computer's hard disk. Imagine carrying a desktop or even a laptop with you to listen to music! As you may know, this is not necessary. To learn about MP3 files, software, and portable players, visit the MP3 site at **www.mp3.com.** Although illegal MP3 copies of copyrighted music are available, why would an artist choose to place free copies of his or her work on the Internet? Explore the software link, determine which application you might purchase, and explain why. Explore the hardware link, choose which MP3 player you might purchase, and explain why.

5. Tired of entering input with a keyboard? One of the new features of Microsoft Office XP is speech recognition. Go to Microsoft's speech recognition site at **www.microsoft.com/office/evaluation/indepth/speech.asp** to learn about this novel method of entering input. Speech recognition will help users with which three actions? According to this Web page, which users will and will not benefit from this technology? Why did Microsoft design a bimodal approach to its speech recognition? That is, why can users not enter dictation and commands simultaneously? How do users switch between dictation and command modes? In addition to voice-recognition training, what are at least two Microsoft suggestions to minimize speech-recognition errors?

   Although most computer systems include a sound card and speakers, a microphone may not be supplied. If you have a computer, was a microphone included in the purchase price? What are the names and costs of the microphone and headset combinations that are suggested by Microsoft to be used with Office XP? Explain why you would or would not consider using speech recognition as a method of entering input.

# FILE MANAGEMENT

You've just finished your term paper—where do you save it? You never know when you may need a writing sample for a graduate school or job application, so you'll want to keep it someplace safe. The secret to finding what you're looking for in the future is good file management now. Managing your computer files is essential to becoming computer competent. Fortunately, you only have to learn two main things: the big picture of file management, and the specific practices of actually managing your files.

For most people, managing files is intuitive—it's simple once they learn the basics. You can think of managing files as being similar to the way you organize and store files and folders in a file cabinet (Figure 3A). You start with a storage device (the filing cabinet), divide it into definable sections (folders), and then fill the sections with things (documents) that fit the defined category. We've always organized the things in our lives, and the principles are the same when managing files in a computer.

# The Big Picture: Files, Folders, and Paths

A **file** is a named unit of related data stored in a computer system. Your data (as well as the programs installed on your computer) is stored in files. Files store things such as Word documents, MP3 music files, photo images, Excel spreadsheets, applications, and a variety of other digital compilations. Every file is stored along with a variety of attributes. An **attribute** is a setting that provides information such as the file's date of creation, its size, and the date it was last modified. Because most programs consist of many files, they are sometimes called packages. A **package** is a set of program files, as well as associated data and configuration files, that are all designed to work together.

Files are organized using **directories** (also called folders). **Folders** help you to organize groups of files that have something in common. Many folders have **subfolders**—or folders within folders—that allow you to organize your files even further. For example, you might create a folder called Classes, and then create subfolders for each school term, and then subfolders within each school term for your individual classes (Figure 3B).

All of the files and folders you create must reside on a storage device, called a **drive**. The primary

### Figure 3A

You can organize digital files on your computer the same way you would organize documents in a filing cabinet.

storage devices on desktop computers are the **hard drive**, **floppy disk drive**, **Zip drive**, and **CD** and **DVD drives**. On PCs, these storage devices are designated by drive letters. A **drive letter** is simply a letter of the alphabet followed by a colon and backslash character. For instance, the floppy disk drive is almost always referred to as A:\. The hard drive is generally referred to as C:\. Other drives, such as an external Zip drive, might be labeled Drive E (E:\). (On the Mac, drives are not labeled with letters. You'll see them as icons appearing on your screen.)

In order for your computer to access a particular file, it needs to know the path it should take to get to the file. A **path** is the sequence of directories that the computer must follow to locate a file. A typical path might look like this:

C:\Classes\Expository Writing 201\Homework#1_draft1.doc

In this case, the C:\ in the path indicates that the file is located on the C:\ drive. The **top-level folder**, "Classes," contains, as the name indicates, things that have to do with classes. The **subfolder** named "Expository Writing 201" contains all of the subfolders and files you will create for your writing class. The file at the end of the path, "Homework#1_draft1.doc," is the first draft of your first homework assignment. The .doc

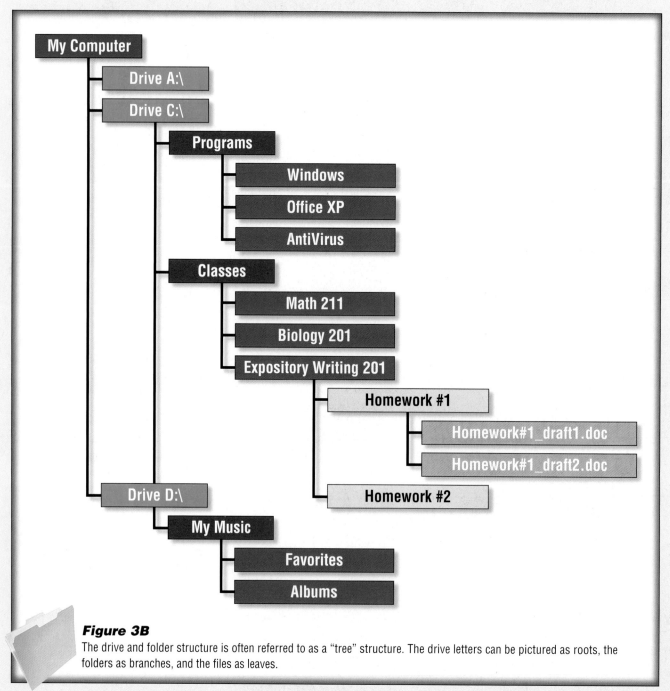

**Figure 3B**
The drive and folder structure is often referred to as a "tree" structure. The drive letters can be pictured as roots, the folders as branches, and the files as leaves.

extension indicates that the file is a Microsoft Word document. We'll discuss filenames in greater depth shortly.

Figure 3B illustrates what a hierarchical drive, folder, and file structure might look like.

## FILE-NAMING CONVENTIONS

As is obvious from our discussion so far, in order to save a file, you need to know where you're going to store it—in other words, on which storage device and in which folder. In addition, each file needs a specific filename. The **filename** is the name that the storage device uses to identify each unique file, so the name must differ from all other filenames used within the same folder. You may use the same name for different files, but they must exist on different drives or in different folders. Be careful to include enough detail in naming a file so that you will be able to recognize the filename when you need it later. The name you use when you create a file is usually very obvious to you at the time--but is often elusive when you try to remember it in the future.

Every filename on a PC has two parts, which are separated by a period (read as "dot"). The first part, the part you're probably most familiar with, is called the **name**. The second part is called the **extension**. In a file called Homework#1_draft1.doc, Homework#1_draft1 is the name and .doc is the extension; together they make up the filename.

Typically, extensions are used to identify the type of data that the file contains (or the format it is stored in), and sometimes the application that created the file. In Microsoft Windows, each application automatically assigns an extension to a file when you save it for the first time. For example, Microsoft Word automatically assigns the .doc extension. Workbooks created

### Commonly Used Filename Extensions

| Extension | File Type |
|---|---|
| .exe | Program or application |
| .doc | Microsoft Word |
| .xls | Microsoft Excel |
| .ppt | Microsoft PowerPoint |
| .mdb | Microsoft Access |
| .pdf | Adobe Acrobat |
| .txt | ASCII text |
| .htm or .html | Web pages |
| .rtf | Files in Rich Text Format |
| .jpeg or .jpg | Picture or image format |

**Figure 3C**

in Microsoft Excel use the .xls extension. When naming files you never need to be concerned about typing in an extension—because all programs attach their extension to the filename by default.

**Program files**, also called **application files**, usually use the .exe extension, which stands for "executable." The term executable is used because when you use an application, you execute, or run, the file. Figure 3C lists the most commonly used extensions and their file types. Note that when using Mac OS, extensions are not needed because Macintosh files contain a code representing the name of the application that created the file. However, it is generally recommended that Mac users add the appropriate three-letter extension to their filenames so that they can more easily exchange them with PC users.

Even Web addresses use file-naming conventions. The ubiquitous term *dot-com* reflects the extension *com,* used to designate commercial Web sites. Other Web site types are .edu for higher education, .net for noncommercial groups, .gov for governmental agencies, and .org for not-for-profit organizations. In 2002, seven new extensions were created: .biz, .info, .name, .pro, .aero, .coop, and .museum.

The initial operating system for all personal computers was the **Disk Operating System**, or **DOS**. In the early days of DOS, and also the earliest versions of Windows, filenames were limited to eight characters for the name and three characters for the extension. Today, you can use up to 250 characters in a filename in Microsoft Windows, and you're also allowed to use spaces. Extensions can now include up to four characters, but most still use three.

Filenames in Microsoft Windows cannot include any of the following characters: forward slash (/), backslash (\), greater than sign (>), less than sign (<), asterisk (*), question mark (?), quotation mark ("), pipe symbol ( | ), colon (:), or semicolon (;). In Mac OS you can use up to 31 characters in a filename, including spaces, and all characters except the colon.

You can use an application to open a file or use a file to launch the application that created it. Let's say you create a document by using Word. You give the file the name "Letter Home" and Word assigns the extension ".doc" by default. Later, you use the My Computer file management utility (discussed in detail in the next section) to locate the file, and then use the mouse to double-click the filename. The file will open in Word. Alternately, you could launch Word and then use the File, Open menu sequence to locate the file and open it. The Open dialog box defaults to showing only files that have the .doc extension. This way, you see only files that were created by Word and are not distracted by the names of other files that Word cannot read. Figure 3D shows the Open dialog box in its default "Word documents" view and also in the "All Files" view.

Now that you understand the basics of paths, folders, and file-naming conventions, let's turn our attention to the business of managing files.

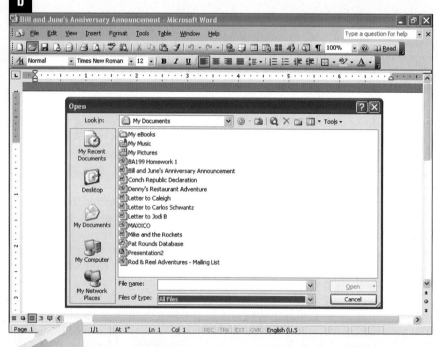

**Figure 3D**
Word's "Open" dialog box in (**a**) Word documents view, and (**b**) All Files view.

# Managing Files

Files can be managed in two ways: with a file management utility such as My Computer, or from within the programs that create them. In the following sections, we'll explore both methods.

## FILE MANAGEMENT UTILITIES

The primary file management utility for PCs is the My Computer program. The My Computer icon is usually available on your desktop as well as on the upper right panel on the Start menu.

My Computer contains the familiar Windows title bar, menu bar, and a toolbar (Figure 3E). The window is split into two panes. The **left pane** displays links to system tasks, such as viewing system information, adding and removing programs, and changing settings. The left pane also displays links to "Other" places besides the available drives, such as My Network Places, My Documents, Shared Documents, and the Control Panel.

The **right pane** contains a listing of available drives and folders. The left pane is dynamic; that is, if you click items in the right pane, the left pane gives you choices that are specific to the particular folder or drive you've clicked. You may sort within the right pane by filename, file type, or file size. Click the Name, Type, or Total Size bars at the top of the window. You can also use this view to manage folders and files. Simply double-click the drive name in the right pane, and the left pane changes to show you the tasks you can accomplish, such as creating, managing, and deleting folders and files.

To use My Computer in strictly file management mode—without a dynamic left pane—click the Folders button on the Standard toolbar. In Folders view, the left pane shows the names of the drives and folders, and the right pane shows the folders and files within the folders (Figure 3F). To view more detail about the drives or folders in the left pane, simply click the icons in the left pane and the detail appears in the right pane. To open folders and files, double-click the icons in the right pane. (You may also use the menu sequence View, Explorer Bar, Folders to toggle between the default view and Folders view.)

You can view the contents of the right pane in several ways. The different views are accessible from the View menu or from the Views button on the Standard toolbar.

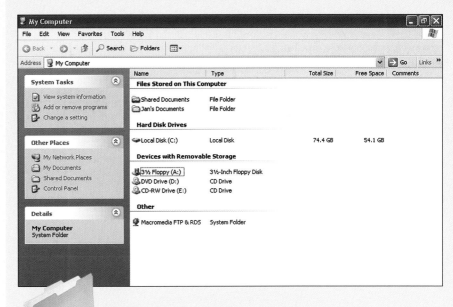

**Figure 3E**
The My Computer program is divided into two panes: the left pane shows system tasks and links to other places; the right pane shows the various files and drives you can currently choose from.

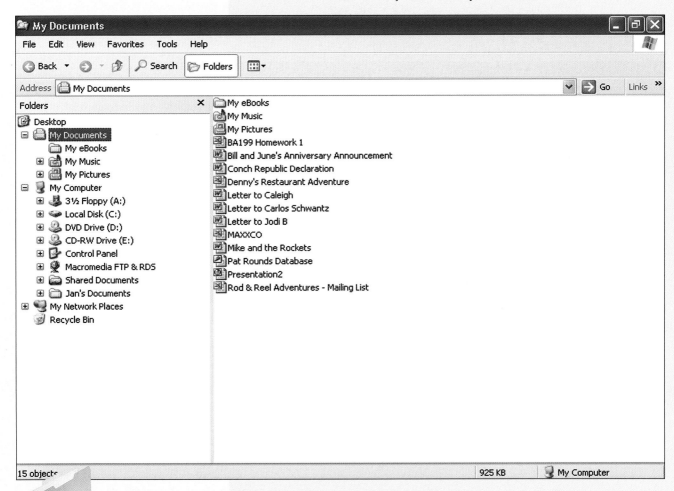

**Figure 3F**
When you click the Folders button on the Standard toolbar in My Computer, you'll see the Folders view.

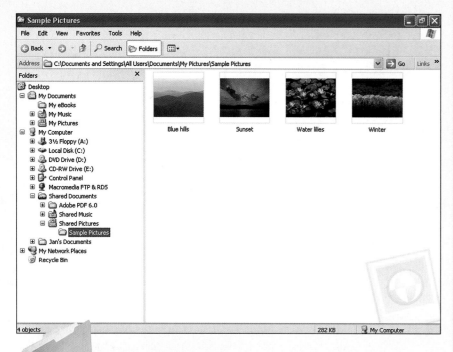

**Figure 3G**
The thumbnail view is especially handy for previewing images.

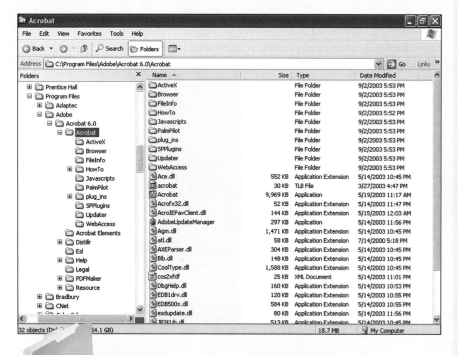

**Figure 3H**
The details view allows you to see the file size, file type, and the date a file was last modified.

The thumbnail view is particularly helpful if you're searching through pictures and photographs because it allows you to preview a thumbnail-sized copy of the images you have in the folder—before you open them (Figure 3G). The list view simply lists the names of the files, whereas the details view offers you information regarding file size, file type, and the date a file was last modified (Figure 3H).

### Creating Folders

To manage your files effectively, you'll need to create a **folder structure**—an organized set of folders within which to save your files. The process of creating a folder structure is accomplished in two steps:

#### STEP 1

Decide what physical storage location, such as a floppy disk, hard disk, or CD-RW disc, you want to create your folder on. Then click the device letter or designator in the left pane of your file management utility.

#### STEP 2

Establish the primary or top-level folder. Choose the File, New, Folder menu sequence to place a new folder at the root of the storage device or in a selected preexisting folder. In other words, if you have selected the C:\ drive, the new folder will be placed at the top level. See Figure 3I for an example of a new folder that has been created at the root of the C:\ drive.

If, however, you selected a top-level folder or subfolder as your starting point, then the new folder will be placed within it (Figure 3J).

You can repeat this process as many times as is necessary to create your desired folder structure. For example, if you're taking three classes, you might want to create three separate subfolders with the appropriate class names under a top-level folder called Winter_2005_Classes. That way, you'll know exactly where to save files each time you create them, and you'll avoid having a cluttered and disorganized storage space.

Of course, creating a well-organized folder structure requires that you add, rename, and move folders as your needs change. For example, if you add a class to your schedule, you'll want to create a new subfolder in your top-level Winter_2005_Classes folder. Next term, you'll create a new folder called Spring_2005_Classes and then create subfolders for each of your spring-term classes. Another organizational scheme might be to create a top-level folder called Classes and then to create subfolders for each term. This way you would have fewer top-level folders on your C:\ drive.

### Transferring Files

Once you've created a useful folder structure, you're ready to transfer already existing files and folders. We will use the example of working with files in this section, but the same rules apply to folders as well. There are two ways to transfer your files and folders: you can copy them or you can move them. The easiest way to accomplish these tasks is simply to right-drag the files you want to copy or move to the new location. When you release the right mouse button, a context-sensitive menu appears, allowing you to choose the result of your right-drag (Figure 3K). The choices on this menu are to copy, move, create a shortcut, or cancel the action.

- **Copying** creates a duplicate file at the new location and leaves the existing file as is.

- **Moving** is similar to cutting and pasting; the file is moved from its original location to the new location.

- **Creating a shortcut** leaves the original file in place and creates a pointer that will take

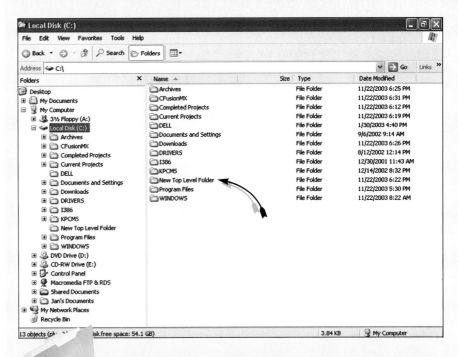

**Figure 3I**

This top-level folder has been created at the root of the C:\ drive on the hard disk.

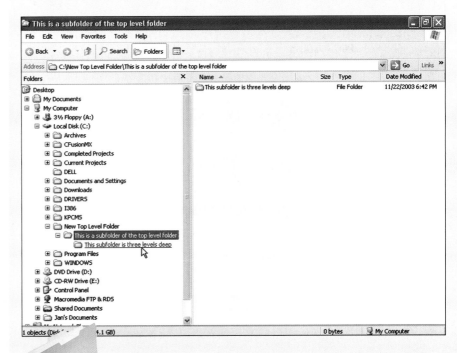

**Figure 3J**

This new subfolder is located three levels deep on the hard disk.

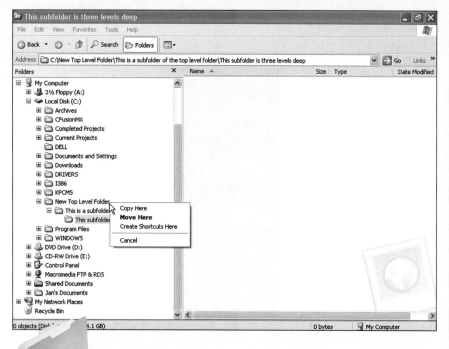

**Figure 3K**
The right-drag context-sensitive menu allows you to copy, move, create a shortcut, or cancel the action.

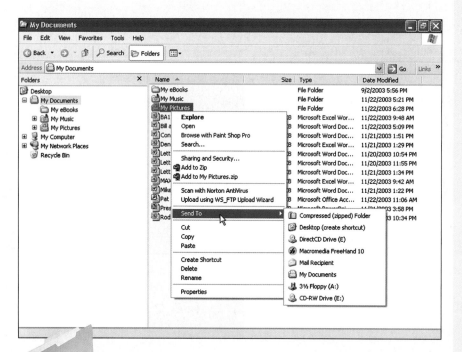

**Figure 3L**
The right-click custom menu provides you with a shortcut to common tasks.

you to the file you've created the shortcut to. This action is handy for files that you access often.

If you **left-drag** a file *within the same drive*, the file is automatically moved to the new location on the drive. Left-dragging *between drives* creates a copy of the file in the new location.

Right-clicking a file invokes a context-sensitive menu that allows you to choose among many common tasks, such as copying, deleting, renaming, and creating shortcuts (Figure 3L). You may also use the File menu or toolbars to accomplish these and other file management tasks.

## Backing Up

There are several ways to create a backup copy of your files. The first, and easiest, way is to create intermediate copies as you work. You can do this by using the File, Save As menu sequence every 15 or 20 minutes. Name your intermediate copies by appending a number or letter to the filename. For example, Writing121_homework.doc would become Writing121_homework1.doc and then Writing121_homework2.doc, and so forth.

Additionally, you can use the My Computer program to drag a copy to a floppy disk or CD/DVD drive. Backing up files to the same drive that the original copy is on introduces the risk of losing both copies in the case of disk failure or other disaster, so you should always use a remote or portable medium for your backups.

A third way to be sure that you don't lose your work is to obtain software that is specifically designed for that purpose. Backup programs are available at your local software store or from sites on the Web such as **www.bakbone.com** and **www.backupsoft.net**. These programs allow you to create a complete backup of your disk or a partial backup of only the files that have changed since the last backup.

## *Getting Help*

If you need help when working within the My Computer program, choose the Help menu selection, click Help and Support, and then type "managing files" into the Search dialog box, which is located in the top left corner of the window. This will bring up Tasks, Overviews, Articles, and Tutorials that will help you to further understand file management practices.

## MANAGING FILES FROM WITHIN PROGRAMS

As we mentioned earlier, all software applications use program-specific filename extensions. The advantage of using a default file extension is that both you and your computer will be easily able to associate the file with the program with which it was created. By using appropriate extensions, you can double-click a file in a file management utility such as My Computer and the program will launch the appropriate application.

The File, Open menu sequence in many programs, including Microsoft Office applications, also allows you to manage files. There are icons for creating new folders and for deleting files, and there is a menu choice called Tools that allows you to copy, rename, and create shortcuts to files. Pointing to a file and pressing the right mouse button within the Open menu also invokes a file management menu with various tasks (Figure 3M).

## SAVE OR SAVE AS?

A critical decision you'll make when managing files is whether to use the Save or Save As command to save files. When you first save a file, the initial File, Save menu sequence always invokes the Save As dialog box because the drive, path, and filename must be designated the first time a file is saved.

But when you're working with a previously saved document, you need to be more careful. When you choose the Save command under the File menu, the program takes what you've created or modified in memory and writes over or replaces the file that is stored on disk. This means that the Save command doesn't allow you to designate a

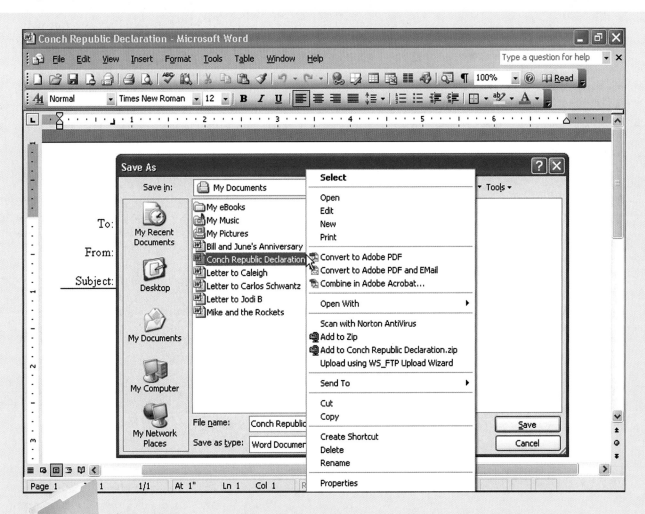

### *Figure 3M*
Right-clicking a file in either the Save As or Open dialog box invokes file management commands.

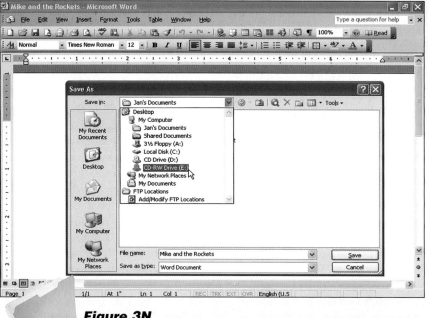

**Figure 3N**
The Save As dialog box allows you to designate the drive or folder you want to save your file in, as well as assign an appropriate filename.

different drive, folder, or filename; it simply replaces what is stored with the contents of memory.

The Save As command, however, does allow you to change one or all of these parameters (Figure 3N). You might also use the Save As command to save a copy of your finished work on a floppy disk or in an alternate folder as backup, just in case something happens to your original work. It's often advisable to save intermediate copies of your work, thus allowing you to go back to a previous version should something go wrong with a subsequent version.

### Intermediate Files

Follow these steps to help prevent the loss of your work.

- Begin work, and then save your file.

- Continue working for an additional 10 to 20 minutes.

- Use Save As to save the intermediate work in the same place, but with a modified filename. (Use the original filename, but add an incremental number.)

So, your original file might be named "resume.doc." You would then name the intermediate copies "resume1.doc," "resume2.doc," "resume3.doc," and so on. Then, when your iterations result in a final document that you are happy with, you can delete the intermediate copies.

# Software Management

Managing files also involves managing the software that creates them. The number one rule in effectively and safely managing your software is to purchase your own copy of every program, or to be sure that any shareware

or freeware is from a reliable source. This is a necessary practice for several reasons:

- It respects the right of the manufacturer to receive compensation for its work.

- It provides programs in their complete and unadulterated form.

- It's the legal way to own software.

- It's your ethical responsibility.

In addition, when you own an original and legitimate copy of a program, you're entitled to certain warranties and guarantees. You often qualify for technical assistance, upgrades, or other forms of support, and you can expect that the manufacturer will stand behind its product if there is a bug or defect.

Once you've purchased software, read the directions before and during installation. Know where the program is being installed, how to access it, and whether shortcuts have been created on the desktop. Shortcuts usually carry the name of the program and use the company logo for an icon. If you don't want these shortcuts on your desktop, delete them by right-clicking the icons and choosing delete. This doesn't affect the program in any way because a shortcut is just a pointer to a program or file. The program will still be available via the Start, All Programs menu sequence.

## INSTALLING AND REMOVING PROGRAMS

When you purchase the right to use a software program you are usually provided with an optical disk (CD) or floppy disks that contain the program and an installer. Most often, you insert the disk into an appropriate drive and the

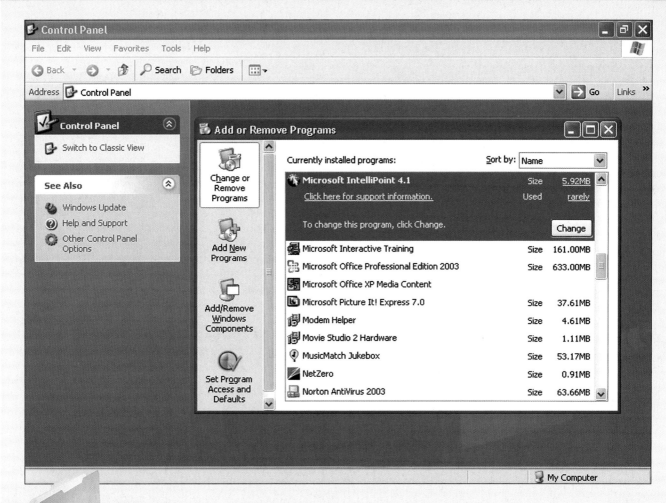

**Figure 3O**
Always use the Add or Remove Programs feature in your computer's Control Panel when you're removing a program.

operating environment automatically senses the insertion and attempts to locate and run an install or startup file. You are then prompted for any necessary input as the program installs.

Should inserting the disk not invoke the install program, you will need to click the Windows Start button and then choose Run from the bottom of the right pane. The Run menu sequence will invoke a dialog box into which you can type a command or choose a button labeled Browse. The Browse button brings up a dialog box, from which you will choose the drive that contains the startup disk. You will then select the install or startup file and click the Open button. The final step is to click the OK button within the Run window.

The proper way to remove a program from your computer is to choose the Add or Remove Programs icon located on the Control Panel, which is listed on the Start menu (Figure 3O). Choose the program that you wish to uninstall from the list of installed programs, and then provide any input the uninstaller asks you for. Since most programs create library files and ancillary files in various directories, they will not all be removed if you simply delete the program icon or delete the program files from within the file management utility. The operating system may not run efficiently if you don't remove all program files correctly, so always use the uninstall utility to remove unwanted programs.

# A Few Last Reminders

Good file management is the hallmark of a competent computer user. There is no need to feel intimidated by or frustrated with managing files. Computers are tremendously complex and powerful devices, but the principles of managing your work are simple. Plan and construct folder structures that make sense to you. Name your files in such a way that you can easily find them. Always begin at the beginning. If something doesn't work, go back to when it did. Read the manual. Follow directions carefully. Make backup copies of your work. And, if all else fails, don't be afraid to ask for help.

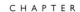

# Networks: Communicating and Sharing Resources

## What You'll Learn . . .

- **Understand basic networking concepts.**

- **List the three major types of physical media and the types of physical connections they support.**

- **Define *bandwidth* and discuss the bandwidth needs of typical users.**

- **Discuss how modems transform digital computer signals into analog signals.**

- **Contrast circuit switching and packet switching networks and explain their respective strengths and weaknesses.**

- **Explain the importance of protocols in a computer network.**

- **Discuss the advantages of networks.**

- **Distinguish between peer-to-peer and client/server LANs.**

- **Name the most widely used LAN protocol and discuss its benefits.**

- **Identify two ways that businesses use WANs.**

Fast forward a few years, and imagine yourself building a house. Everyone in your five-person family wants a computer, a printer, and an Internet connection. You could pay for five computers, five printers, and five Internet accounts. Or you could pay for five computers, one really good printer, one Internet account, and inexpensive local area network (LAN) hardware that enables everyone to share the printer and Internet connection. If you think the LAN route makes sense, you've just joined the huge and growing number of people who've discovered the benefits of networking.

Businesses of all sizes are already convinced that networking is a great idea. They're spending billions of dollars annually on networking equipment. The benefits go far beyond saving money on shared peripherals. Networks enable organizations to create massive, centralized pools of information, which are vital to performing their mission. And networks enable people to communicate and collaborate in ways that aren't possible without some means of connecting the computers they're using (Figure 6.1).

As an informed and literate computer user, you need to know enough about networking to understand the benefits and possibilities of connecting computers. In addition, learning about networking is a good idea for anyone looking for a job these days; employers like to hire workers who grasp networking concepts. This chapter explains the essential concepts of networking and teaches the basic networking terms you'll need to discuss the subject intelligently.

# Network Fundamentals

Although computer networking is increasingly important, most people consider this topic to be highly technical. As this chapter makes clear, however, the *concepts* of computer networking are easy to understand.

A **network** is a group of two or more computer systems linked together to exchange data and share resources, including expensive peripherals such as

**FIGURE 6.1**
Networks enable users to create common pools of data, which employees can access to obtain the information they need.

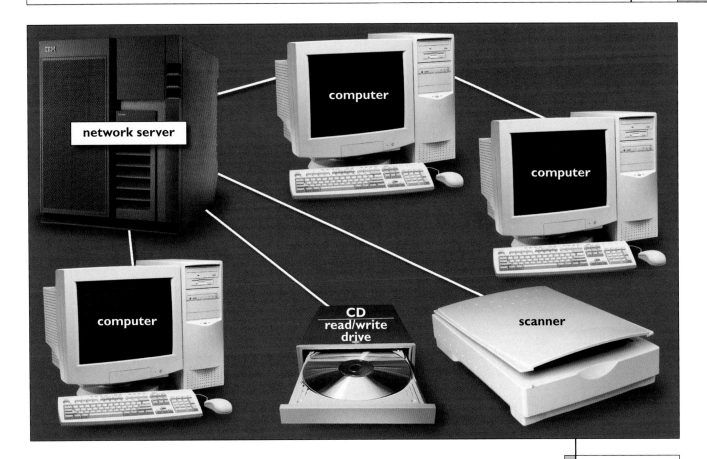

**FIGURE 6.2**
Networks allow
people to share
data and
resources.

high-performance laser printers (Figure 6.2). Networks enable communications. **Communications** (data communications or telecommunications) is the process of electronically sending and receiving messages between two points. Communications takes place over communications channels. **Communications channels** (also referred to as links) are the path through which messages are passed from one network location to the next. In communications, a source encodes messages and sends them over the communications channel to a destination that decodes messages (Figure 6.3). When you send a message from your computer, the data is converted to an electrical signal.

Phones and phone lines send and receive analog signals. **Analog signals** are continuous waves that vary in strength and quality. Computers send and receive digital signals. **Digital signals** are discontinuous pulses in which the presence or absence of electronic pulses represents 1s and 0s (Figure 6.4).

A network also needs communications devices to convert signals that travel over a communications channel.

**Communications devices** include computers (workstations), modems, routers, switches, and network interface cards (NICs). These devices transform data from analog to digital and back again, determine efficient data-transfer pathways, boost signal strength, and facilitate digital communication (Figure 6.5).

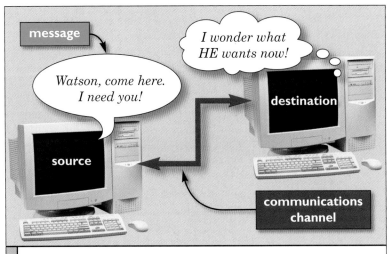

**FIGURE 6.3** In communications, a message is encoded into electrical signals and then decoded at the receiving end.

**FIGURE 6.4**
Digital signals are composed of on/off pulses, whereas analog signals use waveform modulation.

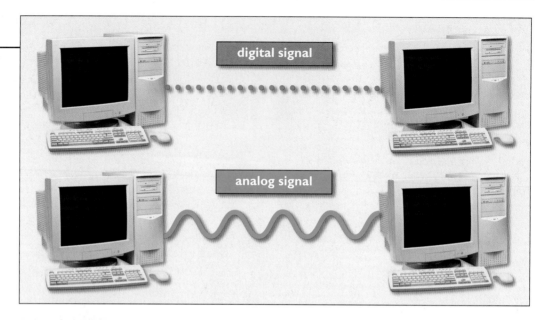

On a network, data travels from one device to another over physical (wired) or wireless transmission media. We'll discuss physical transmission media in the next section. Wireless alternatives to physical network infrastructure such as broadcast radio, cellular radio, microwaves, communications satellites, and infrared will be discussed in Chapter 8.

Now that you understand the fundamentals of networks, let's look at the components that make up a network.

## PHYSICAL INFRASTRUCTURE

Physical infrastructure refers to cables, modems, switches, and routers that guide messages to their destination. Cables provide the pathway for data to travel between computers and peripheral devices. Often, a single message travels over several different physical media, including telephone lines, coaxial cable, and fiber-optic cable, before arriving at its destination. For now, we'll look at each of the types of physical media in more detail. Remember as you read through this section that some of the concepts apply to local networking, where all of the computers and peripherals are physically connected to the network infrastructure, and some of the concepts apply to networks that are made up of computers and peripherals that may be tens or hundreds of miles apart.

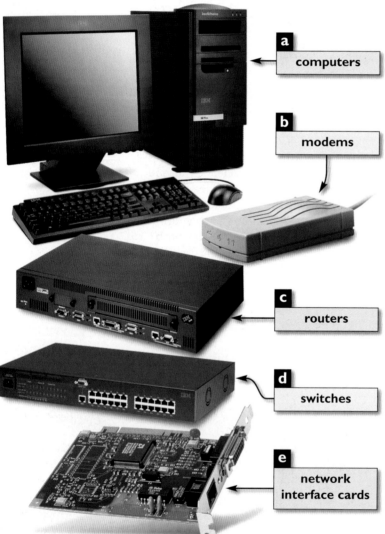

**FIGURE 6.5** Communications devices include: (**a**) computers, (**b**) modems, (**c**) routers, (**d**) switches, and (**e**) network interface cards.

## Twisted Pair

The same type of wire used for telephones, **twisted pair** uses two insulated wires twisted around each other to provide a shield against electromagnetic interference, which is generated by electric motors, power lines, and powerful radio signals (Figure 6.6).

Because twisted pair wiring will be with us for many years, engineers have developed a number of interim technologies that make use of twisted pair wiring:

- A 56 Kbps **leased line** is a specially conditioned telephone line that enables continuous, end-to-end communication between two points. The earliest type of permanent digital connection, 56 Kbps leased lines have declined in popularity as services such as ISDN and ADSL have become more widely available. Larger organizations, such as Internet service providers, corporations, and universities, connect using leased **T1** lines, which are specially conditioned copper wires that can handle up to 1.544 Mbps of computer data. This is a costly service that individuals and small businesses can't afford.

- **Integrated Services Digital Network** (**ISDN**) is a standard that provides digital telephone and data service. ISDN services offer connections ranging from 56 to 128 Kbps (Basic Rate ISDN) or 1.5 Mbps (Primary Rate ISDN) using ordinary twisted pair telephone lines. The cost of an ISDN line is often two to three times

that of an analog phone line, but there's a payoff. With 128 Kbps ISDN services, you get two telephone numbers with one ISDN account; you can use one for computer data and another one for voice or fax. When you're using the connection for computer data only, the system automatically uses both data channels to give you the maximum data transfer rate; if a phone call comes in, the connection automatically drops back to 64 Kbps to accommodate the incoming call. What's more, connection is nearly instantaneous; unlike analog connections with a modem, there's no lengthy dial-in procedure and connection delay.

- **Digital Subscriber Line** (**DSL**, also called **xDSL**) is a blanket term for a group of related technologies, including Asymmetric Digital Subscriber Line (ADSL), that offer high-speed Internet access. ADSL and related DSL technologies are expected to provide 1 Mbps access, again using ordinary twisted pair telephone lines. Already available in major metropolitan markets, ADSL is akin to ISDN in that it uses existing copper wiring. But ADSL is much faster: typically, up to 1.5 Mbps when you're downloading data and up to 256 Kbps when you're uploading data. (Note that downloading speeds are much faster than uploading speeds; the discrepancy explains why the service is called asymmetric. ADSL isn't the best choice if you need to upload huge amounts of data.)

## Techtalk

**cat-5**

Cat-5 wiring is similar to telephone wire but consists of four twisted pairs instead of just two. Cat-5 wiring uses an RJ-45 connector that looks very similar to a telephone jack connector but is a little wider and thicker.

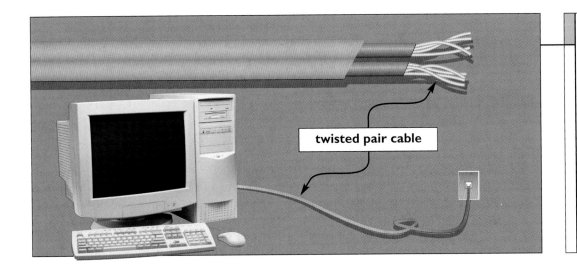

twisted pair cable

**FIGURE 6.6**
Twisted pair cable refers to inexpensive copper cable that's used for telephone and data communications. The cable is twisted to prevent interference from electrical circuits.

**FIGURE 6.7** With coaxial cable, data travels through the center copper wire and is shielded from interference by the braided wire.

**FIGURE 6.8** Fiber-optic cables consist of thin strands of glass that transmit data by means of pulses of light.

### Coaxial Cable

Familiar to cable TV users, **coaxial cable** consists of a center wire surrounded by insulation, which is then surrounded by a layer of braided wire. The braided wire provides a shield against electrical interference (Figure 6.7).

Like twisted pair, interim technologies for coaxial cable do exist, such as cable modems and Ethernet. These will be discussed in subsequent sections.

### Fiber-Optic Cable

**Fiber-optic cable** consists of thin strands of glass that carry data by means of pulses of light (Figure 6.8). A recent innovation in fiber-optic cable is the use of colored light. Instead of carrying one message in a stream of white light impulses, this technology allows for the use of colored impulses. The result is that a single fiber-optic strand can carry multiple signals simultaneously. Eight colors were available in 2000, 16 in 2001, 32 in 2002, and the projection is that there will be 256 colors in use by the turn of the decade.

Engineers have also developed interim technologies to make better use of existing fiber-optic cables. Fiber-optic **T3** lines can handle 43 Mbps of computer data. Another technology requiring fiber-optic cable, **Synchronous Optical Network (SONET)** is a standard for high-performance networks. The slowest SONET standard calls for data transfer rates of 52 Mbps; some enable rates of 1 Gbps or faster. Outside the United States, SONET is known as Synchronous Digital Hierarchy (SDH). SONET is expected to provide the fiber-optic cable services for Broadband ISDN (BISDN), but this service isn't expected to benefit homes and small businesses.

## BANDWIDTH

**Bandwidth** refers to the amount of data that can be transmitted through a given communications channel. Bandwidth is determined by the method used to represent and transmit data via the transmission medium, subject to an upper limit imposed by the physical characteristics of the medium. For analog signals, bandwidth is expressed in cycles per second, or hertz (Hz). Bits per second (bps) measures the bandwidth of digital signals. A transmission medium's bandwidth is measured in kilobits per second (Kbps), megabits per second (Mbps), or gigabits per second (Gbps).

Low bandwidth (narrowband) is considered to be 56 Kbps, while high bandwidth (broadband) is equivalent to 622 Mbps. Fiber-optic cable can carry more data without loss of signal strength for longer distances than twisted pair or coaxial cable. Twisted pair carries data at transfer rates of 1 Kbps, coaxial cable at 10 Mbps, and fiber-optic cable at 1 Gbps.

So how much bandwidth do you need? For text, you can get by with a transmission medium with a low bandwidth of 56 Kbps. That rate, however, is often painfully slow for the highly graphical Web (unless you're *really* patient). Exploring the Web is a more pleasant proposition using a physical medium with a data transfer rate of 128 Kbps or faster.

Broadband digital connections aren't widely available yet. According to one estimate, by 2005 only about five percent of households in the United States will have digital connections operating at speeds of 1.5 Mbps or greater. But fiber-optic infrastructure is being installed across the north-south and east-west corridors of the United States, so high-speed digital may soon be coming to a computer near you!

## MODEMS: FROM DIGITAL TO ANALOG AND BACK

**Modems** are devices that transform digital signals into analog form for transmission through telephone lines. Using a process called modulation, a modem transforms the computer's digital signals into analog tones that can be conveyed through the telephone system. On the receiving end, the process used is demodulation, in which the other modem transforms this signal from analog back to digital. Modems can play both roles, modulation and demodulation, which is where the name modem comes from: it's short for modulator/demodulator (Figure 6.9).

Two types of modems are available: internal and external. An internal modem is designed to fit in one of your computer's expansion slots. It gets its power from the computer's expansion bus. An external modem has its own case and power supply. For this reason, external modems are slightly more expensive.

### Asynchronous Communication

Modems use a method of networking called **asynchronous communication**. In this method, data is sent one bit at a time, in a series (one after the other). Start bits and stop bits are added to the data so that the receiving computer can tell where one byte ends and the next one begins. This networking method is called asynchronous because the start and stop bits eliminate the need for

techtv

To learn about accessing a remote computer, see the video clip at **www.prenhall.com/ cayf2005.**

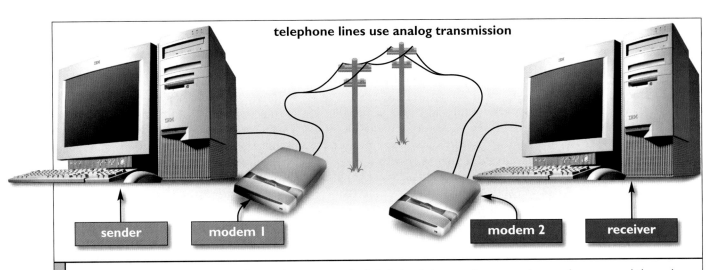

**telephone lines use analog transmission**

sender | modem 1 | modem 2 | receiver

**FIGURE 6.9** A modem transforms the computer's digital signals into analog tones that can be conveyed through the telephone system.

## Destinations

To learn more about the ITU and international telecommunications standards, visit the ITU's home page at **www.itu.int**.

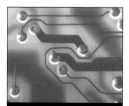

## Techtalk

**negotiation**
When you use your computer's modem to connect to a network, the funny screeching noises and static you hear are called "negotiation." Your modem is communicating with the modem on the other end of the line, figuring out how fast each modem can transfer data and how the bits to be exchanged are going to be handled.

some kind of synchronization signal. In **synchronous communication**, data exchange requires a synchronization signal that identifies the units of data being exchanged.

### Modulation Protocols

To establish communications, modems must conform to standards that are set by international standards organizations. These standards, called **modulation protocols**, ensure that your modem can communicate with another modem, even if the second modem was made by a different manufacturer.

Several modulation protocols are in common use. Each protocol specifies all the necessary details of communication, including the data transfer rate, the rate at which two modems can exchange data. The data transfer rate is measured in bits per second (bps) and is referred to as the bps rate. You may encounter the term *baud rate* when a modem's data transfer rate is discussed. The **baud rate** is the maximum number of changes that can occur per second in the electrical state of a communications circuit. Note that the technical definitions of baud rate and bps rate differ. The correct measurement of a modem's data transfer rate is the bps rate.

Modulation protocols are governed by the Geneva, Switzerland-based International Telecommunications Union (ITU), a division of the United Nations. The most recent modulation protocol, called **V.90**, enables modems to communicate at a maximum rate of 56 Kbps. (In practice, V.90 modems rarely achieve speeds higher than 42 Kbps.) The protocol also includes standards for data compression and error checking.

Two modems can communicate only if both follow the same modulation protocol. When a modem attempts to establish a connection, it automatically negotiates with the modem on the other end. The two modems try to establish which protocols they share, and then they use the fastest rate that both modems have. If a computer with a 9600 bps modem is connected to a computer with a 14,400 bps modem, data is transferred between the two computers at 9600 bps.

Traditional modems that use the telephone system (telephone modems) will be useful only until faster forms of communicating are available. In the next sections you will learn about the high-speed replacement for telephone modems.

### DSL Modems

To connect to a DSL line, your computer needs a DSL modem, as well as a DSL phone line and a DSL service subscription. One problem is that DSL service isn't standardized, so you'll need to select a modem that's compatible with your telephone company's particular type of DSL service. Standardization efforts are under way, however, and these efforts will reduce the cost and complexity of DSL installations.

### ISDN Adapters

To connect computers to ISDN lines, you need an **ISDN adapter** (also called a **digital modem**, although it isn't actually a modem). ISDN adapters are 100 percent digital. Increasingly, small businesses and even homeowners are installing ISDN-capable routers, which enable them to link the ISDN circuit to a local area network (LAN). Using an ISDN router, a small business can connect as many as 32 desktop computers and provide all with on-demand Internet service.

### Cable Modems

Currently, the leading contender in the high-bandwidth sweepstakes is your local cable TV company, which has probably already wired your home with coaxial cable. In contrast to twisted pair, coaxial cable makes it easy to achieve very-high-bandwidth data communications. What's more, about 73 million homes in the United States now subscribe to cable TV service, and an additional 35 million are within easy reach of cable systems.

Does the cable TV industry's huge installed base of coaxial cable hold the key to high-bandwidth digital service delivery? Not yet. The cable TV system was designed to run signals in one direction only: toward the house, not away from it. But data communications requires two-way communication. Only about one-eighth of the homes in the United States have cable service delivery that's capable of two-way data communications; the cable industry is busily upgrading the rest of its infrastructure to provide this capability. And, increasingly, they're offering data communications services—specifically, Internet access.

For computer users, these services offer data transfer rates that leave ISDN in the dust and rival those of DSL. **Cable modems**, devices that enable computers to access the Internet by means of a cable TV connection, now deliver data at bandwidths of 500 Kbps to 1 Mbps or more, depending on how many subscribers are connected to a local cable segment. You'll hear figures stating that cable modems are capable of bandwidths of 30 Mbps or more, but this bandwidth must be divided among the 2,000 or more subscribers in the cable company's service area.

In the next section you will learn what happens once data is transformed into digital signals by the modem and sent on its way.

## SWITCHING AND ROUTING TECHNIQUES

Networks can work with an amazing variety of physical media. But how does the message get through the maze of cables to the right place? Who sorts the mail en route? Networks funnel messages to the correct destination using two basic technologies, called circuit switching and packet switching.

### Circuit Switching
In **circuit switching**, the network creates a physical, end-to-end circuit between the sending and receiving computers. Circuit switching works best when it is essential to avoid delivery delays. In a circuit switching network, high-speed electronic switches handle the job of establishing and maintaining the connection.

### Packet Switching
In **packet switching**, an outgoing message is divided into data units of a fixed size, called **packets** (Figure 6.10). Each packet is numbered and addressed to the destination computer. The sending computer pushes the packets onto the network, where they're examined by routers. **Routers** are devices that examine each packet they detect. After reading the packet's address, the router consults a table of possible pathways to the packet's destination. If more than one path exists, the router sends the packet along the path that is most free of congestion. There's no guarantee that the packets will arrive in

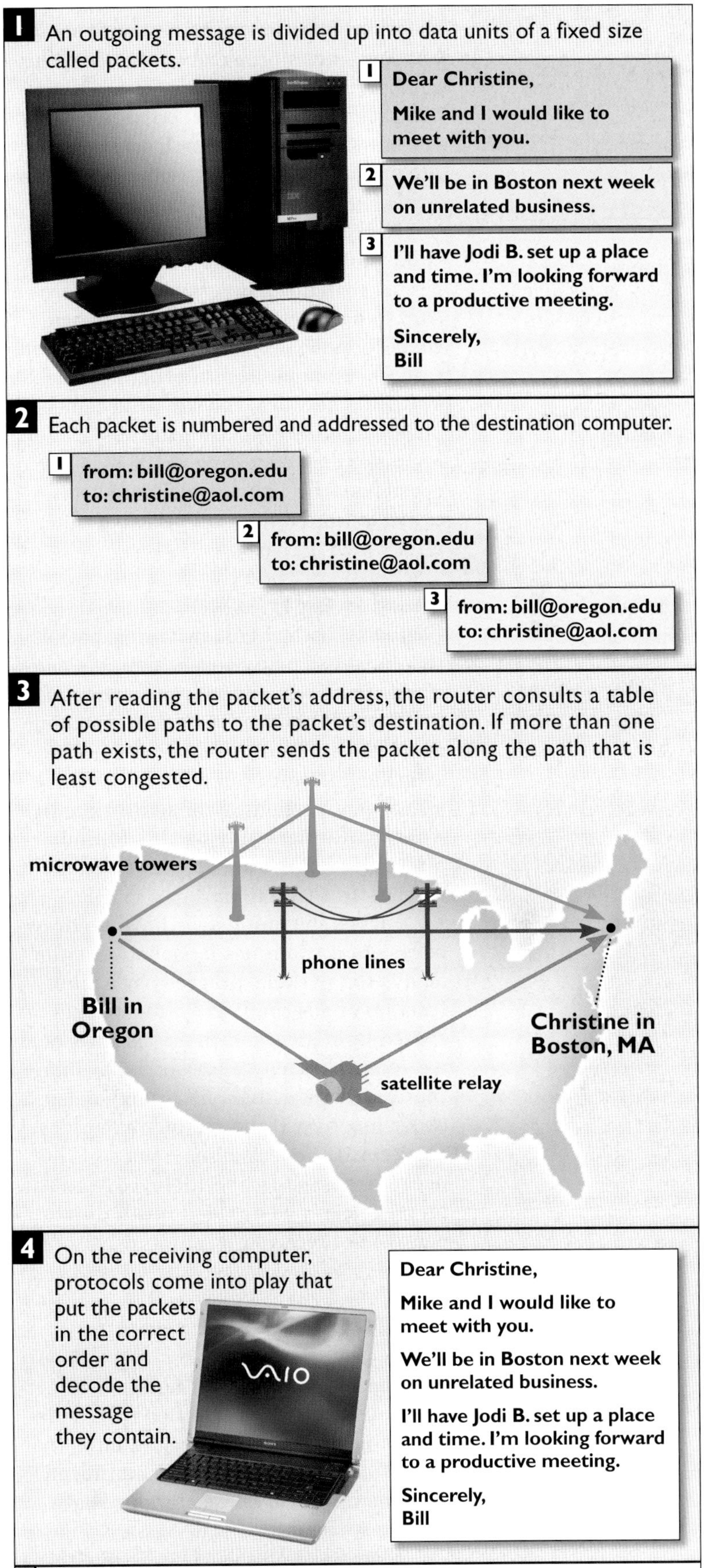

**FIGURE 6.10** Packet Switching

the same order in which they were sent, but that's not a problem; on the receiving computer, protocols come into play to put the packets in the correct order and decode the message they contain. If any packets are missing, the receiving computer sends a message requesting retransmission.

Packet switching networks are often called **connectionless** because, unlike circuit switched networks, it's not necessary to have an active, direct electrical connection for two computers to communicate. For example, the Internet is a packet switching network; you can send somebody an e-mail message even if the destination computer isn't operating. If the message doesn't get through, the software keeps trying to send it for a set period of time, after which it gives up.

### Which Is Best?

Compared with circuit switching, packet switching has many advantages. It's more efficient and less expensive than circuit switching. What's more, packet switching networks are more reliable. A packet switching network can continue to function even if portions of the network aren't working. Routers may be able to find alternative pathways so that the data reaches its destination.

Packet switching does have its drawbacks. As it examines a packet, a router delays the packet's progress by a tiny fraction of a second. In a huge packet switching network such as the Internet, a given packet may be examined by many routers, introducing a noticeable delay called **latency**. If the network experiences **congestion** (overloading), some of the packets may be further delayed, and the message can't be decoded until all its packets are received.

### PROTOCOLS

What makes a network function isn't merely the physical connections. Of fundamental importance are the standards that specify how computers can communicate over the network. These standards are called **protocols**.

What are protocols? They're like the manners you were taught when you were a child. When you're growing up, you're taught to say certain fixed things, such as "It's nice to meet you," when you meet someone in a social situation. The other person replies, "It's nice to meet you too." Such exchanges serve to get communication going. Networking protocols are similar. They are fixed, formalized exchanges that specify how two dissimilar network components can establish communication.

A specific type of network may use dozens of protocols. For example, the Internet uses well over a hundred protocols that specify every aspect of Internet usage, such as retrieving documents through the Web or sending e-mail to a distant computer. The complete package of protocols that specify how a specific network functions is called a **protocol suite**. Collectively, a protocol suite specifies the network's overall design, called the **network architecture**. The term *architecture* may sound daunting, but in the next section, you'll learn that the basic idea isn't much more complicated than a layer cake.

### NETWORK LAYERS

Networks aren't easy to design because they're complex systems, and a lot can go wrong. To make network design easier, engineers divide a network architecture into separate **network layers**, each of which has a function that can be isolated and treated separately from other layers. Because each layer's protocols precisely define how each layer passes data to another layer, it's possible to make changes within a layer without having to redesign the entire network.

### The Protocol Stack

How do layers work? To understand the layer concept, it's helpful to remember that protocols are like manners, which enable people to get communication going. Let's look at an example.

Suppose you're using a Web browser and you click a link that looks interesting. Now imagine that each protocol is a person, and each person has an office on a separate floor of a multistory office building. You're on the top floor, and the network connection is in the basement. When you initiate your request, your browser calls the person on the next floor down, "Excuse me, but

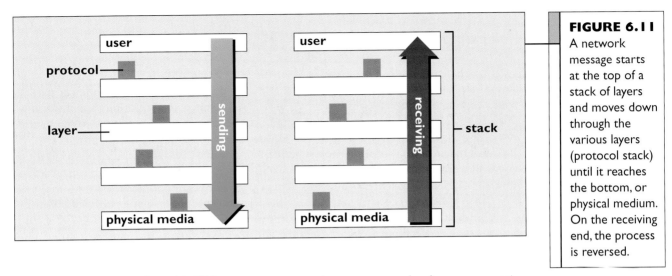

**FIGURE 6.11**
A network message starts at the top of a stack of layers and moves down through the various layers (protocol stack) until it reaches the bottom, or physical medium. On the receiving end, the process is reversed.

would you please translate this Web page request into a form the Web server can process?" The person on the floor below replies, "Sure, no problem," and then calls the person on the *next* floor down. "If it isn't too much trouble, would you please put this translated message in an envelope and address it to such-and-such computer?" And so it goes, until the message finally reaches the physical transmission medium that connects the computers in the network.

At the receiving computer, precisely the opposite happens. The message is received in the basement and is sent *up*. It's taken out of its envelope, translated, and finally handed up to the top floor, where it's acted on.

To summarize, a network message starts at the top of a stack of layers and moves down through the various layers until it reaches the bottom (the physical medium). Because the various layers are seen to be vertically arranged like the floors in an office building, and because each is governed by its own protocols, the layers are called a **protocol stack**. On the receiving end, the process is reversed: the received message goes up the protocol stack. First, the network's data envelope is opened, and the data is translated until it can be used by the receiving application. Figure 6.11 illustrates this concept.

## ADVANTAGES OF NETWORKING

What's the point of having a computer network? When you connect two or more computers, you see gains in every aspect of computing:

- **Reducing hardware costs.** Networks enable users to reduce costs by sharing expensive equipment. For example, dozens of users can share a single high-capacity printer or a common connection to the Internet.

- **Enabling application sharing.** Networks enable users to share software. Network versions of applications are designed to be installed on a high-powered computer, called a **file server**, that makes these applications available to more than one user at a time. For example, at Platt Electric Supply, an Oregon-based industrial electric supply firm, sales representatives upload orders from notebook computers to an order-tracking program installed on the company's file server. After installing the network, employees found that they had up to 20 percent more time to focus on their customers' needs.

- **Building massive information resources.** Networks enable users to create common pools of data, which employees can access to obtain the data they need. At publisher Prentice Hall, for example, a company-wide network makes a vast archive of illustrations available to book designers and greatly reduces the amount of time spent tracking down appropriate photographs for textbooks and other publishing projects.

# Ethernet

On May 22, 1973, Bob Metcalfe sent a memo to colleagues at the Palo Alto Research Center that described a local-area networking standard he called Ethernet. Today, Ethernet is a standard for physically connecting computers into a local area network, and a communications protocol that lets those computers share data.

The Ethernet interface uses a protocol called Carrier Sense Multiple Access/Collision Detection, or CSMA/CD. To be a part of the LAN, every computer needs a network interface that bundles data into chunks that travel across the network, as well as a connection point, or port, for the special wiring that connects all the PCs. The port is either built into the motherboard or provided as an add-in network interface card. It sends data to the network and receives data sent from other computers on the network.

The standard also dictates the communications protocol, or how connected computers send data. Computers linked by Ethernet send data along wires in small chunks called packets. You can think of a packet as a letter, addressed to travel to a different city, moving through the mail system. In addition to the data itself, each packet carries a destination address and your computer's "home" address.

By using the CSMA/CD protocol, the computer first looks for an opportunity to place the packet into the system and then sends it on its way. Every time a packet reaches its destination, the sender gets confirmation and the computer waits for a gap to open to shoot off another packet. Devices along the way read the address and pass the packet along to the next device en route to its destination. Occasionally, two devices send a packet into the same gap at the same time, resulting in a "collision" and the loss of both packets, for the moment. When packets collide, the PCs that sent them are instantly notified, and each chooses a random interval to wait before it resends the packet. This approach helps prevent network gridlock.

The Ethernet specification also details how fast data can travel across the network and the types of wires that must be used. For a long time, 10BaseT Ethernet, capable of passing 10 megabits of data per second, was the fastest and most popular implementation. As people used Ethernet for larger and more complex networks, and as file sizes grew, 100BaseT Ethernet (also known as Fast Ethernet), with 10 times the data transfer speed, became the Ethernet of choice. To get that much more speed, Fast Ethernet uses higher-quality cabling that sends the packets more quickly without degrading the signal. Still newer, but not as widely implemented, is a version that sends data at 1 gigabit per second. And the 10 Gbps version is on the horizon. These super-fast connections are often used to create large networks, as they prevent data bottlenecks, or gridlock.

By creating an Ethernet network, you can transfer files between PCs and file servers, run applications stored on other computers, print to printers in other rooms or parts of a building, and share high-speed access to the Internet. Ethernet is the most popular networking technology for large and small businesses. Its widespread availability and fast transfer speeds have made it the de facto standard for networking.

- **Centralizing data management.** Storing data on a network allows multiple users to access the data, and at the same time it provides data security and integrity assurance through the use of firewalls and password protection. Centralized storage also makes it easier to maintain consistent backup procedures.

- **Connecting people.** Computers create powerful new ways for people to work together. For example, groupware applications enable workers to create a shared calendar for scheduling purposes. Team members can see instantly who's available at a given day and time. What's more, these people don't have to work together in the same building. They can be located at various places around the world and still function effectively as a team.

Now that you know how you can benefit from using networks, let's look at the different types of networks.

# Types of Computer Networks: LANs and WANs

Computer networks fall into two categories: local area networks (LANs) and wide area networks (WANs).

- A **local area network** (**LAN**) uses direct cables, radio, or infrared signals to link computers within a small geographic area, such as a building or a group of buildings. A home network is one example of a LAN. It comprises two or more computers that communicate with each other and with peripheral devices such as a printer or cable modem.

- A **wide area network** (**WAN**) uses long-distance transmission media to link computers separated by a few miles or even thousands of miles. The Internet is a wide area network open to public use. (As you'll see, other WANs, including some that use the same technology that the Internet uses, aren't public.)

## LOCAL AREA NETWORKS (LANs)

LANs transform an organization's hardware into what seems to users like one gigantic computer system. From any computer on the LAN, you can access any data, software,

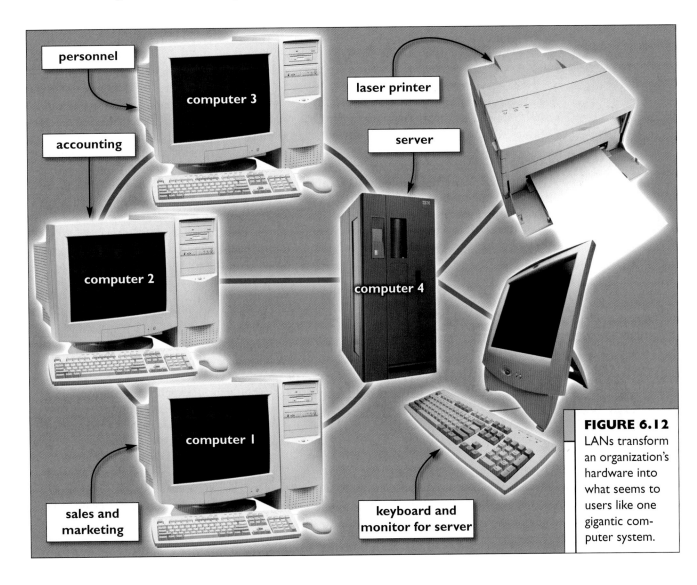

**FIGURE 6.12**
LANs transform an organization's hardware into what seems to users like one gigantic computer system.

or peripherals (such as fax machines, printers, or scanners), as long as the network administrator has made these resources accessible (Figure 6.12).

Network access is controlled by the network administrator. Most of the time a network user will need to provide a user name and a password to access the network. Once logged in, the user will have access to the user's own folders on a server, or other people's folders that the user has permission to see/use. Access will also be granted to peripheral devices such as printers, and to the Internet, if the network is connected.

Like all networks, LANs have all the basic network components—cabling, protocols, and a mechanism for routing information to the correct destination. As you'll see in the following sections, LANs require that the networked computers have special hardware and software. LANs are primarily differentiated by the networking model they use (peer-to-peer or client/server), as well as their cabling, protocols, and the fact that they cover a relatively small service area.

### Networking Hardware: Network Interface Cards (NICs)

The special hardware a computer needs to work with a LAN is a network interface card (NIC), unless this circuitry is part of the computer's design (Figure 6.13). **Network interface cards** (**NICs**) are expansion boards that are made to fit into a computer's expansion slots. Some NICs are designed to work with a specific type

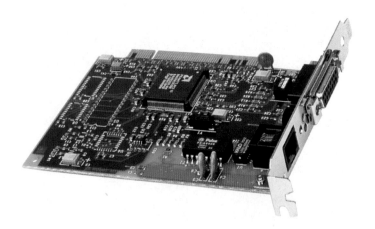

**FIGURE 6.13** A network interface card (NIC) provides the electronic connection between your computer and the network.

of cabling and protocols, but others can work with more than one type.

When a PC is connected to a LAN, the PC is called a **workstation**. The term **node** is used to describe any computer or peripheral (such as a printer) that's connected to the network. Every node on the LAN has a unique name that's visible to LAN users, as well as a unique, numerical network address.

### Networking Software

Each computer on the LAN must also be equipped with additional system software that enables the computer to connect to the network and exchange data with other computers. Most operating systems, including UNIX, Linux, Windows, and Mac OS, now include such software in their standard installations. Using this special networking software, you can set up LANs called peer-to-peer networks and client/server networks. Let's examine the differences between these two types of LANs.

**Peer-to-Peer Networks** In a **peer-to-peer network** (**P2PN**), all the computers on the network are equals—that's where the term *peer-to-peer* comes from—and there's no file server. But there is file sharing. In file sharing, each computer user decides which, if any, files will be accessible to other users on the network. Users may also choose to share entire directories, or even entire disks. They can also choose to share peripherals, such as printers and scanners.

Peer-to-peer networks are easy to set up; people who aren't networking experts do it all the time, generally to share an expensive laser printer or provide Internet access to all the workstations on the LAN (Figure 6.14). Peer-to-peer networks tend to slow down with heavy use, however, and keeping track of all the shared files and peripherals quickly becomes confusing. For this reason, peer-to-peer LANs aren't suitable for networks that connect more than one or two dozen computers.

**Client/Server Networks** The typical corporate LAN is a **client/server network**, which includes one or more file servers as well as networked workstations, called **clients** (Figure 6.15). The file server on a client/server network is a high-capacity, high-speed computer with a large hard disk capacity. The server contains network versions of programs and large data files.

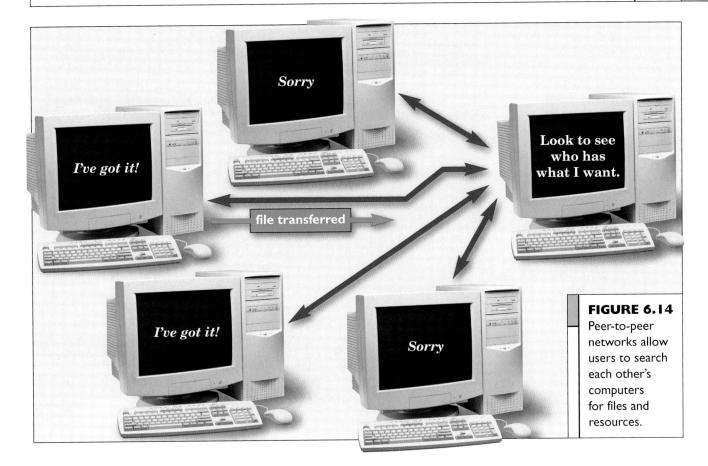

**FIGURE 6.14**
Peer-to-peer networks allow users to search each other's computers for files and resources.

Clients—all the computers that can access the server—send requests to the server. The client/server model works with any size or physical layout of LAN and doesn't tend to slow down with heavy use.

The file server also contains the **network operating system** (**NOS**), the software required to run the network. A network operating system, such as Novell Corporation's NetWare or Microsoft's Windows NT Server, is a complex program that requires skilled technicians to install and manage it. Network operating system services include:

● file directories that make it much easier to locate files and resources on the LAN

● automated distribution of software updates to the desktop computers on the LAN

● support for Internet services such as the Web and e-mail

Now that we know the different kinds of networks that people and businesses use, let's look at the actual physical layouts of various networks.

### LAN Topologies

The physical layout of a local area network is called a **network topology**. What's at stake here isn't just the arrangement of computers in a particular space; topologies provide a solution to the problem of **contention**, which occurs when two workstations try to access the LAN at the same time. Contention sometimes results in **collisions**, the corruption of network data caused by two workstations transmitting simultaneously.

The earliest LANs used a **bus topology**, also called a daisy chain, in which the network cable forms a single bus to which every workstation is attached (Figure 6.16a). At the ends of the bus, special connectors called terminators configure the end of the circuit. To resolve the contention problem, bus networks use some type of **contention management**, a technique that specifies what happens when a collision occurs. (A common technique is to abandon any data that could have been corrupted by a collision.) The underlying design is simple, but bus networks are unwieldy in practice; it's difficult to add users in the middle of the circuit.

A **star topology** solves the expansion problems of the bus topology by

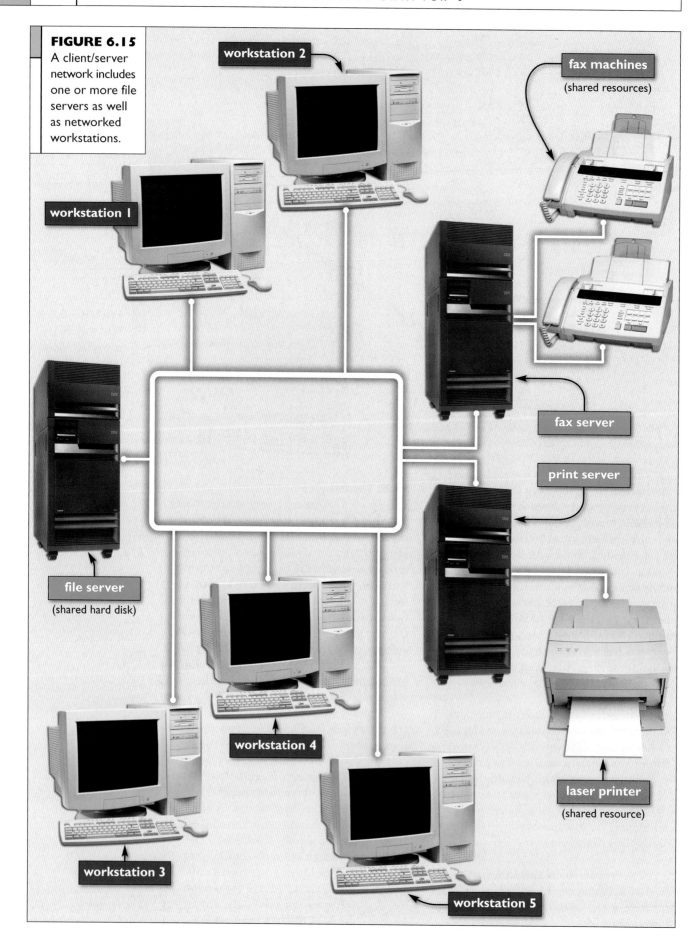

**FIGURE 6.15**
A client/server network includes one or more file servers as well as networked workstations.

workstation 2

fax machines
(shared resources)

workstation 1

fax server

print server

file server
(shared hard disk)

workstation 4

laser printer
(shared resource)

workstation 3

workstation 5

introducing a central wiring concentrator, called a **hub** (Figure 6.16b). Adding users is simple; you just run a cable to the hub and plug the new user into a vacant connector. Star networks also generally use contention management to deal with collisions.

A **ring topology** has all nodes attached in a circular wiring arrangement. This topology makes possible a unique way of preventing collisions (Figure 6.16c). A special unit of data called a **token** travels around this ring. A workstation can transmit only when it possesses the token. Although ring topology networks are circular in that the token travels a circular path, they look more like star networks because all the wiring is routed to a central hub.

### LAN Technologies

Although several LAN technologies specify functions at the lower layers of the protocol stack (Figure 6.17), by far the most popular LAN standard is **Ethernet**. The various versions of Ethernet are used by approximately 80 percent of all LANs. Although early versions of Ethernet (called 10base2 and 10base5) used coaxial cable in bus networks, the most popular versions today are Ethernet star networks that use hubs and twisted pair wire. Two versions are available: 10baseT (10 Mbps) and Fast Ethernet (100 Mbps, also called 100baseT). The hardware to create a 10baseT Ethernet for five PCs can cost as little as $200. The newest LAN technology, **Gigabit Ethernet**, can transfer data at speeds as high as 1,000 Mbps.

Perhaps the simplest LAN technology is **LocalTalk**, the networking system built into every Macintosh computer. You can quickly create a LocalTalk network by buying some LocalTalk connectors and ordinary telephone cables.

Local area networks enable an organization to share computing resources in a single building or a group of buildings. But a LAN's geographic limitations pose a problem. Today, many organizations need to share computing resources with distant branch offices, employees who are traveling, and even people outside the organization, including suppliers and customers. This is what wide area networks (WANs) are used for—to link computers separated by even thousands of miles.

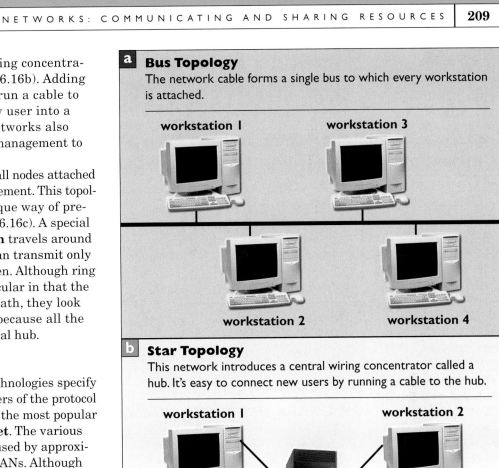

**a Bus Topology**
The network cable forms a single bus to which every workstation is attached.

workstation 1    workstation 3

workstation 2    workstation 4

**b Star Topology**
This network introduces a central wiring concentrator called a hub. It's easy to connect new users by running a cable to the hub.

workstation 1    workstation 2

workstation 4    workstation 3

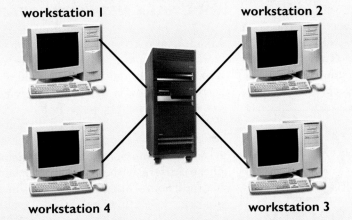

**c Ring Topology**
All the nodes are attached in a circular wiring arrangement.

workstation 1    workstation 4

workstation 2    workstation 3

**FIGURE 6.16 a–c** Most networks use a bus, star, or ring topology.

## Destinations

To learn more about Ethernet, check out Charles Spurgeon's Ethernet Web site at **www.etherman age.com/ethernet/ ethernet.html**. The site covers all the Ethernet technologies used today and includes a practical guide for do-it-yourselfers.

To learn more about how a home network works, go to **computer.how stuffworks.com/ home-network.htm**.

To learn how to set up a home network, see the video clip at **www.prenhall.com/ cayf2005**.

### FIGURE 6.17 Popular LAN Protocols

| Protocol Name | Data Transfer Rate | Physical Media | Topology |
|---|---|---|---|
| LocalTalk | 230.4 Kbps | Shielded twisted pair (phone connector cords) | Bus |
| Ethernet (10base5 and 10base2) | 10 Mbps | Coaxial cable | Bus |
| Ethernet (10baseT) | 10 Mbps | Twisted pair cable | Star |
| Fast Ethernet (100baseT) | 100 Mbps | Twisted pair or fiber-optic cable | Star |
| Gigabit Ethernet | 1,000 Mbps | Fiber-optic cable | Star |
| IBM Token Ring Network | 4–16 Mbps | Twisted pair cable | Star |

## WIDE AREA NETWORKS (WANs)

Like LANs, WANs have all the basic network components—cabling, protocols, and a mechanism for routing information to the correct destination. WANs are like long-distance telephone systems. In fact, much WAN traffic is carried by long-distance voice communication providers, such as AT&T, MCI, and Sprint. Like long-distance phone carriers, WANs have what amounts to a local access number, called a point of presence (POP), and long-distance trunk lines, called backbones (Figure 6.18). So, you can picture a WAN as a local area network that has long-distance communications needs between its servers, computers, and peripherals.

Some WANs are created and maintained for the sole purpose of one organization's internal needs. For instance, The Condon Group, Ltd maintains a wide area network with offices in five states. Other WANs are created to serve the public, like those maintained by online service providers such as AOL and MSN.

### FIGURE 6.18
Wide area networks allow companies, such as The Condon Group, Ltd, to communicate and share resources across great distances.

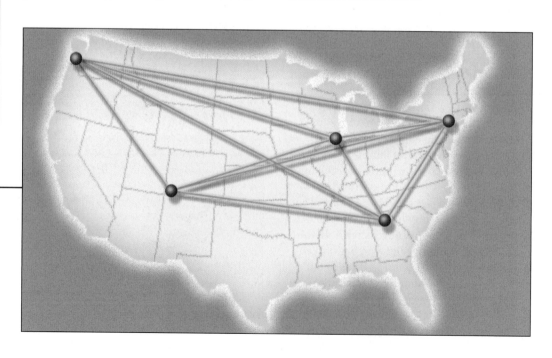

**IMPACTS**

**Milestones**

# Wi-Fi

Wireless networks that use the Ethernet standard are becoming more popular every day. The Wi-Fi Alliance is an organization made up of leading wireless equipment and software providers with the missions of certifying all 802.11-based products for interoperability and promoting the term *Wi-Fi* as the global brand name across all markets for any 802.11-based wireless LAN products.

While all 802.11a/b/g products are called Wi-Fi, only products that have passed the Wi-Fi Alliance testing are allowed to refer to their products as "Wi-Fi Certified" (a registered trademark). Products that pass are required to carry an identifying seal on their packaging that states "Wi-Fi Certified" and indicates the radio frequency band used (2.5 GHz for 802.11b or 802.11g, 5 GHz for 802.11a).

Wi-Fi (for "wireless fidelity," like "hi-fi" for "high fidelity" in audio equipment) offers Ethernet speeds without the wires, but someone has to pay for it. While you may purchase a Wi-Fi-compatible PC card for under $100 that operates in peer-to-peer mode, Wi-Fi networks require access points, which range in cost from about $300 to $1,400. In other words, you can communicate between computers with wireless technology, but to access the Internet or to communicate across distances with computers and printers you need to have a central control point. So, wireless networking may remove the wires, but there is still the need for a central server or control point. Most access points have an integrated Ethernet controller to connect to an existing wired-Ethernet network.

The controller also has an omnidirectional antenna to receive the data transmitted by the wireless transceivers.

Apple sells an inexpensive (under $300) and easy-to-configure access point called Airport. Airport has to be connected to an Apple computer (iMac, PowerMac, iBook), but it will accept signals from any 802.11b-compatible wireless-network card, whether it's PC- or Mac-based.

Wi-Fi networked devices communicate at a speed of 11 Mbps whenever possible. If signal strength or interference is disrupting data, the devices will drop back to 5.5 Mbps, then 2 Mbps, and finally down to 1 Mbps. Though it may occasionally slow down, this keeps the network stable and very reliable.

Here are some advantages of Wi-Fi:
- It's fast (11 Mbps).
- It's reliable.
- It has a long range (1,000 feet in open areas, 250 to 400 feet in closed areas).
- It's easily integrated into existing wired-Ethernet networks.

Here are some disadvantages:
- It can be expensive.
- It can be difficult to set up.
- Speed can fluctuate significantly.

Like home radio-frequency systems, the majority of Wi-Fi wireless transceivers available are in PCMCIA card form. Because these products are not targeted at the home market, they are not typically sold in "do-it-yourself" kits. Instead, everything is a la carte, allowing customers to build a system that exactly meets their needs.

**LAN-to-LAN Connections** In corporate information systems, WANs are often used to connect the LANs at two or more geographically separate locations. This use of WANs overcomes the major limitation of LAN technology: its inability to link computers separated by more than a few thousand feet. New services from WAN service providers such as AT&T, Sprint, and MCI enable companies to connect their LANs at 100 Mbps, the same data transfer rate used in most companies' internal systems. With these connections, users get the impression that they're using one huge LAN that connects the entire company and all its branch offices.

**Transaction Acquisition** When you make a purchase at retail chain stores such as Sears or Starbucks Coffee, information about your transaction is instantly relayed to central computers through WANs. That's because the "cash register" the clerk uses is actually a computer, called a point-of-sale (POS) terminal, that's linked to a data communications network (Figure 6.19). The acquired data are collected for accounting and also analyzed to reveal changing sales patterns.

**Point of Presence (POP)**
To carry computer data over the long haul, a WAN must be locally accessible. For this

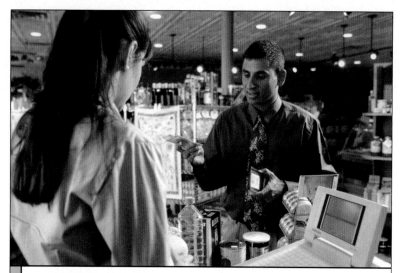

**FIGURE 6.19** POS terminals are fast becoming a part of a company's ability to know its customers.

reason, WANs make a point of presence (POP) available in as many towns and cities as needed. A **point of presence** (**POP**) is a WAN network connection point that enables customers to access the WAN by means of a local analog telephone call (using a modem) or a direct digital hookup that enables a continuous, direct connection. One WAN, called Tymnet, has more than 1,000 local points of presence in the United States.

### Backbones

The high-capacity transmission lines that carry WAN traffic are called **backbones**. Some are regional, connecting towns and cities in a region such as southern California or New England. Others are continental or even transcontinental in scope.

Whatever their scope, backbones are designed to carry huge amounts of data traffic; cross-country Internet backbones, for example, can handle nearly 2.5 gigabits per second, and much higher speeds are on the way. A current U.S. government–funded research project is constructing a backbone network that will operate at speeds of 9.6 gigabits per second.

### WAN Protocols

Like any computer network, WANs use protocols. Some WANs use circuit switching network technology, but most use packet switching. The oldest packet switching protocol for WAN usage, called **X.25**, is optimized for dial-up connections over noisy telephone lines and is still in widespread use. Local connections generally offer speeds of 9.6 to 64 Kbps. X.25 is best used to create a point-to-point connection with a single computer. A point-to-point connection is a single line that connects one communications device to one computer. It is widely used for automated teller machines and credit card authorization devices. New protocols designed for 100 percent digital lines, such as Switched Multimegabit Data Service (SMDS) and Asynchronous Transfer Mode (ATM), enable much faster data transfer rates (up to 155 Mbps).

### WAN Applications

WANs enable companies to use many of the same applications you use on the Internet, such as e-mail, conferencing, document exchange, and remote database access. This section focuses on the ways to take advantage of a WAN's superior security.

**Public Data Networks and Virtual Private Networks**  A **public data network** (**PDN**) is a for-profit data communications network available for use on a per-byte-transmitted fee basis. PDNs charge hefty fees, but they can assure good security and can guarantee that network capacity is available when it's needed.

Large corporations, banks, and governments may construct private data networks, which aren't open to the public or to any other users. These are the most secure WANs, but they're also the most expensive to operate. An alternative developed in the 1980s, called the **virtual private network** (**VPN**), consists of lines that are exclusively leased to a single company, thus ensuring excellent security.

Organizations often take advantage of private networks by using groupware— applications such as e-mail, schedulers, calendars, and file sharing and management utilities. If all of the members of a group keep their personal electronic calendars up-to-date, a groupware application such as Microsoft Outlook can quickly determine an optimum time for a meeting, find an open room, send a notice asking for the meeting, and then coordinate responses to show who has confirmed the meeting. Alternatively, a master document may be shared amongst a group, and then all of the group's comments can be collectively edited by the author of the document.

# Summary

## NETWORKS: COMMUNICATING AND SHARING RESOURCES

- Computer networks link two or more computers so that they can exchange data and share resources. Networks enable communications (electronically sending and receiving data) through the establishment of communications channels.

- Computer networks require physical media, including twisted pair wire, coaxial cable, and fiber-optic cable. Physical connections, including leased lines, ISDN, DSL, and SONET, incorporate new technologies to increase the capacity of existing physical media.

- Bandwidth refers to the data transfer capacity of a communications channel and is measured in bits per second (bps). To transmit text, you can get by with low bandwidth (such as a 56 Kbps connection). That rate, however, is often painfully slow for exploring the Web, which is more enjoyable at a bandwidth of 128 Kbps or faster.

- To send digital data over dial-up phone lines, it's necessary to modulate the signal (transform it into analog form). On the receiving end, the signal must be demodulated (transformed back into digital form). Modems (modulators/demodulators) perform this service.

- Circuit switching creates a permanent, end-to-end circuit that is optimal for voice and real-time data. Packet switching does not require a permanent switched circuit and can funnel more data through a medium with a given data transfer capacity. But packet switching introduces slight delays that make the technology less than optimal for voice or real-time data.

- Protocols define how network devices can communicate with each other. A network requires many protocols to function smoothly. When a computer sends a message over the network, the application hands the message down the protocol stack, where a series of protocols prepares the message for transmission through the network. At the other end, the message goes up a similar stack.

- Computer networks can reduce hardware costs, enable users to share applications, create the means to pool all of an organization's mission-critical data, and foster teamwork and collaboration.

- A peer-to-peer LAN doesn't use a file server and is most appropriate for small networks. Client/server networks offer network navigation tools, shared applications, shared databases, groupware, and e-mail, but trained technicians are required to configure and maintain them.

- By far the most widely used LAN protocol is Ethernet, which is available in 10 or 100 Mbps star topology configurations that use hubs and twisted pair wiring. The newest LAN technology, Gigabit Ethernet, can transfer data at the rate of 1,000 Mbps.

- Businesses use WANs for LAN-to-LAN connections and transaction acquisition. Private data networks and virtual private networks allow organizations the proprietary use of groupware applications.

# Key Terms and Concepts

Go to **www.prenhall.com/cayf2005** to review this chapter, answer the questions, and complete the exercises.

# Matching

Match each key term in the left column with the most accurate definition in the right column.

_____ 1. network operating system (NOS)

_____ 2. network architecture

_____ 3. protocols

_____ 4. Ethernet

_____ 5. SONET

_____ 6. peer-to-peer network

_____ 7. routers

_____ 8. clients

_____ 9. token

_____ 10. packets

_____ 11. latency

_____ 12. bus topology

_____ 13. network topology

_____ 14. collision

_____ 15. node

a. all the computers that access the server

b. a standard for high-performance optical networks

c. a computer or peripheral that is connected to the network

d. a network where all the computers are equal

e. a special unit of data that travels around the ring in a ring topology

f. communications devices that examine each packet they detect

g. delay in packet transmission due to router examination

h. data units of fixed size that are used with packet switching networks

i. the most popular lower-level protocol stack standard

j. standards that specify how the networks function

k. the overall design of a network

l. also known as a daisy chain

m. the physical layout of a local area network

n. software required to run the network

o. the corruption of network data caused by two workstations transmitting simultaneously

# Multiple Choice

Circle the correct choice for each of the following.

1. Which of the following is not a computer network?
   a. local area network (LAN)
   b. leased-line area network (L2AN)
   c. wide area network (WAN)
   d. peer-to-peer network (P2PN)

2. Which technology enables networks to funnel messages to the correct destinations?
   a. circuit switching
   b. packet switching
   c. both a and b
   d. none of the above

3. What type of line uses fiber optics?
   a. T1
   b. T2
   c. T3
   d. 10baseT

4. To connect to a LAN, a computer must be equipped with which of the following?
   a. network interface card (NIC)
   b. backbone
   c. both a and b
   d. none of the above

5. Which of the following media carries more data for longer distances?
   a. digital coax
   b. coaxial cable
   c. twisted pair
   d. fiber-optic cable

6. Which of the following is not a LAN topology?
   a. ring
   b. star
   c. hub
   d. bus

7. What do you call a for-profit data communications network available for use on a per-byte-transmitted fee basis?
   a. virtual private network (VPN)
   b. public data network (PDN)
   c. peer-to-peer network (P2PN)
   d. client/server network (CSN)

8. Which of the following is a WAN network connection point that enables customers to access the WAN through a local phone call?
   a. point of presence (POP)
   b. leased line
   c. permanent virtual circuit (PVC)
   d. frame relay

9. Which of the following is the most popular LAN standard?
   a. ISDN
   b. LocalTalk
   c. Ethernet
   d. Synchronous Optical Network (SONET)

10. Which of the following is the oldest and most widely used packet switching protocol for WAN usage?
    a. 10baseT
    b. category 5 (cat-5)
    c. X.25
    d. T1

# Fill-In

In the blanks provided, write the correct answer for each of the following.

1. A(n) _____ links two or more computers together to enable data and resource exchange.

2. A(n) _____ uses direct cables, localized wireless radio, or infrared signals to link computers within a small geographic area.

3. When a PC is connected to a LAN, the PC is called a(n) _____.

4. A(n) _____ is a PC expansion board needed to connect a computer to a LAN.

5. In _____, an outgoing message is divided into data units of a fixed size called packets.

6. _____ uses two insulated wires twisted around each other to provide a shield against interference.

7. _____ is a standard for high-performance fiber-optic networks.

8. The earliest LANs used a(n) _____ topology.

9. A(n) _____ is a networking standard that has been developed and published by an independent organization such as a standards body.

10. The high-capacity transmission lines that carry WAN traffic are called _____.

11. A _____ is a for-profit data communications network available for use on a per-byte-transmitted fee basis.

12. In a(n) _____, file sharing allows users to decide which computer files, if any, are accessible to other users on the network.

13. _____ protocols ensure that your modem can communicate with another modem.

14. A(n) _____ uses long-distance transmission media to link computers separated by a few miles or even thousands of miles.

15. In _____, the network creates a physical, end-to-end circuit between the sending and receiving computers.

# Short Answer

1. What is bandwidth, and why is it an important consideration in a network connection to the Internet?

2. Explain the difference between peer-to-peer and client/server networks.

3. What are the differences between local and wide area networks?

4. Name three types of LAN topologies, and describe how they work.

5. Explain the difference between the terms *modulation* and *demodulation*. Which of these must a modem be able to perform? Explain why.

6. Explain the differences between circuit switching and packet switching. What are the advantages of each method?

# A Closer Look

1. Visit a campus computer lab and determine what network topology is used. In addition to computer workstations, what other devices are connected to the network? What types of physical media are used to connect the computers and other peripherals in this lab? If your school has more than one lab, what physical media are used to interconnect the labs? How does your school connect to the Internet?

2. If you were responsible for setting up a network for a company that had offices in five different states, how would you do it? What part would the Internet play in your plans?

3. If you live in a highly populated area, you may already have cable television access for your home. Some cable companies also offer one-way (download-only) Internet service through this cable. However, this service still requires the use of a modem and a telephone connection for uploading. Unfortunately, only a fraction of the cable companies can provide the two-way data communications that is needed for full cable Internet access. Contact your local cable company to see if you are one of the lucky cable users who can get a two-way Internet cable connection. What additional hardware is needed for Internet cable connections? What is the monthly cost of this service? Do you already have a two-way Internet cable connection? If not, explain why you would or would not consider this high-speed alternative to telephone service.

4. The number of households that have more than one computer is increasing, and families want to share resources among them. One of these resources is the Internet connection. Although the newer versions of Microsoft Windows use software to allow two computers to share an Internet connection, consumers with high-speed connections such as cable or DSL can use hardware in the form of a router to share Internet access. Go to a local computer store and investigate cable/DSL routers. How many ports do these devices have? How much do they cost? What physical medium is used to connect the devices to the router? Can a printer be shared using a router? What type of network topology is used? What additional hardware is needed to network computers to the router? If you had a high-speed connection and multiple computers, would you purchase a router? Why or why not?

5. Many homes with cable television service have more than one television set. Connecting multiple televisions requires the use of "splitters" to divide the incoming signal and send it to each television set. Some new houses are constructed with coaxial cable running to multiple rooms, but how are multiple television sets connected in older homes? Unfortunately, this usually requires drilling holes in walls, floors, or ceilings, or even running cables on the exterior of the residence, and some homeowners and landlords don't like doing this. The same connection problem exists with home computer networks. Fortunately, there's an alternative to running networking cables: using a wireless access point. Go to a local computer store and investigate wireless networking. What are the prices for these devices? How does the wireless connection speed compare with a wired one? What type of network topology is used? What additional hardware is needed to network computers to the wireless access point? If you had a home network, would you consider this networking alternative? Why or why not?

# On the Web

1. Visit CNET at **www.cnet.com** to see what you can learn about establishing a home network. While you may find information on wireless networking, restrict your research to a wired network. Assume that you have two computers, a printer, and a scanner that you wish to network. What additional hardware and software will you need to purchase? How much will your network cost? Will you connect to the Internet? If so, how, and at what cost? If not, why not?

2. The textbook discusses Gigabit Ethernet technology that allows LAN connection speeds of 1,000 Mbps or 1 Gbps. Go to the "10 GEA" site at **www.10gea.org/Tech-whitepapers.htm** to learn about this promising technology. What does 10 GEA mean, and when was it formed? Name three of the founding member organizations. What is the name of the new standard that is being developed? When is ratification of the new standard expected? What types of companies, organizations, or institutions do you think will use this technology?

3. Assume that you have both a desktop and a laptop computer and you wish to network them together. To do this, you need network interfaces for each computer. Go to **www.pricegrabber.com** to find the best price for a network card for a desktop and a laptop computer. What are the prices for each? Why do you think the cards for a laptop are more expensive? Many desktop computers and laptop computers now include automatic built-in network connectivity. Locate and name specific desktop and laptop models that have internal networking capability. If you currently have a desktop or laptop computer, does your computer have internal networking capability?

4. Because of their small size, personal digital assistants (PDAs) are popular mobile computing devices. Do you own, or have you considered buying, a PDA? Go to **www.dartek.com/Browse/index.cfm** to find information on PDAs. What are the most popular methods for networking a PDA to a desktop computer? Which of these methods require additional PC hardware? Is the use of the word *networking* correct? Explain why it is or is not.

5. One of the oldest and most widely used network operating systems is Novell NetWare. Visit the Novell site at **www.novell.com**. What is the latest version of NetWare? In addition to LAN software, what Internet features does NetWare support? What are the initial purchase and upgrade costs for a small system that supports a server and five workstations? What products qualify for competitive upgrades? In addition to English, name three other languages for which NetWare is available. Does NetWare support Macintosh and UNIX-based computers? Does your school use any Novell networking software?

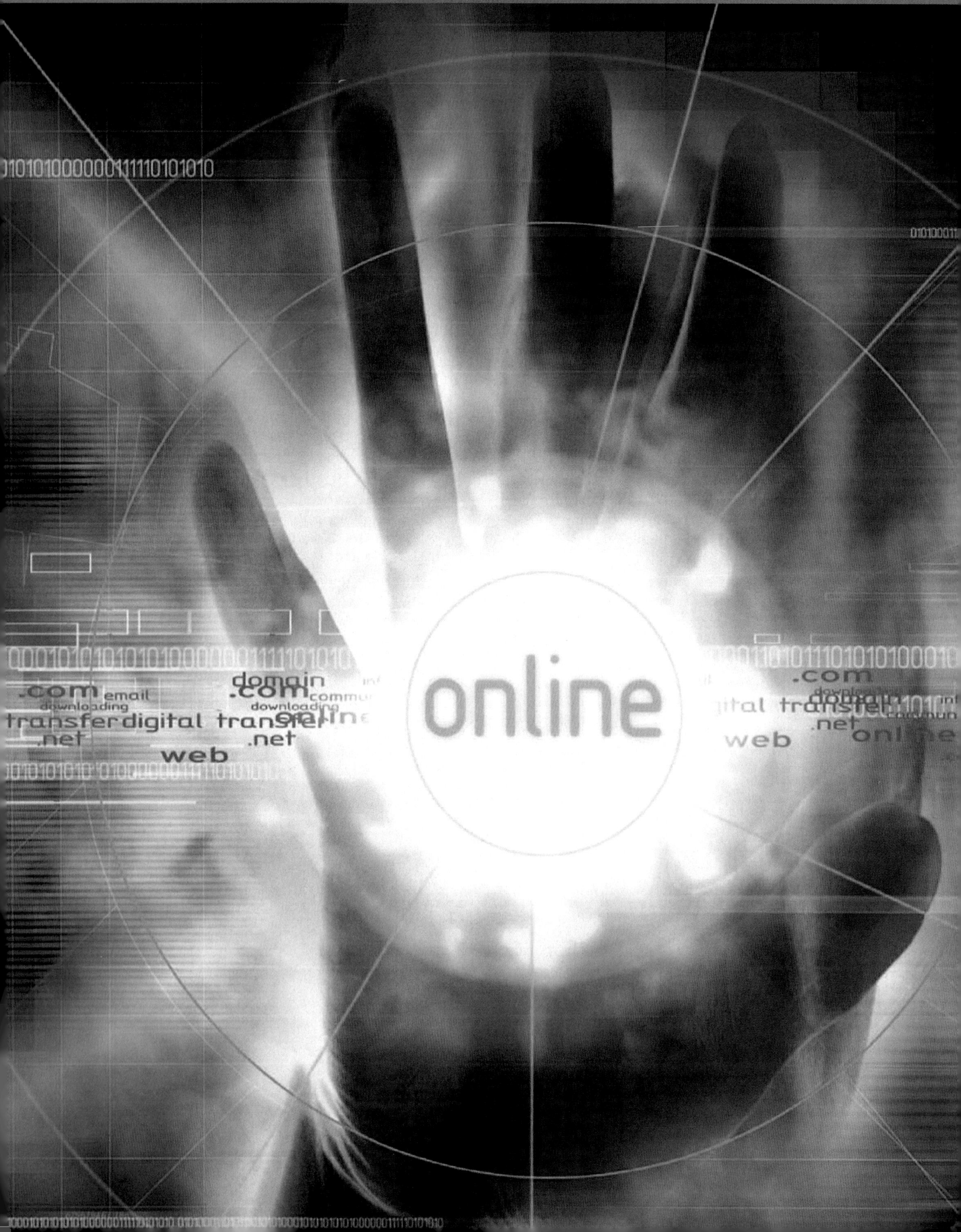

# The Internet and World Wide Web

## What You'll Learn . . .

- Define the Internet and discuss its history.

- Differentiate the Internet from the World Wide Web.

- Explain the concept of hypertext.

- Contrast Web browsers and Web servers.

- Explain the parts of a URL.

- Define the elements of Internet addresses, including domain names.

- List the most popular Internet services and explain what they do.

- Contrast Web subject guides and search engines.

- Explain how search operators can improve Web search results.

- Evaluate the reliability of information on a Web page.

## Destinations

Looking for a radio station? Try "Live Radio" on the Internet at **www.live-radio .net.** This site lists more than 1,500 live Internet radio stations worldwide. You need a player to listen to radio over the Internet, but you can download one for free. Radio station home pages have links that enable you to obtain the software you need.

As you're well aware, the **Internet** is a global computer network with hundreds of millions of users worldwide, and it's growing rapidly. According to one estimate, the total amount of information available on this worldwide network doubles each year. But defining the Internet as a fast-growing global network understates its significance. We're witnessing the birth of the first major mass medium since television; more than 60 percent of U.S. residents between the ages of 16 and 34 are Internet users. What's more, the Internet isn't simply a new mass medium; it's the *first* mass medium that involves computers and uses digitized data. And it's more interactive than TV, radio, and newspapers, which limit user interaction to content selection. With the Internet, people can create information as well as consume it. For this reason, it's the first truly democratic mass medium, one that allows anybody to add their own content to the growing mass of information available online.

Almost all college students have been on the Web—it's hard to imagine students these days not having heard of a Web page, a URL, or a Web link. But no matter how familiar you are with this part of the Internet, it's important that you fully understand the concepts behind the Web and Web browsers, how to effectively use the Web for research, and how to evaluate the quality of the information you retrieve. This chapter discusses these and other topics, helping you become an even more fluent Web user (Figure 7.1).

# The Internet's History

The Internet has become an integral part of our lives. But as we use it on a daily basis to communicate with family and friends, find information, look for jobs, pay bills, and so on, we don't often stop to consider where the Internet originated. This section discusses the evolution of the Internet from a government research program into the mass medium it is today.

## A GALACTIC NETWORK

The Internet was first envisioned by Massachusetts Institute of Technology (MIT) scientist J. C. R. Licklider in August 1962. Licklider, who was President Roosevelt's science advisor during World War II, headed the first computer research program at the Defense Advanced Research Projects Agency (DARPA), as it was then known, a unit of the U.S. Department of Defense. In a series of historic memos, Licklider spoke of a "galactic network," a globally interconnected network through which any computer could directly access any other and exchange data.

Licklider's idea of a galactic network led to 1960s-era work on packet switching theory at MIT. The Internet is also based on studies at a private-sector military think tank, California-based Rand Corporation, which called for the construction of a military network that could continue to function even if enemies knocked out portions of the network. Rand researchers had independently concluded that a packet switching network offered the best chance of surviving during wartime. Under the leadership of Lawrence G. Roberts at DARPA, these researchers formulated the specifications for the Advanced Research Projects Agency Network, **ARPANET**. In 1968, the agency requested bids for development work.

With DARPA's leadership and funding, university and corporate researchers developed the technologies we use today, including routers, WANs, and Internet protocols (standards). ARPANET went online in September 1969 and connected four computers located in California and Utah. Although ARPANET access was initially restricted to universities or research centers with U.S. Defense Department contracts, the network grew rapidly. ARPANET became an international network in 1973, with the addition of computers at defense-related sites in England and Norway. By 1981, ARPANET connected 213 computers. By 1984, it connected 1,000 computers, and by 1987, this figure had risen to 10,000. Universities lacking ARPANET access were clamoring to get it.

## FROM ARPANET TO INTERNET

Why did ARPANET grow so quickly? One reason is that users came to see the network

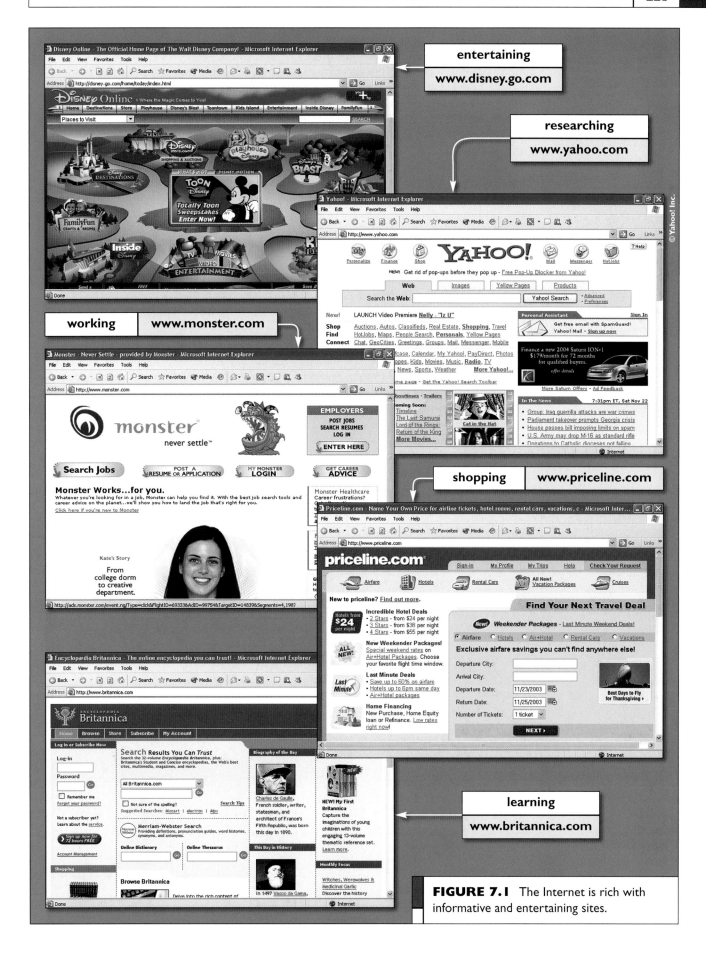

**FIGURE 7.1** The Internet is rich with informative and entertaining sites.

## Destinations

If you'd like to learn more about Internet history, the best place to start is the Internet Society's "Internet Histories" page at **www.isoc.org/ internet/history**. The Internet Society is a professional organization for anyone interested in supporting the Internet's technical development.

as an indispensable means of communication. Although ARPANET's designers thought the network would be used to exchange research data, users saw the network as a communications medium. Invented in 1972 by ARPANET researcher Ray Tomlinson, e-mail quickly became the most popular use of ARPANET. Researchers used e-mail and e-mail discussion groups to stay in touch with colleagues at other institutions. Researchers who lacked ARPANET access felt left out, so they pressured their universities to join the network.

The ARPANET was a test-bed network, designed to serve as the development platform for packet switching technology. The original ARPANET protocols had many deficiencies. As ARPANET researchers Robert Kahn and Vinton Cerf addressed the network's shortcomings, they created the Internet protocols that are now in use throughout the world. On January 1, 1983, the current Internet protocols went online for the first time.

As Internet technology took shape, ARPANET moved steadily away from its military origins. In 1982, the civilian

(ARPANET) network was separated from the military (MILNET) portions. Supervision of ARPANET passed to the U.S. National Science Foundation (NSF), which subsidized ARPANET to aid university researchers. NSF financed the construction of a new long-distance data transmission network, called NSFnet. The old ARPANET backbone was decommissioned in 1990, having performed its research function with spectacular success. Collectively, the NSFnet backbone and the various regional networks connected to it became known as the Internet.

## THE RISE OF A NEW MASS MEDIUM

In the early 1990s, the Internet was still primarily a university network, used mainly for communication and file exchange. By the late 1990s, it was on its way to becoming a new mass medium of global proportions (Figure 7.2).

As computer experts worked to develop software to make the Internet more user

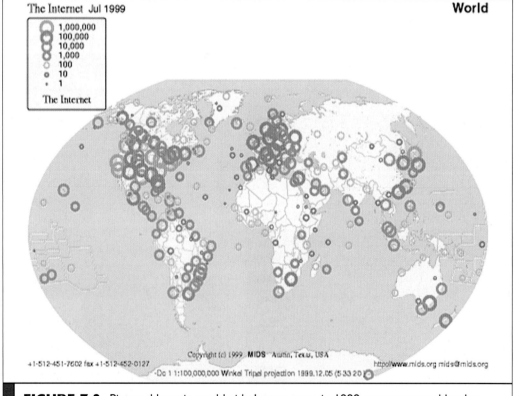

**FIGURE 7.2** Pictured here is worldwide Internet use in 1999 as represented by the Web site **www.mids.org/mapsale/world/index.html**.

friendly, the key transforming event took place in 1995: the elimination of barriers to commercial activity on the Internet. Before 1995, commercial traffic was forbidden on the taxpayer-funded NSFnet backbone. When NSF shut down the backbone and eliminated all Internet subsidies, commercial Internet development took off.

Who controls the Internet today? No one. The Internet is a huge information space made up of thousands of privately owned computers and networks, all of which agree to implement the Internet protocols and share resources on the network. A variety of organizations are responsible for different aspects of the network. For example, the World Wide Web Consortium (W3C) based in Cambridge, Massachusetts, issues standards related to all aspects of the Web. Standards organizations cannot force vendors to follow these standards, but most Internet vendors understand that everyone loses if the standards aren't followed.

## THE FUTURE OF THE INTERNET

Imagine a billion Internet users by 2015. What's more, hundreds of millions of people will be connecting with super-fast connections, using technologies such as cable modems and ADSL (Asymmetric Digital Subscriber Line). Can the Internet handle this growth? According to Internet experts, key changes must take place to ensure that the Internet doesn't become overwhelmed by its own success.

### More Bandwidth

**Internet2 (I2)**, a project of the University Corporation for Advanced Internet Development (UCAID), is a collaborative effort among more than 120 U.S. universities, several U.S. government agencies, and leading computer and telecommunications companies. The I2 project is developing and testing high-performance network and telecommunications techniques. These improvements will eventually find their way to the public Internet. To test I2 ideas, universities participating in I2 are establishing **gigabits per second points of presence (gigaPoP)**. A gigaPoP is a point

of presence (PoP) that provides access to a backbone service capable of data transfer rates in excess of 1 Gbps (one billion bits per second). These network connection points link to various high-speed networks developed by federal government agencies.

Now that you understand the past and potential future of the Internet, let's differentiate the Internet from its most popular entity, the World Wide Web.

# The Internet and Web: What's the Difference?

Imagine an information source that contains billions of documents, each of them almost instantly accessible by means of the computer sitting on your desk. And imagine, too, that this information source is growing at an astonishing rate, with thousands of new documents appearing every day. This resource contains a wealth of useful information, and it's all available when you access the Internet. You guessed it, it's the World Wide Web.

Second in popularity only to e-mail, the World Wide Web is an indispensable information resource. Each day, millions of Internet users turn to the Web to research product purchases, medical decisions, current events, and much more (Figure 7.3).

The **World Wide Web** is a global hypertext system that contains billions of documents and uses the Internet as its transport mechanism. The Web *uses* the Internet for its existence, but it's a separate entity. The Internet is the physical connection of millions of networks, while the Web consists of hypertext embedded on Web pages that are hosted on Web sites.

A **Web site** is a computer that is accessible to the Internet and makes Web pages available. **Web page** refers to any document on a Web site that includes text, graphics, sound, animation, and video. You've undoubtedly visited many Web sites by now. These collections of related Web pages typically contain a **home page** (also called an **index page**),

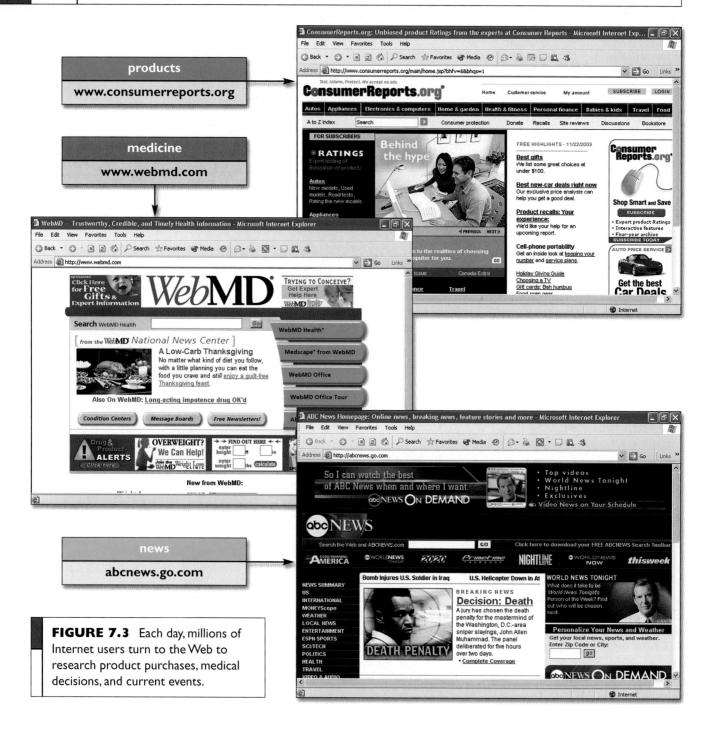

**FIGURE 7.3** Each day, millions of Internet users turn to the Web to research product purchases, medical decisions, and current events.

a default page that's displayed automatically when you enter the site at its top level. Figure 7.4 shows the home pages for several Web sites.

The Web is appealing because of its graphical richness, made possible by the integration of text and graphics. More than 300,000 new Web pages appear every week. Increasingly, Web pages are as well designed as the pages of commercial magazines, and they often feature fonts of the quality you'd associate with desktop publishing.

In the following section, you'll learn how all of these pieces work together on the Web, starting with the concept of hypertext.

## THE HYPERTEXT CONCEPT

**Hypertext** is a method of preparing and publishing text that is ideally suited to be read with a computer. With hypertext, the *sequence* of the information—the order in which it is read—is determined by the

**FIGURE 7.4**

A Web site's home page, like those shown here, is displayed automatically when you enter the site at its top level.

**FIGURE 7.5**
In hypertext, you follow the links to related information.

**FIGURE 7.5**
In hypertext, you follow the links to related information.

reader. You can think of hypertext as active text. That is, the text you read is linked to text or graphics that are contained within the document you are reading or in other documents in cyberspace. Hypertext works by means of hyperlinks. **Hyperlinks** (also called **links**) are words that you can click to bring another document into view (Figure 7.5).

In addition to being a global hypertext system, the Web is a distributed hypermedia system. A **hypermedia system** uses multimedia resources, such as sounds, movies, and text as a means of navigation or illustration. A **distributed hypermedia system** is a network-based content development system. In this system, the responsibility for creating content is distributed among many people. And the more people who create content, the easier hypertext development becomes. For example, if someone has created a document about Queen Isabella and another person has created a document about King Ferdinand, you can link to these documents instead of writing them yourself.

The Web's distribution of content-creation responsibilities does have a drawback: you can link to any page you want, but you can't guarantee that the page's author will keep the page on the Web. The author can delete it or move it, and the author isn't under any obligation to notify other authors who have included links to the page. For this reason, **dead links** (also called **broken links**), links to documents that have disappeared, are common on the Web.

Now that you understand hypertext, let's move on to what enables us to use hyperlinks: browsers and servers.

## WEB BROWSERS AND WEB SERVERS

The first graphical Web browsers (which make hypertext become "live" on your computer screen) were developed in 1994. A **Web browser** is a program that displays a Web document and enables you to access linked documents. Browsers transformed the Internet into something more than a communication and file exchange network: it became a medium for discovering and exploring information that even novices could enjoy. Figure 7.6 illustrates how to connect to the Internet via your browser.

The first successful graphical browser, called Mosaic, helped launch the Web on the road to popularity. Developed by the National Center for Supercomputing Applications (NCSA) at the University of Illinois, Mosaic was followed by two commercial products, Netscape Navigator and Microsoft Internet Explorer, which have since captured virtually the entire browser market (Figure 7.7).

Content on the Web is made available by means of more than one million Web servers located all over the world. When you click a hyperlink, the browser sends a message to a Web server, asking the server to retrieve the requested information and send it back to the browser through the network. A **Web server** is a computer running server software that accepts requests for information, processes these requests, and sends the requested document. If the file isn't found, the server sends an error message.

Simple Web servers are easy to operate, but you need programming skills to configure and maintain the industrial-strength servers that host commercial Web sites. These complex servers use special programs to enhance interactivity and provide access to information stored in databases.

## WEB ADDRESSES (URLs)

An addressing system that precisely states where a resource (such as a Web page) is located is necessary to make the Web work. This system is provided by URLs. A **URL (uniform resource locator)** is a string of characters that precisely identifies an Internet resource's type and location.

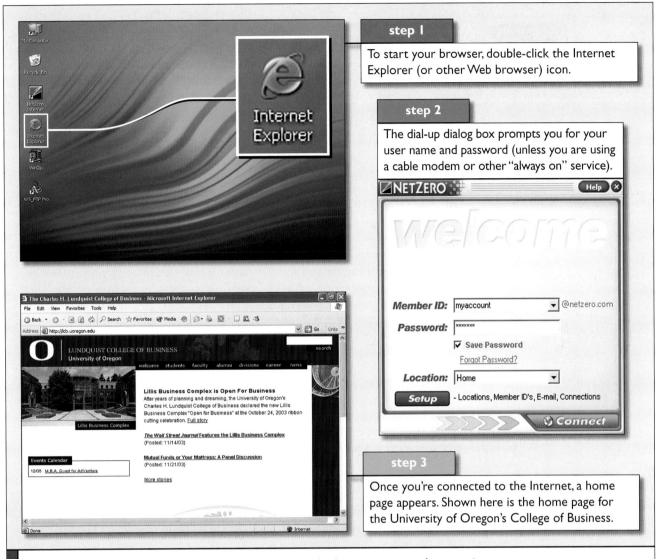

**step 1**

To start your browser, double-click the Internet Explorer (or other Web browser) icon.

**step 2**

The dial-up dialog box prompts you for your user name and password (unless you are using a cable modem or other "always on" service).

**step 3**

Once you're connected to the Internet, a home page appears. Shown here is the home page for the University of Oregon's College of Business.

**FIGURE 7.6** These steps show how to connect to the Internet via your browser icon.

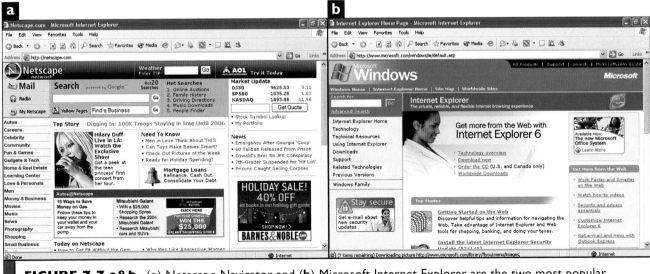

**FIGURE 7.7 a&b** (a) Netscape Navigator and (b) Microsoft Internet Explorer are the two most popular graphical Web browsers.

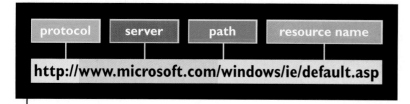

**http://www.microsoft.com/windows/ie/default.asp**

protocol | server | path | resource name

**FIGURE 7.8**
A complete URL has four parts: protocol, server, path, and resource name. This is the URL for the default Internet Explorer home page.

You've seen plenty of URLs, which look similar to the one shown in Figure 7.8.

A complete URL has four parts:

### Protocol

The first part of a complete URL specifies the **Hypertext Transfer Protocol** (**HTTP**), the Internet standard that supports the exchange of information on the Web. Most browsers can also access information using FTP (File Transfer Protocol) and other protocols. The protocol name is followed by a colon and two slash marks (//). With most Web browsers you can omit the *http://* protocol designation when you're accessing a Web page because the browser assumes that you are browsing hypertext Web pages. For example, you can access **http://www. prenhall.com/cayf2005** by typing **www.prenhall.com/cayf2005**.

### Server

The second part of a complete URL specifies the name of the Web server on which the page is located. Early Web servers adopted the name "WWW," but as time has passed, the convention of using WWW as the Web server name has become less common. Also included in the second part of a complete URL is the top-level domain name. The **domain** is the three-letter extension (such as .com or .edu) representing the type of group or institution that the Web site represents.

### Path

The third part of a complete URL specifies the location of the document on the server. It contains the document's location on the computer, including the names of subfolders (if any). In the example in Figure 7.8 the path to the default.asp file on the WWW server at Microsoft.com is /windows/ie/default.asp.

### Resource Name

The last part of a complete URL gives the filename of the resource you're accessing.

A resource is a file, such as an HTML file, a sound file, a movie file, or a graphics file. The resource's extension (the part of the filename after the period) indicates the type of resource it is. For example, HTML documents have the .html or .htm extension.

Many URLs don't include a resource name because they reference the server's default home page. If no resource name is specified, the browser looks for a file named *default* or *index*—a default page that's displayed automatically when you enter the site at its top level. If it finds such a file, it loads it automatically. For example, **www.microsoft.com/windows/ie** displays the default Internet Explorer home page. Other URLs omit both the path name and the resource name. These URLs reference the server's home page. For example, **www.microsoft.com** displays Microsoft's home page on the Web.

## BROWSING THE WEB

Once you have installed browser software and are connected to the Internet (we'll discuss connection options in a subsequent section), you're ready to browse the Web. Both major browser programs use similar features such as navigation buttons, a program icon, an address toolbar, and a status bar as shown in Figure 7.11. One way to customize your browser is to change the default start page (Figure 7.9). You might also decide to use the *default blank* default page choice, which doesn't load a page at all but waits for you to type in an address (Figure 7.10). You can find the default page setting in Internet Explorer under the Tools, Internet Options menu.

As you browse the Web, your browser keeps a list of the pages you've accessed, called the **history list**. If you'd like to return to a previously viewed site and can't find it by clicking the Back button, you can consult the history list and choose the page from there. You'll soon find some Web pages you'll want to return to frequently. To accomplish this easily, you can save these pages as Favorites (Internet Explorer) or Bookmarks (Netscape Navigator) (Figure 7.11). After you've saved these pages as Favorites or Bookmarks, you see the names of these pages in the Favorites or Bookmarks menu.

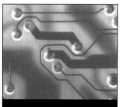

## Techtalk

**spiders**
The Web contains more than just a vast network of information links. "Spiders" exist there, too. A spider is a small piece of software that crawls around the Web picking up URLs and information on the pages attached to them.

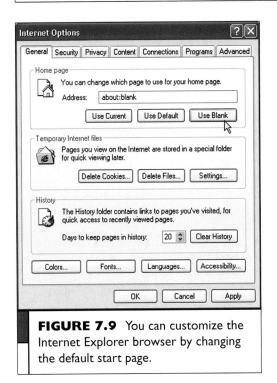

**FIGURE 7.9** You can customize the Internet Explorer browser by changing the default start page.

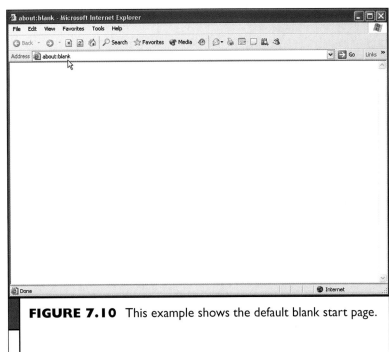

**FIGURE 7.10** This example shows the default blank start page.

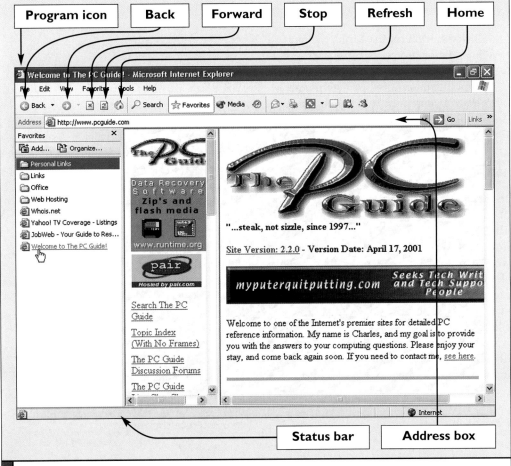

| Program icon | Back | Forward | Stop | Refresh | Home |

Status bar    Address box

**FIGURE 7.11** Both major browser programs use similar features. Also, you can save Web pages to which you'll want to return frequently as Favorites (Internet Explorer) or Bookmarks (Netscape Navigator).

**techtv**

To learn more about customizing your browser, view the video clip at **www.prenhall.com/cayf2005**.

### Accessing Web Pages

To access a Web page, you can do any of the following:

- Click a hyperlink. Hyperlinks are usually underlined, but sometimes they're embedded in graphics or highlighted in other ways, such as with shading or colors. To tell whether a given portion of a Web page contains a hyperlink, position your mouse pointer over it and watch for a change in the pointer's shape. Most browsers indicate the presence of a hyperlink by changing the on-screen pointer to a hand shape.

- Type a URL in the Address box (Internet Explorer) or Location box (Netscape Navigator). You don't need to type http://. Watch for spelling errors, and don't insert spaces. A common mistake is typing a comma instead of a period to separate the components of a URL.

- Click a button on the Links toolbar. Both major browsers come with predefined links on a toolbar, which contains buttons linked to Web pages. You can customize this toolbar with pages you frequently access.

### WEB PAGE DESIGN TOOLS

To create a Web page, Web authors use a markup language called the Hypertext Markup Language (HTML). A **markup language** is a set of codes, called **elements**, which authors can use to identify portions of a document such as a title or a heading. Most elements have two codes, called a **start tag** and an **end tag**, that surround the marked-up text. The following illustrates HTML markup for a level 1 (major) heading, a paragraph of text, and an indented quotation:

```
<H1>This is the text of a major
heading.</H1>
```

```
<P>This is a paragraph of text.
Most browsers display paragraph
text with a blank line before
the paragraph and flush left
alignment.</P>
```

```
<BLOCKQUOTE>This is an indented
quotation. Most browsers display
blockquote material with an
indentation from the left mar-
gin.</BLOCKQUOTE>
```

A document marked up with HTML contains plain text (ASCII text). When browsers access the document, they read the markup and position the various portions of the document in accordance with the markup language's formatting settings.

HTML's simplicity is an important reason for the Web's popularity—nearly anyone can learn how to create a simple Web page using HTML. As a result, it's possible for millions of people to contribute content to the Web. In fact, it may be easier than you imagine; Microsoft Word, Excel, Access, and PowerPoint allow you to save Web-ready documents in HTML format.

# How the Internet Works

The Internet is best defined as *the* overarching network of networks. To understand the Internet, it's important to begin with a solid grasp of just what differentiates the Internet from other networks that traverse huge distances, such as wide area networks (WANs).

In this network of networks, every connected computer can directly exchange data with any other computer on the network. The local and wide area networks that make up the Internet are connected to the Internet backbone. They are maintained by large organizations, such as corporations and universities, as well as by service providers that sell Internet subscriptions to the public (Figure 7.13). Today, hundreds of thousands of networks and more than 50 million computers are connected to the Internet.

### INTEROPERABILITY

If the Internet merely allowed any one of millions of computers to exchange data

# Faces Behind the Web

The Web is the second-largest single part of the Internet and is growing daily. Millions of users browse billions of pages, all sharing information freely and openly.

It wasn't always that way, however. In the world of computing, the Web is not that old. It started as the brainchild of Tim Berners-Lee, a researcher at CERN in Geneva, Switzerland (Figure 7.12). Although many of the concepts behind the Web were laid out in a paper Berners-Lee authored at CERN in 1980, it wasn't until 1989 and 1990 that the protocols and programs were developed to make the Web a reality.

The original Web browsers were text-oriented programs designed for the UNIX environment. This approach more than fulfilled the development goals of Berners-Lee, who saw the Web as a way for researchers to communicate and collaborate. The lack of a graphical interface, however, was in stark contrast to the overwhelming success of Windows, the operating system that was taking the desktop by storm.

In late 1992, two programmers at the National Center for Supercomputing Applications (NCSA) at the University of Illinois developed a new browser called Mosaic. The lead programmer on the project was an undergraduate student named Marc Andreessen. While working at the university's physics research lab, Andreessen saw the potential for bringing multimedia together with the capability to link global resources. At the time, the world had between 30 and 50 Web servers, but that didn't stop the development of Mosaic. The development effort consisted of many all-night sessions to get the C code put together and debugged. The result was released to the public as a free download in 1993. It soon became extremely popular due to its easy-to-use point-and-click interface.

In late 1993, Andreessen moved to California and accepted a job with Enterprise Integration Technologies. After three short months, Andreessen met with Jim Clark, founder of Silicon Graphics, and the two formed a company named Netscape Communications Corporation. The focus of their company was the infant Web, and they decided to create a commercial Web browser that anyone could use.

Andreessen assembled a team of six programmers, who developed the original Netscape Navigator between May and July of 1994. After some testing and refinement, the product was released to the world in October 1994.

Navigator featured several improvements over the original Mosaic. The biggest improvement was continuous document streaming, which meant users could view documents as they were being downloaded.

Netscape followed an unorthodox distribution program for its software: the company gave it away. When released, Navigator was available for free download for educational and nonprofit users. Others could use it for a time but then agree (on the honor system) to pay a modest licensing fee. In this respect, Netscape was following the popular distribution model of thousands of shareware authors.

The marketing model was wildly successful; from the humble beginnings of Netscape in 1994, the company grew into a powerhouse with annual revenues in excess of $525 million. Netscape was subsequently purchased by America Online, where Andreessen worked briefly as the company's chief technology executive.

**FIGURE 7.12** The Web started as the brainchild of Tim Berners-Lee.

**FIGURE 7.13**
LANs and computers connected to the Internet are maintained by corporations, universities, and Internet service providers.

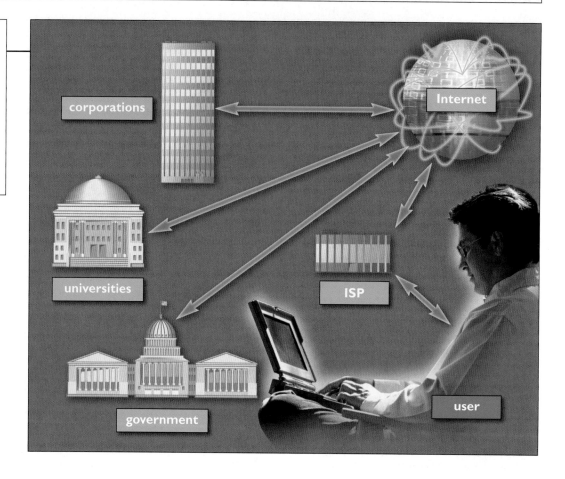

with any other, it would be quite an achievement. But the Internet does more. It enables any connected computer to *operate* a remote computer by sending commands through the network. One key to the Internet's success is called **interoperability**, the ability to work with a computer even if it is a different brand and model. This remarkable characteristic of the Internet comes into play every time you use the network. When you access the Web with a Macintosh, for example, you contact a variety of machines that may include other Macintoshes, Windows PCs, UNIX machines, and even mainframe computers. You don't know what type of computer platform you're accessing, however, and it doesn't make any difference. (A **platform** is a distinct type of computer that uses a certain type of processor and operating system, such as an Intel-based Windows PC.) In other words, the Internet is a cross-platform network (Figure 7.14). A **cross-platform network** is a computer network that includes more than one type or brand of hardware and operating system.

The Internet's cross-platform capability helps explain the network's popularity. No network could match the Internet's success if it forced people to use just one or two types of computers. Many home computer users have PCs, but others have Macintoshes or other types of computers or digital communications and browsing devices. All too many businesses have invested haphazardly in Windows PCs, UNIX workstations, and Macintoshes, only to find that, in the absence of the Internet, these computers don't work together well. Almost magically, the Internet enables these computers to exchange data and even to control each other's operations.

The Internet connects millions of LANs, but a key Internet design principle is that LANs don't all have to work the same way to connect to the Internet. This is an important key to the Internet's success because it means that an organization doesn't have to change its internal computer network to connect to the Internet. In the same way, Internet data can travel over any type of WAN because of Internet protocols.

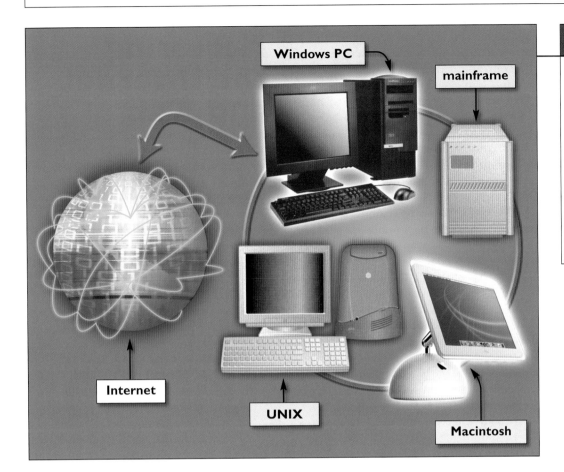

**FIGURE 7.14**
The interoperability provided by the Internet removes the distinctions among different hardware and operating systems, allowing users on all different platforms to work with each other.

## THE INTERNET PROTOCOLS (TCP/IP)

A network is comprised of not only the physical transmission media that carry its signals, but also the protocols (standards) that enable devices connected to the network to communicate with each other. The Internet protocols, collectively called **TCP/IP**, are open protocols that define how the Internet works. TCP/IP is an abbreviation for the Transmission Control Protocol (TCP) and the Internet Protocol (IP). However, more than 100 protocols make up the entire Internet protocol suite.

### Internet Protocol (IP)

Of all the Internet protocols, the most fundamental is the **Internet Protocol** (**IP**) because it defines the Internet's addressing scheme, which enables any Internet-connected computer to be uniquely identified. The Internet Protocol is a connectionless protocol; this means that with IP, two computers don't have to be online at the same time to exchange data. The sending computer just keeps trying until the message gets through.

Since IP enables direct and immediate contact with any other computer on the network, the Internet bears some similarity to the telephone system (although the Internet works on different principles). Every Internet computer has an **Internet address**, or **IP address** (similar to a phone number), and it can directly exchange data with any other Internet computer by "dialing" the other computer's address. An IP address is a four-part number, with the parts separated by periods (such as 128.254.108.7). The Internet works on packet switching principles rather than the circuit switching principles of the telephone system. Still, the Internet does for computers what the telephone system does for phones: it enables any Internet-connected computer to connect almost instantly and effortlessly with any other Internet-connected computer anywhere in the world.

### Transmission Control Protocol (TCP)

The **Transmission Control Protocol** (**TCP**) defines how one Internet-connected computer can contact another to exchange

## Destinations

See for yourself how the domain name service works. Access the "NSLOOKUP" page at **www.infobear.com/ nslookup.shtml** and type a domain name such as **www.microsoft .com**. Click the Run button and you'll see a message showing the IP address associated with the domain name you typed.

For more information on the Internet Corporation for Assigned Names and Numbers, visit **www.icann.org**.

control and confirmation messages. You can see TCP in action when you're using the Web; just watch your browser's status line. You'll see messages such as "Contacting server," "Receiving data," and "Closing connection."

### The Domain Name System

Because IP addresses are difficult to type and remember, the Internet uses a system called the Domain Name System (DNS). The **Domain Name System** (**DNS**) enables users to type an address that includes letters as well as numbers. For example, MSN.com has the numeric address 207.68.172.246. You could type the numeric address into your browser, but most of us find that it's much easier to use text names. A process called **domain name registration** enables individuals and organizations to register a domain name with a service organization called InterNIC.

Domain names can tell you a great deal about where a computer is located. For computers located in the United States, **top-level domain** (**TLD**) **names** (the *last* part of the domain name) indicate the type of organization in which the computer is located (Figure 7.15). Outside the United States, the top-level domain indicates the name of the country in which the computer is located, such as ca (Canada), uk (United Kingdom), and jp (Japan).

**FIGURE 7.15** Common Top-Level Domain Names

| TLD | Used By |
|-----|---------|
| .com | Commercial businesses |
| .edu | Educational institutions |
| .gov | Government agencies |
| .mil | Military |
| .net | Network organizations (such as Internet service providers) |
| .org | Nonprofit organizations |

# Accessing the Internet and Web

To connect to the Internet, your computer must support Internet networking protocols. Today, this support is built into popular operating systems, such as Mac OS, Microsoft Windows, and Linux. Depending on how you're planning to access the Internet, you'll also need communications equipment, such as a telephone, DSL, or cable modem, an ISDN adapter, or an Ethernet card.

You can access the Internet in the following ways:

- **Dial-up access with Point-to-Point Protocol (PPP)** Most home users access the Internet by dial-up access. With this method, your computer is directly connected to the Internet, but it's usually assigned a temporary IP address. For this reason, you can't conveniently run server software on a computer connected to the Internet with PPP; to run a server (in order to host a Web page, for example), you need a system that has a fixed IP address and a registered domain name. Some ISPs use an older protocol, called SLIP, which isn't as efficient as PPP.

- **Digital Subscriber Line (DSL)** Available in many urban areas, DSL connections offer high-speed access and a permanent online connection. One drawback of DSL is that service doesn't extend more than a few miles from a telephone switching station or central office (CO). Although this distance is being extended, DSL service remains unavailable in some rural areas.

- **Cable and satellite access** Cable TV companies are increasingly offering Internet access at speeds much faster than that of dial-up modems. Satellite access enables fast downloads but requires a phone line and a modem for uploading data. Like dial-up access, these access methods give your computer a temporary IP address, so you can't run server programs in such a way that other Internet users can find your content.

- **LAN access** If the company you're working for has a LAN, or if you're attending a university that provides Ethernet access in residence halls, you can access the Internet by means of the local area network. LAN access is generally much faster than dial-up access, but the performance you experience depends on how many LAN users are trying to access the Internet at the same time. With LAN access, your computer probably has a permanently assigned IP address, and you may be able to run server programs.

## ISPs AND BACKBONE SERVICE PROVIDERS

**Internet service providers (ISPs)** are companies that sell Internet accounts and connections (or subscriptions) to home and business users. For home users, they offer dial-up access. Many ISPs also provide direct connections on leased lines for businesses and large organizations.

Looking for an ISP? A good place to start is The List, at **www.thelist.com**, a buyer's guide to ISPs. You can search for an ISP by area code or country. To understand the need for an ISP, it helps to understand how data travels on the Internet. This journey can be compared to an interstate car trip. When you connect to the Internet and request access to a Web page, your request travels by local connections—the city streets—to your Internet service provider's local point of presence (POP). From there, your ISP relays your request to the regional backbone—a highway. Your request then goes to a **network access point (NAP)**—a freeway on-ramp—where regional backbones connect to national backbone networks. And from there, the message gets on the national backbone network, the freeway. Near the destination, your message gets off the national backbone network and travels regional and local networks until it reaches its destination.

The Internet is becoming more complex every day as new backbone service providers expand the network and more ISPs sell this bandwidth to business and residential customers (Figure 7.16). How is this growth accommodated? Because the Internet isn't centrally administered, the network couldn't function without its automated routers, which route Internet messages to their destinations. The Internet's routers are designed to share information with each other automatically. At any given moment, a router automatically possesses up-to-date information about the portion of the network to which it is directly connected. For this reason, new service providers can extend the Internet with a simple registration process; no permission need be obtained from anyone.

As local service providers extend the Internet, traffic grows rapidly. Backbone service providers are expanding capacity at breakneck speed; for example, AT&T is doubling its Internet capacity every three months or so. Still, Internet experts worry that backbone service providers won't be able to construct bandwidth capacity rapidly enough to keep up with the Internet's burgeoning growth.

## INTRANETS AND EXTRANETS

The Internet has developed into a mature technology, and millions of people know how to access and exchange information using

### Destinations

Explore the Internet's physical structure at "An Atlas of Cyberspace," located at **www.cybergeography.org/atlas/atlas.html**. This site is maintained by Martin Dodge at the Centre for Advanced Spatial Analysis, University of London.

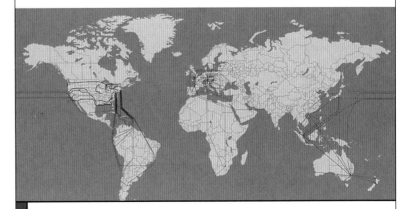

**FIGURE 7.16** AT&T IP Services provides a backbone network in the United States and around the globe.

Internet e-mail and Web browsers. And that's precisely why so many companies are building internal networks based on TCP/IP. Called **intranets**, these networks enable users to use the same familiar tools they use on the Internet. However, these networks are intended for internal use only and aren't accessible from the external Internet without a registered username and password.

Intranets are transforming the way organizations produce and share information. Because it's so easy to create a Web page, companies can distribute Web publishing duties throughout the enterprise. Every department can maintain its own Web page, making its resources available to everyone. By moving expensive print-based publications, such as employee manuals and telephone directories, to the internal Web, companies can realize enormous savings and significantly reduce the amount of trash that goes to local landfills.

Some companies open their intranets to selected allies, such as research labs, suppliers, or key customers. Called **extranets**, these networks can use the Internet to connect, and the data traverses the Internet in encrypted form, safe from prying eyes.

## THE INTERNET VS. ONLINE SERVICES

What's the difference between the Internet and an online service, such as MSN or America Online? An **online service** is a for-profit firm that provides a proprietary network offering e-mail, chat rooms, discussions, and fee-based content, such as magazines and newspapers (Figure 7.17). To enable users to access the service, an online service distributes software that runs on users' computers, makes the connection to the service, and guides them through the available content and activities. As the Internet grew in popularity during the late 1990s, online services began to offer Internet access in an attempt to keep existing customers and attract new ones. While retaining their proprietary network and custom content, they have become Internet service providers (ISPs).

Online services such as MSN, AOL, and Yahoo! are called portals. A **portal** is a gateway that provides a conveniently organized subject guide to Internet content, fast-breaking news, local weather, stock quotes, sports scores, and e-mail (Figure 7.18).

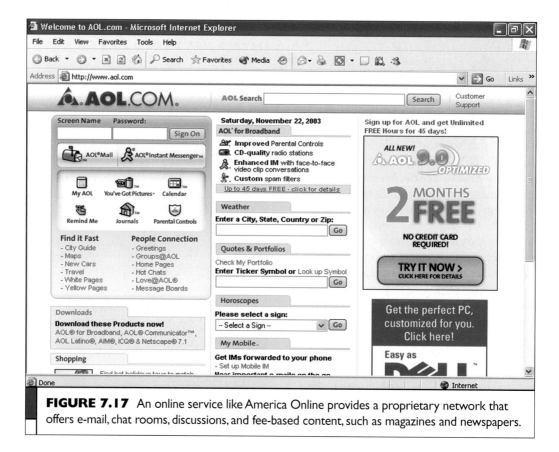

**FIGURE 7.17** An online service like America Online provides a proprietary network that offers e-mail, chat rooms, discussions, and fee-based content, such as magazines and newspapers.

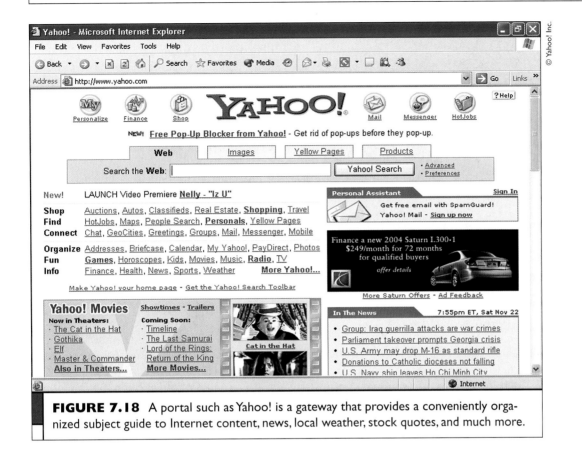

**FIGURE 7.18** A portal such as Yahoo! is a gateway that provides a conveniently organized subject guide to Internet content, news, local weather, stock quotes, and much more.

Now that you know how to access the Internet, let's explore some of the many possibilities available to you once you're there.

# Exploring Internet Services

As we mentioned earlier, the Internet's capacity to work with many types of computers enables users of all popular computers—Macs, PCs, and UNIX systems—to access the Internet. After you're connected, you can take advantage of a lengthy and growing list of Internet services, described in this section.

An **Internet service** is best understood as a set of standards (protocols) that define how two types of programs—a client, such as a Web browser that runs on the user's computer, and a server—can communicate with each other through the Internet. By using the service's protocols, the client requests information from a server program that is located on some other computer on the Internet.

To make use of the most popular Internet services, you need several client programs. That's why the two leading browsers, Netscape Navigator and Microsoft Internet Explorer, are available as part of software suites that include several popular clients in addition to the Web browser. Figure 7.19 lists the clients available in both suites, as well as the services they

**FIGURE 7.19** Clients Available in Popular Browser Suites

| Client | Microsoft Internet Explorer Suite | Netscape Communicator |
|---|---|---|
| Web browser | Internet Explorer | Netscape Navigator |
| E-mail | Outlook Express | Netscape Messenger |
| Usenet | Outlook Express | Netscape Collabra |
| Internet telephony | NetMeeting | Netscape Conference |

**FIGURE 7.20**
E-mail is the most popular Internet service.

support. Most Internet users obtain additional client software to make use of services that these suites don't support, such as Internet Relay Chat (IRC).

## E-MAIL: STAYING IN TOUCH

The most popular application on the Internet is e-mail (electronic mail) (Figure 7.20). In order to send e-mail you need to know the recipient's e-mail address. An **e-mail address** is a unique cyberspace identity for the recipient, such as **myname @someserver.com**. When you receive e-mail you can reply to the message, forward it to someone else, store it for later action, or delete it. Usually, e-mail arrives at the destination server in a few seconds, but it's stored on the server until the recipient

logs on and downloads the message. In addition to sending text messages, you can include attachments such as a word processing document or a photo.

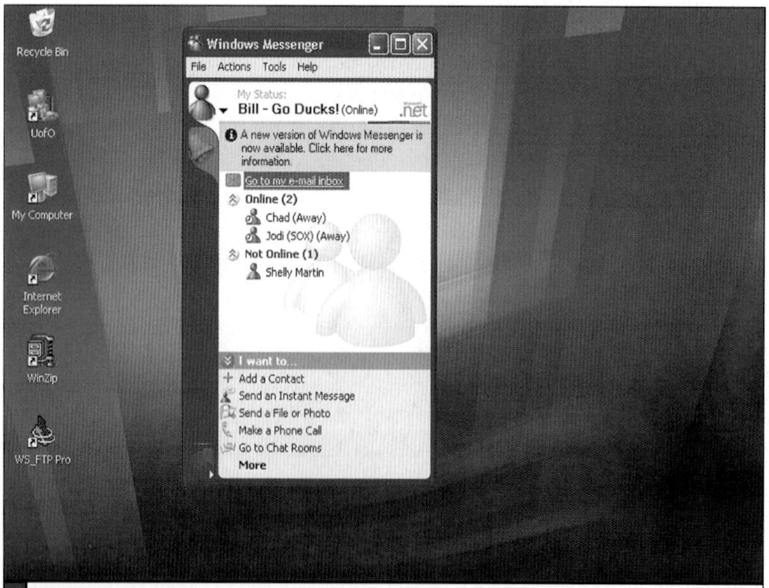

## INSTANT MESSAGING: E-MAILING MADE FASTER

What's faster than e-mail and more convenient than picking up the phone? **Instant messaging (IM) systems** alert you when someone you know who also uses the IM system (a buddy or contact) is online. You can then contact this person and exchange messages and attachments, including sound files.

To use IM, you need to install instant messenger software from an instant messenger service, such as AOL's Instant Messenger or Microsoft's Windows Messenger, onto your computer (Figure 7.21). You can use IM systems on any type of computer, including handhelds. Many instant messenger services also give you access to information such as daily news, stock prices, sports scores, and the weather. You can also keep track of your appointments. At this time, there is no standard instant messaging protocol, which means that you can send messages only to people who are using the same instant messaging service you are.

An increasing number of businesses and institutions are trying out instant messaging services, with mixed results. On the one hand, IM is a novel and convenient way to communicate. But on the other hand, voice communication is faster and richer. Until we can type faster than we can speak, and until we can include timing, inflection, and feeling in the typed word, phone and face-to-face communication will continue to be best.

## IRC: TEXT CHATTING IN REAL TIME

**Internet Relay Chat (IRC)** is an Internet service that enables you to join chat groups, called **channels**, and get into real-time, text-based conversations. IRC servers typically make thousands of channels available; some cover a specific topic, whereas others are gathering places for groups of friends.

**FIGURE 7.21** An IM system alerts you when someone you know who also uses the IM system is online. You can then contact this person and exchange messages.

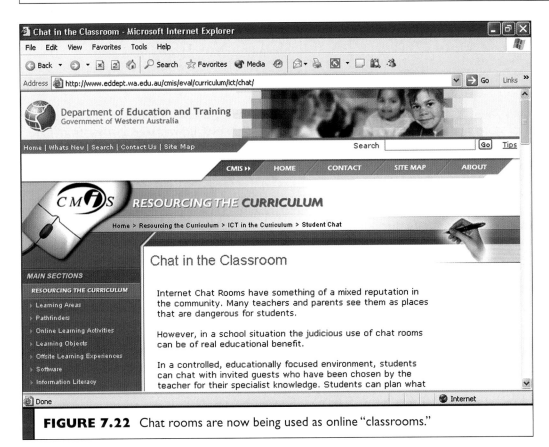

**FIGURE 7.22** Chat rooms are now being used as online "classrooms."

**Destinations**

To get started with IRC, visit the IRChelp.org Help Archive at **www.irchelp.org**. You'll find lots of information devoted to making your IRC experience a rewarding one.

When you join a channel, you'll find that others are already there, chatting away, with their messages appearing on-screen (Figure 7.22). Each message is prefaced with the participant's nickname. Sometimes IRC participants will send a special type of message, called an action, which describes a behavior (such as, "Walker shakes your hand"). Normally, your messages are seen by everyone in the channel, but it's possible to send a whisper, which is seen only by the one person to whom you send it.

Sometimes IRC isn't a friendly place. You may encounter various sorts of antisocial behaviors, including **flooding** (sending repeated messages so that no one else can get a word in edgewise) and **nuking** (exploiting bugs that cause your computer to crash). Bear in mind, too, that some of the "people" in channels aren't people at all, but rather miniprograms called **bots**. Bots are illegal on some servers, but on others they're used to greet newcomers (and sometimes to harass them). Also, every channel has a channel operator who can kick you out of the channel for any reason, or none at all.

## FTP: TRANSFERRING FILES

**FTP (File Transfer Protocol)** provides a way to transfer files via the Internet. With an FTP client, you can transfer files from an FTP server's file directories in an operation called **downloading**. In **uploading**, you transfer files *to* the server and write them to a directory on the remote computer. FTP can transfer two types of files: ASCII (text files) and binary (program files, graphics, or documents saved in proprietary file formats).

To use FTP, you need a user name and a password. An exception is called anonymous FTP. In **anonymous FTP**, files are made publicly available for downloading. It's called anonymous FTP because you log on by typing the word *anonymous* instead of a user name, and you supply your e-mail address as your password. The leading Web browsers, Microsoft Internet Explorer and Netscape Navigator, support file downloading from anonymous FTP sites, so you don't need any special skills to use anonymous FTP. Downloadable files are listed as hyperlinks; when you click such a hyperlink, downloading begins automatically.

# What's Hiding on Your Computer?
# Spyware, Adware, and Pop-Ups

**IMPACTS**

**Privacy**

You're probably already familiar with the dangers of viruses, those insidious files that can damage your computer system. You've probably also heard of cookies, electronic files that are deposited on your hard disk when you visit certain Web sites. But do you know what else may be hiding on your computer?

Spyware is Internet software that is placed on your computer without your knowing it. It helps outside organizations gather information about you (such as your login name and password) and then relays that information to the spyware source. Spyware usually enters your system through the Internet, often when you download software—most often shareware and freeware. Spyware may be launched by individuals, organizations, or the government. Some spyware is capable of recording every keystroke you type and every Internet address you visit. Spyware isn't necessarily always concerned with clandestine activity, but it's always a threat to your privacy.

If you've ever downloaded software and seen a banner advertisement or pop-up, you've also downloaded a form of adware. Adware is like spyware, only it's created specifically by an advertising agency to collect information about your Internet habits. Although ethically questionable, shareware and freeware creators sometimes allow advertisers to tag along and have their adware downloaded onto your computer at the same time you download software.

Spyware and adware are so commonplace that if you've ever downloaded anything from the Internet, you probably have some form of spyware or adware hiding on your computer.

How can you get rid of spyware and adware? One company, Lavasoft (**www.lavasoftusa.com**), offers a free spyware removal utility called Ad-aware that scans your memory, registry, and hard drives for known spyware and eliminates it safely. Because new spyware is created all the time, you should use the utility frequently to scan your system.

And if you hate pop-ups, an Internet privacy company called Panicware (**www.panicware.com**) has a Pop-Up Stopper program that can take care of these annoyances for you. The program lets you adjust the intensity of the pop-up stopping. (Be warned, however: if you download the Pop-Up Stopper but need to use pop-up utilities for online quizzes, for example, the utility can keep such pop-ups from functioning properly.) Both Pop-Up Stopper and Ad-aware have free download versions, but advanced versions, with more options, can be purchased for a small fee.

Knowing that these privacy intrusions exist, and that there is something you can do about them, is an important defense. As you make your way through the Net, know that there are people watching you, and consider taking proactive steps to protect your privacy.

---

Exercise caution when downloading executable program files and data files of unknown origin from the Web. If you download software from a site that doesn't inspect files using up-to-date virus-checking software, you could infect your computer with a virus. Most Internet users believe that it's safe to download software from vendor sites (Web sites maintained by software companies) and from leading shareware sites. However, you shouldn't download software to any computer that contains vital data. Also, be aware that many viruses are spread in the data files of productivity programs, such as Microsoft Word or Excel. These files may contain destructive viruses masquerading as **macros**, miniprograms that automatically carry out a series of

program commands. If you download data files, be sure to check them with an antivirus program that can detect macro viruses.

Most downloadable software is compressed. In **file compression**, lengthy data patterns are replaced with a short code, enabling compression software to reduce the size of program files by 50 percent or more. Compression enables faster downloads, but you must decompress a file after downloading it. In decompression, the compression software finds the short codes and replaces them with the longer data patterns. After decompressing the downloaded software, you can install it on your computer.

Some compressed files are designed to decompress automatically when you

**FIGURE 7.23** Compression Software

| Extension | Compression Software Needed |
|-----------|-----------------------------|
| .exe | None; this file is designed to decompress itself automatically |
| .zip | WinZip (**www.winzip.com**) or ZipIt (**www.maczipit.com**) |
| .sit | StuffIt Expander |
| .hqx | StuffIt Expander (BinHex encoding) |

launch them; others require you to obtain and install decompression software. On Windows systems, the most widely used decompression software is WinZip (**www.winzip.com**). To survive the trip over the Internet, Macintosh software is encoded using BinHex and may also be compressed with a compression program called StuffIt. You can determine how a file was compressed by looking at the file's extension (Figure 7.23).

You can easily download publicly accessible files by using a Web browser, but in some cases, you'll need an FTP client to upload files. If you'd like to publish your own Web pages, you'll need to use FTP to upload your pages to your ISP's Web publishing directories so that your pages are available to other Internet users. The best FTP clients enable you to work with remote file directories as if those directories were on your own computer.

## USENET: JOINING ONLINE DISCUSSIONS

**Usenet** is a discussion system accessible through the Internet. It consists of thousands of topically named **newsgroups**, discussion groups devoted to a single topic. Each newsgroup contains articles that users have posted for all to see. Users can respond to specific articles by posting follow-up articles, and in time, a thread of discussion develops as people reply to the replies. A **thread** is a series of articles that offer a continuing commentary on the same general subject.

To access Usenet, you use a Usenet client that communicates with a Usenet server (also called an NNTP server). Usenet client software comes with most browser suites. To begin using your Usenet client, you download the entire list of newsgroups available on your ISP's server. Then you subscribe to the newsgroups you want to follow. When you open the newsgroup, your client downloads the current article list, which may contain anywhere from a few dozen to several thousand messages.

Usenet newsgroups are organized into categories called **hierarchies**. These categories are further divided into several subcategories (also called hierarchies, if they include more than one newsgroup). These categories include the standard newsgroups, the alt newsgroups, and the biz newsgroups, each of which include many levels of subcategories and hundreds of newsgroups.

- **Standard newsgroups** You're most likely to find rewarding, high-quality discussions in the standard newsgroups (also called world newsgroups), which can't be established without a formal voting procedure. Figure 7.24 lists the standard newsgroup hierarchies. Usenet servers are expected to carry all these standard newsgroups, with the exception of those in the talk hierarchy.

- **Alt newsgroups** The alt hierarchy is much more freewheeling. Anyone with the requisite technical knowledge can create an alt newsgroup (which explains why so many of them have silly or offensive names), but servers aren't under any obligation to make them available.

- **Biz newsgroups** These newsgroups are devoted to the commercial uses of the Internet.

In addition to the standard and alt newsgroups, most servers carry many local newsgroups, which are created to suit the needs of a specific community, such as a

## Destinations

Learn the rules of netiquette by visiting "Dear Emily Postnews," the authoritative voice concerning Usenet manners, at **www.templetons .com/brad/emily .html**.

To learn more about Internet telephony, view the video clip on phoning a friend online at **www.prenhall.com/ cayf2005**.

### FIGURE 7.24 Standard Newsgroup Hierarchies

| Hierarchy Name | Description of Topics Covered |
|---|---|
| comp | Everything related to computers and computer networks, including applications, compression, databases, multimedia, and programming |
| misc | Subjects that do not fit in other standard newsgroup hierarchies, including activism, books, business, consumer issues, health, investing, jobs, and law |
| sci | The sciences and social sciences, including anthropology, archaeology, chemistry, economics, math, physics, and statistics |
| soc | Social issues, including adoption, college-related issues, feminism, human rights, and world cultures |
| talk | Debate on controversial subjects, including abortion, atheism, euthanasia, gun control, and religion |
| news | Usenet itself, including announcements and materials for new users |
| rec | All aspects of recreation, including aviation, backcountry sports, bicycles, boats, gardening, and scouting |

university. Some of these are of interest outside their context, as well; for example, Symantec Corporation, a major software vendor, maintains the Symantec hierarchy. Technical support engineers monitor the groups and offer solutions to problems users encounter with Symantec products.

If you're sure you understand a newsgroup's mission, you can use your Usenet client to post your own messages. But be careful what you say on Usenet. When you post an article, you're publishing in a public medium. Although most Usenet servers erase messages more than a few days old, several Internet services store Usenet messages in Web-accessible archives.

Also, be aware that you'll be expected to follow the rules of **netiquette**, guidelines for good manners when you're communicating through Usenet (or any Internet service). For example, some Usenet clients enable you to post messages using formatting, but this is considered bad manners because people who have text-only clients see a lot of meaningless formatting symbols. If you violate netiquette rules, you may receive **flames** (angry, critical messages) from other newsgroup subscribers.

## LISTSERV: ELECTRONIC MAILING LISTS

A **listserv** manages electronic mailing lists of e-mail addresses. Eric Thomas developed the program in 1986 for BITNET. Similar in many ways to newsgroups and forums, a listserv automatically broadcasts messages to all individuals on a mailing list. However, since the listserv messages are transmitted as e-mail, only individuals who are subscribers to the mailing list can view the messages. Most colleges and universities manage listservs. The most common listserv program is called Majordomo, which is distributed as freeware.

## INTERNET TELEPHONY: REAL-TIME VOICE AND VIDEO

**Internet telephony** is the use of the Internet for real-time voice communication. Although the Internet isn't ideal for real-time voice and video, you can place calls via the Internet in a variety of ways. To place free long-distance calls, you'll need a computer equipped with a microphone, speakers, an Internet connection, and a telephony-enabled program such as Microsoft's NetMeeting. Your calls are limited to people using similarly equipped computers—and they need to be online.

If you and the person you're calling have a digital video camera, you can converse with real-time videoconferencing as well. Don't expect spectacular quality; you'll hear echoes and delays in the audio, and the picture will be small, grainy, and jerky. But there are no long-distance charges! You can try Internet telephony by using the clients supplied with the two most popular browsers.

In addition to Internet voice and video calls, Internet telephony products support real-time conferencing with such features as a shared whiteboard (a space where callers can draw simple graphics or share pictures), file exchange, and text chatting. Current technology doesn't enable you to videoconference with more than one caller at a time, but you can create an audio conference with as many users as you want (Figure 7.25).

Until home users can obtain faster Internet connections, Internet telephony and videoconferencing will prove most useful on corporate intranets, where bandwidth is in ample supply.

What about placing a call to an ordinary telephone? You can't do it for free. However, **Internet telephony service providers** (**ITSPs**) such as Net2Phone are stepping into the act by offering computer-to-phone and phone-to-phone services that use the Internet for long-distance transmission (Figure 7.26). Rates are cheap, but the quality isn't always what subscribers expect.

Still, the basic idea of Internet telephony has an enormous advantage: because the Internet doesn't rely on switches to route messages, it's cheaper to operate. Providers can route dozens, hundreds, or even thousands of calls over the same circuit.

According to one estimate, routing data over a switched network costs more than three times as much as sending the same data over a switch-free computer network such as the Internet. New technologies, such as advanced compression, are making Internet telephony sound better, but you'll still run into delays when you're calling over the public Internet.

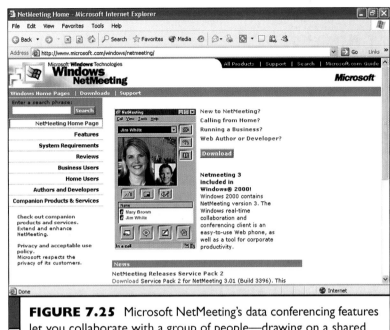

**FIGURE 7.25** Microsoft NetMeeting's data conferencing features let you collaborate with a group of people—drawing on a shared whiteboard, sending text messages, and transferring data.

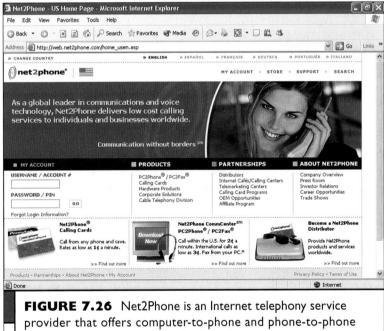

**FIGURE 7.26** Net2Phone is an Internet telephony service provider that offers computer-to-phone and phone-to-phone services that use the Internet for long-distance transmission.

## INTERNET FAXING

If the Internet isn't perfect for voice calls, it has none of those shortcomings for faxes. Faxes don't have to be delivered in real time, like voice does, so slight service delays don't cause a problem.

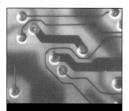

## Techtalk

**clickstream**
As you spend time on the Web, you leave a clickstream in your wake. A clickstream is a trail of Web links that you have followed to get to a particular site. Internet merchants are quite interested in analyzing clickstream activity so they can do a better job of targeting advertisements and tailoring Web pages to your liking.

## Destinations

Using the Web to research a paper? Visit "A Student's Guide to Research with the WWW," created by Craig Branham of St. Louis University, at **www.slu.edu/ departments/ english/research**.

How does Internet faxing work? You need an Internet connection and an account with an Internet fax service provider. From a fax machine or computer, you send the fax through the Internet to the fax service provider, which then automatically routes the fax through the Internet to a local telephone near your fax's destination. The service isn't free, but it's 25 to 50 percent cheaper than sending the fax through the phone system.

Now that you're familiar with some of the Internet's most useful services, let's examine how to conduct research on the Web.

# Finding Information on the Web

Although browsing by means of hyperlinks is easy and fun, it falls short as a means of information research. Web users soon find themselves clicking link after link,

searching for information that they never find. If you can't find the information you're looking for after a bit of browsing, try *searching* the Web. You've no doubt heard of search tools such as Google, Yahoo!, AltaVista, and Lycos. Although these and other Web search tools are far from perfect, knowledge of their proper use (and their limitations) can greatly increase your chances of finding the information you want.

Most search services offer a **subject guide** to the Web, grouping Web pages under such headings as business, news, or travel. These services don't try to include every Web page in the subject categories. Instead, they offer a selection of high-quality pages that they believe represent some of the more useful Web pages in a given category. If you're just beginning your search for information, a subject guide is an excellent place to start.

## USING SEARCH ENGINES

If you can't find what you're looking for in a Web subject guide, you can try searching

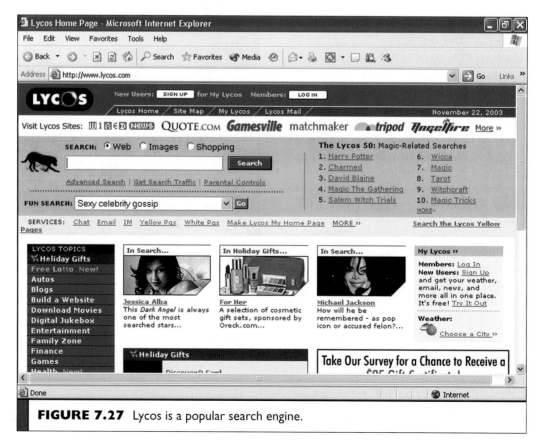

**FIGURE 7.27** Lycos is a popular search engine.

databases that claim to index the full Web. Called **search engines**, these services don't actually maintain databases of every Web page in existence, but the leading ones are known to have indexed about one-third of them (Figure 7.27). That's an enormous pool of information, and chances are that by using these services, you'll find information relevant to the subject you're looking for.

To use a search engine, type one or more words that describe the subject you're looking for. Generally, it's a good idea to type several words (four or five) rather than one or two; most Web searches produce far more results than you can use.

Why do search engines sometimes produce unsatisfactory results? The problem lies in the ambiguity of the English language. Suppose you're searching for information on the Great Wall of China. You'll find some information on the ancient Chinese defensive installation, but you may also get the menu of the Great Wall of China, a Chinese restaurant, information on the Great Wall hotel in Beijing, and the lyrics of a song titled "Great Wall of China" by Billy Joel.

Although you can improve search effectiveness by learning the search techniques we'll discuss later in the chapter, Web searches will continue to be hampered because there remains no framework to describe the content of documents. If such a framework existed, Web authors could describe their documents using such terms as *historical* or *commercial*. Searches would be much more effective because you could specify the *type* of document you want, not just the content it should contain. Several proposals for such frameworks have been made, but no standard exists yet.

### Specialized Search Engines

Full Web search engines generally don't index specialized information such as names and addresses, job advertisements, quotations, and newspaper articles. To find such information, you need to access **specialized search engines**. Examples of such specialized search engines include CareerBuilder.com, a database of over 400,000 jobs, and Infoplease.com, which contains the full text of an encyclopedia and an almanac (Figure 7.28).

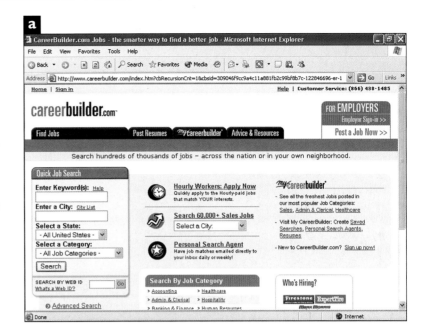

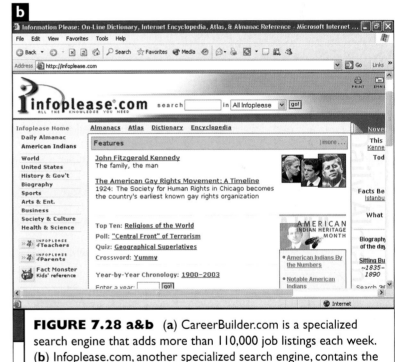

**FIGURE 7.28 a&b** **(a)** CareerBuilder.com is a specialized search engine that adds more than 110,000 job listings each week. **(b)** Infoplease.com, another specialized search engine, contains the full text of an encyclopedia and an almanac.

## USING SEARCH TECHNIQUES

By learning a few search techniques, you can greatly increase the accuracy of your Web searches. One problem with Web search services is that each uses its own unique set of **search operators**, symbols or words that you can use for advanced searches. A trend toward standardization, however, means that some or all of the following

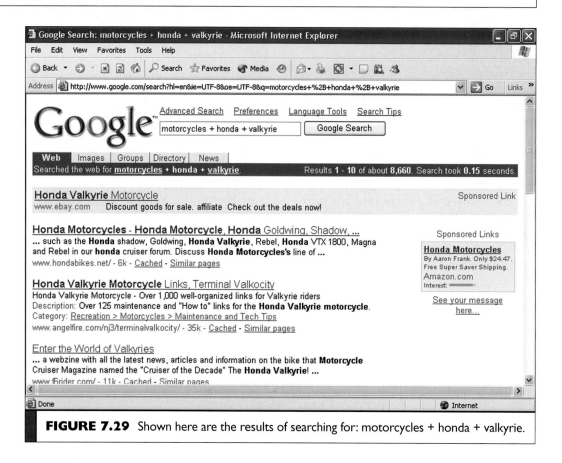

**FIGURE 7.29** Shown here are the results of searching for: motorcycles + honda + valkyrie.

## Destinations

The leading search engines include Google (**www.google.com**), HotBot (**www. hotbot.lycos.com**), AltaVista (**www.altavista. digital.com**), GoTo.com (**www.overture. com**), Excite (**www.excite.com**), and Go.com (**www.go.com**). Most of these also offer subject guides.

techniques will work with most search services. To find out which ones you can use with a given search service, look for a link to a page explaining search options.

### Inclusion and Exclusion

In many search engines, you can improve search performance by specifying an **inclusion operator**, which is generally a plus (+) sign (Figure 7.29). This operator states that you don't want a page retrieved unless it contains the specified word. By listing several key terms with this search operator, you can exclude many pages that don't contain one or more of the essential terms. The following, for example, will retrieve only those pages that contain all three of the words mentioned:

**+kittens +care +Siamese**

If the list of retrieved documents contains many items that you don't want, you can use the **exclusion operator**, which is generally a minus (−) sign. For example, the preceding search retrieves many classified ads for Siamese kittens. You can exclude

them by prefacing the term *classified* with the exclusion operator, as follows:

**+kittens +care +Siamese −classified**

### Wildcards

Many search engines enable you to use **wildcards** (symbols such as ? and * that take the place of one or more characters in the position in which they are used). Wildcards help you improve the accuracy of your searches. In the preceding example, many unwanted pages contain the word *classifieds* and aren't excluded by the singular *classified*. The following example using the asterisk wildcard excludes any document containing the words *classified* or *classifieds*:

**−classified***

### Phrase Searches

Another way to improve the accuracy of your searches involves **phrase searching**, which is generally performed by typing a phrase within quotation marks. This tells the search engine to retrieve only those documents that contain the exact phrase (rather than some or all of the words anywhere in the document).

### Boolean Searches
Some search engines enable you to perform Boolean searches. **Boolean searches** use keywords (AND, OR, and NOT) to link the words you're searching for. By using Boolean operators, you can gain more precise control over your searches. Let's look at a few examples.

### The AND, OR, and NOT Operators
When used to link two search words, the AND operator tells the search service to return only those documents that contain both words (just as the plus sign does). For example, the search phrase "Jamaica AND geography" returns only those documents that contain both terms. You can use the AND operator to narrow your search so that it retrieves fewer documents.

If your search retrieves too few documents, try the OR operator. For example, the search phrase "pottery OR ceramics" retrieves documents that contain either or both of these words. (Most search engines will return both without the OR operator.)

To exclude unwanted documents, use the NOT operator. This operator tells the search engine to omit any documents containing the word preceded by NOT (just as the minus sign does). For example, the search phrase "kittens NOT cats" retrieves pages that mention kittens, but not those that mention cats.

**Using Parentheses**  Many search engines that support Boolean operators enable you to use parentheses to nest Boolean expressions. When you **nest** an expression, the search engine evaluates the expression from left to right, and the material within parentheses is resolved first. Such expressions enable you to conduct a search with unmatched accuracy. Consider this example:

**(growth OR increase OR development) NEAR (Internet or Web)**

This search retrieves any document that mentions the words *growth, increase,* or *development* within a few words of *Internet* or *Web*.

## EVALUATING THE INFORMATION YOU'VE FOUND

After you've found information on the Web, you'll need to evaluate it critically. Anyone can publish information on the Web; Web pages are not subjected to the fact-checking standards found in newspapers or magazines, let alone the peer review process that safeguards the quality of scholarly and scientific publications. Although you can find excellent and reliable information on the Web, you can also find pages that are biased and self-serving.

### Rules for Critically Evaluating Web Pages
As you're evaluating a Web page, carefully note the following:

- Who is the author of this page? Is the author affiliated with a recognized institution, such as a university or a well-known company? Is there any evidence that the author is qualified with respect to this topic? A page that isn't signed may signal an attempt to disguise the author's lack of qualifications.

- Does the author cite his or her sources? If so, do they appear to be from recognized and respected publications?

- Who provides the server for publishing this Web page? Who pays for this page?

- Does the presentation seem balanced and objective, or is it one-sided?

- Is the language objective and dispassionate, or is it strident and argumentative?

- What is the purpose of this page? Is the author trying to sell something or push a biased idea? Who would profit if this page's information were accepted?

- Does the information appear to be accurate? Is the page free of sweeping generalizations or other signs of shoddy thinking? Do you see many misspellings or grammatical errors

### Destinations

If you're using Web sources in a college paper, you'll need to cite your sources. "A Style Sheet for Citing Internet Resources: MLA Style," located at **www.lib.berkeley. edu/TeachingLib/ Guides/Internet/ Style.html,** shows how to cite Internet sources using the Modern Language Association style, which is widely used in the humanities. For the American Psychological Association citation style for Internet sources, see "The Columbia Guide to Online Style: APA-Style Citations of Electronic Sources," located at **www.columbia.edu/ cu/cup/cgos/ idx_basic.html.**

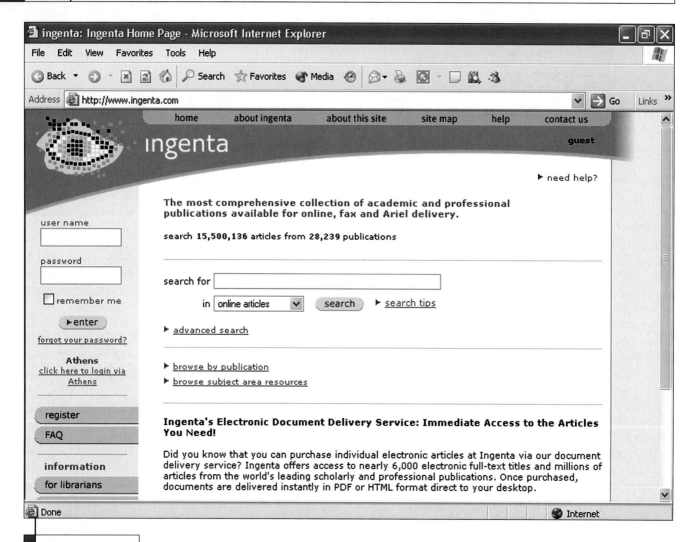

that would indicate poor educational background?

- Is this page up-to-date? When was it last maintained?

### Locating Material in Published Works

Remember that the Web is only one of several sources you can and should use for research. Your best sources of information are respected publications, which you'll likely find in the library. You can use the Internet, however, to locate publications, then obtain them in your college's library. Check your library's home page to find out what Internet services are available. Also, visit Ingenta (**www.ingenta.com**), a free database service that enables you to search for high-quality articles from more than 25,000 published magazines and journals (Figure 7.30). After you search, you'll see

article lists and titles. You can then obtain the source in the library or online.

### Authoritative Sources Online

Some respected magazines and journals have established Web sites that enable you to search back issues, giving you the best of both worlds: the power and convenience of the Internet, plus material that's more reliable than the average Web page. The following respected publications provide a valuable public service by providing free access to their back issue archives:

- *Christian Science Monitor* (**www.csmonitorarchive.com**)

- *Time* magazine (**www.time.com/time/magazine/archives**)

- *Scientific American* (**www.sciam.com**)

# Summary
# THE INTERNET AND WORLD WIDE WEB

- The Internet is the network that connects hundreds of thousands of local area networks (LANs), creating a global medium in which millions of computers can directly dial each other and share resources. It began as a project of the United States Defense Department and evolved into a vast communications channel that is still growing today.

- The World Wide Web is a global hypertext system that contains billions of documents and uses the Internet as its transport mechanism. Millions of users turn to the Web to research current events, general information, product information, scientific developments, and much more.

- In hypertext, related information is referenced by means of links instead of being fully explained or defined in the same location. On the Web, authors can link to information created by others.

- A Web browser is a program that displays a Web document and enables you to access linked documents. A Web server is a computer that retrieves documents requested by browsers.

- A URL consists of the protocol (such as http://), the server (such as www), the path (such as /windows /ie), and the resource name (such as default.htm). URLs enable Web authors

- to state the exact location of a resource available on the Internet.

- An Internet address (IP address) is a four-part number that uniquely identifies one of the millions of computers connected to the Internet. A domain name is an easy-to-type and easy-to-remember equivalent of the numerical address.

- Popular Internet services include e-mail, instant messaging (communication), FTP (file exchange), Usenet, listserv, Internet Relay Chat (text chatting), Internet telephony (phone calls through the Internet and videoconferencing), and Internet faxing (document exchange).

- Web subject guides index a limited number of high-quality pages, whereas full Web search engines enable you to search huge databases of Web documents.

- Most Web searches retrieve too many irrelevant documents. You can improve search results by using inclusion and exclusion operators, phrase searches, and Boolean operators.

- Anyone can publish anything on the Web. Don't accept any information you find until you have critically evaluated the author's credentials and purpose for publishing the page.

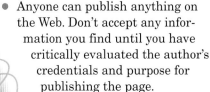
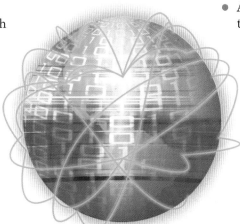

# Key Terms and Concepts

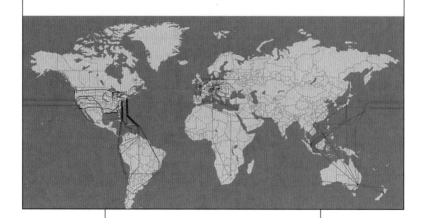

:: AT&T GLOBAL IP BACKBONE NETWORK

Go to **www.prenhall.com/cayf2005** to review this chapter, answer the questions, and complete the exercises.

# Matching

Match each key term in the left column with the most accurate definition in the right column.

_____ 1. Internet

_____ 2. portal

_____ 3. network access point

_____ 4. Web browser

_____ 5. newsgroups

_____ 6. platform

_____ 7. hypertext

_____ 8. netiquette

_____ 9. World Wide Web

_____ 10. TCP/IP

_____ 11. Web server

_____ 12. Web site

_____ 13. Internet Relay Chat

_____ 14. Internet service

_____ 15. markup language

a. guidelines for good manners when you are communicating through Usenet or any Internet service

b. discussion groups devoted to a single topic

c. a global computer network with hundreds of millions of users worldwide

d. open protocols that define how the Internet works

e. a distinct type of computer that uses a certain type of processor and operating system

f. a gateway that provides a conveniently organized subject guide to Internet content and free e-mail

g. a set of standards that define how two types of programs can communicate with each other through the Internet

h. an Internet service that enables a user to join chat groups

i. a program that displays a Web document and enables you to access linked documents

j. where regional backbones connect to national backbone networks

k. uses the Internet for its existence but is a separate entity

l. a computer running software that accepts Web page requests

m. a set of codes that authors can use to identify portions of a document for a Web page

n. a collection of related Web pages

o. a way of presenting information so that its sequence is left up to the reader

# Multiple Choice

Circle the correct choice for each of the following.

1. Which of the following networks best describes the functional structure of the Internet?
   a. metropolitan area network (MAN)
   b. cross-platform network
   c. local area network (LAN)
   d. client/server network

2. Which of the following is a client program?
   a. hypertext
   b. ARPANET
   c. Internet address
   d. Web browser

3. You would use this type of Boolean operator to keep certain values out of the search results.
   a. inclusion
   b. exclusion
   c. *
   d. ?

4. Which of the following is an internal network, based on TCP/IP, that gives users the same familiar tools they use on the Internet?
   a. local area network (LAN)
   b. intranet
   c. extranet
   d. firewall

5. Which of the following alerts you when someone you know is online?
   a. client software
   b. Internet Explorer
   c. online services
   d. instant messaging systems

6. Which of the following provides the slowest Internet connection?
   a. dial-up access
   b. Digital Subscriber Line (DSL)
   c. cable access
   d. LAN

7. Links to documents that have disappeared are known as what?
   a. unknown links
   b. tenuous links
   c. hyperlinks
   d. dead links

8. What is the name of the system that is used to ensure that no two Internet addresses are the same?
   a. domain name
   b. TCP/IP
   c. unicode
   d. registry domain

9. When using a search engine, a minus sign is an example of what?
   a. an exclusion operator
   b. an addition operator
   c. a mathematical operator
   d. an inclusion operator

10. A complete URL does *not* contain which one of the following?
    a. protocol
    b. server
    c. path
    d. author

# Fill-In

In the blanks provided, write the correct answer for each of the following.

1. A(n) _____ is a string of characters that precisely identifies an Internet resource's type and location.

2. A(n) _____ is a gateway that provides a conveniently organized subject guide to Internet content.

3. _____ are internal networks that are based on the TCP/IP protocol.

4. _____ are networks that use the external Internet to allow selected users access to corporate intranets.

5. _____ provides a way for users to transfer files via the Internet.

6. _____ enables any Internet-connected computer to be uniquely identified.

7. A(n) _____ is a number comprising four parts separated by periods.

8. The _____ defines how one Internet-connected computer can contact another to exchange control and confirmation messages.

9. _____ enables individuals and organizations to register domain names with the InterNIC.

10. The Web is a(n) _____, where the responsibility for creating content is distributed among many people.

11. If you can't find what you are looking for using a Web subject guide, you can try a _____, a database that indexes many Web pages.

12. A browser's _____ records the Web pages that you've accessed.

13. _____ are underlined or highlighted words that you can click to bring another document into view.

14. _____ searches use key words such as AND, OR, and NOT.

15. When doing _____, you enclose a phrase within quotation marks.

# Short Answer

1. What is the difference between an Internet address and a domain name? Give examples to illustrate each of the terms.

2. Explain the difference between downloading and uploading files. Have you used the Internet to transfer files? What types of files did you transfer? What type of software did you use? Explain why it is dangerous to download executable (.exe) files.

3. Do you submit any of your assignments electronically? That is, have you submitted an assignment to a "drop box," in the body of an e-mail message, or as an e-mail attachment? If you have, describe the method, the assignment, and the course in which you used electronic submissions.

4. What is the difference between a Web server and a Web browser? What are some rules of thumb for evaluating content on the Web?

5. Now that you have completed this chapter, you should be able to conduct more effective searches. List three search engines that you use most frequently to find information on the Internet, and explain why you prefer these search engines over the others.

Go to **www.prenhall.com/cayf2005** to review this chapter, answer the questions, and complete the exercises.

# A Closer Look

1. Frequently, the IP addresses of an organization's Internet computers begin with the same several digits. For example, all the computers at Buffalo State College have an IP address of the form 136.183.xxx.xxx, and the last two sets of numbers usually denote the building and individual computers. Stop by your school's computing services and find out if your institution has a common set of IP addresses for its computers. If it does, what are the common digits? Now go to one of your school's Windows-based networked computers to determine its IP address. Go to Start, select Run…, in the Open textbox type "winipcfg," and click the OK button. What is the IP address of this computer? Does it begin with the common set of digits?

2. Although present Internet bandwidth does not support high-quality videoconferencing, it provides varying qualities of telephony. Besides computer-to-computer voice communication, you can also make computer-to-telephone connections. Visit the dialpad Internet site at **dialpad.com**. Sign up for the free calls, and make some local and long-distance calls. What was the quality of the phone conversations? What type of connection—modem, satellite, ISDN, xDSL, cable, or LAN—did you use? How does the speed of the connection affect the quality of the call?

3. Explain the difference between a browser's history list and Favorites (Internet Explorer) or Bookmarks (Netscape Navigator). Have you used either one?

Explain how you used them. Did you know that you can place very frequently visited Web sites in your Links Toolbar (Internet Explorer) or in your Personal Toolbar (Netscape Navigator)? Select one of these two browsers and explain how you can place links to Web sites in the appropriate toolbar. If you have never done this, use the browser's help feature to learn how.

4. Use the Internet to find two potential jobs in the field of your current or intended major. Give the URLs of the sites that list the positions, and describe each job—the organization, location, necessary qualifications, benefits, salary, and so on. Explain why you feel that your major coursework does or does not prepare you to assume either of these two positions.

5. As institutions begin to offer distance learning courses, student access to library materials becomes a critical issue. Since students may not be able to visit an institution's library physically, how will they read relevant materials? One method is to make full-text versions of books and periodicals available online. Visit your school's library (either physically or electronically) and determine whether it offers online reference materials. Does your library provide these materials directly, or does it use a third party to provide these services? Can you read the online materials from off-campus as well as on-campus? Are the materials accessible only to faculty and students? If so, how do they gain permission to view the materials?

# On the Web

1. Internet2, or I2, is a collaborative effort among educational institutions, government agencies, and computer and telecommunications companies to increase Internet bandwidth. Visit the I2 site at **www.internet2.edu**. Presently, how many university members are there? Does your school belong to I2? If not, locate and identify the nearest institution that does. What are the annual membership fees and estimated annual institutional costs to participate in I2? What are the annual membership fees and estimated annual corporate partnership costs to participate in I2? Name two corporate partners and two corporate sponsors. In addition to I2, the U.S. government also sponsors its own advanced Internet initiative. Identify this initiative and list two governmental agencies that participate in it and in I2.

2. Have you thought about getting your own domain name? What would you like it to be? Visit the site **register.com** and try different top-level domain names (.com, .net, .org, and so on) to see if they're available. If they are, what is the annual registration cost? If the domain names are already taken, who owns them, when did they acquire them, and when do they expire? What is the minimum bid amount that can be offered to purchase domain names? Visit the Web sites and describe their content.

3. Unlike conventional telephone service, which is available to almost any home, DSL service is limited by the distance from the central office (CO) or switching station to your home. Do you have DSL? Go to the DSL Reports at **www.cognigen.net/ speakeasy** to see if you qualify for this service. How far are you from the CO? Which, if any, of the xDSL services can you get? If you are able to get xDSL service, name at least one ISP that partners with the phone company to provide this service. What are the transfer rates, installation charges, and monthly fees? Based on the increased speed and increased cost, why would, or would you not, use DSL?

4. Suppose one of your instructors requires you to write a research paper for his or her class. Besides referencing printed sources found in books and periodicals, you can use the Internet to find information. However, before using Internet materials, you should critically evaluate them. Since citing Internet-based sources is not the same as citing traditional references, visit UC Berkeley's "Library style" site at **www.lib.berkeley. edu/TeachingLib/Guides/Internet/Style.html** to learn how to properly cite Internet and electronic resources. What are the three general content areas and corresponding style sheets discussed on this site? Although there are minor differences, what are the main components of citations for:

   - WWW sites?
   - e-mail messages?
   - online databases?

   Why do you think that the date the site was last accessed is always included? Have you already had an occasion to "cite a site" in a paper? If you have, list the title of your paper and the style you used.

5. Use the search techniques discussed in this chapter to locate two sites that sell research or term papers. Identify the URLs of these sites, how you find a specific topic, and the costs of purchasing a paper. Do these sites post any disclaimers about students using their papers? Do they provide sample writings? What is the quality of the paper? Do you know anyone who has purchased an online paper? Discuss the ethics of using one of these sites to purchase a research or term paper.

# Wired and Wireless Communication

## What You'll Learn . . .

- Explain the limitations of the public switched telephone network (PSTN) for sending and receiving computer data.

- Describe multiplexing and digital telephony, including their impact on line usage.

- Describe wireless transmission media and explain several transmission methods.

- Provide examples of how convergence is blurring the boundaries that distinguish popular communications devices, including phones, computers, and TVs.

- Provide an overview of home networking using wired and wireless communications applications.

- Discuss what a company should consider before investing in teleconferencing and videoconferencing technology.

- Describe telecommuting and workgroup computing.

Suppose you're on a trip and need to access your e-mail, but you don't have your laptop with you. No problem—you just use your Web-enabled cell phone to retrieve your messages. As for sending e-mail messages back: again, no problem—you can do this, too, with most messaging devices. Back at home, you hop on your ultrafast DSL connection to download and upload files. The whole time, you're experiencing the realities of **connectivity**. Defined broadly, this term refers to the ability to link various media and devices. Connectivity enhances communication and improves access to information. In Chapter 6, we discussed the various technologies involved in communications and networks, such as channels, physical media, and devices. In this chapter, we'll examine all of these pieces, whether they're wired (connected by a physical medium) or wireless (connected through the air or space).

# Wired Communication via the PSTN

Although you frequently use the telephone system to send and receive computer data, the analog service it offers isn't ideal for

**FIGURE 8.1** Most telephone lines provide an analog connection, based on standards that date back more than a century.

data communication. It's important to understand the phone system's limitations for this purpose.

Let's start with the beginning: the public switched telephone network (PSTN), derisively (and somewhat unfairly) called the Plain Old Telephone Service (POTS) by some computer users. The **public switched telephone network (PSTN)** is the world telephone system, a massive network used for data as well as voice communications, comprising various physical media such as twisted-pair wire and fiber-optic cable. The derision comes from the fact that most analog telephone lines are based on standards that date back more than a century (Figure 8.1). As you'll see, though, it's not true that the PSTN is an entirely analog network. In this section, you'll learn enough about how the PSTN works to realize that it's on the verge of becoming a truly digital network, which will mean positive changes for data communications.

Any discussion of the PSTN should begin with praise for its accomplishments. Today's PSTN uses advanced switching technology to create an end-to-end circuit between *any* two telephones in the world. What's amazing about this system is the number of telephones that can be directly and almost instantly connected; nearly a half a billion telephones are connected to the global telephone system today, and most are accessible by means of direct dialing (Figure 8.2). In the United States alone, nearly a billion telephone calls are made *every day*. Despite infrequent service outages, the PSTN is able to pull off these feats with a guaranteed **quality of service (QoS)**: when you need to make a call, you can, and the audio quality is good.

Most home and business telephones in use today are analog devices, which transmit and receive a continuously changing electrical signal that matches the acoustics of the human voice. These telephones are linked to subscriber loop carriers (SLCs) by means of twisted-pair wires. A **subscriber loop carrier (SLC)** is a small, waist-high curbside installation that connects as many as 96 subscribers; you've probably seen one in your neighborhood. The area served by an SLC is called the **local loop**.

From the SLC on, though, the PSTN is increasingly a digital network. The SLC

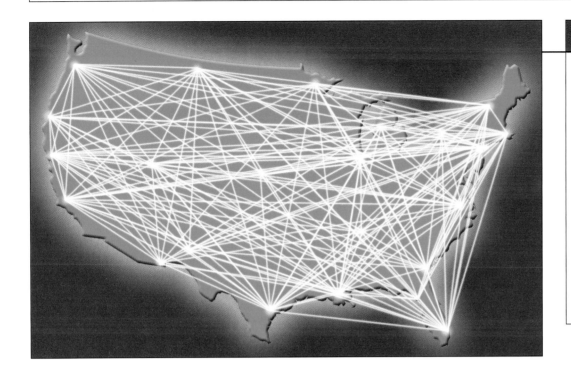

**FIGURE 8.2**
Nearly half a billion telephones are connected to the global telephone system today, and most are accessible by means of direct dialing. In the United States alone, nearly a billion telephone calls are made every day.

transforms local analog calls into digital signals, routing them through high-capacity, fiber-optic cables to the **local exchange switch**, which is also based on digital technology capable of handling thousands of calls. The local exchange switch is located in the local telephone company's central office. From the local phone company's central office, the call can go anywhere in the world. It continues on the digital portion of the PSTN's fiber-optic cables and can even be converted to radio waves and sent out over cellular networks.

Although analog connections are still common, this situation is changing as more and more new digital telephone services become available. **Digital telephony** uses all-digital protocols: the telephones are digital, and the transmission is all handled digitally. As was mentioned earlier, most of the phones in the local loop are analog devices, prone to noise and interference. Digital phones, however, offer noise-free transmission and high-quality audio. You've probably already used a digital phone: large organizations, such as corporations and universities, typically install their own internal digital telephone systems, called private branch exchanges (PBXs). By using a PBX, an organization avoids the high cost of paying for a line to the local telephone company's exchange switch for each employee. Calls to the outside

must be translated into analog signals to connect to the PSTN.

Because long-distance lines must handle thousands of calls simultaneously, techniques called **multiplexing** have been developed to send more than one call on a single line. The electrical and physical characteristics of copper wire impose a limit of 24 multiplexed calls per wire, but fiber-optic cables can carry as many as 48,384 digital voice channels simultaneously. In contrast to the analog local loop, most long-distance carriers use digital signals so that they can pack the greatest number of calls in a single circuit.

The inability of homes or businesses to access the PSTN's high-speed fiber-optic cables, along with the bottleneck of data on the "last mile" of twisted-pair phone lines connecting homes and businesses, is often referred to as the **last-mile problem**. Here's why: In most areas of the United States, only the local loop is still stuck with analog technology, due largely to the fact that nearly all existing buildings were originally constructed with built-in twisted-pair wiring. These analog connections are vulnerable to line noise and can't surpass a theoretical limit of 56 Kbps for analog services on twisted pair. In order for the local loop to change over to digital lines, all of this wiring would have to be redone—an expense that is simply too

**Destinations**

To learn more about the PSTN and new telecommunications technologies, a great place to start is HelloDirect.com's "Get Informed" tutorials at **telecom.hello-direct.com/docs/ Tutorials/ default.asp**.

# Universal Service:
# No More Access for Everyone?

**CURRENTS**

**Changing Times**

It's called universal service—and thanks to the rise of Internet telephony, it may very well be coming to an end. An outgrowth of Depression-era New Deal legislation, universal service has long been a cornerstone of U.S. telecommunications policy.

In the telecommunications industry, universal service ensures that people in all parts of the country have equal access to "reasonably priced" telephone services (Figure 8.3). But there's just one problem: it's much more expensive to provide telephone service in lightly populated rural areas, where wires must be strung dozens or hundreds of miles to serve just a few houses. To pay for local phone service in remote areas, long-distance companies collect surcharges from their customers and kick back most of these surcharges to local telephone companies in the form of access fees. In turn, the local telephone companies use these fees to hold down the cost of residential telephone services.

But all that's changing. Thanks to the U.S. Telecommunications Act of 1996, competitive access providers (CAPs) can sell direct access to the long-distance market without paying access fees—and that's one of the reasons Internet telephony is booming. Internet telephony service providers (ITSPs) such as Net2Phone

don't pay access fees. According to conventional long-distance providers, that isn't fair. Long-distance, regional, and local telephone companies want the U.S. Congress to hit ITSPs with access fee charges—or abandon the idea of universal service altogether.

The 1996 Telecommunications Act does give telephone companies a break; the legislation calls for gradual reductions in access fees until they're completely eliminated. But it doesn't let consumers off the hook; universal service must still be paid for, somehow, and the Telecommunications Act extended the concept of universal service to digital-based services such as the Internet. For now, consumers are taking the hit, as you'll discover if you examine your next phone bill: there's a welter of incomprehensibly named taxes, such as the Presubscribed Interexchange Carrier Charge, the Federal Access Charge, the FCC line charge, state-imposed Universal Service charges, and—chances are—several more. The various taxes and fees can add up to 60 percent to the cost of your monthly phone bill.

At least there's one tax you won't be paying any more. In 2000, the U.S. Congress voted to terminate the Federal Excise Tax on telephone service—a tax that was initially created in 1898 to pay for the Spanish–American War.

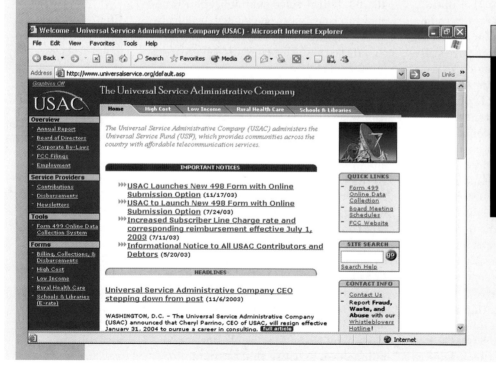

**FIGURE 8.3** The Universal Service Administrative Company is a nonprofit organization dedicated to providing underserved regions of the United States with access to affordable telecommunications.

great. The cost to replace all the twisted pair that currently delivers phone service to homes and offices worldwide would be upwards of $325 billion. That's not going to happen anytime soon. So in the meantime, computer users who desire high-speed data communications can consider a number of "last-mile" technologies as well as wireless options.

## LAST-MILE TECHNOLOGIES

Because the last mile of twisted-pair wiring in the local loop will be with us for many years, phone companies and other telecommunications providers offer a number of interim digital telephony technologies that make use of twisted-pair wiring. Sometimes called **last-mile technologies**, these solutions include digital telephone standards (such as ISDN and DSL, discussed in Chapters 6 and 7) that can use twisted-pair wiring, as well as "always on" high-speed wired services (such as coaxial cable and cable modems).

In addition to adapting twisted-pair wiring and broadband coaxial cable, wireless technologies are helping to solve the last-mile problem as well. Here's a look at two wireless solutions.

Multichannel Multipoint Distribution Service or Multipoint Microwave Distribution System (MMDS) can be thought of as wireless cable. MMDS was originally slated as a wireless alternative to cable television, but now its main application is Internet access. Service providers offer MMDS Internet access within a 35-mile radius at projected speeds of 1 Gbps, about 1,000 times faster than DSL, cable, and satellite. The Federal Communications Commission (FCC) holds exclusive licenses for the frequencies on which MMDS operates. Typically, the FCC allows commercial access to these frequencies, but not in the case of MMDS channels.

In many rural areas where installing new coaxial or fiber-optic cable may be inconvenient or expensive, Local Multipoint Distribution Service (LMDS) is a possible solution. This fixed wireless technology delivers high-bandwidth services on the "last mile" connecting homes and businesses. One LMDS node can supply phone and data services for up to 80,000 customers in a two- to three-mile radius. LMDS can transfer data

at rates of 1.5 to 2 Gbps, but data transfer rates typically average around 38 Mbps.

In mountainous areas or other places where there are obstructions, MMDS and LMDS don't work well because they are line-of-sight technologies. Line of sight means the transmitting and receiving devices have a clear path between them. Other wireless technologies that dispense with the local loop entirely are discussed in the following section.

# Wireless Transmission Media

Unlike networks with wired physical media such as twisted-pair, coaxial, and fiber-optic cable, networks that utilize wireless media don't use solid substances to carry data but do so through the air or space, using infrared, radio (broadcast or cellular), or microwave signals. Why would you want to use wireless media instead of cables? One instance would be in situations where cables can't be installed or costs to do so are prohibitive. More and more colleges are implementing wireless computing capabilities on their campuses because users demand connectivity but the cost of wiring classrooms is too great. The phenomenon is often similar for home networks; it is much easier to set up a wireless network than it is to install new cable for a wired network. We'll discuss these wireless alternatives along with their advantages and disadvantages in the following sections.

## INFRARED

If you use a remote control to change television channels, you're already familiar with infrared wireless signaling. **Infrared** is a wireless transmission medium that carries data via beams of light through the air. No wires are required, but the transmitter and receiver must be in the line of sight or the signal is lost. In other words, infrared signals can only work within a maximum of about 100 feet and when the path between the transmitter and

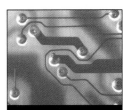

**Techtalk**

**common carrier immunity**
Another important concept underlying the telephone system is **common carrier immunity**. A **common carrier** is a transportation or communications company that provides vital public services; in return, legislation holds these carriers immune from civil or criminal liability for the actions of individuals who misuse these services. If you make a harassing telephone call, for example, you, not the phone company, are personally liable.

the receiver is unobstructed by trees, hills, mountains, buildings, or other structures.

In order to utilize infrared technology with your computer system, you need an IrDA port. You may encounter an IrDA port on mobile computing devices and peripherals such as a PDA, digital camera, laptop, mouse, printer, or keyboard. The most common use of the IrDA port is to transfer data from your PDA to your desktop or laptop computer or another PDA. To allow data transfer, the IrDA port on the transmitting device must be in the line of sight (usually a few feet) of the port on the receiving device. IrDA ports offer about the same data transfer rates as traditional parallel ports (4 Mbps). So why would you want to use infrared with all of these restrictions? If you had a situation where hooking devices together with cables wasn't an option, infrared could be a good choice. Plus, it's more convenient to simply point and transfer than it is to connect wires or cables!

## RADIO

You may not realize the impact that the use of radio waves has on your daily life or on society in general. All kinds of gadgets—from cell and cordless phones to baby monitors—communicate via radio waves. Although humans cannot see or otherwise detect them, radio waves carry data in a variety of forms (music, voice conversations, and photos) through the air.

Radio transmissions offer an alternative to infrared transmissions. You probably experience one type of radio transmission daily by listening to your favorite radio station. In **radio** transmissions, data travels through the air as radio-frequency (RF) signals, or radio waves, via a transmitter and a receiver. Or instead of separate transmitting and receiving devices, radio transmissions can use a wireless transceiver, a combination transmitting and receiving device equipped with an antenna. Data transfer rates via radio transmission are variable but generally fall in the range of 64 Kbps to 720 Kbps.

One application of radio is a wireless LAN in a home or business. Wireless LANs come in handy when users must move around a building instead of staying put. In Veterans Administration hospitals, for example, wireless LANs help hospital personnel track the distribution of controlled substances, a job that's both time-consuming

**FIGURE 8.4**
To learn even more about the possibilities of Bluetooth, visit **www.blue tooth.com**.

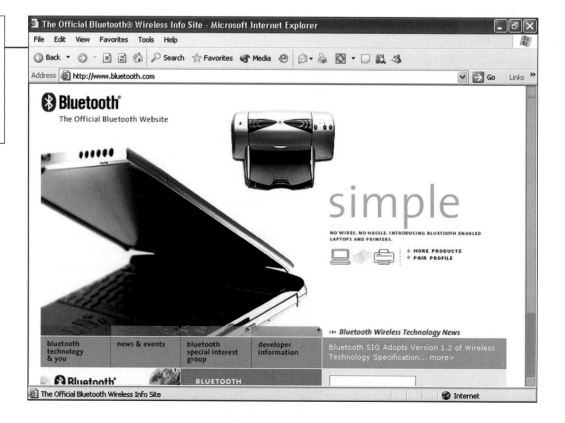

# Sharing Wireless Communities

As cyberspace becomes populated by more and more of the world, the questions posed related to computer ethics become more complex. Should there be new rules for today's wireless world? For example, many people argue that compensation for use rather than access is ethical—that is, you should have to pay for each user on a DSL line, not for the DSL line itself. Others think that if you've subscribed to a DSL line, you should be able to share that line with whomever you see fit.

Imagine the following scenario: You recently decided to pay for fast Internet access by sub-scribing to an expensive DSL provider. You also bought an inexpensive router and now share your bandwidth free of charge with your roommate. You're even thinking of sharing it with your apart-ment building. Why not—it won't cost you any-thing more. After all, you paid for the access and you're not profiting yourself by offering it free to others. Surely there's nothing wrong with that.

Well, there is something wrong with it, in fact. For one, most DSL providers wouldn't allow it, and, more important, you'd be breaking the law even if you didn't earn any money by sharing your bandwidth.

Can bandwidth ever be shared legally? It might be in the case of business access to the Net. There are those who are working on trying to build legal free wireless communities. One idea is to ask businesses to give away a little of their unused bandwidth so that "community members" can access the Internet using laptops and other

wireless devices for free. In such communities, users have to be within a certain distance of the server in order to take advantage of the free bandwidth, but that range can be about as far as a city block. Proponents of this idea suggest that businesses could offer the access at off-peak, after-business hours. In order to make such arrangements legal, businesses would pay a higher flat fee for their bandwidth on the condition that it may be offered freely.

This idea is already taking off. In New York City, for example, NYCWireless provides free "hot spots" of Internet access in parks, coffee shops, and building lobbies. Other cities are fol-lowing suit. Sharing bandwidth certainly makes for a unique way for companies and governments to serve their community. And free wireless access in cities may prove to be the next Internet frontier. Who knows? Perhaps, in the future, businesses will choose their locations based on which cities offer a free wireless zone to their residents.

As you may have guessed, the trick will be to make free wireless network communities safe and secure from malicious users and from those who would bog down the system with hefty downloads. In order for these networks to be feasible, they'll need to allow users access as well as prevent nasty network activities. Whether free networks piggyback off existing commercial networks or are created through altogether separate, new, independent networks, look for these wireless Internet communities in the future.

---

and prone to error without the computer's help. Now nurses use bedside computers, connected to the network through wireless signals, to track the use of these substances. Many campuses also are installing wire-less LANs to serve students seamlessly as they move around campus.

Most wireless LANs (WLANs) use a radio transmission technique that ensures security by spreading the signal over a seemingly random series of frequencies. Only the receiving device knows the series, so it isn't easy to eavesdrop on the signals. Radio-based wireless LAN signals can traverse up to about 1,000 feet.

A major disadvantage of radio trans-mission is noise susceptibility and inter-ference. One of radio's advantages is that

radio signals are long range (between cities, regions, and countries) and short range (within a home or office). Let's take a look at a short-range radio transmission technology that has become very popular in recent years: Bluetooth.

### Bluetooth™

**Bluetooth**, named after the infamous 10th-century Viking Harold Bluetooth, who united Denmark and Norway, was first conceived by Swedish cell phone giant Ericsson (Figure 8.4). Bluetooth technol-ogy relies on a network called a piconet, or a PAN (a personal area network), that allows all kinds of devices—desktop com-puters, mobile phones, printers, pagers, PDAs, and more—within a certain range of each other to communicate automatically and wirelessly.

How exactly does Bluetooth work? Bluetooth-enabled devices identify each other using identification numbers that are unique to each device. When these devices are within a certain range of each other (usually 30 feet or so), they automatically "find" and link to one another. You don't have to worry about being connected to Bluetooth devices you don't want to connect to either: the device requires that you confirm a connection before making it final. Up to eight Bluetooth-enabled devices can be connected to each other in a piconet at any one time, and, unlike infrared technologies, Bluetooth doesn't require a direct line of sight to be connected. Because the frequency used by Bluetooth devices changes often, Bluetooth devices never use the same frequency at the same time and don't interfere with each other. Bluetooth can accommodate data transfer rates of up to 1 Mbps.

Using Bluetooth-enabled devices, you can wirelessly send files from your desktop computer to your printer or to a friend's laptop. You can buy concert tickets online, download the electronic tickets into your Bluetooth-enabled PDA, and then link to the Bluetooth-enabled scanner at the concert house instead of presenting a ticket. You can even equip devices in your own home (such as light fixtures and microwave ovens) with a Bluetooth chip and use your cell phone or other device as a remote control, wirelessly telling your appliances what to do when.

## MICROWAVES

High-frequency radio waves called **microwaves** handled much of the long-distance telephone service before the recent growth of fiber-optic networks. Because microwaves must travel in a straight line with no obstructions like buildings, hills, mountains, and so on, relay stations are built at a distance of approximately every 30 miles (the line-of-sight distance to the horizon), or closer if the terrain blocks transmission. Microwave relay stations are also often situated on the tops of buildings or mountains. Microwave signals are sent from one relay station to the next. These

relay stations are similar to satellite dishes with an antenna, transceivers, and so on.

Microwave transmission bypasses the need for a wired infrastructure. It is useful in areas where the use of physical wires is impractical or impossible. Microwaves are also useful for communities of users who are within the line-of-sight horizon, such as universities, hospitals, and private and government organizations.

## SATELLITES

Essentially microwave relay stations suspended in space, communications **satellites** are positioned in **geosynchronous orbits**, which match the speed of the Earth's rotation and therefore are permanently positioned with respect to the ground (Figure 8.5). The satellites transmit data by sending and receiving microwave signals to and from Earth-based stations. Devices such as handheld computers and Global Positioning System (GPS) receivers can also function as Earth-based stations.

Some satellite systems, called **Direct Broadcast Satellite** (**DBS**), use an 18- or 21-inch reception disk to receive digital TV signals broadcast at a bandwidth of 12 Mbps. Increasingly, DBS operators offer Internet access as well as digital TV service, but at much lower bandwidth. Currently, Hughes Network Systems offers satellite Internet access at 400 Kbps, but there are a couple of drawbacks. To access the Internet using satellite technology, you need a satellite dish and satellite modem card. Additionally, current subscription rates are about double that of land-based services.

One interesting application of satellite communications technology is the Global Positioning System (GPS). The **Global Positioning System** is actually a cluster of 27 Earth-orbiting satellites (24 in operation and three extras in case one fails). The U.S. military developed and implemented this satellite network as a military navigation system but soon opened it up to everybody else. Each of these 3,000- to 4,000-pound solar-powered satellites circles the globe at about 12,000 miles in altitude, making two complete rotations every day. The orbits are arranged so that at any

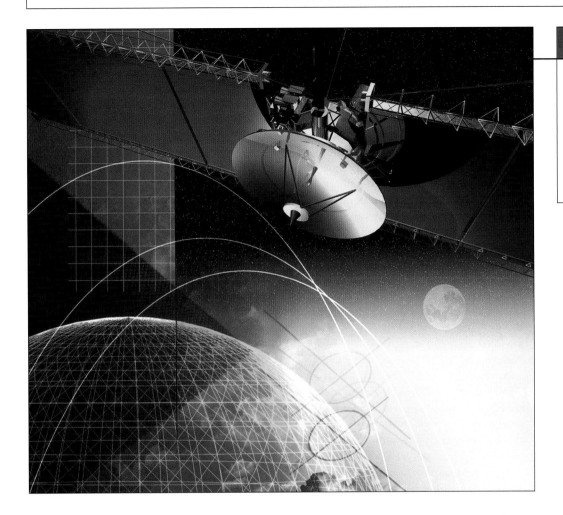

**FIGURE 8.5**
Communications satellites are often permanently positioned with respect to the ground to provide specific area coverage.

time, anywhere on Earth, there are at least four satellites "visible" in the sky. A GPS receiver's job is to locate four or more of these satellites, figure out the distance to each, and use this information to deduce its own location. A GPS receiver can be either handheld or installed in a vehicle. Navigation systems in rental cars are a typical application of GPS. Other applications of satellite technology include air navigation, TV and radio broadcasts, paging, and videoconferencing.

So, what is it about wireless connectivity that is so interesting? Well, one answer is that wireless technology allows us to not be "place specific." Place specificity is needing to be in a certain place in order to receive a service. Wireless technology allows you to be wherever you choose to be and still have the ability to be connected. Furthermore, wireless devices are proliferating at a tremendous pace. It is not unusual today for your phone to talk to your PDA or computer, or for your computer to be controlled by a wireless mouse

or keyboard, or for all of these devices to be wirelessly accessed through your television console.

You can sit in a classroom today and receive instant messages, e-mail, and stock quotes, and even browse the Web— all from your cell phone! In the next section we will explore the phenomenon of the coming together of these communications technologies.

# Convergence: Is It a Phone or a Computer?

We've been examining various technologies that carry computer data over voice lines as well as through the air. At the core of this process is **digitization**, the transformation of data such as voice, text, graphics, audio, and video into digital

form. Digitization enables convergence. **Convergence** refers to the merging of disparate objects or ideas (and even people) into combinations that have never been tried before. Within the IT industry, convergence means two things: the combination of various industries (computers, consumer electronics, and telecommunications), as well as the coming together of products like PCs, TVs, and telephones. Some futurists believe convergence may mark the end point of the digital revolution, in which all types of digital information (voice, video, and data) will travel over the same network.

Digitization also enables media convergence. Media convergence is the unification of all forms of media (including newspapers, TV, radio, and telephones). Former U.S. Vice President Al Gore coined the term *Information Superhighway* to describe this phenomenon of media convergence. The Internet is already a major source of breaking news, rivaling such traditional sources as newspapers and television. And, according to a recent estimate, more than five percent of all long-distance voice telephone calls will someday travel over the Internet, creating a $9 billion industry and posing a genuine threat to the traditional public switched telephone network.

Why should you care about convergence? Because it was predicted to happen, is happening, and will continue to happen in the future. This section explores some of the dimensions of computer-telephony convergence, a process of technological morphing in which previously distinct devices lose their sharply defined boundaries and blend together (Figure 8.6). As you'll see, it's creating some interesting hybrids.

## CELLULAR TELEPHONES, PAGERS, AND WEB-ENABLED DEVICES

As you've already learned, most phones are analog devices tied to the local loop's twisted-pair wiring. That's unsatisfactory for many people, so alternative ways have been devised to gain access to telephone services, such as wireless (cellular) telephones.

The PSTN isn't the only analog phone technology around. First-generation (1G) **cellular telephones**, which enable subscribers to place calls through a wireless communications system (Figure 8.7), use analog cellular technology. A wireless communications system uses radio or infrared signals to transmit voice or text data.

Believe it or not, wireless communications systems were used as far back as World War II. The armed forces used walkie-talkies for mobile, two-way communication. One of the problems with walkie-talkies is that the signal can weaken or disappear completely the farther away you get from the transmitting unit. By 1971, AT&T had found a way to solve this problem by

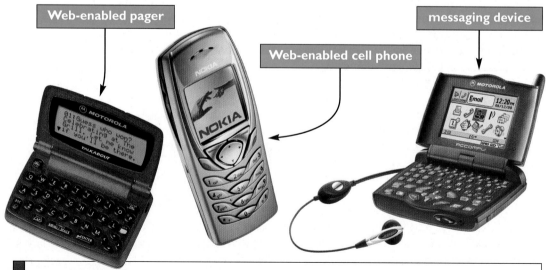

**FIGURE 8.6** Digitization enables convergence, a process of technological morphing in which previously distinct devices lose their sharply defined boundaries and blend together.

building a network of transmitters that automatically repeat signals. This network of transmitters (called **cell sites**) broadcasts signals throughout specific but limited geographic areas (called **cells**). When callers move from cell to cell, each new cell site takes over automatically to maintain signal strength. But who or what monitors your cell phone's signal strength to give you the best reception? That's the job for a **mobile telephone switching office** (**MTSO**), the switching office that connects cell towers to the telephone company's central office (CO) and the PSTN (Figure 8.8). Each cell tower reports signal strength to the MTSO, which then switches your signal to whatever cell tower will provide the clearest connection for your conversation.

In 1983, analog cellular telephone service was introduced to the market. Even

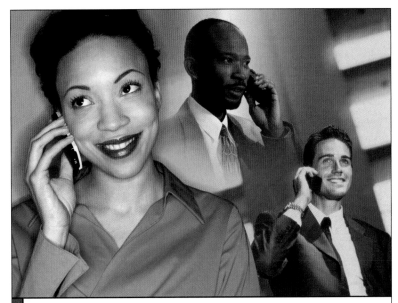

**FIGURE 8.7** Cellular telephones enable subscribers to place calls through a wireless communications system.

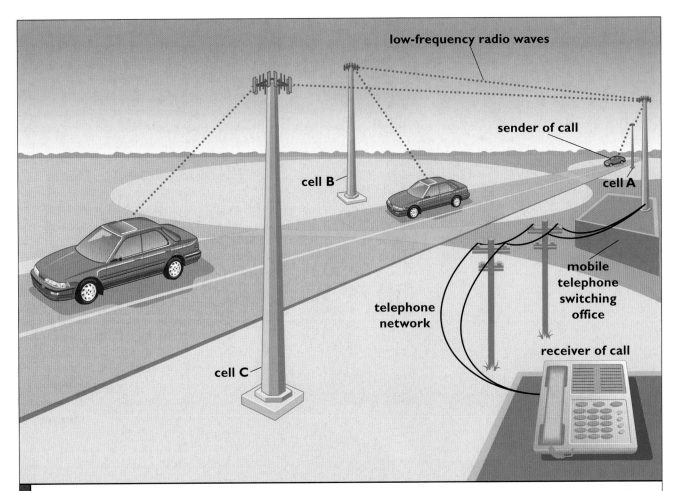

**FIGURE 8.8** When callers move from cell to cell, each new cell site takes over automatically to maintain signal strength. The mobile telephone switching office (MTSO) is the switching office that connects cell towers to the telephone company's central office (CO) and the PSTN.

**Destinations**

To learn more
about cell phones,
go to **www.fda.gov/
cellphones/**

though it is still a predominantly analog
system, more than 500 million people use
cell phones worldwide today.

## PERSONAL COMMUNICATION SERVICE (PCS)

Digitization is bringing the same rapid
change to cellular phone service that you're
seeing in other media. A group of related
digital cellular phone service technologies
called **Personal Communication Service**
(**PCS**) is quickly replacing most analog
cellular services. PCS is also referred to
as 2G, for second-generation technology.
Digital cellular phones offer noise-free
sound and improved coverage, but that's
just the beginning. PCS offers protection
from eavesdropping and cellular phone
fraud, two problems that plague analog
cellular technologies. It also offers a spate
of new, computer-based telephony services,
such as voice recognition technology that
enables users to screen incoming calls or

to place calls without dialing a phone
number. In short, PCS enables computers
and cellular phones to be combined, and
the result is a profusion of technologies
that transform the way we communicate.

PCS is transforming mobile computing
into a reality for millions of people. Because
PCS technology is digital, it's much more
amenable to data communication than
analog cellular services. It's possible to
access the Internet by means of a modem
connected to an analog cellular phone, but
data transfer rates are as low as 4 Kbps
due to line noise and poor connections.
Emerging PCS standards will enable speeds
of up to 384 Kbps for downloads.

Analog cellular service was the first
generation (1G), while digital PCS is
known as the second generation (2G). The
International Telecommunication Union
(ITU) has released a specification for 3G,
or third-generation, mobile communications
technology. 3G offers speeds that vary
depending upon the application—384 Kbps
while walking, 128 Kbps in a moving
vehicle, and 2 Mbps in fixed locations.

### Pagers

Using a signaling concept similar to cell
phones, paging networks use towers to service large regional and national areas. Think
of a pager as a radio that is always tuned to
the same radio station. A **pager** (also called
a beeper) is a small wireless handheld device
that acts as a receiver for radio signals broadcast from a transmitter in the paging network. All pagers within a network are tuned
to the same frequency. The paging network
transmitter sends signals over this frequency.

Every pager in a network has a special
code that uniquely identifies that particular device. When the network transmitter
sends out signals, pagers listen for their
special codes. As long as it is turned on, a
pager "beeps" or emits another sound to
notify the user that it recognizes its code.
Some pagers, like those used by restaurants,
vibrate, whereas more complex pagers
can display phone numbers or brief text
messages, and even enable users to hear
voice messages. There are one-way pagers,
which only receive signals, and two-way
pagers, which allow you to send and receive
signals and messages.

The rise of the cell phone has signaled
the demise of the pager. Before there were

**FIGURE 8.9** Pagers may have
reached their zenith, but they are still a
big part of corporate communications.

cell phones, pagers were everywhere. Now that cell phones are seemingly everywhere, the popularity of the pager has declined (Figure 8.9). However, some benefits of pagers over cell phones are their smaller size, lower price, and longer battery life.

## Web-Enabled Devices

A **Web-enabled device** is any device that can display and respond to the codes in a markup language such as HTML or XML. Web-enabled devices include PDAs, some cell phones, and tablet PCs.

Web-enabled and Web-based are basically synonyms used for describing applications and devices that allow access to the Web. Even though the terms are used interchangeably, they actually have two distinct meanings. If an application or device is referred to as Web-based, this means that it was designed and developed to work only via the Web. Meanwhile, a Web-enabled application or device was conceived before the Web even existed and must be retrofitted with a Web interface to "enable" Web access.

Web-enabled PDAs include the Palm line, which uses the Palm Operating System; Handspring (purchased by Palm in 2003), which features a design that accepts modules such as a camera, software applications, and a phone; the Casio Pocket PC, which uses the Microsoft CE operating system and is often used for bar-code scanning and other business-focused applications; and, finally, the Sharp Zaurus, which is the leading PDA in Japan, with an estimated 10,000 applications due to the plethora of Java and Linux coders who write applications for it (Figure 8.10).

For Web-enabled devices to work over wireless networks requires WAP (short for wireless application protocol). WAP is a standard that specifies how users can access the Web securely using pagers, cell phones, PDAs, and other wireless hand-held devices.

It doesn't matter which operating system your device uses since WAP is supported by them all. However, WAP-enabled devices do require a special software program called a microbrowser, a Web browser that works with small file sizes. Smaller file sizes are necessary due to the low memory capacities of WAP-enabled devices and wireless networks with low bandwidth.

**FIGURE 8.10** PDAs are the most prevalent Web-enabled devices in use today.

## FAX

**Facsimile transmission**—or **fax**, as it's popularly known—enables you to send an image of a document over the telephone lines (Figure 8.11). The sending fax machine makes a digital image of the document. Using a built-in modem, the sending fax machine converts the image into an analog representation so that it can be transmitted through the analog telephone system. The receiving fax machine converts the analog signals to digital signals, converts the digital signals to an image of the document, and prints that image.

Some modems, called **fax modems**, support fax as well as data modulation protocols. If your computer has a fax modem, you can send and receive faxes from your computer instead of a fax machine. However, you'll need a scanner too if you want to fax something that's printed or sketched on paper.

Since computers can send and receive faxes, it is not a far stretch of the imagination to see that sending and receiving documents will soon be accomplished by network-enabled cell phones or personal communications devices, thereby making fax machines as we know them today obsolete.

## TV INTERNET SET-TOPS

You're sitting in front of your TV, and your eyes never leave the screen. The show you're watching is boring, so you spend some time checking your e-mail

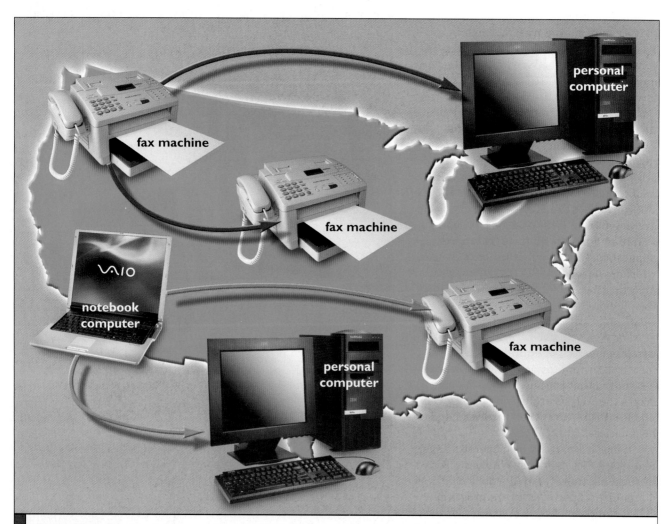

**FIGURE 8.11** Facsimile transmission enables you to send an image of a document over the telephone lines to anyone who has a fax machine. If your computer has a fax modem, you can send and receive faxes from your computer instead of a fax machine.

**FIGURE 8.12**
MSN® TV allows you to access the Internet using your television set as a display.

**Techtalk**

**The Everything PC**
It *looks* like a computer, but it's much more: it's also an audiophile-quality stereo, a TV, a DVD player, and even an answering machine. That's the pitch for a new series of multimedia-enhanced PCs that combine huge monitors (27 or even 31 inches), DVD drives, high-fidelity speakers with surround sound, and voice-capable 56 Kbps modems. If it's equipped with a microphone and the right software, you can even use this PC to place free, long-distance phone calls over the Internet. This could be the ultimate machine for cramped dorm rooms!

and surfing the Web. While you're on the Web, you check an interactive channel guide featuring your local cable TV listings, jump to some TV-related Web sites, and finally find something worth watching. All these tasks are accomplished on your TV set, thanks to **MSN® TV** (formerly **WebTV**), an Internet service that you access using an inexpensive **set-top appliance** (also referred to as an Internet appliance) that enables you to access the Internet using your TV as a display (Figure 8.12). To navigate the Web, you use a wireless keyboard or a remote control unit.

High-definition television (HDTV) is an emerging standard for digital TV that requires a bandwidth of 11 Mbps. It is just beginning to be available in major cities and will someday be the standard for all televisions and broadcast media. HDTV provides extremely high-quality video and audio representation due to its ability to carry so much information to the television receiver (11 Mbps).

Now that you understand the types of wired and wireless media and devices that are available, let's take a look at several ways you can connect and communicate with a home network.

# Wired and Wireless Home Networks

You learned about the broad world of networks and communications in Chapter 6. Home networks, a personal and specific use of network technology, can accommodate both wired and wireless communications. Wired home networks use coaxial cable, telephone wires, cat-5 wires, or your home's electric power wiring; wireless home networks use radio signals.

According to International Data Corporation (IDC), approximately half of all U.S. households owned a computer by the end of 2000. In addition, more than 20 million of those households owned two or more computers. Additional market research indicates that multicomputer households are becoming more common because folks who already own a PC are still buying new ones.

You may decide to implement a home network because you wish to share data or a connection to the Internet, play games on different computers with multiple users, or share peripherals with other computers in your house. It is not unusual for each of the parents and one or more children in a household to have their own computers. Sharing a scanner, printer, or other peripheral is commonplace in home networks.

Keep these three steps in mind when installing a home network:

1. Decide on the network wiring technology. You can choose from the following technologies: standard Ethernet (discussed in Chapter 6), home radio-frequency (RF), home phone-line, and home power-line.

2. Purchase and install the proper hardware.

3. Once the hardware is installed, you must configure the network so that all components function together effectively.

The most important step is Step 3. Once you understand your network's configuration, you will also see that a home network improves your home-computing experience. Some home networking kits come with installation CDs to walk you through the configuration process. You should also consider purchasing and installing personal firewall software to keep your home network safe from viruses and hackers (Figure 8.13).

Now that you understand the basics of a home network, let's look at the different configuration possibilities.

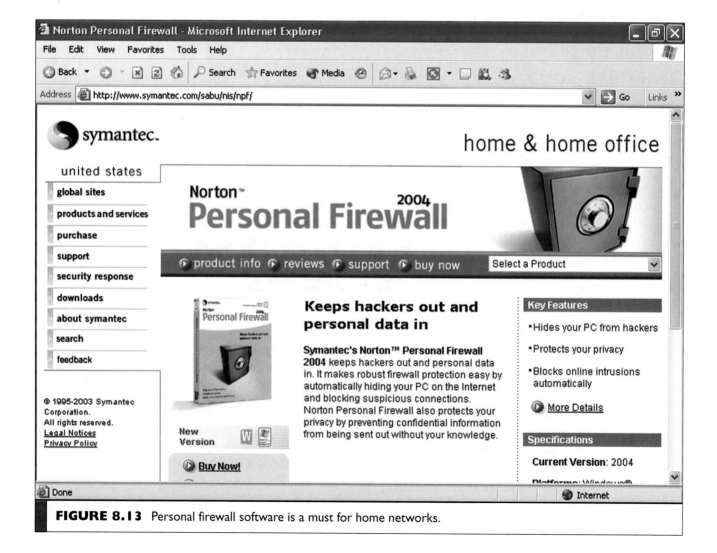

**FIGURE 8.13**  Personal firewall software is a must for home networks.

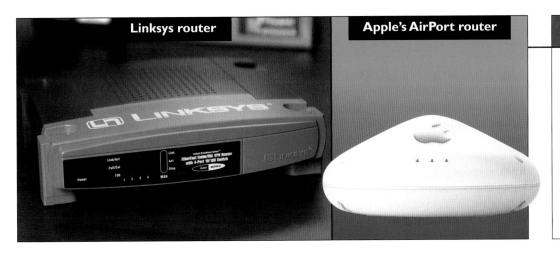

Linksys router

Apple's AirPort router

**FIGURE 8.14**
Linksys network access points and routers are the industry leader in small-office/home-office (SOHO) wireless network routers. The AirPort is Apple's wireless network router.

## HOME RADIO-FREQUENCY NETWORKS

**Home radio-frequency (RF) networks** are wireless networks in which each computer broadcasts its information to another using radio signals. Home RF networks have a **network access point**, which is a communications device used to send and receive data between computers that contain wireless adapters (Figure 8.14). Access points enable you to move a laptop with a wireless adapter from room to room or place computers in different locations throughout the house.

In a home RF network, a peer-to-peer relationship exists among all of the computers in the network. This means that all the computers are equals or "peers" with no particular computer acting as the server. However, some home wireless networks can also be of the client/server type. In a client/server home network, each computer communicates with the server, which then communicates with other computers or peripherals.

## HOME PHONE-LINE NETWORKS

**Home phone-line networks**, also known as **HomePNA**, work off existing phone wiring. Home phone-line networks work best in situations where computers are in different rooms throughout the house. HomePNA offers many advantages, including simple and inexpensive installation, standardization, reliability, and sufficient speed for video applications. Home phone-line networks are compatible with other

home networking technologies and work on all platforms, including Macs and older PCs. Hubs, routers, and network access points are not required with home phone-line networks.

However, there are some disadvantages to HomePNA. Depending on your ISP and type of service, you may need to install special software or hardware. In addition, you must install HPNA network interface cards (NICs) in all the PCs slated for the network. You may also need to run new wiring or additional lengths of phone cord if there isn't a phone jack close to each computer.

The Home Phone Networking Alliance (HPNA), a group of networking-technology companies, created the standards for HomePNA. HPNA 1.0 was the first version of the standard; HPNA 2.0 is the most recent version. HPNA 1.0 operated at a somewhat slow 1 Mbps. Although HPNA 2.0 operates at approximately 10 Mbps, fast Ethernet is still 10 times as fast, with speeds of 100 Mbps.

## HOME POWER-LINE NETWORKS

Like HomePNA, **home power-line networks** run off a home's existing wiring. However, power-line networks use the electrical system instead of phone lines to connect computers through the same electrical power outlet.

One major advantage of home power-line networks is that most homes have an electrical outlet in every room. Inexpensive and easy installation is another advantage. In addition, a peripheral that doesn't have to be directly connected to a computer can

tech**tv**

To learn more about wireless networking, view the video clip at **www.prenhall.com/ cayf2005**.

be located wherever you wish in a home power-line network. For example, whereas a monitor has to be physically near a computer in order to be connected and used, a printer could be located in a completely different room, or on another floor, of a house.

Power-line networking does have some drawbacks. If your home has anything other than 110-volt standard electrical power lines, you can't install a power-line network. In addition, home power usage and older wiring can affect performance. The devices that power-line networks use to access electrical outlets take up a lot of space inside your walls. Connection speeds are rather slow at 50 to 350 Kbps. To ensure network security, you must encrypt all your data. Finally, printer features might be limited, and only Windows-based computers work in a power-line network.

In the next section you will learn how various wired and wireless applications allow the possibilities of group collaboration and shared communication.

# Wired and Wireless Applications

When we talk about wired and wireless applications, we're talking about a combination of technologies that give you the ability to access data using a variety of devices and media, whatever your location. The world of wired and wireless applications is receiving more attention every day. You can't open a magazine, surf the Web, or watch TV without seeing ads for the latest wireless solutions. More and more businesses and home users are implementing these various applications to help them communicate, collaborate, and share text, graphics, audio, and video. And it all happens at increasingly faster speeds, higher data transfer rates, and lower costs.

## TELECONFERENCING

One of the simplest and most secure wired applications for voice communications is

teleconferencing. **Teleconferencing** is simply the conduct of an organization's business by more than two people, separated by distance, through the use of the telephone. Telephone companies like AT&T and other providers offer many services to help facilitate teleconferencing. To use a typical type of conference call service, each caller dials the teleconference number, provides a pass code, and is then connected to the other callers.

## VIDEOCONFERENCING

Before the glut of inexpensive video and Web cameras for PCs hit the market in recent years, talking on the phone and seeing a video image of the person that you're talking to sounded like a pipe dream. Videophones were launched by such companies as AT&T, Sony, Mitsubishi, and MCI as far back as 1964. New models continued to be developed through the 1970s, 1980s, and early 1990s, but they proved to be tremendously unpopular flops. All of that began to change in the mid- to late 1990s, when desktop videoconferencing technology began to enter the scene.

Using the typical forms of communication such as phones, e-mail, instant messaging, and in-person meetings has been sufficient for most people to keep in touch with relatives and friends across the globe, or to conduct business with colleagues in distant offices. But for those who want a more personal interchange with far-flung family, coworkers, and customers, videoconferencing has become a must-have application.

**Videoconferencing** is a technology that transmits sound and video images to enable two or more people to have a face-to-face meeting even though they're geographically separated. There are two categories of videoconferencing: desktop videoconferencing uses PCs equipped with digital video cameras and special software, whereas closed-circuit television videoconferencing requires dedicated hardware. Many PCs today are sold with Intel Videophone or Microsoft's audio- and videoconferencing software, NetMeeting, already installed, as well as cameras like 3Com's Bigpicture.

The events of September 11, 2001, made more people consider videoconferencing for business and personal use than ever before. This increased interest was partially due to fears of terrorism but also was because the airlines' troubles pushed potential travelers to look at other options besides air travel if they didn't want to be forced to put up with flight cancellations and other hassles. Videoconferencing is the best alternative for businesses that require real-time collaboration.

You can implement videoconferencing from almost anywhere, provided your PC has a built-in sound card; speakers; a microphone; a video or Web camera connected to a parallel, serial, or USB port; and a modem. To improve audio quality, you should use a headset or clip-on microphone that remains firmly in place. Although NetMeeting is a popular software choice for videoconferencing, keep in mind that NetMeeting and NetMeeting Server are no longer being updated or supported by Microsoft. However, NetMeeting is still a viable application, and Microsoft has equipped its Windows Messenger software with many of NetMeeting's features.

Conducting a videoconference with two participants is a breeze as long as both parties have all of the aforementioned equipment. If you have a high-speed Internet connection, you can either talk live or record video messages that you can attach to e-mail messages. But what if you want to conduct a videoconference with multiple participants? In those instances, you will need to own, purchase, or rent dedicated conferencing equipment or contact a company or service provider that offers videoconferencing services. CuSeeMe and iVisit are Web-based services that specialize in multiuser videoconferencing. In order to use either of the sites, you must first download and install their software. Both programs provide simultaneous chat and video capabilities for multiple users. CuSeeMe also offers additional functions such as file transfer, application sharing, and writing on whiteboards. The

## Destinations

To learn more about videoconferencing, go to **www.ivisit.info** or **www.cuworld.com**

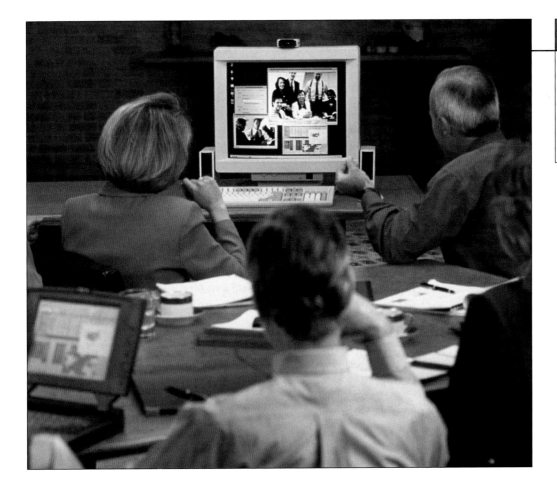

**FIGURE 8.15**
Network-based delivery of high-quality videoconferencing requires a bandwidth of at least 10 Mbps.

program offered by iVisit is more limited and does not offer those additional functions but is significantly less expensive.

To transmit just voice and not video over the Internet, you can use a dial-up modem and connection with 56 Kbps transfer speeds. But for any high-bandwidth Internet application like streaming video, you will need a broadband connection with transfer speeds of at least 128 Kbps. **Broadband** refers to any transmission medium that sends and receives data at high speeds. The bandwidth of traditional twisted-pair telephone lines is too small to carry video, voice, and data simultaneously. Broadband uses fiber-optic or coaxial cable to transmit this data with a technique similar to cable TV. Network-based delivery of high-quality videoconferencing requires a bandwidth of at least 10 Mbps, the speed of a slow hard disk or standard Ethernet local area network (Figure 8.15). Videoconferencing will be a much smoother experience for all participants with broadband's faster upload speeds.

Streaming video or any other new set of Internet applications that require speeds at least 20 times as fast as traditional dial-up phone lines and modems are theoretically possible with broadband. Fiber-optic transmission lines will help to expand this growing communications segment of the market.

If you need to check on an elderly or disabled relative separated from you by distance, you might want to consider purchasing an extremely special type of videoconferencing system called *CareStation 110*. The system, by Motion Media, can connect to various devices that monitor vital signs and transmit this information directly to a patient's health-care provider. You do need to invest in special hardware, but the system connects to and displays images on any television and can be adjusted with a familiar remote control device. CareStation 110 transmits patient data and images over conventional telephone lines. Although low-bandwidth phone lines can affect the quality of the video, costs are the same as a regular phone call.

Motion Media offers another videoconferencing product that provides an alternative for small-business owners who want to keep business travel costs to a minimum but still conduct face-to-face meetings with clients and colleagues. The mm225 videophone can be connected to a television to display a larger image and provides higher-quality video than the CareStation 110 system. However, the videophone requires a high-speed ISDN connection for transmitting calls, an additional expense that business owners must consider.

When small-office/home-office (SOHO) businesses want the capability of sending voice, data, and video over a single broadband connection, they should consider PC-based videoconferencing as a potential solution. PC-based solutions offer a number of benefits over professional-grade videoconferencing systems, such as lower cost and easier installation and maintenance. After implementing PC-based videoconferencing systems, many companies may find that it was well worth the time and money. The principal advantage of videoconferencing is the cost savings in company or personal travel budgets achieved by limiting the need for participants to be physically present. Avoiding rush-hour traffic is an added bonus. Companies also begin to reap the rewards of lower long-distance phone bills and higher productivity. The biggest drawback to the successful implementation of videoconferencing is the fact that the video portion of the medium requires lots of bandwidth. Other concerns include poor video quality, real-time transmission delays, the need for all participants to have access to facilities or equipment, and potential threats to privacy.

Videoconferencing hardware and applications are improving every day. Thanks to inexpensive software and a Web cam, you can attend a meeting you may otherwise have missed. With programs like NetMeeting, you can communicate, interact, and share applications with friends, family, and coworkers. This type of collaboration will otherwise be nearly impossible until broadband Internet service is deployed on a large scale. With the right equipment, you can be present at important meetings within the comfort of your own home. You can even position the camera so you can stay in your pajamas. Speaking of staying in your pajamas, let's look at another application that has received increasing attention with the advent of high-speed, broadband wired and wireless solutions.

## TELECOMMUTING

Due to the burgeoning home network market, another wired or wireless application that has seen a boom in recent years is telecommuting. **Telecommuting** refers to using telecommunications and computer equipment to work from home while still being connected to the office (Figure 8.16). The home system must be able to connect to the company computer system in order to communicate with and transfer data to and from other employees.

Two million Americans telecommuted to work in 1990. By 2000, more than 30 million were doing so at least part-time. However, not all jobs lend themselves to telecommuting. Anyone having to serve or greet the public (bank tellers, waitstaff, office receptionists, and so on) is not a candidate for telecommuting.

Studies have shown that companies experience various benefits by allowing employees to telecommute. Telecommuters tend to be more productive, often working an average of two hours longer per day than traditional office workers. Companies tend to experience lower employee turnover due to employees' higher morale and job satisfaction. Telecommuters also take fewer sick days. Finally, companies save money by paying rent on less office space than they would need for everyone to work on-site. Some disadvantages to a company might be the lack of opportunities for employees to socialize within the company and the lack of direct supervision over an employee's workload.

The main advantages to the telecommuter include quality-of-life issues, such as not having to commute, flexible hours, more family time, and comfortable and

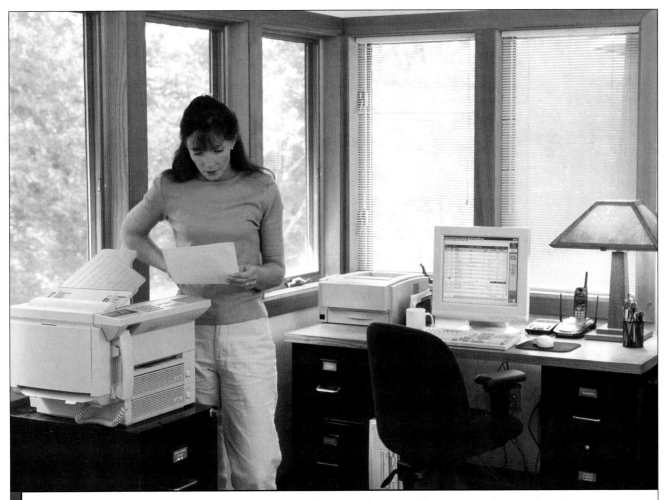

**FIGURE 8.16** Telecommuting allows you to complete work from your home or an alternate location.

familiar surroundings. Telecommuters also save on car expenses (gas, tolls, parking, and so forth) and work clothes. Disadvantages include the lack of social interaction, the need for dedicated work space in the home, and distractions that threaten the separation of the work environment from home activities. The environment and society at large also reap benefits from telecommuting, including fuel conservation and less air pollution.

## WORKGROUP COMPUTING

Workgroup computing is another wired and wireless application for which phone and other communications service providers are striving to provide more bandwidth. Workgroup computing occurs when all the members of a workgroup—a collection of individuals working together on a task—have computers connected to a network that allows them to connect, communicate, and collaborate. **Groupware** is the software that provides computerized support for the information needs of these workgroups. In addition to groupware, specific hardware and networking equipment are necessary for group collaboration. Groupware applications include electronic mail, videoconferencing, group-scheduling systems, customizable electronic forms, real-time shared applications, and shared information databases.

The first successful groupware, Lotus Notes, was designed to run on client/server systems. Newer groupware products, such as Microsoft Exchange and new versions of Lotus Notes, are designed to run on intranets and extranets (Figure 8.17). They make groupware applications available to workgroups that work at geographically separated offices, and even enable organizations to bring in group members who work for other organizations (such as affiliated research labs).

Consider the case of an engineer at a firm who prepares a proposal for an external contract. The proposal goes to the engineer's supervisor for review and approval. The document may need to be seen by several other people before it's finally approved and sent. Groupware helps to facilitate **workflow automation**. Workflow automation is the process of sending documents and data to the next person who needs to see them.

**FIGURE 8.17**
Microsoft Exchange provides remote access to e-mail and contacts.

# Summary
## WIRED AND WIRELESS COMMUNICATION

- The public switched telephone network (PSTN) is predominantly digital, except for the local loop, which uses low-bandwidth twisted-pair wire connected to analog telephones. Even though most computer users utilize the PSTN for data communications frequently, its limitations, such as being an analog network based on century-old standards, susceptibility to line noise, and inability to surpass a data transfer rate of 56 Kbps, make it less than ideal for this purpose.

- Multiplexing is the transmission of more than one telephone call or message on a single line. Digital telephony offers noise-free transmission and high-quality audio.

- Wireless communications media include infrared, radio, microwaves, and satellites. Infrared is low-energy and requires line-of-sight contact; radio frequency is capable of providing broad coverage; microwaves are high-energy radio waves that are limited to line of sight; and satellites are essentially microwave relay stations suspended in geosynchronous orbits, which match the speed of the Earth's rotation and therefore are permanently positioned with respect to the ground.

- Digitization and convergence are blurring the boundaries that distinguish phones, computers, and TVs. MSN® TV brings Internet capabilities to TV viewing, and PCS enables high-bandwidth data communications through cellular telephones. Pagers and faxes are giving way to Web-enabled devices that duplicate their functions.

- A home-based network can be set up with wireless radio-frequency infrastructure (home RF) or by using telephone wire (home phone line), coaxial cable, or your home's electrical wiring (home power line).

- For real-time videoconferencing or other advanced multimedia applications, such as telecommuting and workgroup computing, 56 Kbps is insufficient. For these applications, bandwidths of 1 Mbps or more are needed for good quality.

# Key Terms and Concepts

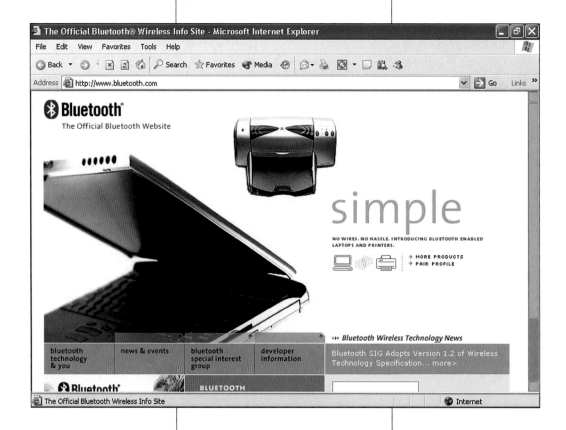

# Matching

Match each key term in the left column with the most accurate definition in the right column.

_____ 1. workflow automation

_____ 2. broadband

_____ 3. groupware

_____ 4. PSTN

_____ 5. wireless

_____ 6. last-mile technologies

_____ 7. convergence

_____ 8. teleconferencing

_____ 9. cell

_____ 10. microwave

_____ 11. set-top appliance

_____ 12. videoconferencing

_____ 13. quality of service

_____ 14. analog

_____ 15. access point

a. the world telephone system, a massive network used for data as well as voice communications

b. a communications medium that uses radio or infrared signals

c. interim digital telephony technologies that make use of twisted-pair wiring to reach the end user

d. the coming together of people, ideas, or things in ways that did not happen before

e. the geographic area in which wireless signals are broadcast

f. an electrical signal that changes continuously to match the acoustics of the human voice

g. high-frequency radio-wave transmissions that are limited to line-of-sight distances

h. a wired controller that receives and transmits data to the wireless adapters installed in computers

i. a technology that enables two or more people to have a face-to-face meeting even though they're geographically separated

j. the process of sending documents and data to the next person who needs to see them

k. enables you to access the Internet using your TV as a display

l. the conduct of an organization's business by more than two people, separated by distance, through the use of the telephone

m. software that provides computerized support for the information needs of workgroups

n. the expectation of completing a high-quality audio phone call

o. digital transmissions in excess of 1.5 Mbps

# Multiple Choice

Circle the correct choice for each of the following.

1. Which of the following transmission media would not be used in a home network?
   a. phone lines
   b. power lines
   c. fiber-optic lines
   d. coaxial cable

2. Which of the following is not a transmission medium used to provide regional and long-distance service between local telephone exchanges?
   a. microwaves
   b. fiber-optic cables
   c. common carrier
   d. copper wire

3. What does POTS stand for?
   a. Pretty Old Telephone System
   b. Plain Old Telephone Service
   c. Partially Operative Telephone Switching
   d. Progressive Open Telecommunications Standard

4. What does DBS stand for?
   a. Digital Band Service
   b. Direct Binary Satellite
   c. Digital Broadband Service
   d. Direct Broadcast Satellite

5. When someone makes a cellular phone call, all the cell sites are connected to which of the following?
   a. public switched telephone network (PSTN)
   b. mobile optical network (MONET)
   c. Mobile Digital Subscriber Line (MDSL)
   d. mobile telephone switching office (MTSO)

6. What is multiplexing?
   a. a multiple-screen movie theater
   b. many interconnected networks
   c. the ability to transmit more than one call on a single line
   d. the ability to send data and faxes with a single device

7. Which of the following services requires broadband digital transmission?
   a. digital television
   b. faxing
   c. sending e-mail
   d. none of the above

8. Which type of port would you use for an infrared keyboard?
   a. parallel
   b. serial
   c. IrDA
   d. InFRA

9. What term describes the process of sending documents and data to the next person who needs to see it?
   a. workflow automation
   b. process automation
   c. document automation
   d. data automation

# Fill-In

In the blanks provided, write the correct answer for each of the following.

1. _____ refers to being able to make a call with good audio quality whenever you need to.

2. _____ is a small, waist-high curb-side installation that connects as many as 96 telephone subscribers.

3. A network of local connections is called the _____.

4. _____ has been developed to send more than one call on a single line.

5. To pay for local phone service in rural areas, long-distance companies collect surcharges called _____ from their customers and pass along most of these funds to local telephone companies.

6. A(n) _____ is a transportation or communications company that provides vital public services; in return, legislation holds these carriers immune from civil or criminal liability for the actions of individuals who misuse these services.

7. _____ is the transformation of data such as voice, text, graphics, audio, and video into digital form.

8. _____ is software that provides computerized support for the information needs of workgroups.

9. If your computer is equipped with a(n) _____, you can send and receive faxes from your computer.

10. _____ is performing work at home while linked to the office by means of a telecommunications-equipped computer system.

11. A(n) _____ enables you to access the Internet using your television as a display.

12. Communication satellites are placed in _____ orbits, which match the speed of the Earth's rotation.

13. When using _____, no wires are required, but the transmitter and receiver must be in line of sight or the signal is lost.

14. _____ is a high-speed, high-capacity data transmission channel that sends and receives information on coaxial cable or fiber-optic cable, giving it the ability to carry video, voice, and data simultaneously.

15. _____ refers collectively to a group of related digital cellular telephone service technologies.

# Short Answer

1. A computer must have a fax modem and a scanner to fully function as a fax device. Explain why the scanner is needed.

2. In terms of the last-mile problem, explain the limitations of the public switched telephone network (PSTN) for sending and receiving computer data.

3. What is the definition of groupware? Provide an example of groupware in action.

4. Define and provide at least one example of technological convergence.

5. Briefly explain how Bluetooth works.

# A Closer Look

1. Examine your most recent telephone bill. What are the various surcharges and taxes? What percentages of your bill are for local calls, long-distance calls, and surcharges and taxes? Is your long-distance company the same as your local one? Are your telephone bills available online? Can you pay them online?

2. Do you own, or have you considered owning, a cellular phone? Contact two communications companies that provide cellular service in your area. What are their various rate plans? Do any of these plans include long-distance service? Do the two companies that you contacted provide Internet access? If they do, describe which Internet services they support and their associated costs.

3. Have you sent or received a facsimile transmission using a computer? Was the fax sent or received from another computer or from an actual fax machine? Could you tell the difference? What was the name of the fax software application that you used? Describe the process for sending and receiving the fax. If you sent a fax, describe how you created the document. If you received a fax, did you print it? Why or why not?

4. Many people have negative feelings about the use of cellular phones. They may be irritated by the careless use of cell phones in public places or concerned about their dangerous use by people driving motor vehicles. Which states have banned drivers from using handheld cell phones? See if you can determine the policies on cellular phone use in aircraft, trains, hospitals, movie theaters, restaurants, and the classrooms on your campus.

5. Teleconferencing is the voice connection of more than two people who are usually far away from each other. For instance, a teleconference might involve coworkers in Denver, Boston, and Orlando. See what you can learn about Internet teleconferencing services. How much do different services charge? Are any of them free? What can you learn about call quality? If you used such a service, would you worry about privacy? Should you? Why?

# On the Web

1. Broadband cable is not readily available in many rural or other low-population areas. But, given a clear view of the southern sky, many of these areas are prime candidates for Direct Broadcast Satellite (DBS). Visit the StarBand Web site at **www.starband.com**. Why do DBS systems require a clear view of the southern sky? Unfortunately, the major weakness of DBS systems is their inability to upload data. The StarBand DBS system by StarBand Communications allows two-way high-speed Internet access. Identify the additional hardware that is necessary to use the StarBand system with a computer. What are the initial hardware costs, installation charges, and monthly service fees? Explain why you would or would not consider using one of these DBS systems for high-speed access. Can these systems also be used to receive television signals?

2. OnStar is a multifaceted communications system that offers a broad range of services. Visit their Web site at **www.onstar.com**. What is the primary function of the OnStar system? Name four automotive manufacturers who supply vehicles with OnStar systems. What are the costs and services provided with the basic and premium service plans? Do you know anyone who has OnStar? What do they think about this service? Would you consider purchasing a vehicle with OnStar? If you would, which plan would you select?

3. Have you tried MSN® TV (formerly known as WebTV)? Visit the MSN® TV site at **resource center.msn.com/access/MSNTV/default.asp** to explore this communications medium.

   - What is needed to connect an MSN® TV?
   - What are the manufacturer's suggested retail prices for the two receivers? Explain which, if either, you would purchase and why.
   - What are the six service plans? Explain which, if any, you would purchase and why.

4. One of the newest technologies in mobile communications is 3G, which stands for *third generation*. Visit the Webopedia site at **webopedia.com** to learn about this new technology. What were the first generations of mobile phones? Although you may think that Sprint created the term "PCS," what organization actually did? What organization developed the specifications for 3G? The present speed for using a cellular phone to connect a computer to the Internet is only 14.4 Kbps. What are the expected transmission rates for 3G connections? When are 3G systems expected to be available? Explain why you would or would not consider purchasing or upgrading to a 3G phone.

5. Go to the Adventure GPS site at **www.gps4fun.com** to examine sophisticated satellite-based communications systems called Global Positioning Systems (GPSs). Who owns the collection of satellites that make up the GPS? How many GPS satellites are there, and how high do they orbit? How does a GPS receiver determine its position? How accurate is a GPS? List a civilian, military, and commercial use of a GPS. Do you know anyone who owns a GPS? Have you tried one? Find a specific model GPS and its price, and explain how you would use it.

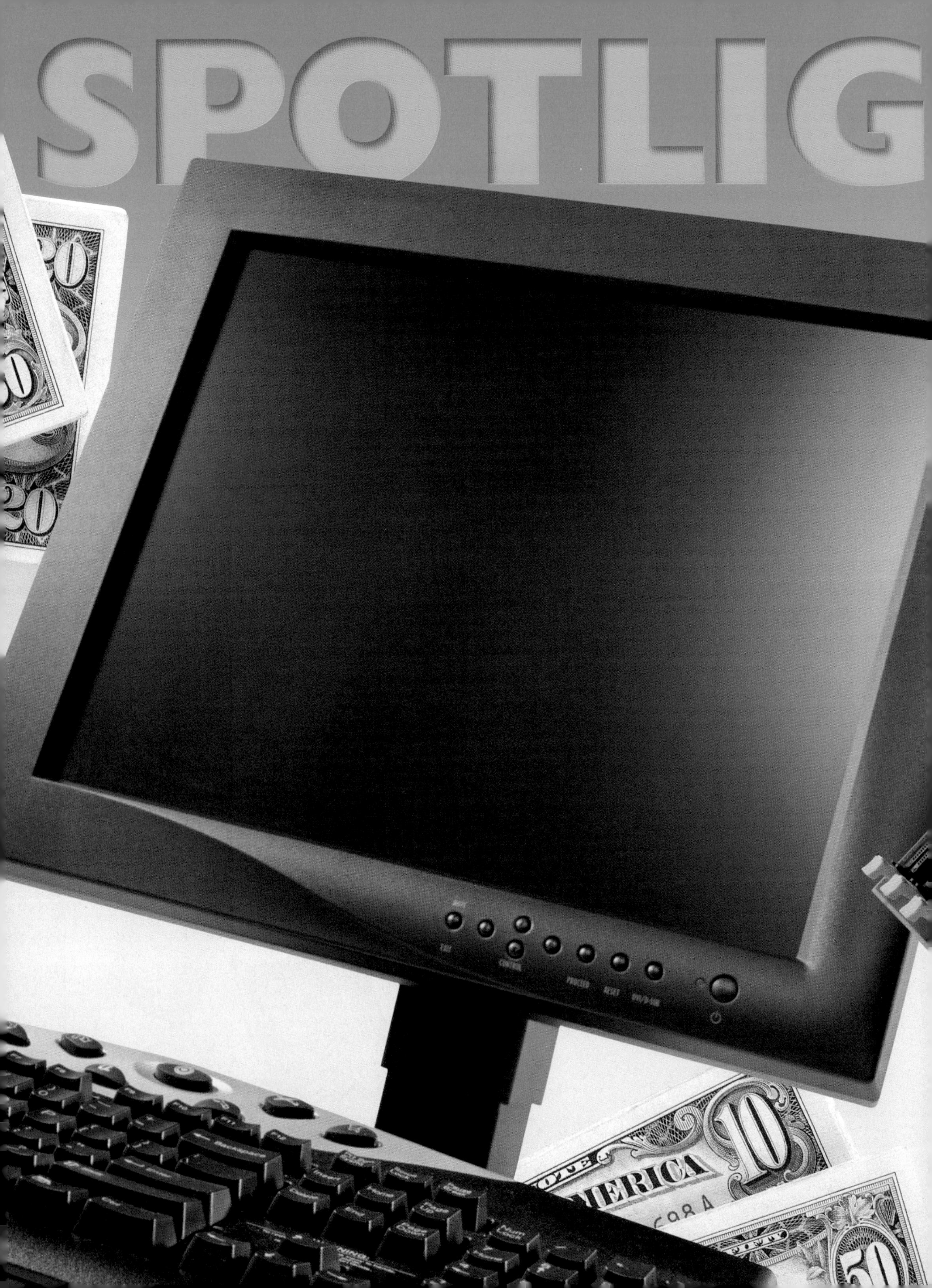
SPOTLIG

# HT

# Buying and Upgrading Your Computer System

When you're buying a computer, there's a lot you need to know in order to make a good decision. But buying a computer doesn't have to be intimidating. Many students successfully purchase and maintain their own computers. In fact, at a typical state university, 80 percent of students own a computer. Having your own PC enables you to type term papers, create slide presentations, and, in many cases, use a high-speed network connection in your own dorm room. In addition, increasing numbers of colleges are encouraging students to purchase a computer upon entering the university. Even though schools still provide computer labs, owning your own computer allows you to work when you want and, in the case of laptops, where you want.

Owning a computer is the best way to ensure computer literacy because, when you own a computer, you are responsible for managing it. And employers are demanding higher levels of computer literacy than ever before. According to a recent study, employers described computer literacy as "important" or "very important" in their hiring decisions. Particularly attractive to employers were the following skills: word processing, e-mail, spreadsheet analysis, database entry and editing, use of presentation software, and Internet searching. If you're in the market for a new computer, you'd be wise to buy a system that can run all this software, and then learn to use as much of it as you can while you're still in school.

This Spotlight will guide you, step by step, through the process of buying your own computer. Read on to learn how to choose the equipment you need for the best prices on today's market.

# Get Started the Right Way

There's a right way and a wrong way to select a computer. The right way involves understanding the terminology and the relative value of the components that make up a computer system. You then determine your software needs and choose the computer that runs this software in the most robust way. What's the wrong way? Buying strictly based on price, being influenced by sales hype, or buying a system you know nothing about.

For these reasons, this Spotlight begins by introducing you to the hardware-first approach. Then we'll move on to system configurations, buying strategies, computer maintenance, and upgrading your system.

# Choose the Right Hardware

Computer systems are made up of many components. The following are the components you need to understand in order to buy a computer wisely:

- ✗ processors
- ✗ memory
- ✗ hard disks
- ✗ internal and/or external drives
- ✗ video cards and monitors
- ✗ network cards
- ✗ modems
- ✗ sound cards and speakers
- ✗ keyboards and mice
- ✗ an uninterruptible power supply

monitor

speakers

CPU

mouse

keyboard

This section introduces you to these components (Figure 4A). Keep in mind as you read that one of the best ways to prepare yourself for buying a computer is to peruse newspaper and magazine ads listing computer systems for sale. Another great source is the Internet. To research particular computer manufacturers (such as Apple, Dell, IBM, Gateway, and so on), simply type the manufacturer's name in the address bar of your Internet browser and add the .com extension. It's also a good idea to visit a good comparison site, such as CNET, MySimon, Yahoo!, AOL, and PCWorld. These sites enable you to perform side-by-side comparisons of different systems.

Let's start our discussion of hardware components by looking at the processor.

**FIGURE 4A** Computer systems include the system unit, monitor, internal and external drives, and input devices such as a keyboard and a mouse.

**FIGURE 4B** Computer systems are named after their processors and clock speed.

## PROCESSORS

Of all the choices you make when buying a computer, which microprocessor to get is the most important. Strictly speaking, the microprocessor (called a processor or CPU for short) *is* the computer, which is why it's the key component in terms of shaping the system's overall performance. In general, the higher the processor's clock speed, the faster the computer (Figure 4B).

As you research processors, keep in mind that you'll pay a premium if you buy the newest and fastest processor available. One approach is to buy the second- or middle-fastest processor on the market. This way

you'll get plenty of speed without paying a penalty for being the first to have the most. In addition, today's processors are so powerful that it's not always necessary to have the fastest one. You only need enough processing power to handle the work or play you intend to accomplish. If you're a heavy game user you may need lots of processing power, but if you use your computer to surf the Net, play audio files, and communicate using e-mail and instant messaging programs, the middle-speed processor on the market will suit you just fine.

## MEMORY

The next item to consider when buying a computer is how much memory you need. Two important issues are the amount of random access memory (RAM) and whether your system is equipped with cache memory. You really can't have too much memory, so a good rule of thumb is to buy as much as you can afford.

### RAM

Windows XP and Mac OS X theoretically require only 64 MB of RAM, but neither system functions very well with so little. When you try to run two or more programs, there's no more room in memory. As a result, the operating system has to store portions of a program on your hard disk, causing sluggish performance. To maximize your computer's performance, you should seriously consider purchasing at least 256 MB of RAM; 512 MB would be even better. Several different types of RAM exist. Currently, the fastest is called synchronous DRAM (SDRAM). For PCs with Pentium IV processors, you need SDRAM capable of running at a speed of 100 MHz. This type of RAM is often called PC100 SDRAM.

### Secondary Cache

Cache memory is built into the processor. As you research this kind of memory, keep in mind that systems with cache memory tend to be faster than systems without it. (Refer to Chapter 4 for an in-depth discussion of secondary cache memory.)

## HARD DISKS

A common mistake made by first-time buyers is to underestimate the amount of disk storage they'll need. Today, 10 GB (gigabytes) sounds like a lot, but you won't believe how quickly you'll fill it up. A good rule of thumb is to use no more than 25 percent of your hard disk space for the operating system and applications. Because Windows XP and Microsoft Office consume up to 2 GB of disk space, a 10 GB drive should be a minimum. The good news is that most entry-level systems on today's market come with a 20 GB hard disk, and it's relatively inexpensive to upgrade to 40 or 60 GB.

Among computer systems that have the same processor, hard disk speed makes the biggest contribution to overall system speed. Suppose you're looking at two Pentium IV systems with 3 GHz processors. The less expensive one might use a slow hard drive, which can slow the system down so much that it isn't much faster than a well-designed 2 GHz system. In particular, pay attention to rotation speed; drives that spin at 5,400 RPM are bottom-of-the-line products. The better drives spin at 7,200 or 10,000 RPM.

## INTERNAL AND/OR EXTERNAL DRIVES

To install new software, most of which is distributed on CD-ROM discs, you'll want a CD-ROM drive. You can get CD-ROM drives with speeds of up to 70x (70 times the original CD-ROM standard of 150 Kbps). You may consider a DVD drive instead of a CD-ROM drive. In addition to reading the same CD-ROM discs, you'll be able to read DVD discs, which can store up to 4.7 GB of data. For example, you'll be able to view movies and store up to 1,300 MP3 files (Figure 4C). It's also a good idea to buy a system that has the ability to write to CDs or DVDs, such as a CD-RW drive, to read and write files to a CD for portable storage of your data.

Increasingly popular are Zip drives for backup and supplemental storage. You can add a Zip drive (with up to 750 MB removable disks) to your system for about $100. Another option is Sony's HiFD, a removable storage drive that uses cartridges capable of holding more than 200 MB. HiFD drives have an advantage over Zip drives: they're downwardly compatible with 3.5-inch floppy disks. However, users are increasingly choosing Zip disks over floppies, so you should make your decision based on how large you expect your files to be and whether other computer systems you work with use floppies or Zip disks.

**FIGURE 4C** DVD discs can store more data than CD-ROM discs, and a DVD drive will also read ordinary CD-ROM discs.

## VIDEO CARDS AND MONITORS

The computer's **video card** determines the quality and resolution of the display you see on your monitor. The current standard display for a Windows PC is a **Super Video Graphics Array** (**SVGA**) monitor with a resolution of either 1024 x 768 or 1280 x 1024. High-end video cards can display resolutions of 1600 x 1200. The higher the resolution, the more memory is required. To display 1600 x 1200 resolution with a color palette of 16.7 million colors, for example, you need to equip

**FIGURE 4D (1&2)**
(1) A 17-inch monitor is considered to be the industry standard. (2) Flat-screen monitors are becoming increasingly popular.

your video card with 8 MB of **video RAM** (**VRAM**), memory that's set aside for video processing.

Advanced systems offer a special bus design that directly connects the video circuits with the microprocessor, increasing performance speed considerably. In Windows PCs, the best systems currently offer an **Accelerated Graphics Port** (**AGP**), which transfers video data much more quickly than the standard PCI interface.

If you plan to run Microsoft Windows, look for a system that has a graphics accelerator built into the video card. A **graphics accelerator** is a display adapter that contains its own dedicated processing circuitry and VRAM, enabling faster display of complex graphics. This accessory can double or triple the performance of Windows.

Monitors are available in different sizes. You can purchase anything from a 14-inch to a 21-inch monitor, but the larger the monitor, the higher the cost. Increasingly, a 17-inch monitor is considered the industry standard (Figure 4D). If you plan to get into desktop publishing or CAD, you may want to upgrade to a 21-inch monitor. Keep in mind that for cathode-ray tube (CRT) displays, the quoted size of the monitor is the size of the CRT's front surface measured diagonally. However, since some of this surface is hidden and unavailable for display purposes, it's important to distinguish between the monitor's quoted size and the viewable area. Although they're more expensive than traditional CRTs, flat-screen monitors have gained recent popularity due to the fact that they have less distortion and therefore cause less eye strain.

The monitor's dot pitch is also an important factor. **Dot pitch** (also called aperture grill) is a physical characteristic that determines the smallest dot the screen can display. Don't buy a monitor with a dot pitch larger than .28mm—the smaller the dot pitch, the better your display.

## NETWORK CARDS

If you're planning to connect your computer to the campus network, you need a **network interface card** (**NIC**). Check with your college's computer center to find out what kind of network card you need. Most colleges run 10 Mbps (10baseT) Ethernets, but a few require you to get a 100 Mbps (100baseT) network card.

On Macintoshes, support for Ethernet networks is built in, but you need a **transceiver**, a device that handles the electrical connection between the cable and the Mac's Ethernet port, to actually connect. On Windows PCs, you need an Ethernet card, which already includes the transceiver (Figure 4E). Look for a card that plugs into your computer's Peripheral Component Interconnect (PCI) bus.

**FIGURE 4E** An Ethernet card is a network interface card designed to work with Ethernet local area networks (LANs).

## MODEMS

If you plan to log on to the campus network by means of a telephone connection, you need a modem. Many computers now come with a modem built into the system, so buying an external modem is unnecessary. Today's standard modem uses the 56 Kbps V.90 protocol. Check with your campus computer center to find out how to connect to your school's system and which modem protocols are supported.

## SOUND CARDS AND SPEAKERS

To take full advantage of the Internet's multimedia capabilities, you need a sound card and speakers.

On Macs, the sound is built in; you need external speakers, though, to hear sounds in stereo. On Windows PCs, you'll need to equip your system with a sound card. Look for a sound card that offers **wavetable synthesis**, which uses stored samples of real musical instrument sounds, as well as a PCI interface, which reduces demands on your processor. For the richest sound, equip your system with a subwoofer, which reproduces bass notes realistically.

Be aware that many computers come with cheap speakers, especially the lowest-priced systems. If sound matters a lot to you—and it does to many college students—consider upgrading to a higher-quality, name-brand speaker system.

## KEYBOARDS AND MICE

Most computers come with standard keyboards. If you use your computer keyboard a lot and you're worried about repetitive stress injury (RSI), consider upgrading to an ergonomic keyboard, such as the Microsoft Natural Keyboard.

Most systems also come with a basic mouse, but you can ask for an upgrade. With Windows PCs, there's good reason to do so, thanks to the improved mouse support built into Windows XP. Any mouse that supports Microsoft's IntelliMouse standard includes a wheel that enables you to scroll through documents with ease. Wheel mice also include programmable buttons that allow you to tailor your mouse usage to the software application you're using (Figure 4F).

In order to choose a good keyboard and mouse, go to a local store that sells computers and try some out. The button placement and action can be quite different from model to model. You'll be using these input devices a lot, so be sure to make an informed decision.

## UNINTERRUPTIBLE POWER SUPPLY (UPS)

"I'm sorry I don't have my paper. I finished it, and then a power outage wiped out my work." If this excuse sounds familiar, you may want to purchase an **uninterruptible power supply** (**UPS**), a device that provides power to a computer system for a short period of time if electrical power is lost. Considering the comparatively low price of today's UPSs—you can get one with surge protection for less than $200—it's wise to consider buying one for your campus computer, especially if you experience frequent power outages where you live or work. A UPS allows you enough time to save your work and shut down your computer properly until the power is back on.

**FIGURE 4F** The wheel mouse includes a scrolling wheel and programmable buttons.

# Notebook or Desktop?

Deciding whether to buy a notebook or a desktop computer is often one of the hardest decisions you'll have to make when considering which computer to buy (Figure 4G). Today's notebook (or laptop) computers rival desktop machines in terms of power. The best of them are truly awesome machines, with big (over 14-inch) displays and fast processors.

The main advantages of having a notebook are portability and size. Since notebooks are portable, you can take them to class in a specially designed carrying case (Figure 4H). Once in class, you can easily fit a notebook on your desk to type notes. As you're probably well aware, campus housing or shared rental units often limit the amount of space for a desk, which makes notebooks even more appealing.

**FIGURE 4G** Notebook computers are convenient but more expensive than comparable desktop models. Deciding whether to buy a notebook or a desktop computer is often one of the hardest decisions college students make.

On the downside, notebook computers cost more than comparable desktop models. You should also consider that notebooks are easy to lose or steal, and if your notebook goes missing, your precious data will go along with it. More than 250,000 notebook computers are stolen each year, mostly at airports and hotels. Recently, however, thieves have been targeting college campuses, making safety another important factor when considering a notebook.

In the end, the decision most often hinges upon convenience versus expense. You might want to pay a visit to your professor to ask his or her advice. In addition, your family, friends, and coworkers may be able to tell you what they have used and preferred. Notebooks have come a long way, but the desktop computer is still the most popular model on the market.

**FIGURE 4H** Notebook computers allow you to take your work with you wherever you go. Special carrying cases protect your computer from the wear and tear of traveling.

# Mac or PC?

No doubt you're aware that there are two main platforms of computer systems: Windows (PC) and Macintosh (Figure 4I). If you ask around, you'll find that some users prefer the Mac, while other users prefer Windows. Each thinks their platform is the best, and rarely do they cross platforms. How do you know which system is best for you?

Here's the truth. *Today's top-of-the-line Macintoshes and PCs are virtually indistinguishable in terms of features and performance.* What's more, excellent software for all the important applications you'll need—word processing, e-mail, spreadsheets, database software, presentation graphics, and Web browsers—is available for both platforms. Macs used to be easier to set up and use, but thanks to improvements in Microsoft Windows, Macs and PCs are now about even.

So is it a toss-up? Not quite. Some minor differences between Macs and PCs can become major issues for some people. Although Macs can read most PC files, and conversion software is available, compatibility within an organization is critical. If your professor or place of work uses PCs, you'll probably have fewer conversion problems if you also have a PC. In some cases the type of computer doesn't make a difference, but oftentimes, compatibility issues can cause real headaches.

Career interests enter into the Mac-versus-PC picture, too. In general, Macs have a strong niche market in artistic fields, such as publishing, music, graphics, illustration, and Web site design. PCs figure prominently on the desktops of engineers and businesspeople. The classic stereotype is that the successful artist has a Mac, but her accountant uses a PC. But like all stereotypes, this is not always the case. For example, you might think that scientists would use PCs, but that's not necessarily true. In the "wet" sciences (chemistry and biology), Macs have many adherents—and for good reason. These sciences involve visual representation, an area in which Macs excel.

If you're on a budget, consider the cost angle, too. Although the price gap is narrowing, Macs and Mac peripherals and software are somewhat more expensive than comparable PC equipment. Another point in favor of the PC is Linux. Although a version of Linux is available for the Mac, the PC version is where you'll find all the action; more than 90 percent of the computers in use today are PCs, and developers are more inclined to develop software for the broadest market. However, you can run Linux on the same hard drive as Windows or Mac OS, giving you the best of both worlds.

What truly distinguishes Macs from PCs is software availability. Far more programs are available for Windows PCs than for Macintoshes. Only about one Macintosh is sold for every 20 Windows PCs. Many software companies that formerly focused on the Macintosh are de-emphasizing Mac software and bringing out Windows products. Other publishers are dropping Mac products altogether. For example, Autodesk, publisher of the top-selling CAD program, AutoCAD, dropped its sluggish-selling Mac version to focus on its Windows products. This fact alone pretty much rules out the Mac if you're interested in architecture or engineering. Even software publishers that continue to support the Mac typically bring out the Mac versions later and don't include as many features.

Does software availability make a difference? If you're planning to use your computer only for basic applications, such as word processing, e-mail, Web

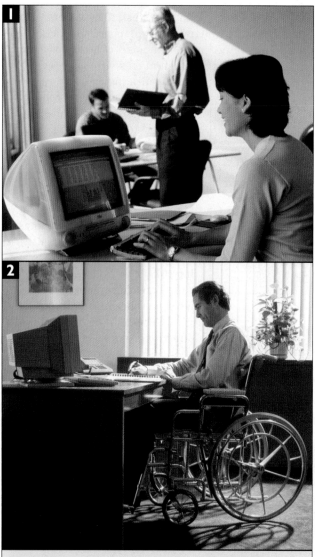

**FIGURE 4I (1&2)** (1) Macs have a strong niche market in artistic fields, such as publishing, music, graphics, illustration, and Web site design. (2) PCs figure prominently on the desktops of engineers and businesspeople.

browsing, and spreadsheets, the Mac-versus-PC issue simply isn't important. But look down the road. What if you declare a major a couple of years from now, only to find that your professors want you to use special-purpose programs designed to run on a different type of computer? Thus, as you decide whether to buy a PC or a Mac, it's important that you anticipate your future software needs. Find out which programs students in your major field of study are using, as well as which programs are used by graduates working in the career you're planning to pursue.

To find out what type of computer is preferred by people working in your chosen career, interview appropriate professionals, or ask students or professors in that department at your school. It might turn out that one of your major's required courses uses analytical software that runs only on a PC capable of crunching numbers at high speed, or uses a design program that runs only on a Mac loaded with memory.

Keep in mind that any computer on the market will handle your basic needs of word processing, e-mail, Web browsing, and basic number crunching. If you can learn what specialized programs you might have the need for, you'll be one step ahead in making sure that the system you purchase can not only run the software, but run it without straining resources.

# Get the Right Printer

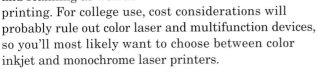

Printers fall into four basic categories: color inkjet printers, monochrome laser printers, color laser printers, and multifunction devices that include faxing and scanning as well as printing. For college use, cost considerations will probably rule out color laser and multifunction devices, so you'll most likely want to choose between color inkjet and monochrome laser printers.

Although laser printers continue to slightly outperform inkjet printers, the difference in print quality is not enough to justify the price differential. As a result, which printer is best depends for the most part on your budget. Although monochrome laser printers are more expensive than color inkjet printers, laser printers are cheaper to use in the long run because

laser toner cartridges, priced on a cost-per-page basis, are cheaper than inkjet cartridges.

Speed matters, too. The slowest laser printers are faster than the fastest inkjet printers, and the slowest inkjet printers operate at a glacial pace. High-end laser printers can print as many as 60 ppm (pages per minute). Still, the best inkjet printers churn out black-and-white pages at a peppy pace—as many as 18 ppm. If you go the inkjet route, look for a printer that can print at least 8 ppm.

Printing technology has come a long way in the past 10 years. Stay with a major brand name and you'll be served well. It's always a good idea to purchase an extra print cartridge and to stash it away with 30 or 40 sheets of paper. This way, Murphy's Law won't catch you at two in the morning trying to finish an assignment without ink or paper.

# Shop Wisely

As you get ready to buy a computer, it's important that you shop wisely. Should you buy a top-of-the-line model or a bargain-bin special? Are mail-order companies safe? What about refurbished or used computers? Let's take a look at some of these issues.

### TOP-OF-THE-LINE VS. BARGAIN-BIN SPECIAL

Should you buy a top-of-the-line system, or try to save some money by getting a slower, older model? A good argument for getting the best system you can afford is that you don't want it to become obsolete before you graduate. In your senior year, do you want to spend time upgrading your hard drive when you should be focusing on your studies? In addition, every time you open the computer's cover and change something, you risk damaging one of the internal components.

The most important consideration here is the type of software you're planning to run. If you'll be using your computer for basic applications such as word processing, you don't need the most powerful computer available. In this situation, a bargain-bin special may be okay, as long as you exercise caution when making such a purchase. But what if you decide to declare a major in mechanical engineering? You might want to run a CAD package, and CAD programs demand a fast system with lots of memory. In that case, you'd be better off paying extra to get the memory you need up front, rather than settling for a bargain-bin special that may end up being inadequate later.

## LOCAL STORES VS. MAIL-ORDER/ONLINE COMPANIES

Whether you're looking for a Windows PC or a Macintosh, you need to consider whether you want to purchase your system locally or from a mail-order or online company. If you buy locally, you can resolve problems quickly by going back to the store (Figure 4J). With a system ordered over the telephone or online, you have to call the company's technical support line.

If you're considering ordering through the mail or online, look for companies that have been in business a long time—and particularly those that offer a no-questions-asked return policy for the first 30 days. Without such a policy, you could get stuck with a "lemon" system that even the manufacturer won't be able to repair. Be aware that the lowest price isn't always the best deal—particularly if the item isn't in stock and will take weeks to reach you. Also, don't forget about shipping and handling charges, which could add considerably to the price of a system purchased online or through the mail.

Also, make sure you're not comparing artichokes and oranges. Some quoted prices include accessories such as modems and monitors; others do not. To establish a level playing field for comparison, use the Shopping Comparison Worksheet in Figure 4K. For the system's actual price, be sure to get a quote that includes all the accessories you want, such as a modem, a monitor, and a UPS.

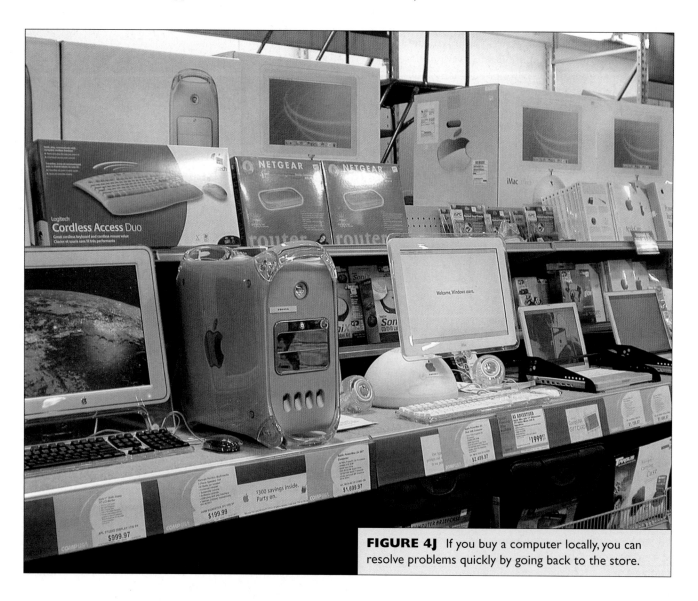

**FIGURE 4J** If you buy a computer locally, you can resolve problems quickly by going back to the store.

# Shopping Comparison Worksheet

**VENDOR** _____  Date _____
  Brand Name _____
  Model _____
  Real Price _____ (including selected components)

**PROCESSOR**
  Brand _____
  Model _____
  Speed _____ MHz

**RAM**
  Type _____
  Amount _____ MB

**HARD DRIVE**
  Capacity _____ GB      Seek time _____ ns
  Speed _____ rpm        Interface _____

**MONITOR**
  Size _____ x _____ pixels   Dot pitch _____ mm

**VIDEO CARD**
  Memory _____ MB        Max. resolution _____ x _____ pixels
  Accelerated? . . . . . . . . . . ☐ yes ☐ no

**FLOPPY/ZIP DRIVE(S)**
  Capacity _____ KB      Number _____

**REMOVABLE DRIVE**
  Type _____
  Location . . . . . . . . . .☐ internal ☐ external

**CD-ROM DRIVE**
  Speed _____

**CD BURNER**
  Included? . . . . . . . . . . . . . . ☐ yes ☐ no

**DVD-ROM DRIVE**
  Included? . . . . . . . . . . . . . . ☐ yes ☐ no

**SPEAKERS**
  Included? . . . . . . . . . . . . ☐ yes ☐ no   Upgraded? . . . . . . . . . . . . . ☐ yes ☐ no

**SUBWOOFER**
  Included? . . . . . . . . . . . . . . ☐ yes ☐ no

**SOUND CARD**
  Included? . . . . . . . . . . . . . . ☐ yes ☐ no

**NETWORK CARD**
  Included? . . . . . . . . . . . . ☐ yes ☐ no   Speed (10/100) _____

**MODEM**
  Included? . . . . . . . . . . . . ☐ yes ☐ no   Protocol _____

**KEYBOARD**
  Upgraded? . . . . . . . . . . . . ☐ yes ☐ no   Model _____

**MOUSE**
  Included? . . . . . . . . . . . . ☐ yes ☐ no   Upgraded? _____

**UPS**
  Included? . . . . . . . . . . . . . . ☐ yes ☐ no

**SOFTWARE**
_____
_____

**WARRANTY** _____
**Service location** _____
**Typical service turnaround time** _____

**FIGURE 4K**
Shopping Comparison Worksheet

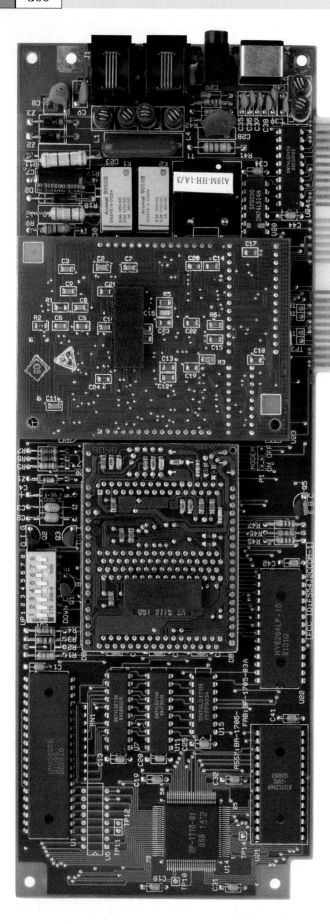

## BUYING USED OR REFURBISHED

What about buying a used system? It's risky. If you're buying from an individual, chances are the system is priced too high. People just can't believe how quickly computers lose value. They think their systems are worth a lot more than they actually are. Try finding some used computer ads in your local newspaper, then see how much it would cost to buy the same system new, right now, if it's still on the market. Chances are the new system is cheaper than the used one.

In addition, there are reputable businesses that refurbish and upgrade systems for resale. National chains such as MacWarehouse have standards that help to ensure that their systems are "as good as new" when you make a purchase. As always, be sure to check out the storefront and stay away from establishments that don't look or feel right. And most important, make sure that your refurbished machine comes with a warranty.

## NAME-BRAND VS. GENERIC PCS

The name-brand PC manufacturers, such as Hewlett-Packard, Dell, and Gateway, offer high-quality systems at competitive prices. You can buy some of these systems from retail or mail-order stores, but some, such as Dell computers, are available only by contacting the vendor directly.

If you're buying extended warranty protection that includes on-site service, make sure the on-site service really is available where you live; you may find out that the service is available only in major metropolitan areas. Make sure you get 24-hour technical support; you'll probably need it.

One disadvantage of name-brand systems is their use of proprietary components. If something breaks down, you have only one repair option: go back to the manufacturer. And, after the warranty has expired, you may end up paying a premium price for parts and repairs. Fortunately, this is becoming less and less of an issue. Almost all of today's name-brand computers run well right out of the box, and in-service failure rates are declining.

What about generic PCs? In most cities, you'll find local computer stores that assemble their own systems using off-the-shelf components. These systems are often just as fast (and just as reliable) as name-brand systems because they use the same components. You save because you don't pay for the name-brand company's marketing and distribution costs.

What you may not get from such stores is adequate technical support. Another thing to consider is that the industry's profit margin is razor-thin; if the company goes bankrupt, your warranty may not mean much.

# Caring for Your Computer System

After your computer is running smoothly, chances are it will run flawlessly for years if you take a few precautions:

✗ Equip your system with a **surge protector**, a device that will protect all system components from power surges caused by lightning or other power irregularities (Figure 4L).

✗ Consider purchasing an uninterruptible power supply (UPS). These devices help to ensure that your system is protected should the computer lose power.

✗ Don't plug your dorm refrigerator into the same outlet as your computer. A refrigerator can cause fluctuations in power, and consistent power supply is critical to the performance and longevity of your computer. Manage it well.

✗ Make sure there's sufficient air circulation around the components. Don't block air intake grilles.

✗ If you connect or disconnect any cables, make sure you switch off the power first.

✗ Make sure the cables aren't stretched or mashed by furniture.

✗ Avoid eating or drinking near your computer. Crumbs can gum up your keyboard, and spilled liquids (even small amounts) can ruin an entire system.

✗ Don't switch off the power without following the proper shut-down procedure.

✗ To keep your hard disk running smoothly, run a disk defragmentation program regularly. This program ensures that related data is stored as a unit, increasing retrieval speed. In Windows, the defragmenting program is usually found under the Accessories menu choice on the Start, Programs menu.

✗ Get antivirus software and run it frequently. Don't install and run any software someone gives you on a disk until you run a virus check on the disk and its contents. If someone gives you a document file on a disk, be sure to check for macro viruses.

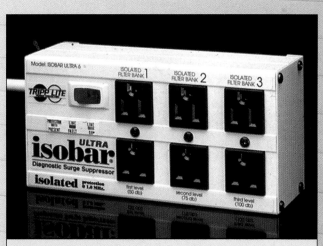

**FIGURE 4L** Surge protectors help prevent costly damage to delicate circuitry and components.

Be sure to keep your computer clean, too:

X *Clean your computer and printer with a damp, soft, lint-free cloth.*

X *To clean your monitor, spray some window cleaner on a soft, lint-free cloth—not directly on the monitor—and then wipe the surface clean.*

X *If your mouse gets gummed up, twist off the ring on the bottom of the mouse, remove the ball, and clean the ball with warm, soapy water. Rinse and dry it thoroughly with a clean, lint-free cloth. Clean the rollers with a cotton swab, and remove any lint that may have accumulated.*

X *To clean your keyboard, disconnect it from the system unit and gently shake out any dust or crumbs. You can also use cans of compressed air to clear dust or crumbs from underneath keys. Also on the market are specially designed vacuums for keyboards. Never use a regular vacuum cleaner on your keyboard, as the suction is too strong and may damage the keys.*

# Upgrading Your System

Many computer owners improve their systems' performance and utility by adding new hardware, such as modems, sound cards, and additional memory. This section discusses the two most common hardware upgrades: adding expansion boards and adding memory.

Before you decide to upgrade your computer on your own, be aware that doing so may violate your computer's warranty. Read the warranty to find out. You may need to take your computer to an authorized service center to get an upgrade. Also, while it can be relatively simple to install new components, doing so can be risky. If you aren't absolutely certain of what you're doing—don't!

## REMOVING THE COVER

To upgrade your system, begin by unplugging the power cord and removing all the cables attached to the back of the unit. Make a note of which cable went where so you can correctly plug the cables back in later. With most systems, you can remove the cover by removing the screws on the back of the case. If you don't know how to remove the cover, consult your computer manual. Keep the screws in a cup or bowl so they'll be handy when you reassemble the computer.

## ADDING EXPANSION BOARDS

To add an expansion board to your system, identify the correct type of expansion slot (ISA, PCI, or AGP), and unscrew the metal insert that blocks the slot's access hole. Save the screw, but discard the insert. Gently but firmly press the board into the slot. Don't try to force it, though, and stop pressing if the motherboard flexes. If the motherboard flexes, it is not properly supported, and you should take your computer to the dealer to have it inspected. When you've pressed the new expansion board fully into place, screw it down using the screw you removed from the metal insert. Before replacing the cover, carefully check to make sure the board is fully inserted.

## UPGRADING MEMORY

Many users find that their systems run faster when they add more memory. With additional memory, it's less likely that the operating system will need to use virtual memory, which slows the computer down. In order to upgrade your computer's memory, you'll find it helpful to learn a few terms and concepts.

Older computers use memory chips supplied on 72-pin **single inline memory modules (SIMMs)**; most newer computers use 168-pin **dual inline memory modules (DIMMs)**. SIMMs and DIMMs are printed circuit boards (with affixed memory chips) that are designed to snap into specially designed sockets on the computer's motherboard. Most motherboards have either four SIMM sockets or two to three DIMM sockets (Figure 4M). SIMMs must be installed in pairs, which limits their flexibility. Since you don't need to install DIMMs in pairs, they're often easier to work with.

SIMMs and DIMMS are available in various capacities, ranging from 8 MB to 128 MB each. You need to consult your computer's manual to determine whether your computer uses SIMMs or DIMMs, and where you can add them. For example, suppose your computer has two 8 MB SIMMs in the first two sockets, leaving two sockets empty. Because you must install SIMMs in pairs, you can add two 8 MB SIMMs (for a total of 32 MB of memory—the original 16 plus the additional 16), two 16 MB SIMMs (for a total of 48 MB of memory—16 + 32), or two 32 MB SIMMs (for a total of 80 MB of memory—16 + 64).

Consult your computer's manual to determine which type of memory technology your computer uses. Older computers use the slowest of these technologies, **fast-page mode** (**FPM**) **DRAM**, which is available only in SIMMs. Newer computers use the faster **extended data out** (**EDO**) **DRAM**, which is available in both SIMMs and DIMMs. Still newer computers

use the fastest available memory technology, called **synchronous dynamic RAM** (**SDRAM**), which is available only in DIMMs.

You also need to consider the memory chips' speed. FPM and EDO DRAM chips are rated in nanoseconds (ns), billionths of a second. The smaller the number, the faster the chip. Pentiums require 60ns chips, while older systems can work with 70ns or 80ns chips. For SDRAM chips, the speed is rated in megahertz (MHz), millions of cycles per second, and this speed must match the speed of the motherboard's data bus (66 MHz, 100 MHz, or 133 MHz).

When you purchase memory modules, a knowledgeable salesperson might help you determine which type of module you need and how much memory you can install. But more often the salesperson won't know any more about installing memory than you do. This further reinforces the case for buying locally if you think that you'll need or want to upgrade your system during its life span.

Before you install memory modules, be aware that memory chips are easily destroyed by static electricity. Do not attempt to install memory chips without wearing a **grounding strap**, a wrist-attached device that

**FIGURE 4M** Memory modules are affixed to slots on the motherboard.

grounds your body so that you can't zap the chips. Remember: don't try to force the memory modules into their receptacles; they're supposed to snap in gently. If they won't go in, you don't have the module aligned correctly, or you may have the wrong type of module.

## REPLACING THE COVER

When you have checked your work and you're satisfied that the new hardware is correctly installed, replace the cover and screw it down firmly. Replace the cables and then restart your system. If you added Plug and Play devices, you'll see on-screen instructions that help you configure your computer to use your new hardware.

# Summary

To be a savvy consumer, you need to become familiar with the terminology and significant components of the system you're buying. Among other components, the processor, memory, hard disk, and monitor will determine both the comfort and quality of your computing experience. Other things you need to consider are whether you want a desktop or a notebook, a PC or a Mac, and what storage devices, printer, and peripherals you'll need.

Research is fairly painless and very powerful. The Internet makes side-by-side comparison easy. For instance, typing "PC comparison shopping" (including the quotes) into the Google search engine returns more than 15 pages of links. Use as many resources as you can, and then remember that no matter how happy or unhappy you are with the result, you'll most likely be doing it all again within three years.

# Acronym Finder

**NOTE: SEE GLOSSARY FOR DEFINITIONS**

**3GL** See third-generation language.

**4GL** See fourth-generation language.

**ADSL** See Asymmetric Digital Subscriber Line.

**AGP** See Accelerated Graphics Port.

**AGV** See automatic guided vehicle.

**AI** See artificial intelligence.

**ALU** See arithmetic-logic unit.

**ASCII** See American Standard Code for Information Interchange.

**ATA** See Advanced Technology Attachment.

**AUP** See acceptable use policy.

**BIOS** See basic input/output system.

**BMP** See Windows Bitmap.

**BPR** See business process reengineering.

**bps** See bits per second.

**BRI** See Basic Rate Interface.

**CA** See certificate authority.

**CAD** See computer-aided design.

**CAI** See computer-assisted instruction.

**CAM** See computer-aided manufacturing.

**CAPE** See computer-aided production engineering.

**CASE** See computer-aided software engineering.

**cat-5** See category 5.

**CAVE** See Cave Automated Virtual Environment.

**CBE** See computer-based education.

**CBT** See computer-based training.

**CCD** See charge-coupled device.

**CD-R** See compact disc-recordable.

**CD-ROM** See compact disc read-only memory or CD-ROM drive.

**CD-RW** See compact disc-rewritable.

**CIM** See computer-integrated manufacturing.

**CIS** See computer information system.

**CISC** See complex instruction set computer.

**CMI** See computer-managed instruction.

**CMI** See copyright management infrastructure.

**CMOS** See complementary metal-oxide semiconductor.

**COM** See Component Object Model.

**CORBA** See Common Object Request Broker Architecture.

**CPU** See central processing unit.

**CRT** See cathode ray tube.

**CS** See computer science.

**CSCW** See computer-supported cooperative work.

**CSS** See Cascading Style Sheet.

**CTD** See cumulative trauma disorder.

**CTS** See carpal tunnel syndrome.

**CVS** See computer vision syndrome.

**DBS** See Direct Broadcast Satellite.

**DIMM** See dual inline memory module.

**DMA** See direct memory access.

**DNS** See domain name server.

**DoS** See denial of service attack.

**DRAM** See dynamic random access memory.

**DSL** See Digital Subscriber Line.

**DSS** See decision support system.

**DTP** See desktop publishing.

**DTV** See digital television.

**DVD** See digital video disc.

**DVD-RAM** See digital video disc-RAM.

**DVD-ROM** See digital video disc-ROM.

**EBCDIC** See Extended Binary Coded Decimal Interchange Code.

**EDI** See electronic data interchange.

**EE** See electrical engineering.

**EIDE** See Enhanced IDE.

**EIS** See executive information system.

**EPIRB** See Emergency Position Indicating Radio Beacons.

**EPS** See Encapsulated PostScript.

**ERD** See entity-relationship diagram.

**ERMA** See Electronic Recording Machine—Accounting.

**ESS** See executive support system.

**FAT** See file allocation table.

**FED** See field emission display.

**FPU** See floating-point unit.

**GIF** See Graphics Interchange Format.

**GPL** See General Public License.

**GPS** See Global Positioning System.

**GUI** See graphical user interface.

**HGP** See Human Genome Project.

**HMD** See head-mounted display.

**HTML** See Hypertext Markup Language.

**HTTP** See Hypertext Transfer Protocol.

**IC** See integrated circuit.

**IDE** See Integrated Drive Electronics.

**IIOP** See Internet Inter-Orb Protocol.

**ILS** See integrated learning system.

**IM** See instant messaging.

**IMAP** See Internet Message Access Protocol.

**IP** See Internet Protocol.

**IS** See information systems.

**ISA** See Industry Standard Architecture.

**ISDN** See Integrated Services Digital Network.

**ISP** See Internet service provider.
**ITS** See Intelligent Transportation System.
**ITU** See International Telecommunications Union.
**IXC** See interexchange carrier.
**JAD** See joint application development.
**JIT** See job instruction training.
**JIT** See just-in-time.
**JPEG** See Joint Photographic Experts Group.
**K** See kilobyte.
**KB** See kilobyte.
**L2** See level 2.
**LAN** See local area network.
**LATA** See local access and transport area.
**LCD** See liquid crystal display.
**LEC** See local exchange carrier.
**LSI** See large-scale integration.
**M** See megabyte.
**MAN** See metropolitan area network.
**MB** See megabyte.
**MICR** See magnetic-ink character recognition.
**MIDI** See Musical Instrument Digital Interface.
**MIME** See Multipurpose Internet Mail Extensions.
**MIS** See management information system.
**MO** See magneto-optic.
**MP3** See MPEG Audio Layer 3.
**MPEG** See Moving Picture Experts Group.
**MRI** See magnetic resonance imaging.
**MSI** See medium-scale integration.
**MTBF** See mean time between failures.
**MUD** See multiuser dungeon.
**NAS** See network attached storage.
**NC** See network computer.
**NIC** See network interface card.
**NOS** See network operating system.
**OCR** See optical character recognition.
**OLAP** See online analytical processing.
**OLE** See object linking and embedding.
**OMR** See optical mark reader.
**OO** See object-oriented.
**OOP** See object-oriented programming.
**OS** See operating system.
**P3P** See Platform for Privacy Preferences.
**PBX** See private branch exchange.
**PC** See personal computer.
**PCI** See Personal Computer Interface.
**PCS** See Personal Communication Service.
**PDA** See personal digital assistant.
**PDL** See page description language.
**PDLC** See program development life cycle.
**PDN** See public data network.
**PICS** See Platform for Internet Content Selection.
**PIM** See personal information manager.

**PNG** See Portable Network Graphics.
**PnP** See Plug and Play.
**PoP** See point of presence.
**POP** See Post Office Protocol.
**POS** See point-of-sale.
**POTS** See Plain Old Telephone Service.
**PSTN** See public switched telephone network.
**PVC** See permanent virtual circuit.
**QBE** See query by example.
**QIC** See quarter-inch cartridge.
**QoS** See quality of service.
**RAD** See rapid application development.
**RAM** See random access memory.
**RBOCs** See Regional Bell Operating Companies.
**RFP** See request for proposal.
**RFQ** See request for quotation.
**RISC** See reduced instruction set computer.
**ROI** See return on investment.
**ROM** See read-only memory.
**RSI** See repetitive strain injury.
**SCSI** See Small Computer System Interface.
**SDLC** See systems development life cycle.
**SDRAM** See synchronous DRAM.
**SIMM** See single inline memory module.
**SMIL** See Synchronized Multimedia Integration Language.
**SMTP** See Simple Mail Transport Protocol.
**SOHO** See small office/home office.
**SONET** See Synchronous Optical Network.
**SQL** See Structured Query Language.
**SSI** See small-scale integration.
**SVGA** See Super Video Graphics Array.
**TCP** See Transmission Control Protocol.
**TFT** See thin film transistor.
**TLD** See top-level domain.
**TPS** See transaction processing system.
**UPC** See universal product code.
**UPS** See uninterruptible power supply.
**URL** See uniform resource locator.
**USB** See universal serial bus.
**VAN** See value-added network.
**VAR** See value-added reseller.
**VB** See Visual Basic.
**VLSI** See very-large-scale integration.
**VPN** See virtual private network.
**VR** See virtual reality.
**W3C** See World Wide Web Consortium.
**WAN** See wide area network.
**WLAN** See wireless LAN.
**WORM** See write once, read many.
**WWW** See World Wide Web.
**XML** See Extensible Markup Language.

# Glossary

## DEFINITIONS

**@** In an e-mail address, a symbol used to separate the user name from the name of the computer on which the user's mailbox is stored (for example, frodo@bagend.org). Pronounced "at."

**10baseT** An Ethernet local area network capable of transmitting 10 megabits of data per second through twisted-pair cabling.

**100baseT** See Fast Ethernet.

**128-bit domestic-level encryption** A level of encryption used for secure Web sites and e-mail that uses an encryption bit length of 128. This bit length prevents the message from being intercepted and decoded, but current U.S. export regulations prevent U.S. companies from exporting software that incorporates this strong level of encryption.

**1394 port** An input-output port that combines high-speed performance (up to 400 Mbps) with the ability to guarantee data delivery at a specified speed, making the port ideal for use with real-time devices such as digital video cameras. Synonymous with FireWire, which is Apple Computer's name for this technology.

**3D graphics adapter** A video adapter that can display images that provide the illusion of depth as well as height and width.

**3-D rendering** Transforming graphic images by adding shading and light sources so that they appear to be three-dimensional.

**40-bit encryption** A minimal level of encryption supplied with most Web browsers. Although this encryption level is insufficient to guarantee confidentiality during Internet information transfers, it is used because it is weak enough to escape U.S. export regulations.

## A

**abacus** A digital computer that originated thousands of years ago. Calculations are performed by using sliding beads to represent figures and by following rules to perform mathematical operations.

**absolute cell reference** A spreadsheet cell reference that doesn't adjust when you copy or move a formula.

**absolute hyperlink** In an HTML document, a hyperlink that fully and precisely specifies the file location of the referenced remote document. An absolute link specifies the protocol (such as http:// or ftp://), as well as the name of the computer and the location of the referenced file in the computer's directory structure.

**Accelerated Graphics Port (AGP)** A port specification developed by Intel Corporation to support high-speed, high-resolution graphics, including 3D graphics.

**accelerator** A circuit board that speeds up some function of your computer.

**acceptable use policy (AUP)** An Internet service provider (ISP) policy that indicates which types of uses are permissible.

**acceptance testing** In information systems development, the examination of programs by users. See also application testing.

**access point** In a home radio-frequency (RF) network, the wired controller that receives and transmits data to the wireless adapters installed in each computer.

**access speed** The amount of time that lapses between a request for information from memory and the delivery of the information. Also called access time.

**access time** See access speed.

**accessible software** Software that is designed to be easily and conveniently used by people with limited vision, hearing, or dexterity.

**account** On a multiuser computer system, a user information profile that includes the user's name, password, and home directory location. Unlike a profile on a consumer-oriented operating system, an account provides basic security features that prevent users from accessing or overwriting each others' files.

**action** A special type of Internet chat group message that describes a behavior.

**active cell** In a spreadsheet program, the cell in which the cell pointer is located. The contents of the active cell are displayed in the formula bar.

**active-matrix LCD** A full-color liquid crystal display (LCD) in which each of the screen's pixels is controlled by its own transistor. Active-matrix displays offer a higher resolution, contrast, and vertical refresh rate than less expensive passive-matrix displays. Also called thin film transistor (TFT).

**active monitoring** In online banking, a security measure in which a security team constantly monitors the system that holds account information for the telltale signs of unauthorized access.

**ActiveX control** A small program that can be downloaded from a Web page and used to add functionality to a Web browser. ActiveX controls require Microsoft Windows and Microsoft Internet Explorer and are usually written in Visual Basic (VB).

**activity light** A light-emitting diode (LED) that illuminates when a disk drive is sending or receiving data.

**ad network** On the World Wide Web, a commercial service that uses cookies to track a user's movements and browsing preferences through all of the network's participating sites. This information is used to present the user with advertisements tailored to the user's interest.

**adapter** 1. A circuit board that plugs into an expansion slot in a computer, giving the computer additional capabilities. Synonymous with card. Popular adapters for personal computers include video adapters that produce video output, memory expansion boards, internal modems, and sound boards. 2. A transformer that enables a computer or peripheral to work with line voltage that differs from its electrical requirements.

**Add or Remove Programs** An icon in a computer operating system's control panel that allows for proper installation and uninstallation of programs.

**advanced intelligent tape (AIT)** An advanced, high-end tape backup standard that is used by organizations to back up the entire contents of a file server or other mission-critical systems.

**Advanced Technology Attachment (ATA)** See Integrated Drive Electronics (IDE).

**adware** A type of Internet spyware created by advertising agencies to collect information about computer users' Internet habits.

**agent** An automatic program that is designed to operate on the user's behalf, performing a specific function in the background. When the agent has achieved its goal, it reports to the user.

**alert box** In a graphical user interface (GUI), a dialog box that appears on-screen to either warn you that the command you've given may result in lost work or other errors, or that explains why an action can't be completed.

**algorithm** A mathematical or logical procedure for solving a problem.

**algorithmic art** In computer art, the use of an unfolding mathematical procedure as a means of artistic expression.

**alias** A secondary or symbolic name for a computer user or group of users. Group aliases provide a handy way to send e-mail to two or more people simultaneously.

**all-in-one computers** A system unit that contains all of the computer's components, including input components and the display.

**alphabetic check** Ensures that only alphabetical data (the letters of the alphabet) are entered into a field.

**American Standard Code for Information Interchange (ASCII)** A standard computer character set consisting of 96 uppercase and lowercase letters along with 32 nonprinting control characters. Developed in 1963, ASCII was the first computer industry standard.

**analog** Based on continuously varying values or voltages. Analog techniques are used for the reproduction of music in standard LP records and audio cassettes. See digital.

**analog computer** A machine that measures an ongoing process using a continuously variable scale. See digital computer.

**analog signal** A signal sent via continuous waves that vary in strength and quality, such as those that phones and phone lines send and receive. See digital signal.

**Analytical Engine** A device planned by Charles Babbage in the nineteenth century. Never completed, this device would have been a full modern computer with an IPOS cycle and punched cards for data input.

**analytical graphics** As opposed to presentation graphics, a type of graphics application in which the user attempts to display all or most of the data so that the underlying patterns become visible.

**anchor text** In the World Wide Web, the on-screen text of a hyperlink.

**animation** A method of creating the illusion of movement by saving a series of images that show slight changes in the position of the displayed objects, and then displaying these images in sequence fast enough that the eye perceives smooth movement.

**anonymity** On the Internet, the ability to post a message or visit Web sites without divulging one's identity. Anonymity is much more difficult to obtain than most Internet users realize.

**anonymous FTP** An Internet service that enables you to contact a distant computer system to which you have no access rights, log on to its public directories, and transfer files from that computer to your own.

**antivirus program** A utility that checks for and removes computer viruses from memory and disks.

**applet** 1. A small- to medium-sized computer program that provides a specific function, such as emulating a calculator. 2. In Java, a mini-program embedded in a Web document that, when downloaded, is executed by the browser. Both leading browsers (Netscape Communicator and Microsoft Internet Explorer) can execute Java applets.

**AppleTalk** A networking protocol developed by Apple Computer that enables Apple Macintosh computers to connect by LocalTalk, EtherTalk, and token ring networks.

**application file** See program file.

**application software** Programs that enable you to do something useful with the computer, such as writing or accounting (as opposed to utilities, which are programs that help you maintain the computer).

**application testing** In information systems development, the examination of programs individually, and then further examination of the programs as they function together.

**application window** The area on-screen that encloses and displays a launched application.

**application workspace** The area within an application window that displays the document.

**archival backup** A procedure in which a backup utility backs up all files on the hard disk by copying them to floppy disks, tape, or some other backup medium. See incremental backup.

**archival storage** See offline storage.

**archive** A file that contains two or more files that have been stored together for convenient archiving or network transmission.

**area chart** See pie chart.

**argument set** In spreadsheet programs such as Microsoft Excel, the part of a mathematical function that contains its passable parameters or variables.

**arithmetic-logic unit (ALU)** The portion of the central processing unit (CPU) that makes all the decisions for the microprocessor, based on the mathematical computations and logic functions that it performs.

**arithmetic operations** One of the two groups of operations performed by the arithmetic-logic unit (ALU). The arithmetic operations are addition, subtraction, multiplication, and division.

**arithmetic operators** A set of symbols corresponding to the standard operations of grade-school arithmetic (addition, subtraction, multiplication, and division).

**ARPANET** An acronym for the Advanced Research Projects Agency Network, from which the Internet developed.

**arrow keys** See cursor-movement keys.

**article** In Usenet, a message that begins discussion on a new subject. Compare follow-up article.

**artificial intelligence (AI)** A computer science field that tries to improve computers by endowing them with some of the characteristics associated with human intelligence, such as the capability to understand natural language and to reason under conditions of uncertainty.

**artificial system** A collection of components constructed by people and organized into a functioning whole to accomplish a goal.

**aspect ratio** In computer graphics, the ratio between an image's horizontal and vertical dimensions.

**assembler** A program that transforms source code in assembly language into machine language readable by a computer.

**assembly language** A low-level programming language in which each program statement corresponds to an instruction that the microprocessor can carry out.

**assistive technology** A technology that helps people with limited vision, hearing, or dexterity use the computer comfortably and productively.

**Asymmetric Digital Subscriber Line (ADSL)** A type of Digital Subscriber Line (DSL) service for Internet access. ADSL enables download speeds of up to 1.5 Mbps.

**asynchronous** Not kept in time (synchrony) by the pulses of a system clock or some other timing device.

**asynchronous communication** A method of data communication in which the transmission of bits of data isn't synchronized by a clock signal, but instead is accomplished by sending bits one after another, with a start bit and a stop bit to mark the beginning and end, respectively, of each data unit.

**AT form factor** A system unit case design that was introduced with IBM's Personal Computer AT (short for Advanced Technology).

**ATA (AT attachment)** A hard disk interface originally designed by IBM for its 1984 Personal Computer AT. More recent versions, such as ATA/66 and Ultra ATA (also called Ultra DMA) offer performance approaching that of SCSI hard drives.

**ATA-2** Current standard IDE/ATA interface for entry-level devices.

**ATA-5** Newest version of the IDE/ATA standard.

**attachment** A binary file, such as a program or a compressed word processing document, that has been attached to an e-mail message.

**attribute** In HTML, an optional or required setting that controls specific characteristics of an element and enables authors to specify values for these characteristics.

**ATX form factor** Developed by Intel, the ATX form factor provides better accessibility to system components, better cooling, more full-sized expansion slots, and a more convenient layout for system upgrades.

**Audio output** A type of computer output that consists of sound, music, or synthesized speech.

**authentication** In computer security, a method of preventing unauthorized users from accessing a computer system, usually by requesting a password.

**authoring tools** In multimedia, application programs that enable the user to blend audio files, video, and animation with text and traditional graphics.

**autocorrect** In a word processing program, a feature that automatically corrects common typographical errors as you type.

**automated teller machine (ATM)** A computer-based kiosk that provides bank customers with 24-hour access to their funds.

**automatic** Able to run without human intervention.

**automatic guided vehicle (AGV)** In computer-integrated manufacturing, a small automated machine that provides supplies where they are needed.

**automation** The replacement of human workers by machines.

**autorepeat** A keyboard function that causes a character to repeat if you hold down the key.

**autosave** A software feature that backs up open documents at a user-specified interval.

**auxiliary storage** See storage.

**avatar** In a graphical MUD, a character that represents the person who is controlling the avatar's appearance, movement, and interaction with other characters.

# B

**back door** A secret decoding mechanism that enables investigators to decrypt messages without first having to obtain a private key.

**backbone** In a wide area network (WAN), such as the Internet, a high-speed, high-capacity medium that transfers data over hundreds or thousands of miles. A variety of physical media are used for backbone services, including microwave relay, satellites, and dedicated telephone lines.

**background application** In a multitasking operating system, any inactive application. Compare foreground application.

**background color** In HTML, the color assigned to the background of a Web page.

**background graphic** In HTML, a graphic displayed as a Web page's background. Most browsers automatically repeat (tile) a background graphic so that the image fills the entire page, even if the browser window is enlarged.

**backside cache** A special type of secondary cache memory that is located on the processor. See secondary cache.

**backup** A file (or group of files) containing copies of important data. These files may be specially formatted so that, should the need arise, they can be used to restore the contents of the hard disk in the event of a hard disk failure.

**backup file** A copy of a file created as a precaution in case anything happens to the original.

**backup utility** A program that copies data from a secondary storage device (most commonly a hard disk) to a backup medium, such as a tape cartridge.

**bad sector** In magnetic storage media such as hard drives, a sector of the disk's surface that is physically damaged to the point that it can no longer store data safely.

**bandwidth** The amount of data that can be transmitted through a given communications channel, such as a computer network.

**banner ad** On the World Wide Web, a paid advertisement—often rectangular in shape, like a banner—that contains a hyperlink to the advertiser's page.

**bar chart** In presentation graphics, a graph with horizontal or vertical bars (rectangles) commonly used to show the values of the items being compared.

**bar code** A binary coding system using bars of varying thickness or position that provide information that can be scanned into a computer.

**bar code reader** An input device that scans bar codes and, with special software, converts the bar code into readable data.

**baseline** The line on which the base (but not the extender, if any) of each character is positioned. An extender is the portion of certain letters (such as p and y) that extend below the baseline.

**BASIC** Acronym for Beginner's All-Purpose Symbolic Instruction Code. An easy-to-use high-level programming language developed in 1964 for instruction.

**basic input/output system (BIOS)** Read-only memory (ROM) built into the computer's memory that contains the instructions needed to start the computer and work with input and output devices.

**Basic Rate Interface (BRI)** In ISDN, the basic digital telephone and data service that is designed for residences. BRI offers two 56 Kbps or 64 Kbps channels for voice, graphics, and data, plus one 16,000 bps channel for signaling purposes.

**batch processing** A mode of computer operation in which program instructions are executed one after the other without user intervention. Batch processing uses computer resources efficiently but is less convenient than interactive processing, in which you see the results of your commands on-screen so that you can correct errors and make necessary adjustments before completing the operation.

**baud rate** The maximum number of changes that can occur per second in the electrical state of a communications circuit. An early modem's data transfer rate may have been given in baud, but a modem's data transfer rate is now correctly measured in bits per second (bps).

**benchmark** A standard measurement used to test the performance of different brands of equipment.

**beta version** In software testing, a preliminary version of a program that is widely distributed before commercial release to users who test the program by operating it under realistic conditions.

**binary digit** See bit.

**binary file** A file containing data or program instructions in a computer-readable format that is unreadable by humans. The opposite of a binary file is an ASCII file.

**binary numbers** A number system with a base (radix) of 2, unlike the number systems most of us use, which have bases of 10 (decimal numbers), 12 (feet and inches), and 60 (time). Binary numbers are preferred for computers for precision and economy. Building an electronic circuit that can detect the difference between two states (high current and low current, or 0 and 1) is easy and inexpensive; building a circuit that detects the difference among 10 states (0 through 9) is much more difficult and expensive. The word *bit* derives from the phrase *binary digit*.

**bioinformatics** A field that develops database software for storing genetic information and making it available for widespread use.

**biological feedback device** A device that translates eye movements, body movements, and brain waves into computer input.

**biometric authentication** A method of authentication that requires a biological scan of some sort, such as a retinal scan or voice recognition.

**BIOS screen** The information seen on the computer screen that provides information about the BIOS software encoded in the computer's ROM.

**bit** Short for binary digit, the basic unit of information in a binary numbering system.

**bit depth** In a scanner, the length (expressed in bits) of the storage unit used to store information about the scanned image. The greater the bit depth, the better the scanner's resolution.

**bit length** In encryption, the length (expressed in bits) of the key used to encode and decode plaintext data. The greater the bit length, the stronger (less breakable) the encryption.

**bitmapped graphics** Images formed by a pattern of tiny dots, each of which corresponds to a pixel on the computer's display. Also called raster graphics.

**bits per second (bps)** In asynchronous communication, a measurement of data transmission speed. In personal computing, bps rates frequently are used to measure the performance of modems and serial ports.

**biz newsgroups** In Usenet, a category of newsgroups devoted to commercial concerns.

**block element** In HTML, one of two basic types of elements (the other is inline element). A block element starts on a new line and comprises a separate paragraph, or block. Block elements include P (text paragraph), BLOCKQUOTE (indented quotation), and UL (bulleted list).

**blue screen of death** A feared error message with a blue background that appears when Microsoft Windows NT has encountered an error condition; typically resolved only by system rebooting.

**Bluetooth** A trademarked personal area network (PAN) technology, conceived by cell phone giant Ericsson and named after a 10th-century Viking, that allows computers, mobile phones, printers, and other devices within a certain range of each other to communicate automatically and wirelessly.

**body** In HTML, one of two elements that make up an HTML document's global structure. The body contains the text and markup that is visible in a browser window.

**body type** The font (usually 8- to 12-point) used to set paragraphs of text. The body font is different from the font used to set headings, captions, and other typographical elements.

**bold** In character formatting, a character style in which the letters of a font appear thicker and darker than normal.

**bookmark** A Web browser navigational tool that allows Internet users to tag or mark favorite sites so they can be easily accessed.

**Boolean search** A database or Web search that uses the logical operators AND, OR, and NOT to specify the logical relationship between search concepts.

**boot** To start the computer. See cold boot and warm boot.

**boot disk** See emergency disk.

**boot sector** A portion of the computer's hard disk that is reserved for essential programs used when the computer is switched on.

**boot sector virus** A computer virus that copies itself to the beginning of a hard drive, where it is automatically executed when the computer is turned on.

**boot sequence** The series of operations that the computer runs through every time the power is switched on or the computer is restarted. See cold boot and warm boot.

**bootstrap loader** A program stored in the computer's read-only memory (ROM) that enables the computer to begin operating when the power is first switched on.

**border** Lines that are added to the top, bottom, left, or right side of a paragraph.

**bots** Miniprograms capable of carrying out a variety of functions on the Internet, such as greeting newcomers to Internet chat groups.

**bounce message** An e-mail message informing the user that another e-mail message could not be delivered to its intended recipient. The failure may be due to an incorrectly typed e-mail address or to a network problem.

**Braille output devices** An output device that prints computer output in raised Braille letters, which can be read by people with severely limited or no vision.

**branch control structure** See selection control structure.

**branch prediction** A technique used by advanced CPUs to prevent a pipeline stall. The processor tries to predict what is likely to happen.

**broadband** A type of data communication in which a technique called *multiplexing* is used to enable a single transmission line to carry more than one signal.

**broadband ISDN (BISDN)** A high-bandwidth digital telephone standard for transmitting up to 1.5 Mbps over fiber-optic cables. See Basic Rate Interface and Integrated Services Digital Network.

**broken link** On the World Wide Web, a hyperlink that refers to a resource (such as a sound or a Web page) that has been moved or deleted. Synonymous with stale link.

**browse view** In a database, a way of viewing records one by one.

**browser** A program that enables the user to navigate the Web. The two leading browsers are Netscape Navigator, part of Netscape Communication's Netscape Communicator package, and Microsoft Internet Explorer. A browser serves as the client for Web and other types of Internet servers.

**brute force** In programming, a crude technique for solving a difficult problem by repeating a simple procedure many times. Computer spell-checkers use a brute-force technique. They don't really "check spelling"; they merely compare all the words in a document against a dictionary of correctly spelled words.

**bubble-jet printer** See inkjet printer.

**bug** A programming error that causes a program or a computer system to perform erratically, produce incorrect results, or crash. The term *bug* was coined when a real insect was discovered to have fouled up one of the circuits of the first electronic digital computer, the ENIAC. A hardware problem is called a glitch.

**build** In a presentation graphics program, a type of bulleted list in which the bullet items appear one by one. Animation effects enable the new items to slide in from the side.

**build-or-buy decision** In the development of information systems, the choice of building a new system within the organization or purchasing it from an outside vendor.

**built-in function** In a spreadsheet program, a complex formula that is automated with a simple command. To add a large column of numbers, for example, you can use the sum function instead of typing each cell address.

**bulleted list** In Microsoft Word, bulleted lists are useful for listing items or giving instructions.

**bus** A term that describes the pathways that are used to move computer data, especially between peripherals or over a network.

**bus mouse** A type of mouse that connects to an expansion board mounted on the computer's expansion bus.

**bus topology** The physical layout of a local area network that does not use a central or host computer. Instead, each node manages part of the network, and information is transmitted directly from one computer to another.

**business process reengineering (BPR)** The use of information technology to bring about major changes and cost savings in an organization's structure. Also called reengineering.

**business-to-business (B2B) e-commerce** A type of e-commerce where one business provides another business with the materials and supplies it needs to conduct its operations.

**byte** Eight bits grouped to represent a character (a letter, a number, or a symbol).

## C

**C** A high-level programming language developed by Bell Labs in the 1970s. C combines the virtues of high-level programming with the efficiency of assembly language but is somewhat difficult to learn.

**C++** A flexible high-level programming language derived from C that supports object-oriented programming but does not require programmers to adhere to the object-oriented model.

**cable modem** A device that enables a computer to access the Internet by means of a cable TV connection. Some cable modems enable downloading only; you need an analog (POTS) phone line and an analog modem to upload data. The best cable modems enable two-way communications through the cable TV system and do not require a phone line. Cable modems enable Internet access speeds of up to 1.5 Mbps, although most users typically experience slower speeds due to network congestion.

**cache memory** A small unit of ultra-fast memory used to store recently accessed or frequently accessed data, increasing a computer system's overall performance.

**calculated field** In a database management program, a query that instructs the program to perform an arithmetic operation on the specified data and display the result.

**calculator** A device designed to help people solve mathematical problems.

**call center** A computer-based telephone routing system that automatically connects credit card authorization systems to authorization services.

**callback system** A method of network control that serves as a deterrent to system sabotage by verifying the user ID, password, and telephone number of the individual trying to access the system.

**cancel button** In a spreadsheet program, a button positioned near the entry bar that cancels the text inserted in the entry bar area.

**Caps Lock** A toggle key that switches the keyboard into a mode in which uppercase letters are produced without pressing the Shift key.

**car navigation system** A computer-based driving accessory that displays digitized maps and tracks the car's location using a satellite-based positioning system.

**card reader** A device capable of reading information on flash memory cards and transferring it to a computer.

**carpal tunnel syndrome (CTS)** A painful swelling of the tendons and the sheaths around them in the wrist.

**Cascading Style Sheet (CSS)** In Web publishing, a way to specify document formats in which specific formatting attributes (such as alignment, text style, font, and font size) are assigned to specific HTML tags, so that all subsequent uses of the tag in the same page take on the same formats. Like a style sheet in a word processing document, CSS enables a Web designer to make a single change that affects all the text marked with the same tag.

**case control structure** In structured programming, a logical construction of programming commands that contains a set of possible conditions and instructions that are executed if those conditions are true.

**CAT (computerized axial tomography) scanner** In health care, a computer-controlled imaging device used to diagnose patients.

**category 5 (cat-5)** A type of twisted-pair cable used for high-performance digital telephone and computer network wiring.

**cathode ray tube (CRT)** A vacuum tube that uses an electron gun to emit a beam of electrons that illuminates phosphorus on-screen as the beam sweeps across the screen repeatedly.

**Cave Automated Virtual Environment (CAVE)** A virtual reality environment that replaces headsets with 3D glasses and uses the walls, ceiling, and floor to display projected three-dimensional images.

**CD-R discs** Compact disc-recordable storage media that cannot be erased or written over once data has been saved; they're relatively inexpensive.

**CD-R drives** Compact disc-recordable devices that can read standard CD-ROM discs and write data to CD-R discs.

**CD-ROM** See compact disc read-only memory.

**CD-ROM drive** A read-only disk drive that reads data encoded on compact discs and transfers this data to a computer.

**CD-ROM jukeboxes** Devices that contain as many as 256 CD-ROM drives, providing storage for massive amounts of data.

**CD-RW drive** A compact disc-rewritable drive that provides full read/write capabilities using erasable CD-RW discs.

**CD-RW discs** Compact disc-rewritable storage media that allows data that has been saved to be erased or written over.

**cell** 1. In a spreadsheet, a rectangle formed by the intersection of a row and a column in which you enter information in the form of text (a label) or numbers (a value). 2. In telecommunications, a limited geographical area in which a signal can be broadcast.

**cell address** In a spreadsheet, a unique identifier associated with each cell.

**cell pointer** The mouse pointer, when moved across the worksheet, becomes a cell pointer and is shaped like a cross. Use the cell pointer to select one or more cells.

**cell reference** In a spreadsheet, a way of specifying the value of one cell in another one by entering its cell address.

**cell site** In a cellular telephone network, an area in which a transmitting station repeats the system's broadcast signals so that the signal remains strong even though the user may move from one cell site to another.

**cellular telephone** A radio-based telephone system that provides widespread coverage through the use of repeating transmitters placed in zones (called cells). The zones are close enough so that signal strength is maintained throughout the calling area.

**centered alignment** In word processing, a way of formatting a block of text so that it is centered on the page, leaving both ends unaligned.

**central processing unit (CPU)** The computer's processing and control circuitry, including the arithmetic-logic unit (ALU) and the control unit.

**certificate authority (CA)** In computer security, a company that verifies the identity of individuals and issues digital certificates attesting to the veracity of this identity.

**certification** An endorsement of professional competence that is awarded on successful completion of a rigorous test.

**channel** In Internet Relay Chat (IRC), a chat group in which as many as several dozen people carry on a text-based conversation on a specific topic.

**character** Any letter, number, punctuation mark, or symbol produced on-screen by the press of a key or a key combination.

**character code** An algorithm used to translate between the numerical language of the computer and characters readable by humans.

**character formatting** The appearance of text, including character size, typeface, and emphasis.

**character set** The collection of characters that a given computer is able to process and display on-screen.

**charge-coupled device (CCD)** A small matrix of light-sensitive elements used in digital cameras and scanners.

**chart** A graphical representation of data, such as is created by spreadsheet programs.

**chart type** In a spreadsheet program, a style of chart, such as column chart, bar chart, line chart, or pie chart.

**check-screening system** A computer system used in point-of-sale (POS) terminals that reads a check's account number and accesses a database of delinquent accounts.

**child directory** A directory inside another directory.

**chip** An integrated circuit (IC) that can emulate thousands or millions of transistors.

**chipset** A collection of supporting components that are all designed to work together smoothly on a computer motherboard.

**chunks** Concise hypertext documents that contain many links to other documents.

**circuit switching** A type of telecommunications network in which high-speed electronic switches create a direct connection between two communicating devices. The telephone system is a circuit-switching network.

**citation** In a word processing document, a reference to a bibliographic item that is referenced within the text. Citation options include footnotes and endnotes.

**citation format** A set of guidelines for typing footnote or bibliographic information. When you write a paper for a college class, you will be asked to follow a certain citation format.

**citing sources** Providing enough information about the source of information you are using so that an interested or critical reader can locate this source without difficulty.

**class** In object-oriented (OO) programming, a category of objects that performs a certain function. The class defines the properties of an object, including definitions of the object's variables and the procedures that need to be followed to get the object to do something.

**click** To press and release a mouse button quickly.

**click-and-mortar** In electronic commerce, a retail strategy in which a Web retail site is paired with a chain of local retail stores. Customers prefer this strategy because they can return or exchange unwanted goods more easily.

**clickstream** The trail of links left behind to reach a particular Web site.

**client** 1. In a client/server network, a program that runs on users' computers and enables them to access a certain type of data. 2. On a computer network, a program capable of contacting the server and obtaining needed information.

**client program** The part of client/server computing that handles interaction with the user and is installed on users' desktop systems. See server program.

**client/server** A method of organizing software use on a computer network that divides programs into servers (programs that make information available) and clients (programs that enable users to access a certain type of data).

**client/server computing** A software application design framework for computer networks in which software services are divided into two parts, a client part and a server part.

**client/server network** A computer network in which some computers are dedicated to function as servers, making information available to client programs running on users' computers.

**clip art** A collection of graphical images stored on disk and available for use in a page layout or presentation graphics program.

**Clip Organizer** In Microsoft Office, a repository of clip art and images that can be inserted into a document or presentation.

**clipboard** A temporary storage location used to hold information after it has been copied or cut. See cut and paste.

**clock speed** The speed of the internal clock of a microprocessor that sets the pace at which operations proceed in the computer's internal processing circuitry.

**clock tick** One "beat" of the computer's internal clock.

**clone** A functional copy of a hardware device, such as a personal computer. Although clones of Apple Macintosh computers exist, this term almost always refers to clones of IBM computers and their microprocessors. Compare IBM compatible.

**close** To remove a window from the desktop. With some applications, closing the last window terminates the application.

**close tag** In HTML, a tag that's used to indicate where the heading text stops.

**closed architecture** See proprietary architecture.

**cluster** On a magnetic disk, a storage unit that consists of two or more sectors.

**CMOS (complementary metal-oxide semiconductor)** A special type of nonvolatile memory used to store essential startup configuration options.

**coaxial cable** A high-bandwidth connecting cable in which an insulated wire runs through the middle of the cable.

**COBOL (Common Business-Oriented Language)** An early, high-level programming language for business applications.

**code of conduct** A set of ethical principles developed by a professional association, such as the Association for Computing Machinery (ACM).

**code-and-fix** In programming, an early method of program development in which the programmer first created a program, and then tried to correct its shortcomings.

**codec** Short for compression/decompression standard. A standard for compressing and decompressing video information to reduce the size of digitized multimedia files. Popular codecs include MPEG (an acronym for Motion Picture Experts Group), Apple's QuickTime, and Microsoft's AVI.

**cold boot** A system start that involves powering up the computer. Compare warm boot.

**collaboratory** A laboratory that is made accessible to distant researchers by means of the Internet.

**collision** In local area networks (LANs), a garbled transmission that results when two or more workstations transmit to the same network cable at exactly the same time. Networks have means of preventing collisions.

**color depth** The number of colors that can be displayed on a monitor at one time.

**color laser printer** A nonimpact high-resolution printer capable of printing in color.

**column** In a spreadsheet, a block of cells going down the screen.

**column chart** In presentation graphics, a graph with vertical columns. Column graphs are commonly used to show the values of items as they vary at precise intervals over a period of time.

**command** A user-initiated instruction that tells a program which task to perform.

**command line** An area where commands are typed in a command-line user interface.

**command-line user interface** In an operating system, a variety of user interface that requires users to type commands one line at a time.

**commercial software** Copyrighted software that must be paid for before it can be used.

**common carrier** A public telephone or data communications utility.

**common carrier immunity** A basic principle of telecommunications law that absolves telecommunications carriers of responsibility for any legal or criminal liability resulting from messages transmitted by their networks.

**Common Object Request Broker Architecture (CORBA)** In object-oriented (OO) programming, a leading standard that defines how objects can communicate with each other across a network.

**communications** The high-speed movement of data within and between computers.

**communications device** Any hardware device that is capable of moving data into or out of the computer.

**compact disc read-only memory (CD-ROM)** A standard for storing read-only computer data on optical compact discs (CDs), which can be read by CD-ROM drives.

**compact disc-recordable (CD-R)** A "write-once" optical storage technology that uses a CD-R drive to record data on CD-R discs. Once you've recorded on the disc, you can't erase the stored data or write over the disc again. You can play the recorded CD on most CD-ROM drives.

**compact disc-rewritable (CD-RW)** A read/write optical storage technology that uses a CD-R drive to record data on CD-RW discs. You can erase the recorded data and write new data as you please. Most CD-ROM drives can read the recorded data. CD-RW drives can also write to CD-R discs, but you can write to CD-R discs only once.

**CompactFlash** A popular flash memory storage device that can store up to 128 MB of digital camera images.

**compatible** The capability to function with or substitute for a given make and model of computer, device, or program.

**compatible computers** Computer systems capable of using the same programs and peripherals.

**compiler** A program that translates source code in a third-generation programming language into machine code readable by a computer.

**complementary metal-oxide semiconductor (CMOS)** A type of semiconductor often used in computers for battery-powered circuits that store the date, time, and system configuration information.

**completeness check** Determines whether a required field has been left empty. If so, the database prompts the user to fill in the needed data.

**complex instruction set computer (CISC)** A type of central processing unit that can recognize as many as 100 or more instructions and carry out most computations directly.

**Component Object Model (COM)** In object-oriented (OO) programming, a standard developed by Microsoft Corporation that is used to define how objects communicate with each other over networks.

**component reusability** In programming, the capability to create a program module that can perform a specific task and be used in another program with little or no modification.

**computer** A machine that can physically represent data, process this data by following a set of instructions, store the results of the processing, and display the results so that people can use them.

**computer addiction** A psychological disorder characterized by compulsive and prolonged computer usage.

**computer crimes** Actions that violate state or federal laws.

**computer ethics** A new branch of philosophy dealing with computing-related moral dilemmas.

**computer fluency** A high level of computer conceptual knowledge and skills sufficient to enable a user to apply the computer creatively in novel situations.

**computer information system (CIS)** A computer system in which all components are designed to work together.

**computer literacy** A standard of knowledge and skills regarding computers that is sufficient to prepare an individual for working and living in a computerized society.

**computer literate** Used to describe persons who are skilled computer and Internet users.

**computer network** A collection of computers that have been connected together so they can exchange data.

**computer science (CS)** A scientific discipline that focuses on the theoretical aspects of improving computers and computer software.

**computer security risk** Any event, action, or situation—intentional or not—that could lead to the loss or destruction of computer systems or the data they contain.

**computer system** A collection of related computer components that have all been designed to work smoothly together.

**computer virus** A program, designed as a prank or as sabotage, that replicates itself by attaching to other programs and carrying out unwanted and sometimes dangerous operations.

**computer virus author** A programmer who creates computer viruses to vandalize computer systems.

**computer vision syndrome (CVS)** An eyesight disorder, such as temporary nearsightedness and blurred vision, that results from focusing closely on a computer screen for long periods of time.

**computer-aided design (CAD)** An application that enables engineers and architects to design parts and structures. The user can rotate the design in three dimensions and zoom in for a more detailed look. Also see computer-aided manufacturing (CAM).

**computer-aided manufacturing (CAM)** Software used to drive computer-controlled manufacturing equipment. CAM systems often use output from computer-aided design applications (CAD).

**computer-aided production engineering (CAPE)** See virtual manufacturing.

**computer-aided software engineering (CASE)** Software that provides tools to help with every phase of systems development and enables developers to create data flow diagrams, data dictionary entries, and structure charts.

**computer-assisted instruction (CAI)** The use of computers to implement programmed instruction. More broadly, CAI describes any use of computers in education.

**computer-based education (CBE)** A generic term that describes any use of computers for educational purposes.

**computer-based training (CBT)** The use of computer-assisted instruction (CAI) programs to educate adults.

**computer-integrated manufacturing (CIM)** The integration of computer technology with manufacturing processes.

**computerized information system (CIS)** A computer-based information system, composed of data, hardware, software, trained personnel, and procedures, that provides essential services to organizations; collects mission-critical data, processes this data, stores the data and the results of processing, and disseminates information throughout the organization.

**computer-managed instruction (CMI)** The use of computers to help instructors manage administrative teaching tasks, such as tracking grades.

**computer-supported cooperative work (CSCW)** A collection of applications that supports the information needs of workgroups. These applications include e-mail, videoconferencing, and group scheduling systems.

**condensed spacing** In character formatting, a character style in which characters are squeezed together more tightly than normal.

**conditional control structure** See selection control structure.

**configuration file** A file that stores the choices you make when you install a program so that these choices are available each time the program starts.

**confirmation** A message originated by a program that verifies that a user command has been completed successfully.

**congestion** In a packet switching network, a performance interruption that occurs when a segment of the network experiences overload.

**congestion management system** In transportation engineering, a computer-based system that reduces traffic congestion by means of traffic light synchronization and other techniques.

**connectionless** Not directly connected to another computer on the network. A connectionless network protocol enables two networked computers to exchange data without requiring an active connection to exist between them.

**connectivity** The ability to link various media and devices, thereby enhancing communication and improving access to information.

**connector** A component that enables users or technicians to connect a cable securely to the computer's case. A male connector contains pins or plugs that fit into the corresponding female connector.

**consistency check** Examines the data entered into two different fields to determine whether an error has been made.

**constructivism** A school reform movement that places emphasis on students constructing knowledge for themselves rather than learning it by rote.

**contact manager** A program that helps you keep track of contacts by maintaining a list of addresses, phone numbers, and fax numbers. Information is also maintained through the use of a notepad, automatic telephone dialing with a modem, and search and sort capabilities.

**content** In HTML, the text of a document.

**content model** In HTML, a specification of the type of information that can be placed between the start and end tags of an element.

**contention** In a computer network, a problem that arises when two or more computers try to access the network at the same time. Contention can result in collisions, which can destroy data.

**contention management** In a computer network, the use of one of several techniques for managing contention and preventing collisions.

**context menu** See popup menu.

**continuous speech recognition** The decoding of continuous human speech (without artificial pauses) into transcribed text by means of a computer program.

**control method** In an information system, a technique used to reduce the flow of information to people who do not need it (such as routing information so that it goes to only those people who really need to see the information).

**control structure** In structured programming, a logical element that governs program instruction execution.

**control unit** A component of the central processing unit (CPU) that obtains program instructions and sends signals to carry out those instructions.

**convergence** The coming together of information technologies (computer, consumer electronics, telecommunications) and gadgets (PC, TV, telephone), leading to a culmination of the digital revolution in which all types of digital information (voice, video, data) will travel over the same network.

**conversion utility** A special translation program that enables a program to read and create files in formats other than those the program normally creates.

**cookie** A text file that is deposited on a Web user's computer system, without the user's knowledge or consent, that may contain identifying information. This information is used for a variety of purposes, such as retaining the user's preferences or compiling information about the user's Web browsing behavior.

**cooling fan** A part of the system unit that prevents components from being damaged by heat.

**cooperative multitasking** In operating systems, a method of running more than one application at a time. If the active application crashes, however, the whole system must be restarted.

**copper wire** In telecommunications, a type of network cabling that uses strands of copper coated with insulation.

**copy** In the editing process, a command that enables the user to duplicate selected text, store this text in a temporary storage location called the clipboard, and insert (paste) the text in a new location.

**copy-protected software** Computer programs that include some type of measure to prevent users from making unauthorized copies.

**copyright infringement** The act of using material from a copyrighted source without getting permission to do so.

**copyright management infrastructure (CMI)** Enables vendors of copyrighted digital media to track and control the use and copying of their products after consumers purchase them.

**copyright protection scheme** A method used by software manufacturers to ensure that users cannot produce unauthorized copies of copyrighted software.

**copyrighted** Protected legally against copying or modification without permission.

**cordless keyboard** A type of keyboard that connects to the computer by means of an infrared port.

**cordless mouse** A type of mouse that connects to the computer by means of an infrared port.

**corporate espionage** The unauthorized access of corporate information, usually to the benefit of one of the corporation's competitors.

**cost/benefit analysis** An examination of the losses and gains, both tangible and intangible, related to a project.

**cracker** A computer user obsessed with gaining entry into highly secure computer systems.

**crash** An abnormal termination of program execution.

**credit card authorization** A system used in point-of-sale (POS) terminals that connects to an authorization service through a call center each time a credit card purchase is made.

**critical thinking** The capacity to evaluate the quality of information.

**cross-functional team** A method of designing products in which people who were formerly separated, such as engineering and finance professionals, work together in a team from the beginning of a project.

**cross-platform network** A computer network that includes more than one type or brand of hardware and operating system. In many colleges and universities, for example, the campus local area network includes Macintoshes, UNIX computers, and Windows PCs.

**cross-platform programming language** A programming language that can create programs capable of running on many different types of computers.

**cross-platform standard** A standard that assures interoperability on two or more brands or types of computers or computer operating systems.

**cryptanalysis** Code breaking.

**cumulative trauma disorder (CTD)** An injury involving damage to sensitive nerve tissue due to motions repeated thousands of times daily (such as mouse movements or keystrokes). Also called repetitive stress injury (RSI).

**cursor** A flashing bar, an underline character, or a box that indicates where keystrokes will appear when typed. Also called insertion point.

**cursor-movement keys** A set of keys on the keyboard that move the location of the cursor on the screen. The numeric keypad can also move the cursor when in the appropriate mode. Also called arrow keys.

**custom software** Application software designed for a company by a professional programmer or programming team. Custom software is usually very expensive.

**cut and paste** An editing operation in which characters or graphics are copied into a temporary storage location (called the clipboard) and then inserted somewhere else.

**cybercrime** Crime carried out by means of the Internet.

**cybergang** A group of computer users obsessed with gaining entry into highly secure computer systems.

**cyberlaw** A new legal field designed to track developments in cybercrime.

**cyberphobia** An exaggerated fear of computing that leads people to avoid computers and may result in physical symptoms.

**cyberstalking** A form of harassment in which an individual is repeatedly subjected to unwanted electronic mail or advances in chat rooms.

**cylinder** A single track location on all the platters of a hard disk. See track and platter.

## D

**data** The raw material of computing: unorganized information represented for computer processing.

**Data Access Page** In the Microsoft Access database management system, the object used to post data to the Web.

**data archiving** The process of transferring infrequently used data to backup devices, where the data will be accessible should the need arise.

**data backup** The process of making copies of data so that it can be restored in the event of a catastrophic system failure, such as the loss of a hard disk drive.

**data bus** A high-speed freeway of parallel connections that enables the CPU to communicate at high speeds with memory.

**data compression** The reduction of a file's size so that the file can be stored without taking up as much storage space and can be transferred more quickly over a computer network. Two types of compression are lossless compression (the compressed file can be decompressed without losing any original information) and lossy compression (some of the original information is permanently removed).

**data dependency** A microprocessor performance problem in which a CPU is slowed in its functioning by the need to wait for the results of instructions before moving on to process the next ones.

**data dictionary** In information systems development, a collection of definitions of all data types that may be input into the system, including field name, data types, and validation settings.

**data diddling** A computer crime in which data is modified to conceal theft or embezzlement.

**Data Encryption Standard (DES)** A commonly used symmetric key encryption developed by U.S. security agencies.

**data file** A named unit of information storage that contains data rather than program instructions.

**data flow diagram** A graphical representation of the flow of data through an information system.

**data glove** A device that translates hand and arm movements into computer input.

**data independence** In a database, the storage of data in such a way that it is not locked into use by a particular application.

**data integrity** In a database, the validity of the stored data; specifically, its freedom from error due to improper data entry, hardware malfunctions, or transmission errors.

**data mart** A large database that contains all the data used by one of the divisions of an organization.

**data mining** The analysis of data stored in data warehouses to search for previously unknown patterns.

**data processing** A professional field that focuses on the use of computers to create transaction processing systems for businesses.

**data projector** An output device that projects a computer's video output onto a large screen so that an audience can see it.

**data redundancy** In a database, a design error in which the same data appears more than once, creating opportunities for discrepant data entry and increasing the chance that the data will be processed incorrectly.

**data storage hierarchy** In data processing, a means of conceptualizing storage that envisions a scale ranging from the smallest unit of data (the bit) to the largest (the file).

**data transfer rate** 1. In secondary storage devices, the maximum number of bits per second that can be sent from the hard disk to the computer. The rate is determined by the drive interface. 2. The speed, expressed in bits per second (bps), at which a modem can transfer, or is transferring, data over a telephone line.

**data type** In a database or spreadsheet program, a particular type of information, such as a date, a time, or a name.

**data validation** In a database, a method of increasing the validity of data by defining acceptable input ranges for each field in the record.

**data warehouse** A very large database, containing as many as a trillion data records, that stores all of a firm's data and makes this data available for exploratory analysis (called data mining).

**database** A collection of information stored in an organized way.

**database file** A file containing data that has been stored in the proprietary file format of a database program.

**database management system (DBMS)** An application that enables users to create databases that contain links from several files. Database management systems are usually more expensive than file management programs.

**database object** In Microsoft Access, a tool for designing and using database components (including tables, forms, and queries).

**database program** An application that stores data so that needed information can be quickly located, organized, and displayed.

**database server** In a client/server computing network, a program that makes the information stored in databases available to two or more authorized users.

**database vendor** 1. A company that compiles information into large databases. 2. A company that creates and sells database software.

**datasheet view** In Microsoft Access and Microsoft Excel, a data viewing option that enables the user to view the numerical data underlying a chart or a table.

**date field** In a database, a space that accepts only date information.

**daughterboard** An auxiliary circuit board that is designed to mount on the surface of a motherboard.

**dead key** A keyboard shortcut that adds a diacritical mark to the next letter you type.

**dead link** See broken link.

**debugging** In programming, the process of finding and correcting errors, or bugs, in the source code of a computer program.

**decision support system (DSS)** A program that helps management analyze data to make decisions on semistructured problems.

**declarative language** A language that can be used to identify the components of a text. Synonymous with markup language.

**decode** One of four basic operations carried out by the control unit of a microprocessor. The decode operation figures out what a program instruction is telling the computer to do.

**decrement** (v.) To decrease. (n.) A specified unit by which a quantity should be decreased.

**defamation** An unfounded attack on the character or reputation of an individual or company.

**default** In a computer program, a fallback setting or configuration value that is used unless the user specifically chooses a different one.

**default folder** In e-mail, a folder that appears automatically when you set up your e-mail account and cannot be deleted. The inbox folder, sent mail folder, and deleted mail folder are all default folders.

**default start page** The Web document that appears when you start your Web browser or click the Home button. Most Web browsers are set up to display the browser company's home page, but you can easily change this setting so that the browser displays a more useful default home page.

**default user interface** In an operating system, the user interface (the means of interacting with the user) that appears automatically, based on preset options in the program. Some operating systems enable users to choose more than one user interface.

**deliverable** In the development of an information system, the outcome of a particular phase of the systems development life cycle (SDLC).

**Delphi** An object-oriented programming compiler based on Pascal. Although Delphi is similar to Microsoft's Visual Basic (VB), it has not been able to match Visual Basic's success.

**demodulation** In telecommunications, the process of receiving and transforming an analog signal into its digital equivalent so that a computer can use the information.

**demote** In an outlining utility, to lower the status of a heading (for example, by moving it from II to B).

**denial of service (DoS) attack** A form of network vandalism that attempts to make a service unavailable to other users, generally by flooding the service with meaningless data. Also called syn flooding.

**deregulation** A type of legislative reform in which government protections or regulations are removed in an effort to spur competition.

**desktop computer** A personal computer designed for an individual's use. Desktop computers are increasingly used to gain access to the resources of computer networks.

**desktop environment** A user interface that simulates a knowledge worker's desktop by depicting computer resources as if they were files and folders.

**desktop publishing (DTP)** The combination of text, graphics, and advanced formatting to create a visually appealing document.

**device driver** A program file that contains specific information needed by the operating system so that a specific brand or model of device will function.

**diacritical mark** A mark added to a character in a language other than English, such as an accent, tilde, or umlaut.

**dialog box** In a graphical user interface (GUI), an on-screen message box used to request information from the user.

**Difference Engine** A clockwork calculating machine created by Charles Babbage in the nineteenth century and capable of solving equations and printing tables. Technology at the time had not advanced enough to produce this invention.

**digital** A form of representation in which distinct objects, or digits, are used to stand for something in the real world, such as temperature or time, so that counting can be performed precisely.

**digital audio tape (DAT)** A magnetic tape backup medium that offers data backup capabilities at relatively low cost.

**digital camera** A camera that records an image by means of a digital imaging system, such as a charged-coupled device (CCD), and stores the image in memory or on a disk.

**digital cash system** A method for using smart cards and prepaid amounts of electronically stored money to pay for small charges such as parking and tolls.

**digital certificate** A form of digital ID used to obtain access to a computer system or prove one's identity while shopping on the Web. Certificates are issued by independent, third-party organizations called certificate authorities (CA).

**digital computer** A machine that represents data by means of an easily identified symbol, or digit. See analog computer.

**digital data storage (DDS)** A digital audio tape (DAT) storage medium that stores up to 40 GB of backup data on a single cartridge.

**Digital Display Working Group (DDWG)** An industry association working to define digital video output.

**digital light processing (DLP) projector** A computer projection device that employs millions of microscopic mirrors, embedded in a microchip, to produce a brilliant, sharp image.

**digital linear tape (DLT)** A tape backup medium that offers faster data transfer rates and more storage capacity than quarter-inch cartridge (QIC) or digital audio tape (DAT) drives, at a significantly higher cost.

**Digital Millennium Copyright Act (DMCA)** A 1998 law that imposes stiff penalties for anyone convicted of disclosing information about how a copyright management infrastructure (CMI) works.

**digital modem** See ISDN adapter.

**digital rights** A type of intellectual property right that gives the holder the lawful ability to sell digital reproductions of a work.

**digital signal** A signal sent via discontinuous pulses, in which the presence or absence of electronic pulses represents 1s and 0s, such as computers send and receive. See analog signal.

**digital signatures** A technique used to guarantee that a message has not been tampered with.

**Digital Subscriber Line (DSL)** A general term for several technologies that enable high-speed Internet access through twisted-pair telephone lines. Also called xDSL. See Asymmetric Digital Subscriber Line (ADSL).

**digital telephony** Telephone systems using all-digital protocols and transmission, offering the advantage over analog telephony of noise-free transmission and high-quality audio.

**digital video** Digital technologies for capturing and displaying still photography and full-motion images.

**digital video camera** Camera that uses digital rather than analog technologies to store recorded video images.

**digital video disc (DVD)** The newest optical disc format, DVD is capable of storing an entire digitized movie. DVD discs are designed to work with DVD video players and televisions.

**digital video disc-RAM (DVD-RAM)** A digital video disc (DVD) format that enables users to record up to 2.6 GB of data.

**digital video disc-ROM (DVD-ROM)** A digital optical disc format capable of storing up to 17 GB on a single disc, enough for a feature-length movie. DVD is designed to be used with a video player and a television. DVD discs can be read also by DVD-ROM drives.

**Digital Video Interface (DVI)** The standard created by the Digital Display Working Group that provides connections for LCD and other flat panel devices.

**digitization** The transformation of data such as voice, text, graphics, audio, and video into digital form, thereby allowing various technologies to transmit computer data through telephone lines, cables, or air and space.

**digitizing tablet** In computer-aided graphics, a peripheral device used with a pointing device to convert hand-drawn graphics into data that a computer can process.

**direct access file** In business data processing, a type of data file in which the computer can gain direct and immediate access to a particular unit of storage, without having to go through a sequence of data.

**Direct Broadcast Satellite (DBS)** A consumer satellite technology that offers cable channels and one-way Internet access. To use DBS for an Internet connection, a modem and phone line are required to upload data.

**direct conversion** In the development of an information system, the termination of the current system and the immediate institution of the new system throughout the whole organization.

**direct memory access (DMA) channels** Set of circuits that enable peripheral devices to access the computer's main memory (RAM) directly, without having to go through the CPU.

**directory** A logical storage unit, often represented as a folder, that enables computer users to group files in named, hierarchically organized folders and subfolders. In magnetic and optical disks, a file that contains a list of all the files contained on the disk and information about each file.

**disaster recovery plan** A written plan, with detailed instructions, specifying an alternative computing facility to use for emergency processing until a destroyed computer can be replaced.

**discrete speech recognition** A speech recognition technology that is able to recognize human speech only when the speaker pauses between words.

**disgruntled employee** A current or former employee who has real or imagined grievances. Most computer crime and sabotage stems from disgruntled employees and embezzlers rather than external intruders.

**disintermediation** The process of removing an intermediary, such as a car salesperson, by providing a customer with direct access to rich information and warehouse-size selection and stock.

**disc** A portable storage optical media, such as CD-ROM.

**disk** A portable storage magnetic media, such as floppy disks, that provides personal computer users with convenient, near-online storage.

**disk cache** A small amount of memory (up to 512 KB), usually built into the electronics of a disk drive, used to store frequently accessed data. Disk caches can significantly improve the performance of a disk drive.

**disk cartridge** A removable cartridge containing one or more rigid disks similar to those found in hard disks.

**disk cleanup utility** A utility program that removes unneeded temporary files.

**disk drive** A secondary storage mechanism that stores and retrieves information on a disk by using a read/write head. Disk drives are random-access devices.

**disk scanner** A utility program that can detect and resolve a variety of physical and logical problems related to file storage.

**diskette** See disk.

**display** The visual output of a computer, usually portrayed by a monitor or a liquid crystal display (LCD).

**display adapter** See video adapter.

**display type** In word processing or desktop publishing, the typeface or font used for titles and heading text. Sans serif fonts are usually chosen for display type.

**distance learning** The use of telecommunications (and increasingly the Internet) to provide educational outreach programs for students at remote locations.

**distributed hypermedia system** A network-based content development system in which individuals connected to the network can each make a small contribution by developing content related to their area of expertise. The Web is a distributed hypermedia system.

**DMA conflict** A common cause of system instability that was caused when users inadvertently configured peripherals so that they competed for the same DMA channel. Occurred before plug-and-play peripherals came into use.

**DNS server** See domain name server.

**document** A file created with an application program, such as a word processing or spreadsheet program.

**document formatting** In a word processing document, options that alter the appearance of the entire document, such as orientation and paper size.

**document map** In a word processing program, an on-screen window that provides a visual guide to the document's overall organization.

**documentation** In information systems development, the recording of all information pertinent to the development of an information system, usually in a project notebook.

**document-centric** In a software suite, a user interface concept in which what counts is the document the user is creating rather than the software being used to create a portion of the document. Menus and toolbars dynamically and automatically change to those relevant to the type of data being edited.

**domain** In a computer network, a group of computers that are administered as a unit. Network administrators are responsible for all the computers in their domains. On the Internet, this term refers to all the computers that are collectively addressable within one of the four parts of an IP address. For example, the first part of an IP address specifies the number of a computer network. All the computers within this network are part of the same domain.

**domain name** On the Internet, a readable computer address (such as www.microsoft.com) that identifies the location of a computer on the network.

**domain name registration** On the Internet, a process by which individuals and companies can obtain a domain name (such as www.c34.org) and link this name to a specific Internet address (IP address).

**domain name server** An Internet server program that maintains a table showing the current IP addresses assigned to domain names. Also called DNS server or name server.

**Domain Name System (DNS)** The conceptual system, standards, and names that make up the hierarchical organization of the Internet into named domains.

**dongle** A small peripheral that must be connected to a user's computer for the particular copy-protected program to function.

**dot-com** The universe of Internet sites, especially those doing electronic commerce, with the suffix com appended to their names.

**dot pitch** On a monitor, the space (measured in millimeters) between each physical dot on the screen.

**dot-matrix printer** An impact printer that forms text and graphic images by hammering the ends of pins against a ribbon in a pattern (matrix) of dots. Dot-matrix printers produce near–letter quality printouts.

**double data rate (DDR) SDRAM** A type of SDRAM that can both send and receive data within a single clock cycle.

**double-click** To press and release a mouse button twice quickly.

**double-density (DD)** A floppy disk format that offers up to 800 KB of storage.

**download** To transfer a file from another computer to your computer by means of a modem and a telephone line. See upload.

**downsizing** In corporate management, a cost-reduction strategy involving layoffs to make a firm leaner and more competitive. Downsizing often accompanies technology-driven restructuring that theoretically enables fewer employees to do the same or more work.

**downwardly compatible** Capable of running without modification when using earlier computer components or files created with earlier software versions.

**drag** To move the mouse while holding down a mouse button.

**drag handle** In a graphics program, a small rectangular mark that appears on an image's border that enables the user to drag, scale, or size the graphic image.

**drawing program** An application program used to create, edit, and display vector graphics.

**drill-and-repeat test** In programmed instruction, a method of testing students and ensuring that they learn the material. If students miss questions on a drill-and-repeat test, they are guided back to the material that explains the missed questions.

**drill-down** A technique used by managers to view information in a data warehouse. By drilling down to lower levels of the database, the manager can focus on sales regions, offices, and then individual salespeople, and view summaries at each level.

**drive** A computer storage device, such as the hard disk drive. The name is derived from the motors that "drive" the movement of the media that store data.

**drive activity light** A light on the front panel of most computers that signals when the hard disk is accessing data.

**drive bay** A receptacle or opening into which you can install a floppy drive, a CD-ROM or DVD-ROM drive, or a removable drive.

**drive interface** The electrical pathway between a secondary storage device, such as a hard disk, and the computer. The drive interface is a leading factor in determining the speed of a storage device.

**drive letters** On PCs, the storage device designation, such as Drive A for the floppy disk and Drive C for the hard disk.

**driver** A utility program that is needed to make a peripheral device function correctly.

**dual inline memory module (DIMM)** A plug-in memory module that contains RAM chips. DIMMs use a 64-bit bus to transfer data between the memory and the processor, which is required for many new computers.

**dual-inline packages (DIP)** Chip packages that are affixed to a socket by means of two parallel rows of downward-facing pins.

**dual scan LCD** See passive matrix LCD.

**dumpster diving** A technique used to gain unauthorized access to computer systems by retrieving user IDs and passwords from an organization's trash.

**DVD players** Digital video disc devices for watching movies.

**DVD-R discs** Digital video disc-recordable optical storage media that, like CD-R discs, cannot be erased or written over once data has been saved.

**DVD-RAM** See digital video disc-RAM.

**DVD-ROM** See digital video disc-ROM.

**DVD-ROM discs** Optical storage media that can hold up to 17 GB of data.

**DVD-ROM drive** A read-only disk drive that reads the data encoded on DVD-ROM discs and transfers this data to a computer.

**DVD+RW discs** Digital video disc-read/write optical storage media that allow you to write, erase, and read from the disc many times.

**dye sublimation printer** A thermal transfer printer that produces results that rival high-quality color photographs. Dye sublimation printers are slow and extremely expensive.

**dynamic random access memory (DRAM)** A random access memory chip that must be refreshed periodically; otherwise, the data in the memory will be lost.

# E

**e-book** A book that has been digitized and distributed by means of a digital storage medium.

**e-book reader** A book-sized device that displays an e-book.

**e-commerce** See electronic commerce.

**economically feasible** Capable of being accomplished with available fiscal resources. This is usually determined by a cost/benefit analysis.

**edit menu** In a graphical user interface (GUI), a pull-down menu that contains standard editing commands, such as Cut, Copy, and Paste.

**edutainment** Software combining education and entertainment that provides educational material in the form of a game so that the education becomes entertainment.

**effect** In a graphics program, a processing option that changes the appearance of an image. For example, some graphic programs can manipulate a photograph so that it looks like a watercolor painted on textured paper.

**electrical engineering (EE)** An engineering discipline that is concerned with the design and improvement of electrical and electronic circuits.

**electronic commerce** The use of the Internet and other wide area networks (WANs) for business-to-business and business-to-consumer transactions. Also called e-commerce.

**electronic data interchange (EDI)** A communications standard for the electronic exchange of financial information through information services.

**electronic mail** See e-mail.

**Electronic Recording Machine— Accounting (ERMA)** A computer system developed in 1959 by General Electric that could read special characters. ERMA had a major effect on the banking business, where it was used to digitize checking account information.

**electronic vault** In online banking, a mainframe computer that stores account holders' information.

**electronic warfare** In information warfare, the use of electronic devices to destroy or damage computer systems.

**electronics** A field within electrical engineering that is concerned with the use of transistors to amplify or switch the direction of electrical current.

**element** In HTML, a distinctive component of a document's structure, such as a title, heading, or list. HTML divides elements into two categories: head elements (such as the document's title) and body elements (headings, paragraphs, links, and text).

**element name** In HTML, the code name used to differentiate an element, such as a level-one heading (H1) or a paragraph (P).

**e-mail** Electronic mail; messages sent and received through the use of a computer network.

**e-mail address** A series of characters that precisely identifies the location of a person's electronic mailbox. On the Internet, e-mail addresses consist of a mailbox name (such as jsmith) followed by an at sign (@) and the computer's domain name (as in jsmith@hummer.virginia.edu).

**e-mail attachment** A computer file that is included with an e-mail message.

**e-mail client** A program or a program module that provides e-mail services for computer users, including receiving mail into a locally stored inbox, sending e-mail to other network users, replying to received messages, and storing received messages. The better programs include address books, mail filters, and the capability to compose and read messages coded in HTML. Also called user agent.

**e-mail server** An application that sends mail across the Internet and stores incoming mail until it is downloaded by an e-mail client.

**embedding** See object linking and embedding (OLE).

**emergency disk** A disk that can be used to start the computer in case the operating system becomes unusable for some reason.

**Emergency Position Indicating Radio Beacons (EPIRB)** A yachting safety device that emits a radio signal indicating the device's precise position, which the device determines by using signals from geographical positioning system (GPS) satellites.

**emoticon** See smiley.

**empty element** In HTML, an element that does not permit the inclusion of any content. The <BR> element is an example of an empty element.

**Encapsulated PostScript (EPS)** A graphics format used to print images on PostScript printers.

**encapsulation** In object-oriented programming, the hiding of all internal information of objects from other objects.

**encryption** The process of converting a message into ciphertext (an encrypted message) by using a key, so that the message appears to be nothing but gibberish. The intended recipient, however, can apply the key to decrypt and read the message. See also public key cryptography and rot-13.

**encryption algorithm** A step-by-step method for encrypting and decrypting a message.

**encryption key** A formula that is used to make a plaintext message unreadable.

**end tag** In HTML, the closing component of an element, such as </A>. All elements begin with a start tag; most require an end tag.

**endnote** In a word processing program, a feature that automatically positions and prints footnotes at the end of a document, rather than the bottom of the page.

**Enhanced IDE (EIDE)** An improved version of the IDE drive interface offering faster data transfer rates, access to drives larger than 528 MB, and access to four secondary storage devices instead of two. Also called ATA-2.

**enhanced keyboard** A keyboard with 101 keys that is typically supplied with desktop computers in the United States.

**enhanced parallel port (EPP)** A type of parallel port that, unlike the older Centronics parallel port standard, supports bidirectional communication between the computer and printer and offers significantly faster transmission speeds (up to 2 Mbps). EPP is a standard defined by an international standards body. Compare extended capabilities port (ECP).

**ENIAC (Electronic Numerical Integrator and Computer)** Considered the first large-scale electronic digital computer ever assembled, created in 1946 by Dr. John Mauchly and J. Presper Eckert.

**Enter button** In a spreadsheet program, a button that confirms the text typed in the entry bar area and inserts this text into the active cell.

**enterprise storage system** The collection of online, nearline, and offline storage within an organization. The system typically makes use of servers connected to hard disks, massive RAID systems, tape libraries (high-capacity tape systems), optical disc libraries, and tape backup systems.

**enterprise-wide system** An information system available throughout an organization, including its branch offices.

**entity-relationship diagram (ERD)** In the design of information systems, a diagram that shows all the entities (organizations, departments, users, programs, and data) that play roles in the system, as well as the relationships between those entities.

**entry-level drive** A storage device typically found on the least expensive computers marketed at a given time.

**ergonomic keyboard** A keyboard designed to reduce (but not eliminate) the chance of a cumulative trauma disorder (CTD), an injury involving damage to sensitive nerve tissue caused by motions repeated thousands of times daily.

**error message** A message originated by a program that warns the user about a problem of some kind. The user's intervention may be required to solve the problem.

**Esc** A key that is often used to interrupt or cancel an operation.

**Ethernet** A set of standards that defines local area networks (LANs) capable of operating at data transfer rates of 10 Mbps to 1 Gbps. About 80 percent of all LANs use one of several Ethernet standards.

**Ethernet card** A network interface card (NIC) designed to work with Ethernet local area networks (LANs).

**ethical principle** A principle that defines the justification for considering an act or a rule to be morally right or wrong. Ethical principles can help people find their way through moral dilemmas.

**ethics** The branch of philosophy dealing with the determination of what is right or wrong, usually in the context of moral dilemmas.

**e-tickets** Tickets for airline flights that are purchased online and can be picked up at small self-serve kiosks in airport terminals.

**e-trading site** On the Internet, an online brokerage that enables investors to buy and sell stocks without a human broker's intervention.

**even parity** An error-checking technique that sets an extra bit to 1 if the number of 1 bits in a byte adds up to an odd number.

**event-driven** In programming, a program design method that structures the program around a continuous loop, which cycles until an event occurs (such as the user clicking the mouse).

**exception report** In a transaction processing system (TPS), a document that alerts someone of unexpected developments, such as high demand for a product.

**exclusion operator** In database and Internet searching, a symbol or a word that tells the software to exclude records or documents containing a certain word or phrase.

**executable** See executable file and executable program.

**executable file** A file containing a script or program that can execute instructions on the computer. Program files usually use the .exe extension in the filename.

**executable program** A program that will run on a certain type of computer.

**execute** One of four basic operations carried out by the control unit of a microprocessor. The execute operation involves performing a requested action, such as adding or comparing two numbers.

**execution cycle** In a machine cycle, a phase consisting of the execute and write-back operations.

**executive information system (EIS)** A system that supports management's strategic planning function.

**executive support system (ESS)** A type of decision support system designed to provide high-level executives with information summarizing the overall performance of their organization on the most general level.

**expanded spacing** In character formatting, the provision of extra space between each character.

**expansion board** A circuit board that provides additional capabilities for a computer.

**expansion bus** An electrical pathway that connects the microprocessor to the expansion slots. Also called I/O bus.

**expansion card** See expansion board.

**expansion slot** A receptacle connected to the computer's expansion bus that accepts an expansion board.

**expert system** In artificial intelligence (AI), a program that relies on a database of if-then rules to draw inferences, in much the same way a human expert does.

**Extended Binary Coded Decimal Interchange Code (EBCDIC)** A character encoding scheme developed by IBM and used on its mainframe computer systems.

**extended capabilities port (ECP)** A parallel port standard that is virtually identical to the enhanced parallel port (EPP) standard, except that it was defined by two companies in advance of the issuance of the EPP standard.

**extended character set** A set of characters that can be accessed only by increasing the number of bits per character from the standard seven bits to eight bits (one byte). The extended character set was never standardized, so the PC and Macintosh versions are not compatible.

**extended data out (EDO) DRAM** A type of dynamic RAM (DRAM) that provides faster speeds because it can begin fetching the next item to be stored in memory at the same time that it is sending an item to the CPU.

**extended keyboard** A Macintosh keyboard that closely resembles the enhanced keyboard sold with most desktop PCs.

**Extensible Markup Language (XML)** A set of rules for creating markup languages that enables Web authors to capture specific types of data by creating their own elements. XML can be used in HTML documents.

**extension** A three-letter suffix added to a DOS filename. The extension is often supplied by the application and indicates the type of application that created the file.

**external drive bay** In a computer case, a receptacle designed for mounting storage devices that is accessible from the outside of the case.

**external modem** A modem with its own case, cables, and power supply that plugs into the serial port of a computer.

**extranet** A corporate intranet that has been opened to external access by selected outside partners, including customers, research labs, and suppliers.

**eye-gaze response system** A biological feedback device that enables quadriplegics to control computers by moving their eyes around the screen.

## F

**facsimile machine** A device that transmits scanned images via the telephone system (also known as fax machine).

**facsimile transmission (fax)** The sending and receiving of printed pages between two locations, using a telephone line and fax devices that digitize the page's image.

**fair use** An exception to copyright laws made to facilitate education, commentary, analysis, and scholarly research.

**fall back** In modems, to decrease the data transfer rate to accommodate communications with an older modem or across a dirty line. Some modems also fall forward if line noise conditions improve.

**Fast ATA** An entry-level hard drive interface standard that offers data transfer rates of up to 16 Mbps. Synonymous with Fast IDE and ATA-2.

**Fast Ethernet** An Ethernet standard for local area networks (LANs) that enables data transfer rates of 100 Mbps using twisted-pair cable; also called 100baseT.

**Fast IDE** See Fast ATA.

**fast-page mode (FPM) DRAM** A type of dynamic RAM (DRAM) that provides faster speeds because it can replace data stored within a row of a data page without having to replace the entire page.

**fault tolerance** The ability to continue working even if one or more components fail, such as is found in a redundant array of independent disks.

**fault-tolerant system** A computer system under development by computer scientists that can keep running even if it encounters a glitch in programming.

**fax modem** A modem that also functions as a fax machine, giving the computer user the capability of sending word processing documents and other files as faxes.

**fax software** A utility program that transforms a modem-equipped PC into a device capable of sending and receiving faxes.

**fax-on-demand** An information service in which faxes can be requested by means of a telephone call, and then automatically sent to the caller.

**female connectors** Connectors with receptacles for external pins.

**fetch** One of four basic operations carried out by the control unit of a microprocessor. The fetch operation retrieves the next program instruction from the computer's memory.

**fiber-optic cable** A network cable made from tiny strands of glasslike material that transmit light pulses with very high efficiency and can carry massive amounts of data.

**field** In a database, an area for storing a certain type of information.

**field code** In a word processing program, a code that, when inserted in the text, tells the program to perform an operation specified by the code, such as inserting the time and date when the document is printed.

**field emission display (FED)** A flat-panel display technology that uses tiny CRTs to produce each on-screen pixel.

**field name** Describes the type of data that should be entered into the field.

**file** A document or other collection of information stored on a disk and identified as a unit by a unique name.

**file allocation table (FAT)** A hidden on-disk table that keeps vital records concerning exactly where the various components of a given file are stored. The file allocation table is created at the conclusion of the formatting process.

**file compression** The replacement of lengthy data patterns with short code, reducing the size of a file without harming the data and thereby enabling faster downloads.

**file compression utility** A program to reduce the size of files without harming the data.

**file defragmentation utility** A program used to read all the files on a disk and rewrite them so that files are all stored in a contiguous manner. This process almost always improves disk performance by some degree.

**file finder** A utility that enables one to search an entire hard disk for missing file.

**file format** See format (definition 1).

**file infector** A computer virus that attaches to a program file and, when that program is executed, spreads to other program files.

**file management program** An application that enables users to create customized databases and store in and retrieve data from those databases.

**file menu** In a graphical user interface (GUI), a pull-down menu that contains standard file-management commands, such as Save and Save As.

**file server** In client/server computing, a computer that has been set aside (dedicated) to make program and data files available to client programs on the network.

**file sharing** In a local area network (LAN), the modification of a file's properties so that other users may read or even modify the file.

**File Transfer Protocol (FTP)** An Internet standard for the exchange of files between two computers connected to the Internet. With an FTP client, you can upload or download files from a computer that is running an FTP server. Normally, you need a user name and password to upload or download files from an FTP server, but some FTP servers provide a service called anonymous FTP, which enables anyone to download the files made available for public use.

**file viewer** A utility program that can display the contents of a certain type of file.

**filename** A unique name given to a stored file.

**fill** In a spreadsheet program, a copying operation that copies the contents of the current cell to the specified range.

**fill handle** In a spreadsheet program, a fill handle is a rectangular box on a cell corner that can be used to specify the size of a fill area. The fill command fills a range of cells with values from selected cells.

**filter** In e-mail, a rule that specifies the destination folder of messages conforming to certain criteria.

**filtering software** A program that attempts to prevent minors from accessing adult material on the Internet.

**firewall** A program that permits an organization's internal computer users to access the Internet but places severe limits on the ability of outsiders to access internal data.

**FireWire port** Synonymous with 1394 port. FireWire is Apple Computer's name for 1394 port technology.

**first sale doctrine** A principle of copyright law stipulating that a person who legally obtains a copyrighted work may give or sell the work to another person without the author's permission.

**fixed disk** A hard disk that uses nonremovable platters.

**flame** In Usenet and e-mail, a message that contains abusive, threatening, obscene, or inflammatory language.

**flash BIOS** See flash memory.

**flash memory** A special type of read-only memory (ROM) that enables users to upgrade information contained in memory chips. Also called flash BIOS.

**flash memory card** Wafer-thin, highly portable solid state storage system that is capable of storing as much as 1 gigabyte of data. Used with some digital cameras, the card stores digitized photographs without requiring electrical power to maintain the data.

**flash memory reader** A slot or compartment in digital cameras and other devices into which a flash memory card is inserted.

**flat file** A type of file generated by a file management program. Flat files can be accessed in many different ways but cannot be linked to data in other files.

**flatbed scanner** A device that copies an image (text or graphics) from one side of a sheet of paper and translates it into a digital image.

**flat-panel display** A low-power, lightweight display used with notebook computers (and increasingly with desktop computers).

**flicker** An eye-straining visible distortion that occurs when the refresh rate of a display is below 60 Hz.

**flight simulator** A program that acts like the aircraft on which a pilot is training.

**floating-point notation** A method for storing and calculating numbers so that the location of the decimal point isn't fixed but floating. This allows the computer to work with very small and very large numbers.

**floating-point unit (FPU)** A portion of the microprocessor that handles operations in which the numbers are specified in floating-point notation.

**flooding** A type of antisocial behavior found on Internet Relay Chat characterized by sending repeated messages so that no one else can engage in the conversation.

**floppy disk** A removable and widely used data storage medium that uses a magnetically coated flexible disk of Mylar enclosed in a plastic envelope or case. Although 5.25-inch floppy disks were standard, they became obsolete due to the development of the smaller, more durable 3.5-inch disk.

**floppy disk drive** A mechanism that enables a computer to read and write information on a removable medium that provides a convenient way to move data from one computer to another.

**flowchart** In structured programming, a diagram that shows the logic of a program.

**flush left alignment** In word processing, a way of formatting a block of text so that the left side is aligned but the right side is not.

**flush right alignment** In word processing, a way of formatting a block of text so that the right side is aligned but the left side is not.

**fly-by-wire system** In an aircraft, a computer-based control system that eliminates the pilot's direct physical control over the aircraft's control surfaces (such as flaps and rudders) in favor of computer-controlled mechanisms.

**FM synthesis** A method of generating and reproducing music in a sound card. FM synthesis produces sound similar to an inexpensive electronic keyboard.

**FMD-ROM (fluorescent multilayer disc–read-only memory) disc** A type of high-capacity storage disc with multiple layers whose fluorescent coating allows for storage of up to a terabyte of data.

**folder** A graphical representation of a directory. Most major operating systems display directories as though they were file folders.

**folder list** In an e-mail program, a panel that shows the default and personal mail folders, including the inbox.

**folder structure** An organized set of primary and secondary folders within which to save your files.

**follow-up article** In Usenet, a message posted in reply to another message.

**font** A set of characters that has a name (such as Times Roman) and a distinctive design that falls into one of two broad categories, serif (characters that have small finishing strokes) and sans serif (characters that lack finishing strokes).

**foot mouse** A type of mouse that is controlled by motions of the feet rather than the hands.

**footer** An area at the bottom of the page, but above the bottom margin, that can be used for page numbers or for text that appears on each page of the document.

**footnote** A type of citation that pairs an in-text (and usually numbered) reference with a source citation that appears at the bottom of the page.

**footprint** The amount of room taken up by the case on the desk.

**foreground application** In a multitasking operating system, the active application.

**Form** In the Microsoft Access database manage-ment system, the object used to collect data.

**form factor** A specification for mounting internal components, such as the motherboard.

**form letter** A generic message sent to many people that uses database output to create the illusion that the message is individually written and addressed. Business word processing programs can generate form letters using a feature called mail merging.

**format** 1. A file storage standard used to write a certain type of data to a magnetic disk (also called file format). 2. To prepare a magnetic disk for first use. 3. In word processing, to choose the alignment, emphasis, or other presentation options so that the document will print with an attractive appearance.

**format menu** In a graphical user interface (GUI), a pull-down menu that allows you to modify such features as font style and paragraph settings.

**formatting** The process of modifying a document's appearance so that it looks good when printed.

**Formatting toolbar** In Microsoft Office, a default-loaded toolbar that includes icons for various functions, including choosing document font size and style.

**formula** In a spreadsheet program, a mathematical expression embedded in a cell that can include cell references. The cell displays the formula's result.

**formula bar** In a spreadsheet program, an area above the worksheet that displays the contents of the active cell. The formula bar enables the user to work with formulas, which normally do not appear in the cell.

**Fortran** An early third-generation language that enabled scientists and engineers to write simple programs for solving mathematical equations.

**fourth-generation language (4GL)** A programming language that does not force the programmer to consider the procedure that must be followed to obtain the desired result.

**fractal geometry** The study of a certain type of irregular geometric shapes, in which the shape of internal components is similar to the overall shape. Fractal shapes are common in nature.

**fragmentation** A process in which the various components of a file are separated by normal reading and writing operations so that these components are not stored close together. The result is slower disk operation. A defragmentation utility can improve a disk's performance by placing these file components closer together.

**frame** 1. In a word processing program, a unit of text or a graphic image that has been formatted so that it will appear and print in a precise location on the page. Material placed within frames does not "float" when text is inserted or deleted above the frame. 2. A capability of Web browsers, frames can show more than one HTML page simultaneously.

**frames** In a video or animation, the series of still images flashed on-screen at a rapid rate.

**frame rate** In a video or animation, a measurement of the number of still images shown per second.

**frame relay** A type of packet-switching network that enables an organization to connect to an external network's point of presence for a lower cost than a permanent leased line.

**free e-mail service** A Web-based service that provides e-mail accounts free of charge. The service is supported by advertising.

**freeware** Copyrighted software that can be freely copied but not sold.

**frequently asked questions (FAQ)** A document that contains topical information organized by the questions that are commonly asked concerning the topic.

**front panel** An area on the front of most computers containing various indicator lights and controls.

**FTP client** A program that is able to assist the user to upload or download files from an FTP site. There are many standalone FTP clients, and FTP downloading capabilities are built into Web browsers such as Netscape Navigator. Microsoft Internet Explorer 5.0 can upload files to FTP servers as well as download files.

**FTP server** On the Internet, a server program that enables external users to download or upload files from a specified directory or group of directories.

**FTP site** An Internet-accessible computer that is running an FTP server.

**full backup** The process of copying all files from a secondary storage device (most commonly a hard disk) to a backup medium, such as a tape cartridge.

**full-motion video** A video presentation that gives the illusion of smooth, continuous action, even though it consists of a series of still pictures. The key to full-motion video is a frame rate fast enough to create the illusion of continuous movement.

**function** In spreadsheet programs such as Microsoft Excel, one of the two basic types of formulas (along with mathematic expressions). In a function, operations can be performed on multiple inputs.

**function keys** A row of keys positioned along the top of the keyboard, labeled F1 through F12, to which programs can assign various commands.

**fuzzy logic** A branch of logic concerned with propositions that have varying degrees of precision or confidence.

# G

**G or GB** Abbreviation for gigabyte, approximately one billion (one thousand million) bytes or characters.

**Gantt chart** A bar chart that summarizes a project's schedule by showing how various activities proceed over time.

**gas plasma display** A flat-panel display technology. Although gas plasma displays have excellent image quality, they are very expensive and consume too much power to be used on portable computers.

**gate** An electronic switch; same as transistor.

**Gbps** A data transfer rate of approximately one billion bits per second.

**genealogy program** A special-purpose application program to assist in tracing and compiling family trees.

**General Public License (GPL)** A freeware software license, devised by the Open Software Foundation (OSF), stipulating that a given program can be obtained, used, and even modified, as long as the user agrees to not sell the software and to make the source code for any modifications available.

**general-purpose computer** A computer that can run a variety of programs, in contrast to an embedded or dedicated computer, which is locked to a single function or set of functions.

**genetic algorithm** An automated program development environment in which various alternative approaches to solving a problem are introduced; each is allowed to mutate periodically through the introduction of random changes. The various approaches compete in an effort to solve a specific problem. After a period of time, one approach may prove to be clearly superior to the others.

**geosynchronous orbit** A circular path around the Earth in which a communications satellite, for example, has a velocity exactly matching the Earth's speed of rotation, allowing the satellite to be permanently positioned with respect to the ground.

**GIF animation** A graphics file that contains more than one image stored using the GIF graphics file format. Also stored in the file is a brief script that indicates the sequence of images, and how long to display each image.

**gigabit** A unit of measurement approximately equal to one billion bits.

**Gigabit Ethernet** An Ethernet local area network (LAN) that is capable of achieving data transfer rates of 1 Gbps (one billion bits per second) using fiber-optic cable.

**gigabit per second (Gbps)** A data transfer measurement equivalent to one billion bits per second.

**gigabits per second points of presence (gigaPoPs)** In Internet II, a high-speed testbed for the development of next-generation Internet protocols, a point of presence (PoP) that provides access to a backbone service capable of data transfer rates in excess of 1 Gbps (one billion bits per second).

**gigabyte (G or GB)** A unit of measurement commonly used to state the capacity of memory or storage devices; equal to 1,024 megabytes, or approximately one billion bytes or characters.

**glass cockpit** In aviation, a cockpit characterized by a profusion of data displays.

**Global Positioning System (GPS)** A satellite-based system that enables portable GPS receivers to determine their location with an accuracy of 100 meters or less.

**global structure** In an HTML document, the top-level document structure created by using the HEAD and BODY tags.

**global unique identifier (GUID)** A uniquely identifying serial number assigned to Pentium III processor chips that can be used by Web servers to detect which computer is accessing a Web site.

**graphical browser** On the World Wide Web, a browser capable of displaying graphic images as well as text. Early browsers could display only text.

**Graphical MUD** A multiuser dungeon (MUD) that uses graphics instead of text to represent the interaction of characters in a virtual environment.

**graphical user interface (GUI)** An interface between the operating system and the user. Graphical user interfaces are the most popular of all user interfaces but also require the most system resources.

**graphics accelerator** A display adapter (video card) that contains its own dedicated processing circuitry and video memory (VRAM), enabling faster display of complex graphics images.

**graphics file** A file that stores the information needed to display a graphic. Popular graphics file formats include BMP (Windows Bitmap), JPEG, and GIF.

**Graphics Interchange Format (GIF)** A bitmapped color graphics file format capable of storing images with 256 colors. GIF incorporates a compression technique that reduces file size, making it ideal for use on a network. GIF is best used for images that have areas of solid color.

**graphics output** A type of output that consists of visual images, including charts and pictures.

**graphics tablet** A graphics input device used with CAD applications to enter graphic data precisely.

**grayscale monitor** A monitor that displays black, white, and dozens or hundreds of shades of gray. Grayscale monitors are often used to prepare copy for noncolor printing.

**grounding strap** A wrist strap worn when repairing or upgrading computer components. The strap can be connected to an electrical ground to prevent the discharge of static electricity, which can ruin computer components that contain semiconductor chips.

**group e-mail address** An e-mail address that directs an e-mail message to more than one person.

**groupware** The software that provides computerized support for the information needs of individuals networked into workgroups.

**gutter** In document formatting, extra space on the side of each page that allows for binding.

# H

**hacker** Traditionally, a computer user who enjoys pushing his or her computer capabilities to the limit, especially by using clever or novel approaches to solving problems. In the press, the term hacker has become synonymous with criminals who attempt unauthorized access to computer systems for criminal purposes, such as sabotage or theft. The computing community considers this usage inaccurate.

**hacker ethic** A set of moral principles common to the first-generation hacker community (roughly 1965–1982), described by Steven Levy in *Hackers* (1984). According to the hacker ethic, all technical information should, in principle, be freely available to all. Therefore, gaining entry to a system to explore data and increase knowledge is never unethical. Destroying, altering, or moving data in such a way that could cause injury or expense to others, however, is always unethical. In increasingly more states, unauthorized computer access is against the law. See also cracker.

**handheld computer** See personal digital assistant.

**handheld scanner** A scanner used to digitize images of small originals, such as photographs or small amounts of text.

**handle** In a spreadsheet program, a rectangular box on a cell corner that can be used to specify the size of a fill area.

**handwriting recognition software** A program that accepts handwriting as input and converts it into editable computer text.

**hanging indent** A type of indentation that does not indent the first line but does indent the following lines.

**haptics** A field of research in developing output devices that stimulate the sense of touch.

**hard copy** Printed computer output, differing from the data stored on disk or in memory.

**hard disk** A secondary storage medium that uses several rigid disks (platters) coated with a magnetically sensitive material and housed in a hermetically sealed mechanism. In almost all modern computers, the hard disk is by far the most important storage medium. Also called hard disk drive.

**hard disk controller** An electronic circuit that provides an interface between a hard disk and the computer's CPU.

**hard disk drive** See hard disk.

**hardware** The physical components, such as circuit boards, disk drives, displays, and printers, that make up a computer system.

**hardware MPEG support** Circuitry built into a computer to improve MPEG video playback speed and quality.

**hashing** In data processing, the process in which the position of a record is determined through the use of a mathematical computation to produce an address where the unique key field is stored.

**hashing algorithm** A mathematical formula used to determine the address of a record in a direct access file.

**head** In HTML, one of two main portions of the document (the other is the body). The head contains elements that do not appear in a browser's display window.

**head actuator** Mechanism on a floppy disk drive that moves the read/write head to the area that contains the desired data.

**head crash** In a hard disk, the collision of a read/write head with the surface of the disk, generally caused by a sharp jolt to the computer's case. Head crashes can damage the read/write head, as well as create bad sectors.

**header** In e-mail or a Usenet news article, the beginning of a message. The header contains important information about the sender's address, the subject of the message, and other information.

**head-mounted display** See headset.

**headset** A wearable output device with twin LCD panels for creating the illusion that an individual is experiencing a three-dimensional, simulated environment.

**heat sink** A heat-dissipating component that drains heat away from semiconductor devices, which can generate enough heat in the course of their operation to destroy themselves. Heat sinks are often used in combination with fans to cool semiconductor components.

**help menu** In a graphical user interface (GUI), a pull-down menu that provides access to interactive help utilities.

**help screen** In commercial software, information that appears on-screen that can provide assistance with using a particular program.

**help utilities** Programs, such as a table of contents of frequently requested items, offered on most graphical user interface (GUI) applications.

**hexadecimal number** A number that uses a base 16 number system rather than a decimal (or base 10) number system.

**hierarchy** In Usenet, a category that includes a variety of newsgroups devoted to a shared, general topic.

**hierarchy chart** In structured programming, a program planning chart that shows the top-down design of the program and the relationship between program modules. Also called structure chart.

**High Definition Television (HDTV)** The name given to several standards for digital television displays.

**high FD (HiFD)** A Sony removable disk storage format that can store up to 200 MB using a drive that is also capable of reading 3.5-inch floppy disks.

**high-density (HD)** A floppy disk storage format that can store up to 1.44 MB of data.

**high-level programming language** A programming language that eliminates the need for programmers to understand the intimate details of how the computer processes data.

**history list** In a Web browser, a window that shows all the Web sites that the browser has accessed during a given period, such as the last 30 days.

**home and educational programs** General-purpose software programs for personal finance, home design and landscaping, encyclopedias and other computerized reference information, and games.

**home directory** In a multiuser computer system, a directory that is set aside for an individual user.

**home page** 1. In any hypertext system, including the Web, a document intended to serve as an initial point of entry to a Web of related documents. Also called a welcome page, a home page contains general introductory information, as well as hyperlinks to related resources. A well-designed home page contains internal navigation buttons that help users find their way among the various documents that the home page makes available. 2. The start page that is automatically displayed when you start a Web browser or click the program's Home button. 3. A personal page listing an individual's contact information, and favorite links, and (generally) some information—ranging from cryptic to voluminous—about the individual's perspective on life.

**home phone-line network (HomePNA)** A linked personal communications system that works off a home's existing phone wiring, thus being easy to install, inexpensive, and fast. The acronym PNA is derived from the Home Phone Networking Alliance.

**home power-line network** A linked personal communications system that works by connecting computers to one another through the same electrical power outlet, thus providing the convenience of not having to locate each computer in the home next to a phone jack.

**home radio-frequency (RF) network** A linked personal communications system that connects computers using wireless radio signals, making computers portable throughout the house.

**horizontal application** A general-purpose program widely used across an organization's functional divisions (such as marketing and finance). Horizontal applications are also popular in the consumer market.

**horizontal scroll bar** A scroll bar that enables the user to bring areas of a document into view that are hidden to the left or right.

**host** In a computer network, a computer that is fully connected to the network and is able to be addressed by other hosts.

**hostile environment** In laws concerning sexual harassment in the workplace, a working environment characterized by practices (such as sexually explicit jokes or calendars) that make some workers feel as though the workplace is offensive or oppressive.

**Hot swapping** Connecting and disconnecting peripherals while the computer is running.

**HTML editor** A program that provides assistance in preparing documents for the Web using HTML. The simplest HTML editor is a word processing program that enables you to type text and add HTML tags manually. Standalone HTML editors provide automated assistance with HTML coding and display some formats on-screen.

**hub** In a local area network (LAN), a device that connects several workstations and enables them to exchange data.

**Human Genome Project (HGP)** A research project seeking to identify the full set of genetic instructions inside human cells and find out what those instructions do.

**hyperlink** In a hypertext system, an underlined or otherwise emphasized word or phrase that, when clicked, displays another document.

**hypermedia** A hypertext system that uses various multimedia resources, such as sounds, animations, and videos, as a means of navigation as well as decoration.

**hypermedia system** A hypertext system that uses various multimedia resources, such as sounds, movies, and text, as a means of navigation as well as illustration.

**hypertext** A method of preparing and publishing text, ideally suited to the computer, in which readers can choose their own paths through the material. To prepare hypertext, you first "chunk" the information into small, manageable units, such as single pages of text. These units are called *nodes*. You then embed hyperlinks in the text. When the reader clicks a hyperlink, the hypertext software displays a different node. The process of navigating among the nodes linked in this way is called *browsing*. A collection of nodes interconnected by hyperlinks is called a web. The Web is a hypertext system on a global scale.

**Hypertext Markup Language (HTML)** A language for marking the portions of a document (called elements) so that, when accessed by a program called a Web browser, each portion appears with a distinctive format. HTML is the markup language behind the appearance of documents on the Web. HTML is standardized by means of a document type definition in the Standard Generalized Markup Language (SGML). HTML includes capabilities that enable authors to insert hyperlinks, which when clicked display another HTML document. The agency responsible for standardizing HTML is the World Wide Web Consortium (W3C).

**Hypertext Transfer Protocol (HTTP)** The Internet standard that supports the exchange of information on the Web. By defining uniform resource locators (URLs) and how they can be used to retrieve resources anywhere on the Internet, HTTP enables Web authors to embed hyperlinks in Web documents. HTTP defines the process by which a Web client, called a browser, originates a request for information and sends it to a Web server, a program that responds to HTTP requests and provides the desired information.

## I

**I/O bus** See expansion bus.

**I/O device** Generic term for any input or output device.

**IBM compatible personal computer** A computer that can use all or almost all software developed for the IBM personal computer and accepts the IBM personal computer's cards, adapters, and peripheral devices. Compare clone.

**icon** In a graphical user interface (GUI), a small picture that represents a program, a data file, or some other computer entity or function.

**IDE/ATA** See Integrated Drive Electronics (IDE).

**identify theft** A form of fraud in which a thief obtains someone's Social Security number and other personal information, and then uses this information to obtain credit cards fraudulently.

**image editor** A sophisticated paint program for editing and transforming complex bitmapped images, such as photographs.

**image processing system** A filing system in which incoming documents are scanned and stored digitally.

**impact printer** A printer that generates output by striking the page with something solid.

**inbox** In e-mail, a default folder that contains any new mail messages, as well as older messages that have not been moved or deleted.

**inclusion operator** In database or Web searching, a symbol or keyword that instructs the search software to make sure that any retrieved records or documents contain a certain word or phrase.

**increment** (v.) To increase. (n.) A specified unit by which a quantity should be increased.

**incremental backup** The process of copying files that have changed since the last full backup to a backup medium, such as a tape cartridge.

**indecency** In U.S. law, the use of four-letter words or any other explicit reference to sexual or excretory acts that violates community decency standards.

**index page** In Web publishing, the page that the Web server displays by default (usually called index.html or default.html).

**indexed file** See indexed sequential file.

**indexed sequential file** A file with records that can be accessed either directly (randomly) or sequentially. Also called indexed file.

**Industry Standard Architecture (ISA) bus** A bus architecture used for expansion slots introduced in the IBM PC/AT. Although they are slower than the PCI bus architecture, ISA expansion slots continue to appear in new computers for compatibility.

**information** Processed data.

**information hiding** A modular programming technique in which information inside a module remains hidden with respect to other modules.

**information kiosk** An automated presentation system used for public information or employee training.

**information literacy** The capability to gather information, evaluate the information, and make an informed decision.

**information overload** A condition of confusion, stress, and indecision brought about by being inundated with information of variable value.

**information processing cycle** A complete sequence of operations involving data input, processing, storage, and output.

**information system** A purposefully designed system that brings data, computers, procedures, and people together to manage information important to an organization's mission.

**Information Superhighway** A term coined by former U.S. Vice President Al Gore to describe the phenomenon of media convergence.

**information systems (IS) department** In a complex organization, the division responsible for designing, installing, and maintaining the organization's information systems.

**information terrorism** The intimidation of a person, an organization, or a country by means of sabotage directed at information systems.

**information warfare** A military strategy that targets an opponent's information systems.

**information-literate person** Someone who knows how to gather information, evaluate the information, and make an informed decision.

**infrared** A data transmission medium that uses the same signaling technology used in TV remote controls.

**inheritance** In object-oriented (OO) programming, the capacity of an object to pass its characteristics to subclasses.

**inkjet printer** A nonimpact printer that forms an image by spraying ink from a matrix of tiny jets.

**inline element** In HTML, an element that can be included in a block element. Some inline elements enable Web authors to choose presentation formats such as bold or italic.

**input** The information entered into a computer for processing.

**input device** Any device that is capable of accepting data so that it is properly represented for processing within the computer.

**input/output (I/O) bus** See expansion bus.

**input/output (I/O) port** A circuit that enables a peripheral device to channel data into and out of the computer.

**insert mode** In word processing, a text insertion mode in which the inserted text pushes existing text to the right and down.

**insertion point** See cursor.

**install** To set up a program so that it is ready to function on a given computer system. The installation process may involve creating additional directories, making changes to system files, and other technical tasks. For this reason, most programs come with setup programs that handle the installation process automatically.

**instant messaging (IM) system** Software program that lets you know when a friend or business associate is online. You can then contact this person and exchange messages and attachments.

**instruction** A unique number assigned to an operation performed by a processor.

**instruction cycle** In a machine cycle, a phase consisting of the fetch and decode operations.

**instruction set** A list of specific instructions that a given brand and model of processor can perform.

**intangible benefits** Gains that have no fixed dollar value, such as access to improved information or increased sales due to improved customer services.

**integer** A whole number.

**integrated circuit (IC)** A semiconductor circuit containing more than one transistor and other electronic components; often referred to as a chip.

**Integrated Drive Electronics (IDE)** A popular secondary storage interface standard commonly found in PCs that offers relatively good performance at a low cost. Although IDE is a commonly used interface, newer computers use either Enhanced IDE (EIDE) or Ultra ATA. Also called Advanced Technology Attachment (ATA).

**integrated learning system (ILS)** A mainframe-based system used to bring computer-assisted instruction (CAI) to schools.

**integrated program** A program that combines three or more productivity software functions, including word processing, database management, and a spreadsheet.

**Integrated Services Digital Network (ISDN)** A worldwide standard for the delivery of digital telephone and data services to homes, schools, and offices using existing twisted-pair wiring. The three categories of ISDN services are Basic Rate Interface (BRI), Primary Rate Interface (PRI), and Broadband ISDN (BISDN).

**Intelligent Transportation System (ITS)** A system, partly funded by the U.S. government, to develop smart streets and smart cars. Such a system could warn travelers of congestion and suggest alternative routes.

**interactive multimedia** A presentation involving two or more media, such as text, graphics, or sound, and providing users with the ability to choose their own path through the information.

**interactive processing** A type of processing in which the various stages of the information processing cycle (input, processing, storage, and output) can be initiated and controlled by the user.

**interactive TV** Features that enable users to engage in two-way communication with a digital television set. Interactive TV will enable broadcasters and cable TV providers to implement features such as user-selectable movies, weather broadcasts selected by ZIP code, and news on selected topics.

**interexchange carrier (IXC)** In the public switched telephone network (PSTN), a company that provides long-distance or regional trunk services between local telephone exchanges.

**interface** A means of connecting two dissimilar computer devices. An interface has two components, a physical component and a communications standard, called a protocol. The physical component provides the physical means for making a connection, while the protocol enables designers to design the devices so that they can exchange data with each other. The computer's standard parallel port is an example of an interface that has both a distinctive physical connector and a defining, standard protocol.

**interlaced monitor** A monitor that refreshes every other line of pixels with each pass of the cathode gun. This often results in screen flicker, and almost all monitors now are noninterlaced.

**internal drive bay** In a computer's case, a receptacle for mounting a storage device that is not easily accessible from outside the computer's case. Internal drive bays are typically used to mount nonremovable hard drives.

**internal modem** A modem that fits into the expansion bus of a personal computer. See also external modem.

**internal speaker** One of the components inside a computer's system unit, typically for emitting beeps and other low-fidelity sounds.

**International Telecommunications Union (ITU)** A branch organization of the United Nations that sets international telecommuni-cations standards.

**Internet** An enormous and rapidly growing system of linked computer networks, worldwide in scope, that facilitates data communication services such as remote logon, file transfer, electronic mail, the World Wide Web, and newsgroups. Relying on TCP/IP, the Internet assigns every connected computer a unique Internet address (called an IP address) so that any two connected computers can locate each other on the network and exchange data.

**Internet 2** The next-generation Internet, still under development.

**Internet address** The unique, 32-bit address assigned to a computer that is connected to the Internet, represented in dotted decimal notation (for example, 128.117.38.5). Synonymous with IP address.

**Internet client** A user program for accessing information on the Internet, such as e-mail or a Web site.

**Internet hard drive** Storage space on a server that is accessible from the Internet.

**Internet Inter-Orb Protocol (IIOP)** In object-oriented (OO) programming, a standard that allows Web browsers to request information from objects by using the Common Object Request Broker Architecture (CORBA).

**Internet Message Access Protocol (IMAP)** In Internet e-mail, one of two fundamental protocols (the other is POP3) that governs how and where users store their incoming mail messages. IMAP4, the current version, stores messages on the mail server rather than facilitating downloading to the user's computer, as does the POP3 standard. For many users, this standard may prove more convenient than POP3 because all of one's mail is kept in one central location, where it can be organized, archived, and made available from remote locations. IMAP4 is supported by Netscape Messenger, the mail package in Netscape Communicator; Microsoft Outlook Express; and by other leading e-mail programs.

**Internet programs** General-purpose software programs for e-mailing, instant messaging, Web browsing, and videoconferencing.

**Internet Protocol (IP)** One of the two core Internet standards (the other is the Transmission Control Protocol, TCP). IP defines the standard that describes how an Internet-connected computer should break data down into packets for transmission across the network, and how those packets should be addressed so that they arrive at their destination. IP is the connectionless part of the TCP/IP protocols.

**Internet protocols** The standards that enable computer users to exchange data through the Internet. Also called TCP/IP.

**Internet Relay Chat (IRC)** A real-time, Internet-based chat service, in which one can find "live" participants from the world over. IRC requires the use of an IRC client program, which displays a list of the current IRC channels. After joining a channel, you can see what other participants are typing on-screen, and you can type your own repartee.

**Internet service** A set of communication standards (protocols) and software (clients and servers) that defines how to access and exchange a certain type of information on the Internet. Examples of Internet services are e-mail, FTP, Gopher, IRC, and Web.

**Internet Service Provider (ISP)** A company that provides Internet accounts and connections to individuals and businesses. Most ISPs offer a range of connection options, ranging from dial-up modem connections to high-speed ISDN and ADSL. Also provided is e-mail, Usenet, and Web hosting.

**Internet telephony** The use of the Internet (or of nonpublic networks based on Internet technology) for the transmission of real-time voice data.

**Internet telephony service providers** A long-distance voice messaging service that provides telephone service by means of the Internet or private data networks using Internet technology.

**InterNIC** A consortium of two organizations that provide networking information services to the Internet community, under contract to the National Science Foundation (NSF). Currently, AT&T provides directory and database services, while Network Solutions, Inc., provides registration services for new domain names and IP addresses.

**interoperability** The ability to work with computers and operating systems of differing type and brand.

**interpreter** In programming, a translator that converts each instruction into machine-readable code and executes it one line at a time. Interpreters are often used for learning and debugging, due to their slow speed.

**interrupt handlers** Miniprograms in an operating system that kick in when an interrupt occurs.

**interrupt request (IRQ)** Lines that handle the communication between input or output devices and the computer's CPU.

**interrupts** Signals generated by input and output devices that inform the operating system that something has happened, such as a document has finished printing.

**intranet** A computer network based on Internet technology (TCP/IP) that meets the internal needs of a single organization or company. Not necessarily open to the external Internet and almost certainly not accessible from the outside, an intranet enables organizations to make internal resources available using familiar Internet tools. See also extranet.

**IP address** A 32-bit binary number that uniquely and precisely identifies the location of a particular computer on the Internet. Every computer that is directly connected to the Internet must have an IP address. Because binary numbers are so hard to read, IP addresses are given in four-part decimal numbers, each part representing 8 bits of the 32-bit address (for example, 128.143.7.226).

**IPOS cycle** A sequence of four basic types of computer operations that characterize everything computers do. These operations are input, processing, output, and storage.

**IPv6** The Next Generation Internet Protocol, also known as IPng, is an evolutionary extension of the current Internet protocol suite that is under development by the Internet Engineering Task Force (IETF). IPv6 was originally intended to deal with the coming exhaustion of IP addresses, a serious problem caused by the Internet's rapid growth. However, the development effort has broadened to address a number of deficiencies in the current versions of the fundamental Internet protocols, including security, the lack of support for mobile computing, the need for automatic configuration of network devices, the lack of support for allocating bandwidth to high-priority data transfers, and other shortcomings of the current protocols. An unresolved question is whether the working committee will be able to persuade network equipment suppliers to upgrade to the new protocols.

**IPX** See IPX/SPX.

**IPX/SPX** In local area networks (LANs), a suite of network and transport layer protocols developed by Novell for use with the NetWare network operating system.

**IrDA port** A port housed on the exterior of a computer's case that is capable of sending and receiving computer data by means of infrared signals. The standards that define these signals are maintained by the Infrared Data Association (IrDA). IrDA ports are commonly found on notebook computers and personal digital assistants (PDAs).

**IRQ conflict** A serious system failure that results if two devices are configured to use the same IRQ but are not designed to share an IRQ line.

**ISDN adapter** An internal or external accessory that enables a computer to connect to remote computer networks or the Internet by means of ISDN. (Inaccurately called an ISDN modem.)

**italic** A character format in which characters are slanted to the right.

**iteration control structure** See repetition control structure.

# J

**Java** A cross-platform programming language created by Sun Microsystems that enables programmers to write a program that will execute on any computer capable of running a Java interpreter (which is built into today's leading Web browsers). Java is an object-oriented programming (OOP) language similar to C++, except that it eliminates some features of C++ that programmers find tedious and time-consuming. Java programs are compiled into applets (small programs executed by a browser) or applications (larger, standalone programs that require a Java interpreter to be present on the user's computer), but the compiled code contains no machine code. Instead, the output of the compiler is bytecode, an intermediary between source code and machine code that can be transmitted by computer networks, including the Internet.

**Java Virtual Machine (VM)** A Java interpreter and runtime environment for Java applets and Java applications. This environment is called a virtual machine because, no matter what kind of computer it is running on, it creates a simulated computer that provides the correct platform for executing Java programs. In addition, this approach insulates the computer's file system from rogue applications. Java VMs are available for most computers.

**JavaScript** A scripting language for Web publishing, developed by Netscape Communications, that enables Web authors to embed simple Java-like programming instructions in the HTML text of their Web pages.

**Jaz drive** A removable drive from Iomega that can store up to 2 GB.

**jewel boxes** Plastic protective cases for storing CD-ROM discs.

**job instruction training (JIT)** A method of on-the-job training where decision-making is eliminated as much as possible.

**joint application development (JAD)** In information systems development, a method of system design that involves users at all stages of system development. See also prototyping.

**multiple series** In a chart such as a bar chart or line chart, the use of more than one data series to compare two or more items.

**multiple undo** A feature of many of today's application programs that enables the user to undo more than one editing change. Some programs offer unlimited undo.

**multiplexing** A technique that enables more than one signal to be conveyed on a physical transmission medium.

**multiprocessing** The use of two or more processors in the same computer system at the same time.

**Multipurpose Internet Mail Extensions (MIME)** An Internet standard that specifies how Internet programs, such as e-mail programs and Web browsers, can transfer multimedia files (including sounds, graphics, and video) through the Internet. Before the development of MIME, all data transferred through the Internet had to be coded in ASCII text.

**multiscan monitor** A monitor that automatically adjusts its refresh rate to the output of the video adapter.

**multisession PhotoCD** A standard for recording PhotoCD information onto a CD-ROM during several different recording sessions. Unlike standard CD-ROM drives, drives that are Multisession PhotoCD-compatible can read information recorded on a disk during several different pressings.

**multitasking** In operating systems, the capability to execute more than one application at a time. Multitasking shouldn't be confused with multiple program loading, in which two or more applications are present in random access memory (RAM) but only one executes at a time.

**multithreading** In multitasking, the capability of a computer to execute more than one task, called a thread, within a single program.

**multiuser** Designed to be used by more than one person at a time.

**multiuser dungeon (MUD)** A text-based environment in which multiple players can assume online personas and interact with each other by means of text chatting.

**Musical Instrument Digital Interface (MIDI)** A standard that specifies how musical sounds can be described in text files so that a MIDI-compatible synthesizer can reproduce the sounds. MIDI files are small, so they're often used to provide music that starts playing automatically when a Web page is accessed. To hear MIDI sounds, your computer needs a sound card. MIDI sounds best with wavetable synthesis sound cards, which include sound samples from real musical instruments.

# N

**name** The first part of a filename. It is separated by a period, or dot, from the second part of the name, called the extension.

**name box** In a spreadsheet program, an area that displays the name of the active cell.

**nanometer** A billionth of a meter.

**nanorobots** Atoms and molecules used to perform certain tasks in nanotechnology.

**nanosecond (ns)** A unit of time equal to one billionth of a second.

**nanotechnology** Manipulating materials on an atomic or molecular scale in order to build microscopic devices.

**National Television Standards Committee (NTSC)** The organization that defines the display standards for broadcast television in the U.S.

**native application** A program that runs on a particular brand and model of processor or in a particular operating system.

**natural language** A human language, such as English or Japanese.

**near-letter-quality printout** Print quality that is almost as good as printed text.

**near-online storage** A type of storage that is not directly available, but can be made available by a simple action such as inserting a disk.

**nest** In structured programming, to embed one control structure inside another.

**NetBEUI** This LAN protocol defines Microsoft Windows NT–based networks.

**netiquette** Short for network etiquette. A set of rules that reflect long-standing experience about getting along harmoniously in the electronic environment (e-mail and newsgroups).

**Netscape extensions** Additions to standard HTML added in the mid-1990s by Netscape Communications, Inc., in an effort to provide Web designers with more presentation options.

**network** A group of two or more computer systems linked together to enable communications by exchanging data and sharing resources.

**network access point (NAP)** In a wide area network (WAN), a location where local and regional service providers can connect to transcontinental backbone networks.

**network architecture** The overall design of a computer network that specifies its functionality at every level by means of protocols.

**network attached storage (NAS) devices** High-performances devices that provide shared data to clients and other servers on a local area network.

**network computer (NC)** A computer that provides much of a PC's functionality at a lower price. Network computers don't have disk drives because they get their software from the computer network.

**network effect** An economic term for the rewards consumers get when they purchase a popular product rather than a less popular, even if technologically superior, one.

**network interface card (NIC)** An adapter that enables a user to connect a network cable to a computer.

**network laser printer** A nonimpact, high-resolution printer capable of serving the printing needs of an entire department.

**network layers** Separate divisions within a network architecture with specific functions and protocols, allowing engineers to make changes within a layer without having to redesign the entire network.

**network medium** A physical condition that links two or more computers.

**network operating system (NOS)** The software needed to enable data transfer and application usage over a local area network (LAN).

**network topology** The physical layout of a local area network (LAN), such as a bus, star, or ring topology, that determines what happens when, for example, two workstations try to access the LAN or transmit data simultaneously.

**network version** A version of an application program for use by more than one person at a time on a local area network (LAN).

**network warfare** A form of information warfare characterized by attacks on a society's information infrastructure, such as its banking and telecommunications networks.

**neural network** In artificial intelligence, a computer architecture that attempts to mimic the structure of the human brain. Neural nets "learn" by trial and error and are good at recognizing patterns and dealing with complexity.

**newsgroup** In Usenet, a discussion group devoted to a single topic. Users post messages to the group, and those reading the discussion send reply messages to the author individually or post replies that can be read by the group as a whole.

**NNTP server** See Usenet server.

**node** In a LAN, a connection point that can create, receive, or repeat a message.

**nonimpact printer** A printer that forms a text or graphics image by spraying or fusing ink to the page.

**noninterlaced monitor** A monitor that refreshes the entire screen with each pass of the cathode gun. Because this reduces flicker and eye strain, almost all monitors today are noninterlaced.

**nonprocedural** Not tied down to step-by-step procedures. In programming, a nonprocedural programming language does not force the programmer to consider the procedure that must be followed to obtain the desired result.

**nonresident** Not present in memory. A nonresident program must be loaded from secondary storage when it is needed.

**nonvolatile** Not susceptible to loss. If power is lost, the data is preserved.

**normal layout** In an application program, an on-screen rendition of the document's appearance that does not attempt to show all of the features that will appear in the printout.

**normal view** A view available in Microsoft PowerPoint that shows the outline view on the left side of the screen and the slide view on the right side of the screen.

**normalization** In database management, a formal process of database design that assures the elimination of duplicate data entry (data redundancy).

**notebook computer** A portable computer that is small enough to fit into an average-size briefcase but includes nearly all peripherals commonly found on desktop computers.

**notes view** In a presentation graphics program, a view of the presentation that enables you to see your speaker's notes.

**NTSC converter** A device needed to connect a computer to a TV.

**NuBus** A 32-bit wide expansion bus used by older Macintosh computers. Newer Macintoshes use the Personal Computer Interface (PCI) bus.

**nuking** A type of antisocial behavior found on Internet Relay Chat characterized by exploiting bugs that cause computer crashes.

**Num Lock** A toggle key that determines whether the numeric keypad functions in cursor movement mode or number entry mode.

**numbered lists** In Microsoft word, numbered lists are useful for listing items or giving instructions.

**numeric check** Ensures that numbers are entered into a field.

**numeric field** In a database, a space that accepts only numbers.

**numeric format** In a spreadsheet program, the way values appear in cells. Examples of numeric formats are currency and date.

**numeric keypad** A set of keys, usually on the right side of the keyboard, for entering numeric data quickly. The numeric keypad can also move the cursor.

## O

**object** 1. In object-oriented programming (OOP), a unit of computer information that contains data and all the procedures or operations that can process or manipulate the data. 2. Nontextual data. Examples of objects include pictures, sounds, or videos.

**object code** In programming, the machine-readable instructions created by a compiler from source code.

**object linking and embedding (OLE)** A Microsoft Windows standard that enables applications to exchange data and work with one another dynamically. A linked object, such as a graphic or paragraph, is dependent upon, or linked to, the source file such that if the object changes in the source file it also changes in the destination file. An embedded object is simply copied into a program.

**object-oriented database** The newest type of database structure, well suited for multimedia applications, in which the result of a retrieval operation is an object of some kind, such as a document. Within this object are miniprograms that enable the object to perform tasks such as displaying graphics. Object-oriented databases can incorporate sound, video, text, and graphics into a single database record.

**object-oriented (OO) programming** A programming technique that creates generic building blocks of a program (the objects). The user then assembles different sets of objects as needed to solve specific problems. Also called OOP, for object-oriented programming.

**obscenity** In U.S. law, a literary or artistic work that is obviously designed to produce sexual arousal, violates established community standards, and has no literary, artistic, or scientific value.

**odd parity** An error-checking protocol in which the parity bit is set to 1 if the number of 1 digits in a byte equals an even number.

**office application** An application program that is useful for anyone working with words, numbers, graphic images, and databases in a contemporary office setting. This category includes word processing, spreadsheet, and presentation graphics software, as well as database management programs designed for use by untrained users.

**Office Clipboard** In Microsoft Office, a feature that temporarily stores in memory whatever has been cut or copied from a document, allowing for those items to be used within any Office application.

**office suite** A collection of separate office applications that have been designed to resemble each other as closely as possible and to exchange data smoothly. The leading office suite package is Microsoft Office. Compare integrated program.

**offline storage** A type of storage that is not readily available and is used to store infrequently accessed or backup data.

**off-the-shelf software** See packaged software.

**on-board video** Video circuitry that comes built into a computer's motherboard.

**online** Directly connected to the network.

**online analytical processing (OLAP)** In a decision support system (DSS), a method of providing rich, up-to-the-minute data from transaction databases.

**online banking** The use of a Web browser to access bank accounts, balance checkbooks, transfer funds, and pay bills.

**online processing** The processing of data immediately after it has been input by a user, as opposed to waiting until a predetermined time, as in batch processing.

**online service** A for-profit firm that makes current news, stock quotes, and other information available to its subscribers over standard telephone lines. Popular services include supervised chat rooms for text chatting and forums for topical discussion. Online services also provide Internet access.

**online stock trading** The purchase or sale of stock through the Internet.

**online storage** A type of storage that is directly available, such as a hard disk, and requires no special action on the user's part to enable.

**online travel reservations** A rapidly growing area of e-commerce that allows consumers to use the Internet to research, book, and purchase airline flights, hotel rooms, and rental cars.

**on-screen keyboard utility** An accessibility feature that displays a graphic image of a computer keyboard on-screen so that people with limited dexterity can type conveniently.

**open** To transfer an existing document from storage to memory.

**open architecture** A system in which all the system specifications are made public so that other companies may develop add-on products, such as adapters.

**open protocol** A network standard placed in the public domain and regulated by an independent standards organization.

**open source software** Software in which the source code is made available to the program's users.

**operating platform** See operating system.

**operating system (OS)** A program that integrates and controls the computer's internal functions and provides a user interface.

**operationally feasible** Capable of being accomplished with an organization's available resources.

**optical character recognition (OCR)** Software that automatically decodes imaged text into a text file. Most scanners come with OCR software.

**optical mark reader (OMR)** A reader that senses magnetized marks made by the magnetic particles in lead from a pencil.

**optical mice** A type of mouse that uses a low-power laser to determine the mouse's position.

**optical resolution** A measure of the sharpness with which a scanner can digitize an image.

**optical storage** A storage system in which a storage device retains data using surface patterns that are physically encoded on the surface of plastic discs. The patterns can be detected by a laser beam.

**optical storage device** A computer storage device that retains data in microscopic patterns, detectable by a laser beam, encoded on the surface of plastic discs.

**options** Choices within an application that allow users to change defaults and to specify how they want the program to operate.

**order of evaluation** In any program that evaluates formulas, the order in which the various operations are performed. Some programs evaluate formula expressions from left to right, while others perform operations in a given order.

**organization** A collection of resources (personnel and equipment) arranged so that they can provide some kind of product or service.

**orientation** In document formatting, the layout of the page (either portrait or landscape).

**outline view** In a word processing or presentation graphics program, a document display mode that enables you to see an outline of the document or presentation.

**output** The results of processing information, typically shown on a monitor or a printer.

**output devices** Monitors, printers, and other machines that enable people to see, hear, and even feel the results of processing operations.

**outsourcing** The transfer of a project to an external contractor.

**overclock** To configure a computer system so that it runs a processor faster than it is designed to run; it may make the system unstable.

# P

**package** A collection of programs. A common example of a package is Microsoft Office, which bundles a word processing program and a spreadsheet program with other applications.

**packaged software** Ready-to-use software that is sold through mass-market channels and contains features useful to the largest possible user base. Synonymous with off-the-shelf software and shrink-wrapped software.

**packet** In a packet-switching network, a unit of data of a fixed size—not exceeding the network's maximum transmission unit (MTU) size—that has been prepared for network transmission. Each packet contains a header that indicates its origin and its destination. See also packet switching.

**packet sniffer** In computer security, a device that examines all traffic on a network and retrieves valuable information such as passwords and credit card numbers.

**packet switching** One of two fundamental architectures for a wide area network (WAN); the other is a circuit-switching network. In a packet-switching network such as the Internet, no effort is made to establish a single electrical circuit between two computing devices; for this reason, packet-switching networks are often called connectionless. Instead, the sending computer divides a message into packets, each of which contains the address of the destination computer, and dumps them onto the network. They are intercepted by devices called routers, which send the packets in the appropriate direction. The receiving computer assembles the packets, puts them in order, and delivers the received message to the appropriate application. Packet-switching networks are highly reliable and efficient, but they are not suited to the delivery of real-time voice and video.

**page** In virtual memory, a fixed size of program instructions and data that can be stored on the hard disk to free up random access memory.

**page description language (PDL)** A programming language capable of precisely describing the appearance of a printed page, including fonts and graphics.

**page formatting** In word processing applications, page formatting allows you to format text, which involves specifying the font, alignment, margins, and other properties.

**page layout** In an application program, an on-screen rendition of the document's appearance that shows all or almost all of the features that will appear in the printout.

**pager** A personal communications device, once widespread but now mostly replaced by more versatile cell phones, that receives (and may send) signals or short messages.

**paging** An operating system's transference of files from storage to memory and back.

**paint program** A program that enables the user to paint the screen by specifying the color of the individual pixels that make up the screen display.

**paper size** The size of the paper that is available for use in the printer. Most programs can work with a variety of paper sizes, but you must configure the program to work with nonstandard sizes.

**paragraph** In word processing, a unit of text that begins and ends with the Enter keystroke.

**paragraph formatting** In a word processing document, presentation options that can be applied to a block of text, such as justification and indentation.

**parallel conversion** In the development of an information system, the operation of both the new and old information systems at the same time to ensure the compatibility and reliability of the new system.

**parallel port** An interface that uses several side-by-side wires so that one or more bytes of computer data can travel in unison and arrive simultaneously. Parallel ports offer faster performance than serial ports, in which each bit of data must travel in a line, one after the other.

**parallel processing** The use of more than one processor to run two or more portions of a program simultaneously.

**parent directory** In the relationship between a directory and a subdirectory, the directory that contains the subdirectory.

**parity bit** An extra bit added to a data word for parity checking. See even parity and odd parity.

**parity checking** A technique used to detect memory or data communication errors. The computer adds the number of bits in a one-byte data item, and if the parity bit setting disagrees with the sum of the other bits, the computer reports an error. See even parity and odd parity.

**parity error** An error that a computer reports when parity checking reveals that one or more parity bits are incorrect, indicating a probable error in data processing or data transmission.

**partition** A section of a storage device, such as a hard disk, that is prepared so that it can be treated as if it were a completely separate device for data storage and maintenance.

**passive matrix LCD** An inexpensive liquid crystal display (LCD) that sometimes generates image flaws and is too slow for full-motion video. Also called dual scan LCD.

**password** A unique word that a user types to log on to a system. Passwords should not be obvious and should be changed frequently.

**password guessing** In computer security, a method of defeating password authentication by guessing common passwords, such as personal names, obscene words, and the word "password."

**paste** In the editing process, a command that inserts text stored in the clipboard at the cursor's location.

**path** The sequence of directories that the computer must follow to locate a file.

**pattern recognition** In artificial intelligence, the use of a computer system to recognize patterns, such as thumbprints, and associate these patterns with stored data or instructions.

**PC 100 SDRAM** A type of SDRAM capable of keeping up with motherboards that have bus speeds of 100 MHz.

**PC card** Synonymous with PCMCIA card. A computer accessory (such as a modem or network interface card) that is designed to fit into a compatible PC card slot mounted on the computer's case. PC cards and slots are commonly used on notebook computers because they offer system expandability while consuming a small fraction of the space required for expansion cards.

**peer-to-peer network** A computer network design in which all the computers can access the public files located on other computers in a network.

**pen** Input device that looks like a writing pen except that its tip is equipped with electronics instead of ink.

**pen computer** A computer operated with a stylus, such as a personal digital assistant (PDA).

**Pentium** A 64-bit microprocessor manufactured by Intel, introduced in 1993. The Pentium introduced many improvements over the 80486, including a superscalar architecture and clock speeds up to 200 MHz. Also called Pentium Classic.

**Pentium II** A 64-bit microprocessor manufactured by Intel, introduced in 1998. The Pentium II includes the MMX instruction set, contains 7.5 million transistors, and runs at clock speeds of 233 MHz and higher.

**Pentium MMX** A 64-bit microprocessor manufactured by Intel and introduced in 1997. The Pentium MMX includes a set of multimedia extensions, 57 processor instructions that run multimedia applications faster. It contains 4.5 million transistors and runs at clock speeds up to 233 MHz.

**Pentium Pro** A 64-bit microprocessor manufactured by Intel, introduced in 1995. The Pentium Pro introduced many new features, such as enhanced pipelining and a large on-board cache. Because it is optimized to run only 32-bit software, however, the Pentium Pro is found mainly in servers and engineering workstations.

**performance animation** See motion capture.

**peripheral** A device connected to and controlled by a computer, but external to the computer's central processing unit.

**Peripheral Computer Interface (PCI) bus** A bus architecture used for expansion slots and introduced by Intel in 1992. It has displaced the VESA local bus and has almost displaced the ISA bus.

**permanent virtual circuit (PVC)** A high-speed network connection that enables organizations to connect to external data networks at a cost lower than that of a leased line.

**personal certificate** A digital certificate attesting that a given individual who is trying to log on to an authenticated server really is the individual he or she claims to be. Personal certificates are issued by certificate authorities (CA).

**Personal Communication Service (PCS)** A digital cellular phone service that is rapidly replacing analog cellular phones.

**personal computer (PC)** A computer system that meets the computing needs of an individual. The term PC usually refers to an IBM-compatible personal computer.

**Personal Computer Interface (PCI) bus** A bus architecture that supports Plug and Play (PnP) and is used in today's PCs and Macs.

**Personal Computer Memory Card International Association (PCMCIA) card** See PC card.

**personal digital assistant (PDA)** A small, handheld computer that accepts input written on-screen with a stylus. Most include built-in software for appointments, scheduling, and e-mail. Also called palmtop.

**personal finance program** A special-purpose application program that manages financial information. The best personal finance programs manage many types of information, including checking accounts, savings and investment plans, and credit card debt.

**personal firewall** A program or device that is designed to protect home computer users from unauthorized access.

**personal identification number (PIN)** A number used by a bank customer to verify identity when using an ATM.

**personal information manager (PIM)** A program that stores and retrieves a variety of personal information, such as appointments. PIMs have been slow to gain acceptance due to their lack of convenience and portability.

**personal laser printer** A nonimpact high-resolution printer for use by individuals.

**personal productivity program** Application software, such as word processing software or a spreadsheet program, that assists individuals in doing their work more effectively and efficiently.

**phased conversion** In the development of an information system, the implementation of the new system in different time periods, one part at a time.

**photo communities** Web-based communities that enable users to upload their pictures and make them available to friends and family at no charge.

**photo printer** See snapshot printer. Specially designed printers with flash memory card readers that enable users to bypass the computer completely.

**PhotoCD** See Multisession PhotoCD.

**photo-editing program** A program that enables images to be enhanced, edited, cropped, or sized. The same program can be used to print the images on a color printer.

**phrase searching** In database and Web searching, a search that retrieves only documents that contain the entire phrase.

**physical modeling** A technique used to simulate what occurs when a real musical instrument produces a sound, such as a plucked guitar string.

**pie chart** A graph that displays a data series as a circle to emphasize the relative contribution of each data item to the whole. Also known as area chart.

**pilot conversion** In the development of an information system, the institution of the new system in only one part of an organization. When that portion of the organization is satisfied with the system, the rest of the organization then starts using it.

**pin grid array (PGA)** A complex pattern of downward-facing pins designed to fit into a compatible receptacle.

**pipelining** A design that provides two or more processing pathways that can be used simultaneously.

**pit** A microscopic indentation in the surface of an optical disc that absorbs the light of the optical drive's laser, corresponding to a 0 in the computer's binary number system.

**pixel** Short for picture element, the smallest element that a device can display and out of which the displayed image is constructed.

**placeholder** An area that is set aside to receive data of a certain type when this data becomes available.

**plagiarism** The presentation of somebody else's work as if it were one's own.

**Plain Old Telephone Service (POTS)** A term used to describe the standard analog telephone service.

**plaintext** A readable message before it is encrypted.

**platform** A distinct type of computer that uses a certain type of processor and operating system, such as a Macintosh or an Intel-based Windows PC.

**Platform for Internet Content Selection (PICS)** A voluntary rating system, widely endorsed by companies contributing to the Internet, used to inform users of cyberporn on the Internet.

**Platform for Privacy Preference Project (P3P)** A set of standards developed by the World Wide Web Consortium (W3C) for informing Web users of a site's use of personal data.

**platter** In a hard drive, a fixed, rapidly rotating disk that is coated with a magnetically sensitive material. High-capacity hard drives typically have two or more platters.

**plotter** A printer that produces high-quality output by moving ink pens over the surface of the paper.

**Plug and Play (PnP)** A set of standards jointly developed by Intel Corporation and Microsoft that enables users of Microsoft Windows–based PCs to configure new hardware devices automatically. Operating systems equipped with plug-and-play capabilities can automatically detect new PnP-compatible peripherals that may have been installed while the power was switched off.

**plug-in program** Software that directly interfaces with a particular program and gives it additional capabilities.

**point** A standard unit of measurement in character formatting and computer graphics that is equal to 1/72 inch.

**point of presence (PoP)** A locality in which it is possible to obtain dialup access to the network by means of a local telephone call. Internet service providers (ISPs) provide PoPs in towns and cities, but many rural areas are without local PoPs.

**point-and-shoot digital cameras** Digital cameras that typically include automatic focus, automatic exposure, built-in automatic electronic flash with red eye reduction, and optical zoom lenses with digital enhancement.

**point-of-sale (POS) terminal** A computer-based cash register that enables transaction data to be captured at the checkout stand. Such terminals can automatically adjust inventory databases and enable managers to analyze sales patterns.

**pointer** An on-screen symbol, usually an arrow, that shows the current position of the mouse.

**pointing device** Any input device that is capable of moving the on-screen pointer in a graphical user interface (GUI), such as a mouse or trackball.

**pointing stick** A pointing device introduced by IBM that enables users to move the pointer around the screen by manipulating a small, stubby stick that protrudes slightly from the surface of the keyboard.

**POP3** Also spelled POP-3. The current version of the Post Office Protocol (POP), an Internet standard for storing e-mail on a mail server until you can access it and download it to your computer.

**popup menu** A menu that appears at the mouse pointer's position when you click the right mouse button.

**port** An interface that controls the flow of data between the central processing unit and external devices such as printers and monitors.

**port conflict** A serious system instability that occurs when two input/output devices attempt to use the same I/O port.

**portable** Able to be easily removed or inserted or transferred to a different type of computer system.

**portable keyboard** A small folding keyboard often used with a handheld computer.

**Portable Network Graphics (PNG)** A graphics file format closely resembling the GIF format but lacking GIF's proprietary compression technique (which forces publishers of GIF-enabled graphics software to pay a licensing fee).

**portal** On the Web, a page that attempts to provide an attractive starting point for Web sessions. Typically included are links to breaking news, weather forecasts, stock quotes, free e-mail service, sports scores, and a subject guide to information available on the Web. Leading portals include Netscape's NetCenter (www.netcenter.com), Yahoo (www.yahoo.com), and Snap! (www.snap.com).

**portrait mode** In document formatting, a page layout in which text runs down the narrow orientation of the page.

**positioning performance** A measure of how much time elapses from the initiation of drive activity until the hard disk has positioned the read/write head so that it can begin transferring data.

**post** To submit a message to an online newsgroup; the message itself may be referred to as a post or posting.

**Post Office Protocol (POP)** An Internet e-mail standard that specifies how an Internet-connected computer can function as a mail-handling agent; the current version is POP3. Messages arrive at a user's electronic mailbox, which is housed on the service provider's computer. You can then download the mail to a workstation or computer and print, store, or reply to it.

**post-implementation system review** In the development of an information system, the ongoing evaluation of the information system to determine whether it has met its goals.

**PostScript** A sophisticated page description language (PDL) widely used in desktop publishing.

**Power Macintosh** A line of Macintosh computers based on the Motorola Power PC processors, which use RISC design principles.

**power-on light** A light on the front panel of most computers that signals whether the power is on.

**power-on self test (POST)** The series of system integrity tests that a computer goes through every time it is started (cold boot) or restarted (warm boot). These tests verify that vital system components, such as the memory, are functioning properly.

**power outage** A sudden loss of electrical power, causing the loss of all unsaved information on a computer.

**Power PC** A series of processors developed by Motorola that utilize RISC design principles. Apple Computer's Power Macintosh systems use Power PC processors.

**power supply** A device that supplies power to a computer system by converting AC current to DC current and lowering the voltage.

**power surge** A sudden and sometimes destructive increase in the amount of voltage delivered through a power line.

**power switch** A switch that turns the computer on and off. Often located in the rear of a computer.

**precedence** The position of a given operation, such as addition or multiplication, within a program's default order of evaluation.

**preemptive multitasking** In operating systems, a method of running more than one application at a time. Unlike cooperative multitasking, preemptive multitasking allows other applications to continue running if one application crashes.

**preferences** A list of the user's preferences for an application program's configuration. Preferences are stored so that they remain in place the next time the program is opened.

**preformatted** A floppy disk that has been formatted before it is packaged and sold.

**presentation graphics** A software package used to make presentations visually attractive and easy to understand.

**Pretty Good Privacy (PGP)** The most widely used digital signature and certificate system.

**primary cache** A small unit (8 KB to 32 KB) of ultra-fast memory included with a microprocessor and used to store frequently accessed data and improve overall system performance.

**primary folder** A main folder such as is created at the root of a drive to hold further subfolders. Also called top-level folder.

**Primary Rate ISDN (PRI)** An ISDN connection designed for medium-sized organizations that offers twenty-three 64 Kbps data/voice channels.

**primary storage** See online storage.

**print area** In a spreadsheet program, a user-defined area that tells the program how much of the spreadsheet to print.

**print driver** Files placed on a hard drive after a printer install that contain the printer's instruction set.

**print layout view** In a word processing program, an on-screen view of the document in which all or most printed features are visible. The print layout view is fully editable.

**print preview** In a word processing program, an on-screen view of the document in which all printed features are visible. The document is not editable in this view.

**printed circuit board** A flat piece of plastic or fiberglass on which complex patterns of copper pathways have been created by means of etching. These paths link integrated circuits and other electrical components.

**printer** An output device that prints computer-generated text or graphics onto paper or another physical medium.

**privacy** The right to live your life without undue intrusions into your personal affairs by government agencies or corporate marketers.

**private branch exchange (PBX)** An organization's internal telephone system, which is usually digital.

**private key** A decryption key.

**procedural language** A programming language that tells the computer what to do and how to do it.

**procedure** The steps that must be followed to accomplish a specific computer-related task.

**processing** The execution of arithmetic or comparison operations on data.

**processing cycle** See machine cycle.

**processor** See central processing unit (CPU).

**processor socket** In contemporary motherboard designs, a socket that enables a knowledgeable user to mount a microprocessor chip without damaging the chip or the motherboard.

**productivity software** Programs that help people perform general tasks such as word processing.

**professional workstation** A very powerful computer system for engineers, financial analysts, and other professionals who need exceptionally powerful processing and output capabilities. Professional workstations are very expensive.

**profile** In a consumer-oriented operating system such as Windows 98, a record of a user's preferences that is associated with a user name and password. If you set up two or more profiles, users see their own preferences. However, profiles do not prevent users from accessing and overwriting each others' files. Compare account.

**program** A list of instructions telling the computer what to do.

**program development life cycle (PDLC)** A step-by-step procedure used to develop software for information systems.

**program file** A file containing instructions written in a programming language to tell the computer what to do; also called an application file.

**program listing** In programming, a printout of the source code of a program.

**program specification** In software development, a technical description of the software needed by the information system. The program specification precisely defines input data, the processing that occurs, the output format, and the user interface.

**programmable** Capable of being controlled through instructions that can be varied to suit the needs of an individual.

**programmed instruction** A method of introducing new material by means of controlled steps in a workbook.

**programmer** A person skilled in the use of one or more programming languages. Although most programmers have college degrees in computer science, certification is an increasingly popular way to demonstrate one's programming expertise.

**programming language** An artificial language composed of a fixed vocabulary and a set of rules used to create instructions for a computer to follow.

**project dictionary** In the development of information systems, a compilation of all terminology relevant to the project.

**project management program** Software that tracks individual tasks that make up an entire job.

**project notebook** In the development of an information system, a place where information regarding system development is stored.

**project plan** A specification of the goals, scope, and individual activities that make up a project.

**promote** In an outlining utility, to increase the importance of a heading by moving it up in the hierarchy of outline categories (for example, by moving it from B to II).

**proportional font** A font in which the shape of each character determines how much space it requires and in which more characters fit on a line than in a monospace font; a proportional font closely resembles printed text.

**proprietary architecture** A design developed by a company and treated as a trade secret; the design can be copied only on payment of a licensing fee. Also called closed architecture.

**proprietary file format** A data-storage format used only by the company that makes a specific program.

**proprietary protocol** In a network, a communications protocol developed by a company and not available for public use without payment of a licensing fee.

**protected mode** A processing mode, first offered on Intel's 32-bit 80386 microprocessor, the enables users to access virtually unlimited amounts of memory.

**protocol** In data communications and networking, a standard specifying the format of data and the rules to be followed. Networks could not be easily or efficiently designed or maintained without protocols; a protocol specifies how a program should prepare data so that it can be sent to the next stage in the communication process. For example, e-mail programs prepare messages so that they conform to prevailing Internet mail standards, which are recognized by every program involved in the transmission of mail over the network.

**protocol stack** In a computer network, a means of conceptualizing network architecture in which the various layers of network functionality are viewed as a vertical stack, like the layers of a layer cake, in computers linked to the network. When one computer sends a message to the network, the message goes down the stack and then traverses the network; on the receiving computer, the message goes up the stack.

**protocol suite** In a computer network, the collection of network protocols that defines the network's functionality.

**prototyping** In information systems development, the creation of a working system model that is functional enough to draw feedback from users. Also called joint application development (JAD).

**proximity operator** In database and Web searching, a symbol or keyword that tells the search software to retrieve records or documents only if two specified search words occur within a certain number of words of each other.

**PS/2 mouse** A type of mouse that connects to the computer by means of the PS/2 port.

**PS/2 port** An input/output port that enables users to attach a specially designed mouse (called a PS/2 mouse) without requiring the use of the computer's built-in serial ports.

**pseudocode** In structured programming, a stylized form of writing used as an alternative to flowcharts to describe the logic of a program.

**public data network (PDN)** A network that builds its own high-speed data communications network using microwaves, satellites, and optical fiber, and sells network bandwidth to companies and government agencies.

**public domain software** Noncopyrighted software that anyone may copy and use without charge and without acknowledging the source.

**public key** In public key cryptography, the encoding key, which you make public so that others can send you encrypted messages. The message can be encoded with the public key, but it cannot be decoded without the private key, which you alone possess.

**public key cryptography** In cryptography, a revolutionary new method of encryption that does not require the message's receiver to have received the decoding key in a separate transmission. The need to send the key, required to decode the message, is the chief vulnerability of previous encryption techniques. Public key cryptography has two keys: a public one and a private one. The public key is used for encryption, and the private key is used for decryption.

**public key infrastructure (PKI)** A uniform set of encryption standards that specify how public key encryption, digital signatures, and CA-granted digital certificates should be implemented in computer systems and on the Internet.

**public switched telephone network (PSTN)** The world telephone system, a massive network used for data communication as well as voice.

**pull-down menu** In a graphical user interface (GUI), a named item on the menu bar that, when clicked, displays an on-screen menu of commands and options.

**pumping and dumping** An illegal stock price manipulation tactic that involves purchasing shares of a worthless corporation and then driving the price up by making unsubstantiated claims about the company's value in Internet newsgroups and chat rooms. The perpetrator sells the shares after the stock price goes up but before other investors wise up to the ploy.

## Q

**quality of service (QoS)** In a network, the guaranteed data transfer rate. A major drawback of the Internet for real-time voice and video, as well as for time-sensitive data communication, is that it cannot assure quality of service. Network congestion can delay the arrival of data.

**quarter-inch cartridge (QIC)** A tape cartridge using quarter-inch wide magnetic tape widely used for backup operations. QICs can hold up to 5 GB on a single cartridge.

**Query** In the Microsoft Access database management system, the object used to ask questions of the database.

**query by example (QBE)** In a database, a method of requesting information by using a blank form that corresponds to the record form. You fill out one or more fields in the form, and the search software uses your response to try to match any records in the database that contain the data you supplied.

**query language** A retrieval and data-editing language for composing simple or complex requests for data.

**QuickTime** An Apple Computer–developed file and compression format for digital video.

**quote** In e-mail, text from a previous message that is copied into a reply message.

**quoted size** The front surface measured diagonally on a cathode-ray tube monitor, a figure that is greater than the viewable area, since some of the surface is hidden and unavailable for display purposes. See viewable area.

**QWERTY keyboard** A keyboard that uses the standard keyboard layout in which the first six letters on the left of the top row spell "QWERTY."

## R

**radio** A wireless signaling technology that sends data by means of electromagnetic waves that travel through air and space between separate or combined transmitting and receiving devices.

**radio transmission** A signaling technique now being used by some wireless local area networks (WLANs) for greater security.

**RAID (Redundant Array of Independent Disks)** A storage device that groups two or more hard disks containing exactly the same data.

**Rambus DRAM** Type of RAM that uses a narrow but very fast bus to connect to the microprocessor.

**RAMDAC** Abbreviation for Random Access Digital to Analog Converter. This chip converts a video card's digital output to the analog output required by most monitors.

**random access** An information storage and retrieval technique in which the computer can access information directly, without having to go through a sequence of locations.

**random access file** See direct access file.

**random access memory (RAM)** Another name for the computer's main working memory, where program instructions and data are stored to be easily accessed by the central processing unit through the processor's high-speed data bus. When a computer is turned off, all data in RAM is lost.

**random access storage device** A storage device that can begin reading data directly without having to go through a lengthy sequence of data.

**range** In a spreadsheet, a rectangular group of cells treated as a unit for a given operation.

**range check** Verifies that the entered data fall within an acceptable range.

**range expression** In a spreadsheet program, a statement that indicates a group of cells to be treated as a unit for an operation.

**rapid application development (RAD)** In object-oriented programming, a method of program development in which programmers work with a library of prebuilt objects, allowing them to build programs more quickly.

**raster graphics** See bitmapped graphics.

**ray tracing** A 3D rendering technique in which color intensity on a graphic object is varied to simulate light falling on the object from multiple directions.

**read** To retrieve data or program instructions from a storage device such as a hard or floppy disk.

**read/write** The capability of a primary or secondary storage device to record (write) data and to play back (read) data previously recorded or saved.

**read/write device** A device that can read and write.

**read/write head** In a hard or floppy disk, the magnetic recording and playback device that travels back and forth across the surface of the disk, storing and retrieving data.

**read/write medium** A storage medium that enables users to write as well as read data. Compare read-only.

**read-only** Capable of being displayed or used but not altered or deleted.

**read-only memory (ROM)** The part of a computer's primary storage that contains essential computer instructions and doesn't lose its contents when the power is turned off. Information in read-only memory cannot be erased by the computer.

**real-time processing** A type of processing that deals with data as it is generated by an ongoing process, such as a live video feed or text chatting.

**record** In a database, a group of one or more fields that contains information about something.

**redo** In the editing process, a command that reverses the effect of the last undo command or repeats the last editing action.

**reduced instruction set computer (RISC)** A type of central processing unit in which the number of instructions the processor can execute is reduced to a minimum to increase processing speed.

**reengineering** See business process reengineering (BPR).

**reflector** See list server.

**refresh rate** The frequency with which the screen is updated. The refresh rate determines whether the display appears to flicker.

**Regional Bell Operating Companies (RBOCs)** The local and regional telephone companies created after the divestiture of telephone monopoly AT&T.

**register** 1. In a microprocessor, a memory location used to store values and external memory addresses while the microprocessor performs logical and arithmetic operations on them. 2. In commercial software and shareware, to contact the software vendor and submit a form that includes personal information such as the user's name and address. Registering allows the software vendor to inform the user of important information and software updates.

**registration fee** An amount of money that must be paid to the author of a piece of shareware to continue using it beyond the duration of the evaluation period.

**registry** 1. A database that contains information about installed peripherals and software. 2. In Microsoft Windows, an important system file that contains configuration settings that Windows requires in order to operate.

**regular weight** In character formatting, a darkness level that is normal for a given font.

**relational database** A type of database that uses the contents of a particular field as an index to reference particular records.

**relative cell reference** In a spreadsheet program, a cell reference that is automatically adjusted when it is relocated.

**relative file** A special type of direct-access file that does not use a mathematical formula (hashing algorithm) to determine the address of records, but bases the address on the key field, which is numbered with an integer.

**relative URL** In HTML, a URL that refers to a file located in the same directory as the referring file or in a nearby directory.

**removable drive** A hard disk that uses a data cartridge that can be removed for storage and replaced with another.

**removable hard disk** A hard disk that uses a removable cartridge instead of a sealed unit with a fixed, nonremovable platter.

**repetition control structure** In structured programming, a logical construction of commands repeated over and over. Also called looping or iteration control structure.

**repetitive strain injury (RSI)** See cumulative trauma disorder (CTD).

**replication** In a spreadsheet program, the duplication of a group of cells into another group of cells. Formulas are automatically adjusted to account for the new cell addresses.

**Report** In the Microsoft Access database management system, the object used to present data.

**report file** A file that holds a copy of a report in computer-accessible form until it is convenient to print it.

**report generator** In programming, a programming language for printing database reports. One of four parts of a database management system (DBMS) that helps the user design and generate reports and graphs in hard copy form.

**report language** In database management, a computer language that enables the user to specify which information to display or print.

**request for proposal (RFP)** In the development of information systems, a request to an outside vendor to write a proposal for the design, installation, and configuration of an information system.

**request for quotation (RFQ)** In the development of information systems, a request to an outside vendor or value-added reseller (VAR) to quote a price for specific information components.

**reset switch** A switch on the front panel of most computers that can restart the computer in the event of a failure.

**resolution** A measurement, usually expressed in linear dots per inch (dpi) both horizontally and vertically, of the sharpness of an image generated by an output device such as a monitor or a printer.

**resource** In a network, any useful device or program that can be shared by the network's users. An example of a resource is a network-capable printer.

**restore** To return a window to its size and position before it was maximized.

**résumé manager** A program that provides expert assistance in the preparation of résumés.

**return on investment (ROI)** The overall financial yield of a project at the end of its lifetime. ROI is often used by managers to decide whether a project is a good investment.

**right pane** In the My Computer primary file management utility for PCs, one of two main default windows. It displays the various files and drives you can choose from. See also left pane.

**ring topology** The physical layout of a local network in which all nodes are attached in a circle, without a central host computer.

**rip and tear** A confidence scam that involves convincing people that they have won a large sweepstakes prize but they cannot obtain the needed information unless they pay a fee. The prize never materializes, and the perpetrators disappear.

**robot** A computer-based device that is programmed to perform useful motions.

**robotics** A division of computer science that is devoted to improving the performance and capabilities of robots.

**ROM BIOS (basic input/output system)** See basic input/output system (BIOS).

**root directory** The top-level directory in a secondary storage device.

**rot-13** In Usenet newsgroups, a simple encryption technique that offsets each character by 13 places (so that an e becomes an r, for example).

**rotational speed** In hard disks, the number of revolutions the disks make in one minute (rpm). Rotational speed is the largest single factor in determining drive speed. Currently, hard disks have rotational speeds as high as 10,000 rpm.

**router** In a packet-switching network such as the Internet, one of two basic devices (the other is a host). A router is an electronic device that examines each packet of data it receives and then decides which way to send it toward its destination.

**row** In a spreadsheet, a block of cells going across the screen.

**RS-232 standard** A standard maintained by an international standards organization that defines the operation of the serial ports commonly found on today's computers. Synonymous with RS-232C.

**RS-422 standard** A standard maintained by an international standards organization that defines the operation of the serial ports found on Apple's Macintosh and some other computers. The RS-422 is a more recent version of the earlier RS-232 standard. It offers higher data transfer rates than its predecessor.

**rule** A straight line.

**ruler** A bar that measures the document horizontally or vertically with reference to the printed page's edges or margins. Typically, the ruler shows the cursor's current position, margin settings, indentations, and tab stops.

**runtime** Able to run without having the original installed application. A runtime version of a PowerPoint presentation, for example, can run on a computer that does not have Microsoft PowerPoint installed.

## S

**safe mode** An operating mode in which Windows loads a minimal set of drivers that are known to function correctly.

**safety-critical system** Any computer system that could subject human beings to death or injury if it fails to operate correctly. The Federal Aviation Administration's air traffic control (ATC) system is an example of a safety-critical system.

**salami shaving** A computer crime in which a program is altered so that it transfers a small amount of money from a large number of accounts to make a large profit.

**sampling** In sound cards, a sound synthesis technique that modifies sound samples of musical instruments.

**sans serif font** A typeface style for letters that does not include finishing strokes.

**SATAN** A network security diagnostic tool that exhaustively examines a network and reveals security holes. SATAN is a double-edged sword: In the hands of network administrators, it is a valuable tool for detecting and closing security loopholes. In the hands of intruders, it is an equally valuable tool for exposing remaining loopholes and gaining unauthorized access to a network.

**satellite** In data communications, a communications reflector placed in a geosynchronous (stationary) orbit.

**save** To transfer data from the computer's memory to a storage device for safekeeping.

**save as** A command that enables the user to store a document with a new name.

**saving** In an application software program, the process of transferring a document from the computer's temporary memory to a permanent storage device, such as a hard disk, for safekeeping.

**scale** To increase or decrease the size of an image without affecting the image's aspect ratio.

**scaling** In graphics, to adjust the scale of a chart to make sure that it conveys information effectively.

**scanner** A device that copies the image (text or graphic) on a sheet of paper and translates it into a digital image. Scanners use charge-coupled devices to digitize the image.

**scientific visualization** The use of computer systems to discover hidden patterns in large amounts of data.

**screenreader** An accessibility program that reads text appearing on various parts of the computer screen for people with limited or no vision.

**script** A short program written in a simple programming language, called a scripting language.

**scripting language** A simple programming language that enables users to create useful programs (scripts) quickly. VBScript is one example of a scripting language.

**scroll** To bring hidden parts of a document into view within the application workspace.

**scroll arrow** An arrow appearing within the scroll bar that enables the user to scroll up or down (or, in a horizontal scroll bar, left and right) by small increments.

**scroll bar** A vertical or horizontal bar that contains scroll arrows and a scroll box. The scroll bar enables the user to bring hidden portions of a document into view within the application workspace.

**scroll box** A rectangular control positioned within the scroll bar that enables the user to bring hidden portions of a document into view. Unlike scroll arrows, the scroll box is used to scroll by large increments.

**search engine** Any program that locates needed information in a database, but especially an Internet-accessible search service (such as AltaVista or HotBot) that enables you to search for information on the Internet.

**search operator** In a database or a Web search engine, a word or a symbol that enables you to specify your search with precision.

**secondary cache** A small unit (256 K to 1 MB) of ultra-fast memory used to store frequently accessed data and improve overall system performance. The secondary cache is usually located on a separate circuit board from the microprocessor, although backside cache memory is located on the processor. Also called level 2 (L2) cache.

**secondary folder** See subfolder.

**secondary storage** See near-online storage.

**section** In a word processing document, a portion of a document that is separated from the others so that it can contain unique formats, such as column layout or footnote numbering.

**section break** A nonprinting symbol that can be placed within a word processing document to create sections within the document.

**sector** A pie-shaped wedge of the concentric tracks encoded on a disk during formatting. Two or more sectors combine to form a cluster.

**secure mode** In a Web browser, a mode of operation in which all communication to and from the server is encrypted.

**security** The protection of valuable assets stored on computer systems or transmitted via computer networks.

**seek time** In a secondary storage device, the time it takes for the read/write head to reach the correct location on the disk. Seek times are often used with rotational speed to compare the performance of hard drives.

**select** To highlight something on-screen, usually with the mouse and other times with the keyboard.

**selection control structure** In structured programming, a method of handling a program branch by using an IF-THEN-ELSE structure. This is more efficient than using a GOTO statement. Also called conditional or branch control structure.

**selective availability** In the U.S. Geographical Positioning System (GPS), a Defense Department imposed signal degradation intended to make GPS signals useless for enemy missile guidance systems.

**semiconductor** A material that can selectively conduct or impede the flow of electrical current. By fabricating devices made of differing semiconductor materials arranged in layers, electronics manufacturers can mass-produce highly complex electronic devices at very low cost per unit.

**sequence control structure** In structured programming, a logical construction of programming commands executed in the order in which they appear.

**sequencer** A program that enables composers to write, record, edit, and play back musical notation on a computer.

**sequential access** An information storage and retrieval technique in which the computer must move through a sequence of stored data items to reach the item to be retrieved.

**sequential file** A file in which the entries are processed in the order in which they were encoded.

**sequential storage device** A storage device that cannot begin reading data until the device has moved through a sequence of data in order to locate the desired beginning point.

**serial mouse** A type of mouse that connects to the computer by means of a serial port.

**serial port** An input/output (I/O) interface that is designed to convey data in a bit-by-bit stream. Compare parallel port.

**series** In a spreadsheet program, a range of values used to generate a chart.

**serif font** A typeface style for letters that includes finishing strokes.

**server** A computer dedicated to providing information in response to external requests.

**server address** In a mailing list, the e-mail address of the list server, rather than the address of the list itself. For subscribing and unsubscribing to a mailing list, send messages to the server, not the list.

**server program** The part of client/server computing that runs on a high-powered, centralized minicomputer that everyone on the network can access with the appropriate security clearance. See client program.

**set-top appliance** A computer-based unit that works with cable TV data and enhances the television viewing experience (in some cases, by enabling Internet access).

**setup program** A utility program provided by a computer's manufacturer that enables users to specify basic system configuration settings, such as the correct time and date and the type of hard disk that is installed in the system. Setup programs are accessible by pressing a special key (such as Delete) during the computer's power-on self test (POST).

**shading** A formatting option in which a color or pattern appears in the background of a paragraph, table cell, or some other formatting unit.

**shadow** A type of character formatting in which characters appear with a simulated shadow.

**shareware** Copyrighted software that may be tried without expense but requires the payment of a registration fee if you decide to use it after a specified trial period.

**sheetfed scanner** A device that draws in single sheets of paper, copies an image (text or graphics), and translates the image into a digital image.

**sheets** In Microsoft Excel workbook files, the 255 sets of columns and rows intersecting at cells.

**shell** In an operating system, the portion of the program that provides the user interface.

**shell access** An inexpensive Internet access, through the user interface of a UNIX computer.

**shill** In an auction, an accomplice of the seller who drives up prices by bidding for an item that the shill has no intention of buying.

**shoulder surfing** In computer security, a method of defeating password authentication by peeking over a user's shoulder and watching the keyboard as the user inputs his or her password.

**shrink-wrapped software** See packaged software.

**shutter** The sliding metal piece on a floppy disk the protects the disk from fingerprints, dust, and dirt.

**signature** In e-mail and Usenet newsgroups, a brief file (of approximately three or four lines) that contains the message sender's name, organization, address, e-mail address, and (optionally) telephone numbers. You can configure most systems to add this file automatically at the end of each message you send. Netiquette advises against long, complicated signatures, especially when posting to Usenet.

**signature capture** A computer system that captures a customer's signature digitally, so that the store can prove that a purchase was made.

**Simple Mail Transport Protocol (SMTP)** An e-mail communication standard specifying how servers should send plaintext messages across the Internet.

**simulation** A method used to discover something about the real world by creating a working model of it, which can then be explored by varying its characteristics to see what happens.

**single-edge contact (SEC)** Chip packages that are designed to be pressed into a slot; the connectors are aligned along one of the package's edges.

**single inline memory module (SIMM)** A plug-in memory module that contains RAM chips. SIMMs use a 32-bit bus to transfer data between the memory and the processor. Many newer computers have 64-bit buses that require DIMMs.

**single-lens reflex (SLR) digital camera** Expensive digital camera that offers features such as interchangeable lenses, through-the-lens image previewing, and the ability to override the automatic focus and exposure settings.

**single-session CD** A CD that can accept only one "burn" (recording) session.

**single-tasking** Capable of running only one application at a time.

**site license** An agreement with a software publisher that allows multiple copies of the software to be made for use within an organization.

**site registration** On the World Wide Web, a process used to gain entry to a Web site that requires you to provide your name, e-mail address, and other personal information, which may be disclosed to marketing firms.

**size** To increase or decrease the size of one of the dimensions of an image. Compare scale.

**slack space** Space that is wasted when a disk's cluster size is too large.

**slide** In a presentation graphics program, an on-screen image sized in proportion to a 35mm slide.

**sleep** See standby.

**slide layout** In a presentation graphics program, a view of the document that shows each slide individually.

**slide show view** In a presentation graphics program, a view of the document that displays the slides in a sequence.

**slide sorter view** In a presentation graphics program, a view of your presentation in which all your slides are represented by small thumbnail graphics. You can restructure your presentation by dragging a slide to a new location.

**slide view** In a presentation graphics program, a view of your presentation that enables you to see your slides, just as they will appear when displayed for presentation purposes.

**small caps** In character formatting, a formatting option in which the lowercase letters appear as small capital letters.

**Small Computer System Interface (SCSI)** A bus standard for connecting peripheral devices to personal computers, including hard disks, CD-ROM discs, and scanners.

**small office/home office (SOHO)** Small businesses run out of homes or small offices—a rapidly growing market segment.

**small-scale integration (SSI)** A technology used to assemble integrated circuits (ICs). SSI was the first integration technology used to build ICs and could fit only 10 or 20 transistors to a chip.

**Smalltalk** An early object-oriented programming language that many OO promoters believe is still the only pure OO language.

**smart car** A car with microprocessors that provide more control and interaction with the environment. A smart car can diagnose internal problems, operate safely, warn the driver of potential problems, and help with navigation.

**smart card** A card that resembles a credit card but has a microprocessor and memory chip, enabling the card to process as well as store information.

**smart tags** In Microsoft Office, icons attached to items, allowing various choices for how text is treated when pasted within an application or between applications.

**SmartMedia** A flash memory storage device designed for digital cameras that is capable of storing up to 128 MB of digital image data.

**smiley** In e-mail and newsgroups, a sideways face made of ASCII characters that puts a message into context and compensates for the lack of verbal inflections and body language that plagues electronic communication. Also called emoticon.

**snapshot printer** A thermal transfer printer that prints the output of digital cameras at a maximum size of 4 by 6 inches. Snapshot printers are less expensive than other thermal transfer printers.

**social engineering** A method of defeating password authentication by impersonating a network administrator and asking users for their passwords.

**socket** In Internet and UNIX, a virtual port that enables client applications to connect to the appropriate server. To achieve a connection, a client needs to specify both the IP address and the port address of the server application.

**soft copy** A temporary form of output, as in a monitor display.

**software** One of two basic components of a computer system (the other is hardware). Software includes all the instructions that tell the computer what to do.

**software crisis** A period of time in the 1960s when programming was extremely inefficient due to poor programming practices.

**software engineering** A new field that applies the principles of mainstream engineering to software production.

**software license** An agreement included with most commercial software that stipulates what the user may and may not do with the software.

**software piracy** Unauthorized duplication of copyrighted software.

**software programs** Input that gives the computer specific instructions of what to do.

**software suite** A collection of full-featured, standalone programs that usually share a common command structure and have similar interfaces.

**software upgrading** The process of keeping a version of an application current with the marketplace, whether through patches, service releases, or new versions.

**sole proprietorship** A business run and owned by only one person.

**solid state device** An electronic device that relies solely on semiconductors (rather than vacuum tubes) to switch or amplify electrical current.

**solid state disk (SDD)** A storage device that is composed of high-speed RAM chips.

**solid state storage device** This device consists of nonvolatile memory chips, which retain the data stored in them even if the chips are disconnected from their current source.

**sort** In a database, to rearrange records according to a predetermined order, such as alphabetical or chronological order.

**sound board** See sound card.

**sound card** An adapter that adds digital sound reproduction capabilities to an IBM-compatible PC. Also called a sound board.

**sound file** A file containing digitized sound that can be played back if a computer is equipped with multimedia.

**sound format** A specification of how a sound should be digitally represented. Sound formats usually include some type of data compression to reduce the size of sound files.

**source code** The typed program instructions that people write. The program is then translated into machine instructions that the computer can execute.

**source data automation** The process of capturing data at its source, eliminating the need to file paper documents or record data by keying it manually.

**spaghetti code** In programming, source code that contains numerous GOTO statements and is, in consequence, difficult to understand and prone to error.

**spam** Unsolicited e-mail or newsgroup advertising.

**spammer** A person who sends unsolicited e-mail messages containing advertisements.

**speaker** A device that plays the computer's audio output.

**specialized search engines** Web location programs that index particular types of information, such as job advertisements.

**special-purpose program** A program that performs a specific task, usually for a specific profession. Examples include printing greeting cards and calculating stresses in an engineering project.

**speculative execution** A technique used by advanced CPUs to prevent a pipeline stall. The processor executes and temporarily stores the next instruction in case it proves useful.

**speech recognition** The use of a computer system to detect the words spoken by a human being into a microphone, and translate these words into text that appears on-screen. Compare speech synthesis.

**speech recognition software** A computer program that decodes human speech into transcribed text.

**speech synthesis** The capability of a computer to speak through synthesized computer-generated voices.

**spider** A small piece of software that crawls around the Web picking up URLs and information on the pages attached to them.

**spindle speed** The rotational speed of a hard disk, measured in revolutions per minute (rpm).

**spinoff technology** Devices based on discoveries originally made in military or space research.

**spreadsheet** A program that processes information in the form of tables. Table cells can hold values or mathematical formulas.

**spreadsheet programs** The computer equivalent of an accountant's worksheet.

**SPX** See IPX/SPX.

**spyware** Internet software that is placed on a computer without the user's awareness, usually during a shareware or freeware download.

**SQL** Abbreviation for structured query language. SQL is a standardized query language for requesting information from a database.

**stale link** On the Web, a hyperlink that refers to a document that has been moved or deleted. Synonymous with broken link.

**standalone e-mail client** A program sold commercially that provides e-mail services for computer users. Most people use e-mail capabilities built into Web browsers rather than buying commercial programs.

**standalone program** An application sold individually.

**standard newsgroups** In Usenet, a collection of newsgroups that every Usenet site is expected to carry, if sufficient storage room exists. The standard newsgroup hierarchy includes the following newsgroup categories: comp.*, misc.*, news.*, rec.*, sci.*, soc.*, and talk*. A voting process creates new newsgroups within the standard newsgroup hierarchies.

**standard toolbar** In Microsoft Office, a default-loaded toolbar that includes icons for various functions, including opening, closing, and printing files.

**standby** A low-power state that allows an operating system to be restored to full power quickly without going through the lengthy boot process; called sleep in the Mac OS.

**star topology** The physical layout of a local network in which a host computer manages the network.

**start tag** In HTML, the first component of an element. The start tag contains the element's name, such as <H1> or <P>.

**statistical function** In a spreadsheet program, a built-in function that performs a useful task such as determining an average.

**status bar** An area within a typical application's window that is reserved for the program's messages to the user.

**status indicator** A small indicator light on a keyboard that shows when a toggle key keyboard function is turned on.

**storage** A general term for computer components that offer nonvolatile retention of computer data and program instructions.

**storage area network (SAN)** Links high capacity storage devices to all of an organization's servers, which makes any of the storage devices accessible from any of the servers.

**storage device** A hardware component that is capable of retaining data even when electrical power is switched off. An example of a storage device is a hard disk. Compare memory.

**storage hierarchy** A classification scheme that divides storage devices into three categories: online (directly available), near-online (easily available), offline (not easily available).

**storage media** A collective term used to describe all types of storage devices.

**stored-program concept** The idea underlying the architecture of all modern computers that the program should be stored in memory with the data.

**streaming audio** An Internet sound delivery technology that sends audio data as a continuous, compressed stream that is played back on the fly.

**streaming video** An Internet video delivery technology that sends video data as a continuous, compressed stream that is played back on the fly. Like streaming audio, streaming video begins playing almost immediately. A high-speed modem is required. Quality is marginal; the video appears in a small, on-screen window, and motion is jerky.

**striping** In RAID drives, a method of duplicating the data in which each disk contains a portion of every disk's data.

**strong AI** In artificial intelligence, a research focus based on the conviction that computers will achieve the ultimate goal of artificial intelligence, namely, rivaling the intelligence of humans.

**strong encryption** Methods of encrypting text so that it is very difficult or impossible to break.

**structural analysis and design tools** Methods of graphical analysis that systems analysts can use to convey a description of an information system to managers, programmers, and users.

**structural sabotage** In information warfare, attacks on the information systems that support transportation, finance, energy, and telecommunications.

**structural unemployment** Unemployment caused by advancing technology that makes an entire job obsolete.

**structure** In HTML, the overall pattern of a document's organization into units containing information of a certain type, such as titles, headings, or an abstract.

**structure chart** See hierarchy chart.

**structured programming** A set of quality standards that make programs more verbose but more readable, more reliable, and more easily maintained. A program is broken up into manageable components, each of which contributes to the overall goal of the program. Also called top-down program design.

**style** In word processing programs, a collection of formatting options that have been grouped and saved under a distinctive name so that they can be easily applied subsequently.

**style sheet** In word processing, desktop publishing, and Web publishing, a formatting method in which named styles are defined in a separate document. When changes are made to the style sheet, these changes are reflected in all the documents linked to the style sheet for formatting.

**stylus** A pen-shaped instrument used to draw on a graphics tablet or to input commands and handwriting to a personal digital assistant (PDA).

**subdirectory** A directory created in another directory. A subdirectory can contain files and additional subdirectories.

**subfolder** A folder within a folder, usually created to allow for better file organization. Also known as secondary folder.

**subject guide** On the World Wide Web, an information discovery service that contains hyperlinks classified by subjects in broad categories and multiple levels of subcategories.

**subnotebook** A portable computer that omits some components (such as a CD-ROM drive) to cut down on weight and size.

**subscribe** To sign up to receive regular postings, such as from a newsgroup on the Internet.

**subscriber loop carrier (SLC)** A small, waist-high curbside installation of the public switched telephone network that transforms local home and business analog calls into digital signals and routes them through high-capacity cables to the local exchange switch.

**subscript** A character formatting option that places characters below the line.

**summary report** In a transaction processing system (TPS), a document that provides a quick overview of an organization's performance.

**Super Video Graphics Array (SVGA)** An enhancement of the VGA display standard that can display as much as 1,280 pixels by 1,024,768 lines with as many as 16.7 million colors.

**supercomputer** A sophisticated, expensive computer that executes complex calculations at the maximum speed permitted by state-of-the-art technology. Supercomputers are used mostly by the government and for scientific research.

**SuperDisk** A removable hard disk made by Imaton that can store up to 120 MB of data per disk. The drive can also work with 3.5-inch floppy disks.

**superscalar** A measure of microprocessor performance characterized by the ability to execute more than one instruction per clock cycle.

**superscalar architecture** A design that lets the microprocessor take a sequential instruction and send several instructions at a time to separate execution units so that the processor can execute multiple instructions per cycle.

**superscript** A character formatting option that places text above the line.

**superuser status** In multiuser operating systems, a classification normally given only to network administrators, enabling them to access and modify virtually any file on the network. If intruders obtain superuser status, they can obtain the passwords of everyone on the network.

**supervisor program** See kernel.

**surge** A momentary and sometimes destructive increase in the amount of voltage delivered through a power line.

**surge protector** An inexpensive electrical device that prevents high-voltage surges from reaching a computer and damaging its circuitry.

**swap file** In virtual memory, a file on the hard disk used to store pages of virtual memory information.

**swapping** In virtual memory, the operation of exchanging program instructions and data between the swap file (located on the hard disk) and random access memory (RAM).

**symmetric key encryption** Encryption techniques that use the same key for encryption and decryption.

**syn flooding** See denial of service (DoS) attack.

**Synchronized Multimedia Integration Language (SMIL)** A scripting language that enhances Web browsers with multimedia capabilities without the use of plug-in programs.

**synchronous communication** In a computer network, the use of a timing device to demarcate units of data.

**synchronous DRAM (SDRAM)** The fastest available memory chip technology.

**Synchronous Optical Network (SONET)** A standard for high-performance networks using optical fiber.

**syntax** The rules governing the structure of commands, statements, or instructions given to a computer.

**syntax error** In programming, a flaw in the structure of commands, statements, or instructions.

**synthesizer** An audio component that uses FM (frequency modulation), wavetable, or waveguide technology to create sounds imitative of actual musical instruments.

**system** A collection of components purposefully organized into a functioning whole to accomplish a goal.

**system administrator** In a multiuser computer system, the individual who is responsible for keeping the system running smoothly, performing backup and archiving operations, supervising user accounts, and securing the system against unauthorized intrusions.

**system bus** Also called memory bus.

**system clock** An electronic circuit in the computer that emits pulses at regular intervals, enabling the computer's internal components to operate in synchrony.

**system requirements** The stated minimum system performance capabilities required to run an application program, including the minimum amount of disk space, memory, and processor capacity.

**system software** All the software used to operate and maintain a computer system, including the operating system and utility programs.

**system unit** A boxlike case that houses the computer's main hardware components and provides a sturdy frame for mounting and protecting internal devices, connectors, and drives.

**system utilities** Programs such as speaker volume control and antivirus software that are loaded by the operating sytem.

**system utility programs** Programs, such as file management and file finder, that provide a necessary addition to an operating system's basic system-management tools.

**systems analysis** A discipline devoted to the rational and organized planning, development, and implementation of artificial systems, including information systems.

**systems analyst** A computer professional who helps plan, develop, and implement information systems.

**systems development life cycle (SDLC)** An organized way of planning and building information systems.

**systems engineering** A field of engineering devoted to the scientific study of artificial systems and the training of systems analysts.

# T

**T1** A high-bandwidth telephone trunk line capable of transferring 1.544 megabits per second (Mbps) of data.

**T3** A high-bandwidth fiber-optic line capable of handling 43 megabits per second (Mbps) of computer data.

**tab stop** In a word processing program, a position within the current paragraph to which the cursor will move when the Tab key is pressed.

**table** 1. In HTML, a matrix of rows and columns that appears on a Web page, if the user is browsing with a table-capable browser (such as Netscape Navigator). 2. In database terminology, a table stores information in a list of records, each of which has one or more fields.

**table** In the Microsoft Access database manage-ment system, the object used to store data.

**tactile display** A display that stimulates the sense of touch using vibration, pressure, and temperature changes.

**tag** In HTML, a code that identifies an element (a certain part of a document, such as a heading or list) so that a Web browser can tell how to display it. Tags are enclosed by beginning and ending delimiters (angle brackets). Most tags begin with a start tag (delimited with <>), followed by the content and an end tag (delimited with </>).

**tangible savings** Reduced labor, service, and material costs due to the replacement of a system.

**tape libraries** High-capacity tape systems often found in enterprise storage systems.

**task pane** In Microsoft Office, a feature that usually appears on the right side of an opened application window and that provides various options, such as for opening or formatting work.

**tax software** An application capable of preparing tax payments using on-screen simulations of tax forms. Some tax programs include specialized tax forms and content-based advice to assist the user.

**TCP/IP** The two most important Internet protocols. See Transmission Control Protocol and Internet Protocol.

**technically feasible** Able to be accomplished with respect to existing, proven technology.

**telecommunication** The use of the public switched telephone network (PSTN) and public data networks (PDNs) for data communication.

**telecommuting** Performing work at home while linked to the office by means of a telecommunications-equipped computer system.

**teleconferencing** A simple and secure wired voice communications application in which more than two distant people conduct business by conference call.

**telemedicine** The use of computers and the Internet to make high-quality health care available to underserved populations.

**template** A standard format used to create standardized documents.

**tendonitis** A physical disorder in which tendons and their sheaths become irritated from repeated exertion.

**terabyte (T or TB)** A unit of measurement commonly used to state the capacity of memory or storage devices; equal to 1,024 gigabytes, or approximately one trillion bytes or characters.

**terminal** An input/output device consisting of a keyboard and a video display that is commonly used with mainframe and minicomputer systems.

**tertiary folder** A folder within a subfolder.

**tertiary storage** See offline storage.

**testbed** In engineering, a small-scale version of a product that is developed in order to test its capabilities.

**text box** An area capable of containing text that can be inserted into a graphic image.

**text field** In a database, a space that accepts only characters (letters, numbers, and punctuation marks).

**text file** A file containing nothing but standard characters, that is, letters, punctuation marks, and numbers.

**text-only browser** A Web browser that cannot display graphics.

**text output** A type of computer output that consists strictly of characters (letters, numbers, and punctuation marks).

**text slide** In a presentation, a slide that contains nothing but text.

**thermal transfer printer** A printer that uses a heat process to transfer colored dyes or inks to the paper's surface. Although thermal transfer printers are the best color printers currently available, they are very expensive.

**thin film transistor (TFT)** See active-matrix LCD.

**third-generation language (3GL)** A programming language that tells the computer what to do and how to do it but eliminates the need for understanding the intimate details of how the computer works.

**thread** 1. In multithreading, a single type of task that can be executed simultaneously with other tasks. 2. In Usenet, a series of articles on the same specific subject.

**thumbnail** A small version of a graphic image that enables you to see what it looks like before you spend time opening the much larger file containing the full version of the image.

**tile** To size graphics or windows so that they are all the same size and take up all the available screen space.

**time bomb** A destructive program that sits harmlessly until a certain event or set of circumstances makes the program active.

**time-limited trial versions** Internet-offered commercial programs capable of being used on a trial basis for a period of time, after which the software is unusable.

**time series** A type of column chart that shows changes over a period of time.

**timesharing** A technique for sharing the resources of a multiuser computer in which each user has the illusion that he or she is the only person using the system.

**title bar** In a graphical user interface (GUI), the top bar of an application window. The title bar typically contains the name of the application, the name of the document, and window controls.

**toggle key** A key on a keyboard that functions like a switch. When pressed, the function is turned on, and when pressed again, the function is turned off.

**token** A handheld device used to gain access to a computer system, such as an automated teller machine (ATM).

**toolbar** In a graphical user interface (GUI), a bar near the top of the window that contains a row of graphical buttons. These buttons provide quick access to the most frequently used program commands.

**tools menu** In a graphical user interface (GUI), a menu that provides access to special program features and utilities, such as spell-checking.

**top-down program design** See structured programming.

**top-level domain (TLD) name** The last part of an Internet computer address. For computers located in the United States, it indicates the type of organization in which the computer is located, such as commercial businesses (com), educational institutions (edu), and government agencies (gov).

**top-level folder** See primary folder.

**topology** The physical layout of a local area network.

**touch screen** A touch-sensitive display that enables users to input choices by touching a region of the screen.

**touchpad** An input device for portable computers that moves the pointer. The touchpad is a small pad in front of the keyboard that moves the pointer when the user moves a finger on the pad.

**tower case** A tall and deep system unit case designed to sit on the floor next to a desk and easily accommodate add-on components.

**track** One of several concentric circular bands on computer disks where data is recorded, similar to the grooves on a phonographic record. Tracks are created during formatting and are divided into sectors.

**trackball** An input device, similar to the mouse, that moves the pointer. The trackball looks something like an inverted mouse and does not require the desk space that a mouse does.

**trackpad** See touchpad.

**trackpoint** An input device on some notebook computers that resembles a tiny pencil eraser; you move the cursor by pushing the tip of the trackpoint.

**trade show** A periodic meeting in which computer product manufacturers, designers, and dealers display their products.

**tracks** The concentric circular bands on a hard disk. Data is recorded in the tracks, which are divided into sectors to help keep track of where specific files are located.

**traditional organizational structure** In an organization, a method used to distribute the core functions of the organization into divisions such as finance, human resources, and operations.

**transaction** An exchange of goods, services, or funds.

**transaction file** A file used to store input data until it can be processed.

**transaction processing system (TPS)** A system that handles the day-to-day operations of a company; examples include sales, purchases, orders, and returns.

**transceiver** A device used to regulate the electrical connection between a computer and a local area network (LAN).

**transfer performance** A measure of how quickly read/write heads are able to transfer data from a hard disk to memory.

**transistor** A device invented in 1947 by Bell Laboratories that controls the flow of electricity. Due to their small size, reduced power consumption, and lower heat output, transistors replaced vacuum tubes in the second generation of computers.

**Transmission Control Protocol (TCP)** One of two basic Internet protocols (the other is Internet Protocol, IP). TCP is the protocol (standard) that permits two Internet-connected computers to establish a reliable connection. TCP ensures reliable data delivery with a method known as Positive Acknowledgment with Re-transmission (PAR). The computer that sends the data continues to do so until it receives a confirmation from the receiving computer that the data has been received intact.

**transparency** A clear acetate sheet used with an overhead projector for presentations.

**trap door** In computer security, a security hole created on purpose that can be exploited at a later time.

**Trojan horse** An application disguised as a useful program but containing instructions to perform a malicious task.

**Turing test** A test developed by Alan Turing and used to determine whether a computer could be called intelligent. In a Turing test, judges are asked to determine whether the output they see on computer displays is produced by a computer or a human being. If a computer program succeeds in tricking the judges into believing that only a human could have generated that output, the program is said to have passed the Turing test.

**turnover line** In an indentation, the second and subsequent lines.

**twisted pair** An inexpensive copper cable used for telephone and data communications. The term *twisted pair* refers to the braiding of the paired wires, a practice that reduces interference from electrical fields.

**two-megapixel** Type of digital camera that can produce sharp images at higher enlargements such as 8 by 10 inches.

**typeface** A complete collection of letters, punctuation marks, numbers, and special characters with a consistent and identifiable style. Also called font.

**typeover mode** In word processing, a text insertion mode in which new material replaces (types over) existing text.

## U

**ubiquitous computing** A scenario for future computing in which computers are so numerous that they fade into the background, providing intelligence for virtually every aspect of daily life.

**Ultra ATA** A drive interface that offers data transfer rates twice as fast as its predecessor, Enhanced IDE (EDIE). Also called Ultra DMA (Direct Memory Access).

**Ultra DMA (Direct Memory Access)** See Ultra ATA.

**Ultra DMA/100** The latest version of the Ultra DMA/66 standard enables data transfer rates of up to 100 MHz, but these drives require a special cable.

**Ultra DMA/66** An IDE hard disk standard capable of transferring data at speeds of up to 66 Mbps.

**Ultra Wide SCSI** A SCSI (Small Computer Systems Interface) standard that enables hard disk data transfer rates of up to 40 Mbps.

**Ultra160 SCSI** See Ultra3 SCSI.

**Ultra3 SCSI** A SCSI standard that can transfer data at speeds of up to 160 Mbps. Synonymous with Ultra160 SCSI.

**unauthorized access** In computer security, the entry of an unauthorized intruder into a computer system.

**undo** In the editing process, a command that reverses the action of the last editing change.

**undocumented feature** A program capability not mentioned in the program's documentation.

**Unicode** A 16-bit character set capable of representing almost all of the world's languages, including non-Roman characters such as those in Chinese, Japanese, and Hindi.

**uniform resource locator (URL)** In the World Wide Web, one of two basic kinds of Universal Resource Identifiers (URI), a string of characters that precisely identifies an Internet resource's type and location. For example, the fictitious URL http://www.wolverine.virginia.edu/~toros/winerefs/merlot.html identifies a World Wide Web document (http://), indicates the domain name of the computer on which it is stored (www.wolverine.virginia.edu), fully describes the document's location in the directory structure (~toros/winerefs/), and includes the document's name and extension (merlot.html).

**uninstall** To remove a program from a computer system by using a special utility.

**uninterruptible power supply (UPS)** A device that provides power to a computer system for a short period of time if electrical power is lost.

**universal product code (UPC)** A label with a series of bars that can be either keyed in or read by a scanner to identify an item and determine its cost. UPC scanners are often found in point-of-sale (POS) terminals.

**universal serial bus (USB)** An external bus architecture that connects peripherals such as keyboards, mice, and digital cameras. USB offers many benefits over older serial architectures, such as support for 127 devices on a single port, Plug and Play, and higher transfer rates.

**universal service** A basic principle of U.S. telecommunications law, which holds that service providers have an obligation to provide service in areas where it is not economically attractive to do so, such as remote rural regions. Taxes are used to subsidize the extension of service to such areas.

**UNIX** A 32-bit operating system that features multiuser access, preemptive multitasking, multiprocessing, and other sophisticated features. UNIX is widely used for file servers in client/server networks.

**upgrade processor** A microprocessor that upgrades older systems.

**upgrade socket** A receptacle on a motherboard for an upgrade processor.

**upload** To send a file to another computer by means of a computer network.

**Usenet** A worldwide computer-based discussion system that uses the Internet and other networks for transmission media. Discussion is channeled into more than 50,000 topically named newsgroups, which contain original contributions called articles, as well as commentaries on these articles called follow-up posts. As follow-up posts continue to appear on a given subject, a thread of discussion emerges; a threaded newsreader collates these articles together so readers can see the flow of the discussion.

**Usenet client** Software that comes with most browser suites that communicates with a Usenet server.

**Usenet server** A computer running the software that enables users to read Usenet messages, post new messages, and reply to existing messages. The server software also ensures that new messages are shared with other servers so that all participating servers are able to make the same messages available. Also called an NNTP server.

**user** A person who uses a computer and its applications to perform tasks and produce results.

**user agent** See e-mail client.

**user ID** A word or name that uniquely identifies a computer user. Synonymous with user name.

**user interface** The part of system software that interacts with the user.

**user name** A unique name that a system administrator assigns to you that you use as initial identification. You must type this name and also your password to gain access to the system.

**user response** Input the computer requires from the operator for a process to continue.

**utilities** See system utility programs.

**utility program** A program that is designed to assist the user with tasks related to computer system maintenance, such as defragmenting the hard drive.

# V

**V.34** An ITU modulation protocol for modems transmitting and receiving data at 28,800 bits per second (bps). An addition to the protocol enables transmission rates of up to 33.6 Kbps.

**V.90** An ITU modulation protocol for modems transmitting and receiving data at 56 Kbps.

**vaccine** See antivirus program.

**vacuum tube** A device that controls the flow of electrons. Vacuum tubes were used extensively in first-generation computers, but they failed often and were replaced shortly thereafter by transistors.

**validation** In a database, a method of increasing data integrity by ensuring that users enter the correct data type in each field.

**value** In HTML, most attributes require a value, which is usually surrounded by quotation marks and preceded by an equals sign.

**value-added network (VAN)** A public data network that provides value-added services for corporate customers, including end-to-end dedicated lines with guaranteed security. VANs, however, also charge an expensive per-byte fee.

**value-added reseller (VAR)** An independent company that selects system components and assembles them into a functioning system.

**VBScript** A scripting language used to write short programs (scripts) that can be embedded in Web pages.

**vector graphic** An image composed of distinct objects, such as lines or shapes, that may be moved or edited independently. Each object is described by a complex mathematical formula.

**vendor** A company that sells goods or services.

**vertical application** A program for a particular line of business or for a division in a company.

**very-large-scale integration (VLSI)** A level of technological sophistication in the manufacturing of semiconductor chips that allows the equivalent of up to 1 million transistors to be placed on one chip.

**VGA connector** A physical connector that is designed to connect a VGA monitor to a video adapter.

**video accelerators** Video adapters with fast processors.

**video adapter** Video circuitry that fits into an expansion bus and determines the quality of the display and resolution of your monitor. Also called display adapter.

**video capture board** See video capture card.

**video capture card** An expansion board that accepts analog or digital video signals, which are then compressed and stored.

**video card** See video adapter.

**video editor** A program that enables you to view and edit a digitized video and to select special effects.

**Video for Windows** A Microsoft video and compression format for digital video.

**video graphics adapter (VGA)** A video adapter that conforms to the VGA specification, which is capable of displaying data at a resolution of 640 x 480.

**Video Graphics Array (VGA)** A display standard that can display 16 colors at a maximum resolution of 640 pixels by 480 pixels.

**video output** A type of computer output that consists of a series of still images that are played back at a fast enough rate to give the illusion of continuous motion.

**video RAM (VRAM)** A random access memory chip that maximizes the performance of video adapters.

**videoconferencing** A technology enabling two or more people to have a face-to-face meeting even though they're geographically separated.

**view menu** In a graphical user interface (GUI), a menu that provides access to document viewing options, including normal layout, print layout, and document magnification (zoom) options.

**viewable area** The front surface on a cathode-ray tube monitor actually available for viewing, which is less than the quoted size. See quoted size.

**viewable size** The area of a monitor display used to display an image.

**virtual manufacturing** A design process in which a powerful computer assembles digitally drawn parts to ensure that they fit well and function as planned. Also called computer-aided production engineering (CAPE).

**virtual memory** A means of increasing the size of a computer's random access memory (RAM) by using part of the hard disk as an extension of RAM.

**virtual private network (VPN)** A method of connecting two physically separate local area networks (LANs) by using the Internet. Strong encryption is used to ensure privacy.

**virtual reality (VR)** A computer-generated illusion of three-dimensional space. On the Web, virtual reality sites enable Web users to explore three-dimensional virtual reality worlds by means of VR plug-in programs. These programs enable you to walk or "fly" through the three-dimensional space that these worlds offer.

**Virtual Reality Modeling Language (VRML)** A scripting language that enables programmers to specify the characteristics of a three-dimensional world that is accessible on the Internet. VRML worlds can contain sounds, hyperlinks, videos, and animations as well as three-dimensional spaces, which can be explored by using a VRML plug-in.

**virus** Hidden code within a host program that may be destructive to infected files.

**vision technology** See eye-gaze response system.

**visual aids** Graphical supplements to a presentation, such as slides or transparencies.

**Visual Basic (VB)** A programming language developed by Microsoft based on the BASIC programming language. Visual Basic is one of the world's most widely used program development packages.

**visual display system** The video adapter and monitor that generate a computer's images.

**vocabularies** In XML, sets of elements and tags designed for use in a particular field.

**voice recognition** See speech recognition.

**volatile** Susceptible to loss; a way of saying that all the data disappears forever if the power fails.

# W

**warm boot** To restart a computer that is already operating.

**warm start** See warm boot.

**waterfall model** A method in information systems development that returns the focus of the systems development project to a previous phase if an error is discovered in it.

**waveform** A type of digitized audio format used to record live sounds or music.

**waveguide synthesis** A method of generating and reproducing musical sounds in a sound card. Waveguide synthesis simulates what happens when a real musical instrument produces a sound; it is superior to wavetable and FM synthesis.

**wavetable synthesis** A method of generating and reproducing musical sounds in a sound card. Wavetable synthesis uses a prerecorded sample of dozens of orchestral instruments to determine how particular notes should sound. Wavetable synthesis is far superior to FM synthesis.

**Web** See World Wide Web (WWW).

**Web browser** A program that runs on an Internet-connected computer and provides access to information on the World Wide Web (WWW).

**Web cam** A low-cost video camera used for low-resolution videoconferencing on the Internet.

**Web-enabled devices** Devices that have the ability to connect to the Internet and e-book readers.

**Web layout** In Microsoft Word, a document view that approximates the document's appearance if it were saved as a Web page and viewed by a Web browser.

**Web integration** A variety of techniques used to make information stored in databases available through Internet or intranet connections.

**Web page** A document you create to share with others on the Web. A Web page can include text, graphics, sound, animation, and video.

**Web server** On the Web, a program that accepts requests for information framed according to the Hypertext Transfer Protocol (HTTP). The server processes these requests and sends the requested document.

**Web site** A computer that is accessible to the public Internet and is running a server program that makes Web pages available.

**Web technology** In application software, the capability to save files in a form that contains a Web document's underlying HTML codes, greatly facilitating file conversion.

**Webmaster** A person responsible for the visual layout of a Web site, its written content, its links to other locations, and often the techniques to follow up on customers' inquiries.

**WebTV** See MSN® TV.

**weight** The darkness or thickness of a character.

**what-if scenario** In business, an experiment using make-believe data to see how it affects an outcome, such as sales volume.

**wheel mouse** A type of mouse that has a dial that can be used to scroll through data on-screen.

**whisper** A special type of Internet chat group message that, instead of being seen by everyone on the channel, is seen by only the one person to whom it is sent.

**whistleblowing** Reporting illegal or unethical actions of a company to a regulatory agency or the press.

**whiteboard** A separate area of a videoconferencing screen enabling participants to create a shared workspace. Participants can write or draw in this space as if they were using a chalkboard in a meeting.

**wide area network (WAN)** A commercial data network that provides data communications services for businesses and government agencies. Most WANs use the X.25 protocols, which overcome problems related to noisy analog telephone lines.

**wildcard** A symbol that stands for any character or any group of characters.

**Win 95** See Microsoft Windows 95.

**Win 98** See Microsoft Windows 98.

**window border** The outer edge of a window on a graphical user interface (GUI); in Microsoft Windows it can be dragged to change the size of the window.

**window controls** In a graphical user interface (GUI), a group of window management controls that enable the user to minimize, maximize, restore, or close the window.

**Windows Bitmap (BMP)** A bitmapped graphics format developed for Microsoft Windows.

**wireless communication** A means of linking computers using infrared or radio signals.

**wireless keyboard** Battery-powered keyboards that use infrared or radio waves to send signals to a computer.

**wireless LANs (WLANs)** Local area networks that use a radio signal spread over a seemingly random series of frequencies for greater security.

**wireless mouse** See cordless mouse.

**wizard** In a graphical user interface (GUI), a series of dialog boxes that guide the user through a complex process, such as importing data into an application.

**word completion prediction program** An accessibility feature designed for people with limited dexterity that presents a menu of possible word completions.

**word processing program** An office application that enables the user to create, edit, format, and print textual documents.

**word size** The number of bits a computer can work with at one time.

**word wrapping** A word processing feature that automatically moves words down to the beginning of the next line if they extend beyond the right margin.

**workbook** In a spreadsheet program, a file that can contain two or more spreadsheets, each of which has its own page in the workbook.

**workflow automation** An information system in which documents are automatically sent to the people who need to see them.

**workgroup** A team of two or more people working on the same project.

**worksheet** The graphical accounting pad that appears in spreadsheet programs. Also called spreadsheet.

**worksheet tab** In a spreadsheet program, a tab that enables the user to determine which worksheet to display within a workbook.

**workstation** A powerful desktop computer that meets the computing needs of engineers, architects, and other professionals who require detailed graphic displays. In a LAN, a workstation runs application programs and serves as an access point to the network.

**World Wide Web (WWW)** A global hypertext system that uses the Internet as its transport mechanism. In a hypertext system, you navigate by clicking hyperlinks, which display another document (which also contains hyperlinks). Most Web documents are created using HTML, a markup language that is easy to learn and that will soon be supplanted by automated tools. Incorporating hypermedia (graphics, sounds, animations, and video), the Web has become the ideal medium for publishing information on the Internet. See also Web browser.

**World Wide Web Consortium (W3C)** An independent standards body made up of university researchers and industry practitioners devoted to setting effective standards to promote the orderly growth of the World Wide Web. Housed at the Massachusetts Institute of Technology (MIT), W3C sets standards for HTML and many other aspects of Web usage.

**worm** A program resembling a computer virus that can spread over networks.

**write** To record data on a computer storage device.

**write once, read many (WORM)** An optical disc drive with storage capacities of up to 15 G. After data is written, it becomes a read-only storage medium.

**write-back** One of four basic operations carried out by the control unit of a microprocessor. The write-back operation involves writing the results of previous operations to an internal register.

**write-protect notch** See write-protect tab.

**write-protect tab** On a floppy disk, a tab that prevents the computer from overwriting or erasing the disk's contents.

**WWW** See World Wide Web (WWW).

**WYSIWYG** A type of on-screen document view in which the user sees the results of formatting choices on-screen. WYSIWYG stands for "what-you-see-is-what-you-get."

# X

**X.25** A packet-switching network protocol optimized for use on noisy analog telephone lines.

**X-10** A standard for computer-controlled home automation devices.

**xDSL** See Digital Subscriber Line (DSL).

**Xeon** A 64-bit microprocessor manufactured by Intel. Introduced in 1998, the Xeon uses a wider socket with more contacts to increase communication speed between the processor and components on the motherboard. Due to its high cost, the Xeon is used mostly in servers and high-end workstations.

# Z

**zero-insertion force (ZIF) socket** A receptacle for microprocessors that makes it easy to remove and install them without the risk of bending pins.

**Zip disk** A removable storage medium that combines the convenience of a floppy disk with the storage capacity of a small hard disk (100 to 200 MB).

**Zip disk drive** A popular removable storage medium, created by Iomega Corporation, that provides 100 to 200 MB of storage on relatively inexpensive ($10 each) portable disks.

**zoom** To increase or decrease the magnification level of a document as displayed in the application workspace.

**zoom level** The degree of magnification of a document within the application workspace.

# Illustration Credits

## CHAPTER I

**Figure 1.1, top**
© Tim Pannell/Corbis

**Figure 1.1, bottom left**
© Robert Levine

**Figure 1.1, bottom right**
© Tom Stewart/Corbis

**Figure 1.2**
© Jose Luis Pelaez/Corbis

**Figure 1.3, PC**
Courtesy of International Business Machines
    Corporation. Unauthorized use not permitted.

**Figure 1.3, Macintosh**
© 2003 Apple Computer, Inc. All rights reserved.

**Figure 1.3, notebook**
Courtesy of Sony Electronics Inc.

**Figure 1.3, PDA**
Courtesy of Sony Electronics Inc.

**Figure 1.5b**
Courtesy of Sony Electronics Inc.

**Figure 1.5a, b, c, d, e, f**
Courtesy of International Business Machines
    Corporation. Unauthorized use not permitted.

**Figure 1.5h**
Courtesy of Creative Labs.

**Figure 1.5j**
© Paul Hardy/Corbis

**Figure 1.5k**
Courtesy of International Business Machines
    Corporation. Unauthorized use not permitted.

**Figure 1.6**
© Japack Company/Corbis

**Figure 1.8**
Courtesy of Intel Corporation.

**Figure 1.9a**
Courtesy of International Business Machines
    Corporation. Unauthorized use not permitted.

**Figure 1.13a**
© Reuters NewMedia/Corbis

**Figure 1.13b**
Courtesy of PaPeRo.

**Figure 1.16**
© George Hall/Corbis

**Figure 1.17, top**
© 2003 Apple Computer, Inc. All rights reserved.

**Figure 1.18, top to bottom**
Courtesy of International Business Machines
    Corporation. Unauthorized use not permitted.
Courtesy of International Business Machines
    Corporation. Unauthorized use not permitted.
Courtesy of International Business Machines
    Corporation. Unauthorized use not permitted
Courtesy of Cray, Inc.

**Figure 1.19**
© Lester Leftkowitz/Corbis

## SPOTLIGHT I

**Figure 1A**
© Tom Stewart/Corbis

**Figure 1B**
Courtesy of the Software Publishers Association.

**Figure 1C**
© AFP/Corbis

**Figure 1D**
© Ed Wheeler/Corbis

**Figure 1E**
© Jim Erick/Corbis

## CHAPTER 2

**Figure 2.1d**
Photo courtesy of Iomega Corporation. Copyright © 2003
    Iomega Corporation. All Rights Reserved. Zip is a
    registered trademark in the United States and/or
    other countries. Iomega, the stylized "i" logo and
    product images are property of Iomega Corporation
    in the United States and/or other countries.

**Figure 2.8a**
Courtesy of Gateway Computers.

**Figure 2.8b**
© 2003 Apple Computer, Inc. All rights reserved.

**Figure 2.15a**
© James Leynse/Corbis Saba

**Figure 2.15b**
© James A. Sugar/Corbis

**Figure 2.15c**
© Judy Griesediek/Corbis

**Figure 2.17**
© 1995-2003 Symantec Corporation

## SPOTLIGHT 2

**Figure 2B**
Courtesy of Microsoft Coporation.

**Figure 2P**
Courtesy of Infocus.

## CHAPTER 3

**Figure 3.1**
© 2003 Tucows Inc.

**Figure 3.4**
© Jose Luis Palaez/Corbis

**Figure 3.5**
© AFP/Corbis

**Figure 3.7**
Screen shot(s) reprinted by permission from Microsoft
Corporation.

**Figure 3.9**
Screen shot(s) reprinted by permission from Microsoft
Corporation.

## CHAPTER 4

**Figure 4.4**
Courtesy of Intel Corporation.

**Figure 4.5**
Courtesy of Intel Corporation.

**Figure 4.6**
Courtesy of Advanced Micro Devices.

**Figure 4.7a**
© 2003 Apple Computer, Inc. All rights reserved.

**Figure 4.8a**
© 2003 Apple Computer, Inc. All rights reserved.

**Figure 4.8b**
© 2003 Apple Computer, Inc. All rights reserved.

**Figure 4.9**
© Bonnie Kamin/Photo Edit

**Figure 4.13**
© Mark M. Lawrence/Corbis

**Figure 4.14**
© Bonnie Kamin/Photo Edit

**Figure 4.16**
Courtesy of International Business Machines
Corporation. Unauthorized use not permitted.

**Figure 4.19**
© AFP/Corbis

**Figure 4.23**
Courtesy of Intel Corporation.

## CHAPTER 5

**Figure 5.1, bottom**
© William Whitehurst/Corbis

**Figure 5.6, trackball**
Courtesy of International Business Machines
Corporation. Unauthorized use not permitted.

**Figure 5.6, pointing stick**
Courtesy of International Business Machines
Corporation. Unauthorized use not permitted.

**Figure 5.6, joystick**
Courtesy of International Business Machines
Corporation. Unauthorized use not permitted.

**Figure 5.6, touchscreen**
© Kim Kulish/Corbis Saba

**Figure 5.6, stylus**
Courtesy of International Business Machines
Corporation. Unauthorized use not permitted.

**Figure 5.7**
Courtesy of Microsoft Corporation.

**Figure 5.9**
AP/Wide World Press

**Figure 5.10**
Polaroid digital camera images provided by World Wide
Licenses Ltd. Exclusive licensee of Polaroid
Corporation, Pembroke, Mass.

**Figure 5.11b**
© Reuters NewMedia/Corbis

**Figure 5.14a**
Courtesy of International Business Machines
Corporation, Unauthorized use not permitted.

**Figure 5.14b**
AP/Wide World Press

**Figure 5.14c**
© Stocker Mike/Corbis Sygma

**Figure 5.17a**
Lexmark International, Inc.

**Figure 5.17b**
© Bill Aron, Photo Edit

**Figure 5.18**
Xerox Corporation

**Figure 5.19**
Courtesy of Canon, Inc.

**Figure 5.20, left**
AP/Wide World Press

**Figure 5.20, middle**
© AFP, Martin Athenstaldt/Corbis

**Figure 5.20, right**
© AFP/Corbis

**Figure 5.25, right**
Courtesy of Intel Corporation.

**Figure 5.25, center**
Courtesy of International Business Machines
Corporation. Unauthorized use not permitted.

**Figure 5.26**
Courtesy of Advanced Computer and Network
Corporation.

**Figure 5.27a**
Courtesy of International Business Machines
Corporation. Unauthorized use not permitted.

**Figure 5.27b**
Courtesy of International Business Machines Corporation. Unauthorized use not permitted.

**Figure 5.28**
Photo courtesy of Iomega Corporation. Copyright © 2003 Iomega Corporation. All Rights Reserved. Zip is a registered trademark in the United States and/or other countries. Iomega, the stylized "i" logo, and product images are property of Iomega Corporation in the United States and/or other countries.

**Figure 5.29**
© Michael Keller Studios/Corbis

**Figure 5.31**
Courtesy of International Business Machines Corporation. Unauthorized use not permitted.

**Figure 5.32**
Santac Corporation

**Figure 5.33**
Courtesy of International Business Machines Corporation. Unauthorized use not permitted.

## CHAPTER 6

**Figure 6.1**
© William Taufic/Corbis

**Figure 6.5a**
Courtesy of International Business Machines Corporation. Unauthorized use not permitted.

**Figure 6.5c**
Courtesy of International Business Machines Corporation. Unauthorized use not permitted.

**Figure 6.5d**
Courtesy of International Business Machines Corporation. Unauthorized use not permitted.

**Figure 6.7**
© Digital Art/Corbis

**Figure 6.8**
© Digital Art/Corbis

**Figure 6.10d**
Courtesy of Sony Electronics Inc.

**Figure 6.15, file server, fax server, print server**
Courtesy of International Business Machines Corporation. Unauthorized use not permitted.

**Figure 6.19**
© Chuck Savage/Corbis

## CHAPTER 7

**Figure 7.1a**
© Disney. All rights reserved.

**Figure 7.1b**
Reproduced with permission of Yahoo! Inc. © 2003 by Yahoo! Inc. YAHOO! and the YAHOO! logo are trademarks of Yahoo! Inc.

**Figure 7.1c**
© 2003 Monster.com

**Figure 7.1d**
© 1998–2003 priceline.com Incorporated, all rights reserved.

**Figure 7.1e**
Reprinted with permission from Britannica.com. © 2003 by Encyclopaedia Britannica, Inc.

**Figure 7.3a**
© 2003 by Consumers Union of U.S., Inc., Yonkers, NY 10703. Used by permission. Log on to www.ConsumerReports.org.

**Figure 7.3b**
© 2003 WebMD Inc.

**Figure 7.3c**
Copyright © 2003 ABCNEWS Internet Ventures

**Figure 7.4a**
© 2003 REI

**Figure 7.4b**
© 2003 WebCam.com

**Figure 7.4c**
Copyright © 1968–2003 Mountain News Corp.

**Figure 7.6c**
© 2003 University of Oregon

**Figure 7.7a**
Netscape website © 2003 Netscape Communications Corporation. Screenshot used with permission.

**Figure 7.7b**
Screen shot(s) reprinted by permission from Microsoft Corporation.

**Figure 7.11**
© Copyright 1997–2003 Charles M. Kozierok

**Figure 7.12**
AP/Wide World Photos

**Figure 7.17**
© America Online, Inc.

**Figure 7.18**
Reproduced with permission of Yahoo! Inc. © 2003 by Yahoo! Inc. YAHOO! and the YAHOO! logo are trademarks of Yahoo! Inc.

**Figure 7.20**
© Dennis Novak, Image Bank/Getty Images

**Figure 7.25**
Screen shot(s) reprinted by permission from Microsoft Corporation.

**Figure 7.26**
© 2003 Net2Phone, Inc.

**Figure 7.27**
© Copyright 2003, Lycos, Inc. All Rights Reserved. Lycos® is a registered trademark of Carnegie Mellon University.

**Figure 7.28a**
© 2003 CareerBuilder

**Figure 7.28b**
© 2000–2003 Pearson Education, publishing as
    Information Please®

**Figure 7.29**
© 2003 Google Inc.

**Figure 7.30**
© 2003 Ingenta, Inc.

## CHAPTER 8

**Figure 8.1**
© Corbis

**Figure 8.3**
© 2003 Universal Service Administrative Company

**Figure 8.4**
© 2003 Bluetooth SIG, Inc.

**Figure 8.6, left**
Courtesy of Motorola.

**Figure 8.6, middle**
Courtesy of Nokia.

**Figure 8.6, right**
Courtesy of Motorola.

**Figure 8.9**
© Jack Chenet

**Figure 8.10, top**
© Jean Nelson/Corbis

**Figure 8.10, middle**
AP/Wide World Photos

**Figure 8.10, bottom**
AP/Wide World Photos

**Figure 8.11f**
Courtesy of Sony Electronics Inc.

**Figure 8.12**
© Corbis/Sygma

**Figure 8.13**
© 1995–2003 Symantec Corporation

**Figure 8.14, left**
AP/Wide World Photos

**Figure 8.14, right**
© 2003 Apple Computer, Inc. All rights reserved.

**Figure 8.15**
© John Feingush/Corbis

**Figure 8.16**
© Robert Llewellyn/Corbis

**Figure 8.17**
Screen shot(s) reprinted by permission from Microsoft
    Corporation.

## SPOTLIGHT 4

**Figure 4A**
Courtesy of International Business Machines
    Corporation. Unauthorized use not permitted.

**Figure 4B**
Courtesy of Intel Corporation.

**Figure 4D.1**
Courtesy of International Business Machines
    Corporation. Unauthorized use not permitted.

**Figure 4D.2**
Courtesy of International Business Machines
    Corporation. Unauthorized use not permitted.

**Figure E**
Courtesy of Intel Corporation.

**Figure 4F**
Courtesy of Microsoft Corporation.

**Figure 4G**
© Jose Luis Pelaez/Corbis

**Figure 4I.1**
© LWA-JDC/Corbis

**Figure 4I.2**
© Jose Luis Palaez/Corbis

**Figure 4J**
© Susan Van Etten/Photo Edit

**Figure 4L**
Courtesy of Isobar.

**Figure 4M**
Courtesy of Intel Corporation.

# Index

## SYMBOLS AND NUMBERS